D1274441

STALINGRAD

Attack. Stalingrad, 1943. *Photographer: Natalya Bode*

STALINGRAD

.....

THE CITY THAT DEFEATED THE THIRD REICH

JOCHEN HELLBECK

Translated by Christopher Tauchen and Dominic Bonfiglio

PUBLICAFFAIRS
New York

This book has been prepared as part of a joint agreement between the Institute of Russian History of the Russian Academy of Sciences and the German Historical Institute in Moscow.

Copyright © 2015 by Jochen Hellbeck.

First published in Germany in 2012 by S. Fischer Verlag GmbH.

Published in the United States by PublicAffairs™,
a Member of the Perseus Books Group

All rights reserved.

Printed in the United States of America.

No part of this book may be reproduced in any manner whatsoever without written permission except in the case of brief quotations embodied in critical articles and reviews. For information, address PublicAffairs, 250 West 57th Street, 15th Floor, New York, NY 10107.

PublicAffairs books are available at special discounts for bulk purchases in the U.S. by corporations, institutions, and other organizations. For more information, please contact the Special Markets Department at the Perseus Books Group, 2300 Chestnut Street, Suite 200, Philadelphia, PA 19103, call (800) 810-4145, ext. 5000, or e-mail special.markets@perseusbooks.com.

Book Design by Pauline Brown

Library of Congress Cataloging-in-Publication Data

Hellbeck, Jochen.
[Stalingrad-Protokolle. English]
Stalingrad : the city that defeated the Third Reich / Jochen Hellbeck.—First edition.
pages cm
"First published in Germany in 2012 by S. Fischer Verlag GmbH"—Title page verso.
Includes bibliographical references and index.
ISBN 978-1-61039-496-3 (hardcover)—ISBN 978-1-61039-497-0 (electronic) 1. Stalingrad, Battle of, Volgograd, Russia, 1942–1943. 2. Stalingrad, Battle of, Volgograd, Russia, 1942–1943—Personal narratives, Russian. 3. Stalingrad, Battle of, Volgograd, Russia, 1942–1943—Personal narratives, German. I. Title.
D764.3.S7H4513 2015
940.54'21747—dc23

2015002880

First Edition

10 9 8 7 6 5 4 3 2 1

CONTENTS

1

THE FATEFUL BATTLE

The battle of Stalingrad—the most ferocious and lethal battle in human history—ended on February 2, 1943. With an estimated death toll in excess of a million, the bloodletting at Stalingrad far exceeded that of Verdun, one of the costliest battles of World War I. The analogy with Verdun was not lost on German and Soviet soldiers who fought at Stalingrad. As they described the "hell of Stalingrad" in their private letters, some Germans saw themselves trapped in a "second Verdun." Many Soviet defenders meanwhile extolled Stalingrad, a city with a prehistory of bloody warfare, as their "Red Verdun," vowing never to surrender it to the enemy. But, as a Soviet war correspondent reporting from Stalingrad in October 1942 remarked, the embattled city differed from Verdun: it had not been designed as a stronghold and it possessed

> no fortresses or concrete shelters. The line of defense passes through waste grounds and courtyards where housewives used to hang out the laundry, across the tracks of the narrow gauge railway, through the house where an accountant lived with his wife, two children and aging mother, through dozens of similar houses, through the now deserted square and its mangled pavement, through the park where just this past summer lovers sat whispering to one another on green benches. A city of peace has become a city of war. The laws of warfare have placed it on the front line, at the epicenter of a battle that will shape the outcome of the entire war. In Stalingrad, the line of defense passes through the hearts of the Russian people. After sixty days of fighting the Germans now know what this means. "Verdun!" they scoff. This

is no Verdun. This is something new in the history of warfare. This is Stalingrad.[1]

Lasting six months, the battle also unfolded as a global media war. From the very beginning observers on all sides were fixated on the gigantic clash at the edge of Europe, heralding it a defining event of World War II. The fight for Stalingrad would become the "most fateful battle of the war," a Dresden paper wrote in early August 1942, just when Hitler's soldiers were preparing their assault on the city. The British *Daily Telegraph* used virtually the same terms in September. In Berlin, Joseph Goebbels read the papers of Germany's enemies attentively. The battle of Stalingrad, the Nazi propaganda chief declared with a nod to the British daily, was a "question of life or death, and all of our prestige, just as that of the Soviet Union, will depend on how it will end."[2] Starting in October 1942, Soviet newspapers regularly cited western reports that extolled the heroism of the soldiers and civilians defending the city against Germany's mechanical warriors. In pubs throughout England the radio would be turned on for the start of the evening news only to be turned off after the report on Stalingrad had aired: "Nobody wants to hear anything else," a British reporter noted. "All they talk about is Stalingrad, just Stalingrad."[3] Among the Allied nations, people euphorically commented on the performance of the Soviets at Stalingrad. This sentiment not only reflected the spirit of the antifascist alliance; it also owed to the fact that the western Allied soldiers could not offer any comparable feats: for over a year the British army had suffered defeat after defeat.[4]

In November, a Soviet counterattack trapped more than 300,000 German and Axis soldiers in the Stalingrad pocket, or *Kessel*. German media abruptly stopped reporting on the battle and did not resume until late January 1943, when Nazi leaders realized they could not pass over the rout of an entire German army in silence. They cast the battle as one of heroic self-sacrifice, fought by German soldiers defending Europe against a superior Asian enemy. The propaganda of fear, reinforced by appeals to German citizens to embrace total war, worked imperfectly. The German security police reported that people spoke of the last bullet, which they would save for themselves once "everything was over."[5] One German official undertook particular precautions in the wake of Stalingrad: SS Chief Heinrich Himmler visited the Treblinka death camp in eastern Poland in early March 1943. He urgently instructed the camp authorities to exhume all the bodies of the 700,000 Jews who had been killed there and cremate the corpses.[6] For the next months until Treblinka was shut down, camp workers carried out their grim task while continuing to kill on a reduced scale. Himmler's order grew out of an awareness that a time of reckoning for Germany was drawing near.[7] While it would be another year and a half before the Red Army liberated the camps in Poland, the battle on the Volga disrupted the Nazi death machine. The Dresden newspaper was right, if for the wrong reasons: Stalingrad did mark a turning point in world history.

As long as the battle was raging, no foreign correspondents in Moscow were allowed to travel to Stalingrad. Secretive and distrustful, the Soviet authorities waited until February 4, 1943, before bringing in a first batch of international reporters—British, Americans, French, Czechs, Chinese.[8] Among them was Paul Winterton, who aired this report for the BBC:

> The streets of Stalingrad, if you can give the name to open spaces between ruins, still bear all the marks of battle. There's the usual litter of helmets and weapons, stacks of ammunition, papers flattering in the snow, pocketbooks from dead Germans, and any number of smashed corpses, lying where they fell, or stacked up in great frozen heaps for later burial. Stalingrad can never be repaired. It will have to be rebuilt from the beginning. But even though all its buildings are wrecked there is life in it still. Along the narrow stretch of cement, which the Russians held through long months of assault, there is a city of dugouts—dugouts occupied by the soldiers who have not yet left, and by a few women who stayed behind to launder and cook for the men. There is a real party atmosphere among these people today. They are the proudest men and women I've ever seen. They know they've done a terrific job, and they've done it well. Their city has been destroyed, but they have smashed the invader by sheer stubbornness and unconquerable courage. These men and women fought and worked for months, with their backs to the river that they had sworn never to retreat across, facing an enemy who held the only dominating height in Stalingrad and who pounded them with shells and mortars, unceasingly by day and night. They clung to their narrow foothold, and their feet never slipped.[9]

Winterton opened with a panoramic account of the city and the detritus of war and then moved to what interested him and other journalists most: the defenders of Stalingrad. To Winterton, it was Russian "stubbornness and unconquerable courage" that decided the outcome of the battle; Alexander Werth, a reporter for the *London Times*, celebrated Red Army soldiers' "extraordinary [. . .] individual achievements," and for *New York Times* correspondent Henry Shapiro, Stalingrad symbolized the "triumph of men over metal"—Soviet men over German metal, to be exact.[10] Valuable as these reports are as repositories of wartime views and emotions, they are also perfunctory and one-sided. The foreign correspondents were given only a quick tour of Stalingrad, and their Soviet guides were keen for them to meet the captured German generals rather than talk with Soviet citizens.[11]

The journalists touring the battleground in February 1943 did not know that more than a month earlier, a delegation of historians from Moscow had begun a large-scale project to document for posterity the voices of the Stalingrad defenders. They belonged to the Commission on the History of the Great Patriotic War, which had been founded by Isaak Mints, a professor at Moscow State University.

The historians arrived in Stalingrad in late December 1942, and they took up their work on January 2, 1943. They visited various locations along the front line running through the embattled city: the steelworks in the north, General Vasily Chuikov's command post, the Beketovka settlement at Stalingrad's southern edge. In trenches and bunkers they spoke with commanders, officers, and soldiers of the Red Army. A stenographer accompanying them transcribed the interviews. The historians had to leave Stalingrad on January 9, a day before the Red Army began its final offensive, and they returned in February to resume their work just days after the Germans surrendered. In the following weeks and months, they conducted many one-on-one interviews, eventually collecting 215 eyewitness accounts: from generals, staff officers, troop commanders, simple foot soldiers, commissars, agitators, sailors of the Volga Military Flotilla, nurses, and a number of civilians—engineers, laborers, and a cook among them—who worked in the bombed-out city or were just struggling to survive there.

Their interviews bring the reader close to the battle and paint a vivid picture of the actions, thoughts, and feelings of the Soviet participants that is unique among known sources. Soldiers spoke off the cuff about their lives, delivering rich and colorful descriptions (some in vernacular idiom) with the immediacy of an audio recording. The interviewees talked about their hometowns, how they ended up in Stalingrad, and their assignments. Candid and firsthand, authentic and nuanced, they described moments of terror and exhilaration, discussed the strengths and weaknesses of the Soviet military leadership, boasted of the honors they received, and depicted the deeds of heroes and cowards. These interviews are also unique in that many of the participants fought side by side and mention each other by name. Regarded as a whole, the interviews convey a unity of place, time, and action, the likes of which are found only in literature.

The historians went about their work systematically. In some cases they interviewed dozens of members of a single division: the commander, the political representative, staff officers, regimental commanders, company leaders, and infantry. These include twenty-four soldiers from the 308th Rifle Division, a unit that suffered heavy losses northwest of the city before being reassigned to Stalingrad to protect the Barricades munitions plant. The historians also spoke with engineers in charge of planning the reconstruction of the Red October steelworks, and with more than twenty soldiers from the 38th Motorized Rifle Brigade who had captured General Paulus and the rest of the 6th Army command. Taken together, these individual perspectives give rise to a finely woven, multifaceted picture of soldiers in battle. Alongside this impressive specificity, the transcripts reveal shared spheres of experience and elucidate—credibly—how the Red Army operated as a combat force. The candor and complexity of the Stalingrad interviews sealed their fate, however. The historians were unable to obtain approval for publication from state censors during the war, and the documents they collected later disappeared in an archive.[12] They are presented here in English for the first time.

Like the journalists who toured Stalingrad in early 1943, the historians around Isaak Mints were drawn to the city's defenders. They hoped to find in their testimony answers to the question that observers around the world were asking: exactly how had the Red Army been able to prevail against an enemy who was considered superior in operational planning, soldierly discipline, and fighting skills? Which resources did the defenders of Stalingrad bring to bear that stopped the unbeatable Germans who had until now forced Europe to its knees? These questions occupy researchers to the present day. The perhaps most debated issue surrounds the motivation of Red Army soldiers at Stalingrad. Did they act freely or were they coerced into battle, even at gunpoint? Did they draw from traditional Russian values, or were they animated by specifically Soviet ones? How did love for the homeland, hatred toward the invader, and devotion to Stalin figure in Red Army soldiers' willingness to fight and die? The wartime interviews that lie at the center of this book provide rich and at times startlingly new answers to these questions.

Featuring a panoply of Soviet voices from wartime, this book allows English readers for the first time to imagine Red Army soldiers and other defenders of the city as thinking and feeling individuals. As it gives these voices a forum, the book adds substantially to writing on World War II that—in part for lack of access to personal documents—portrays the Red Army as a depersonalized machine and often feeds on unverified clichés about "the Russian soldier." The book also provides a corrective to the many studies on Stalingrad that present the clash largely through the eyes of the Germans who were trapped in the city. By contrast, the Stalingrad interviews show in compelling detail how Soviet citizens made sense of the battle and located themselves in it.

This first chapter presents a historical context to enable readers to better understand the transcripts generated by the Mints commission. It begins with an overview of the battle and its treatment by historians, followed by a short history of the Red Army and Soviet society that culminates with the war. It then observes political and military events at the Stalingrad front through a microscopic lens. The chapter also features the creation of the Historical Commission, its aims and methods, and its journey to Stalingrad. It closes with a discussion of the interviews included in this book and the form of their presentation.

These interviews were prepared for publication jointly by the German Historical Institute in Moscow and the Russian Academy of Sciences. Under my direction, a small team of historians spent two years accessing and inventorying thousands of pages of interview transcripts, internal commission documents, and other relevant sources. Space limitations dictated that only a portion of the interviews found entry into this volume.[13] Ten of them are presented verbatim; many others are woven into veritable tapestries—they tell the story of the battle in the form a chorus of soldierly and civilian voices (Chapters 2–3).

As they talked about how they had experienced the battle of Stalingrad, many of the interviewees shared impressions and thoughts about their German adversary. The historians of the Mints commission were interested in this question, and they additionally collected documents that illuminated the personal horizons of German soldiers at Stalingrad. These documents, which include the transcripts of captured Germans who were interrogated in early February 1943 and the diary of a German soldier that was found on the battlefield, form the bulk of Chapter 4.

The final, fifth chapter covers the aftermath of the Soviet victory at Stalingrad and follows the dramatic fate of the Soviet historians and writers who chronicled the battle.

A CITY UNDER SIEGE

The battle of Stalingrad marked a turning point in World War II. For six months, two massive army groups, each under orders not to cede an inch to the enemy, fought for control of the city that bore the Soviet dictator's name.[14] The battle ended with the encirclement and destruction of an entire German field army. At the time it was the worst military defeat in Germany's history—and, in the immediate aftershock, the writing was on the wall for clear-eyed German observers.[15] For the Soviet Union, Stalingrad represented its greatest victory to date over the German invaders. It shifted the war's momentum in favor of the Red Army; after Stalingrad, its divisions would push steadily westward, their sights set on Berlin.

After German advances on Leningrad, Moscow, and Sevastopol had ground to a halt in the fall of 1941 and the Soviets launched their winter counterattack, Hitler started planning a sweeping offensive for the following summer code-named Operation Blue. It began on June 28, 1942, with a major assault along the Russian-Ukrainian front to take control of the region's strategically important natural resources—the coal mines of the Donets basin and the oil fields outside Maykop, Grozny, and Baku. The German panzer and motorized infantry divisions gained ground quickly, but the pincer tactics they employed often missed their mark: whenever faced with encirclement, the Red Army divisions broke into rapid retreat. Hitler, assuming that the enemy troops had already dispersed, divided Army Group South into two parts: Army Group A, which was ordered to push toward the Caucasus, and Army Group B, which was to head northeast and secure the flanks. The spearhead of Army Group B was the 6th Army, under the command of General Friedrich Paulus. Its mission was to capture the city of Stalingrad, a key center for industry and weapons manufacturing on the Volga River.

By July 1942, the gravity of the situation—as even a cursory glance at a map made plain—had become apparent to many Soviet citizens. The writer Vasily Grossman noted in his diary, "The war in the south, on the lower reaches of the Volga, feels like a knife driven deep into the body."[16] The regime responded to the crisis with severe measures. After Rostov-on-Don fell into German hands with little resistance, Stalin issued Order no. 227, notorious for the line "Not one step back!"[17] Henceforth, anyone who retreated from the enemy without an express order to do so would be branded a traitor to the fatherland and subjected to a military tribunal. This draconian edict was enforced at the battle of Stalingrad. The city extended like a ribbon twenty-five miles along the western bank of the Volga. Here "Not one step back!" meant that the river was the farthest point of retreat for the city's defenders.

From the outset of the battle, Soviet leaders impressed on soldiers the symbolic significance of Stalingrad. It was the place where Stalin had staved off the enemies of the Soviet system during the Russian Civil War. Losing Stalingrad to the Germans would damage the myth of the city and its eponymous hero, and had to be prevented by all means. For the same reasons the city was crucially important to Hitler. Banking on the psychological blow that a Soviet defeat would deliver to Stalin, he framed it early on as a battle between two opposing worldviews. On August 20, 1942, Joseph Goebbels wrote in his diary that the Führer "has made the city a special priority. [. . .] Not one stone will be left on another."[18]

At the western bend of the Don curve, some distance from Stalingrad, German forces encountered heavy resistance from the Soviet 62nd Army. The Germans took 57,000 prisoners, however, and crossed the Don on August 21. By the twenty-third, the first German panzers reached the Volga, some forty miles away, and barred access to Stalingrad from the north. The news set off alarms in Moscow. Three days later, Stalin appointed General Georgy Zhukov deputy supreme commander of the Red Army and put him in charge of the city's defense.

At the beginning of the war, the population of Stalingrad was just under half a million, and the city was considered a safe haven far behind the front lines; by the summer of 1942 it was teeming with refugees. The city's administrators implored Stalin to permit the evacuation of factories and civilians—to no avail. Lazar Brontman, a *Pravda* correspondent present during these discussions, recorded in his diary "how the boss [Stalin] declared with a glum expression: 'Where should they be evacuated? The city must be held. That's final!' he shouted, and pounded his fist on the table."[19] Only after German bombers had laid waste to the city did Stalin allow women and children to leave.

After two weeks of bombing, Stalingrad was stormed by German troops. On September 14, a regiment broke through the inner city and reached the Volga.[20] In the heavy street fighting that ensued over the following weeks, the Germans managed to push the soldiers of the 62nd Army back to the riverbank. Once the Wehrmacht's shock troops had cleared a path, the German occupation authority set up headquarters, began executing communists and Jews, and prepared to deport the civilian population. On the other side, the Soviet defenders, dug in on the Volga's steep western bank, held no more than a few bridgeheads. They received supplies, soldiers, and weapons by boat and cover from artillery positions on the east bank of the Volga. The 62nd Army in Stalingrad was part of the Southeastern Front,[21] commanded by General Andrei Yeryomenko,[22] which consisted of the 64th, 57th, and 51st Armies, the 8th Air Army, and the ships and sailors of the Volga Military Flotilla, all stationed south of the city; it also included the 1st Guards Army and the 25th and 66th Armies, located to the north and northwest. In September the latter cluster tried repeatedly to break through Germany's northern barricade and meet up with the city's defenders but never succeeded.

The Soviet plan for a comprehensive counteroffensive took shape in mid-September during the critical phase of the defense of Stalingrad. Zhukov and Alexander Vasilevsky, the chief of the general staff of the Soviet armed forces, proposed to Stalin an operation adopting the German *Blitzkrieg* method—a combined application of massive force, speed, and surprise—to envelop and rout the enemy. Over the next two months the Soviets prepared for the offensive: another formation (the Southwestern Front), under the command of General Nikolai Vatutin, secretly moved to a position on the upper Don; meanwhile, the armies in Stalingrad (divided since the end of September into two fronts: the Don Front, under the command of Lieutenant General Konstantin Rokossovsky,[23] and the Stalingrad Front, under the command of Yeryomenko) received reinforcements of soldiers and equipment. These maneuvers did not go undetected by the Germans, but intelligence officers, believing that the Soviet Union's reserves of materials and soldiers had been exhausted, assigned them no special importance.[24]

After a number of concerted drives in October, the 6th Army still had not taken complete control of Stalingrad. German observers strained to explain the enemy's unexpectedly bitter resistance. The lead article in the October 29, 1942, edition of the official SS newspaper *Das Schwarze Korps* began with an assessment of Soviet morale: "The Bolshevists attack until total exhaustion, and defend themselves until the physical extermination of the last man and weapon. [. . .] Sometimes the individual will fight beyond the point considered humanly possible." Everything the soldiers of the Wehrmacht had experienced in their campaigns in Europe and North Africa was like "a child's game compared with the elementary event of war in the East." The article accounted for this difference by evoking German racial biology. The Soviet soldiers originated from a "baser, dim-witted humanity" unable "to recognize the meaning and value of life." Owing to their purported absence of human qualities, the soldiers of the Red Army were thought to fight with a disregard for death that was foreign to culturally superior Europeans. The article concluded by depicting the threat for

Europe contained in the "power of this unleashed inferior race," and turned the battle of Stalingrad into a question of world historical destiny. "It is up to us to decide whether we remain human beings at all."[25]

On November 19, 1942, the Red Army finally began its counteroffensive, known as Operation Uranus, with a contingent of over 1 million soldiers. Motorized divisions advanced through the Romanian-controlled Don heights 150 kilometers west of Stalingrad. On November 24, the Soviet tank vanguard joined forces with Yeryomenko's tank divisions, which four days earlier had begun to push west from the area south of Stalingrad. The Germans and their allies were surrounded, trapped in what they referred to as a *Kessel*, or cauldron.

The 6th Army command deliberated whether to attempt a breakout, but Hitler ordered "Fortress Stalingrad" to be held at all costs. He called for an air bridge to supply the soldiers in the *Kessel* with food and munitions. This was not the first time Hitler had taken this route. In December 1941, when the Red Army began its counteroffensive outside Moscow, Hitler, who had recently named himself supreme commander of the army, issued an order forbidding retreat under the threat of severe punishment. Shrouding himself in the mystique of the strong-willed military leader whose job was to embolden his generals whenever they succumbed to "neurasthenia" and "pessimism," Hitler credited his decision with preventing the collapse of the Eastern Front despite strong attacks from the Red Army in the ensuing weeks.[26] In January 1942, Soviet forces nevertheless managed to encircle six German divisions—almost 100,000 soldiers—farther north near Demyansk at Lake Ilmen. Hitler responded by sending in planes to drop supplies. This continued for two months until a relief force broke through the Demyansk pocket from the outside at the end of March. It was this successful precedent that General Paulus thought of when he sought to reassure the trapped men of the 6th Army, concluding his November 27 communiqué with the line, "Hold on! The Führer will get us out!"[27]

But severe weather and heavy shelling hampered the Stalingrad airlift; the 300,000 encircled soldiers began to suffer from shortages of food and munitions. General Erich von Manstein launched Operation Winter Storm (December 12–23, 1942) in an effort to break through the encirclement with a panzer advance from the southwest,[28] but it became bogged down midway in the face of strong Soviet resistance. In the meantime the Red Army had initiated an offensive on the Don farther west known as Little Saturn. Its objective was to break through to Rostov in the south, stymieing the German relief force and cutting off the entire army group, along with the 400,000 troops stationed in the Caucasus. The offensive succeeded in part: although it forced Manstein to abort Operation Winter Storm, he was able to protect the army in the Caucasus from imminent strangulation.

At the end of November Soviet leaders began a massive propaganda campaign to persuade the Germans and their allies to surrender. Soviet aircraft dropped hundreds of thousands of leaflets written in German, Romanian, and Italian, describing the hopelessness of the situation. A delegation of German communist exiles in Moscow traveled to Stalingrad and broadcast political messages by loudspeaker, but their efforts to prevail on their countrymen on the other side of the front line were for naught. On January 6, two weeks after Manstein aborted his relief operation, General Rokossovsky offered Paulus terms for an honorable surrender. Under intense pressure from Hitler, the 6th Army commander ignored the deal.

The Soviets' final push to crush the encircled German troops, code-named Operation Ring, began on January 10. From the west, soldiers on the Don Front gradually drove the enemy back into the city. At the same time, the 62nd Army intensified its attacks from the banks of the Volga, and on January 26 it joined the Don Front at Mamayev Kurgan,[29] a strategic elevation south of the city's industrial district and for months the scene of fierce fighting. The Soviets cut the Germans into two pockets, one in the

Operation Ring. Soviet military drawing.

north, the other in the south. General Paulus, repeatedly forced to give up his quarters as the Red Army closed in, sought refuge for himself and his staff on January 26 with the 71st Infantry Division, the first unit to reach the Volga at Stalingrad; its commanders were now headquartered beneath a department store on the Square of the Fallen Heroes. On January 30, the tenth anniversary to the day when the Nazis assumed power, Hermann Göring gave a radio address that reached the soldiers in Stalingrad. Göring compared the Germans in Stalingrad to the heroes in the Song of the Nibelungs. Like those who "fought to the last man" during an "unmatched battle in a hall of fire and flame," the Germans in Stalingrad would fight—would have to fight—"for a people who can fight like this must win." On the night of January 31, Paulus received a signal from Hitler's headquarters saying that he had been promoted to field marshal. Everyone involved understood the message: never before had a German field marshal been taken prisoner; to avoid ignominy, Paulus would have to kill himself. Instead, he chose to defy his Führer.

In the morning hours of January 31, Soviet soldiers of the 64th Army surrounded the Square of the Fallen Heroes. A German officer emerged with a white flag and offered terms of surrender. A group of Red Army soldiers were escorted into the basement below the department store, where Paulus's army staff was assembled. (Chapter 2 contains a detailed eyewitness account of this encounter.) Several hours later, the German soldiers in the southern pocket threw down their weapons. In the northern pocket, intense fighting continued for two more days. It died down after the Red Army showered the German soldiers with photographs telling them of Paulus's surrender.[30] After the Soviet counteroffensive started but before the battle ended, 60,000 German soldiers died and 113,000 German and Romanian survivors were taken prisoner, many of them injured or exhausted. All in all, the battle and the subsequent imprisonment cost 295,000 German lives (190,000 on the battlefield, 105,000 in captivity). On the Soviet side, conservative estimates place the number of dead at 479,000, though one scholar has put the death toll at over a million.[31]

Nazi leaders responded to the defeat of the 6th Army by ramping up their propaganda and mass mobilization efforts. The sacrifice in Stalingrad, they believed, would motivate German soldiers in the fight to stem the "red tide" now moving west. No sooner had the three-day period of national mourning ended than Joseph Goebbels delivered his total war speech, met with frenzied applause from an audience of party loyalists. With the Red Army threatening to cross into Europe, the specter of "Bolshevik hordes" from "Asia," long invoked by Nazi propagandists, had become a real possibility; for the terrified population, fighting on seemed to be the only way out—and that's what happened, with greater intensity than before, as the war raged for two more years.

The Soviet side also ramped up the political pressure. The captured German generals and officers were held in a special camp and called on to publicly renounce Hitler. Their Soviet captors foresaw for them a role as leaders of a Soviet-friendly postwar German state. Most other prisoners were kept in work camps, where they received little to eat and poor medical care. By July 1943, three-quarters of all German prisoners in Soviet captivity had died.

When Red Army soldiers recaptured the city, they counted 7,655 civilian survivors.[32] As the cleanup began, the Soviets discovered mass graves filled with civilians the German occupiers had shot or hanged. Several thousand captured Germans were put to work in February 1943, clearing bodies and defusing bombs and mines. Eventually they would help rebuild the city.[33]

By the end of the battle, the scolding Stalin gave commanders in July 1942 had turned to praise, and he bestowed numerous honors on the Soviet military for its achievements. He complimented the Red Army as a "cadre army" and granted four field armies—the 62nd, the 64th, the 24th, and the 66th—the coveted Guards status. Stalin also rewarded himself, assuming the title Marshal of the Soviet Union on February 6, 1943.

INTERPRETATIONS OF THE BATTLE

Though widely researched and recounted, the battle of Stalingrad in most western depictions is a story of Germany's demise.[34] This narrative usually doesn't start until November 19, 1942, the day the Soviets encircled the 6th Army. This chronological framework transforms the aggressors into desperate victims—cold, hungry, fighting to defend themselves[35]—and omits the German attack on Stalingrad and the long trail of blood the soldiers of the 6th Army left behind as they forced their way through the Ukrainian cities of Berdichev, Kiev, and Kharkov.[36] Even the more comprehensive accounts, which start in June 1941 and include Soviet eyewitness reports, follow a German script, perfectly exemplified by the three-part TV documentary *Stalingrad: The Attack—The Kessel—The Doom* (2003).[37] The human drama of Stalingrad is often reduced to four numbers: the 300,000 German soldiers trapped in the *Kessel*, the 110,000 survivors taken into Soviet captivity, the 6,000 who eventually returned home, and the twelve years it took

Stalingrad, 1943. *Photographer: Natalya Bode*

them to get there. The extent of Soviet losses, by contrast, is rarely reported in the west. Unlike the overall portrayal of the Wehrmacht's activities on the Eastern Front, which in the past two decades has received significant critical reexamination (though not without some blanket simplifications), views on Stalingrad remain to this day strikingly complacent and insular, emphasizing the suffering of German soldiers and seldom bothering to mention their adversary.

Over the years, scholarly and public opinion in the west has offered a number of different narratives of Stalingrad. In the 1950s and 1960s, attention was focused on the figure of the battlefield soldier who upheld martial values to his dying breath. The former field marshal Erich von Manstein wrote in 1955 that the memory of the "unparalleled heroism, fidelity, and devotion to duty" of the soldiers who "starved, froze, and died" in Stalingrad will "live on long after the victors' cries of triumph have died away and the bereaved, the disillusioned, and the bitter at heart have fallen silent."[38] Their memory would not endure nearly as long as Manstein predicted. As society underwent changes—best symbolized by the student movements of the late 1960s—and as the field of *Alltagsgeschichte* (everyday history) emerged, the image of the valiant soldier was replaced by that of the antihero. The soldiers of Stalingrad became simple, clueless young men, who sometimes expressed themselves awkwardly in their letters, who were hurled into war, who seemed to share nothing of the Nazis' grand ambitions.[39]

In German popular memory, Stalingrad also connotes anti-Nazi resistance from within. Some historical evidence for this indeed exists. In February 1943 Hans and Sophie Scholl, members of the White Rose resistance group, distributed copies of what would be the group's final leaflet to students and faculty at the University of Munich. "The dead of Stalingrad implore us to take action," it read, calling for Germans to free themselves from the tyranny of National Socialism.[40] (This appeal fell on deaf ears, as did the antifascist manifestos later written by German prisoners of war in the Soviet Union.) Another possible source of resistance came from the Stalingrad veterans who claimed to have renounced Hitler and National Socialism amid battle.[41] But are their assertions credible? Did their disavowal really take place at the point they describe, or was it a view they first expressed in their memoirs?[42] One thing is certain: after Stalingrad, countless Germans followed the regime in a redoubled effort to prevent the tide of war from turning against them.[43]

The focus on the German drama at Stalingrad has left the Soviet side without well defined contours. Part of the problem was that the Germans who fought in Stalingrad didn't really know their adversary. For them, the

Soviets were a tawny-colored horde that rushed its opponent while crying out "Hurrah!" driven by pistol-waving political officers. These ideas carried over into official military studies of the postwar era. This should come as no surprise. The misconceptions were fed by propagandists of the Third Reich, and people like Franz Halder, Hitler's chief of general staff, later drew on racially fueled anticommunism to teach Americans about "the Russian soldier."[44]

Consequently we still lack a clear picture of how Red Army soldiers fought, of the cultural impressions they brought to bear on the war, what drove them as they fought against forces they believed were superior to their own, and what Stalingrad meant to them. Though Soviet historians cite the actions of many heroes, they fail to shed light on the specifics and the context. One exception is the Stalingrad veteran Alexander Samsonov. His study of the military strategy employed in the battle not only provides such details but is the only major work from a Soviet author to consider the German side as well.[45]

Many archives have opened since the dissolution of the Soviet Union, dramatically expanding our understanding of what is known in Russia as the Great Patriotic War, and the place of the battle of Stalingrad within it. This is largely owing to the efforts of Russian archivists and scholars, including those working in the Russian Security Service (FSB), who have presented a wealth of previously classified materials. These include detailed data on desertion, arrests, and executions inside the Red Army as well as secret reports by NKVD Special Section officers with analyses of the political moods among Soviet rank-and-file soldiers.[46] Moreover, a good number of uncensored memoirs, letters, and diaries from the war have been published, including the revealing diaries of Vasily Grossman and Konstantin Simonov, two writers who worked as war correspondents on the Stalingrad Front.[47] And yet, when it comes to the thoughts and attitudes Soviet citizens held during the war, the overall picture remains sketchy. The problem lies in part with the strictures of Soviet censorship, which ensured that with few exceptions Soviet wartime letters lacked exact place-names or detailed portrayals of events and beliefs. The other and larger part of the problem is that scores of human documents from the war—personnel files, secret surveillance materials, interrogation protocols, confiscated letters—continue to remain off-limits in the massive archival collections of Russia's Ministry of Defense.[48]

Historians continue to debate the motivations of Soviet soldiers. To what extent did they fight of their own free will, impelled by love of country, loyalty to the Soviet system, or to Stalin personally? To what extent was their engagement coerced? Antony Beevor argues for the latter. In his best-selling account of the battle he sharply criticizes the Soviet system for its "barely believable ruthlessness."[49] Beevor portrays the fighting in Stalingrad as not only a clash between Germans and Russians, but also a battle that Soviet leaders waged against their own population. From his perspective, one number in particular illustrates the inhuman character of the regime: General Chuikov's decision to execute around 13,500 Red Army soldiers unwilling to fight in the 62nd Army. Beevor refers to these killings in his preface and concludes his book by noting that "the thousands of Soviet soldiers executed at Stalingrad on his [Chuikov's] orders never received a marked grave."[50] But he does not provide convincing proof. He merely cites the military historian John Erickson, who speaks of 13,500 "reportedly" executed by firing squad.[51] Recently declassified materials, however, show that in the period from August 1 to October 15, 1942—one of the most critical phases of battle for the Red Army—278 Soviet soldiers were executed by the Soviet security police (NKVD) on the Stalingrad Front, of which the 62nd Army was only one part.[52]

The interviews published in this book make clear that violence, and especially the threat of violence, were widely applied in the Red Army, but they also suggest that western notions of mass executions on the Stalingrad Front need to be revised. Such notions are fully on view in the film *Enemy at the Gates* (2001). In the opening scene soldiers of the 284th Siberian Rifle Division are thrown into battle with insufficient weapons and munitions. Not surprisingly, the attack stalls and the soldiers retreat. They are immediately gunned down by an NKVD blocking detachment firing away with automatic weapons. The Stalingrad transcripts, which include conversations with two soldiers from the 284th Siberian Rifle Division, Major Nikolai Aksyonov and the celebrated sniper Vasily Zaytsev, the protagonist in *Enemy at the Gates,* show how far from reality this scene is.

In addition to presenting the battle predominantly from a German perspective, Beevor's book transports a number of clichés that originated in Nazi-era propaganda. For instance, he describes the will of soldiers to defend the Soviet Union to the point of self-sacrifice as "almost atavistic," an expression that recalls the "primitive" eastern enemy described by Goebbels and others.[53] Beevor is also convinced, without providing solid evidence, that Soviet troops in Stalingrad lived in permanent fear of political officers, the so-called commissars. By contrast, he praises Wehrmacht officers for their cultivation and gallantry, and revels in the image of "German gunners in shorts, with their bronzed torsos muscled from the lifting of shells" who "looked like athletes from a Nazi propaganda film."[54]

Had Beevor taken more time to study the other side, he would have read how Soviet citizens saw the shirtless German invaders as disrespectful and uncivilized.[55] As concepts, "primitive" and "civilized" are nothing more than free-floating, culturally dependent attributes.

If Beevor describes the Soviet soldiers as terrorized subjects, the British historian Catherine Merridale portrays them as betrayed victims. While the soldiers believed they were part of a struggle to liberate the Soviet Union from Nazi invaders, Stalin's regime kept them permanently oppressed in conditions tantamount to enslavement.[56] Merridale's social history of the Red Army offers vivid descriptions of the privation and hardship in soldiers' everyday lives, but she is less convincing when writing about their experiences of war. She argues that Soviet troops lived two different wars: "The first, the one that they alone could know, was the war of the battlefield, the scream war of shells and smoke, the shameful one of terror and retreat. But the other war, whose shape was crafted by writers, was the one that propaganda created."[57] The ideology that appealed to morality and promised a just war had, in Merridale's view, nothing to do with the soldiers' primary experience of war; it was something imposed externally. Yet as a method of analysis, the attempt to separate experience from ideology is dubious, for it assumes that individuals conceive experience outside values and linguistic expression. More to the point, the soldiers who speak in her book strongly identify with the public language and ideals of the time.[58]

In seeking to uncover the Soviet soldier's "real" experience, freed of state ideology, Merridale interviewed dozens of World War II veterans. Ironically, she discarded most of their testimony on the grounds that it parroted official views—as if the veterans had all succumbed to false consciousness.[59] Their association of moral ideals and patriotism with the war did not fit into Merridale's preconceived notion of war as nothing but suffering and disturbing violence. There was no place in her understanding for Red Army troops who identified with the state, the homeland, or socialist values.

Anyone who, like Merridale or Beevor, depicts the Soviet population as enslaved by the system cannot persuasively explain why millions of people fought against the Germans until they literally collapsed. More recent studies such as those by Yelena Senyavskaya, Amir Weiner, Lisa Kirschenbaum, and Anna Krylova address the central undying questions: how did the state convince large segments of the population to join the war effort, and what intellectual and psychological reserves did it unleash in the process? They describe how journalists, writers, and artists helped draft and distribute inspiring slogans; they investigate how the civil population wrested meaning from the hardship of war thanks to heroic appeals from the state; and they show how frontline soldiers began to understand themselves as actors in the Soviet regime.[60]

The Stalingrad transcripts make it possible for the first time to hear the voices of Red Army soldiers, hitherto virtually unknown, across a varied, nuanced spectrum. They give three-dimensional shape to the emotions, motives, and actions of individual soldiers—soldiers who saw themselves as active participants and embraced their combat roles, and thus provide support for the recent trend among scholars to see the Great Patriotic War as a people's war. But the interviews also reveal an element at odds with most western depictions: the Communist party's enormous effort to condition the troops.[61] The party was an ever-present institutional force in the form of political officers and ideological messages. It permeated all military levels and sent its emissaries—political officers, agitators, party and youth league secretaries—into the trenches, where they sermonized, provided counsel, encouraged and rallied the troops, explained the current state of affairs, and created meaning. The interviews show how this apparatus functioned, how it mobilized the soldiers, and how it responded to crises. The political officers denounced every trace of weakness as cowardice and counterrevolutionary treason while preaching self-discipline and heroism. Together with the secret police, the party placed the army in an iron yoke. But even when party officials doled out punishment, the intentions were corrective, seeking to instruct, motivate, and remake the troops.

Historians in the west have overlooked the Communist party's mobilizing function. This is partly because their access has been limited to official documents from political headquarters, which offer little insight into the everyday working of the political apparatus. But it is also because they tend to understand the party as solely repressive in nature, regarding its ideological work as a mere demonstration of political power. Also contributing to this oversight is the view of many military historians that the Communist party hampered the military, and that the Red Army did not become an effective combat force until the political officers were removed.[62] But in reality the party never left; indeed, its presence in the armed forces increased as the war continued.

The American historian Stephen Kotkin understands power and ideology in the early Soviet era in a way that helps illuminate conditions in the Red Army during World War II. Kotkin's local study on building socialism in a Soviet industrial city illustrates how the communist state, through targeted forms of speech and behavior, recast millions of rural immigrants and refugees in a socialist mold. Party agitators saw to it that workers not only met quotas but understood the political significance of the international class struggle. The regime grouped individuals into "shock brigades" and pitted them against each other in socialist competitions. Those who learned how to "speak Bolshevik" went on to have careers and felt part of the communist society and the grand future advertised by the regime.[63] But as many diaries and letters from the 1930s record, the internalization of socialist values did not take place by party directive alone; many Soviet citizens, especially the younger and better educated, saw the 1930s as a world-historical battle between an emergent communism and a crisis-shaken capitalism (of which fascism was part), and tried to shape their own lives in keeping with these high standards.[64] Many believed that they needed to prepare themselves for an inevitable conflict.[65]

These ideals, like indoctrinated forms of behavior and speech, did not vanish when war broke out; on the contrary. The Stalingrad transcripts document the further evolution of classic Soviet character traits from the 1930s: willful, optimistic, collectively minded, and accepting of violence.[66] After war erupted, the party brought its ideological conditioning to the factories and the work floors, pushing workers (by then mostly women) to meet the needs of the war industry. It put more of its agitators in battlefield trenches and shelters and sponsored new socialist competitions to see who could kill the most Germans. Judging by the medals and other distinctions awarded during the war, this renewed wave of subjectivation in Soviet society encompassed thousands of civilian workers and Red Army soldiers.

Kotkin's perspective emphasizes the interlocking nature of a party and society that reinforced each other. This characterization is at odds with the conviction of many researchers that Soviet society opposed the party and during the war years temporarily freed itself from the chains of Stalin's regime. The Russian literary scholar Lazar Lazarev, himself a veteran of the war, speaks of "spontaneous destalinization." He and others point out how, after the war began, the regime opened up greater freedoms in intellectual life; even the party newspaper *Pravda* became more honest in its reporting.[67] The chief proponent of this view was Vasily Grossman, a war correspondent in Stalingrad in the fall of 1942 who stayed longer than any other observer. His epic novel *Life and Fate* (1950–1959) is a monument to the Red Army soldiers who fought there.[68] Paradoxically, the novel describes the ruined city as a place of freedom. Party officers, stationed at the general staff command post at a safe distance from the fighting, have lost control of the city. As the old hierarchy breaks down, a commissar is sent to the city to inspect the situation. The open political conversations he hears horrify him, but he is fascinated by how the soldiers vouch for each other and by the sense of community that unites them. This spirit of fraternity and democracy reminds him of his youth and the early stages of the Russian Revolution. Grossman describes the flame of human freedom that burned for a short time in Stalingrad but went out again after the Germans were defeated and Stalin's state regained control over society.

Such thoughts are absent from Grossman's wartime writing. Even in his more candid and critical war diary he writes admiringly of communists who used their moral authority to raise the spirits of despondent Red Army soldiers. One diary entry describes a meeting with brigade commissar Nikolai Shlyapin. During a combat operation in Belorussia in July 1941 Shlyapin galvanized the surviving soldiers from his division and broke through the German lines. He was a man Grossmann described as "intelligent, strong, calm, big, and slow. People sense his inner power over them."[69] In the English translation of the diary, edited by Antony Beevor, Grossman's interview with Shlyapin is not included. Beevor removed the interview on the grounds that it was drenched in "contemporary Soviet clichés" and thus unimportant for modern readers. Grossman's interview with Shlyapin's adjutant, the political commissar Klenovkin, is also missing in Beevor's editions. The adjutant describes Shlyapin as a savior: "In combat the commissar walks calmly and slowly. 'Get over here, like this!' He acts as if there were no fighting at all. Everyone looks at him expectantly. 'The commissar is with us.'"[70] Klenovkin served as the inspiration for a key figure in Grossman's novel *The People Immortal* (1942).[71]

The spirit of Stalingrad, as Grossman understood it, consisted in the moral strength of ordinary soldiers who attained heroic status when they risked their lives to fulfill their civic duty. Some, though not all, of the commissars set a glowing example. For Grossmann, the war contained the promise of a moral renewal of the party and its relationship with Soviet society. Only years later did he realize that his hopes had been illusory, forcing him to rethink his experiences.[72] In *Life and Fate* Grossman's original enthusiasm for Soviet war heroes faded into a declared belief in individual freedom, as opposed to Stalin's regime.

Grossman, however, was not wrong about the political atmosphere during the war years: it had indeed become more liberal, as the party began to open itself to the outside (as the Stalingrad transcripts show). In particular, the party changed its criteria for admission. Earlier the litmus test had been knowledge of Marxist theory and a working-class background, but now it was military achievement. The party opened its doors to anyone who could demonstrate having killed Germans in battle. This is how many of the best soldiers were admitted to the party. Between 1941 and 1944, the number of party members in the army rose continuously, and by the end of the war the vast majority of commanders carried a membership book. In the process, not only did the composition of the party change but also the meaning of involvement. The party assumed more of a military quality and became closer to the people.[73] As the end of the war neared, however, the party leadership reversed course, tightening admission requirements and increasing vigilance within the ranks.[74]

Relying on incessant training and supervision, party officers generated a unified worldview among Red Army troops. The pervasiveness and effectiveness of political involvement in military units set the Red Army apart from other modern armies. Recent historical studies that discuss the question of why and how soldiers fight often point to loyalties and relationships built up within the most basic, "primary" fighting groups—the platoon or the company. They deem comradeship, or the "band of brothers" concept, of utmost importance and sometimes believe it to have universal value.[75] And yet these notions played a subordinate role in the Red Army. For one, the terrible casualty rate on the Soviet side consumed whole units in a matter of days and made it impossible for soldiers to develop personal cohesion. Moreover, communist authorities actively sought to suppress such ties: they feared that soldiers' particularist visions and desires might undermine their larger Soviet identity. Unlike the German army that filled its units with soldiers from the same region so as to buttress their regional identity (*Landsmannschaft*), the Soviet military mixed recruits from different nationalities, lest they turn nationalistic.[76] The cement that the Red Army command used to bind together diverse soldiers and motivate them to fight was ideology. Preached incessantly and targeting every recruit, it was made up of accessible concepts with an enormous emotional charge: love for the homeland and hatred of the enemy.

Several German observers in the war were impressed by the Soviet example. After the battle of Stalingrad they demanded that political training in the Wehrmacht be radically expanded, arguing that such training planted the decisive seed of military morale. In December 1943 Hitler created the position of National Socialist leadership officer (NSFO), which, unlike the commissars, came from the army but had to be confirmed by party leaders.[77] Because the military identity of soldiers and officers in the Wehrmacht lay outside politics, the reforms did not find acceptance. People poked fun at the leadership officer, calling him the "NSF zero." Political questions had a very different status in the Red Army, as even its name makes clear.[78]

REVOLUTIONARY ARMY

On February 23, 1943, three weeks after its victory at Stalingrad, the Red Army commemorated its twenty-fifth anniversary. A young army, it still showed traces of its origins in the Russian Revolution and the Civil War that followed (1917–1921). How present the revolutionary era was for many Soviet soldiers in Stalingrad can be illustrated by the interviews with General Vasily Chuikov and General Alexander Rodimtsev, who tell how they joined up with the Red Army in the commotion of the revolution and earned their spurs in the Civil War. But other links, institutional and intellectual, also existed between the Civil War and World War II. The Red Workers and Peasants Army—renamed the Soviet Army in 1946—understood itself as a new kind of revolutionary organization. It was "the world's first political army," equipped with an arsenal of words as well as weapons.[79] This ambition found striking expression in an early emblem of the Red Army, which depicted a gun and a book alongside the hammer and sickle.[80]

The Red Army began as a volunteer army fueled by the revolutionary spirit of armed workers, the so-called Red Guards. In the summer of 1918, when enemies closed around Soviet Russia, Leon Trotsky, as war commissar of the Red Army, introduced general conscription, opening the army for millions of soldiers from the countryside. Lenin was appalled as he watched the ragged recruits march across Red Square on the first anniversary of the October Revolution.[81] Yet from the outset the Bolsheviks tried to mold the members of the Peasants Army. They initiated mandatory instruction in reading, writing, and math and appealed constantly to the recruits' political consciousness in the hope they would fight for the new system from personal belief and conviction.[82] Toward the end of the Civil War, the Red Army consisted of 5 million soldiers, far more than necessary to defeat the Whites. For the Soviet leadership, the crucial motivation lay elsewhere: making sure that as many people as possible acquired the rudiments of socialism.

As Marxists, the Bolsheviks brought to the recruits a broad understanding of politics. Each was an actor on the world-historical stage; every thought and action carried political significance. The Bolsheviks wanted the recruits to internalize the message and fight of their own free will because they believed this would make them better soldiers and citizens. Their idea of humanity was thoroughly voluntarist: a person with a fully developed will could achieve anything. Soviet communists understood people as products of their environment and hence saw human nature as adaptable. Peasants unskilled in war were ignorant but they could learn. Deserters who showed remorse and recognized the error of their ways got a second chance. By contrast, deserters in the White Army were summarily executed, as was common practice in tsarist Russia.[83]

To monitor troops in their beliefs, Soviet leaders introduced a comprehensive system of political surveillance. During World War I many governments kept tabs on troop morale, but none went as far as the Bolsheviks. In the 1920s and 1930s and throughout World War II and after, military censors under the direction of the secret police screened all letters written by Red Army soldiers.[84] The letters were not sealed but folded into triangles, each bearing the censor's stamp and signature. In contrast, Wehrmacht mail inspectors made do with spot checks.[85]

The Soviet practice of surveillance always included an educational mission. The Bolsheviks wanted to educate the ignorant, convert the skeptical, and root out die-hard "counterrevolutionaries." Because the system of surveillance and education reached deeply into everyday life, Red Army soldiers were familiar with the moral categories of Soviet leaders. Faintheartedness, bourgeois values, and political indifference were anathema; open criticism of superiors in mail correspondence, inadvisable; selfless and heroic action, the ideal.

The Communist party had a strong institutional presence in the Red Army from the outset. The Bolsheviks formed party cells at all levels of the army down to the company. Commissars (*politruks* at the company level and *voenkoms* at the higher echelons) served as direct representatives of the government. Initially, their primary task was to monitor the military commander to whom they were assigned and with whom they held equal military rank. All orders issued by commanders required the express approval of their respective commissar.[86] This dual system of military and political leadership grew out of Trotsky's decision in the spring of 1918 to enlist thousands of former tsarist officers in the Red Army.[87] Trotsky believed that the military expertise of these "bourgeois specialists" would benefit the Soviet regime because the Red Workers and Peasants Army had so few experienced commanders. (Trotsky and other Bolsheviks purposely avoided the terms "officer" and "soldier," which they associated with the hierarchies and class differences of the tsarist army. Instead, they spoke of "Red Army men" or "fighters." Any mention of "soldiers" referred to enemy troops.) Many other Bolsheviks, including Stalin and his associate Kliment Voroshilov, disagreed with Trotsky. They found former members of the tsarist army repulsive both personally and politically. The conflict between Stalin and Trotsky smoldered for several years before erupting publicly.

A portrayal of the relationship between the commissar and the commander is found in Dmitri Furmanov's autobiographical novel *Chapayev* (1923). Furmanov was a provincial teacher before joining the Bolshevik party in 1918 and entering the Red Army the following year. There he served as the commissar for divisional commander Vasily Chapayev as they fought side by side against Admiral Alexander Kolchak's White Army in the Urals. In his novel, Furmanov depicts Chapayev as a brash go-getter, brimming with a peasant's anarchistic fervor. The unit's commissar, a disciplined fighter and a patient teacher, must harness Chapayev's energy if the backwoods commander is to benefit the revolution. Over the course of many conversations the commissar instills a higher political consciousness in the physically powerful but mentally malleable Chapayev.

In 1934 the novel was adapted into a film, establishing Chapayev as a heroic Soviet icon. Stalin had seen the film dozens of times within a year and a half of its release. He knew the scenes and dialogue by heart and reanalyzed the actors and plot at every screening.[88] Several of the soldiers interviewed in Stalingrad mentioned Chapayev, and a gunboat in the Volga Military Flotilla bore his name.

Interestingly, the film contains a subplot not found in the novel: a budding romance between two supporting characters, Chapayev's adjutant Petya and a machine gunner named Anka. Initially not taken seriously by Petya, Anka proves herself by valiantly repelling an attack by the Whites. In a pivotal scene, the enemy troops, dressed in regal uniforms and marching in full formation—as the film makes clear, the purpose is intimidation—close in on the outnumbered Reds. Anka's comrades are eager to fire their guns and storm the enemy troops, but Anka waits until they are almost on top of her before opening fire, furiously cutting them down with a Maxim machine gun. Her actions inspired many young women to enlist in 1941[89] and symbolized the presence of mind and strength of will vaunted by the Bolsheviks. But the psychological intimidation depicted in the film was a fantasy, fed by the belief that the enemy sought to break communist will. Red Army soldiers in Stalingrad spoke repeatedly of German "psychic attacks." In all likelihood this impression had more to do with *Chapayev* than with the actual intentions of the enemy.[90]

The culture of the Red Army during the Civil War was marked by not only political mobilization but also raw physical violence. Many of the commanders interviewed in Stalingrad cut their teeth as young men in the Civil War. The future army commander Vasily Chuikov learned how to cement his authority with beatings and executions. Writer Isaak Babel, working as a war correspondent, described how the commander Semyon Timoshenko, "a colossus in red half-leather trousers, red cap, well-built," whipped his regiment officers with a riding crop and shot at them with his pistol to drive them into battle. Babel also observed Kliment Voroshilov—later a confidant of Stalin's and part of the Soviet political and military leadership in World War II—berating a divisional commander in front of his troops while riding to and fro on horseback.[91] Babel recorded brutal violence among the troops, executions of Polish prisoners of war, and assaults on Jews and other civilians. Although horrified, he continued to express his admiration for the soldiers' heroic deeds and convictions, which he helped foster in his reports from the war zone.

STALIN'S CITY

Joseph Stalin and the city named after him had their own Civil War experiences. Until 1925 Stalingrad bore the name Tsaritsyn, a Tatar word meaning "city on the yellow river" in reference to the Tsaritsa, which flows into the Volga at Stalingrad. The city's location on the Volga and on a railway line stretching from Moscow to the Caucasus made it into a transportation and trade hub for southern Russian and had promoted industrial development there since the nineteenth century. The weapons factory in Tsaritsyn, founded in 1914 and renamed the Red Barricades after the revolution, was the largest munitions manufacturer in Europe. The area around Tsaritsyn was one of the first burning points in the Civil War. After the Bolsheviks seized power, many tsarist officers fled to the Cossack settlements in the Don and Kuban regions where they formed a volunteer army in the spring of 1918 to mobilize against the new rulers. They received logistical support from the German occupying powers in the Ukraine. In May 1918 Stalin, as people's commissar of nationalities, was tasked with boosting the food supply from the northern Caucasus. Due to fighting, the train carrying Stalin and his Red Army troops got stuck in Tsaritsyn, where they joined forces with the 10th Army, which had been cobbled together from partisans under the command of Voroshilov. Meanwhile, the White Army, together with an allied Cossack army under the direction of Ataman Pyotr Krasnov, had pushed forward from the south and the west toward the city. Although Stalin's assignment was civilian in nature and he had no military experience, he seized the reins. In a letter to Lenin, he demanded that General Andrei Snesarev, the commander of the Red Army in the northern Caucasus military district who still wore his tsarist epaulets, be fired. Lenin gave in to Stalin's pressure. In the middle of August 1918 Stalin declared the city under siege and ordered the city's bourgeoisie to dig trenches. The Soviet defenders spoke of Tsaritsyn as a "Red Verdun" that would never surrender to the Whites and the foreign meddlers who backed them. A counterattack pushed the enemy troops behind the Don, but by September Krasnov's troops had recovered their ground. Once again, there was a conflict between Stalin and a former tsarist commander in the service of the Red Army, and once again it ended with the commander's dismissal. Trotsky, furious, ordered Stalin back to Moscow immediately. Yet by the middle of October the Red Army had ended the White assault on Tsaritsyn.[92]

Stalin's role in saving the city is contested. First after his death, and again after the Soviet Union fell apart, critics have raised doubts about Stalin's military acumen in view of the heavy losses.[93] But at the time, some admired Stalin for his brutal approach. Writing in 1919, an officer in the White Army who had infiltrated the Red Army as a spy during the siege of Tsaritsyn stressed the effectiveness of Stalin's ruthless measures. He cites one example where Stalin, convinced that the city's bourgeoisie harbored counterrevolutionary sentiments, had several dozen officers and civilians placed on a barge, which he threatened to blow up if city residents did not side with the Red Army. The officer also attested to Stalin's great skills as an agitator:

> He would often say in his arguments about military skill: "It's fine if everyone is talking about the need for military skill, but if the most talented general in the world does not have a conscientious soldier educated by the right kind of agitation, believe me, he won't be able to do anything with a bunch of motivated revolutionaries, however few in number." And Stalin, in accordance with his conviction, spared no means on propaganda, on the publication and distribution of newspapers, on dispatching agitators.[94]

Thanks to Stalin, the White spy continued sadly, the city bore the name "Red Tsaritsyn." The officer also explained the many casualties on the Soviet side: they had resulted from his successful disinformation.

By the end of the Civil War, Tsaritsyn had been besieged multiple times, yet in Soviet memory the defense of the city was associated with Stalin even before it was renamed in 1925. In the 1930s the Stalingrad cult began to bloom. After the success of *Chapayev*, the Vasiliev brothers began work on a movie about the defense of Tsaritsyn. The filming encountered delays, and the first part was not released in theaters until April 1942.[95] The film follows the same template as *Chapayev*, with Voroshilov behind a Maxim gun, single-handedly fending off an attack designed to intimidate the Reds. But here it was not the Whites but the Germans (equipped anachronistically with Wehrmacht helmets) on the opposing side. The tsarist general serving under the Bolsheviks wants to give up Tsaritsyn, but Stalin resists. "In order to be victorious, one has to fight." The film culminates with Stalin delivering an address to the workers of Tsaritsyn: "An honest death is better than mean, slavish life. [. . .] Onward for the motherland!"

The striking parallels between the *Defense of Tsaritsyn* and the defense of Stalingrad may be coincidental, but they also suggest that the Civil War era and its legends acted as a template for World War II. As in the battle of Tsaritsyn, Stalin prohibited the evacuation of his namesake city, declared a state of siege, and demanded self-sacrifice from residents. Civil War veterans gave rousing speeches in the city and on the front, and one of the City Defense Committee's first appeals to city residents after the German assault began with the following call to arms:

> Like 24 years ago, our city is again experiencing hard times. [. . .] In the momentous 1918 our fathers held Red Tsaritsyn against the onslaught of the gangs of German hirelings. And we ourselves shall hold Red Stalingrad in 1942. We shall hold it so that then we may drive back and destroy the bloodthirsty gang of German occupiers [. . .] Everybody to the construction of barricades! Everybody capable of bearing arms to the barricades, to the defense of the native city, the native home![96]

On November 6, 1942, one day before the public holiday commemorating the October Revolution, Soviet newspapers printed an open letter to Stalin signed by commanders and soldiers from the 62nd Army. The signatories swore to Stalin and their "fathers, the gray-haired defenders of Tsaritsyn," that they would defend Stalingrad "till the last drop of blood, till the last breath."[97] The Moscow historians who visited Stalingrad in December 1942 were not immune to the spell of the Civil War. Several were recognized specialists in the field; one had published a documentary history on the defense of Tsaritsyn several months earlier.[98] In the historical memory of many Soviet participants to the battle, the Civil War figured very prominently, shrouded in a mystique of heroic magnitude and revolutionary zeal.

PREWAR ERA

In the years after the Civil War the Red Army shrank from 5 million soldiers to 1.5 million. But this did not deter the Soviet government from preparing for a global showdown between capitalist and socialist camps. In Bolshevik fashion, Stalin spoke to an assembly of industrial executives in 1931, pointing out that Soviet Russia was currently lagging "fifty to one hundred years behind" developed nations and exhorting the managers to close the gap by 1941: "We must cover this distance in ten years, or we will be crushed."[99]

Like other governments, the Soviet Union made three major investments that enabled it to wage war effectively in the twentieth century. It launched a national industrialization campaign to equip a large army; it prepared its population for impending war; and it created human reserves to feed the industrial cycle of mass production and mass killing. The nationalized economy and the one-party system enabled Soviet leaders to take measures that were more sweeping and more ruthless than those of rival states during the interwar period. Socialist planners approached industrialization like a war. They deployed superproductive "shock workers," achieved "breakthroughs," celebrated "triumphs" over nature, and fought against the machinations of "class enemies." The backbone of this campaign consisted of the Communist party and its youth organization, the Komsomol. The party dispatched armed delegations from an "army of revolutionary warriors,"[100] whose job was to force recalcitrant populations in rural areas onto collective farms. This violent expansion of socialism took place at the expense of much of the population, who had to learn to live with rationing and privation—while increasing productivity. In 1940 the government passed laws punishing tardiness at work as severely as desertion. Though the system demanded much from citizens, it also held out a promise. Every worker who took part could become a "builder of socialism," a part of the system and an actor on the world-historical stage.

Like other states in the interwar period, the Soviet government encouraged citizens to start families in an effort to increase the birth rate, but it also tied these pro-family policies to a comprehensive premilitary education. In 1931 the Komsomol introduced a military sports program in which millions of adolescents learned how to shoot rifles and throw grenades. By 1933, a Komsomol offshoot, the Society for the Assistance to Defense, Aviation, and Chemical Construction, had 10 million men and 3 million women members, who received flight training and practiced parachuting.[101] The Soviet new person—an ideal that expressly included women—was strong of will, full of fight, fearless, and optimistic. Even the youngest Soviet citizens were sworn to military discipline and allegiance to the collective as members of the party's pioneer organization.[102] Their literary paradigm was another hero from the Civil War: Pavel Korchagin, from Nikolay Ostrovsky's bestselling novel *How the Steel Was Tempered* (1934). Korchagin was a Komsomol and a soldier who strove to "work on himself" and benefit society even after being severely wounded in battle.

Ever since Japan invaded Manchuria in 1931, war had been a real danger for the Soviet Union. Beginning in 1935 the Soviet press portrayed fascist Germany as the main enemy. The Spanish Civil War (1936–1939)—in which Stalin supplied the Republicans with weapons and advisers—received sympathetic coverage, and even found its way into the diaries of village residents.[103] The successful play *The Final Battle* (1931) showcased Soviet citizens' belief that war was imminent. The final scene shows a group of twenty-seven Red Army soldiers defending the border against an imperialist enemy. In a hail of machine gun fire, all die but one. The injured survivor drags himself to a blackboard, where, just before collapsing, he writes, "162,000,000-27 = 161,999,973." At that point a man walks out on stage and addresses the audience. Invariably the following exchange would take place. The man would ask, "Who is in the army?" and a few members of the audience would stand up. Then he would ask, "Who is a reservist?" and more would stand up. Finally he would ask, "Who will defend the Soviet Union?" and the entire audience would stand up. "Show's over," the man would announce. "To be continued on the front."[104] The avant-garde device—tearing down the barrier between the stage and the audience—sought to activate spectators as militarized participants. "The final battle" were words straight out of "The Internationale," an anthem familiar to every Soviet child.

War preparations included a massive expansion of the Red Army, but the process was erratic and tense. In 1937 the deputy people's commissar of defense, Marshal Mikhail Tukhachevsky, together with seven other generals, was accused of high treason and espionage and sentenced to death. Stalin's distrust of Tukhachevsky, a brilliant military strategist but also the son of a noble family and a former lieutenant in the tsarist army, seems to have precipitated the purge. The confessions of the accused, extracted under torture, led to further arrests. By 1939 more than 34,000 officers had been expelled from the Red Army. In the meantime the regime had broadened the original 1925 mandate of the people's commissar for the purposes of monitoring military commanders deemed politically unreliable.[105]

The scope of the Red Army purges was probably less than has long been assumed, however.[106] It is certainly the case that Nikita Khrushchev exaggerated their extent in order to pin the blame for the devastating defeats in 1941 on his predecessor. In truth, most of the 34,000 officials excluded from the Communist party escaped execution: 11,000 had reentered the party by 1939 after lodging successful appeals; less than half of the remaining 23,000 became caught in the tentacles of the NKVD, but most cases were not political and resulted in minor sanctions. Many of the dismissed officers later sought to prove their loyalty. Guards General Major Nestor Kozin was among the soldiers interviewed in Stalingrad. Like most victims of Stalin's terror, Kozin sincerely believed that the purges were meant for enemies and a mistake had been made in his case:

> Why I was kicked out of the party. The formal reason for the expulsion was that divisional commander Balakiryev turned out to be an enemy of the people, and they accused me of not being vigilant enough. All I said was that the political chief, the deputy, the entire political department, along with the top commanders—all of them party members—missed that he was an enemy of the people. But here I—a platoon commander—was meant to see what kind of man he was. They called it "spreading anti-Soviet rumors." Long story short—they kicked me out of the party.[107]

Further in his defense, Kozin explained that he was unable to command his troops during the 1939 Soviet invasion of Finland because, having been deemed politically unreliable, he had to prove himself first as an instructor (which he did with flying colors). He joined the Great Patriotic War immediately and was awarded the Order of Lenin within several months. In December 1941 he was reaccepted into the party. Most commanders interviewed in Stalingrad were young, part of a group of majors and captains who advanced after their superiors were demoted and went on to have impressive careers.

ARMY AND PARTY IN WAR

Despite—or because of—its massive expansion between 1938 and 1941, the Red Army was poorly equipped for the German attack in June 1941. The impressive number of Red Army soldiers enlisted by that time—5 million versus 1.6 million in January 1938[108]—obscured the fact that most of the recruits, assembled near the Polish border, were inexperienced and poorly trained. When the Hitler-Stalin pact put half of Poland in the Soviet Union's sphere of influence, the Red Army positioned its soldiers close to the new border, where they could repel an enemy attack quickly and decisively. They erected a wall immediately behind the border, mostly with materials taken from the old line of defense, known by the Germans as the Stalin line. When war broke out, the new wall was still incomplete and the old one half demolished; neither provided significant protection.

The first phase of the Soviet Union's wartime production favored quantity over quality, especially when it came to aerial forces. When the Germans invaded, Soviet warplanes lacked radio equipment, making effective communication with ground troops and other aircraft impossible,[109] and the pilots and airplane mechanics were inadequately trained. As a result, in the first year of the war Germany managed to immobilize almost the entire Soviet air force, a large part on the ground in the Blitz raids of June 1941. By the end of 1941, the Soviet Union had lost more than 10,000 aircraft. Another 10,000 machines were inoperative due to breakdowns and mechanical defects. Germany incurred fifteen times fewer losses during the same period.[110] Many of the Red Army soldiers interviewed in Stalingrad noted the poor performance of the Soviet air force and Germany's absolute air superiority in the summer and fall of 1942. The soldiers criticized the poor coordination within the armed services and the lack of experience in mechanized and mobile warfare. In 1942 the Red Army improved its coordination, as well as its military hardware, especially with the introduction of the T-34 tank and the Pe-2 dive bomber, which the Germans came to respect and fear.[111]

The Soviets were up against a 4 million man army that possessed superior technology, well-rehearsed tactical maneuvers, and almost two years of uninterrupted combat experience. The Wehrmacht's arsenal comprised first-rate reconnaissance, tested coordination between tank troops, air force, and infantry, and a proven artillery that could unleash devastating barrages. Hitler and his generals believed that they could deliver a death blow to the Red Army with deep pincer movements. This strategy yielded hundreds of thousands of prisoners, but it did not break the Red Army's will. The Wehrmacht lost 185,000 men on the Eastern Front in the first three months of battle, almost twice as many as it had since June 1941.[112]

The German leadership was oblivious to the strong backing the Soviet regime received from its people and its ability to mobilize a seemingly inexhaustible number of troops. Just as Nazi Germany was skilled militarily, the Soviet system was well versed politically: with a push of a button it could launch a political campaign, exhorting citizens to go above and beyond. One example was the evacuation of industry after the German invasion on June 22, 1941. Within six months, the Soviets completely dismantled 1,500 large plants and relocated their machinery and workers to the east. As Soviet leaders had not reckoned with the Germans advancing so far into the country, no evacuation plans had been drawn up in advance. The massive campaign worked because it was executed in the command economy style that the Soviets had employed successfully for many years.[113] The regime sought to raise the fighting spirit of civilians and soldiers against the "fascist aggressors," just as the Russian empire had in the Patriotic War of 1812. Stalin appealed to his people's love for country, calling on his "brothers and sisters" to fight a "just war" that would end in either Soviet liberation or German enslavement. The many thousands of Soviet citizens, men and women alike, who volunteered for the front in the first weeks of the war confirmed the effectiveness of his appeal.

Owing to the enormous losses sustained by the Red Army in the initial months—by December 1941, 3 million soldiers had been killed or captured[114]—the military leadership kept expanding the pool of potential recruits. From late 1941 on, it began sending non-Slavic soldiers to the front, though their political loyalty and military ability were considered suspect. By 1945, 8 million people besides the Slavs—Uzbeks, Kazaks, Tatars, Latvians, and others—had joined the Red Army, close to one-fourth of the 34 million who enlisted during the war.[115] The high number of casualties compelled Stalin to conscript women into the Red Army, in particular female Komsomols who had volunteered in the summer of 1941 but had yet to be cleared for armed combat. Over the course of several recruitment waves beginning in 1942, a total of 1 million women entered the armed forces.

The inexperience of the recruits led to panicked retreats, especially in the first months of war, prompting Soviet commanders to take drastic measures. Following a method implemented in the Civil War and then again in the Winter War,[116] they deployed blocking squads ordered to shoot soldiers who were unwilling to fight and could not be persuaded in any other way.

Order no. 270, issued by Stalin in August 1941, branded any Red soldier captured alive a traitor to his country.[117] The family members of imprisoned troops saw their benefits cut; wives of captive officers were often sent to labor camps. At the same time, the regime appealed to the soldiers' sense of honor and sought to raise the morale of the commanders. As in the tsarist army, units that distinguished themselves through bravery and perseverance were granted Guards status. Leading the way in September 1941 were four divisions, "divisions of heroes," as the army newspaper *Red Star* put it, their ranks "welded together like steel, firm and unshakable."[118]

Soviet leaders put most of their stock in the political mobilization of Red Army soldiers. They banked on the influence of the Communist party and sought to increase it at every turn. As the war progressed, the number of party members in the Red Army rose steeply, and by July 1945 there were 2,984,750 party members, more than one in four, up from 654,000 at the war's onset. Between 1941 and 1945 membership in the Young Communist League tripled to 2,393,345 soldiers who were Komsomol members. Taken together, these figures amount to a strongly communist army by war's end.[119] This development was consistent with

General Chuikov (pictured on the far left) presents the commander and the commissar of the 39th Rifle Division (both kneeling) with the Guards title in Stalingrad, January 3, 1943. The ceremony took place on the steep banks of the Volga. The division soldiers (outside the picture) kneel before the commanding officers. *Photographer: Georgy Samsonov*

the party's earlier expansions—during the Civil War, when party membership increased by 600 percent, and once again during the first five year plan. By contrast, party membership contracted in the wake of the political purges (in 1921, 1933–1939, and starting again in 1944).

To acquire as many new members as possible in a short period of time, the party simplified its admission criteria. In December 1941 the Central Committee shortened the trial period for new candidates from one year to three months. Moreover, applicants no longer needed to submit recommendations from longtime party members. Pragmatic considerations dictated some of these changes. The previous system was time-consuming and impractical in wartime, especially when the objective was to increase membership. Another obvious factor was the changing character of the party.[120] Soldiers who before the war had stood no chance of membership were now achieving glory and honor as party comrades. Captain Alexander Olkhovkin, the propaganda instructor for the 39th Guards Division, spoke of one such soldier in his interview. On November 19, 1942, some men from his division met to discuss the circulation of the general attack order. Olkhovkin joined the meeting as a sniper was speaking. The sniper, Olkhovkin remarked, was "completely uneducated. This is how he talks: 'We was about to go on the attack.' He'd say, 'I knowed I was gonna be a sniper today.' Before that he was a runner for the battalion commander. This man—Afonkin was his name—started working as a sniper. Over the course of eighteen days he racked up thirty-nine Hitlerites. Now he's been admitted to the party and decorated."[121]

In the war years the idea of a good party comrade was quite simple. A successful candidate had to prove that he had killed a German soldier, shot down an enemy plane, or taken out a panzer. Soldiers received forms known as "vengeance accounts" to record the number of opponents they killed and the number of weapons they destroyed. A soldier with an empty account had no chance of being admitted to the party.[122] By contrast, someone like the sniper Vasily Zaytsev rose immediately to communist status—the number of Germans he killed was recommendation enough. As Zaytsev explained, "I thought, How can I join the party when I don't know the program? I read the program and wrote my application right there in a trench. Two days later I was summoned to a party commission. By then I'd killed sixty Germans. I'd been decorated."[123]

The ideal communist in wartime was occasionally described as bloodthirsty. Consider Colonel Nikolai Glamazda's description of the final battle of a commissar named Yudayev, who led an assault unit in the 253rd Regiment of the 45th Division. When storming a German bunker, his:

> rifle was knocked out of his hands by a grenade fragment. Comrade Yudayev rushed at one of the unarmed Germans, grabbed him by the throat, and strangled him. The Germans threw in some reinforcements and again pounced on that handful of heroes. Yudayev was raised by the Germans on their bayonets but wouldn't let go of his victim. Impaled and raised on bayonets, he was still holding on to his strangled German. So he had strangled him and died on the bayonets himself. The Germans overran that trench but after some time that company kicked them out of the dugout, took that hero Yudayev, and buried him by the third workshop of the Red October plant.[124]

Colonel Dobryakov, the deputy director of the political department of the 64th army, described a similarly violent scene:

> The battery commander of the 154th Marine Brigade was put in charge of the defense. He had thirteen men including himself. He was ordered not to engage the Germans under any circumstances because he had so few men and the Germans were already advancing. He couldn't bring himself to stay put, yelled "Hurrah!," and attacked a company that was supported by machine guns. He drove them out, killing seven Germans himself. During that assault a piece of flesh was torn from his side. He went up to the brigade commander, Colonel Smirnov, and asked: "Comrade Colonel, can I have a little something to drink?"
>
> "Yes, of course," said the colonel.
>
> And then the wounded battery commander held up that piece of flesh and asked: "Do you suppose this is worth seven Germans?"[125]

Needless to say, the missing flesh from the commander's body guaranteed his admission to the party.

As the war raged on, the party extended its influence by tailoring its political efforts to circumstances on the battlefield. Retaliation for the suffering inflicted by the enemy and the will to victory constituted a common denominator among the soldiers. "We are communists; we will avenge our murdered soldiers, commanders, and political officers." To the mind of Ivan Vasiliev, commissar of the 62nd army, this expressed the overwhelming mood in the battle for Stalingrad.[126] General Chuikov relayed to Vasily Grossman the hands-on quality of political education: "Political work:

everything has only one purpose, and everything is done together with the soldiers. As for isms—communism, nationalism—we weren't doing that." Nevertheless, as Chuikov stressed when interviewed by historians, Soviet soldiers in Stalingrad demonstrated a high level of political consciousness.[127] He meant that Red Army soldiers had internalized the "patriotic duty" promoted by the party to hold Stalingrad at all costs. For Chuikov, this was the essential reason for Soviet victory.

During the battle of Stalingrad the Communist party made an extra effort to deepen its influence. Between August and October 1942, the number of party members on the Stalingrad Front increased by 25,000, reaching a total of 53,500.[128] By November membership surpassed 60,000.[129] These numbers do not take into account battlefield losses and need an upward correction for an accurate total. Major Yakov Serov, the political department director of the 45th Division, provided some unit-level specifics. In the first months of the battle of Stalingrad, the 45th Division had 840 party members, of whom 163 died in battle and 405 were sidelined by injuries. During the same period, 659 additional soldiers joined the party. "People took joining the party very seriously and applied only when they had six, seven, ten Fritzes[130] to their name. One would show up and claim: I have killed ten Fritzes. Here is my certificate. No commando would apply before opening his [vengeance] account." Conveying what party membership meant for soldiers, Serov quoted from their applications:

> Junior Sergeant Ivan Sleptsov of the 178th Artillery Regiment expressed this wish: "In the fight with beastly fascism I want to be a communist. I will smite the enemy until my eyes can see and my hands can rotate the elevation and traverse wheels of my cannon. I will not disgrace the lofty rank of a Bolshevik warrior in the fight for the motherland. I ask to be admitted to the ranks of the Communist party, I ask that my request be granted. In these trying times when the destiny of mankind lies in the balance, our party is leading us to victory. I want to become its member, and under its banner my strength and hatred for the occupiers will grow ever more. The single-mindedness of the party is my own single-mindedness, and should I fall in battle, the party will avenge me. I swear to be its faithful member, to be its faithful defender to my last drop of blood."
>
> And here is the application of Novitsky, a sergeant-major in our reconnaissance unit: "In these trying times when the destiny of mankind lies in the balance, our party is leading us to victory.

> I want to become its member, and under its banner my strength and hatred for the occupiers will grow ever more. The single-mindedness of the party is my own single-mindedness, and should I fall in battle, the party will avenge me. I swear to be its faithful member, to be its faithful defender to my last drop of blood."[131]

The high casualty rates in the battle of Stalingrad supplied additional impetus to join the party. Party functionaries tried to persuade soldiers to submit their applications before combat. This way they could be certain of finding a place in the communist pantheon if they were killed. "They don't want to join the Komsomol before entering combat," reported 2nd Lieutenant Nikolai Karpov, the Komsomol secretary in the 38th Motorized Rifle Brigade. "They start looking for an excuse—'let's wait till after this fight.' I put it to them bluntly: 'How can you go fight? If you're killed, you'll die without being politically conscious. But if you die as a member of the Komsomol, you will die in glory.' I got six people to join the Komsomol that way."[132] Several political officers reported that seriously injured soldiers asked to enter the party so they could die as communists. Sergeant Alexander Duka, also of the 38th Rifle Brigade, explained how the thought of death motivated him to join the party.[133]

COMMANDERS AND COMMISSARS

The Communist party was ultimately governed by Joseph Stalin, the general secretary of the Central Committee. Known as the "boss" (*khozyain*) and the "leader" (*vozhd*), Stalin headed every institution relevant to the war effort from 1941 on: the State Committee for Defense, the People's Commissar for Defense, and the Supreme High Command of the Red Army (the Stavka). The party made its influence felt in the military through the Main Political Administration of the Red Workers and Peasants Army (GlavPURKKA). In the war's first year the administration was led by the former *Pravda* editor and communist rabble-rouser Lev Mekhlis. In 1942 the Moscow party secretary Alexander Shcherbakov succeeded him. That same year, Shcherbakov became a Politburo candidate member, a promotion that underlined the prominence of his office in the Red Army.

The political administration exerted its power primarily via the commissars. At the highest levels, at the front and in the army, the commissar served on the military council, a cooperative body consisting of commanders, political delegates, and the chief of staff. Stalin's confidant Nikita

Military council of the Stalingrad Front, 1942. *Left to right*: Commissar Nikita Khrushchev, Lieutenant General Alexei Kirichenko, regional party secretary Alexei Chuyanov, and Colonel General Andrei Yeryomenko. *Photographer: Oleg Knorring*

Khrushchev served as the commissar for the Stalingrad Front. Along with front commander Yeryomenko, he was the most important figure in the military council. This dual system extended to all levels of the army, though most of the political work took place in the regiments. The system provided for two offices and their respective secretaries, one for the party, the other for the Komsomol, as well as a club for the soldiers and a library, all under the oversight of the regiment's commissar. In the companies the politruks served as agitators in political discussions with soldiers and were responsible for finding suitable candidates for party membership. In 1942, the political administration installed party cells in the companies as well.[134]

All Red Army newspapers, from *Red Star* (*Krasnaya Zvezda*), the official military broadsheet, to division newsletters, were under the control of GlavPURKKA. The Main Political Administration also recruited war correspondents, among them the notable Soviet writers Ilya Ehrenburg, Vasily Grossman, Konstantin Simonov, Vsevolod Vishnevsky, and Alexei Tolstoy—and pursued a variety of cultural initiatives to raise the morale of Red Army soldiers such as the circulation of army songs and literary works. The Soviet secret police, the NKVD, also had a broad presence in the Red Army. In every division, a Special Department (*Osoby otdel*) of uniformed secret police officers investigated cases of murder, suicide, theft, espionage, and desertion, made arrests, and delivered suspects to military tribunals—tasks that in other armies fell to the military police. The Special Department was also charged with ensuring the political loyalty of soldiers, commanders, and political officers and with reporting signs of counter-revolutionary sentiment. Working together with the military censor, also under the control of the NKVD, and with secret informers, the Special Department prepared weekly reports (sometimes more frequently) about the troops' "political-moral moods" for Stalin's desk.[135] The men of the Special Department, known as Osobists, were widely feared.[136] Every soldier and officer, regardless of rank, faced general political and moral suspicion. In an anonymous letter to Stalin, Mekhlis, and several leading military brass, a commander described the allure of being an Osobist. The letter, written in May 1943, provides insights (some unintended) into the habits of powerful men in the Red Army.

> A commander cannot make a decision without an Osobist. Women have been taken away from commanders, and each Osobist has one or two. At each step they threaten Mekhlis, and the commanders now are in quite an unenviable state. Most of them have been defending their motherland, risking life and limb, and are decorated with four to eight orders. Why is it so? Can it be that 1937, 1938 is back?[137]

Being interviewed by a historian in Stalingrad, Major Anatoly Soldatov, of the 38th Motorized Rifle Brigade, described how he nearly shot an Osobist during the capture of General Paulus. The intelligence officer had brashly inserted himself into the action in a bold attempt to claim Stalingrad's greatest trophy for the NKVD.[138]

On October 9, 1942, Stalin issued an order that eliminated the system of Red Army commissars and reinstituted single command authority. Many historians have argued that Stalin intended the order to strengthen the status of army officers and weaken the party's influence on the Red Army.[139] It is true that the decision bolstered the authority of commanders—former commissars now served as subordinate "deputies for political affairs"—and that the commissars' vague mandate (keeping military officers in line) ran the risk of "trammeling" effective troop leadership, as stated explicitly in the order.[140] But the reform contained no barbs directed at the party or its presence in the military. Ever since the Red Army's establishment, the commissar system had come into effect whenever the political climate grew uncertain—during the Civil War, in the period from 1937 to 1940, and then again starting in July 1941. Abolishing the commissars in 1942—the wording of the edict left no doubt—expressed Soviet leaders' confidence that the army had become stable enough ideologically to obviate external supervisors. Another reason for the reform arose from the constant demand for capable officers. A separate order issued by Stalin the same day mandated special training for eight hundred erstwhile commissars to prepare them as battalion and regimental commanders.[141]

Several of the Stalingrad interviews made plain that the military commanders now called the shots, with the new political deputies only assisting.[142] Others described a harmonious cooperation.[143] Yet some political officers continued to call themselves commissars in defiance of the reform, trying, as before, to set the tone in their relations with the military command.[144] One outspoken example was Brigade Commissar Vasiliev, who referred to himself by his old rank when he was interviewed in 1943. Vasiliev demanded that commanders be subject to aggressive "ideological education" from the political apparatus, a task he believed had faded into the background because the political apparatus prioritized infantry in the initial phases of the war.

He cited numerous cases in which he observed political officers fighting in an exemplary manner while the military commanders assigned to

The commander of the 45th Rifle Division, Major General Vasily Sokolov *(left)*, and his political deputy, Colonel Nikolai Glamazda *(right)*.

them left the troops high and dry. "I have always thought and I still maintain that a commander has to be trained. If a soldier is trained and a commander is not, some things won't get done and we'll fall short of the desired results." Despite the differing perspectives, the degree to which almost every interviewee understood himself as a part of a single unit joined by common interests is striking. Political officers also provided technical training and input on military tactics, just as commanders also looked out for the ideological and moral well-being of their troops.[145]

POLITICS, UP CLOSE

The current understanding of political activity in the Red Army draws mostly on the orders and directives of the Main Political Administration. Thanks to the Stalingrad transcripts, we now have a vivid description of the continuing efforts of political officers and commanders to commit soldiers to their combat missions and shape them into fearless, self-surpassing heroes in the Bolshevik voluntarist mold. The interviews also describe the coercive measures that accompanied these mobilizing efforts and the impact of officers' entreaties in battle.

Persistence and improvisation alike characterized the modus operandi of the political administration on the Stalingrad Front. Pyotr Molchanov, battalion commissar of the 38th Rifle Division, explained that during the defensive struggles of summer 1942 in the protected ravines of the Don steppes, political assemblies, singers, and accordionists strengthened morale. In Stalingrad such things were not possible. The incessant fighting forced the cancellation of the regular meetings and lectures stipulated by the communist playbook.[146] Colonel Glamazda, the political representative of the 45th Division, depicted the situation of his men on the west bank of the Volga as follows:

> It is hard to imagine that bombing: low-flying airplanes that kept coming in exact thirty-minute intervals from September to November. It was a real hell. Everything was covered in smoke. At night the planes didn't fly and it was possible to move. It was cold and damp but that didn't get to you as much as the planes, the shells, and the mines.

He then explained how the political officers carried out their work:

> What we did was talk to the men in person and then lead by example, showing them how to fight. And in absolutely every battle the party members were the first ones to throw themselves into the fight. I could give you dozens of examples from the lives of communists and Komsomol members who demonstrated how to fight and were then killed in combat.[147]

For particularly critical zones of combat, commanders made sure to distribute communists, Komsomols, and battle-tested soldiers among the companies. According to Lieutenant Colonel Yakov Dubrovsky, director of the political department of the 39th Guards Rifle Division, it was the communists, the Komsomols in particular, who provided the army's moral backbone:

> We established a standing practice that an assault group would always include Komsomol members. How was it done? The secretary of a Komsomol bureau, knowing that a storm group was being formed, would approach the battalion commander and tell him to include two or three Komsomol members. He would then personally instruct them, as well as the squad commanders. The idea was to have the Komsomol members, in addition to carrying out the combat mission itself, undertake all measures to ensure that that mission is transmitted to the personnel.[148]

Brigade Commissar Vasiliev seconded Dubrovsky's views about the young communists: "As for the leading role of communists [. . .] It was considered disgraceful if a communist didn't take a step forward and lead his soldiers."[149]

With the front under relentless fire by day, political work in the trenches moved to night. Alexander Levykin, commissar of the 284th Rifle Division, explained how he prepared his staff:

> This is what I used at divisional headquarters. I would listen to the latest news from all fronts, and then would go out at one or two in the morning and order the loudspeakers turned on. I would then inform the communications people, and from them company politruks would go to the battalions and inform people about the latest developments at the front. [. . .] They would distribute newspapers to the men. [. . .] Only at night was it possible

> to conduct political work individually with every soldier. The political department would brief its instructor staff and dispatch them to the units. A political officer would be able to cover two or three trenches in a night, but no more than that.[150]

Captain Olkhovkin reported that his regimental commander assembled the political officers and directed the agitators to inspect individual companies:

> I was sent to the 2nd Battalion. In the evening we made it to the 4th Company. There were four people in the dugout. I talked to the people at night when it was quieter. We gathered low-ranking agitators at the company command post, which was in a school basement. It was at three o'clock in the morning. The enemy was about forty meters away from the school. A front-page article had just appeared in *Pravda* about the fighting in Stalingrad.[151] I instructed them on that subject. I explained how significant Stalingrad was, why Hitler was pushing so hard for it. I connected it with the order to set up an unbreakable defense.

The night has another benefit, remarked Lieutenant Colonel Dubrovsky, his words revealing the total penetration to which the political administration aspired. "At night a soldier is more disposed to speak candidly, you can really make him spill his guts." Dubrovsky and his colleagues redoubled their efforts whenever their units were about to mount an assault or an enemy attack was expected.

Political officers repeatedly emphasized the frequency of their talks with individual troops. Each Red Army soldier had to be convinced of the war's necessity, each had to become politically aware, able to act on his or her on own initiative. "I consider personal talks the best mode of political work during the defense," noted Battalion Commissar Molchanov. "So, a soldier is sitting in his little trench for a whole month, he sees no one other than his neighbor, and suddenly a commissar or somebody else drops in on him and tells him something or just greets him or says a friendly word—that has great importance. To get him a sheet of paper so that he can write to his loved ones or to write a letter for him—that really cheers a soldier up." Commissars saw themselves as responsible for not only the mental health of the soldiers but also their physical well-being, and took note whenever food rations and warm clothing ran low. During crisis moments, they handed out delicacies—chocolate bars, mandarin oranges—sent to the front by workers' organizations. As Brigade Commissar Vasiliev put it, "It's not so much the food itself as the soldier's moral gratification because he feels that people care for him." The arsenal of the political officer also included military counsel, with instruction on how, say, to perform a hedgehog defense or build sturdy shelters. "We clarified every detail, every moment, every tactical move to the soldiers, doing our best to aid the soldiers and the commanders so that they may be more successful in combat," explained Vasiliev. The agitator[152] Izer Ayzenberg of the 38th Rifle Division employed a curious instrument of political education known as the "agitcult case." Procured by his regimental commissar, this portable device resembling a magician's case was especially well suited for use in the trenches. When open, the words of the Soviet military oath, presented on red velvet, could be read on the left; a command from Stalin and the portraits of Lenin and Stalin were displayed on the right. In the middle were brochures, books "about our proletarian commanders," a topographical map, and a political world map, in addition to a checker set and dominos. Ayzenberg explained how soldiers used the case's contents:

> This is how it works: one group takes a map, hangs it up, and circles with a finger the cities that our bombers and the German bombers are attacking. The soldiers show interest in other military theaters. They ask what's happening in Tunisia,[153] and so on. Another group is playing checkers, another is reading brochures, riddles, and songs—soldiers are laughing cheerfully. Serious brochures are being read in the corner. Also in the briefcase there are envelopes and paper, so they take paper and put together a newsletter. There is also a large mirror. Sometimes when you got it out a line would form up: one would ask to take a look, another would say 'I think I need a shave, let me see.' In the heat of such work the agitator asks for attention and conducts a ten- or fifteen-minute talk or reads an interesting article. We had one of these in each regiment. That's how we used it: I would come to the 1st Battalion headquarters, leave them the briefcase for a day, then take it to the 2nd Battalion, and so on.[154]

The political officers taught soldiers what they were fighting for and what motivated the enemy. They exploited Stalingrad's symbolic capital, spinning the battle into a world-historical event with the aid of voices from the international press. Even a "person with a modicum of awareness knew that the enemy wanted to encircle our capital from the east, take the Volga, take our oil sources—Baku. We knew that thanks to the work of political officers," remarked Senior Sergeant Mitrofan Karpushin of the 39th Guards Rifle Division. Karpushin then explained how the information reached him and the other soldiers: "We still were able to read newspapers, albeit by fits and starts. There were enough newspapers for each soldier. We were reading the division and army newspaper, the central newspaper *Pravda* and *Red Star*. The latter two were particularly numerous. When there was fighting, the newspapers would arrive seven or eight days late. I always managed to take a look at the front page. There was enough light: transformer oil was available—as much as you needed."[155]

In addition to emphasizing the historical importance of the battle of Stalingrad, political officers provided information about combat operations in the surrounding region to give all soldiers a sense of active participation. "I have to say," Major Serov observed, "that even when it was reported that, say, Gorshechnaya railway station or Urazovo railway junction was taken, even such minor victories made people happy. [. . .] When they hear or read in a bulletin that our guys have advanced even a little bit there was this feeling: 'we are gaining ground.' And when rapid advances like in the North Caucasus began, that's when folks really cheered up. Enthusiasm was plainly visible: 'so it's like that—they are pummeling them there, aren't we just as good? Let's get started!'"

Soldiers of the 284th Rifle Division receive letters and newspapers in Stalingrad, 1942.

THE HERO STRATEGY

In Soviet Marxist ideology, human beings were inherently malleable, shaped by their surroundings; through social conditioning anyone could become a hero. The political advisers were entrusted with this task. Brigade Commissar Vasiliev recounted the story of a soldier in the 45th Division who fought well but showed so little discipline that his politruk wrote the parents a letter to complain. Before posting it, he read the offending soldier its contents: "He felt really bad about it, and by then he'd won a medal, but his parents sent him a terrible dressing down from home. So we had to write another letter telling them how he'd put things right and distinguished himself, that he'd received a decoration from the government. Now he was a completely new man. Serov, chief of the political department, had taken him under his wing. The soldier was constantly getting better and never acted up again. It was like he'd been that way his whole life." Major Serov described the incident in greater detail from his vantage point:

> There was one Kiselyov in our 157th Regiment's 1st Company—a real madcap. We talked to him, we arrested him, locked him up—nothing helped. He was an exceptional discipline-breaker. Just wouldn't listen. So then Narovishnik, deputy political officer of the company, decided to write to his parents: "That's how outrageously your son behaves; perhaps you can help." That letter was read to the company. The company knew that the letter had been sent to his parents, and so did he. The very fact of sending the letter to the parents got him thinking. He got their reply when he got to the front: "Why are you bringing shame upon our gray heads? We can't look our neighbors in the eye. Have you forgotten what we were saying when we were seeing you off—be worthy!" Then his sister writes that it's embarrassing to receive such a report about him: "If you want to consider me your sister, fight like our older brother who died." This is when the guy wised up. He killed nine Fritzes and wounded seven more, or the other way around. He was wounded and sent off for treatment.

Heroic deeds—usually defined as actions in which soldiers held their own against a force with superior troops and weapons—were often documented and propagated via leaflets distributed in the sectors where they occurred, on the assumption that readers would know the "heroes of the

Red Army soldiers read a wall newspaper in Stalingrad, 1942. *Photographer: Natalya Bode*

day" personally and strive to emulate them.[156] The 13th Guards Rifle Division handed out leaflets with photos of the honored soldiers and brief descriptions of their deeds. "This creates an extraordinary impression," observed Brigade Commissar Vasiliev. As a political officer in the division explained, the leaflets were read out loud to the units and then sent to parents and family members.[157] In this way the political administration exploited the influence of soldiers' families and hometowns to reinforce punishments and commendations.

Brigade Commissar Vasiliev credited a Komsomol from his unit with embodying the Bolshevik ideal of the war hero. The soldier consciously emulated the feats of celebrated predecessors and wanted his example of self-sacrifice to inspire others to follow the heroic tradition:

> Voronov, for example, a Komsomol member, had read Ostrovsky's How the Steel Was Tempered and lived only by the idea of Ostrovsky's machine gunner. He received twenty-five wounds on the battlefield and it was only when his arms, shot through in several places, would no longer obey him that he left the battlefield. He was commanding a machine-gun detail. He was literally bleeding out and they offered to take him to the medical unit. He said, "No, you keep on fighting. I'll go there myself." He crawled three hundred meters bleeding out. When they got him to the medical

> battalion he was completely torn to shreds and he said: "Now I am that machine gunner from Ostrovsky." Here's this man living by an idea, and you realize that we were doing work without always seeing what we had accomplished.

Vasiliev implied that the work of the political officers was what put the novel *How the Steel Was Tempered* into Voronov's hands.

While some soldiers modeled their behavior on idealized notions of the hero, others drew motivation from more basic sources. "People were fed and informed about the significance of those heights," explained Regimental Commissar Dimitri Petrakov of the 308th Rifle Division. "They were promised a reward: for a captured German soldier an Order of the Red Star, for an officer—an Order of the Red Banner, and to the first one on the height the Order of Lenin."[158] Many of the interviewees corroborated that countless heroic feats did indeed occur on the Stalingrad Front. "Without any exaggeration," relayed Major Pyotr Zayonchkovsky, of the 66th Army, "one can justifiably say that throughout the fighting at Stalingrad all but a handful of commanders and soldiers displayed enormous heroism."[159] General Chuikov reported that "we know about so many heroes produced by the battle of Stalingrad that you've got to marvel at the capabilities of our Russian people, our Soviet people. And to think how many heroes we haven't heard of," he wondered. "There must be ten times more of those." According to an internal memo, by June 1943 the military had bestowed 9,601 medals on soldiers of the 62nd Army for distinction in battle.[160] Army newspapers regularly paid tribute to honored soldiers, and many editions of *Red Star* consisted mostly of the names and ranks of those recently decorated and the medals awarded to them. This echoed the practice used for shock workers in the 1930s, whose achievements Soviet newspapers cited individually.

In promoting heroism in battle, military commanders and political officers conditioned their soldiers to be fearless. Captain Andrei Afanassyev of the 36th Rifle Division summarized the task in a few words: "After the first baptism [of fire] I decided to foster a contempt for death among the personnel."[161] Two terrors received repeated mention: fear of enemy panzers and fear of air raids. Commanders taught soldiers how to protect themselves from tanks by burrowing into the ground and demonstrated how to use bazookas and other antitank weapons.[162] They preached that fear was an animal instinct that could be overcome through mindful thought and action. Alexander Sikorsky, a military hydrographer in the 62nd Army, described how the Soviet soldier "has shown that fear is no longer a part of him, that he is fearless. Each man is born with fear, fear is a quality that every human being possesses, but fear will abandon heroes and remain with cowards."[163]

This emphasis on human willpower received constant mention in the Stalingrad interviews.[164] When soldiers talked about fear, it was usually as something conditional, something felt initially or intermittently that they could actively tune out and overcome. Captain Afanassyev, despite resolving to teach his men fearlessness, confessed the panic he felt during a strong German attack on August 20, 1942:

> In fact, it was terrifying. When I stepped outside for a look I was overcome by doubt: the advancing German army was enormous. You'd look into the binoculars or periscope and think to yourself: there's no way we can hold out against this. That was how I felt then. One look in the periscope would send me into a panic. It wasn't exactly cowardice but the feeling that destroying everything that was moving at us was impossible. Endless black dots. Four to five hundred tanks and other vehicles. And they weren't moving one after another—they were moving in echelon formation.

The scene described here resembles what communist soldiers understood by a "psychic attack." Afanassyev later stressed that he had passed the test.

Lev Okhitovich, an infantryman in the 308th Rifle Division, described his first open-field battle and the paralyzing fear he felt when German fire forced him to the ground. But he also noted that the fear evaporated the moment he realized that he had to stand up if he wanted to avoid a senseless death: "I realized that we might die for nothing. It wasn't bravery or courage (which I had none of). I simply realized that I was going to die unless I did something. And the only chance I had to save myself and others was to advance." Okhitovich picked himself off the ground and was surprised by the galvanizing effect of the battle cry that reflexively crossed his lips: "I couldn't say anything other than what anyone would have said in my place. 'For the motherland! For Stalin!'"[165]

GOOD AND BAD SOLDIERS

Those unable to keep their fear in check were deemed craven and often subjected to harsh punishment. For soldiers on the Stalingrad front the leadership introduced severe disciplinary measures. The most prominent were the sanctions against "cowards" and "traitors" spelled out in Order no. 227. Drafted by Stalin personally, the order commanded soldiers to "tenaciously, to the last drop of blood, defend each position, each meter of Soviet territory, to clutch at each patch of Soviet land and hold it to the very end."[166] Anyone who abandoned a position without explicit orders to do so was to be executed or sent to a penal unit.[167] Inherent in these brutal measures was a strong didactic element. Soldiers deported to penal companies, the order explained, were to be given an "opportunity to redeem their crimes against the motherland with blood." This gave banished soldiers the hope of being rehabilitated and returning to their unit.

Many of those interviewed spoke at length about what was widely known as the "not one step back" policy. Their statements reveal how differently Order no. 227 was interpreted and implemented. General Chuikov took extreme steps for restoring discipline:

> Honestly, most of the divisional commanders didn't have the stomach to die here. The second something happens, they start saying: Permit me to cross the Volga. I yelled "I'm still here" and sent a telegram: "If you take one step I'll shoot you." [. . .] We immediately began to take the harshest possible actions against cowardice. On September 14 I shot the commander and commissar of one regiment, and a short while later I shot two brigade commanders and their commissars. This caught everyone off guard. We made sure news of this got to the men, especially the officers.

The executions, Chuikov added, produced immediate effects.

Major Serov described breaches of discipline in his unit, which forced him to take similarly drastic action. Particularly egregious was the behavior of company commanders, the very people who were supposed to set an example:

> It wasn't all clear sailing, of course. I should note that party members, commanders, and political workers were too bold, reckless even. They were always getting into things they shouldn't. That's why the commanders and political officers, especially at the company level, were getting knocked out so early on. So here's the situation: the enemy is pressing, behind us is the Volga, there is nowhere to retreat. But the leadership of our company commanders

> and their political deputies isn't felt because they're all gone, dead or wounded. And the others, the less resilient ones, who knows where they've gone. [. . .] They're off looking for a hole somewhere to sit this one out. They know this is not the time to sit it out, but they do. Some go for self-inflicted wounds, hoping to preserve their honor by pretending to be wounded and get across to the east bank. This was happening in the beginning. We started exposing these ones publicly and had them shot in front of their units. The number of similar cases started dropping rapidly. That was the only type of desertion. You couldn't do anything else: the Volga behind us let no one get by.

The effort necessary to carry out the order—in extreme cases it required executing one's own soldiers—was expressed by Sergeant Mikhail Gurov of the 38th Motorized Rifle Brigade: "They issued us this order: let no one pass, those who disobey should be simply [*sic*] We read the order of comrade Stalin: 'Our land is vast, but there is nowhere else to go. We must hold it.' And that's what we decided. The order had to be carried out—we didn't let them, hard as it was."[168] The commander of the 36th Rifle Division, Colonel Mikhail Denisenko, devised a Solomonic solution that neither violated the order nor required enforcing it with the utmost rigor. During the large-scale German attack on September 14, many soldiers of the 64th Army fled the front lines, crossing the division's positions "disorderly, moving in a mass." As Denisenko recalls, "I issued an order: stop them, do not allow disorderly movement, and so on. Then they tell me: comrade Colonel, it's our people. It doesn't feel right to shoot! I gave orders to allow them to pass while maintaining the defensive."[169]

While the above accounts tell of troops being disciplined with violence or the threat of it, others emphasize the didactic effect of Order no. 227. Vasiliev reported that his efforts to "inculcate the order into the people's consciousness" yielded results on the very first day of battle. Senior Lieutenant Nikolai Voronin, a crew member on the gunboat *Chapayev*, explained how the political department circulated official news from the front with the proviso that "we mustn't make a single step back even if we have to die."[170] Divisional Commissar Kuzma Gurov (62nd Army) stated for the record that after educating his soldiers about the order they "realized their role as people of the state. Soldiers held their position even though the Germans overran them."[171]

According to Lieutenant Ivan Kuznetsov, a gunboat commander in the Volga flotilla, disciplinary measures and education went hand in hand: "We were feeling the mood. Certainly there were moments when individual soldiers became pale as death during a bombing raid. I warned them, I told them straight up: 'Comrades, this is war. I'm warning you that if anyone abandons ship or shows cowardice—I'll shoot them!'" Kuznetsov recalled a doctor named Petrov who, on all sorts of pretexts, kept jumping off a gunship docked on the riverbank. "I summoned him again and told him that if this happens again he'll be the first one to die and I also asked the Osobist to have a talk with him on that subject." Exhortations peppered with threats of violence achieved a measure of success: "Of course he continued to be afraid—that could be felt—but he was already in a psychological state of knowing that he'll be worse off if he abandons ship. Not only was he saved from cowardice, but the other troops too, who were saying that the medic was about to run off. After that no one would deliberately abandon ship or neglect his duties."[172]

Commanders and political officers demanded discipline not for its own sake but to teach self-control. Their conception of military order also shone through their appraisals of the enemy. Several intelligence officers in Stalingrad spoke about the Wehrmacht's unusually strong discipline, which forged a special bond between soldiers and commanders. One officer observed that during the Soviet barrages in the final days of January 1943 not a single German emerged from a bunker to surrender as long as the commanding officers remained.[173] His approving remark contained an admission: discipline in the Red Army was far from ideal.[174] Yet the intelligence officers also mentioned the "blind" and "mechanical" quality of German discipline.[175] In their eyes, it seemed like slavish obedience, an attribute of the prerevolutionary era in contrast to the discipline born of conscious self-control. Unimaginable in the Wehrmacht, they thought, was the case of a Red Army soldier named Kurvantyev who killed his platoon leader for surrendering. Battalion Commissar Molchanov tells the story: "This is how it was. During the German advance the platoon commander raised his hands when the Germans ran up to him. Seeing that the platoon commander has his hands in the air, Kurvantyev with a machine gun burst mowed down both the Germans and the commander. He assumed command of the platoon, repelled the German attack that had broken through our lines in that place, and retook the position. We admitted him to the party [. . .] and spread his example in talks, lectures, and in the division press."[176]

Even penal units in the Red Army were created for the express purpose of reforming soldier offenders. Deployed in areas along the front line with high casualty rates, these units consisted of "cowards," deserters, and self-mutilators picked up by the blocking squads, together with captured

Red Army soldiers liberated after the Soviet counteroffensive and a large contingent of gulag prisoners. The historians in Stalingrad did not interview a single penal unit serviceman. Indeed, as the words of one staff officer reveal, commanders and soldiers in the other units were reluctant to speak about these formations: the officer reported that the troops of Guards divisions bristled when they heard that their ranks were to be replenished with former *strafniki* from the penal companies. Their biographies were "stained," said one agitator as he admonished the former penal servicemen in his regiment at dawn before a combat operation, "but you must now prove that in one fight you can not only remove this stain but also enter the ranks of the decorated." He reminded them of Ilya Ehrenburg's dictum, "The blood spilled in battle is sacred. Each drop of it is a precious sacrifice on the altar of the motherland. If a man has guilt before the people, he removes it with blood in combat. I said that they were to wash away the guilt with blood. Shouting 'Hurrah!,' several people stepped forward and said, 'You'll see, we will prove it.'"[177]

Almost every mention of the penal companies included an assertion that their men had proven themselves in battle. Senior Lieutenant Alexei Kolesnik, of the 204th Rifle Division, recalled: "We received reinforcements comprised of those sentenced to ten years for self-inflicted wounds and for retreating without orders; there were even commanders among them. We've expunged the records of sixty people for exemplary conduct in combat. Take this one junior lieutenant. He has personally killed thirteen Fritzes and has been put in charge of the regimental engineering service. He was court-martialed for neglecting his duties, got himself blown up by mines."[178] Battalion Commissar Alexander Stepanov (308th Rifle Division) expressed similar sentiments: "About 25 percent of people in our regiment had a conviction in the past. All of them, with a few exceptions, had that conviction removed for courageous conduct and action in combat. We considered that one of the ways to stimulate people toward excellent work."[179] Senior Lieutenant Ayzenberg, the agitator who drove home the image of the blood sacrifice on the altar of the motherland, recounted, "Toward the end of the day, when we checked the casualties, we noticed that Vasiliev was still there, also a former prisoner of war. Not only had Vasiliev washed away his shameful stain, but he was there till the end. He had remembered my words so well he passed them on to his comrades. That evening he approached me and said: 'The battalion commander has just told me that I'm being nominated for a decoration.'"[180]

The enormous losses of the penal companies at the front figured in the depictions of the men's heroic deeds only in passing, if at all.[181] Lieutenant

Alexei Zimin (38th Motorized Rifle Brigade) alluded to the death toll when he said that after one battle "pursuant to Order no. 227 the rest of the offenders had their stain of shame removed."[182] Brigade Commissar Vasiliev was more explicit: "Guryev's division has some convicts. The majority of them have been killed in battle; there are some wounded. [. . .] About six of them are left and their convictions have been removed. Now we're working on the issue of posthumously removing the convictions of those who were killed because they fought and died heroically."

Nowhere else was the idea of reeducation—*perekovka*, literally "reforging"—more present than in the descriptions of soldiers who arrived at the front from the gulag. (*Perekovka* was a common notion in the Soviet penal system in the early 1930s.)[183] Battalion Commissar Stepanov remembered well the ninety prisoners assigned to him when forming his regiment: "people in rags, hungry, covered in lice," the sight of whom initially frightened him. "These were real 'cons,' to use their own slang." How would he break up this close-knit community and "educate" the men? Stepanov showed the results of his efforts by citing some of the paths taken by the men after serving time: "Shafranov is now a party member in the regiment, a decorated field officer, one of our finest commanders. Gavronsky deserted while the regiment was being formed. He was rounded up near Stalingrad and shot. Of all the ninety convicts who came to our regiment, only two of them were unable to reform themselves and ended up being shot. All the rest were reeducated and turned into good honest soldiers."

Some of the offenders sent to the front earned the admiration of their commanders for their determination in battle. Major Andrei Kruglyakov, of the 45th Rifle Division, spoke about a former pickpocket named Chuvakhin. "The day after he arrived at the front in Stalingrad his friend, comrade Ivanov, was killed. He promised that for his friend he would kill no fewer than thirty-five Fritzes. And in a short period of time he killed thirty-three or thirty-two Fritzes. Later he was wounded."[184] "Madcap fellows, real daredevils," said Major Soldatov, referring to the offenders assigned to the 38th Rifle Brigade. "On their first day at the front line they burst into some dugout, captured a German, dragged him here."

The Soviet command also regarded non-Russian recruits, non-Slavs in particular, with suspicion, believing them to hold nationalist aspirations.[185] At the same time, the Main Political Administration also thought about strategies for winning over these unpredictable "cantonists." An October 1942 report to GlavPURKKA head Shcherbakov listed all the non-Russian soldiers fighting at Stalingrad: 5,688 Ukrainians, 1,787 Byelorussians, 2,146 Uzbeks, 3,152 Kazakhs,[186] 187 Turkmen, 181 Kyrgyz, 2,047 Jews, and 3,354

Tatars. The author of the report suggested publishing special newspapers for these soldiers, printed centrally in Moscow since there were no facilities for doing this in the field.

This suggestion implicitly called attention to the communication difficulties in ethnically mixed divisions.[187] Many non-Russian soldiers did not understand the orders issued by their (mostly Russian) superiors, and sometimes had to rely on hand gestures when coordinating battle movements. The 62nd Army tried to surmount the problem by recruiting the best-educated non-Russians and training them as commanders. Those from urban areas with a good command of Russian were used as interpreters and instructors. Lieutenant Nikolai Karpov of the 38th Motorized Rifle Brigade talked about the services of non-Russians when the Square of the Fallen Heroes was stormed in the early hours of January 31, 1943:

> Komsomol members played a leading role in the attack. We had a lot of minorities, and they were generally hard to mobilize. That Ivanov was a Chuvash, but he understood Uzbek and Russian well, in addition to Chuvash. When we were attacking and there were some twenty meters to the building, we hit the ground, as the Germans were laying down heavy fire that night. Ivanov shouts to me: "How about it, comrade Lieutenant, we will keep going?" I immediately got up and shouted: "Forward! For the motherland!" And he shouted to the minorities. We took that building by storm. We got there on January 27 and fought for four days until January 31.[188]

Several of the commanders interviewed attested to the "fighting spirit" of the non-Russians. For instance, Colonel Matvei Smolyanov (64th Army) noted that "there were times when Uzbeks displayed no less courage than that of Russians, Ukrainians, and others."[189] But the depictions also betrayed how little commanders expected from non-Russians. "We had pretty good folks," recalled Captain Ivan Bukharov, of the 38th Rifle Brigade, "including some non-Russians, but the majority were Russians—professionals who had been under fire before."[190] Others bluntly asserted that the non-Russian soldiers fought poorly and were fearful, justifying the brutal punishment they sometimes received. "They'd gotten reinforcements, but they wouldn't move—they were Uzbeks, extremely bad soldiers. The ones who didn't go were shot."[191] General Rodimtsev, the one who delivered this assessment, went on to underscore the outstanding fighting spirit of the Russians in his division, especially those who came from Siberia.

Divisional Commander Stepan Guryev (39th Guards Rifle Division) also criticized the non-Russians, though not across the board. "Among the minorities there were Uzbeks, Kazakhs, and others, but they fought poorly. There are of course those who were able to handle it—good, decorated guys—but that's a small percentage."[192]

These "nationalities"—to Russian commanders and political officers at Stalingrad—were what the Russian peasantry had been to Soviet activists of the first hour: an uneducated, backward throng who could be fashioned into effective soldiers only by dint of enormous effort. Curiously, none of the commanders in Stalingrad spoke critically of Russian soldiers with peasant backgrounds; such a category never occurred to them. The line of division no longer ran between classes, as during the Civil War, but between nationalities, and everyone took it as self-evident that Russians best embodied the communist ideal of the battle-conscious soldier. It was also clear that more than any other Soviet ethnic group they were led by hate for the German invaders.[193]

Political and moral education played an important role in the Red Army units fighting at Stalingrad. Most of the political officers and commanders who spoke with the Moscow historians confirmed that these mobilizing measures began to take effect there. The early phases of the battle critically tested the army's effectiveness, but most of the interviewees affirmed that by October 1942 the city's defenders were standing firm and fighting with conviction. (Senior Lieutenant Alexei Smirnov of the 308th Rifle Division stated that "during the retreat to Stalingrad we would catch individual cowards, but in Stalingrad itself that wasn't the case. Our army blocking units did not have a single case of that.")[194] By that time, the mythology surrounding the pivotal battle on the Volga had taken shape. A slogan like "There is no land beyond the Volga!" imbued Order no. 227 with a tangible, vivid significance for local troops. Combined with the threat of fierce punishment, such rallying cries proved effective, especially after the series of military victories beginning on November 19. Many of those interviewed corroborated the description provided by Major Georgy Spitsky of the Volga flotilla: "By the way, I've been in the service for a long time. It's my fourth war, but I've never seen such a display as that of the ship rallies. It was an exceptional display of enthusiasm. Even the most backward—and we had a few of those—were transformed. They would speak at gatherings, rallies."[195]

These reports of soldiers' behavior at Stalingrad tally with information that has emerged from Soviet secret archives. By August 1, 1942, the military had formed forty-one blocking squads on the Stalingrad and Don Fronts. Over the course of September and August they detained 45,465 soldiers who had left the front lines without authorization: 699 were arrested, and of them, 664 "cowards, panickers, and self-mutilators" were executed on the spot. Another 1,292 were sent to penal companies and battalions. The overwhelming bulk of the deserters—41,472 soldiers—was returned into their units.[196] The figures make clear that the Red Army had a huge problem with internal discipline especially during the early, defensive phase of the Stalingrad campaign. The sources also suggest that the NKVD troops operating behind the front lines with the goal of stemming desertion had two specific tasks. The first was to detain the soldiers who fled from the battlefield and to ensure that their behavior did not spread to other troops: "Today during the enemy's offensive breakthrough two companies of the 13th Guards division froze and began to withdraw," an internal NKVD report of September 23, 1942, stated. "The commander of one of these companies, Lieutenant Mirolyubov, also fled the battlefield in panic, abandoning the company. The blocking unit of the 62nd Army contained the retreat of these units and restored the position." Another report states that a blocking unit opened fire on the fleeing troops, while a third specifies that the NKVD agents aimed over their heads.[197]

The second task was to establish who among the detained was a trustworthy soldier and who wasn't. NKVD officers performed interrogations to "filter out" the "obvious enemies"—incorrigible cowards or "anti-Soviet elements." These needed to be "finished off with an iron hand." But the interrogation could also reveal that an individual had succumbed to a "momentary weakness that most often was the result of not being accustomed to combat conditions—and that in the future he will act with courage, energy, and dignity."[198] This political reading of the personality of individual Red Army soldiers fully conformed with how the NKVD had persecuted purported "enemies of the people" during the prewar Stalinist terror, with the only exception that before the war the sanctions were harsher: few people who ended up in the hands of the secret police got away without a gulag term.[199] In wartime, however, and especially as the war progressed, the regime urgently required soldiers at the front. It even opened the gulag to increase the ranks of the military.

Many of the executions meted out as a consequence of Order no. 227 were conducted in front of all the assembled soldiers of a division. Such exemplary violence was to function as a deterrent, and it was widely publicized.[200] The executions disproportionately affected Red Army commanders and commissars. Multiple sources describe how commanders of troops that buckled under their leadership were later shot in front of their troops.[201] This lot also fell to Lieutenant Mirolyubov, the company commander in General Rodimtsev's division. He had failed to lead by example and to transform ordinary recruits into fearless fighters. The vulnerability of Soviet commanders contrasted starkly with the German armed forces, where officers were practically immune from physical violence. Soviet rank-and-file soldiers, on the other hand, stood a smaller chance of suffering from Order no. 227.[202] As military leaders realized by summer 1942, the supply of Soviet recruits was not endless. By June of that year army orders were issued that called on commanders to "spare their soldiers."[203] Back in August 1941 Stalin's Order no. 270 had decreed indiscriminate violence. Enacted nearly a year later, Order no. 227 had evolved: the bulk of those soldiers who would have been summarily shot under Order no. 270 were now sent to penal units instead. There they were considered probationary fighters, under orders to redeem themselves within a short time frame by fighting in the most dangerous sectors of the front.[204] Even with these qualifications, the penal culture in the Red Army was extremely—and by many accounts, excessively—violent.[205] Over the course of the war, tens of thousands of Soviet soldiers were sentenced to death and executed—the exact number remains a matter of debate.[206]

The brutal measures that were taken at the Stalingrad Front in late summer and fall 1942 seemed to be effective, as later internal documents suggest. In February 1943 the NKVD reported that between October 1942 and the following January, a total of 203 "cowards and panic mongers" were arrested from the six armies that made up the Don Front; 169 of them were shot and the rest were sent to penal companies. The report mentions only "sporadic cases of mass flight from the battlefield."[207]

FORMS OF COMBAT

For all the mobilizing force of political education, the army's initiatives were often inconsistent and contradictory, less products of a single unified theory than of conflicting temperaments and viewpoints. For instance, military leaders differed greatly on whether soldiers should receive vodka to steel themselves for battle. On August 22, 1941, Stalin decreed that every soldier should receive one hundred grams of vodka a day. The directive was repealed on May 11, 1942, and then reintroduced on November 12, 1942.

From May 1943 until the end of the war, unit commanders made their own decisions about alcohol allowances for troops.[208] Senior Lieutenant Vasily Leshchinin of the 39th Guards Rifle Division spoke openly about giving alcohol to his men when preparing them and some recently arrived reserve units for an assault on Stalingrad's industrial district. "We got to know the new reinforcements, talked to every one of them, organized assault teams. We spread our seasoned soldiers among them, cooked them a hot supper, gave them their hundred grams and said 'All right guys, go and get it.' We didn't tell them how, but they went ahead and took that plant."[209] Other officers warned of the dangers of intoxication in battle. Here is Major Spitsky's account:

> Some say the one hundred grams handed out by order of the People's Commissar was a necessity. I would say it was just the opposite. The more complicated the situation, the more we would choose to do without. For example, we commanders simply didn't want to drink. Conducting an operation with a clear head is better. [. . .] There were indeed some small individuals who would credit the alcohol with actions that went beyond what was humanly possible, that were heroic, saying that nothing was impossible for someone who has had a few. But that of course wasn't typical of the general opinion on that subject—just a minor aberration.

The admonition to avoid inebriation appears in an early 1943 report from Stalingrad: "[Enemy intelligence] can meet its objectives successfully only when [. . .] both the commander and soldiers are brave and resourceful, if their mind is clear and sober." The wording of the report suggests that alcohol was widely used to prepare soldiers for their combat missions.[210]

There were also differences in combat style. Political officers urged soldiers to stand tall and proud as they marched into battle in the belief that the heroic posture would encourage others to follow suit. The agitator Izer Ayzenberg remembered how he assumed control of his battalion after the commander sustained an injury while preparing the unit to storm a hill. He called over a soldier named Polukhin, pressed the regiment flag into his hands, and told him to plant it on top of a water tower held by the enemy, in the hope that the waving flag would rally the troops. "When the enemy began retreating, covering us with fire, that Polukhin rose to full height and went across the battle line, carrying the flag. Infantry, not waiting for the flag to be placed, also rose up tall and threw themselves into the offensive. Our divisional commander watched that scene and said that it was exceedingly beautiful how the infantry, standing tall and crying hurrah, followed the flag. Polukhin did place the flag." Ayzenberg does not specify the number of soldiers who lost their lives during this assault.

The sight of his soldiers falling in a shower of enemy bullets exhilarated Brigade Commissar Alexander Yegorov, of the 38th Motorized Rifle Brigade. He was thrilled by his men's willingness to put themselves in harm's way. Earlier, a Soviet attack had stalled when the infantry refused to leave the trenches after an initial artillery barrage. At that point Yegorov's reserve brigade received the order to step in: "As soon as the enemy noticed movement on our line they opened fire. But the joyful thing—my heart rejoiced at it—was that our people were resilient. Shrapnel was ripping our men out of line, there were huge bloodstains on the snow (the first snow had just fallen), but still they didn't get down, they kept advancing."[211]

Writer Vasily Grossman displayed similar enthusiasm when describing a battle in which an entire regiment of the 308th Rifle Division perished: "An iron wind struck them in the face, yet they kept moving forward. The enemy was likely possessed by a superstitious fear: Are these people who are attacking us? Are they mortal? [. . .] [They] were indeed mortal, and while few of them made it out alive, they had all done their duty."[212] Both Grossman and Yegorov were in thrall to the hero cult, convinced of every man's ability to transform himself into a self-sacrificing warrior. Soviet ideas of heroism permeated all levels of warfare, from the upright bearing of the troops as they entered battle to infantrymen pitting themselves against German panzers to pilots crashing into enemy airplanes in midflight. These ideas came at a price: many of the Red Army's enormous losses were a direct result. Yet as cultural norms they also had a great motivating power. Fighter pilot Ivan Sapryagayev summed it up in conversation with Grossman: "I always get into a fight. I don't want distinction. I want to defeat the Germans, sacrificing my life. The battering ram—that is the character of a Russian; that is Soviet upbringing."[213]

Major Zayonchkovsky shared this heroic disposition, but he also pointed out its dark side: the "rash, senseless courage, and the sometimes unnecessary risks. Here's the kind of thing that happens during a day on the front lines: 'Vanka, give me a smoke,' and he gets up and runs over to him. Or people are walking normally in places where they need to crawl, and the next second they're dead." The flamboyant display of heroism that Zayonchkovsky criticized was, for General Chuikov, an indispensible linchpin in his authority as commander:

Attack. Stalingrad, 1943. *Photographer: Natalya Bode*

> We don't have heroes who aren't afraid of anything. No one sees or knows what Chuikov does when he's by himself, when there's no witnesses, nobody to see him, to see what's going on in his head. The idea that a commander would go to his subordinates and bare his poor little soul—you could find them, but they are the rejects. We're in a bunker, and shell fragments are flying at us. But what, you just sit there, and that doesn't get to you? I don't believe it. The survival instinct is still there, but a man's pride—an officer's especially—is of vital importance in combat.

By contrast, General Mikhail Shumilov of the 64th Army repeatedly stressed that the first job of a good commander was to protect his troops. He recounted a successful attack that began with a fifty-five-minute artillery bombardment: "First there was a five-minute fire raid on the front line that was then taken deeper for ten minutes. At that time the infantry started firing heavily from all weapons, stuck out mannequins, and cried 'Hurrah!,' imitating a mass infantry attack. That disoriented the enemy, who decided that we were already attacking and started leaving the dugouts to go into the trenches. Just then, all of our artillery again concentrated on the enemy's front line."[214] Other experienced commanders also noted the effectiveness of subterfuge. The fighter pilot Stepan Prutkov defended this furtive, ignoble form of warfare by arguing that the Germans did it too: "That is how we began tricking the Germans. [. . .] You shouldn't fight them head-on. They're crafty and sly, so you've got to be clever about it."[215] Since these maneuvers lacked the expressive and electrifying power of heroic, straight-backed soldiers striding into battle, they received little attention from political officers and war correspondents.

Shumilov acknowledged an important fact corroborated by other interviewees: for most of 1942 his soldiers lacked weapons and equipment. By January 4, 1943, when Shumilov gave his interview, the situation had changed. "Now that the army is saturated with machinery," he said, the ability to operate them was paramount. The hero cult, filled with tales of soldiers who threw themselves into the path of oncoming German panzers, grew in part out of this scarcity. Consider Lieutenant Colonel Svirin's depiction of the bloody battle on the northwest outskirts of Stalingrad in September 1942: "We educated the soldiers using the example of the brave defenders of Sevastopol, five of whom threw themselves under the tanks, and the example of the twenty-eight Panfilov soldiers who managed to hold back an avalanche of armor."[216]

But the officers interviewed also noted a growing divide within the military. General Shumilov cited *Front*, a play by Alexander Korneychuk that premiered in the summer of 1942. It portrayed the conflict between the obstinate veterans of the Civil War and the younger generation of officers who had graduated from military academies in the 1930s. After the battle of Stalingrad, the soldiers' confidence had become palpable. The defeat of an opponent previously considered invincible testified to their own military prowess. Many officers criticized superiors who relied on brute force alone, without military expertise. Regimental commander Alexander Gerasimov took an indirect swipe at his division head, Vasily Glazkov.[217] When talking about divisional commander Ivan Afonin, the sailors of the Volga flotilla did not mince words.[218] An especially severe rebuke was reserved for General Vasily Gordov, who commanded the Stalingrad Front in July and August 1942. Divisional commander Stepan Guryev of the 39th Guards Division, who had served under Gordov, believed that he was "chiefly responsible" for the heavy losses in the 62nd and 64th Armies on the Don steppes: "History will never forgive him. [. . .] Gordov completely lacks talent." Senior Lieutenant Dubrovsky also pinned the blame on Gordov. "To be honest," he said, "what happened on the Don in August could only be described as a catastrophe." He too

General Mikhail Shumilov (*center*) and members of his military council (S. T. Serdyuk, *front*; Konstantin Abramov, *rear*) in Stalingrad, January 1943.

pinned the blame on General Gordov. General Chuikov noted that he saved the 64th Army from annihilation by disobeying Gordov's commands and ordering a rapid retreat; the 62nd Army held its position and was nearly destroyed by German panzers and aircraft. "The front command," Chuikov summed up, "did not take the direction into consideration, even though Comrade Stalin had warned Gordov and the rest that Tsymlyanskaya was the foremost and most important direction for the enemy." Gordov was relieved of command and demoted in August 1942, allowing the eyewitnesses interviewed in 1943 to criticize him without fear of reprisals. Yet Stalin, who time and again goaded commanders on the front to initiate bloody offensives and threatened them with severe punishment if they failed, escaped criticism of any kind. (It is not known how many Red Army soldiers in Stalingrad knew of Stalin's leadership style or mistrusted it.)

Despite the emphasis on military expertise and strategy after 1942, many of the command forms from the Civil War survived. Stalin valued commanders like Gordov, who did not hesitate to sacrifice entire divisions for a spectacular offensive. The vilified ex-commander made a comeback in 1943, rising to colonel general and later taking part in the attacks on Berlin and Prague. In April 1945 he was awarded the title Hero of the Soviet Union.[219]

PEOPLE IN WAR

The communist wager on the boundless reserves of the human will was shared by scores of Red Army soldiers fighting at Stalingrad, especially by those born after 1917 and brought up in the Soviet education system. In keeping with this voluntarist conception, they distinguished between two basic dispositions—the heroic and the cowardly—and admitted few shades of gray between them. The primacy the Bolsheviks placed on fully developed consciousness expressed itself in how soldiers dealt with the psychological stress of war. In an interview filling twenty-eight pages, army commander Chuikov devoted only one sentence to this matter: "Just understand this one thing: all of this [the months of defensive battles in Stalingrad] has made an impression on our psyches." Then he abruptly changed subjects. Sniper Vasily Zaytsev described his suffering in physiological terms—a common tendency in Soviet psychology at the time—while underscoring the ever present will to fulfill his mission:

> We didn't know fatigue. Now I get tired just walking around town, but then we had breakfast from 4:00 to 5:00 A.M. and dinner from 9:00 to 10:00 P.M., going without food all day without getting tired. We'd go three or four days without sleeping, without even feeling sleepy. How can I explain this? [. . .] Every soldier, including myself, was thinking only of how he could make them pay more dearly for his life, how he could slaughter even more Germans. [. . .] I was wounded three times in Stalingrad. Now I have a nervous system disorder and shake constantly.[220]

Vasiliev mentioned Mikhail Mamekov, who was also a sniper: "In a short period of time he had already killed 138 Fritzes. If he spends a day without killing a Fritz, he can't eat and really starts fretting. He is a typical Tatar and speaks poor Russian, but he is always studying it, even in battle."

Dozens of Red Army soldiers from different ethnic backgrounds told how they attempted to meet the demands placed on them: defending their "home" and the "socialist fatherland," keeping their "self-preservation instinct" in check, surmounting their fear of death, seeing loss of life in battle as a meaningful act or even as life's fulfillment, and constantly fanning their hate of Germans. As the soldiers' stories about their families showed, these attitudes surfaced far away from the front as well. Senior Lieutenant Molchanov, sidelined by a stomach ulcer, taught at a military academy when

Lieutenant Colonel Pyotr Molchanov

war broke out. "I have a daughter, Nina, who is seven. She kept asking, 'Papa, why are you not at the front? Everybody is fighting and you are not.' That had a powerful effect on me. What can I answer the child? Tell her I am sick? But that was not the time for sickness! After that I went to the head of the political department of the district and told him about my wish to go to the front."

Characteristically, talk of resignation or fortune surface nowhere in the interviews, even though fatalism, in the positive sense of the word, once counted as a virtue among soldiers in the Russian empire, lending them their legendary tenacity and endurance.

The question remains how to assess the language of the Stalingrad transcripts in relation to how Soviet soldiers talked or wrote in an unofficial setting. Many historians believe they can best uncover the reality of war in the words of those who speak freely about it. They mistrust official sources, regarding them as outlets of propaganda that yield little for understanding actual individual experience.[221] Indeed, some Soviet wartime letters speak a very different language. We know of their existence because they were recorded by NKVD agents in search of "anti-Soviet" subjects—soldiers who despaired over their fate or voiced defeatist positions. In October 1942, Special Section officers at the Stalingrad Front presented a report containing these excerpts (the agents were not concerned with the letters as a whole, only with passages in them that fit the categories they were searching for):

"The majority no longer believes in victory. The masses are no longer sympathetic to us. And now the allies are delaying the opening of a second front.[222] Seeing all this, I have reached an impasse with my convictions."

"I am in the south where it is very hot, but in a day I'll have to ship out and join the fight with the Germans at Stalingrad. That means waving good-bye to my life. I am writing this letter on a steamship, and these are certainly the last minutes of my life. I have information about the front: when an echelon reaches the front, out of the four thousand men, only fifteen or twenty will make it, and those are the ranking commanders. Only fifteen minutes are needed to destroy a division."

The report also flagged as anti-Soviet several letter writers with anti-Semitic views who claimed the Soviet government was Jewish.[223]

Voices like these are important for understanding the soldiers' experience of war, but they can only be fruitfully studied within their political context. For the NKVD operatives who collected them, these statements represented a pole of hostility they were bent on eradicating. They did so by confiscating the letters and sometimes arresting the authors and addressees as well. Letter writers who voiced despair but did not expound a political platform were left untouched, but their letters confiscated, so as not to contaminate Soviet society. On an aggregate level the work of the NKVD looked like this: "after checking the letters, texts were detected that voiced complaints about exhaustion from the war and the hardship of military service. A number of letters reflected defeatist sentiments. During the period from June to August 1942, out of 30,237,000 examined letters, 15,469 contain such statements."[224] Reports always concluded that the overwhelming majority of letters sent from the Soviet front lines "reflected the healthy morale and political reliability of the personnel."[225] Critics might contend that in making this assertion the NKVD agents did not account for the fact that Red Army soldiers knew their letters were being censored and hence did not confide their true thoughts to them. But such criticism misses the bigger point: that a huge, costly censorship apparatus was at work, scanning every single letter that passed from the front to the rear—a unique feature among all warfaring nations in World War II—in an effort to transform Red Army soldiers' thinking and behavior in wartime.

This work was performed with equal zeal by NKVD censors and by the political officers at the Stalingrad Front who kept explaining to soldiers why they were fighting until minutes before battle. They resumed their task as soon as fighting was over, summarizing and interpreting the day's events. The political officers trained soldiers to speak about themselves in a way that, they believed, would decisively influence thought and action in war. An account of subjective experience in wartime remains incomplete if it fails to take into account the pervasive monitoring and conditioning performed by the Soviet ideological state apparatus and its structuring effects.

And so, when the Moscow historians arrived at the Stalingrad front in late December 1942 they encountered soldiers who had fully incorporated Soviet notions of heroism and cowardice and were conversant about the battle's political and historical significance.

HISTORIANS OF THE AVANT-GARDE

The historians who conducted the interviews in Stalingrad not only documented the work and impact of the ideological apparatus but participated in it. As Soviet citizens they felt called on to help the Red Army defeat Hitler's Germany. They understood their project as an important contribution to the education and mobilization of Soviet society in time of war. Like the writers and artists who volunteered as war correspondents and photographers in the Red Army, the historians wanted to make themselves useful. They did this by reviving the avant-garde documentary style that Russian critics, writers, and filmmakers had developed after the 1917 revolution.[226] The participants in this avant-garde movement took as their subject the Soviet world, where, from their vantage point, a drama of monumental importance was unfolding. They believed it was misguided and senseless to retain traditional art forms such as the novel, whose invented world turned its back on the real one. The critic Sergei Tretyakov argued that writing a work like *War and Peace* in the Soviet era would be anachronistic. The preferred medium was the newspaper, which day after day and page after page reported news of Soviet industrialization and fostered it in the process. News coverage and eyewitness interviews not only represented reality; they also ordered raw facts into a meaningful framework. As documentarians, artists, and intellectuals were "operatives" participating in the "life of the material" and engineering a new world.[227]

Historians and Communist party representatives alike embraced the documentary aesthetic at the beginning of the 1920s, and together initiated a series of large-scale historical projects. The first was the Commission for the Study of the October Revolution and of the Russian Communist Party

(*Istpart*). Founded in 1920, it recorded the history of the Bolshevik uprising for future generations. In Moscow, Petrograd, and numerous other Russian cities, "commemorative evenings" were held in which people relayed their experiences of the 1917 upheaval. The directors of the commission served as mediators in a system of history workshops run through local party bureaus, municipal administrations, and newspaper offices. The directors wanted to gather as many eyewitnesses as possible; they believed that bearing witness to the founding moment of Soviet history would make them active participants in the revolution as well as inspire readers.[228] Despite these high expectations, however, the commission's publication output was meager. As the history of the revolution became entangled in the battle for Lenin's legacy, party leaders began to censor the eyewitness accounts. By the time *The Short Course of the History of the All-Union Communist Party* appeared in 1938, most *Istpart* documents had been expunged from the official record and confined to state archives.

In 1931, in the midst of the first five year plan, the writer Maxim Gorky conceived of a grand literary project: every large factory in the Soviet Union—he had over three hundred in mind—would write its own history and include as many workers as possible as coauthors. A staff of almost one hundred writers and journalists working full-time supervised the mammoth project. Their job was to teach factory workers documentary techniques and expand their historical consciousness by encouraging them to record their own experiences. Gorky asked the editors to collect memories primarily from "shock workers," working-class heroes who far surpassed their work quotas. Gorky embraced the ideas of Nietzsche but interpreted them in a socialist vein. He believed that every person came into the world a hero, but that heroic essence would unfold only if it received proper support. In Gorky's eyes the hero had an important function as a teacher, "a HUMAN BEING in capital letters" who showed others how to become more human than they already were. The project's staff members were to foster a society-wide emergence of socialist heroes while learning from the stories they collected and reforging themselves in a collectivist spirit.[229] By the time war broke out in 1941, twenty volumes had been published in the series *History of the Factories and Plants*. Among them was the well-received volume *People of the Stalingrad Tractor Factory* (1934). It presented a variety of literary sketches and photographic portraits of factory workers, and included an introduction by Gorky and a closing essay by the writer Leopold Averbakh. The work showcased the many functions of the project's authors: observers, creators, participants, and literary engineers of mass transformation.[230]

In 1931 another historical project began under Gorky's supervision: the history of the Russian Civil War. Aesthetically and institutionally similar to his previous work but much larger in scale, it was not intended to be a military history in the traditional sense. Rather, it aimed to depict the heroic individuals who fought in the Civil War, be they workers, peasants, or soldiers. It was to be the start of a new Marxist historiography of the masses that upended traditional hierarchies and mobilized each and every participant. Fifteen narrative volumes were planned, supplemented by documents, scholarly analysis, memoirs, art books, and photo albums. The project was fueled in part by Gorky's concern that the millions of peasants entering the urban industrial workforce in the 1930s could undermine the spirit of the proletarian revolution; all the more reason to invoke this spirit in the life histories of working-class heroes for the political education of "unfinished" workers from rural provinces.[231] The Civil War project eventually acquired gigantic dimensions, with local commissions in the Caucasus, Central Asia, and the Far East. By 1933, three thousand eyewitness accounts had been recorded. The commission directors in Moscow created a catalog of 100,000 index cards and a bibliography of more than 10,000 books.[232]

The project's chief editor was the young historian Isaak Mints. The work, full of intense exchanges with Gorky, was no doubt a formative experience for Mints, who had served as a commissar in the Civil War. [233] He learned to manage a large-scale historical study with multiple field offices and countless workers, to conduct eyewitness interviews, and to embrace Gorky's idea of the socialist hero. The Commission on the History of the Great Patriotic War, which Mints founded in December 1941, primarily relied on the institutional and intellectual resources of the Civil War project.[234]

Isaak Mints was born in 1896 in the Ukrainian mining region of Dnepropetrovsk. The son of a Jewish merchant, he wanted to study at the University of Kharkov but was denied admission on account of his religious background. Instead, he joined the revolutionary movement, becoming a member of the Bolshevik party in April 1917, and fighting in the Red Army when the Civil War broke out in early 1918. Mints quickly rose to commissar in a Cossack division, where he was in charge of political education. In 1920 he was named head commissar in a prestigious Cossack corps.[235] (One can only imagine the chutzpah required of Mints to hold his own among the Cossacks, who were infamous for their anti-Jewish hatred.)[236] After the Civil War he completed a degree in history at the Institute for the Red Professors and later became its deputy director. In the 1920s he wrote about the history of the Civil War. In 1935 he completed his doctoral work, and by 1936 he had become a corresponding member of the Academy of the Sciences.[237]

In 1935 the first large volume of the Civil War history appeared. But it was soon withdrawn and pulped, as many of the eyewitnesses and several of the editors were swept up in Stalin's purges. The revised edition appeared in 1938. Neither it nor the second volume, published four years later, bears any resemblance to Gorky's idea of a workers' history.[238] Instead, they describe the political conflicts of 1917, glorify Stalin, and demonize those denounced in the show trials of 1936–1938. In the run-up to the first volume's publication, Stalin met frequently with Gorky, Mints, and the other editors, eventually making seven hundred corrections to the manuscript.[239] By then, Mints must have understood the political implications of historical publishing in the Soviet Union. The materials he assembled portrayed Stalin and his comrade in arms Voroshilov as revolutionary liberators. From here it was only a small step to Stalin's apotheosis as the agent of world history in *The Short Course of the History of the All-Union Communist Party*. Many researchers have alleged that Mints coauthored *The Short Course*, but available sources provide no supporting evidence.[240]

Isaak Mints, late 1920s

In 1984, looking back, Mints recalled that the idea to write the history of the Great Patriotic War occurred to him several weeks after fighting broke out.[241] Napoleon's invasion of Russia in 1812—Russia's *first* Patriotic War—had been on his mind. He may have been influenced by *War and Peace*, Tolstoy's novel about the events of 1812, which in the summer of 1941 was reprinted in large numbers and consulted by many Soviet citizens looking for historical and moral orientation:[242]

> How did that business start? It was July 1941, a hard time. Our armies were retreating, fighting their way out. At that difficult time I wrote a letter to the Central Committee: I understand that conditions are tough. But think how much better our understanding of the Patriotic War of 1812 would have been if its participants had left us their stories. We must not waste time now. We must record current events. Later mankind will ask how it all happened. I proposed that we create a commission that would gather materials, study, analyze, and create a chronicle of this great epic. Weeks went by. There was no answer. I realized that history was probably the last thing we needed to worry about. That would be true if there were no connection between history and the present. But there is a connection—a direct one. I was very worried, called several times, and then lost hope.

On August 27, 1941, the Central Committee—possibly at Mints's urging—discussed creating a chronicle of the Great Patriotic War but rejected the idea as impractical.[243] The timing was inopportune: by the summer of 1941 the Wehrmacht had pushed far into the Soviet Union's interior, with German troops surrounding Smolensk, just 220 miles from Moscow. Even for historical optimists—which all communists were—spinning these circumstances into a Soviet success story would be difficult. The situation continued to worsen in the following weeks. On October 8, General Zhukov reported to Stalin that the last Soviet line of defense around Moscow was crumbling, and on October 15 Stalin ordered the evacuation of the capital. The tide did not begin to turn until November, when the Germans had to halt their pincer offensive and fresh Soviet troops were deployed on the Moscow front. Stalin's decision to stay in the city, together with his public speeches on the anniversary of the revolution on November 6 and 7, also did their part to boost Soviet morale. On December 5 the Red Army began its counteroffensive against Army Group Center.[244]

Most institutes of the Academy of Sciences and their staff were evacuated farther east in October. Mints and some of his coworkers refused to leave. It was a courageous decision: as later became known, German intelligence agents had listed the editorial office of the "History of the Civil War," located on 9 Comintern Street, among the "strategic objects" that were to be seized following the conquest of Moscow.[245] In his diary Mints merely noted that on November 25, Georgy Alexandrov, party secretary for agitation and propaganda, mandated the creation of a commission to collect documents and materials for a chronicle of the Patriotic War.[246] Two weeks later, on December 10, the Moscow Regional Party Committee, with First Secretary Shcherbakov presiding, passed a directive creating the Commission on the Establishment of a Chronicle of the Defense of Moscow.[247] Alexandrov was appointed to chair the commission, with Mints as his deputy. Other members included Communist party philosopher Pavel Yudin, GlavPURKKA official Fyodor Kuznetsov, Pravda's editor in chief Pyotr Pospyelov, and other representatives of the Moscow Regional Party Committee. Mints was entrusted with building a task force of around twenty researchers from the Academy of Sciences to gather documents on the war and write a daily chronicle of events. According to the directive, local party administrations were to assist the commission with collecting the materials. It also mentioned installing commission branches in large factories to document wartime output. Journalists, writers, war illustrators, and other artists were to provide advice and assistance, while the Main Political Administration of the Red Army was to supply the commission with newspapers, brochures, reports on the political climate, and documents from army life. The directive bore the hallmarks of Gorky's grand historical projects. Mints confirmed this in his brief diary entry for December 11: "In a word, it was suggested to use all the editorial experience of *The History of the Civil War*."

Before the commission was officially established, Mints began searching for staff. On November 30 he gave a lecture to a packed crowd of six hundred researchers at the House of Scholars, outlining the commission's goals and calling on audience members to participate. "One could feel," he subsequently noted in his diary, "that the audience was seeking and expecting to be used in work, to be instructed what to do. They were waiting for leadership."[248] One week later Mints visited the Moscow front. In a division made up of Moscow communists he met historian Arkady Sidorov and three associates from his Civil War project.[249] The next day Mints ran across two earlier staff members in another division: he asked army command to place them in different units to ensure maximum benefit for the commission.[250] Over the next weeks Mints assembled a small task force. By July 1942 the Civil War research unit had returned to Moscow after being evacuated, and Mints had gathered forty permanent staff members—historians, literary scholars, bibliographers, and stenographers.[251]

In the first months the commission mainly focused on the defense of Moscow. As new branches were set up, the staff began to collect materials from other battle sites: Leningrad, Tula, Odessa, Sevastopol, and, in December 1942, Stalingrad. A separate chronicle for each city was planned. Early on, Mints had envisaged two further publications. One was the history of the Red Army beginning with the units that had received the coveted Guards status (awarded for extraordinary valor in combat). In March 1942 an internal commission memo declared, "It is paramount to ensure that all Guards units and all divisions have their combat history recorded. That is the most important order of business of the day, as the history of a military unit is excellent material for educating soldiers, and for transmitting experience, knowledge, and military tradition. That will help in the creation of a great history of the Great Patriotic War in the future, after victory."[252] The troops in the Guards divisions were accorded a similar function to the shock workers in Gorky's history of the Soviet industry. Just as the most productive workers served as role models for laborers from rural villages, the Guards units were to show regular troops how to be heroes. Gorky's heroic model found even clearer expression in the second publication Mints was planning: an encyclopedia of Soviet heroes—a collection of short biographies assembled from interviews and other documents for every Soviet soldier who had been awarded a gold star. The purpose of this encyclopedia was to identify shining examples and encourage readers to emulate them.

The commission's other areas of concentration were the partisan movement, the war economy, Soviet women and non-Russian nationalities in battle, and the German occupation. Mints turned to the last subject immediately after the Historical Commission was established. On December 26, 1941, he traveled with a delegation of scientists and engineers to Yasnaya Polyana, Leo Tolstoy's estate outside Tula that had temporarily fallen into German hands. The delegation was to inventory the destruction wreaked by the invaders on the estate and the state museum there. Mints and his staff, accompanied by a stenographer, spoke with museum personnel and farmers from the neighboring *kolkhoz* who had witnessed the Germans firsthand. The resulting publication provided a key impetus for the creation, in November 1942, of the Extraordinary Commission for the Investigation of Crimes of the German-Fascist Invaders. (At the

Nuremberg trials the Soviets presented the documentary evidence collected by this commission.)[253]

Notably for the Stalin era, Mints acted mostly without official mandate. He quickly renamed the Commission on the History of the Defense of Moscow the Commission on the History of the Great Patriotic War. He even recruited workers for his expanded project, though he was unable to get the blessing of party heads, and with them their resources and authorization.[254] (It should be remembered that Gorky's projects of the 1930s were formed by Central Committee decrees and thus stood under the supervision of the party.)[255] In his diary Mints complained about the bureaucracy and the lack of support from the Academy of Sciences.[256] His protests and the uncertain state of the commission show how much personal control Mints had over the project and how much depended on his initiative, though nominally he was only its vice president.

According to a staff member, Mints traveled to the front multiple times during the war and held hundreds of lectures for political officers and soldiers. Again and again, he impressed those present with his tireless energy.[257] Mints's signature appears frequently in the handling of the source materials. He repeatedly reminded his staff to collect materials impartially and focus on documents and materials normally left out of the archive: army newspapers, brochures, leaflets, political reports, film spools, personal

Professor I. I. Mints lecturing to Red Army commanders near Mozhaisk, February 16, 1942. *Illustrator: A. I. Yermolayev*

letters, diaries, oral histories.[258] Their task was to record civilian war efforts as well as combat operations. Following the documentary spirit of Gorky's projects, Mints envisioned an *histoire totale* encompassing all the war's participants through a variety of media.

In the beginning interviews were only one of many sources of information used by the commission; over time they came to dominate its work.[259] This was not least because of their popularity among the eyewitnesses. Soldiers and partisans pressed for interviews. As one said, they believed that "we have earned attention and our place in history."[260] Due to the many staff members and institutions involved in the project, Mints had guidelines drawn up for carrying out interviews: "It is necessary to record live stories of individual commanders, political workers, and soldiers about specific combat episodes, and about entire time periods of their lives, their encounters, thoughts, feelings, and so on." Mints recommended that a unit's commander and chief of staff be interviewed first. This top-down view would give historians helpful perspective when later questioning individual soldiers, commanders, and political workers who had heroically distinguished themselves. Each interview, the guidelines explained, must contain basic information on the respondent: "biographical details about each storyteller: brief information about the date and place of birth, name, patronymic, home address, party affiliation, and work prior to the war. In certain cases (of particular interest) the biography should be taken down in detail. Such work is best carried out with the help of stenography or, in case and a stenographer is unavailable, by brief hand notation. If the circumstances permit, the notation should be read back to the interviewee and signed by him. It should be indicated when, where, and by whom the notation was made."[261]

The central idea was to shed light on the "living person," "his thoughts, feelings, and experiences, and in connection with that, his place and role in combat." "It is necessary," the guidelines underscored, "to collect the notes of individuals on any 'free' subject bearing on the history of the unit (a combat episode, a report of some encounter, the enemy, the fighting spirit, etc.)." Mints stressed the importance of encouraging soldiers to speak freely without interruption: "for historians, their private feelings, thoughts, and observations are valuable, and therefore they should be able to say anything they like."[262] The guidelines noted the importance of preserving the memory of the fallen, in addition to recording the voices of war: "It is important to take down the stories about fallen comrades at arms, subordinates, commanders, as well as eyewitness accounts of heroic acts and deaths, in order to most fully preserve the glorious image of the fallen."[263] For Mints, a committed communist, politics was a self-evident part of documentary work. But he believed that it should not be "detached" from individuals and combat, as was often the case, but integrated into the entire complex of events. The guidelines concluded with the following points:

10. Do not gloss over difficulties and shortcomings. Reality should not be made more presentable. Remember the instruction of comrade Stalin that "only in a struggle with difficulties are true cadres forged."
11. Show the daily routine of the unit (its life, leisure, connection with the home front, correspondence, joy, and grief).
12. Maintain strict historical truth throughout. Carefully check all events, dates, names, and facts by cross-examining people and documents.[264]

THE COMMISSION IN STALINGRAD

Equipped with these general guidelines, four members of the commission—historians Esfir Genkina, Pyotr Beletski, and Abram Belkin, as well as stenographer Alexandra Shamshina—set off for Stalingrad in late December. They stayed in the besieged city for just under two weeks. To judge from the variety and scope of the transcripts, they carried out interviews almost nonstop. They departed one day before the Soviets launched their final offensive, but returned again in February with more staff. By March they had conducted 130 interviews with soldiers from thirteen rifle divisions, an air force division, a motorized brigade, and a mechanized corps. They spoke with staff officers from different field armies, with representatives from local party offices, and with workers and engineers from two factories. Among the first persons to be interviewed were Generals Chuikov and Shumilov. Many of the interviewees were high in the chain of command (twelve field army staff officers, twelve divisional commanders, twenty-five staff officers at the division and brigade levels, and thirty-three officers at the regiment, battalion, and battery levels); only twelve were sergeants and infantrymen.[265] The historians were not interested in finding as many eyewitnesses as possible but in obtaining in-depth testimony. To this end, they focused on troops from the 62nd, the 64th, and the 57th Armies who had fought in close proximity with one another since retreating from the Don steppes in the summer of 1942. The historians interviewed multiple members of the same unit (divisions, regiments, and, in a few cases, companies) to merge individual narratives into a larger story (the course of the battle in general, but also clashes and other local events) told from a variety of perspectives.[266]

The first few interview transcripts completed by the commission contained the questions and insertions of the historians along with the responses. These were omitted from later transcripts to give them the character of a closed narrative.[267] But the questions can be reconstructed from the recurring narrative patterns in many of the interviews. Sometimes the interviewees began with a question, repeating the words of the interviewer. Interviews with renowned commanders or decorated soldiers usually started with a request to hear about their personal biography: childhood, education, profession, and how they came to join the army and the Communist party. (Most of the commanders had been members for years; the soldiers, usually much younger, did not join until the war.) Afterward came a detailed description of military assignments and responsibilities.

The historians asked them about the "most memorable period" in their lives (as with Colonel Nikolai Batyuk and Lieutenant Colonel Kolesnik). Sometimes they were disappointed by the responses. Regimental Commander Genrikh Fugenfirov said, "How can I single out a characteristic detail or the particular features of a fight if bombs kept raining on us and the regiment was under aerial bombardment for days on end?" They wanted to know when the battle for the city raged most intensely, and how it differed from combat operations elsewhere (as with Lieutenant Colonel Smirnov and Regimental Commander Fugenfirov). Many questions were about what happened before, during, and after battle: "How did we train the soldiers for combat?" (Battalion Commissar Stepanov); "How did we deal with the fear of tanks?" (Lieutenant Colonel Svirin); "How did we work with snipers?" (Captain Olkhovkin); "What was the significance of the river crossing?" (Captain Semyon Ryvkin); "What did the pioneer battalion do during combat?" (Lieutenant Kolesnik); "What did we do following the attack?" (Colonel Smolyanov); "What are we doing now?" (Junior Lieutenant Ayzenberg). Almost every interview inquired about soldiers whose acts set them apart. For instance: "I don't exactly remember who distinguished themselves in that fighting. Some were killed, others wounded" (Sergeant Karpushin). Political officers were asked about the effectiveness of their work: "How did we conduct political and party work?" (Divisional Commissar Levykin); "How did the soldiers feel about our events? What kind of people came to join our party?" (Colonel Smolyanov), "How did communists conduct themselves [in battle]?" (division party secretary Alexander Koshkarev). They were also interested in hearing about deficiencies of the Red Army and they questioned commanders about their "own mistakes"

(General Chuikov). Toward the end of conversations they often asked about promotions or medals soldiers had received. Infantryman Alexei Pavlov summed up his record: "All in all I killed eleven Germans and destroyed one machine gun."[268]

Some soldiers were very communicative, others more reserved. Linguistic hurdles were partly to blame. As one Latvian soldier explained, "Perhaps I could tell more, but my command of Russian is poor. Besides, talking about oneself doesn't feel right."[269] Rural dialects colored the language of some eyewitnesses, in particular the commanders, who spoke more openly than their subordinates. Soldiers for the most part spoke quickly and to the point. The shortest of the interviews ran two to three pages typed out in long form, but most ranged between eight and fifteen pages, with some reaching twenty or thirty. Some of the soldiers interviewed stuck to the fighting in Stalingrad; others went into great length about their family background and how they came to the Red Army. This variety suited the historians; they wanted to show "living people," not just lump together various accounts.

The Stalingrad staff worked diligently, completing many more interviews than other delegations of historians on the front. The total output of the commission during the war was nevertheless considerable: more than five thousand interview transcripts with soldiers, partisans, and civilians, covering broad areas of the war, from the front and the countryside to the occupied territories.[270]

This massive collection of documents is unique in military and social history research. This becomes apparent when it is compared to an ostensibly similar project undertaken by the US armed forces during World War II.[271] The chief US Army combat historian, Lieutenant Colonel Samuel Marshall, and a staff of workers interviewed groups of soldiers within hours after combat in the Pacific and European theaters.[272] Marshall stated that he interviewed a total of four hundred companies, each made up of 125 men. Marshall did not see himself primarily as a documentary historian, however. The project's purpose was to strengthen the army's combat effectiveness. From the interviews he concluded that most soldiers—he put the number between 75 and 85 percent—were so overcome by fear in battle that they wouldn't use their weapons.[273] Marshall recommended drilling the soldiers to overcome their instinctive fear of death. Indeed, it was because of Marshall's influential studies that later generations of US soldiers underwent more live-fire training, increasing the percentage of those who used their weapons in war. But Marshall's work has drawn much criticism from historians. Roger Spiller believes that Marshall greatly exaggerated the number he claimed to interview and contends that he invented his data on the rate of fire. Spiller and others point out that Marshall was trained as a journalist before being promoted to army historian.[274] Instead of having a stenographer transcribe the interviews, he based his work on shorthand notes.

Marshall's approach stands in contrast to the care exercised by professional Soviet historians, who used stenographers to record all the interviews and then archived the transcripts. But comparing Marshall with Mints reveals more than the difference between simple journalism and scholarly rigor. It underscores the emotion that fueled the Soviet historians as they went about their work, their trust in the universal principles governing history, and their confidence that these laws would inevitably lead to Soviet victory. For instance, the decision to record the interviews in the first person followed a Gorky-esque aim: respondents were meant to see themselves as actors on a world-historical stage. Equipped with a new subjective awareness, they would push the envelope of individual achievement and advance the objective course of history.

THE TRANSCRIPTS

In view of the commission's enormous efforts, it published astonishingly little. To this day, virtually none of the thousands of interviews transcribed by stenographers have gone to press. The few publications the commission produced appeared during the war and portrayed events mostly from a bird's-eye view, largely omitting the individual voices. The sparse output was due in part to Mints's own conviction that as long as the Soviet Union remained at war, interviewing eyewitnesses and collecting other documentary materials ought to take precedence. Another difficulty lay in bringing the views expressed by the respondents into line with the ideals of the historians. Gorky's earlier projects generated relatively few publications on similar grounds: few of the interviewed factory workers spoke in the heroic categories attributed to them; most accounts were either edited or hidden away in archives. So too in the case of the Mints commission. Internal discussions reveal that the staff argued about whether to show persons with all their frailties or disclose only their heroic deeds. But the outcome of the debate was a foregone conclusion, for it was not the commission staff that ultimately decided the contents but the Communist party, specifically the powerful censorship office known as Glavlit.

The extent of Glavlit's influence is illustrated by the first large project of the Mints commission—the study of the German occupation of Tolstoy's estate. Germans controlled the Tolstoy museum at Yasnaya Polyana for six weeks, from October 30 to December 14, 1941. As already noted, Mints traveled there at the end of December with historians from the Academy of the Sciences to assess the damage. The delegation's report informed the note on German atrocities in occupied Soviet territory issued by foreign affairs minister Vyacheslav Molotov on January 6, 1942. In it Molotov specifically mentions Tolstoy's estate, a "glorious memorial of Russian culture, wrecked, befouled, and finally set on fire by the Nazi vandals."[275] Joseph Goebbels categorically denied Molotov's public accusations,[276] and Alexandrov gave Mints the task of preparing a response. Mints suggested a book documenting the crimes at Yasnaya Polyana. Though his idea met with Stalin's approval,[277] when the finished book was later submitted to Glavlit for review, it set off alarm bells. The censor took particular offense at diary entries by museum employee Maria Shchegoleva that filled a large portion of the book. Citing Molotov's description of pillaging vandals, the censor complained that Shchegoleva's diary did not do justice to the defilement that occurred at Yasnaya Polyana. The author's "quiet" tone came across as "pedantic" and lacked the outrage befitting a Soviet citizen.[278] In the same breath the censor criticized the book's editors for their "totally irresponsible" work: "They didn't even bother to separate everything that was valuable in Shchegoleva's diary from the obviously useless material which as a result not only fails to increase hatred for the fascist enslavers but actually weakens it."[279] The censor believed that the editors were politically obligated to intervene in the accounts of eyewitnesses, preserving the ideologically compliant views and suppressing everything else. Not surprisingly, the book was rejected. When a revised form later appeared, it did not include Shchegoleva's diary.

In 1943 the commission published two pieces on the battle for Stalingrad, a short study and a separate brochure containing an interview with sniper Vasily Zaytsev.[280] In "Heroic Stalingrad" historian Esfira Genkina portrays Stalingrad as the most important battle of the war, where the heroic spirit of the city's defenders forced Hitler's elite forces to their knees. In Genkina's telling, the valor displayed by Red Army soldiers did not spring from a political education in heroism and cowardice nor from fear of coercive measures—she makes no mention of Order no. 227—but from their very being. Genkina cherry-picks passages from the transcripts that paint the defenders as one-dimensional heroes with deeply held communist convictions, soldiers who without batting an eyelash took on a superior German army. Her narrative sings the unity of Red Army soldiers and ends with an ode to Stalin: "The glory of Stalingrad is the glory of our chief, the leader of the Red Army. To Stalin, to victory!"[281] Like "Heroic Stalingrad," the interview with Zaytsev was also heavily edited, as comparing the stenographic transcripts and the published version shows. The editors omitted from the interview all statements that made Zaytsev seem less than heroic, rewriting his story into an unconditional affirmation of the Communist party.

The editors may well have undertaken these interventions without Glavlit's insistence. It should not be forgotten that Mints and his colleagues understood their project as aiding Soviet victory. Indeed, one finds in their work the revolutionary sweep of the documentary movement. They wanted to become "operative" by engaging with the raw material and extracting from it the fighting spirit needed to excite their readers. In the same breath, however, they strove toward meticulous scholarship. They handled historical documents with the utmost respect, and the clarity of their methodology impresses scholars to this day. Their rigor suffuses each and every interview as well as the enormous archive the commission assembled during its four-year existence (historians continued to maintain the archive after the commission was dissolved). The raw material for the Stalingrad transcripts, presented seventy years later, ultimately owes its existence to this scholarly ethos.

EDITORIAL PRINCIPLES

The transcripts from the 215 interviews conducted by the Mints commission in Stalingrad fill thousands of typed pages. This book presents only a selection. A unique feature of these transcripts is the historians' decision to interview numerous members of the same cohort, be it a division, regiment, or factory. Viewed in their entirety, the transcripts offer a detailed illumination of local events from multiple perspectives. But their three-dimensionality does not materialize when individual interviews are read in succession. To recreate it here, I have arranged the interviews in a way that brings out the common experiences of each cohort while exposing the rifts between them. Specifically, I have woven strands of conversation out of the individual responses and grouped them chronologically and by location.

For instance, I present the combat operations of the 308th Rifle Division as described by both commanders and infantry, providing a single picture from several vantage points within the unit. For some operations, such as a September 18, 1942, attempt to take an important hill that resulted in heavy losses, the storytelling becomes more concentrated, with each eyewitness recalling the intense fighting of that day. Another set of individual accounts—a chorus of voices across diverse parts of Soviet society—provides rich descriptions of the fate of Stalingrad and its people from July 1942, when frantic work began to fortify the frontline city, until the spring of 1943, when engineers returned to plan the reconstruction of its ruined factories.

This type of narrative montage recalls Akira Kurosawa's *Rashomon.* The film is about a criminal trial, recalled in flashback, in which four witnesses take the stand and submit different versions of what happened. The film employs this technique to shed light on the unreliability of subjective statements.[282] But unlike the testimony in *Rashomon*, the interviews from Stalingrad are strikingly consistent down to the smallest detail, from their ideas of heroism, fear, and self-actualization to their accounts of combat and the conduct of fellow soldiers. The extensive agreement among respondents indicates that the events they described were not after-the-fact inventions of Soviet propaganda. A reading of the Stalingrad transcripts invalidates any claim that the public statements of Red Army infantry consisted of Soviet clichés, isolated from the reality of war. Rather, one finds a language shared by foot soldiers and officers alike, informed by the same ideas and horizons of experience. At the same time, it is apparent that political officers emphasized specific modes of speech for talking about both oneself and the enemy. The language of the interviews was thus twofold: a description of the battle and a mark of ideological conditioning.

Following the group conversations are nine individual interviews printed in their original form and for the most part in full.[283] The selection comprises soldiers of different ranks and forms of expression. It begins with the self-serving and confident accounts of Generals Chuikov and Rodimtsev. It also includes the minutely detailed report of staff officer Nikolai Aksyonov, the chatty narrative of the sniper and Hero of the Soviet Union Vasily Zaytsev (by then already a legend), and the artlessly delivered testimony of Private Alexander Parkhomenko. The only woman in the group (the commission interviewed few women in Stalingrad) is Vera Gurova, a medic in General Rodimtsev's division. The last interview is with Captain Pyotr Zayonchkovsky, who, drawing on his work in enemy propaganda, provides interesting insights into Soviet perceptions of Germans at Stalingrad.

The book then switches sides, shedding light on the German perspective. The first part of this chapter contains transcripts from interrogations of imprisoned Germans officers that Captain Zayonchkovsky carried out in February 1943. The second part consists of excerpts from a diary kept by a German soldier in the *Kessel*. The materials for both parts stem from the Historical Commission archive. As with all the previous sections, short introductions provide background and context. Additional information can be found in the endnotes. I conclude with a chapter on the fate of the Mints's commission after the end of the war and discuss why the documents remained under lock and key for decades.

The transcripts are presented with all their stylistic idiosyncrasies intact; only obvious typos have been corrected. The parentheses in the documentary text contain remarks from commission staff; brackets indicate comments and abbreviations by the editors. Except when Latin letters were handwritten in the transcripts, German names in the documents have been reverse translated from the Russian and could not always be reconstructed with certainty. For instance, the soldier referred to in Cyrillic as "Geynts Khyunel" (Гейнц Хюнель) is rendered as "Heinz Hühnel" but could also be spelled "Heinz Hünel."

Interspersed among the transcripts are Soviet photographs, leaflets, and posters that illuminate the battle of Stalingrad and document the mind-set of their creators. Just as the interviews ideologically shaped the respondents while describing the war, the photographs are interventions, conscious attempts by the photographers to attune themselves and their beholders to the exigencies of war. With certain restrictions this also applies to the small-format portraits made by Red Army soldiers and frontline photographers. Alongside a physical impression of the eyewitnesses, they convey an expression of the pride felt by soldiers conscious of doing their part in a people's war.

2

A CHORUS OF SOLDIERS

Soldiers of the 308th Rifle Division

THE FATE OF THE CITY AND ITS RESIDENTS

The German advance on Stalingrad had the stated aim of annihilating the city and forcing the surviving population into slave labor. Yet Stalin forbade the evacuation of residents, ordering that the city be held whatever the cost. The following interviews—carried out between January 1943 and January 1944 with city and regional administrators, party officials, factory managers, engineers, and a professor at the city's medical institute—explain how the city armed for its defense before being reduced to rubble and how, to cite one respondent, the "pulse" of Stalingrad changed over the course of the battle.

The Wehrmacht's basic strategy in Stalingrad was the same one it used to attack Moscow and Leningrad the previous year: use aerial bombardment and artillery fire to destroy the city before occupying it in order to protect the lives of German soldiers on the ground.[1] Luftflotte 4—a fleet of 780 bombers and 490 fighter planes—flew endless sorties over Stalingrad between August 23 and September 13, 1942.[2] The fleet was under the command of General Wolfram von Richthofen, who had been the chief of staff for the Condor Legion when it introduced carpet bombing, a tactic that destroyed Guernica in the Spanish Civil War.[3] Richthofen also commanded the bombing of Belgrade in April 1941 that killed an estimated seventeen thousand residents[4] and was responsible for the attack on Sevastopol in the summer of 1942. The air campaign in Stalingrad, the most violent on the Eastern Front, marked what Beevor described as the "natural culmination of Richthofen's career."[5] German planes dropped the first bombs on Stalingrad in October 1941 and carried out isolated strikes in early 1942. In the second half of July the full-blown campaign began; from that point on air raid sirens in the city sounded almost daily.[6]

At the beginning of July regional officials made plans to evacuate the city and other areas near the front. Representatives from ministries in Moscow, charged with relocating key industries farther east, visited the Stalingrad Tractor factory (refitted for tank production), the Red October steelworks, and the Barricades munitions plant. In mid-July the commanders of the Stalingrad military district, better informed than everyone else about what was happening, decamped with their families. Their actions did not go unnoticed by the city's population, and NKVD officers observed a growing panic, fueled by rumors that the Germans had reached the city limits.[7]

In the early morning hours of July 20 regional party secretary Alexei Chuyanov received a call from Stalin. He ordered military district commanders to be called back immediately, the anxiety quelled, and the city kept out of enemy hands. Chuyanov passed on these orders to his party colleagues the next evening, stressing their responsibility for the city's defense.[8] Coming a week before the fall of Rostov and the issuing of Order no. 227, the call evinced the hard line that Stalin had pursued from the outset. All able-bodied persons not already involved in military production had to help dig trenches. Accompanied by a contingent of activists—in one sector ninety-six politruks supervised the work of four thousand residents—they built three defensive rings around the city. Persons were permitted to leave the city only if it served the war effort: fifty thousand injured soldiers, attending medical personnel, and children from city orphanages.[9] An order evacuating all nonworking women and their children saved the families of local officials, the only ones who could afford to keep their wives at home. Working women could leave the city only if their factory was evacuated. By mid-August almost eight thousand families from the city elite had been sent away. These precautions were not announced publicly but could not be concealed from city residents. Communist agitators in the factories were hard-pressed to explain matters to irate workers and had difficulty convincing people to hold out. Still, until August 22 life in Stalingrad carried on more or less normally: parents prepared their kids for the new school year, audiences packed movie houses and theaters, and communist leaders assured the population that the Germans would never take the city.[10]

The number of people killed in the devastating air raid of August 23 and the ones that followed daily until September 12 is contested. Most researchers put the figure at forty thousand—the number cited in documents presented at the Nuremburg trials.[11] The city commandant, Vladimir Demchenko, told the historians in 1943 that two thousand air strikes took place in the afternoon and evening of August 23, killing ten thousand people.[12] Many injured on the first day of bombing could not be treated because most of the available medical personnel had been sent to the northernmost part of the city, which German panzers had infiltrated the same afternoon. The 8th Soviet Air Fleet focused its attacks on the encroaching panzer troops, leaving the rest of the city exposed.[13]

In the late evening of August 23, military leaders met at General Yeryomenko's headquarters with local party bosses, NKVD officers, and industry representatives. Also present was the head of the Soviet general staff, Alexander Vasilevsky. Two items were on the agenda: the immediate evacuation of the Stalingrad workforce and the mining of industrial facilities. After

Fires in Stalingrad, August 1942. *Photographer: Emmanuil Yevzerikhin*

midnight Chuyanov called Stalin and informed him about their discussion. As Yeryomenko later reported, Stalin continued to rule out large-scale evacuation and banned all further discussion of the matter on the grounds that it would encourage defeatism.[14]

Many people who fled the city in panic were detained at the ferry stations by the NKVD. Others were able to cross the river, either with approval from local officials or not. On August 24 the City Defense Committee ordered the evacuation of women and children to the countryside. The decision was motivated not by humanitarian concerns but by a need to save the scarce food resources in the beleaguered city.[15] The next day party leadership declared a state of siege and started ruthlessly rounding up looters in the burning city. The agitators also stepped up their efforts. The local party committee printed a million leaflets in the final days of August and blanketed the city with rousing slogans: "We will hold our native city!" "Not a step back!"[16]

When a citywide evacuation effort finally started on August 25, specialists and workers whose factories had burned to the ground went first. The mass departure did not commence until August 29, but even then workers took precedence, and in some instances they had to leave their families behind because of the lack of space on the boats. On August 27 three steamers conveying civilians upriver to Saratov—*Mikhail Kalinin*, *In Memory of the Paris Commune*, and *Joseph Stalin*—came under enemy fire. The *Joseph Stalin* ran aground, heavily damaged. Of the 1,200 passengers, only 186 were saved.[17] By September 14—the day German troops pushed forward through the city to the central ferry slip—315,000 people had been evacuated. According to one estimate, just as many were still in the city.[18] At this point Chuyanov and most of the other local party heads and NKVD commanders fled the city.

The city's largest industries continued to operate much longer. In the summer of 1942, the Red October steelworks produced 10 percent of Soviet steel, mostly for aeronautics and tank manufacture, and built rocket launchers on the side. After a state of siege was declared, it switched to the manufacture of machine-gun clusters, tank traps, and shovels, and to the repair of tanks and rocket launchers. The works stayed in operation until October 2; several days later it was gutted.[19] From October 1942 to early January 1943 Germans were mostly in control of the plant, though fighting was severe throughout this period. The Barricades munitions factory had produced large numbers of antitank canons since the Great Patriotic War began. The director left the factory on September 25; the last technicians departed on October 5, one day after the Germans attacked the factory.[20]

The massive Stalingrad Tractor factory—employing some twenty thousand workers—had been refitted for tank production in the late 1930s, and by the time war broke out it was the largest producer of T-34 tanks in the Soviet Union. On August 23, the 16th Panzer Division moved to within striking distance of the plant, but it kept churning out tanks until September 13, when the Germans began the siege. In the following days the vast majority of workers were evacuated; the 62nd Army retained a small contingent to carry out repairs for the tank regiments. The large German offensive on October 14 (described in detail by General Chuikov in his interview) concentrated on the Tractor factory. From there, German divisions planned to head south and take the last stretches of the Volga still held by the Soviets. After what Soviet and German eyewitnesses alike described as the heaviest fighting in the entire battle—the 62nd Army lost 13,000 soldiers and the Wehrmacht, 1,500—the Germans gained complete control of the plant on October 17. The Red Army did not retake the factory until February 2, 1943.[21]

Stalingrad's power plant, StalGRES, was located south of the city, near Beketovka. Situated a few miles from the front line, Beketovka was protected from the brunt of the fighting. It was the site of the main headquarters of the 64th Army, and in October Chuyanov moved the party headquarters there. Once the Germans reached Stalingrad, StalGRES came under daily artillery and mortar fire but remained in operation. A major attack on November 5 forced the power plant to close.

On October 12, Chuyanov noted in his diary that the plant's chief engineer, Konstantin Zubanov, married Dr. Maria Terentyeva in the basement of the plant while artillery fire thundered above.[22] In Zubanov's interview with the historians he described his ties to the plant and likened the factory's electrically generated pulses to the pulse of the city. The pulse metaphor recalls futuristic currents of the early twentieth century that had deep roots in the Russian workforce.[23] Zubanov might also have been referring to the well-known metronome beat that was broadcast over Leningrad radio. Engineers had originally introduced the sound in the 1930s for broadcasting pauses. After the war began, it was used as an early warning system, the speed of the beat quickening whenever enemy planes approached. During the Leningrad blockade radio stations had to restrict their programming and used the metronome to assure the people of Leningrad that the city was still alive.[24]

The interviews with Zubanov and the two dozen other eyewitnesses begin with descriptions of the city's industrialization in the 1930s and its transition to war production. They focus on the efforts to defend the city, the devastating air raids, and the dramatic evacuation of civilians. Worth noting is the severe criticism that General Chuikov and Commissar Vasiliev directed at party officials in Stalingrad for their failings during the city's defense and evacuation. In part, it was unjustified; Stalin bore some of the blame as well. Moreover, it was not about the military's dissatisfaction with the communists. Rather, it reflected the belief of those who fought on the front (which included communists such as Vasiliev) that those who did not only wanted to save their own hides.

The earliest recorded interviews were with Chuikov, Vasiliev, and the engineers Venyamin Zhukov and Pavel Matevosyan; they took place on January 8, 1943, at the destroyed Red October steelworks. Party officials were not interviewed until the historians visited again in March 1943. Woven into the interviews are excerpts from Alexei Chuyanov's war diary, published in 1968. These passages are set in italics. Chuyanov, a local party head, did not take part in the interviews.

THE SPEAKERS

City and Regional Administrators

Pigalyov, Dmitri Matveyevich—Chairman of the Executive Committee of the Stalingrad Soviet of Workers Deputies

Polyakov, Alexei Mikhailovich—Deputy chairman of the Executive Committee of the Stalingrad Regional Soviet of Workers Deputies

Romanenko, Grigory Dmitrievich—First secretary of the Barricades District of Stalingrad

Zimenkov, Ivan Fyodorovich—Chairman of the Stalingrad Regional Soviet of Workers Deputies

Party Officials

Babkin, Sergei Dmitrievich—First secretary of the Kirov District Party Committee

Chuyanov, Alexei Semyonovich—First secretary of the Stalingrad Regional Party Committee (excerpts from his published diary)

Denisova, Claudia Stepanovna—Secretary of the Yermansky District Party Committee

Kashintsev, Semyon Yefimovich—Secretary of the Red October District Party Committee

Petrukhin, Nikolai Romanovich—Chief of the war department of the Stalingrad Regional Party Committee

Piksin, Ivan Alexeyevich—Secretary of the Stalingrad City Party Committee

Prokhvatilov, Vasily Petrovich—Secretary of the Stalingrad Regional Party Committee

Odinokov, Mikhail Afanasievich—Secretary of the Voroshilov District Party Committee

Vodolagin, Mikhail Alexandrovich—Secretary of the Stalingrad Regional Party Committee

Specialists, Workers, Residents

Ioffe, Ezri Izrailevich—Acting director of the Stalingrad Medical Institute

Matevosyan, Pavel Petrovich—Chief engineer of the Red October steelworks

Zhukov, Veniamin Yakovlevich—Foreman of Workshop no. 7 at the Red October steelworks

Zubanov, Konstantin Vasilievich—Chief engineer of the Stalingrad Power Station (StalGRES)

Military Personnel

Burin, Ilya Fyodorovich—Former mechanic at the Barricades factory, scout in the 38th Motor Rifle Brigade

Burmakov, Ivan Dmitrievich—Major general, commander of the 38th Motor Rifle Brigade

Chuikov, Vasily Ivanovich—Lieutenant general, commander of the 62nd Army

Demchenko, Vladimir Kharitonovich—Major, commandant of Stalingrad

Gurov, Kuzma Akimovich—Lieutenant general, member of the Military Council of the 62nd Army

Vasilev, Ivan Vasilevich—Brigade commissar, chief of the political section of the 62nd Army

Zimin, Alexei Yakovlevich—Lieutenant, former worker at the Barricades factory, headquarters commandant of the 38th Motor Rifle Brigade, 64th Army[25]

Dmitri Matveyevich Pigalyov (Chairman of the Executive Committee of the Stalingrad Soviet of Workers Deputies): There were about 25,000 people living in Stalingrad in 1930—400,000 during the war, 550–560 thousand if you count evacuees. The city grew quite rapidly after 1930. As soon as the Tractor factory was completed, the population immediately grew by seventy to eighty thousand. We had a beautiful city center. There were two train stations, one down by the Volga and another in the city center. The recent growth was because of the factories.

From 1934 to 1935, the city was greatly improved. Those years saw the construction of the Great Stalingrad Hotel (370 rooms), the Intourist Hotel on the Square of the Fallen Heroes, the grand Univermag department store, which opened in 1938 or 1939, and the first and

The center of Stalingrad, summer 1942. *Photographer: Emmanuil Yevzerikhin*

second House of Soviets, on the square across from the Intourist Hotel, the Regional Executive Committee building (an extension). The House of Books was built, and the five- or six-story Lesprom building next to Intourist. These new buildings really livened up the whole square. [. . .] In the center we had the big new Gorky Drama Theater, a musical theater, and a youth theater. These were theaters with a permanent acting staff. Lovely buildings—the Palace of Pioneers, the printing institute. There was a good Palace of Sport that looked out over the Volga. In the Yermansky district[26] alone there was a whole bunch of cultural institutes. The art and music schools, the physical education training college—they were in that district, and the Komsomolets cinema, and also the excellent Spartak cinema, and the Red Star. The Tractor factory was home to a mechanical institute. There were 1,500 to 2,000 students. There they trained workers for the Tractor factory. Later they began sharing them with other factories. There was a large medical institute, with around 1,500 students.

Ezri Izrailevich Ioffe (Acting director of the Stalingrad Medical Institute): The Stalingrad Medical Institute was established in

1935. Its first class numbered 160 students. A young but very energetic faculty came together in a very short time. By the beginning of the war we had in our midst twenty-two doctors of medical science and upward of ten docents and candidates of medicine. The institute was located in a large, newly built four-story building, which contained three large auditoriums, ten classrooms, a library with thirty thousand volumes and a reading room, anatomy and pathology museums, and well equipped laboratories. We had more than three hundred microscopes, about a dozen kymographs,[27] radiological equipment, and so on. [. . .] Our first class of doctors graduated in 1940, some 150 of them. The second class, around three hundred doctors, graduated in the early days of the war, and after that there were four more classes that graduated before the city was destroyed.

Konstantin Vasilievich Zubanov (Chief engineer of the Stalingrad Power Station, StalGRES): I was born in 1911. I've been working at StalGRES for more than five years. Graduated from the institute in 1934. From Ordzhonikidze I was sent to Moscow, to a design firm. The three years I spent working there was the low point of my life. Being a designer isn't what I'm cut out for. I always wanted to be in a power station. They sent me here, to Stalingrad. I've worked here at every level: in December 1937 I was one of the station's shift engineers, then the lead supervisor, and from 1939 I was chief engineer of the complex. I trained as an electrical engineer, but now I'm more of a thermal engineer, or, rather, a specialist in power engineering.

Dmitri Matveyevich Pigalyov (Chairman of the Executive Committee of the Stalingrad Soviet of Workers Deputies): What cultural institutions did we have? In the factory settlements there were clubs and palaces of culture. At the Tractor factory there was the Gorky Club, the Shock Worker cinema, and a lot of smaller clubs. And several schools, all of them beautiful. The Derzhinsky School no. 3 was really nice, a small four-story building. There were eight or nine schools altogether, not counting the small ones. At the Barricades factory there was a house of culture, and the club for engineering and technical workers in the Lower Settlement. It wasn't that big, but it was nice. They'd laid out their own park, had a summer theater. They also had a club at Red October and a good technology center.

Konstantin Vasilievich Zubanov (Chief engineer of the Stalingrad Power Station, StalGRES): Basically, the power station is the center of a city's industry—I'd even say it's the center of its culture. A city that is electrified—a city where electricity has become an integral part of its daily life and infrastructure—sees more cultural and economic development than cities where there isn't enough electricity. The power station is to industry what a heart is to a man. The heart beats with a steady pulse, and so the power station maintains a pulse, a pulse of fifty cycles per second. One faint or missing beat is enough to bring all the city's activity to a halt—lights go out, factories stop working, and theaters and cinemas close. In today's world, however, this is extremely unusual. The Stalingrad Power Station was just such a heart to the city of Stalingrad.

Ivan Alexeyevich Piksin (Secretary of the Stalingrad City Committee): Stalingrad is an industrial city, and it has around ten enterprises of national significance, such as the Tractor factory, the 221st (Barricades), Red October, the 264th, and a number of others. During the war, these and all the other factories were refitted to produce ammunition and military equipment.

Veniamin Yakovlevich Zhukov (Foreman of Workshop no. 7 at the Red October steelworks): I made my way up at the factory beginning in 1932. I grew up here, started out as a driver and advanced to workshop foreman. This place has grown before my eyes. [. . .] The plant worked, and I worked. The factory grew, and I grew with it. The party organization raised me. Lately there's been interesting work mastering the Katyusha rocket.[28] [. . .] On the first day of the war we gave the army about forty vehicles, which were given a rating of excellent by the regional military organization, despite the fact that they'd been used in extremely difficult conditions.

The sixty people in the workshop crew put everything they had into mastering the rocket system. So when the decision was made to take the vehicle off the line, we felt awful. Weren't we good enough to keep producing this weapon? It was nice to have a part to play in the war.

Konstantin Vasilievich Zubanov (Chief engineer of the Stalingrad Power Station, StalGRES): For the phase of combat operations, the first stage was the period of time from the outbreak of war until the siege of our city. During this time we tried to do all we could to provide our city—and especially factories of particular military importance—with a sufficient supply of high-quality electricity. [. . .] We tried to breathe as one with our country, to match its rhythm as it repelled the assaults of the fascist horde. The war drastically changed the way we did things. When the Germans took the Donbass region, we found ourselves without coal. We had to find something else to burn: fuel oil. But this didn't faze us. There were no power restrictions at all, meaning that we didn't even notice the switch. We made the move from coal to fuel oil in a very short time frame. Fitters such as master Sergei Vasilievich Ivlev and Mudrenko, the supervisor of the boiler shop—they made it so they city didn't notice the switchover. And our power station safely used the new fuel to provide electricity to its customers without restrictions.

Alexei Yakovlevich Zimin (Lieutenant, former worker at the Barricades factory, headquarters commandant of the 38th Motor Rifle Brigade, 64th Army): The factories were working at full capacity. All kinds of weaponry were set up right there in the compounds, lifted up to the rooftops by crane. Tanks rolled in. People in the workers settlements were feeling lively and cheerful. They constructed bunkers and bomb shelters, made water reservoirs. Apart from that liveliness, there was nothing unusual about them.

Ezri Izrailevich Ioffe (Acting director of the Stalingrad Medical Institute): The institute played an active role in the city's defensive preparations. In the autumn of 1941 and from July to August 1942 the institute built lines of defense. Under the direction of professors and instructors, hundreds of students erected fortifications outside the city and within the city itself.

Alexei Semyonovich Chuyanov (First secretary of the Stalingrad Regional Committee): July 12 [. . .] It's becoming clearer and clearer that combat operations are soon to begin on the immediate approaches to Stalingrad. [. . .]

July 19. As usual, the regional committee sat until dawn, which comes early during the summer. It was past two in the morning when we got a call on the hard line: "Please hold the line for comrade Stalin."

"Has the city decided to surrender to the enemy?" said Stalin angrily. "Why have you moved the military district HQ to Astrakhan? Who gave the order? Answer me!" J.V. Stalin inquired about conditions in the city. He wanted to know about the output of the factories producing military goods. Then he issued directives from the Central Committee regarding the difficult military situation. In conclusion he said: "Stalingrad will not be given to the enemy. You let everyone know that."

Long after I hung up the receiver I stayed under the spell of the conversation. I didn't feel like going home, though it was late. I stood by an open window, breathed in the fresh morning air, and felt a great surge of strength. The main thing was clear: the city was not going to surrender to the Nazis.

Ivan Alexeyevich Piksin (Secretary of the Stalingrad City Committee): Long before the enemy was nearing the city, each factory had formed destruction battalions.[29] The destruction battalions were composed of all the factories' best people—the party and Komsomol members, and the best non-party workers.

All of these military activities took place after exhausting manufacturing work. It must be said that these skills were useful during the war when things became difficult for our city.

Alexei Semyonovich Chuyanov (First secretary of the Stalingrad Regional Committee): August 11. This morning Ivan Fyodorovich Zimenkov dropped by and asked: "How much longer will we keep burdening our families?"

I understood what he meant: "What do you suggest we do?"

"Today we should send the families of all managerial staff in the city and region across the Volga, to a state farm. Or to the koumiss production facility in the Palassovsky district.

This wasn't a simple matter. It's true that many families had already been evacuated, but if our own families were sent away, the enemy might exploit this in their propaganda. But there seemed to be no other choice. When it comes down to it, Valery, who's only a year and a half old, shouldn't have to pay for the fact that his father is a regional committee secretary. He'd already developed a nervous stutter. I approved Zimenkov's proposal. That night our families departed for Srednyaya Akhtuba by boat and later went by car to the Palassovsky district.

Claudia Stepanovna Denisova (Secretary of the Yermansky District Committee): Most of the party activists' families were taken across the river in advance.

Ivan Fyodorovich Zimenkov (Chairman of the Stalingrad Regional Soviet of Workers Deputies): Some rural districts and their livestock were evacuated to the east side of the Volga. We evacuated the collective farms' entire stock apart from parts of the Voroshilov and Kotelnikov district, where we had to leave everything behind. Horses, oxen, sheep, pigs from all the districts later occupied by the Germans were taken across the Volga. We didn't evacuate animals that were for the personal use of the farmers and other workers. From the thirty-eight machine and tractor stations later occupied by the Germans all but 750 tractors were evacuated (from a total of 3,080).[30] We sent tractors across the Volga, some to the Olkhovsky, Molotov, and Nizhne-Dobrinsky districts.

This was at the beginning of the grain harvest. All fourteen districts were effectively occupied by the peak of harvest season. All the grain was left behind. We got all of the government milled grain from Kalach. We got everything from the grain-collection stations on the railway running from Kalach and Nizhny Chir to Stalingrad, and from the warehouses as well.

Ivan Alexeyevich Piksin (Secretary of the Stalingrad City Committee): The enemy caught us unawares, and just about no one—certainly none of the workers—were evacuated from the city.

Ivan Fyodorovich Zimenkov (Chairman of the Stalingrad Regional Soviet of Workers Deputies): We immediately set up four defensive lines. Those who couldn't go far from home because of children worked on the lines inside the city. This was women for the most part. The rest of the city's population—nearly 28,000—worked on the second line, on the third and fourth Don lines. All the 1,500 kilometers of defensive lines were completed by the beginning of August. The whole region was full of lines, all the way to Astrakhan. Along the Don, the Volga, the Medveditsa—defensive lines were everywhere. [. . .]

When I was in Moscow I met the executive committee chairman for the Tula Regional Soviet. He said that they were digging defensive lines, bringing in scrap metal to place in specific locations to keep enemy tanks from getting through. I told this to comrade Chuyanov, the

Stalingrad civilians dig antitank ditches, August 1942. The only man in the picture (*bottom right*) is probably a communist agitator. *Photographer: L. I. Konov*

chairman of our city defense committee, and we started to think about lines in the city and elsewhere, and then we set about doing it.

Dmitri Matveyevich Pigalyov (Chairman of Stalingrad Soviet Committee): On the recommendation of the City Party Committee, we built the so-called internal city line along the perimeter. This was a line the Stavka didn't manage to sign off on. All the others had all been established out of strategic considerations.

This line played an important role during the battle. Our forces couldn't get to the intermediary line, but they held this one. We asked all the women to come build this line, even those with two- to eight-year-old children and women over fifty-five, though it went against every labor law. We were basically asking for anyone who could to come and work. The remainder of the population was mobilized and sent to work on the perimeter.

Vasily Ivanovich Chuikov (Lieutenant general, commander of the 62nd Army): The fortifications surrounding Stalingrad were under construction. We had great plans, but only 10 percent of them were completed.

Kuzma Akimovich Gurov (Lieutenant general, member of the Military Council of the 62nd Army): There was a lack of combat preparations in Stalingrad. We really felt this when we found ourselves fighting to defend the city.

Ivan Alexeyevich Piksin (Secretary of the Stalingrad City Committee): Certain Red Army commanders took offense at not being told about our defensive lines. The commander of the 64th Army [Shumilov] remarked on this several times. What can I say? The people who worked there, on the line, did an excellent job keeping it a secret. Lieutenant General Shumilov said: "If I'd known that line was there, I'd have deployed my troops differently."

Dmitri Matveyevich Pigalyov (Chairman of Stalingrad Soviet Committee): In those first days, before all of the bombing, we constructed barricades in the city. We didn't have any before then. We'd built lines, but no barricades. We didn't think they would get here from the Don in a single day.

Vasily Ivanovich Chuikov (Lieutenant general, commander of the 62nd Army): And those barricades—all you had to do was nick one with your fender, and it'd fall apart. Some construction.

Ivan Vasilevich Vasilev (Brigade commissar, chief of the political section of the 62nd Army): We had nothing to fall back on. The city was not protected. They'd built these "hedgehogs" that would collapse if only grazed by a light vehicle. There were no fortifications. By the station they'd put up camouflage that the Germans later used, so we ended up having to fight against it. And then the workers were complaining, saying how much they'd done for the soldiers, digging bunkers, earth-and-timber emplacements, concrete pillboxes. All of it was lost.

Vladimir Kharitonovich Demchenko (Major, commandant of Stalingrad): Our headquarters had a lot more work because of the large troop movements. A number of units had to be detained. Tens of thousands of men were detained within a few weeks. In the first ten days of August, 17,360 people were detained. That's within the city itself; 85,000 were arrested outside the city—a whole army's worth.[31] I reported this to the front commander. We immediately set up a transfer station to the front line. These people—both officers and soldiers—were dispatched to the transfer station, where they were sent straight to the front line. Our task was to make sure these people did not manage to get across to the east bank of the Volga. We set up outposts along the major roads. Blocking detachments stood on the edge of the city. Nearly every street was covered with checkpoints. We checked civilians' documents too. We checked everyone.

Alexei Semyonovich Chuyanov (First secretary of the Stalingrad Regional Committee): I spent the night of August 22–23 at the offices of the regional committee. I'd been waiting for a call from the Central Committee, so I was late getting back from HQ. [. . .] I left the regional committee building and headed toward the Volga. Even though the front was so close, life went on as usual. Caretakers were still watering the plants. Housewives, having grown used to frequent enemy air raids, hurried to get to the shops and the market. Women would take their children with them. It broke my heart to see this: What would become of them? The enemy is already at the gate.

Ivan Alexeyevich Piksin (Secretary of the Stalingrad City Committee): It was August 23 at around four in the afternoon. I was with the city defense committee when I got a call from the regional committee. The enemy had broken through to Rynka. I say, "That's just talk." "No—Gorgelyad, the deputy people's commissar for tank production, was there. Give him a call." So I call him. "What's going on, comrade Gorgelyad?"[32] "What's going on is that I've seen enemy tanks with my own eyes." Well, what was there to do? Right then we handed over command to the destruction battalions.

Dmitri Matveyevich Pigalyov (Chairman of Stalingrad Soviet Committee): As this formidable threat hung over the city, no military units were in place before it. Our closest forces were seventy or eighty kilometers away from the Tractor factory. Considering the growing threat of the enemy's assault on Stalingrad, on the factory, and beyond, it was basically: "Come on in, the door's open." But when the tanks attacked, the antiaircraft units showed them more than enough resistance, and a significant number of the tanks were taken out. The Germans seemed to get the idea that if we continued to engage them on their approach, then we would resist all the more fiercely when they attacked the city itself. It was evening, so they didn't risk entering the city. If they'd wanted to, they could have done so. We had antiaircraft artillery outside the city, but here we had none. There were some placed on rooftops, but you couldn't hit a tank in the street from there. The Germans didn't come into the city, they stopped there for the night. They'd come as far as Rynka and Spartakovka. At a distance measured not in kilometers but in meters.

During the night [of August 23–24] the City Defense Committee and the City Party Committee brought out whatever forces they could muster. All the destruction battalions and whatever forces could be found in the workers settlements were issued arms and sent in as support, as the armed forces set up to defend the city. We were lucky to have the Tractor factory there producing tanks and artillery. Workers at the factory pulled out all the stops and had sixty tanks ready to go by morning. They took everything that hadn't been entirely completed: some were on stands awaiting repairs, some were ready to go. Tank crews were somehow assembled. Many of them were made up of the Tractor factory workers who had conducted tests, inspections, and so on. They also included people who received the tanks. In any case, the crews were assembled. And then there was the tank school, which also had several tanks. The Barricades workers brought their cannons and brought out their artillery to set up the line of defense. They took anyone and everyone to man the guns. Military representatives, workers who were present during the testing—everyone was sent there, everyone we had at our disposal. By morning some NKVD units had been brought in.

This is how we cobbled together a defense of the city by morning. But you couldn't call it a defense in the full sense of the word.

Ivan Alexeyevich Piksin (Secretary of the Stalingrad City Committee): These destruction battalions held the enemy back until the morning of August 24, at which point the regular Red Army units had arrived. Because of this, the bulk of these destruction battalions were absorbed into the Red Army.

Semyon Yefimovich Kashintsev (Secretary of the Red October District Committee): This destruction battalion lost party member Olga Kovalyova,[33] the only woman in the unit. She hadn't been part of the battalion, but when they were sent to the front line, she left her work and her factory to go to the regional party committee office, where she declared that she wanted to go with the destruction battalion to the front line. At first she helped out as a nurse. Later, when everyone around her was dead, she set off with a rifle to the front line. She died there too.

Olga Kovalyova was a senior party member (from 1925 to 1926) and a senior worker at the Red October factory. When she first came to the factory she was a laborer, worked at the stone crusher. She came to the factory between 1921 and 1923—we're not entirely sure when—then joined the party and started to display a particular zeal for social and party work. She was sent to one of the political departments as either a women's organizer or the deputy for women's affairs. When she returned to the factory, she expressed a desire to learn how to cast steel. She was the only woman in the works who did this, and one of four, I discovered, in the Soviet Union. Three were in Magnitogorsk,[34] and she was the fourth. This is what she did for the last three years, did a good job at this incredibly difficult physical labor.

Olga Kovalyova

Before the siege she was temporarily appointed the workshop's deputy chief for leisure activities, and she was a member of the Stalingrad Party Committee Plenum. She was so easy to work with, so kind-hearted. On top of all that, she adopted a boy and proved to be exceptionally caring with him. She didn't hold anything back—she gave everything to her work and her party life.

Ivan Alexeyevich Piksin (Secretary of the Stalingrad City Committee): She was supporting this boy and her own mother, but still she left to defend her native city. Olga Kovalyova died a hero's death while fighting the enemy. [. . .] The destruction battalion pushed the enemy back to Mechyotka. The enemy certainly lost a lot of men. How did Olga Kovalyova die? She was lying there waiting and waiting, and then she said: "Come on, guys, let's go!" But there were also Germans lying and waiting ahead of her who she couldn't see. She was cut down the moment she got up.

[. . .] Some of the workers took up arms and set off to defend their city, while the others remained at the factories and literally performed miracles. In a single day, from the evening of August 23 through 24, workers at the Tractor factory sent out more than sixty tanks, forty-five trucks, and a great quantity of spare parts for tanks and other vehicles. Some of the tanks were brand-new, while the rest were undergoing major or medium overhauls. Through their intensive work, the factory collective managed to get these tanks to the front line. After they left the factory gates, these tanks were engaging the enemy in only five to ten minutes.

Vladimir Kharitonovich Demchenko (Major, commandant of Stalingrad): On August 23 I received word that the enemy had come as far as the Tractor factory. This was at 2:00 P.M. [. . .] I watched the German advance through my binoculars. The factory workers were the first to be hit.

Nikolai Romanovich Petrukhin (Chief of the war department of the Stalingrad Regional Committee): The sustained bombardment of the city began on August 23 at 6:00 P.M. and continued intensively until August 27, 1942.

Dmitri Matveyevich Pigalyov (Chairman of Stalingrad Soviet Committee): The first raid took place in October 1941 at Beketovka, in the Kirov district. Three Stukas came and dropped a dozen bombs. The bombs struck near the rail station. People had been feeling relatively safe—the enemy was far away. Many people were gathered at the station, so we suffered several dozen casualties. These were our first casualties of the war. Later in the winter, there were only occasional air raids. There was quite a heavy raid in April 1942. Around fifty aircraft took part. We had very few casualties. We'd set up rather strong anti–air installations, and the AA artillery had been brought in. The raid didn't cause much damage, the buildings were unscathed. A few small houses were destroyed, and we lost a few men. Until July there were no mass air raids, though there were small isolated attacks on Krasnoarmeysk. For the most part, the air raid sirens were rarely followed by bombing. Most of the bombing occurred when the sirens were silent. Because of the frequency of the enemy raids, we decided not to raise the alarm for one airplane attacking on its own. Otherwise, the whole city would have panicked. The factories, the plants—it would've caused untold damage. We'd have had to close the factories! So people said you could rest easy whenever you couldn't hear the sirens. It's an odd thing, but life's like that.

That's how it was until August 23, when the siege of the city began. It was a sunny day. Everything was in its place, the city was full of life, and the factories were producing at full speed. Actually, I should mention that we hadn't evacuated the city, even though the front had come as close as the Don, even past Abganerovo from the south. Just two weeks before the siege of the city proper we sent tens of thousands of people out of the city—women with children, who weren't working at the factories. None of the workers were released, with few exceptions. The city was ready. Every company and organization was working at full speed.

Then came August 23. It was a Sunday. Everyone was at work—we didn't have a weekend. It was a fine day. All day the enemy was bombing the stations northwest of the city, starting with Panshino, then Don, Ilovla, the Konny junction, Gorodishche, and then back again. They started bombing the stations in the morning. We didn't think much of it, didn't pay it much attention.

At about noon I left with my deputy, Lebedev, to observe the construction of the ring roads. [. . .] We drove for three hours. During that time the air raid sirens started up. Enemy aircraft had come as far as the city, but hadn't bombed it. They started bombing Orlovka on the other side of the Tractor factory. The general feeling was that so long as the alarm was sounded, there wouldn't be any bombs.

We had come to share this feeling. We decided not to get back to our command post immediately, but to see how the city was doing under the alert. You can't see everything from your command post; you can only gauge the situation from the reports of others. We decided to take a look ourselves. We drove around the city for about an hour during the alert. Then we went to our post. As the head of the local anti–air defense, I took my seat, as did my deputy. These were proven men here. We took our seats and stayed put. Everything was more or less quiet in the city. The city was not being bombed. I established communication with our air defense stations. Communications weren't very good, so I decided to go out to them. The sirens had been going for two hours. By then it was about 5:00 P.M. on August 23.

Claudia Stepanovna Denisova (Secretary of the Yermansky District Committee): There had never been an air raid like that

Residents flee from the bombing, August 1942. *Photographer: Emmanuil Yevzerikhin*

before. It actually looked like the sky was covered with airplanes. There didn't seem to be anywhere that didn't get hit. They started bombing at around five or six. Factory no. 687, a solid-tire factory, was the first place to catch fire. It had just been rebuilt but hadn't started production yet. That same night a lot of places went up in flames: most of the apartment buildings and institutes, the construction trust, the railway depot, and buildings all the way down to the Volga. I stayed at the phone because I wasn't permitted to leave. I couldn't even go to the headquarters of the anti–air defense. I was told to inform the City Party Committee of what damages we had sustained.

I remember that like it was only yesterday. It was a bit frightening. They would announce: "Still under alert. Still under alert." The alert was not removed, so it kept going.

Ezri Izrailevich Ioffe (Acting director of the Stalingrad Medical Institute): The evacuation [of the medical institute] had been set for August 23. It was a Sunday. It had taken us two days to prepare. That evening we were supposed to take a steamer. We were to evacuate the first-year students, the library, and the whole of the theory department. It was beautiful and sunny. All day we loaded the trucks and took everything to the riverbank. The heavy bombing started at around 2:00 P.M., and the air raid sirens kept going and going. Our steamer was meant to disembark at 7:00 P.M., but by around 6:00 P.M. we were being hit unrelentingly by a hundred bombers. Everyone was running for it. My family had already left, and I returned hungry to the institute at 6:00 P.M. It was empty: windows were open, doors and walls were missing, everywhere was covered with shrapnel. There was a dreadful whirlwind. It was terrifying. I stayed at the institute with four Komsomol orderlies. Professor Tsyganov's orderly, who had come from Odessa as an evacuee, was very frightened, so I let him go. The bombs came in waves: they would drop bombs for twenty minutes, then fly away. I stayed there until ten o'clock, when I received a call from the regional committee telling me to send them these Komsomol members because some tanks had been parachuted down north of the Tractor factory. I heard this from the committee secretaries, who had seen planes dropping tanks.[35] I had four students at my disposal whom I sent around the city to gather party and Komsomol members. We ended up with about fifteen people. We were looking until 2:00 A.M. Some we managed to get on the phone, and the others were reached at home.

Claudia Stepanovna Denisova (Secretary of the Yermansky District Committee): They bombed us mercilessly, and there was fire all around. It was like this: one of them flies in, bombs a street, and then the next one's right behind. This goes on and on like a conveyor belt, and all the while with the wailing sirens. The bombing went on through the night. The wounded were taken to the party offices, which were located downstairs. There didn't seem to be much point in taking them there. [. . .] Then we got hold of a car. We loaded the wounded and drove them to the river crossing. All of this was done by our political staff. Afterward, once we'd gotten the wounded to the ferry, I went to the district committee offices. I'd just arrived when it was hit by a bomb. [. . .] It was terrifying. [. . .] The shock wave knocked me through the building and pinned me to a wall, and I was covered in white plaster. One wall of the building was missing. Thankfully, no one was hurt.

When I got to the basement, the State Bank—the building next door—burst into flames. That was a direct hit. [. . .]

The State Bank and the city committee building were on fire. I saw that all the party members had returned. "Where can we go? There's fire everywhere, everything's burning." Our district was a sea of flame. It was hot. We couldn't go outside, but we couldn't stay in this building. There was a wall of smoke—the walls of the city committee building were already on fire.

Ivan Fyodorovich Zimenkov (Chairman of the Stalingrad Regional Soviet of Workers Deputies): On [August] 24 there was heavy bombing in the morning, and the workers gathered at a park in the city center. We held a meeting with the workers to discuss how to defend the city. The park was a good place to distribute arms. It was the rallying point where we armed the worker battalions, which took place on August 24 and 25. The workers would come to get their weapons and assignments, then they'd be handed over to a junior lieutenant, and they'd all go to the front line to defend the city. There were workers from the Tractor factory, from Factory no. 221. This wasn't the only rallying point—it only held four to five hundred men. You couldn't imagine what we were feeling then.

This one steelworker who'd been at the works for thirty or forty years, he picks up a submachine gun, but he'd never picked up one before, so we showed him what to do. We taught men how to load the drum magazines, how to set them to single-fire, and so on. On August 23, 24, and 25, enemy aircraft conducted an especially brutal bombardment of the city. It was during this brutal bombardment that the people came together, took their weapons, and were immediately sent to the front line. We delivered these workers battalions to Front HQ.

Semyon Yefimovich Kashintsev (Secretary of the Red October District Committee): The 1st Destruction Battalion returned from the front at the end of August with only twenty-two men. [. . .] Why so many losses? One survivor, Commissar Sazykov, explained it like this: In those early days it was only our unit and the guys from the Tractor factory bearing the brunt of the main strike, before the regular army units arrived, and the destruction battalion was poorly equipped. The only weapons they had were rifles.

Vladimir Kharitonovich Demchenko (Major, commandant of Stalingrad): At that time there was a great shortage of weapons. We didn't even have rifles. I went all over the place to get rifles for these men. [. . .] Wherever we came across captured enemy weapons, we used them to arm our detachments.

Ezri Izrailevich Ioffe (Acting director of the Stalingrad Medical Institute): In those first two days there was great confusion among the regional organizations, it was the 26th before they put themselves back together. [. . .] On the 24th and 25th we had no newspapers, electricity, or water, and, because of the lack of water, the fire crews could do nothing about the burning buildings. On the night of the 25th I could see an enormous column of smoke on the wooded banks of the Volga—the oil tanks were on fire.

Claudia Stepanovna Denisova (Secretary of the Yermansky District Committee): Putting out the fires was impossible because the Germans had taken out the water supply system. They'd cut off the main pump at Mechyotka—it was destroyed, there was no water. We fought the fires with whatever we had. The self-defense groups and others were not working at all badly and within half an hour they'd manage to extinguish a fire—but then it would flare up again. A lost cause [. . .] I sent all our command staff across the Volga. I did this on my own initiative because otherwise we might have had casualties. Not one person in the district committee died. The people were still alive, and they could be of use. The chairman and three secretaries from the district committee were still there. One secretary was a man, the others women. They called us the "women's district committee." [. . .]

Within three or four days everything was turned into the ruins you're looking at right now.

Vladimir Kharitonovich Demchenko (Major, commandant of Stalingrad): About ten thousand people were dead after the first bombardment. That figure also includes military personnel sent here. Cellars were packed with hundreds of people. There were some I know that held two or three hundred. [. . .] On the first day, thirty-seven aircraft bombed us until evening.[36] Can you imagine? Twenty to thirty dive-bombers trying to take out the AA batteries.

Dmitri Matveyevich Pigalyov (Chairman of Stalingrad Soviet Committee): My opinion—as a nonmilitary man—is that the enemy hoped to demoralize the people. They knew that we hadn't evacuated anyone. There were bombs everywhere, fires everywhere. People were stunned. There was a mass panic, no leadership. It was up to me to take control of the city until the military forces got here.

Because we'd built defensive lines and the enemy hadn't broken through from the north or south, we had a chance to get organized.

Three days after the bombing started in this area, we dragged people out from their trenches and shelters and began making repairs. We decided to repair the water system and the bread factory, to reestablish electricity production, and even to get the trams running. An extraordinary city commission was formed.

Vladimir Kharitonovich Demchenko (Major, commandant of Stalingrad): A commission was established during the bombardment to take decisive measures to reestablish the city's economy. [. . .] Sure, there were bombs, but we still had to feed the people. We still had to organize the economy. Chuyanov chaired this commission, which also included Zimenkov, Voronin, and me, the commandant of the city.

Mikhail Alexandrovich Vodolagin (Secretary of the Stalingrad Regional Committee): In the very first minutes of the raid, bombs severed our main artery, the power line that supplied the factories in the north and center of the city, and in many sectors the 110-kV line was cut off. The city was left without light, water, bread. We were ordered by the city defense committee to do everything we could to restore the city's water supply. The fires that raged throughout the city were stifling. Sometimes it was difficult to get to the river for a quick drink of water. We understood our mission. It was technically difficult but of great importance. Under constant attack from the air—later from artillery and mortar fire—our people threw themselves into their work. At any time day or night—for days on end, actually—they worked to fix the power line. There were times when they'd just finish resupplying a sector only to have it destroyed, the blast sending people ten or twelve meters into the air. But after the initial shock they'd go right back to repairing the line.

Dmitri Matveyevich Pigalyov (Chairman of Stalingrad Soviet Committee): Once we'd restored the water system, the bread factory, and the mills, we started to provide supplies for the population. We opened trade stalls, two or three canteens in the center and outlying areas. We started feeding children at the canteens. Life went on, in a way. Trade resumed, stalls were set up in basements to sell groceries and bread. We set a new goal of rebuilding the bathhouses so people could wash themselves. From August 23 to 28 they'd been staying in shelters, basements, trenches—they needed to wash. We worked for two and a half days to repair a few bathhouses and get them up and running. On the first day about two thousand people used one of the bathhouses. A day after that we launched a radio station and played music from tapes. But amid all the fires and the bombs the music sounded like a funeral march. After a day of this we decided to quit broadcasting the music—we just played the latest news bulletins. Whenever it started playing, the radio lifted people's spirits. If the radio is saying that the bread factory is operating and so on, then the city is alive. People felt better, and that meant that all was not lost. That's the reason for the radio, so the people could listen. [. . .]

In the Yermansky district, in the basement of block 7, two women were trapped for four or five days. Nobody knew they were there. Someone heard moaning and crying as they were passing by. They dug them out, got them out alive. I was there too. Turns out they recognized

Children in Stalingrad during an air raid. *Photographer: L. I. Konov*

me, the chairman of the Executive Committee, and showered me with kisses of joy. [. . .]

A mother and daughter had been buried in this one basement. The mother had managed to dig herself out, but the daughter was buried in such a way that she had no hope of escaping. She was alive, but her legs were stuck in the rubble and she couldn't get up. Several engineers arrived, and they all agreed that they wouldn't be able to dig her out. I found out about this a few days later. I thought, there's got to be some way to save her. So I go there with an engineer. He said he would give it a try. And, sure enough, he did it. When they started digging, she began to sing. Meanwhile, the mother, in complete calm, said to the daughter: "When they've got you dug out, don't forget your things."

Ivan Alexeyevich Piksin (Secretary of the Stalingrad City Committee): There were some terribly gruesome scenes. City committee secretary Khlynin tells of one example. He goes into a cellar just in case, because there were times when there'd be a collapse, but the beams and walls would hold, and the people inside were still alive. He enters the dark cellar and yells, "Is anyone there?" And then there's this humanlike scream of wild profanity. He says it made his hair stand on end. He lights a match and he sees this man, burned all over, no eyes even, nothing at all. Can you imagine a man in such a state? They called for a medic right away. [. . .]

Some people cracked up. It didn't matter how much they tried to restrain themselves or keep it under wraps—they lost it all the same. There is, in the end, only so much one can get used to.

Showing up at the factory never used to be a big deal because you were there all the time. But now when you arrive it's a great event. People greet you warmly, as if it's been ages. When I went to Red October, I went straight into the courtyard, and what a reception! A sturdy-looking man is brought to me, along with some armed workers.

"What's going on here, comrades?"

"What's going on, comrade Piksin, is that the enemy is bombing the city. We're losing the city to them, we're losing the factory, and this bastard here is taking advantage of the situation by looting."

"Tell me what's going on."

"He worked in the auto shop. There were work clothes there, overalls. See for yourself how many he's put on."

He was in fact wearing six sets of overalls. He had hidden underneath his shirt 115 packs of tea and wrapped around himself some eight meters of good drive belt, the kind that can be used as shoe soles. One worker asked: "Why'd you do it? This is government property."

"That's my business."

"Who'd you get it from?"

"Some guy."

"Were you selling them?

"No."

"He's a thief, a looter."

"What are we going to do with him? Send him to the front?"

"You can't send his kind to the front. He'd just do the same thing there. He must be shot!"

I said: "Even so, couldn't we still send him to the front?"

"No—he's got to be shot."

There was a meeting: a district committee secretary, the NKVD chief, a party organizer, and me—at that time I was also a deputy people's commissar.

But then all the workers came out. They took everything from him. He had boots, good box calf boots. They wanted to take them, but other workers said: "Don't bother. We don't need anything of his. Let him die with all his stuff."

They were put in formation, spaced three paces apart. By order of the workers, the man was shot. [. . .] They said: He was well provided for, a good master vulcanizer, childless, had a wife who worked in

Factory no. 221. What else did he need? He couldn't be trusted. He couldn't be sent to the front.

[. . .] Some looting occurred, beginning on the second or third day of the bombing. Flour was being taken, basements were being broken into. This necessitated extraordinary measures. In some districts people were shot on sight. Several people were shot. Afterward, the problem more or less stopped, though incidents of illegal looting still cropped up. We took extreme measures and were rid of our looting problem.

Alexei Yakovlevich Zimin (Lieutenant, former worker at the Barricades factory, headquarters commandant of the 38th Motor Rifle Brigade, 64th Army): [. . .] The factories withstood most of the bombing. This was when two of the Barricades workshops were destroyed. None of the other workshops were hit directly, but they had windows broken and roofs torn off. The Barricades Factory Training School took a direct hit. From August 23–24, three workshops at the Tractor factory were destroyed. When that happened, everyone ran for it. The managers led the way. Workshop foremen loaded their vehicles and headed out, but then after a short break in the bombing the NKVD forces made them turn around, and the factories started up again.

Mikhail Afanasievich Odinokov (Secretary of the Voroshilov District Committee): There was a dark stain on the work of the district party organizations—certain cases in which individual factory directors and party secretaries lost their heads during the bombardment, got scared, and fled the district and the city, leaving their enterprises without leadership. By doing this they helped not the motherland but the enemy.

These directors and party secretaries were Alexei Ivanovich Brilevsky, director of the Stalingrad Cannery, party secretary Sevryugin; Moskalyov, acting director of the confectionary plant; Martynov, director of Factory no. 490; party bureau secretary Maksimov; and Mezentsev, director of Bread Factory no. 5. All of these men left without the permission of the district committee. The coward Samarin, who was in charge of district food provisioning, transformed himself into a cattle driver on the east bank of the Volga and set off for a destination unknown to the regional committee.

Claudia Stepanovna Denisova (Secretary of the Yermansky District Committee): Factories were being destroyed, people were fleeing. Some of the enterprises got some things out, but many were unable to save anything because the bombing raid had been so unexpected. The Krupskaya 8th of March Textile Factory burned down on the 23rd. It had caught fire twice. The first was put out, but the second fire destroyed the whole factory. They'd removed equipment and raw materials. There was still one workshop where they worked on transmission mechanisms. About seventy-five sewing machines were still there. Once they'd gotten out the raw materials, neither the director nor the party secretary came back. They abandoned the workshop, leaving the transmissions and machines to the Germans. This is why the factory's director and party organization secretary were expelled from the party for desertion and cowardice.

Ivan Alexeyevich Piksin (Secretary of the Stalingrad City Committee): From August 23—at the onset of the bombardment—we began evacuating the population. It was an orderly evacuation. Mostly it was the workers' families and the workers themselves who were leaving. We organized ferries across the Volga. [. . .]

The conditions for the evacuation were extremely difficult. Evacuating across the Volga was hard because the boats were being bombed. Many people died. When we sent them out on the Saratov rail line, many of the trains were bombed out. A train carrying workers from the Red October factory sustained very heavy bombing at Leninsk, and again on the way back at the Elton and Pollasovka stations. [. . .]

The evacuation took place under exceptionally difficult conditions, especially since the only way out was the Volga. We had to cross it. Arms and food supplies had to cross the river continuously, at the same time as the population was being evacuated. Hundreds of thousands of people had to get out, mostly women and children. Approximately 60 to 70 percent were women, children, and the elderly. And there were the wounded, who complicated the evacuation.

Ezri Izrailevich Ioffe (Acting director of the Stalingrad Medical Institute): The crossing was made with small ferries and twin-engine military boats. For two or three days everything was done haphazardly, but by the 27th the crossing was organized. Everything the institute had intended to evacuate had burned on the banks of the Volga. The institute itself had burned down on August 25. Nothing was saved. Professor Kolosov carried a lone imported microscope with him to Saratov. We all set off on foot toward Cheborksar, our gathering point. Everyone met again in Saratov.

Alexei Mikhailovich Polyakov (Deputy chairman of the Executive Committee of the Stalingrad Regional Soviet of Workers Deputies): There were two active crossings near the statue of Kolzunov.[37] Quite a large number of people crossed by the ferry near the central waterworks, which was being bombed constantly. In addition to the municipal ferries, there were two large motor boats that had been linked together—this fast, powerful vessel could cross the Volga in eight to ten minutes. They could take ten or twelve vehicles with 200–250 people in the spaces between them. A deck of planks was laid over the two joined boats. The vehicles would go on these planks.

There were some really long days, such as August 27, 28, and 30, when we transported thirty to forty thousand people within a twenty-four-hour period. About one thousand rowboats had been given to us, but they were too disorganized. They were eager to go to the east bank, but once they got there it was difficult to get them to return to the west bank. [. . .]

I was there day and night. [. . .] Having some leadership on the riverbank brought a certain amount of calm. [. . .] I was in command of a militia platoon, the entire force of militiamen on the river. We maintained order and assisted the people as needed. I was there until September 5. Then I was in Krasnaya Sloboda. Though I would go to the right bank several times a day—specifically, to the central command post in the park—most of my time was spent on the east bank because of the enormous crowds of evacuated people who needed to be transported farther.

Ivan Dmitrievich Burmakov (Major general, commander of the 38th [7th Guards] Motor Rifle Brigade): Our arrival at the west bank—that was an interesting moment. The masses of people there! So many kids, so many women! Men seeing off their wives and children. Piles of belongings everywhere. We were crossing at night. Everyone wanted to get across quickly, to hurry. We started to establish order. We wanted to send them as fast as possible. We'd put five women and children on a boat and send them on. Then they had to cross the islands, about a kilometer and a half. I carried two children myself. Everyone was on foot. Soldiers carried people's belongings and children to lighten the load. You'd see a woman with a bunch of stuff and two or three kids. It's heartbreaking to see that. Tons of people at the riverbank, tons of children. I couldn't bear it—the next day I sent ten trucks. I gave orders for the children to be brought to the river first. With these small children running around, you think about your own children in Siberia. Over in Siberia things were all right, but the suffering in Stalingrad was terrible.

Ivan Vasilevich Vasilev (Brigade commissar, chief of the political section of the 62nd Army): We were getting them out, across the Volga, but this evacuation, as we called it, was just as deadly. It was a dreadful sight, especially the children. They're let out onto the sand without water or any kind of food provisions. How could a worker bring anything, what with the explosions all around, the bombs from above, and children going in the boats? You'd often come across some terrible scene on the island. If only some government representative had been present—there were plenty of vehicles coming through that could have taken them. This was well within our capabilities, but once the permission had been given—literally an hour later—they couldn't be found, and at the same time we had to take care of the local population. [. . .]

As a communist, I cannot look at children with indifference. They were going around collecting scraps of bread. I telegrammed Chuyanov, telling him to send Soviet authorities to bring this matter to rest. Things couldn't be so bad that we couldn't feed these children. We got them fed. A private's family—the father's at the front, mother's dead, leaving an infant, a four-year-old, an eight-year-old, and the sick old grandfather. How could you not help a family like that?

Mikhail Alexander Vodolagin (Secretary of the Stalingrad Regional Committee): There were children turning up with no parents, children of all ages, from infants to teenagers. It was decided that the Komsomol would be responsible for gathering these children and transporting them to the east bank of the Volga. Comrade Bykov, secretary of the Yermansky District Komsomol, played a very active role in this work. Komsomol members began searching for unaccompanied children in courtyards, apartments, trenches, and basements. We brought these homeless children to the shelter in the basement of the City Theater. Then at three or four in the morning, or some other suitable time, we'd send them across the Volga. Supplies were being sent at the same time, so we gave them everything they needed.

Konstantin Vasilievich Zubanov (Chief engineer of the Stalingrad Power Station, StalGRES): It was only September 13 when the Germans broke through to the Volga at Kuporosnoye, definitively breaking the link between Stalingrad's heart and brain. The artery was severed. We had a job to do: provide electricity to the southern part of the city, specifically to the industrial and residential areas in the Kirov district. [. . .] The Germans were entrenched in the hills of Yelshanka and Kuporosnoye[38] Evidently they had heard about our work at the station, and they placed us under fierce artillery fire. After a few test shots, the Germans concentrated fire on us with exceptional force.

Refugees from Stalingrad, September 1942.

Claudia Stepanovna Denisova (Secretary of the Yermansky District Committee): On September 14 we held a meeting of the bureau of the district committee. This meeting took place in a trench. We listened to reports on barricade construction and the evacuation of minors.

We stopped the meeting because everything went quiet. Those attending were the chief of the militia, the chief of staff of the local anti–air defense, and the director of the Krasnaya Zastava factory. Someone took minutes in a notebook, everything was preserved. The chief of staff said: "I'll go see what the trouble is." The day before, the 13th, they enemy bombed us heavily, maniacally. [. . .] While he was out seeing what was going on, why there was this strange, ominous silence, some militiamen in black clothing walked by. Submachine guns, satchels, and all of them dressed the same. They walked on. We thought they were our own militiamen and said: "Didn't we see them earlier going toward the House of Specialists?" It turned out that they were German soldiers who later took over the House of Specialists, and here we were about fifty meters away. This was around three o'clock. The chief of staff came back and said: "I suggest we leave immediately. There are German tanks on First of May Street." The tanks were coming from a bridge in the Dzerzhinsky district, and the submachine gunners were already in the House of Specialists.

Vladimir Kharitonovich Demchenko (Major, commandant of Stalingrad): On September 14 German soldiers entered the city and occupied the NKVD building. At that time I received a message from the garrison commander saying that groups of submachine gunners were moving from the central airfield onto the southern slopes of Mamayev Kurgan. My orders were to verify this. I set out on reconnaissance with three men. I decided to stop at my HQ at the Red October factory to get a dozen or so more men, because I had heard all kinds of rumors. [. . .] I went along the riverbank, thinking I'd soon be getting some more men. We reached the north docks, and it turned out that the Germans were firing at the crossing. We spent two hours exchanging fire with them. I gathered my men. At the crossing there were about a hundred vehicles that couldn't be ferried across because of all the German machine guns and submachine guns. I gathered about fifteen men at the House of Specialists. The shooting began—them firing from over there, us from over here. A junior political officer got wounded. I could tell we weren't getting anywhere. I went back with my men to the command post on the Tsaritsa. We got as far as Kholzunov Square. There were antiaircraft guns on the square and right on the riverbank. Five enemy dive-bombers were attacking them. One gun was fifteen meters from the bank. Five planes were coming right for it. The gun started firing. We saw the bombs fall. Two of my men were lying in the water, and I jumped into a ditch. A bomb fell about ten meters away from me. I was thrown into the air, hit the ground, took quite a beating. Put me out of action for a week. I got up but fell down again. I felt like something had snapped inside me. My two comrades grabbed me and got me to our command post. The bombing started up again. A bomb struck the back wall of the building and started a fire. A high-explosive bomb. When I saw that I figured that everyone was probably dead. I got up. I could see that the building was burning.

Alexei Semyonovich Chuyanov (First secretary of the Stalingrad Regional Committee): September 14[39] [. . .] The city defense committee's command post is a few meters back from the front line. Telephone and telegraphic communication with the northern and southern sections of the city has been cut off. In several places the fascists have reached the Volga, dividing the city into isolated defense sectors. It was decided that the command post should be removed to the east bank of the Volga. I. V. Sidorov, the regional committee secretary for transportation, was charged with organizing the crossing. [. . .] Late at night two boats came to the command post from Krasnaya Sloboda, and we started crossing. I left on the last ferry with my assistants and comrades Voronin and Zimenkov. It was relatively calm until we reached the middle of the river. We'd just gotten there when we saw flares overhead. That was when the machine-gun fire began.

We hit the deck. The engineer decided to muffle the engine, but in his haste he went too far and killed it. The current was taking us straight toward the statue of Kholzunov, where the German machine-gun fire was coming from. [. . .] Sidorov left the helm to go down to the engineer.

"Come on!" he said, sighing heavily. "Look what you've done! Do you see where we're headed?"

"To visit the fascists!" joked Zimenkov, deadpan.

But this was no laughing matter. The boat taking fire from machine guns. There was only one way out: to swim for it. And it was just at that moment that the engine started up. Ivan Vasilievich ran back to the helm and turned the vessel sharply toward Krasnaya Sloboda.

Vladimir Kharitonovich Demchenko (Major, commandant of Stalingrad): The [Extraordinary City] Commission existed until

September 14. After September 14 the Regional Committee and the Executive Committee moved to the east bank. The Commandant's Office stayed on the west bank, but all other city and regional authorities moved to the east bank. [. . .] After our building on Communist Street was bombed, the Commandant's Office worked and received people at several different locations. For a few days we were at the hospital, then we moved to October Street, then to the Tsaritsa, and from September 18 we were at General Rodimtsev's command post. We stayed there until September 25. On September 25 we left with the 62nd Army and went to the Barricades district. From there we moved to the Red October district under the direction of the commander of 62nd Army. We built bunkers and stayed in them all the time. [. . .]

I should mention that I was the only one with a map, which was on tracing cloth. Front headquarters had ordered us to show them where certain streets were, where they were located, because the city was not like other cities. We directed people. Someone would come to us at one in the morning, say, some army subunit, and they'd need help with a street or heading. Or there would be ammunition or guns that had to be picked up from the station. We'd go and show them the way. Because of all the ravines here, streets and roads aren't that easy to find.

Vasily Ivanovich Chuikov (Lieutenant general, commander of the 62nd Army): The army's commander and military council defended Stalingrad while based at Mamayev Kurgan. Sometimes when we were surrounded by submachine gunners we'd run down to the riverbank. There were times when we were 150 meters from the enemy's forward positions. Were there any local party organizations there? [. . .] Yes, indeed! I remember comrade Chuyanov, secretary of the regional committee, who was made chairman of the defense committee, I saw him myself—Would you like to know when? It was on February 5, 1943, at the victory rally. And as for Secretary Piksin—I saw him, if I'm not mistaken, in mid- to late January 1943. Until then I had seen no one at all.

[. . .] Then, when things had more or less calmed down, the commandant of Stalingrad showed up on the riverbank.

"How can I help you?"

"Who are you?"

"Commandant of the city."

"Where are you based?"

"Across the river—Leninsk, Akhtuba, Krasnaya Sloboda—everyone's there [. . .]."

I think that with the right leadership, the situation here would have been different.

An army is made up of men, and the Bolshevik leadership ought to be located where the greatest danger is.

[. . .] The enemy had forced his way into Stalingrad. At the Tractor factory there were hundreds of tons of fuel. Transporting fuel across the Volga is not at all easy to do. It is extremely dangerous. I said: get that fuel! I met the director of the factory, who informed me that their regulations prohibited taking anything from the factory. I ordered armed soldiers to take the fuel. These men encountered armed security, who pointed machine guns at them. What was I to do? I gave up and let it go. The fuel stayed there for the enemy.

Alexei Yakovlevich Zimin (Lieutenant, former worker at the Barricades factory, headquarters commandant of the 38th Motor Rifle Brigade, 64th Army): When we arrived to hold the line at the Barricades factory, when we took up positions at the Upper Settlement, I got a chance to visit the offices of the factory [party] committee and the district committee. The only one there from the factory committee was Skorikov, but I did see Secretary Kotov from the district committee. The district soviet was gone—they'd already gone across. The factory management was gone. The factory's director had come back on September 25. Actually, he was brought back and told to stay put until told otherwise.

They did assembly work at the factory. The assembly workshop was undamaged apart from its glass roof, which had fallen in, and this is where the assembly work was done. When they started returning, the managers and foremen had to be forced to organize the work. They organized the assembly of finished parts and weaponry. After that they started making repairs. The Tractor factory had also been blown up, but then their people organized the assembly work and repaired tanks returning from the field.

Ivan Vasilevich Vasilev (Brigade commissar, chief of the political section of the 62nd Army): Party activists could have been left here, so that every apartment and building would return fire, and when the Germans entered the city we'd have been right on top of them. We had no other support. The city was undefended. [. . .] If you've got 400,000 workers, what if you just took 100,000—that's a whole army! We'd have even been able to arm them. We'd have posted them on high ground, and the Germans never would have entered Stalingrad. We would have stopped them on the approach, just like we did in the city. We'd have an easier task now if we'd stayed there, but in the city, even with all our skill, it was a difficult and complex job that took a lot of blood. This much is clear: the city was abandoned, not defended.

Pavel Petrovich Matevosyan (Chief engineer of the Red October steelworks): On September 15 we were with General Chuikov and Gurov, a member of the military council. They demanded that we get our people out, saying that people were dying—they're shooting us, we're shooting them. That's when we started moving out.

Ilya Fyodorovich Burin (Former mechanic at the Barricades factory, scout in the 38th [7th Guards] Motor Rifle Brigade): All the workers began evacuating across the Volga. Then the order came for us to drive to Leninsk with all the machinery. They took everyone. We went across to Leninsk. From there we were to evacuate to Novosibirsk. Some of us were late, and they didn't let us go. Later we got the order: any worker with evacuation papers who stays behind will be detained and sent into combat. We were detained and sent there.

Our unit was formed in Solyanka. I was the only one from my workshop. Later I met a comrade from the same factory, but from Workshop no. 16, Neznamov was his name. Since then we've always been together. [. . .] At first we were the Factory Emergency Rifle Regiment. We were trained there. When our training was completed, we were asked what we wanted to do. I volunteered to be a submachine gunner, and later I was transferred to reconnaissance.

Vladimir Kharitonovich Demchenko (Major, commandant of Stalingrad): Lately we've had to force people to leave. Some of them think: I've been living here twenty years, where will I go? We'll defend our city to the very end; the city will not surrender. There were some, of course, who were waiting for the Germans. [. . .]

From September 23 to October 15 we evacuated 149,000 families [from the population in the factory districts]. We did have to send in the militia to do this. They went into every trench and bomb shelter to take people out and send them to the east bank. Not much of the population remained in the city. Most of those who remained were in the Dzerzhinsky and Voroshilov districts, which had been occupied suddenly. Very few remained elsewhere—frail old people, sick people. In the area where 62nd Army was, they stayed until the very end. There were quite a few children left. The mothers died, the kids remained. Some children were found in bunkers.

This one time we kicked the Germans out of a bunker and destroyed the firing position, but didn't go inside that day. The next evening we entered the bunker. There was a girl, eight or nine years old, lying there among the bodies. As soon as we came in she cried: Take me with you, it's cold in here with them. Her mother had been killed. General Sokolov, commander of the 39th Division,[40] took the girl.

Pavel Petrovich Matevosyan (Chief engineer of the Red October steelworks): We planted mines throughout the factory three times, and each time we removed them. We were in direct communication with army HQ and with the division that was protecting us. At first we had an NKVD division. They'd warned us how difficult things were. The last time we went to General Chuikov he said there was no order from Moscow. He doubted that we were going to blow up the factory: we were going to fight it out to the end. Hopefully we wouldn't lose the city, but if it came down to it, we'd have to abandon Stalingrad. So we removed the mines. Afterward we put them back—after all, that was just his personal opinion. No one had ordered us not to. [. . .] Then we got the order from Moscow to clear the mines. It had apparently come from Beria[41] himself. [. . .] We left there on October 4, and we were the last to leave.

Konstantin Vasilievich Zubanov (Chief engineer of the Stalingrad Power Station, StalGRES): The artillery fire was at its heaviest on September 23, when about four hundred shells hit our power station. That was an intense day, and a difficult period for the workers. It turned out to be a fatal moment for the station.

At first there were isolated shots, then a barrage (which military personnel usually call a fire assault). Our station was rendered completely useless. [. . .] Even without counting the shrapnel, the shells that stuck the station brought destruction to the building assemblies and the units, and there was this entire mass of shrapnel, components, glass, wood, brick, metal—all of this came down on top of people at their work stations. It was especially bad at the boiler shop. [. . .] That day a dud landed at the feet of the boiler technician Dubonosov. He didn't know the shell wouldn't go off right away. He risked his life but never left his station. I saw myself what he went through. He calmed down only once the shell had been carefully removed from his spot and made safe.

In any case, the station was shut down. We had to figure out what to do. The Germans had zeroed in on us well, and their shooting was precise. Working under such conditions was dangerous. [. . .] I met the workshop foreman to discuss the work before us. Later we jokingly called this meeting the Council of Fili.[42] We asked ourselves: What can we do? If we stop, then the factories nearby won't be repairing tanks or making shells, it will mean that the entire area will go without water and that the army will go without bread. Getting the place running again, on the other hand, would expose our workers and all of the managerial staff to considerable danger. It came as no surprise when not a single one of the foreman said no. Very modestly and calmly, and under the unrelenting music of artillery, each of them reached their verdict: the station must continue operating. The station was up and running that very day, September 23.

The onset of darkness at first reduced, then completely eliminated the artillery fire. It appeared that the Germans had been aiming at the cloud of smoke coming from the station. Artillery fire continued straight through to November 10. After the lesson of September 23, our regional authorities decided that the station should operate only at night.

Ivan Alexeyevich Piksin (Secretary of the Stalingrad City Committee): There was this one incident that sounds like a joke. The artillery fire was unbelievable. Zemlyansky, the director of the power station, makes a written address to the army commander: "I request that you immediately neutralize the enemy artillery, as it is making it impossible for Stalingrad Power Station to operate. Should this request be denied, I will appeal to your superiors." Shumilov recalled this recently: "When I got that request, I wrote to the artillery commander: 'Comrade so-and-so, you are to immediately neutralize the artillery so the station can operate.'"

Konstantin Vasilievich Zubanov (Chief engineer of the Stalingrad Power Station, StalGRES): Something surprising: people we had ordered to places less exposed to falling debris and exploding shells often found these heavy barrages very difficult. But if you went along to the main panel, you would see, or rather hear, something extraordinary: against the background of the artillery music you could hear classical music. This was comrade Karochansky playing records on a gramophone.

Sergei Dmitrievich Babkin (First secretary of the Kirov District Committee): When the planes first came and flew over the settlement, people ran and hid in trenches. Now everyone's used to it. They see a group of planes in the air, and people can already tell what they're going to attack. In Staraya Beketovka there were about thirty or forty Katyushas. When they fired, the windmill would immediately start turning. In October, when we were at the collective farm, we watched the Katyushas get hit. A Messerschmitt showed up, turned around, and flew away. I said that more German planes would come in ten minutes. After fifteen minutes, the German planes appeared and started their bombing runs. We were about 250 meters away, and we saw one plane drop eight bombs, then the others made their drops and flew away. We could hear cries and moans. We saw that the planes were coming for us and we took cover behind a building. Two bombs landed three meters away, another at five meters. The driver and I were covered in dirt. We saw a third group. They attacked like that all day long, but everyone held up just fine, no panicking. There was some long-range artillery there, and children would wait on skis and sleds, and when they fired, the shock waves from the guns would push them down the slope.

Konstantin Vasilievich Zubanov (Chief engineer of the Stalingrad Power Station, StalGRES): November 4, 1942. At the end of the night shift at the station, after we shut down, all personnel (incidentally, no one had been allowed to leave since the first days of the siege), went to bed. People were so used to this new way of life that no amount of artillery fire kept them from undressing and going to bed as usual. But on November 4 at 8:30 A.M., fascist vultures unexpectedly spread their wings over the station. Forty-nine Stukas—or, as we called them, "musicians"—started a methodical bombardment. The intention was to destroy our station once and for all. Every one of the forty-nine dive-bombers made multiple runs. The wail of their sirens was particularly unpleasant. I never believe people who say they get used to artillery fire or bombs. I just can't find any truth in it. For me every bomb or shell is hard to take, it's painful. What's important is how you conduct yourself, how much you can contain your feelings. I have never since experienced anything like what I experienced then. You often hear it said that Red Army soldiers were less afraid of the bombs than of the sirens. I'm certain that's the truth. The Stukas' sirens really were incapacitating. So you can imagine what things were like at the station. Half-naked men jumping out of bed and running to the shelters, some running toward the power assemblies to make sure they were "prepared" for such an attack.

The bombing didn't last long—maybe twenty or twenty-five minutes—but for us this seemed like an eternity. When the planes had left we recognized the unusually devastating effects of the bombing. Before then we hadn't had any serious casualties, but that day there were two dozen. Many of the units were lost. In operational terms, the station was put out of action for quite some time.

Secretary Ilin from the regional party committee arrived. The committee finally had us evacuate to the east bank so that these last few brave men might be saved.

Nikolai Romanovich Petrukhin (Chief of the war department of the Stalingrad Regional Party Committee): Regarding the partisans [. . .] By the time of the German invasion we had created thirty-four partisan reconnaissance detachments comprising a total of 839 men. About sixty caches with provisions had been placed to supply these units with food. They were also issued equipment, and the caches also contained weapons and ammunition. Most of the partisans had been trained in units of the destruction battalions or in units created by the regional council of OSOAVIAKhIM,[43] in so-called training groups. We trained some of them in a special school. [. . .]

All the partisan detachments were located on the open steppe. No good cover, no water. That is why the detachments tended to be small, no more than seven, ten, or fifteen men. The fascist hordes conducted harsh inspections and committed atrocities against the civilian population in the occupied districts (fourteen of the regional districts were occupied), which also made it difficult for these detachments to conduct their operations.

In early September 1942 a group of partisans went to Ulyana Vasilievna Sochkova in the village of Kamyshki and asked for water. While citizen Sochkova was fetching the water, two German patrols approached the partisans, who then killed the Germans and disappeared. The next day, German soldiers took the sixty-year-old Sochkova and her thirty-year-old daughter. They conducted a manhunt in the area near the village with a large number of riders, and they found some regular Red Army soldiers who happened to be there after breaking through the encirclement. The Germans gathered all of the men from the village and made them dig a grave. Then they brought over the Russian soldiers and the two women and shot them in front of everyone. A German officer warned the villagers, saying that this would happen to them, that for each murdered German soldier one hundred of them would be shot. [. . .] In the village of Averino in the Kalachevsky district they arrested seventeen children ranging from eight to fifteen years old. They were taken into the road and publicly whipped. For seven days they were given no food or water. On November 7 the fascists shot ten of these defenseless boys as part of a bloody and malicious reprisal. The bodies were taken to the pit silo of the collective farm. It was said that the boys had been shot because an officer was missing a pack of cigarettes, and suspicion had fallen on one of the boys. In the village of Plodovitoye, the wife of a former collective farm manager who had been expelled from the party in 1938 and sentenced to five years for anti-Soviet agitation denounced Natalya

Nikolayevna Ignatievna, a party member, who was then executed by the German occupiers. Her body was left there for a week.

Ezri Izrailevich Ioffe (Acting director of the Stalingrad Medical Institute): Already by December 1942, while Stalingrad was still under occupation, steps were being taken to return a core group of professors. Faculty from the Stalingrad Medical Institute started moving there by the end of January. Four faculty members were in place by February 25.

Veniamin Yakovlevich Zhukov (Foreman of Workshop no. 7 at the Red October steelworks): I'd watched the plant grow up, so it's not easy for me now [This interview was conducted on January 8, 1943, at the site.] to see it destroyed. It's like leaving your parents at home, alive and well, and coming back later to find them dead—that's what it feels like. [. . .] Now all I see are ruins. You can't even walk through them, let alone drive. I just can't take it in. A team from my shop, twenty-two of us, have come to work. We're waiting to get in there so we can help put things back in shape.

Alexei Semyonovich Chuyanov (First secretary of the Stalingrad Regional Committee): February 4. Today we're celebrating our victory on the Volga. The austere and majestic Square of

Major General Stepan Guryev hands over the Red October factory to its director, Pavel Matevosyan, in January 1943. *Photographer: G. B. Kapustyansky*

Clearing the Volga embankment. *Photographer: L. I. Konov*

the Fallen Heroes is covered in red bunting. [. . .] Twelve o'clock noon. Front and army military council members appeared on an improvised rostrum, including V. I. Chuikov, M. S. Shumilov, A. I. Rodimtsev, and the leaders of regional and city organizations. [. . .] By request of the regional committee, the regional soviet of workers deputies, and the city defense committee, I gave an address to the rally: "As we fought against this vicious enemy, the fascist German occupiers decimated our city. But today, in the name of the motherland, of the party, and of our government, let us vow that we will restore our beloved city." [. . .] I said good-bye to my comrades at arms. Their path takes them westward, while I will remain in the city. I was an ordinary civilian once again. The front has moved hundreds of kilometers away. The army is moving out. It wasn't easy to see them go, these comrades I had shared so much with.

Vasily Petrovich Prokhvatilov (Secretary of the Stalingrad Regional Committee of the AUCP[b]): There was a public rally on February 4.[44] Other rallies took place throughout the region. We'd heard from the Sovinformburo that Chuyanov had eliminated the surrounding forces, and I received many congratulatory telegrams from within the region, then from everywhere in the Soviet Union. Not long ago I got one from a certain Pletnev, naming his unit and congratulating us on our victory. This meant something to Stalingrad. Not just Stalingrad, but the entire country. There were a lot of messages like that.

Ivan Alexeyevich Piksin (Secretary of the Stalingrad City Committee): Right after we had completely eliminated the German forces in Stalingrad, we focused our efforts on clearing the bodies. Every district had several thousand corpses.

Alexei Mikhailovich Polyakov (Deputy chairman of the Executive Committee of the Stalingrad Regional Soviet of Workers Deputies): Our main task now is to clear the streets as fast as we can. We've been at it for a month and have barely made a dent. It's not that we aren't working. Thousands of people are helping with the work.

Laborers from the Srednaya Akhtuba and Praleyksky collective farms have been providing a lot of assistance. They each sent around fifty carts, along with workers on camels and oxen. These men and women have removed tens of thousands of bodies.

Vasily Petrovich Prokhvatilov (Secretary of the Stalingrad Regional Committee of the AUCP[b]): [. . .] The collective farmers tried to aid every district that had been occupied by the Germans. I was in Kotelnikovo[45] three days after its liberation. The Poperechensky collective farm is in that area. The workers there had saved nearly the entire herd by concealing them in a hollow, where the Germans didn't find them. The workers there hid their grain in a pit silo and informed the Red Army when they arrived. Now this farm has seed for this year's planting. They held on to twelve tractors. How did they do it? When the Germans were closing in it was impossible to get the tractors out, so the workers removed certain parts from their tractors to render them inoperable. Once the Germans had left, the operators returned with the parts and were able to get them running again in ten days. Now the tractors are all working again. The tractor fleet at this collective farm will be just fine because the people here are Cossacks. The Germans tried to win over the Cossacks, but nothing came of it. We learned this from the farm workers. [. . .]

In the Perelazovsky district I drove out to Lipovsky and spoke with the farm workers there. They told me of atrocities committed by the Germans and Romanians there. A few cows were still in the village. All the rest had been taken by the Germans, and this was a settlement of 170–180 households—not a small place. The villagers were particularly outraged by the POW camp. In Lipovsky there is a pig farm that borders a small river. Nearly all the farms had been burned down. The goat, sheep, and pig farms were all that remained, and these had been fenced in with barbed wire and used to keep prisoners of war. They fed them rye chaff. The day before I arrived there was a burial. Twenty-three Russian officers with frostbitten feet. The Germans couldn't take them away, so they covered them with straw in a pigpen and set them on fire. Six Russian prisoners were being kept in a small hut, another five in a dugout in the yard. The locals helped them, and when the district committee secretary arrived they were brought to the hospital, most of them frostbitten, emaciated from the lack of food.

Grigory Dmitrievich Romanenko (First secretary of the Barricades district of Stalingrad): Of the many thousands of people who had been living in our district before August 23, we came across only 130—they were gaunt, frostbitten, stomachs bloated from starvation. Many of them said that if we'd taken another two or three weeks, they'd have starved to death or died from mistreatment by the Germans.

Ilya Fyodorovich Burin (Former mechanic at the Barricades factory, scout in the 38th [7th Guards] Motor Rifle Brigade): My family stayed in Stalingrad. I had no father, but my mother was killed there. When I got there I went home and found out that she died on September 8. She was in the kitchen cooking at four in the morning when the bomb hit. The building burned down, my mother was killed.

Public kitchen in Stalingrad, March 1943. *Photographer: Georgy Zelma*

Claudia Stepanovna Denisova (Secretary of the Yermansky District Committee): Right now the district has a population of sixty-two. Some people were kicked out by the Germans, some stayed behind. The ones that stayed were close to the Germans, they worked for them. They were allowed to stay here. It was a restricted area.

Now we're going around block by block. We've counted the population three times, determining who's who and what's what. When appropriate, we report them to the relevant authorities.[46]

Ezri Izrailevich Ioffe (Acting director of the Stalingrad Medical Institute): Anyone who couldn't hide was driven westward by the Germans. Only those who could hole up in the nooks and crannies remained. It was easy to identify the people who worked with the Germans—they were the ones who had lost all self-respect. I met a great number of people while seeing patients, and I could recognize these unsoviet people at a glance.

They didn't speak openly, they weren't determined or direct, perhaps because they felt anxious and demoralized. One doesn't get over this easily. These people are psychologically different from the rest.

Konstantin Vasilievich Zubanov (Chief engineer of the Stalingrad Power Station, StalGRES): When I was evacuated to the east bank they asked me to relocate to Moscow. It seemed like the thing to do—work in Moscow, get an apartment. For a certain sort of person this would have been great, but I had to turn it down. They need me here more than they do in Moscow. I couldn't leave the station at such a difficult time. This station raised me when things were good, so I've got to do what I can for it during this difficult time. This is where I came up the ranks, starting as nothing and working my way up to chief engineer. My conscience tells me I have to repair the station and see that it returns to its prewar capacity.

Ezri Izrailevich Ioffe (Acting director of the Stalingrad Medical Institute): [The interview was conducted on February 1, 1944.] Our main difficulty is housing. The students are still sleeping two to a bed. Even though we have plenty of sheets, mattresses, and beds, we have nowhere to put them. [. . .]

There's been a great influx of people in Stalingrad. The population has already reached 250,000, and about ten thousand more are coming every month, according to the "Rebuilding Stalingrad" section of *Stalingradskaya Pravda*. This influx of people causes serious problems for housing, food distribution, schooling, and medical care.

Residents returning to Stalingrad find shelter in the abandoned dugouts of the 62nd Army, 1943. *Photographer: Georgy Zelma*

Population growth is not being factored in when it comes to public services. The schools have begun running several shifts, with lessons running from 8:00 A.M. to midnight. The earlier grades are going only every second day. Though I must say that this influx of people is a sign of the city's recovery. Many still live in varying conditions—in basements, trenches, bunkers, with dozens staying in a single room. But they are still coming, despite the obstacles. Very few are leaving, mostly those who are not from here originally. People come to fight for Stalingrad's recovery. [. . .] The mood here is a cheerful one—we want to live truly and do good work. The victories of the Red Army have given us the elixir of life.

Dmitri Matveyevich Pigalyov (Chairman of Stalingrad Soviet Committee): There was this one telephone operator. Her switchboard wasn't hidden. It was on the second floor. If a bomb comes, they're all finished. Our command post was made of concrete. Sometimes you'd just sit there rocking, like on a boat, while these poor girls were up there sitting at the switchboard. They couldn't leave, they had to connect people. When you called you could hear their voices trembling:

"Get me so-and-so!"

"Putting you through now."

Red Army telephone operators at work in Stalingrad, December 1942. *Photographer: Georgy Zelma*

Her voice trembles, but she connects you. You hear her crying into the receiver, but she doesn't leave her post without an order, she stays put. At the time this seemed an ordinary occurrence. Now that things have calmed down, you think back and it seems different. But at the time you're saying: "What the hell's wrong with you, sitting there crying?" Now you think about it and it's just plain awful. Everything's rumbling, and you're safe under concrete, miserable. But what about her up there on the second floor? She's a woman, after all, not some seasoned fighter. An ordinary woman, an ordinary telephone operator—what did you expect?

AGRAFENA POZDNYAKOVA

I discuss the interview with the cook Agrafena Posdnyakova separately because she is the only one who witnessed the German occupation firsthand.

Posdnyakova shared her fate with approximately 150,000 to 200,000 other residents.[47] Some were denied permission to leave in time, but most stayed to care for sick family members or were reluctant to leave their homes with winter drawing near. Very few gained an accurate picture of the occupiers; if anything, they dismissed Soviet reports of German atrocities as exaggerations.[48]

The destruction of the city wore on after the heavy aerial bombardments in the final days of August. The Luftwaffe continued its air strikes and Soviet artillery shelled the war-ravaged districts from the east bank of the Volga. Residents—mostly the elderly, women, and children—sought shelter in cellars, sheds, foxholes, and drainage pipes.[49] Indiscriminate grenade fire killed many during the street fighting, and the Soviet press published outraged articles about Wehrmacht soldiers who used civilians as human shields.[50]

The Germans built military administrations in the occupied districts and the surrounding areas. Major Hans Speidel, the commandant of Stalingrad, explained to his Red Army captors in February 1943 the goals of the German occupation: "complete destruction of the party and Soviet cadres, eradication of all the Jews," the exploitation of the population, and the security of the soldiers occupying the city.[51] In April 1943 the NKVD reported that "those involved in uncovering the Jews were mainly members of the German field gendarmerie and the Ukrainian auxiliary police. Traitors among the local population played a considerable role in this. To flush out and exterminate Jews, all dwellings, cellars, niches, and dugouts were checked."[52] Few Jews lived in the Stalingrad region, however. The Soviets counted 855 murdered Jews, refugees from Ukraine most likely; some were killed in sadistic fashion.[53] Major Speidel explained to his interrogators that the Germans shot Jews and communists immediately because they did not know where to put them.[54] The number of those murdered would have been higher, were it not for the last-minute evacuation of civilians.

The Germans required all city residents to register at local military headquarters. Anyone who could not produce a registration card risked being shot or sent to a concentration camp. Men fit for military service were preventatively incarcerated with other war prisoners.[55] A special staff under the command of the chief quartermaster of the 6th Army organized the evacuation of residents deemed suitable for economic exploitation. Starting around October 1, the Germans mustered eight thousand to ten thousand residents each morning and sent them on a sixty-mile march—without food, water, or nighttime shelter from the cold—to the nearest railway stop, in Kalach. There they were sent by train to the Forshtat detention center,

180 miles west of Stalingrad, and were inspected by the German authorities.[56] A Wehrmacht soldier described in a letter dated November 20 the lines of deportees walking toward Kalach in zero-degree cold: "On both sides of the road lie frozen women and children. They also lie in trenches and ditches where the refugees are seeking protection at night. Their only food is dead horses. Each such horse is stripped to the very bones."[57]

The Red Army began its counteroffensive at the end of November. By then there were only fifteen thousand civilians in the German-controlled areas of Stalingrad.[58] Their situation worsened rapidly in the following weeks. Since arriving in September, German soldiers had routinely looted households for jewelry and other valuables. In December soldiers began ransacking shacks and cottages, looking for hidden food and warm clothing. Cold, hungry, and exasperated, the invaders intensified their violent attacks on civilians. Units stationed in the barren steppe outside Stalingrad sent commandos into the city to get wood. They demolished whole dwellings without regard for the inhabitants. As the 6th Army fell back, officers and soldiers took up lodging in undamaged residences and threw the inhabitants out into the street. Some German officers confiscated the quarters of their Romanian allies; many of them raped female civilians.[59]

The chief inspector of the 71st Infantry Division for Stalingrad South ordered all remaining civilians to register on January 1, 1943. To receive a registration card, each resident had to give the local military headquarters four and a half pounds of grain. All in all, 2,500 residents registered, yielding the invaders four tons of grain. In some instances marauding soldiers robbed residents of their meager reserves on the way. The inspector, believing that only a small segment of the remaining population had reported for registration, ordered a second registration for January 10. This time, the charge was four and a half pounds of wheat or six and a half pounds of rye. Three hundred additional residents registered.[60]

In her interview Agrafena Posdnyakova described this mandatory levy along with other experiences and impressions of the German occupiers. Her husband and two of her children died during the battle. The story of how she and her four remaining children survived for almost six months of fighting and austerity is astonishing. I was unable to find written documents or photographs giving more information about the cook and her family. But here is how a municipal employee described other civilian survivors she saw on returning to her destroyed neighborhood in February 1943: "We were walking around our liberated district, along little paths, among the mines and encountered people who had lost their memory, who were afraid of the sound of their own voice. You would look at such a person—a boy's figure, but the temples are completely white."[61]

Ulitsa mira (Peace Street), Stalingrad, 1943. *Photographer: L. I. Konov*

COMMISSION ON THE HISTORY OF THE GREAT PATRIOTIC WAR

Stalingrad, March 14, 1943

Agrafena Petrovna POZDNYAKOVA, an employee of the City Committee[62]

At first I worked for the city committee as a cleaner, and then I worked in the kitchen. It's been five years already. My husband was a worker. We had six children. My oldest girl also worked for the city committee, in the library. She was in the Komsomol. My husband was a shoemaker. He worked at a shoe factory, then in a workshop for invalids. I lost my husband and two of my children during the fighting in Stalingrad.

The enemy started bombing on August 23, in the evening, of course. All of us were at work. It was a good day, everything was all right. In the evening we got back home—and before we'd even sat down, *he* dropped by for a visit.

I could have gotten out of the city, but all my children were sick at the time. That's why we stayed here. When our people were here it wasn't so bad, even with the bombs. We were getting bread, and when the bombs came we hid in basements. Sometimes we stayed underground day and night. There were times when it would quiet down a bit, and we'd jump out to grab something, to get some bread, or bake some, and then it was right back down to the basement. We went to the railway for water. Bullets flying overhead. It wasn't easy getting water. It happened a lot that someone would go for water and not come back. We took the water from a tank, and it often came mixed with fuel oil.

We lived on Solnechnaya Street. It was a small two-story building. We were staying in the basement. On the evening of September 14 our basement was taken by the Germans. On September 17 everything was burned. The entire block was burned to the ground. We were driven out of the basement. Me and my family stayed in some trenches in the courtyard, but the house was intact.

Around eleven a fire broke out. It was just awful. Terrible. We stayed, had our supper in the house. We were getting ready to leave, taking some things, getting the children. The Germans closed the doors and shouted: "Sleep, Rus, sleep!" We had to pass the children through a window and then crawl out ourselves. We had to leave everything behind. All that was left of the place was the walls. We spent the night within those walls. That morning the Germans came and announced that we had to leave this place immediately. So we went back to our trench. We cleared it out a bit, got down, and stayed put. That's where we were until September 26. There was heavy shelling on the 27th. My husband and daughter were killed, and we were covered in dirt. This boy here (she points) was wounded. We got dug out, and we left. We went to the basement of this girl, the one who's come with me today. We stayed there until October 12, which was when the Germans drove us out of the area for good, out from the center to the outskirts of the city. Some left with bags over their shoulders, but I had this wounded boy, small children, and my own legs were also injured. We relocated to the outskirts of the city behind the Soviet Hospital, in the Dzerzhinsky district. We've been living there ever since. The Germans came and kicked us out of this place too. We went to the commandant's office, we begged them. I'm sick, I've got children. They came to take a look and shrugged: you've got too many as it is. They'll all die anyway.

They roughed us up pretty good, hit us, shot at us.

There was still a lot of grain in the elevator.[63] The Germans were taking the grain from the elevator. There were these terrible trains of carts. The men moving the carts were Russian prisoners. If you asked one of them for something, they'd bring you a bag or half a bag of flour. We'd pay him two or three hundred rubles for it. There was a German for every Russian prisoner. We'd buy from one of them, and in an hour, hour and a half, another German would come [take it away] because he knew that we'd bought it. That did it: we were ruined. We had no money, no bread. While our people were here, until September [unintelligible] we were getting bread, flour, some white bread for the children. We somehow managed to keep going. Then we started eating horses. There was nothing to feed them with, so the horses started dying. Out on the road by the Soviet Hospital there were these barracks, terrible places. We'd go there, to the barracks, and ask the Russian prisoners. [. . .] You could tell the horse was going to die anyway. So he shot her. We took the meat and ate it. Later, when the Germans were surrounded, they were eating horses too. They left us the legs, heads, entrails. But by the end we didn't even get that. They took everything, left us only hooves and guts. If they saw you had any horsemeat, they took it. Especially when the Romanians got pushed here from Kalach, when our guys took Kalach—we thought they were going to eat us all alive. They were starving. It was so cold, and they were practically naked. It was awful to see. These scarecrows were always on the move. They took anything and everything they came across.

Back when they first took Stalingrad, they could get what they wanted. They needed clothes, good shoes, gold, watches, and they got everything. In the German commandant's office, for example, they offered transportation out of the city in exchange for gold watches, good boots, men's suits or coats, good carpets. But of course we didn't have any of these things. So the only way we could go was on foot. The Germans did other things too. They'd take what you gave them, drive you out of the city, and then leave you there to fend for yourselves. [. . .]

A lot of people stayed in Stalingrad. Girls, young women, children under fourteen, men under fifty-five or sixty, and women up to fifty were packed off to Germany. Many young women and girls worked and even lived with them. Real patriots, those ones. At the start people who worked here in the city center were allowed to go home, but with a German escort. They stopped letting people do this recently. They got special insignia and documents so the places they were living in didn't get destroyed. Some of them did laundry, some of them cleaned.

When our boys came on January 28 our building was again hit by two shells.

They'd knock on the door and ask to come in and get warm. You'd let them in, and they'd toss the place and take your stuff. Towards the end, if you'd made some flat bread with bad flour, they'd take that as well. You'd make something for the children—horse soup. Or you'd have extra pieces of horsemeat—which you cut up in pieces instead of bread—they'd even take this from you. We stopped letting them in. So then it would go like this: They'd come in a group of two or three. One would stand at the door with a revolver. The others said: give us what you've got. My husband isn't here, I'd say. Look for yourself. They'd look and they'd look and they'd find nothing, and if there was anything to find they'd take it. Every night the same story. We stopped letting them in for a while, but then they started shooting.

Then there was an announcement saying that we had to bring bread to the commandant's office, two kilos' worth. If you didn't have bread, then you could bring meat. If you didn't have meat you could bring horsemeat, salt, soap, or tobacco. I didn't have anything at all. I went to the commandant's office and said that I had nothing. So what? You've got to give us something. If you don't, we'll take your pass. I said that I didn't have a pass. You can take me and my children and do what you like with us.

This girl's mother had some spoiled rye flour that mice had gotten into. I picked it over, sifted it, poured it into a bag, and said that was everything I had. That'll do, they said, give it here.

When we lived on Ninth of January Square,[64] this boy, Gera, was going to school. Two Russian soldiers gave him a little wheat. We had nowhere to put it, so we stashed it. When we got kicked out of that apartment, we didn't get a chance to get it. Then they posted a notice saying that the area beyond the railway was restricted. Going there was punishable by death.

Four Germans were quartered in our place. They stayed with us for two whole weeks. Taichka's sister was working on Communist [Street]. She worked for the Germans. She came with a patrolman. We arranged for him to accompany me to where the wheat was buried. It had gotten to the point where the children were dying from starvation. He said of course he would. He spoke good Russian. They were having a hard time of it because of the lack of bread. He said: "Lady, let's split it fifty-fifty." I agreed. He comes to get me the next day. We set off. We got to the bridge by the fire tower. The policemen there let him through, but not me. They told him to either get me a pass or get lost. There were skirmishes constantly going on in this district. He said: "Let's go, lady, let's get you a pass!" The two of us went to the prison. They had some sort of military headquarters there. He wasn't allowed in. He said: "Let's try the commandant's office." And so we went. When we got there he explained the situation. There were generals there, officers. They call for me: Do you have any grain? I say I used to have a bit, but that it might be gone by now. They assign another German to us, a *gendarme*, they called him. With the *gendarme* we were let through. The patrolman was sent home, and I went with the *gendarme*. We crossed the bridge, went down Communist Street, kept going farther. There's more and more shooting. He says: "Lady, that's the front line!" I say: "Go back, then." He sticks to the walls while I walk right down the middle of the street with my sledge. Again he says: "You can't walk in the street, this is the front." I say: "Go back then, why don't you? I'm not afraid." I kept going, forgot all about him. When I glanced back I could see him sneaking his way forward. We make it to Shilovskaya Street. There used to be an enlistment office there. There was a rope stretched across the street with a patrolman standing nearby. That meant we couldn't go this way. He says something to him in German. "Lady, you can't go there, that's the front line."

I looked: it had snowed. You couldn't even see any footprints, let alone people. I told him we were nearly there, that he could stay here while I kept going. It was open all around, you could see everywhere. Someone started shooting, but I keep going with my sledge. Then they must've seen that I was a woman because the shooting stopped, and then our soldiers were shooting. I got to my place marker and dug up the wheat. Then I tidied up the grave where my husband and daughter were buried. I stayed for quite a while. I'd already put the sack on the sledge. He came up and said: "Show me where it was buried!" Maybe there's some more left. I say: "Go ahead, take a look!" He looked. I left, and he crawled after me. We made it to Communist Street. When we got to the bridge, I turned onto another road. He says: "No, we're going to the commandant's office, the grain must be given to them." I think to myself, does that mean I went through all that for the commandant? Turns out I had. There was a notice posted there in Russian: Anyone with knowledge of stores of grain or clothing must report it to the office of the commandant. They'd send a patrolman or two, who would then go dig up the stash and divide it between them. I never got my share. They didn't give me so much as a single grain. They took all of it and then brought me home. I had lost two buckets' worth of wheat.

After returning to Stalingrad, refugees sit on the ruins where their home once stood, March 1943. *Photographer: N. Sitnikov*

On the 26th, when our forces were about to enter the city, the Germans occupied our building, which became their headquarters. They kicked us out into the courtyard at four in the morning, with all the kids and our things. We stayed in the trenches for two days until our soldiers arrived.

GURTYEV'S RIFLE DIVISION IN BATTLE

In September and October 1942, the 308th Rifle Division, under the command of Leonty Gurtyev, saw almost uninterrupted combat. It fought at two key positions: first at the Kotluban heights,[65] twenty-four miles northwest of Stalingrad, and later at the Barricades munitions plant in the city's industrial district. The division, composed of ten thousand soldiers from Siberia, suffered heavy losses in the fighting. By the time the division was placed on reserve status in early November awaiting reinforcements, the roster had shrunk to 1,727 men, of whom in Chuikov's estimation only a few hundred were fit for battle.[66] These eight weeks of intense combat are described in the following conversational strand composed of interviews with commanders, political officers, foot soldiers, and nurses of the 308th Rifle Division.

The German panzer advance north of Stalingrad to the Volga on August 23 took the Soviets completely by surprise. It drove a wedge in the line of defense formed by the Southeastern and Stalingrad Fronts, enabling the 6th Army to cross the Don and disperse units from the 62nd Army in short order. Meanwhile, the 4th Panzer Army approached the city from the southwest, forming a pocket with the 6th Army that pushed the leftovers of the Soviet 64th Army eastward. On September 3 the spearheads of each army joined forces near Pitomnik on the western outskirts of Stalingrad. With Soviet troops still regrouping, the city was vulnerable to the combined German armies. The battle that the Soviets had planned for the fortified line of defense along the Don River would now take place along the Volga, under far worse conditions.

Stalin, who had been tracking these developments from Moscow, pressured his generals to take immediate action. On August 26, General Zhukov, the new deputy commander in chief of the Red Army, departed for Stalingrad, tasked with launching a diversionary attack by September 2.

The 1st Guards Army, with support from the 24th and 66th Armies and from the 4th Tank Army, was to punch a hole in the Wehrmacht's northern cordon stretching from the Don to the Volga, encircle the Germans, and link up with the beleaguered 62nd Army. Zhukov began preparations but objected to the time frame, which he regarded as too narrow, since several of the divisions planned for the offensive had yet to arrive. He believed that a coordinated attack could take place no sooner than September 6. On September 3 the front commander, Yeryomenko, reported to Stalin of heavy bombing in the city, signaling that the German armies were about to strike. In response Stalin cabled an urgent telegraph to Zhukov: "Stalingrad may be taken today or tomorrow if the Northern Army Group doesn't offer immediate assistance. [. . .] Delay at this point is equal to a crime."[67] Zhukov had no choice but to launch the attack the following morning, with the additional units joining the next day.

Though Soviet troops outnumbered their opponents, they were at a disadvantage in several respects. The flat and treeless steppes offered no shelter, and the Soviet rifle divisions, lacking sufficient air and armored support, were exposed to German artillery fire and air attack. The German soldiers of the 76th and 113th Infantry Divisions had entrenched themselves in the *balkas*, deep gullies common in the region, making them hard to hit. What also proved fatal was Yeryomenko's stubborn insistence on daytime fighting.[68] Nevertheless, the Soviets were able to push two and a half miles into the five-mile deep cordon. On September 8 the 308th Rifle Division was taken off reserve status and deployed to Kotluban, at the heart of the offensive, in a bid to seize a strategic hill.

By September 10 Zhukov realized that the intended breakthrough would not succeed. He called Stalin to demand more troops and time for a "more concentrated blow." Stalin summoned him to Moscow so they could deliberate the next move.[69] On September 12 Zhukov, Chief of Staff Vasilevsky, and Stalin discussed how the Red Army could avoid imminent catastrophe. Zhukov wanted at minimum another army, more tanks, and an air force. He also presented ideas for a large-scale counteroffensive. It was here that the plan to encircle the Germans was hammered out.[70]

Meanwhile, the Kotluban offensive continued to exact a high toll. By September 15, as many as a third of the 250,000 soldiers were wounded or dead. On September 18, a second offensive began, this time with more troops and a new formation. The 308th Rifle Division had been absorbed by the 24th Army but continued to fight near Kotluban. During the heavy fighting on September 18–19, the Soviets suffered thirty-two thousand wounded and dead. Nevertheless, the operation succeeded in pinning down several German divisions and elements of the Luftwaffe, reducing the force of the German attack on Stalingrad.[71]

At the end of September, the worn-down 308th Rifle Division was posted to Stalingrad. After marching a hundred-mile detour around the front, they arrived at the eastern bank of the Volga on the night of October 1. They crossed in waves and entered the burning city with a mission to recapture the worker settlements in front of the Barricades munitions plant. On October 3 Paulus started a large offensive to capture the entire industrial district in the north. The advancing soldiers of the 24th Panzers had arrived at the Barricades plant on October 4 and decimated an entire regiment of the 308th Rifle Division. That evening Chuikov removed the remaining soldiers in the division from the line of fire.[72] Stalin was not pleased. On October 5 he issued a strong rebuke to Yeryomenko: Stalingrad would fall if the sections of the city lost to the Germans were not retaken. "For that, it is necessary to turn each house and each street in Stalingrad into a fortress. Unfortunately, you haven't been able to do that and continue surrendering block after block to the enemy. That shows you are acting poorly."[73]

In mid-October fighting in the industrial district reached its zenith. On October 14 the Germans began a large-scale assault on the Stalingrad Tractor factory, with the aim of pushing southward along the Volga to the city center. On October 17 German soldiers infiltrated the Barricades munitions plant defended by the 308th Rifle Division. The following day a Stuka pilot summarized the fighting in his diary: "We were plowing over the burning ruin of Stalingrad all day. I don't understand how people are still able to live in this hell, but the Russians are firmly lodged in the ruins, the cracks, the basements and the chaos of the distorted factory frames."[74]

After ten days of fighting—participants on both sides described it as the most hellish of the battle—the 62nd Army had been pushed back to three shallow bridgeheads: a pocket held by Colonel Sergei Gorokhov's group; the parts of the Barricades plant along the Volga (held by the soldiers of the 138th, 308th, 193rd, and 45th Rifle Divisions and of the 39th Guards Rifle Division); and a strip of land that stretched from the eastern edge of Mamayev Kurgan to the city center (held by the 284th Rifle Division and the 13th Guards Rifle Division).[75] Altogether, these Soviet positions comprised around fifteen thousand able-bodied soldiers. By mid-November their number had shrunk by half.[76] The wounded in the 308th Rifle Division had been carried off the battlefield and those remaining joined the 138th Rifle Division, who had assumed a hedgehog formation—their guns facing outward in all directions—on the banks of Volga under the command of Colonel Ivan Lyudnikov.[77] On November 17, two days before Operation Uranus commenced, Hitler gave up hope of taking Stalingrad before winter. Instead, he urged his commanders "to take at least the areas from the munitions plant and the steelworks to the Volga."[78]

In April and May 1943, the Moscow historians interviewed twenty-four members of the 308th Rifle Division who fought at Stalingrad—from Commander Leonty Gurtyev and Divisional Commissar Afanasy Svirin to military engineers, switchboard operators, and nurses. The interviews provide vivid depictions of combat and death, both inside and outside the city. Above all, they show how the division persevered despite constant attrition. This was partly due to the division's self-confidence and the troops' loyalty to their commander. But it was also helped by the political officers, whose entreaties and encouragement provided a moral compass amid the tumult of battle. Again and again, they called on soldiers to show their mettle and uncover the hero within. If someone died while performing a heroic act—such as the nurse Lyolya Novikova, of whom Captain Ivan Maksin spoke—the example spurred on others to hate the enemy and sacrifice themselves for their country. Many of the interviews attest to how deeply the political conditioning the soldiers received informed their speech and behavior. Medic Nina Kokorina emulated the war heroes celebrated in her Komsomol group. The infantrymen Vasily Boltenko and Vasily Kalinin seem to have internalized the message that the inner strength of the Soviet soldier could prevail in the duel between man and machine that characterized the contest between the Red Army and the Wehrmacht. Soviet military training told soldiers that they could shoot down German aircraft or incapacitate a panzer through willpower alone. The confidence in the collective force of the soldiers finds symbolic expression in Fyodor Skvortsov's description of how a human chain reestablished a broken telephone line.

The first interviews, with Mikhail Ingor and Nina Kokorina, took place in Moscow on April 30, 1943; the remaining ones occurred between May 11 and 14 in the village of Laptyevo.

THE SPEAKERS (in the order they appear)

Gurtyev, Leonty Nikolayevich—Major general, commander of the 308th Rifle Division

Kokorina, Nina Mikhailovna—Senior sergeant, medical company nurse, assistant deputy for political affairs for the medical company of the 347th Rifle Regiment

Belugin, Vasily Georgievich—Major, commissar in the 347th Rifle Regiment

Smirnov, Alexei Stepanovich—Lieutenant colonel, chief of the divisional political section

Ryvkin, Semyon Solomonovich—Captain, commander of an independent field engineering battalion

Svirin, Afanasy Matveyevich—Lieutenant colonel, deputy divisional commander for political affairs

Petrakov, Dmitri Andrianovich—Commissar in the 339th Rifle Regiment

Maksin, Ivan Vasilievich—Captain, chief of the divisional political section in charge of the Komsomol

Boltenko, Vasily Yakovlevich—Junior lieutenant, platoon commander, and deputy battalion commander for combat units of the 347th Rifle Regiment

Seleznev, Gavriil Grigorievich—Private, field engineering battalion

Stoylik, Anna Kipriyanovna—Nurse, medical company platoon commander

Vlasov, Mikhail Petrovich—Senior lieutenant, commissar in the artillery battalion of the 351st Rifle Regiment (no date given)

Koshkarev, Alexander Fyodorovich—Party bureau secretary, 339th Rifle Regiment

Kushnaryov, Ivan Antonovich—Lieutenant colonel, commander of the 339th Rifle Regiment

Chamov, Andrei Sergeyevich—Lieutenant colonel, commander of the 347th Rifle Regiment

Kalinin, Vasily Petrovich—Senior lieutenant, deputy chief of staff for intelligence, 347th Rifle Regiment

Skvortsov, Fyodor Maksimovich—Private, telephone operator

Sovchinsky, Vladimir Makarovich—Major, deputy commander for political affairs, 339th Rifle Regiment

Brysin, Ilya Mironovich—Junior lieutenant, sapper platoon commander, independent field engineering battalion

Dudnikov, Yefim Yefimovich—Private, sapper platoon, independent field engineering battalion

Ingor, Mikhail Lazarevich—Captain, politruk, 347th Rifle Regiment

Trifonov, Alexander Pavlovich—politruk, 1011th Artillery Regiment

Stepanov, Alexander Dmitriyevich—Battalion commissar, 1011th Artillery Regiment

Fugenfirov, Genrikh Aronovich—Commander of the 1011th Artillery Regiment[79]

Major General Leonty Nikolayevich Gurtyev (Commander of the 308th Rifle Division):[80] The division was made up of Siberians for the most part. [. . .] Our unit was recruited in March, April, May. In May we set off for the training camp. We left there in early June and went to the Saratov region. For a while we stayed at Karamyshevka, near the Tatishchevo rail station, where we completed our combat training.

There we were visited by representatives from the region and from the People's Commissariat of Defense. [. . .] In July comrade Voroshilov came and spent two days with us. We conducted a join exercise with the 120th Division. Comrade Voroshilov was pleased with our division, met with our command staff, and gave instructions regarding weaknesses that needed attention. Then he gathered the divisional commanders and the chiefs of staff of the regiments on their own, got to know them, sat with them for two hours in one of the classrooms, talked with them, and then he left. Not long afterward we were sent to the front.

Senior Sergeant Nina Mikhailovna Kokorina (Nurse, assistant deputy for political affairs, 347th Rifle Regiment): I finished [school] in 1941. I'd been planning to go to Sverdlovsk University, but then the war broke out. I got a letter from my sister who had already volunteered. She was headed to the Volkhov Front. I don't know where she is now. My older brother is also at the front, got transferred from the east. My father is at home, works at the Gosrybtrest[81] fish factory. My mother, grandmother, and younger brother stayed at home. All of them are in Tobolsk.

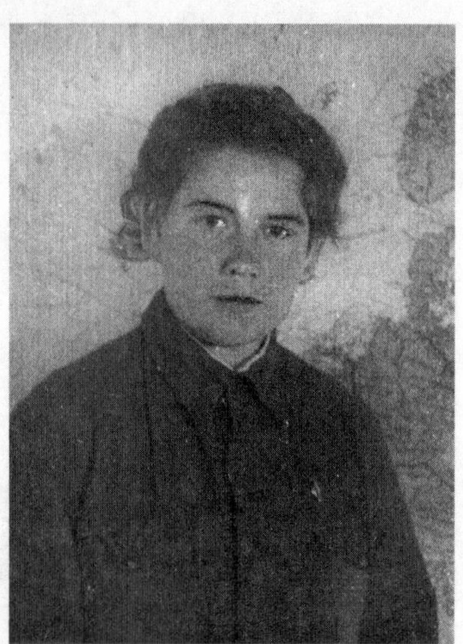
Nurse Nina Kokorina

When I got that letter from my sister, I went home to tell my mother I was going to nursing school. I became a member of the Komsomol there in 1939. In October [1941] I completed nursing school. We tried to sign up after graduation, but they wouldn't take us. "Come back again when you turn nineteen." I wrote a letter to comrade Stalin. They showed me the letter with his decision: to be sent to the front immediately. I was also working with the Red Cross.[82] Sixty of us went to the enlistment office after we learned that a detail was going to arrive, and we all signed a petition. They took about forty-five of us girls, mostly medical orderlies. Then we came to this unit.

I'd also like to talk about when we left. I'll never forget that moment. Usually when they come to see you off, it's nothing but tears. Our mothers stayed strong, it was amazing. In one of her letters Mama said that women often say to her: "Anna Vasilievna, you've sent two daughters and a son to the front—how are you still happy?" She answers them: "I didn't raise them to stay at home."[83]

Major Vasily Georgievich Belugin (Commissar in the 347th Rifle Regiment): I was born in 1897. I've been a member of the party since 1919. The first time I joined the army was in 1916. I was in the old army for nine months until 1917. In December 1916 I was arrested for spreading revolutionary propaganda and weakening army morale. They released me in February 1917. In September 1917 I started working as an inspector in the bakers' union. In 1918 I was drafted into the Rogozhsko-Semyonov battalion. From August 1919 to 1924 I worked for special departments in the Cheka and GPU.[84] At the same time I began my studies. In 1931 I finished technical college and worked as the head of the personnel department at the Supreme Soviet of the National Economy,[85] then as director of the Industrial Transport Institute for the People's Commissariat of Heavy Industry, and then I was named director of the All-Union Industrial Academy by order of the Central Committee in 1935. After that I was sent to work at the People's Commissariat until the beginning of the war. On June 22 I tendered my resignation so I could volunteer for the army.

The Moscow city and regional party committees approved my application on the 25th, so I was free to go. I volunteered, and my daughter accompanied me. She was nineteen. She was carrying a duffel bag when she came to the station to see me off. She'd made up her mind to come with me. No matter what I said she wouldn't leave the station, she just kept asking over and again for me to take her along. At that time we were approached by a member of the military council of the Siberian Military District. Once he understood the situation, he said: "Just let her go." I asked whether I could really take her with me. "You both can and should." And so the two of us set off together.

Captain Semyon Solomonovich Ryvkin (Commander of an independent field engineering battalion): The battalion was set up in March 1942. On March 25 we celebrated our one-year anniversary. I was with the battalion right at its formation. Most of the people were Siberians. Inexperienced youths with no combat experience. We worked with them for a long time. After two months of training we all went to the front, so we were actually working with these soldiers for about five months. By then every one of them could be trusted with all sorts of combat missions.

Senior Sergeant Nina Mikhailovna Kokorina (Nurse, assistant deputy for political affairs, 347th Rifle Regiment): We were very thoroughly trained by General Gurtyev. Nearly every day we were marching thirty to sixty kilometers. There were days when you'd never get dry after it rained, when you'd have just gotten to sleep and the alarm would go off. When you hear it, you get up and go again. The girls held up wonderfully. Sometimes we'd be on the go for three days running, no rest, and we were always singing songs. During halts we danced. Regimental commander Mikhailov really liked our medical company.

Lieutenant Colonel Afanasy Matveyevich Svirin (Deputy commander for political affairs, 308th Rifle Division): The division's previous commissar had been removed. General Medvedyev came and told me I had fifteen minutes: An airplane was waiting at the airfield, he said, and it was taking me to the 308th Division, which was on its way to the front. A car came and took me to the airfield. We went directly to the air base in Omsk. On June 10 we arrived in Saratov. Now I had to get to know the division's political staff. A week later we held a party meeting, where we discussed our party-political work and the objectives of the party organization. I gave a report on the status of the party-political work and set a number of specific tasks—what needed to be done and how—so that the division would be completely prepared. The work of the party organization was to be the basis of everything. The first issue concerned everyday welfare—namely, the operation of the mess hall. After the party meeting we inspected the mess hall and discovered a number of shortcomings. We outlined several measures that would address this. The next problem concerned the soldiers' hygiene. They needed to wash, to get clean clothes. These questions were dealt with sensibly. Finally there was the question of the division's combat training. For this we undertook a wide range of party-political work.

This work took the form of meetings at the regiment and company level, and quite a lot of people would come to take part and speak on a number of issues.

Political deputy of the divisional command, Lieutenant Colonel Afanasy Svirin

During combat training we set ourselves the task of eliminating the soldiers' fear of tanks, and also of planes—issues that we soon enough had to deal with in reality.

What practical methods are there for eliminating a fear of tanks?

First of all, we made each antitank soldier aware of the merciless power and strength of their antitank gun. We gave each soldier the chance to shoot through some metal plates we picked up from the railway. Every soldier convinced himself that a tank could be penetrated and that he was well able to handle his antitank gun. As for the other aspect, what we did was drive tanks over the soldiers as they crouched down in trenches. They were reassured that these narrow trenches provided a safe location, and afterward they could get out and throw grenades.

We also educated them using the examples of the courageous men at Sebastapol, who threw themselves under tanks in groups of five, and of the heroic deeds of Panfilov's men, the twenty-eight who kept an avalanche of vehicles at bay. [. . .]

We taught them our Russian military traditions. We often quoted our great military leaders, who said that to protect your wives and children you must defend the fatherland, you must give everything to defend the fatherland. We told them about the heroic deeds of Ivan Susanin and gave many other examples from the history of the Russian people. All of this enters the consciousness of every soldier, giving him confidence in our victory. Several times on the road I gave speeches on the challenges that our soldiers would be facing in upcoming battles. Other party workers spoke too. Whenever we stopped we held discussions, gave lectures and reports. We did all this so they would arrive at the front in a state of full combat and political readiness. [. . .]

About the fear of planes—we knew we were going to the front, and that we'd come across them even before we got there. We drove home the idea that it wasn't just antiaircraft artillery that could hit planes. You can also shoot one with a rifle, submachine gun, or antitank weapon. We gave examples from newspapers of planes being shot down by rifle fire, and made it perfectly clear that the fear of planes was something they must eliminate in themselves.

Our third task was to get them all, and especially the Komsomol members, to shoot well. During our combat training period we had around three thousand Komsomol members. We set them a goal: a quarter of them to become snipers, and the rest to qualify at no less than "good" or "excellent." [. . .]

Before deploying to the front we conducted a great amount of party-political work. We held a meeting of all the political staff where we set ourselves the task of reaching the front without losing a single soldier or political worker on the way. We also held Komsomol meetings in the companies. Because of this work, we arrived at the front without having a single deserter. There was one incident where a private from our headquarters company dropped his weapon. The commander of the headquarters battery told us that the soldier had lost his carbine about three kilometers back. We sent him back to look for it, and after about five hours he returned, drenched in sweat, with his carbine. That's how we managed not to lose anyone. We brought twelve thousand people to the front. It took seven days.

Major General Leonty Nikolayevich Gurtyev (Commander of the 308th Rifle Division): Our disembarkation point was Kumalga.[86] Some of us got off at Kumalga, and the rest got off at various locations to the north and south, and then we regrouped. We arrived safely. Only one train had been shot at, and one platoon commander was wounded. We gathered at Kumalga and then marched toward the village of Eterevskaya. From there we set off toward Kotluban and Samokhvalovka.[87] For several days we marched without incident. It was a rather difficult march. It was hot, and because we didn't have much time we were covering great distances, and our transportation was delayed. We were always in column formation. We deployed quickly and got there safely. At one point we lost a few men and four horses. [. . .]

In the first couple of days our division suffered very heavy losses. We lost a lot of people to enemy aircraft. A lot of shrapnel wounds. We also lost men from heavy enemy mortar fire. Within a few days more than five thousand men were treated by the medical battalion. All day, from dawn till dusk, there were fifteen to twenty, or as many as forty enemy aircraft, and that whole time we were being shelled by mortars. We didn't have many planes. They joined the fight, but only for general missions. The Luftwaffe was in control of the skies.

Lieutenant Colonel Afanasy Matveyevich Svirin (Deputy commander for political affairs, 308th Rifle Division): On September 1–2 we came to the area of Kotluban. For a few days our division was under the command of the Stavka, but then we were made part of 24th Army. Then we got the order about combat operations in the area of Kotluban. We were ordered to attack at night. Before our departure we held meetings again in all the regiments and battalions. Comrade Yudin, a representative of the Central Committee, gave a speech, as did many other political workers, myself included.

Airplanes were prowling everywhere, illuminating the area all around. We often had to interrupt our meetings. It was as if the enemy had found out about our meetings, were lighting the area with flares and then dropping bombs. Comrade Yudin had come from Moscow only to end up in this mess, and we were the ones who were told to protect him. After our speeches the soldiers pledged that they would carry out their orders, liberate Stalingrad, and link up with the Stalingrad units. The group decided to send a letter to comrade Stalin in which every regiment swore that when these Siberian soldiers were ordered into battle they would give everything they had to execute those orders and defeat the enemy.

That morning when the division left for battle it was good spirits all around, you couldn't help feeling uplifted.

They ordered us to take Hills 132, 154.2, and 143.8, and the 339th and 347th Rifle Regiments moved in with artillery support. We'd been promised tank support for the offensive but hadn't gotten any, so on the 8th, 9th, 10th, and 11th our regiments attacked these hills without tanks. These hills were of great importance because they commanded a view of the entire city. Comrade Stalin knew these hills,[88] and we set ourselves the task of taking them no matter what. Also, these hills would allow further advancement on Gumrak and eventual contact with the people in Stalingrad.

The hills were taken on September 19. Holding them wasn't easy, but we held out until the 27th.

Dmitri Andrianovich Petrakov (Commissar in the 339th Rifle Regiment): On September 4, 1942, we were Lesnichestvo, in the Stalingrad region. We got the order to set out for the Kotluban station. We were on the march from the 5th to the 8th, around three hundred kilometers, and by daybreak on the 9th we reached the Kotluban station. That is when the air raids began. It was a massed air raid. Our regiment didn't have a chance to break formation, so we were still marching in a long column when they started dropping bombs and pounding us with mortars and artillery. That was when we joined the battle. We didn't have any intel beforehand. The area was completely flat and open, and only thing we could see in front of us was the hills, where the enemy was firing at us from his entrenchments. People started to dig in right then and there. We deployed in combat formations and began the assault of Hill 143.9 and Hill 154.2. There were lot of casualties.

That evening 2nd Battalion led the first attack wave and pressed the enemy. That first day we lost about 50 percent of our staff, and nearly all of the political staff. A German sniper and two tank operators remained in some shot-out tanks to keep an eye on 2nd Battalion, but when the battalion advanced those Germans were left behind. We saw someone from the political command staff aiming at the Germans. The Germans eventually worked out that they were being shot at from behind.

That evening something terrible happened. Men were rushing into a ravine without knowing where they were. The division lost about a thousand men altogether. The political workers had to work all night under fire.

Senior Sergeant Nina Mikhailovna Kokorina (Nurse, assistant deputy for political affairs, 347th Rifle Regiment): On our way to Stalingrad we covered 260 kilometers in three days. We did wonderfully on this trip. The girls always kept up with the soldiers. We'd march, ford rivers. The soldiers were often getting sores on their feet. We treated them. The girls were being thanked nearly every day.

We arrived in the area of the Kotluban station. I'll never forget that first day. The attack began at five o'clock. There were two hills: 143.8 and 154.2. A few divisions had come before us, but none of them could take these hills. This was on September 10. It's not something you're used to, you don't understand it. You can't imagine what war is like. This was when the Germans threw their planes into the battle and started bombing our positions. We went around one of the hills and down into a ravine. That's where we took our first casualties. We could feel it immediately. Before that, I didn't really sense that this was something serious. It was like we were in training. The first casualty was from an antitank company. I rushed over to him. His guts were all coming out. I put everything back inside and bandaged him up. [. . .]

A German submachine gunner wearing a Red Army uniform infiltrated our ranks. He didn't shoot at the soldiers or medics, but he immediately shot the first officer who appeared.

Lieutenant Tarnyuk, the battalion commander, ordered me to go dress the wounded and see where the shooting was coming from. I crawled to the right of 2nd Battalion's position and noticed that someone was shooting toward us from that direction. Then I saw this private run off, and after a little while the shooting was coming from the left. I determined roughly where he was shooting from. There was a wounded soldier from 3rd Platoon. I sent him to report what I'd seen. I stayed behind to keep an eye on the gunner and our soldiers. While the soldier was gone, the submachine gunner disappeared and climbed into a tank that was blocking our path, about five hundred meters from the ravine. He took out the commander of 8th Company. My platoon commander, Ganchenko, took command. Half our platoon went there. But the enemy was covering a large area, we couldn't cross it. Ganchenko ordered his men to go around the tank and kill that submachine gunner. They carried out his order quickly.

Nearly all the girls in our battalion were sent up for medals.

I want to talk about Sonya Fateyeva, who was wounded in that battle. She was from Tobolsk. Such a tall and robust girl. This one time in class, when we were still in Yazykovka, this officer showed up, and when she brought her hand down on his shoulder he lost his balance and fell over. We thought very highly of her. A wonderful girl, so friendly. If she saw that someone was a bit down, she'd make them feel better right away.

The Germans had been bombing our ravine since 5:00 P.M. I decided to try slipping through the firing line to get to our people. And I made it. There I discovered that Motya Gurina, a medic, had been wounded. The Germans had the area covered with mortar fire, and there were also airplanes and shelling. I'd nearly gotten to the last trenches. I could see a medic lying there. I crawled over and saw that it was Sofya. Her head was bandaged. She'd been shot in the head, no exit wound. Our sergeant major had tended to her. She'd been brought there from the front line. I don't know how she made her way through the no-man's-land.

I asked her: "Sofya, what happened?" "Well, I got hit. Lost a lot of blood." I said: "You've got to get to the ravine." She said—and I'll never forget it—"I know that life is there, but I'm not going." I didn't try to order her. I didn't have the right to.

Captain Ivan Vasilievich Maksin (Chief of the divisional political section in charge of the Komsomol): As a Komsomol worker, and having earlier been an educator of secondary school students, I strove to make myself into a true frontline Komsomol worker. I used the examples of Arnold Meri,[89] Ilya Kuzin,[90] and Zoya Kosmodemyanskaya[91]—Komsomol members who proved themselves to be heroes of the Patriotic War—in order to bring out the very best in people. In this way I made myself into a true frontline soldier while at the same time teaching the model of these heroic Komsomol members during discussions with Komsomol subunits and organizations, discussions with female members. [. . .]

The situation we found ourselves in near Kotluban made it quite difficult to maintain order among the Komsomol members, and our leaders were not always active in our Komsomol organizations. Comrade Sheiko was the model of a true Komsomol organizer. Every day he knew when and how many of our members were out of action, whether they were wounded, killed, sick, and so on. Every evening the Komsomol would sum up the day's work. They would gather at an appointed place, usually after heavy fighting, during a moment of relative calm, and determine the outcomes of the day's fighting: how many casualties there were in which Komsomol organization, how many were left, which heroic deeds were carried out by whom in what organization. At this meeting we summarized the Komsomol members' heroic deeds, and then we developed a plan for publicizing them, so that these heroes could be known throughout the Komsomol. Members of the regimental bureau went back to their units, to the lowest-level Komsomol organizations, and relayed the topics and outcomes of the meeting, and the heroic spirit of the Komsomol, to the masses, to the front. We gathered small groups of Komsomol members in trenches, on the front lines, sometimes at night, and we reported the outcomes of the meeting and told them about the heroic deeds of members from other Komsomol units. The very next day everyone in the Komsomol knew who among them was a hero of the day.

These gatherings where we announced the heroes of the day—both men and women—one good example would be one that Bureau Secretary Sheiko himself convened at a medical company after the death of Lyolya Novikova, who was a member of the Komsomol, a hero, and a posthumous recipient of the Order of the Red Banner.

Everyone knew Lyolya Novikova. She didn't immediately inspire the confidence that she would later show herself worthy of at the front. She looked more like a ballerina. During combat training she wore high heels. She worked as a draftsman, but she was always so eager to go to the front lines. Because she didn't want to pursue her main profession, many people thought that she lacked discipline. But she kept asking to serve in the battalion as a medic so she could carry the wounded back from the front line. Her lack of discipline ended up being the very reason she was sent to the front.

September 11, 1942 was the division's heaviest day of fighting, especially for the 339th Rifle Regiment. For many hours of intense fighting Lyolya Novikova displayed exceptional heroism. She tended to the wounded and dragged them to back to cover while under heavy machine-gun and mortar fire, never considering which unit or company they were from. That day she used more than fifty packs of bandages, one pack for every wounded soldier, meaning that she dressed and recovered fifty wounded men and officers from the battlefield. That evening she came back from the field. I'd been in that regiment before, during combat training, and the two of us had a conversation: "Lyolya, you're a good Komsomol member, you're well educated, and you've got real talent for reciting poetry. If only you were more disciplined you would be able to join the party. We would recommend you. Show us you can do it." She said that she couldn't join the party because she hadn't yet proved herself in battle. "I don't know how I'll do in really heavy combat," she said. "If I do well at the front and prove myself, I'll join the party, but first I've got to get to the front." She got what she wanted.

Her sleeves were rolled up when she returned from the heavy fighting, and her forearms were plastered with dried blood clear up to her elbows, and there was nowhere to wash because of a problem with the water situation, not just for washing but for drinking as well. She came back to us at sunset, by which time I'd already got word of her display of heroism in battle. The men nearly had to drag her away from the heavy fighting. The first thing she said when she arrived was: "Now I can ask that you enroll me in the party. Now that I've proved myself, proved that I'll never be afraid of heavy combat." She was so delighted as she told us about the shells and bullets flying around her, and how the soldiers would yell: "Help me, sister!" And about how she dragged the wounded soldiers from the field. She was full of these impressions from that life at the front, and she begged so earnestly to be enrolled as a member of the party.

There was more heavy fighting the next day. The battalion commander, whose life Lyolya Novikova had saved when she dragged him out of harm's way at night, gave her a pistol. She slung it over her shoulder and set off for her second day of heavy combat. Two hours into the fight she was shot by a German submachine gun: three bullets to the head. And Lyolya was dead.

So when comrade Sheiko came to the company's Komsomol organization, the first item on the agenda was this, the heroic deeds of Lyolya Novikova. I should also mention that this was an exemplary meeting as far as the education of Komsomol members is concerned. Comrade Sheiko entered the room. All the Komsomol members stood up. He greeted them and said: "This meeting of the medical company Komsomol is now in session. There is one item for today's agenda: the heroic deeds of Komsomol member Lyolya Novikova." After bringing the meeting to order, he rose to speak, seeing as he knew what she had done and was able to tell the story. First he asked everyone to rise and honor the memory of Lyolya Novikova, a hero who was killed in action while fighting the German aggressors. Everyone stood up, many with tears in their eyes, and everyone felt bad for Lyolya. She'd been so cheerful and lively. Comrade Sheiko recounted her heroic deeds. Then some young women spoke, and they vowed to fight the Germans just as Lyolya had. After these oaths, the Komsomol meeting resolved that all its members would prove themselves worthy of the memory of Lyolya Novikova as they fought the German occupiers of their socialist motherland. The meeting likewise resolved to ask the party bureau to accept her application, to take her into the ranks of the Bolsheviks and count her among the members of the Communist party.

The heroic deeds of Lyolya Novikova immediately became the heritage of Komsomol members in all the regimental organizations. There were articles about Lyolya Novikova in our frontline and divisional newspapers, including one that I wrote. Afterward the Komsomol petitioned for her posthumous decoration. Lyolya Novikova was posthumously awarded the Order of the Red Banner. We wrote her mother a heartfelt letter, but there was no reply because she had since been evacuated from Voronezh.

Lieutenant Colonel Afanasy Matveyevich Svirin (Deputy commander for political affairs, 308th Rifle Division): In Kotluban, on Hill 154.2, we encountered tanks for the first time. There were about forty of them. On September 17 my divisional commander and I were at the observation post. The tanks were moving toward the 351st and 347th Regiments. I called two instructors from the political section, told them to go provide moral support to the antitank units before they engaged the tanks, to help them stay firm. They accepted their orders and tried to convince everyone to fight to the death, to not let those tanks past. We opened fire as soon as the tanks came, gave them a heavy barrage of antitank fire. All of the regiment's artillery was there on that hill, and we took out about a dozen tanks right then. The rest of them turned around and went back. The tanks were on fire for everyone to see, and every soldier could see for himself that tanks weren't all that scary if you took the fight to them. While the soldiers were in their slit trenches, we told them that the guys in a tank can't see someone in a trench, and within five meters they can't even shoot at him. After that we began our assault of the hill.

Major Vasily Georgievich Belugin (Commissar in the 347th Rifle Regiment): The 347th Rifle Regiment had been placed in reserve to support the divisional commander. The regimental commander and I had put in five long months of productive work getting this regiment well trained, and we could not agree to our assignment in this order of battle. We had a detailed plan of how the division could complete its objectives, and on September 10 we took these suggestions to the divisional commander. Our plan was accepted, the 351st Regiment was held back, and we became part of the main strike force. Our mission was to attack and defeat the enemy on Hill 154.2, take control of the hill, and then move on to Brovkin and Novaya Nadezhda. On September 18 we set about completing this mission. [. . .] We dug in under the cover of darkness, and despite the horrific amounts of enemy fire that morning of September 18—and with the men in exceptionally high spirts—we took Hill 154.2 in one strong push.

1st and 2nd Battalions went on to complete the regiment's next tasks. They attacked Brovkin and Novaya Nadezhda, and by eleven o'clock they'd taken Brovkin and continued further, despite heavy losses. 3rd Battalion secured our gains by organizing a defensive perimeter of Hill 154.2. This Hill commanded a view of the entire area. You could see eight to ten kilometers away from there. From 10:00 A.M. there was enemy mortar and artillery fire that almost never stopped, and a whole fleet of low-flying aircraft coming in groups of ten to fifteen bombed us until dark without ever letting up. They dropped an incredible amount of deadly metal.

[. . .] A report from the observation post said that more than twenty enemy vehicles had arrived and were unloading infantry. Enemy infantry units were getting into battle formations before our eyes. The first enemy counterattack had begun. This is where our commander's plan was revealed. Regimental commander Barkovsky threw everything he had at the enemy column: all of 3rd Battalion's firepower, including the reserves. The regiment's mortar company on Hill 154.2 had already shot the last shells from their third ammunition reserve. Vasily Boltenko brought up his 45mm guns to the firing line and started to set the enemy vehicles on fire.

Junior Lieutenant Vasily Yakovlevich Boltenko (Platoon commander and deputy battalion commander for combat units of the 347th Rifle Regiment): The fighting moved to a hill that was of great significance: Hill 154.2. The 347th Rifle Regiment was tasked with fighting for this hill from the 17th to the 18th. The situation was grim, and there was a large concentration of enemy forces. I was with 1st Battalion during these fights. Heavy enemy fire was coming from our right flank. As soon as the gunner fired at the bunker, the breach man was killed. Our battery commander was killed two hundred meters away from me. My helmet was hit by a projectile.

Senior Sergeant Vasily Boltenko, recipient of the Order of the Patriotic War, First Class

Our guns didn't retreat after the infantry had taken the hill. I had two Kazakhs drag the guns. Regimental commander Barkovsky was near the hill when eight German tanks came on the counterattack. I disabled two of them, and some antitank riflemen got the rest. They were all ours. The one tank I shot three times, and two shots stopped the other one dead in its tracks.

Major Vasily Georgievich Belugin (Commissar in the 347th Rifle Regiment): A new threat was moving in from the left flank: a formation of thirty enemy tanks was slowly advancing on Hill 154.2. Enemy infantry were following close behind. Submachine gunners were on top of the tanks. The regimental commander decided to use everything we had on that hill. With weapon in hand, he had us take the firing positions of the neighboring division's mortar company. I got about ten antitank rifles. Major Barkovsky, the regimental commander, wanted to set up some powerful close-range machine-gun fire.[92] He gathered all the antitank guns, checked them over himself, indicated the targets, and right at that moment he was mortally wounded. He wanted to tell us something but couldn't finish what he was saying. [. . .]

The tanks were getting closer. I called Igor Mirokhin, the chief of staff and regiment favorite: "Well, my friend, the regiment's yours. Remember back in Cheremushka when you said, 'I'll be on staff for a year or two, and then they'll trust me with a regiment.' It's only been two months!" "I hereby take command of the regiment." Igor Mirokhin checked the firing positions and then used his antitank rifle to shoot at the tanks from the foxhole next to mine.

Dive-bombers and low-flying planes attacked our hill like ravens. But that wasn't the most important thing. The most important thing was to stop that first tank. Then everything else would fall into place. Igor Mirokhin was an excellent shot. He was the first one in our division to shoot down a Messerschmitt with an antitank rifle. And now he shot at the tank on the right and stopped it with his first shot, and with the second shot he set the middle tank on fire. It's a shame the cartridges for antitank guns aren't lubricated. Getting them out of the magazine can be difficult. "You need a shovel." And Igor Mirokhin used his entrenching tool to open the lock, fired, and then a third enemy tank burst into flames. Two hundred meters. At 150 meters the enemy changed his battle formations. The flanking tanks came into the main line and began moving right up to the front line. Igor Mirokhin stopped a fourth tank. "Come on, let's see some fire!" The tank caught fire. And on his sixth shot at the fifth tank, the two shots converged: Mirokhin's and that of the enemy tank. And that was it for Mirokhin. It hit him right in the head. This excellent man, this brave warrior, this soldier with nerves of steel, was decapitated instantly. His brains were all over me.

Four and a half hours of this infernal attack! Four and a half hours of such superhuman effort! I took command of the regiment. Our 45mm guns and the antitank rifle platoon had completely routed the enemy. The tank attack had been repelled.

It was getting dark. I started to bring together the commanders. It was quiet on the hill. A handful of submachine gunners, ten men, two antitank rifles, and fourteen mortars, only one of which was working. I decided to report our situation to divisional command immediately. A representative of the 1st Guards Army, a battalion commissar whose name I can't remember, was sent to division as a messenger for the 347th Rifle Regiment.

Tanks were burning all around like giant candles. We had to assist the wounded right away. We had to get help from division right away.

The fight continued at the same level of intensity until the 19th. Division brought its reserves into battle. The antitank battalion and the training battalion got into combat formations. Heads of departments, a chemical platoon, a sapper platoon, artillery horsemen—everyone fought directly as soldiers on the front line.

On the 19th Colonel Gurtyev, the divisional commander, came over to my command post. He was directly leading the battle together with Svirin, the divisional commissar. They give the preliminary signal to attack. What was going on? There was no indication that the commander of the training battalion had got the order. Did it get to him in time? Get him on the line right now! There's no connection. Despite their best efforts the signalmen were unable to reestablish communication. Again and again the communication line was cut off by enemy fire.

"Belugin, have you got someone you can count on?" asked Gurtyev. "We're attacking in five minutes. The training battalion is located over there." He pointed to the northwest. "We've got to find the training battalion and get them my message."

I called Seligeyev. A long-distance runner, a member of Spartak.[93] He'd also been known to repeatedly cover a hundred kilometers a day during combat training. His mission was to get the order to the commander of the training battalion, and also to report back to say whether the order had been carried out.

Seligeyev crawled off in that direction to carry out the divisional commander's order. I still don't know how he covered that kilometer and a half so quickly, but he got back in time to report to the commander with written confirmation that the training battalion commander had received the orders and would begin attacking as planned.

A red flare shot up into the sky. The artillery extended its fire in depth. The attack began. The special units hung back. They were pushed forward. The attack was successful. We had finally secured the hills.

I was wounded during the attack, and on September 19 at five o'clock my daughter Maya pulled me into a tent. She told me joyfully that the order had been carried out, and she whispered to me: "You'll get better and be back here in no time."

I ended up in a field hospital.

Senior Sergeant Nina Mikhailovna Kokorina (Nurse, assistant deputy for political affairs, 347th Rifle Regiment): On September 1 [*sic*] we took up defensive positions. We did this at night, and apparently we'd come quite close to the German positions. It was me, Zina Reshetova, Anya Shuvanova, and two other girls, Roshina and Arkhatova, and were on guard duty, protecting our commanders. At dawn we heard a shout from the German side: Halt! It turned out that we were surrounded on three sides. The ravine we were in had only one narrow way out, and it was being covered by a tank and was occupied by German submachine gunners. We were almost surrounded, with no chance of help. There were maybe sixteen of us left, no more. We stayed there until September 18. Didn't get food or water for two days. There were a lot of wounded. It was impossible to get them out. We dressed their wounds. There were canteens with water rations. We gave this water to the wounded, looked after them, dug a little trench. The Germans were closing in. On September 17 we asked for reinforcements but none came. The regimental commander ordered our battalion to hold our positions. The whole battalion stayed and did not leave.

We had to do a lot of work with the soldiers. Many of the soldiers were doubting themselves, unsure whether we could take it. We talked with them. You'd crawl into a trench and start telling them about the heroic deeds of soldiers and officers. We'd tell them about Private Kosykh,[94] who was part of a group of six Komsomol members that held back an assault of sixty Germans. That was in our own battalion. He let the Germans come within ten meters, and then started throwing grenades. Meanwhile a machine gun was shooting at them from their flank. He took a soldier, Yefimov, and sneaked over to the trench where the shooting was coming from. When he got there he chucked in a few grenades and yelled: "Battalion, after me!" Six men (the supposed battalion) followed him. He brought back two German machine guns, a lot of rifles, and thirty prisoners. Now he's on a course for senior lieutenants. He was given the Order of the Red Star. Those are the kinds of things we talked about.

On September 18 we got our orders: our group, such as it was, was to attack and occupy Hill 143.6. Our soldiers were in great spirits. They'd been there for two days and held back the German onslaught. That really raised their spirits. We didn't have any casualties. We'd only had casualties on the first day. On September 17 the girls managed to get through to the ravine and carry back the wounded. We worked all night long.

On September 18 we attacked.

Dmitri Andrianovich Petrakov (Commissar in the 339th Rifle Regiment): September 18 marked the peak of our efforts to take the hill, and we still had about ten kilometers of even terrain to get there. I'd been with the company on several attacks, and we'd suffered great losses. On September 18 we were ordered to take the hill. [. . .] Our orders were to reach the battalion's position that night no matter what and to get to work—bearing in mind that the artillery preparation would begin at five o'clock—and then we'd attack at night. We made our way through literally all of the trenches. Our men only had tracer rounds to shoot with. We got them fed and explained the importance of these hills, and we promised them decorations: an Order of the Red Star for a captured German soldier, the Order of the Red Banner for an officer, and the Order of Lenin for whoever gets to the top first. Many of the men said that even this wouldn't encourage them to take prisoners—as soon as they found a German, he'd be a goner. We were assigned an artillery regiment and two Katyusha rocket battalions, in addition to our own battalion. Then we started to fire on the Germans, going on the offensive at six o'clock.[95]

Major General Leonty Nikolayevich Gurtyev (Commander of the 308th Rifle Division): We didn't complete every part of our mission, but we did take those hills.

We were summoned by the front commander, comrade Malenkov,[96] and Yeryomenko, and they talked with us until the beginning of the attack. After we took those hills they didn't have much to say against our division.

It's not easy to say why we didn't complete the mission. Maybe it's because we didn't get any help from the neighboring units on our left. But you've got to know the overall situation in the sector. Generally, though, we didn't catch a lot of flak over it, which I've got to say is something to be proud of, because there were people at that time who did. [. . .]

The blocking detachment didn't get any work on our account. There were isolated cases of desertion and self-mutilation, but nothing on a large scale. [. . .] Most of the soldiers carried themselves well and bravely. You might even say that they weren't restrained enough: once they got going, you couldn't hold them back. [. . .]

Interestingly, we acquired these hills via a committee decision. We'd taken possession of Hill 143.8, but our neighbor thought that he had taken it. I told General Moskalenko[97] that I had taken Hill 143.8, but he didn't believe me. We ended up having to send over a surveyor, who got the hill back in our possession.

There was still more controversy and trouble with Hill 154.2. Our neighbor on the left was interfering, claiming that he was the one who'd taken it. His training battalion had taken the slope on our left, but our units were the ones that took the hill itself. Their chief of staff was Shulgin, who I'd served with before, but we nearly came to blows over this hill. [. . .] On September 26–27 we were pulled back and sent to Stalingrad. We marched for three days.

Lieutenant Colonel Afanasy Matveyevich Svirin (Deputy commander for political affairs, 308th Rifle Division): On September 27 we got the order to withdraw from the front line, and on the 28th we got the order to leave for Stalingrad, and to be there by the 30th at the latest. We took a look at the map: 250 kilometers. But orders are orders. Things ended up just as we'd hoped: we were going to Stalingrad. When people found out that we were going straight to Stalingrad, that we'd be crossing from the west to the east bank of the Volga and then right back to the west again, they took this news with joy.

We had to take the long way. We started telling people the traditions of the defense of Tsaritsyn. In Stalingrad we made comrade Stalin's role in the defense of Tsaritsyn the fundamental pillar of our political work, along with that of comrades Voroshilov and Parkhomenko. When Malenkov and Zhukov visited us, they said that comrade Stalin had said that Stalingrad would not surrender, no matter the cost. You can die, but you cannot leave Stalingrad. Later they explained why. Beyond Stalingrad was the steppe, then Kuybyshev and Moscow. We repeated all of this to the soldiers and warned them what would happen if we surrendered Stalingrad. [. . .]

Before our crossing to the west bank there were meetings in every regiment, battalion, and company. We said: "Take a look—Stalingrad. There are the factories, and there is the Volga, the wide Russian river, and over there are the buildings of Stalingrad, the city where the great Stalin once lived. Our division came into being on the banks of the long, gray Irtysh River, and now we come to the wide banks of this Russian river, the Volga. Back there we learned, and now we're going to put that learning into practice. It was here that comrade Stalin once gave the order for all the rafts and boats to be moved away from the bank so that they wouldn't trouble the men or inspire fear. We too have crossed to the west bank of the Volga, and we too are sending back all of the boats, so that they don't trouble the men, who must only go forward."

That was how the meetings went, always on a high ideological and political level, and the soldiers came forward and swore that they would defend Stalingrad to the very end.

Major General Leonty Nikolayevich Gurtyev (Commander of the 308th Rifle Division): By daybreak we were still ferrying everyone across, and I was gone to army HQ. We ended up having to move into an area that was being bombed by the Germans. This didn't turn out well. Some of us moved along the embankment, including me and my commanders, Stafeyev, Smirnov, my adjutant, and the NKVD chief. Others took an indirect route. It was not going to be easy for us to reach our destination safely. We had about three kilometers to go. The enemy spotted us. This narrow strip of land along the riverbank—the only land still held by Soviet forces by the time we reached Stalingrad—the enemy could see all of it from the height he occupied. We weren't in formation, but the enemy still spotted us and started bombing so we couldn't get through. There were German submachine gunners in this museum-type building, and we were under fire from various mortars. By the time we got to where we were going we'd lost two or three dozen men.

All day long I was busy with reconnaissance matters and the line. My sapper battalion, communications battalion, mortar battalion, and the 351st Regiment had come here with me. Two of my regiments were still on the west [*sic*] bank. [. . .] The 351st Regiment held the line at the Silikat factory. Our regiments were around 300–350 people. The enemy concentrated artillery fire on them, bombed them from planes, and they kept on fighting.

I personally led the 351st Regiment to our initial positions at night, when we still hadn't gotten our bearings in this area. At army HQ we were assigned guides from the division already there. At first we advanced successfully and took over the entire Silikat factory. We'd already made it to its western walls. We stopped after some heavy fire from the Germans, who had now gone on the offensive. All day we were under heavy enemy fire, we'd been taking losses since that morning, and the regiment was weary from the march. There were a lot of wounded in the regiment. Their chief of communications came to me at my command post in the Gastronom store. He was the last one. He was frightened as he ran up to me. He reported that everyone in the regiment was dead. I gave him one of my officers and sent him back to Markelov with a message. He didn't make it back. Afterwards the 339th Rifle Regiment moved in here, and then the fighting went on both day and night against superior enemy forces.

Lieutenant Colonel Alexei Stepanovich Smirnov (Chief of the divisional political section): The 351st Regiment was lost on October 5. [. . .] On October 4 this sector had to be held no matter what. We got an order saying that the regiment had to stay put. At around 11:00 P.M., Markelov, the regiment's commander, was killed. Frolov took command of the regiment and kept up the defense. Eventually the Germans managed to surround the regiment and destroy it completely. Only two men escaped the encirclement, but apparently they'd run away, so I sent them back. We got word on how the regiment fought from regimental commander Frolov.

Lieutenant Colonel Afanasy Matveyevich Svirin (Deputy commander for political affairs, 308th Rifle Division): There were eleven men left in the regiment. The last of them to fall was regimental commissar Frolov, and the regimental commander was severely wounded. Those eleven soldiers had survived because they'd been sent on errands to divisional HQ, regimental HQ, and so on. [. . .]

We felt very bad about Colonel Mikhalyov, the 339th Rifle Regiment's chief of staff, who died together with the entire staff. He was a remarkable officer, competent and strict, and he was well-liked in the regiment. The young nurses talked about him as if he were their own father. You could follow him anywhere, follow any order.

Head of the political department of the 308th Rifle Division, Lieutenant Colonel Alexei Smirnov

On October 6 I got a message from Mikhalyov requesting that I reconcile him with Sandin, the regimental commissar. I knew Mikhaylov well and decided to take Varshavchik, our chief of political affairs, and go to the

Lieutenant Colonel Mikhalyov

regiment immediately. But we'd gone no more than fifty meters when we came across a messenger from the divisional commander with a request to come resolve some kind of argument. I went, and I got held up with the commander and two majors trying to determine the exact positions of our units. I'd just passed through the door on my way to the regiment when I got the report that a bomb had hit them directly, killing the entire staff of the 339th Rifle Regiment. Seventeen people died, including a representative from army HQ.

Alexander Fyodorovich Koshkarev (Party bureau secretary, 339th Rifle Regiment): Our unit arrived in Stalingrad, and we were ferried to the west bank of the Volga on October 1 and 2. [. . .] On the night from the 2nd to the 3rd our subunit took over the main defense at the Airport Garden. We were able to equip our defensive lines at night. Enemy aircraft were constantly in operation during the day. From the 3rd to the 4th our units continued entrenching and improving our defenses.

Our regimental HQ was in the Gastronom building. To the left of that building was the Airport Garden, where our battalion was located. The special units were to the right of the building (a company of submachine gunners, a group of antitank riflemen). We had no artillery, they were still coming. Divisional HQ had been in this building, but they left on the night of the 3rd because the Germans were trying to shell the building.

On October 4 the Germans launched an attack on our combat units in the Airport Garden and on this building that housed our regimental staff and subunits of the headquarters company. At around eleven o'clock, fifteen tanks and infantry launched a heavy assault. The Germans were constantly trying to break through our defenses on the right side. [. . .] On October 4 the fighting continued all day long. Our units held their ground, and the building that the Germans were pressing on stayed in our hands. Lieutenant Shonin, a Komsomol member, demonstrated

Lieutenant Boris Shonin

exceptional heroism there.[98] He'd applied for admission to the party, but we didn't get a chance to take him: he was killed on the 5th. He'd taken out three tanks himself.

By nightfall we had left the Gastronom building because we thought it was a bad idea to stay there. We'd lost some of our soldiers and officers, and we knew that the Germans wanted to take the building at any price, but we didn't get any reinforcements. We moved to a new place about 100–150 meters down from the factory clinic, a T-shaped building. [. . .] During a planning meeting of the unit commanders, a bomb fell directly on the headquarters, and everyone there was killed: the regimental commander and commissar, the chief of staff, two deputy regimental commanders, the deputy chief of the political department, a senior battalion commissar, a front representative, an adjutant, and others. I just happened to be away because I was supposed to go across the Volga for some documents. The survivors included me, Zhigalin,[99] and Fugenfirov.[100] Zhigalin took command. I hadn't been in the regiment for long. I knew Zhigalin and asked him to take command, and we established communication with the battalions and with divisional HQ. I remained at the building to organize the work of digging out bodies.

Major Vasily Georgievich Belugin (Commissar in the 347th Rifle Regiment): On the evening of October 19 I reported to the divisional commander and told him that I had recovered and wished to resume my duties. After the commander's warm and joyful greeting, and the heartfelt reception from Commissar Svirin and all the staff workers, I felt inspired with a renewed courage and certainty in our just cause, in our resistance.

They brought me up to speed on the situation. "This is quite different than it was at Kotluban at Hill 154.2," Colonel Gurtyev told me. "By the way, did you know we had a dispute over Hill 154.2? Everyone was denying that we took it, and we had to drag out a whole army commission to set the record straight. It's too bad you weren't there.

Things are different here. Take a look—the Volga is fifty meters back, and the enemy is 150 meters in front of us. Not a lot of room to maneuver! Every day this two-hundred-meter strip is peppered with any number of shells, mortars, bullets. We're used to it, but you've been laid up in a quiet hospital. Wait, don't go to the regiment, stay with us for a while."

Every minute either Colonel Gurtyev or Commissar Svirin tried to convince me to stay a little longer. I remained their guest at the command post until late at night. "Stay with us a bit longer." "No, I'm off." "Off you go then. Chamov is the new commanding officer over there. Get to know him. It's a difficult sector. Did you know that the 351st Regiment is gone? What's left of them got transferred to 347th and 339th Rifle Regiments. None of their officers survived. Savkin died bravely right after Barkovsky. A wonderful commander, tireless fighter. Colonel Mikhalyov died, the commander of 339th Rifle Regiment. He died stupidly in a building that took a direct hit from a two-ton bomb. He was buried together with his staff workers."

"Don't use a building for a command post. Better to have it on open ground—but with plenty of camouflage. Buildings are dangerous. Use them as strong points and dig communication lines between them. Make forward exits that point toward the enemy, deep slit trenches, and use them. You've got to be cunning and change your firing positions often."

And with those parting words I went to see my new commanding officer at the 347th Rifle Regiment.

Lieutenant Colonel Andrei Sergeyevich Chamov (Commander of the 347th Rifle Regiment): In Stalingrad our regiment took up the defense of the southern section of Airport Garden, Petrozavodskaya Street, and the southern section of the Barricades factory. We were up against the enemy's 305th Infantry Division, which included the 276th, 277th, and 278th Regiments. On October 17 the enemy launched an aerial bombardment of our combat formations, in combination with a massive artillery and mortar barrage. It was clear that the enemy was going to advance and attack the sector our regiment had been ordered to defend.

By 10:00 A.M. enemy tanks broke through the sector on our left, where the 685th Infantry Regiment was, and continued along Buguruslyanka Street to my regiment's command post. There were twenty tanks with submachine gunners.

At 11:00 A.M. another group of tanks broke though the southern perimeter of Airport Garden and the northern part of the Barricades factory, and they had us surrounded.

Fighting in Stalingrad's industrial district, October 1942. *Photographer: Georgy Samsonov*

The divisional commander ordered me not to withdraw but to keep fighting inside the encirclement. [. . .] The men in our regiment's antitank battery, commanded by Sergeant Boltenko, distinguished themselves in this fight. They took out six tanks. With his guns destroyed, his crew continued fighting from slit trenches, using antitank grenades and petrol bombs.

This fight left our regiment divided by the enemy, and 1st Battalion was cut off from 2nd Battalion. About eight tanks attacked the 1st Battalion command post, which was located in a building at the Sormovskaya Power Station. Captain Zalipukhin was the commissar then. The German tanks destroyed the station. They shot at the doors and windows from sixty to seventy meters away. The building caught fire. They stormed the station—infantry at about company-strength. Zalipukhin, two medics, and two signal corps men were in the building. They repelled seven attacks from 4:00 P.M. to 7:00 P.M. Captain Zalipukhin himself killed thirty-two fascists with his pistol, some grenades, and a submachine gun. With this commissar in the lead, this group of soldiers kept up the fight for three hours in the power station under siege.

All of them were wounded, including Zalipukhin, but they did not leave that command post until I ordered them to. Zalipukhin carried the wounded battalion commander and chief of staff from the battlefield. The two medics and one of the signals corps men died in that building, asphyxiated by smoke.

At 6:00 P.M., some thirteen enemy tanks were approaching my command post, where our headquarters staff was located. They began firing directly at us from eighty to ninety meters away. We were taking submachine-gun fire at the same time. That was when our deputy chief of staff for reconnaissance, Lieutenant Vasily Kalinin, came back from a scouting mission. He crawled up to the command post, grabbed an antitank rifle, and went to fight the German tanks on his own. In twelve to fifteen minutes, he burned out five German tanks and disabled six. Then he took a group of seven submachine gunners to launch a counterattack against the paratroopers trying to break into the command post. This counterattack resulted in the deaths of more than a hundred fascists, and Kalinin advanced about 150 meters and dug in.

Senior Lieutenant Vasily Petrovich Kalinin (Deputy chief of staff for reconnaissance, 347th Rifle Regiment): On October 16–17 our combat formations and rear positions were taking a lot of heavy fire from enemy mortars, machine guns, and airplanes. The bombs made the earth groan. The bombing started up again the morning of the 17th, and they launched an attack at about 2:00 P.M. Right then I was in a bunker, on the telephone. I was asking about the condition of our units and about enemy activity. They told me that enemy machine-gun and mortar fire had stopped. I started transferring movements of enemy firepower from my situation map to my notebook where I keep track of these things. I lit a cigarette, and right then I could hear the sound of engines. I rushed out and heard the rumbling of tanks coming from the railway line. I ran to the command observation post, which was about three or four hundred meters away. I could see about ten tanks approaching in dispersed formation. The enemy had managed to take out the observation post, which I still hadn't been informed of. Down below there were antitank soldiers from a neighboring unit. I went down to them and grabbed an antitank rifle. It had been raining a lot the day before, and because of someone's lax standards, the rifle was rusty. I got the thing set up and aimed at a tank. I fired, but was short by a hundred meters or so. Then I lined up the coarse sight and hit the tank head-on. It started sparking like an arc welder. But I could see that it was still coming and that its turret was rotating. I adjusted my aim, thinking that I could hit him first, but we ended up firing at the same time. I hit their gas tank, and their shell hit the upper gable of the building.

The tank caught fire, and after three or four minutes it went up like a box of matches. I saw another tank come out from the same building and try to tow the first. I shot the second tank when it had just come out, and it too caught fire. After I'd set two tanks on fire I thought I'd change my position in this building. I saw another tank coming out. I wanted to take my weapon and see what was going on at the command post, so I got out of there, and right then the tank shot straight at me, hit my antitank rifle and bent it out of shape. I hadn't managed to shoot first. Anyway, it was slow going because of all the rust: after I fired I'd have to open the lock with my foot, which made it difficult and slowed down my rate of fire. I was stunned from the shell, and I felt a sharp pain and sort of lost consciousness for a while. There were clouds of dust everywhere and I couldn't see anything. I thought, I've got to get out of here or he'll finish me off. Nothing from the command post, as if there was no one there. I took my rifle, my runner took some cartridges, and we left. On the way I helped a wounded soldier and ordered the runner to get him out of there. He carried him off and returned with more armor-piercing cartridges, which I'd told him to get. I was stunned, couldn't hear much, my hands were bloody. The tanks were advancing slowly, with a group of submachine gunners right behind. When I shot, the infantry ran down into a ravine that leads to a cemetery. The runner pointed out that the tank was crossing the railway line and was [*sic*] meters away from the command post. I grabbed my antitank rifle and shot the front section of the tank nine times, but I couldn't get through the armor. I decided to shoot at his side, and I let him have it. The tank stopped moving but kept shooting. Then I took an antitank grenade and a petrol bomb, and I told the runner to open fire if they opened the hatch. The tank commander opened the hatch, and the runner shot at him. I crawled up to the tank, threw the bottle and then the grenade. The tank caught fire. [. . .]

Someone showed me that a tank was coming, but the antitank gun was two hundred meters away. I rushed toward the tank. I thought it was just a small tank, I'd take care of it quickly. But you know, this tank was coming at us on an asphalt road, it had broken through our defenses and was coming at us from the rear. The tank came up and started shooting at our combat formations as it collected his own men and sent them back from the front line. Then I took thirteen men. It wasn't easy working out the boundaries between the Germans' positions and our own, and we were often mistaken about who was where. I crawled to the next building, where there was a fork in the railway line, and I set up my antitank rifle. I shot twice, and the fourth tank caught fire. There was a tank down past the school, too far away. I didn't think I could reach it, but I thought I'd try. It turned out that I was out of cartridges, and I didn't know how to reload the antitank rifle because I'd never had to learn. I was really annoyed that I couldn't open the rifle. Then I accidentally pushed a button that opened the chamber, and I put in the cartridges. There were tanks in the area where the others were on fire, and one tank was firing at the building I was in. I listened, and I could hear someone else shooting at the tank with another antitank rifle. There were sparks, but nothing was taking. Then I crawled across the railway line with my rifle, climbed down into the ravine, and went the 150 meters to their forward line, about a hundred meters from the tank. "Now," I thought, "I'm going to get you if it's the last thing I do." I fired once, then twice—nothing. I got closer and fired again, but the rifle couldn't penetrate the armor. I fired twelve times from every direction. It wouldn't burn. Then I crawled back with my rifle, took a runner to carry a grenade and a petrol bomb, and then we crawled back to my last position near the tank. We were about forty meters away. Only one chance to get this right. I crawled up closer, tossed one at the front of the tank. It immediately caught fire. I took advantage of this and threw two grenades, before hurrying back to our own forward positions with my runner.

Private Fyodor Maximovich Skvortsov (Telephone operator, 308th Rifle Division): There were bombs and shells going off all the time. They would sever our communications, and we didn't have enough wire. We had to make connections with used wires. This affected the sound quality, but it still did the job. One time during an enemy attack our communications suddenly stopped working. A submachine gunner had crawled up to our line and cut our wire into bits. I started reconnecting the line, and he started shooting at me. I lay down by the railway, stayed put about fifteen minutes, and then crawled back to the command post, the communication line still intact. [. . .]

One time I had to run a current through a bare rod. The current went right up my arm and through my teeth. There were times when we used barbed wire. You can even complete a circuit by stringing together a few men holding hands.

Senior Sergeant Nina Mikhailovna Kokorina (Nurse, assistant deputy for political affairs, 347th Rifle Regiment): At first our medical company was on the island. The girls had a lot of work to do there. It was eight hundred meters over the island to the ferry, and we took the wounded only as far as the shore. From there they were taken and loaded onto boats, then carried with straps or stretchers to the regimental aid station on the sand. [. . .] We couldn't build fires, so everything had to be done in the dark. There were some first aid workers who did nothing but carry the wounded. The island was under a constant mortar barrage because the enemy knew that our support units were here and that our reinforcements were coming through this island. [. . .]

They forced us back on October 18. We had to move back together with the battalion command post. The Germans had cut off the regimental command post, and we didn't know where our regiment was. We went straight to a workshop at the Barricades factory. This was the morning of October 19. We spent the day there, because it was impossible to get the wounded across the river. [. . .]

That evening it turned out that we were surrounded. We spent a whole night and day at the Barricades factory, but we had no chance of leaving because there was nowhere to go, the enemy had set up machine guns all around, they were even throwing grenades. The Germans had come within five meters of us. We used grenades just like the soldiers. That night we decided to fight our way out of there. There were a lot of Germans, according to the intelligence report, and there wasn't that many of us. So we had to use our brains. We knocked out an enormous hole in one of the walls of the workshop, and we all crawled out through this hole to escape without losing anyone. We made it to the riverbank. [. . .] On October 21 I was wounded on the riverbank and got sent to the medical battalion. At first they were going to send me eighty kilometers away from our field hospital, but there were rumors that our unit was leaving; I was afraid I'd be separated from my unit, so I simply ran away from the field hospital and went to our command post. They packed me off that very night because there was no way they could let me stay—I had a serious head injury. I was wounded when there was a direct hit to our bunker, and battalion commander Posylkin was wounded at the same time. He had to be packed off too. I haven't been back to Stalingrad since October 21.

Private Fyodor Maximovich Skvortsov (Telephone operator, 308th Rifle Division): On the 22nd the 351st Regiment started to retreat. The regimental commander wrote a note to the general saying that the regiment wanted to pull back. This note was taken to the command post, and from there Tarasov ordered me to deliver it to the general. I set off with machine-gun fire and mortar shells coming from all around. Everything was coming apart, buildings were falling down. I crawled about three hundred meters to the general and handed him the message. The general refused to retreat and kept his men where they were, but it wasn't long before we had to leave anyway because we were out of options.

Major Vladimir Makarovich Sovchinsky (Deputy commander for political affairs, 339th Rifle Division): On October 22 we received an address from the Military Council of the Stalingrad Front to all communists and defenders of Stalingrad. We started to go through this address in the units. Party members were brought together in the workshop for an all-regimental meeting. There were around seven or eight people. We didn't manage to get through everything because the enemy launched an attack on the workshops. All the communists, including the party bureau secretary, who had only just arrived, were dismissed. It was ordered that a party member must be in each workshop and that no one was to leave without permission. We held the workshops for two days. At one of them, half of the shop was ours, and the other half was the enemy's. We'd never used as much ammunition as we did on those days. When we ran out of cartridges, we used F-1 grenades. We had a lot of casualties. There were around three or four people left per battalion.

Anna Kipriyanovna Stoylik (Nurse, medical company platoon commander, 308th Rifle Division): We were right on the riverbank on [October] 26. The enemy was shelling us, heavy mortar fire. There was no chance of escape. This one soldier got hit. I ran over to him. The enemy had just begun firing rapidly all at once. I ducked into a bunker, and then I jumped out. This one mortar man nearby was hit in six places. I stripped him and dressed his wounds, but I didn't have enough strength to get him out. Then Robinova ran over, and together we dragged him to the bunker. He came to and asked us for water. Getting water from the Volga meant passing through open ground, which meant that the soldiers' canteens were empty. I ran to the river for water, carried it back, gave it to the wounded man, and left him in the bunker. At night I used a tarp to drag him the two kilometers to the medical company. We didn't have any stretchers. We'd tie up the corners of a tarp and carry the wounded out on our shoulders. The Germans were sweeping the ravines with mortar and submachine-gun fire. [. . .] In Stalingrad I carried out ninety-seven wounded altogether. [. . .] For my work I was awarded the Order of the Red Banner.

Lieutenant Colonel Andrei Sergeyevich Chamov (Commander of the 347th Rifle Regiment): On October 27 the enemy spent the day carrying out a massive barrage of artillery and mortar fire, along with aerial bombardment. The aerial preparations typically began at dawn and stopped, according to all our data, at 6:30 and 6:45 P.M. A German attack was usually expected at that time. At 12:30 I heard from the command post of the divisional commander that there was going to be a "concert." Indeed, this "concert" began at 12:40 P.M. and lasted until 1:20 P.M., forty minutes long. This was the artillery preparation. Then our own artillery, which was on the other side of the Volga, started firing intensively. As a result of this concentrated, competent, and well-planned artillery fire, every attempt by the Germans to advance further was paralyzed. Their communications were cut off, their firepower crushed, and for two hours after the artillery preparation there was no sound of mortar or machine-gun fire. It went completely quiet.

Major Vasily Georgievich Belugin (Commissar in the 347th Rifle Regiment): October 27 was a day I'll never forget. The enemy started acting up early in the morning. They unleashed a constant barrage of fire from artillery, mortars, machine guns, submachine guns, and rifles; they scattered bombs like peas from the sky; and through this assault on both the physical body and the spirit, the enemy was able to unhinge even the most battle-hardened of men. The soldiers said this was hell. I remember a picture of hell from Dante's *Divine Comedy.* In that hell people could celebrate at a wedding and at least feel okay. But here, when mortar fragments, stone, sand, and dirt are always coming down on you deep in your trench; when your eardrums feel like they've burst because of the exploding shells and mortars; when you stick the handle of a shovel out of your trench for only a second before it's hit by a sniper's bullet—try repelling an enemy attack in conditions like that.

Then came the climax. Everything was covered with dirt. Our firing positions were buried, our trenches fell in, our command post was destroyed. We had got out of the trenches only two minutes before, and at that moment we thought that this unstoppable avalanche of enemy manpower and machinery would crush us. But it didn't. Silence—this was the strictest command: prepare yourself. Right now, right this second. Now pull yourself back together, get ready to fight, and even if you're half dead, if you've only got one good arm, use it to shoot the enemy. Deal with that first one coming on the attack. Just deal with that first one. Your first shot will encourage your comrades.

And the silence of this unconditional command starts to lift the men out from their buried trenches, it starts to prepare them for the decisive battle. Everyone is thinking the same thing: this is it. "I'm not letting the enemy in my sector, there's nowhere for me to fall back to. I told comrade Stalin that there's no place for me on the east bank of the Volga. I signed a letter to comrade Stalin in my own hand saying that I would not take one step back, and that I would give all my strength and skill to fight for the motherland."[101] This is what everyone was thinking as they silently prepared themselves to repel the attack.

And then it started. The thundering of the first artillery salvo. Where was it coming from? And why? It was odd, unbelievable that this powerful salvo was coming from the east, from the east banks of the Volga. There was a second and third salvo, and then they began firing at will.

General Chuikov, commander of the 62nd Army, took on the full burden of repelling the enemy attack. A wise decision! He unleashed the firepower of his army's entire artillery corps, hurling it toward his opponent's main strike force. A thousand guns fired for forty minutes, during which time our soldiers—representatives of the 347th Rifle Regiment—were celebrating. They left their trenches, eyes wide, with big, tender smiles. Everyone understood that today the artillery was working for us. I've never seen or heard in my life such a monstrous force of artillery fire as what was unleashed on the enemy by our army commander. Everything burst into flame. The air was full of smoke, ash, dust, and rubble, and we celebrated this day's victory. But what was the enemy up to now? He was all broken up, all his formations were destroyed, his leadership disrupted—there weren't going to be any attacks or counterattacks today. We sent for our dinner, made tea. And during this artillery barrage the soldiers sat down to dinner.

The artillery stopped. There was a silence, the silence of victory. Until evening there wasn't a single shot. Not one Fritz in the observation sector, not one aircraft.

But on November 1, when our regiment was pulled back to the east bank of the Volga, the soldiers felt no less of a burden, no less anxiety, than they felt on that unforgettable day. After we were relieved by a rifle regiment, the enemy broke through in our sector and reached the Volga. It took a lot of strength, resources, and sacrifice to restore things.

Now when I think about the defense of Stalingrad I feel again like saying: "Great Mother Russia. You have a people who are unyielding, who love you, who for your beauty, Mother Russia, will give everything, even their own lives, if the army needs us to."

Major General Leonty Nikolayevich Gurtyev (Commander of the 308th Rifle Division): On November 1 the Germans came at us all at once, and they could only be fought with artillery fire. The artillery batteries were directed from the west bank via radio. The artillery regiment fired reliably and supported the entire division. We were all, I think, satisfied with their work. Once they'd been firing for half an hour everything went quiet in our sector. The Germans really wanted to break into the area of the Barricades factory. They pressed particularly hard on a little ravine that led to the industrial area, and eventually, on about November 9–10, after we'd already left, they broke through, separating the 138th Division from the 95th. Divisional commander Lyudnikov, who was cut off on two sides, was in a difficult spot, and it was only when the river iced over that things improved somewhat.

Lieutenant Colonel Afanasy Matveyevich Svirin (Deputy commander for political affairs, 308th Rifle Division): [October] 28, 29, and November 2 were very difficult for us because there were so few of us remaining. We got a call from army asking about our men: Where are they? How many are there? How spread out? We said we had seventeen men covering a great distance.

Junior Lieutenant Ilya Mironovich Brysin (Sapper platoon commander, independent field engineering battalion, 308th Rifle Division): At 2:00 A.M. [October 28] I got the order from Lieutenant Pavlov to attack. By that time we had only nine men. There was a rampart we couldn't climb over. Pavlov went ahead while I supported. The Germans had superior numbers, and they destroyed nearly all of Pavlov's group. Only two came back: Kostyuchenko and Barannikov. When I heard that Lieutenant Pavlov was killed and all his men were lost, Kostyuchenko and Barannikov joined my group.

On the 28th at 6:00 P.M. I put observers on the second floor of a building: Dudnikov and Kayukov.[102] Me and Sergeant Pavlov took up position in another building, and my men were nearby. At dawn I could see the Germans standing on a hill, yelling: "Come on, Rus, give up! To the Volga!" I was at a loss, didn't know what to do. Then my men ran back to me from the other buildings. But Dudnikov and Kayukov couldn't get down from the second floor because a mortar had destroyed the staircase. I could see that I only had seven men, and I decided to go to the riverbank, where there were entrenchments. We ran in that direction. The Germans occupied the first and second buildings we'd been in. We took up a defensive position twenty meters from the Germans and twenty meters from the water. I didn't tell my men that two of our own were in that building. My men were tough, they didn't panic. They had some antitank grenades. They started chucking them at the Germans so they could get out of there. Once there was a smokescreen they ran out and regrouped by me. After a while Dudnikov and Kayukov showed up. They'd managed to get away from the Germans. We were really glad to see them.

Private Yefim Yefimovich Dudnikov (Sapper platoon, independent sapper battalion, 308th Rifle Regiment): We were always together, me and Private Kayukov. We made ourselves a two-man firing trench. It was tough digging because of the slag, so we took these chunks of rock to make something like a shield and dug down a little bit, so you could shoot on your knees. I noticed a German sniper on the day that Skripka was killed. The sniper was hiding in a pile of rocks and blown-up reinforced concrete. He kept changing positions in the rocks, but there was nowhere else for him to go. I had a German rifle with a good sight, but the few times I shot at him I missed. Toward evening the German sniper decided to move to the building next door. I was watching him the whole time through my binoculars. That's when I shot and killed him. Me and Kayukov spent the night in a crater. Turns out

Pioneers in the 308th Rifle Division: (*left to right*) Ilya Brysin, Yefim Dudnikov, and Alexei Pavlov

we were only a few meters away from the Germans. They made a run for it when it started getting dark. I shot at them. I killed one, Kayukov killed another, and the third one got away. When it was dark I went up to them: one was an officer, the other a soldier. I took a flare gun and a revolver off them and crawled back to our crater.

After a while we got an order from Brysin, telling us when we were to attack, when me and Kayukov were to get back to the building and take up positions on the rampart. But then the Germans attacked, and we had to get up to the second floor. Then a mortar hit and destroyed the staircase. I don't know how it happened, but we were on our own. We were hoping that our buddies were down below, but they weren't. We could hear Germans yelling all around. We started throwing grenades, but it was tough because there was a wall in the way. Then we decided to get down from the second floor. The ceiling was bombed through, the metal bars were broken. We tied two German ponchos to one rod and climbed down one by one. We walked quietly down the corridor. I looked out and wanted to run to join the others, but then I saw some Germans dragging something five or six meters away. I threw two grenades at them and ran back into the building. They started to panic. While they were still confused, Kayukov ran to join the others, and I stayed in the building by myself. I ran down the corridor, peeked in another door—there's Germans there too. I could tell that there were too many of them for me to do anything. I crawled around this pile of rock, made a run for it, and reached the second building. From there I was able to get back to Brysin. Everyone was very happy to see me.

I took a minute to catch my breath. Then I spotted a machine gun and tossed a grenade at it, destroying the gun and its crew. Then we went on the offensive, and Private Kostyuchenko got hit. He was wounded and faint from losing so much blood, but he kept shooting, even with his left arm dead at his side. He threw grenades and went on attacking the fascists until the very end. He was awarded the Order of the Red Banner. He displayed exceptional discipline and self-sacrifice in battle. I bandaged him up. He gave me his gun and three F-1 grenades. Then he was taken to the field hospital.

I made quick use of those grenades. I could see Pavlov and Kayukov running toward me with a satchel of grenades. I was glad to see this. Kayukov and me were friends, if we weren't together in combat we missed one another. I yelled, "Come on, hurry up!" A German machine gun was covering the open space between the building and the rampart, but they had to get across. Pavlov lay down in the rocks, and Kayukov started running, but he got hit in the abdomen and spine. I crawled over to him quickly, gave him my hand and dragged him along a little way. Then I crawled under him to get him on my back and carried him out. They tried to bandage him up three times, but it was no use. He was dead. [. . .]

Kayukov lost his cap when he got hit, so I gave him mine, and I put on my helmet. Then I decided to go back for that cap because the helmet was uncomfortable. Right then a bomb went off, and I was so stunned that I had trouble hearing for days. Shells were exploding all around, and there was a constant rumble from them—but me and Brysin wanted something to eat. We got some black bread. Several of our men were wounded at that time.

Junior Lieutenant Ilya Mironovich Brysin (Sapper platoon commander, independent field engineering battalion, 308th Rifle Division): At ten o'clock on October 28 there were three of us left: me, Dudnikov, and Glushakov. I was summoned by a company commander from 2nd Battalion, 347th Rifle Regiment. I hadn't shaved in a while, and I had a big mustache. The commander named me Sergeant Mustache: "Mustache, go scout out the Germans' locations and find out where their firing positions are." I wanted to point out that you can't go on reconnaissance during the day—it's light, and everything can be seen—but orders are orders, so I went out on reconnaissance with two of my men, Dudnikov and Glushakov. We hooked up with the 10th Regiment, 37th Division.

They showed me where the Germans were. I went back to report the situation to company commander Kuznetsov. I'd discovered the location of their firing positions from the second floor, where I watched them setting up mortars and machine guns on the square. Lieutenant Kuznetsov, the company commander, instructed me to take out those firing positions. I told Dudnikov and Glushakov what we had to do. We got some grenades and ammunition and set off for the 10th Regiment, 37th Division. We found six men in the regiment and one field-grade officer. I told him I was on my way to complete this mission, and I asked if he would help by providing covering fire. That was around midday. We sat for a while and smoked, and they gave me some good advice. My two comrades and I agreed on the plan. I took off my overcoat and crawled forward. I climbed up this high point where I could see the railroad, where there was a big crater with a trench that led into a dugout. There were two machine guns by the crater. I crawled about three meters to the rail line and wanted to go into the crater. But I looked into the trench and saw the Germans. First I threw an F-1 grenade, then another, and then I crawled down into the trench. Both of the Germans were dead. I waved at Dudnikov and Glushakov to tell them to come. We took a satchel from the Germans that had pictures and papers, and we hid all of it under the tracks.

I started thinking about how to take out the mortar, which was [*sic*] meters away from the machine gun crater. I decided to go forward again. I had Dudnikov and Glushakov crawl into the crater and provide supporting fire. I set off. There were German snipers in the area, and I hadn't gone more than a few dozen meters when a sniper landed a shot on my helmet. I turned back. I started out again and crawled like that for two hours. Then I started to throw grenades, and Glushakov killed a sniper with his rifle. I took out the mortar with some grenades and started crawling back. Later we returned and took the German corpses. I had them brought back to regimental HQ, and I went to the company commander to tell him that his orders had been carried out. They let me get some rest in the bunker, seeing as I hadn't slept in four days. [. . .] I didn't get a chance to sleep because this regiment engineer arrived after us, and he was going to help defend the headquarters because they didn't have enough men. So we went to regimental HQ and defended it. [. . .] In the three days from October 26 to October 29, my platoon eliminated eighty-seven soldiers, four machine guns, and a mortar, and we killed one sniper and one officer. I killed twenty-five Fritzes myself. I was given the Order of the Red Banner.

They took me from the aid station to a field hospital where I stayed two days, and then I went back to my unit, where I was taken care of by our medic. It wasn't a serious wound. Later, when reinforcements arrived, I was put in command of a platoon. A pretty decent platoon. I instructed them in accordance with the experience I had already acquired in the Great Patriotic War.

After the battle on October 29 I submitted my application to the party, and now I'm a member.

Senior Lieutenant Vasily Petrovich Kalinin (Deputy chief of staff for reconnaissance, 347th Rifle Regiment): In just two days I destroyed seven tanks and their crews.

Captain Semyon Solomonovich Ryvkin (Commander of an independent field engineering battalion): Those of us who were still alive—thirty men—all of us were decorated. Eight received the Order of the Red Banner, three got the Order of the Red Star, and the rest got medals.

Captain Ivan Vasilievich Maksin (Chief of the divisional political section in charge of the Komsomol): There was also the heroic deed of Zoya Rokovanova, one of our Siberian Komsomol members. Zoya Rokovanova was a civilian typesetter working in the editorial offices of the regional newspaper.[103] She volunteered for the army and came to our division with the same drive and desire to get to the front line as Lyolya Novikova had. She was brought in to work on our newspaper, but she wanted to be on the front line. And so here she was in Stalingrad with a medical company she'd joined, and they were holding a defensive line—a single building. There was only a handful of people left from her unit, including two midgrade Komsomol officers. [. . .] When the Germans came in overwhelming force to cut off and storm the building, Zoya Rokavanova and one of the officers kept throwing grenades at them from a window. The Germans took cover. Their path to the building was obstructed by these grenades, so they withdrew. A few minutes later the building was peppered with incendiary shells and caught fire. As smoke came pouring out of the windows of the building our units tried to break through the German blockade and get our people out of there, but we couldn't do it. And when the Germans were coming right up to the building, our men could hear them yelling "Surrender, Rus!" to those who were still inside, and again they could see grenades being thrown down onto the Germans from the smoking window. Then it went quiet. All you could hear was the Germans yelling, but no one came out of the building to answer their awful cries.

Three days later we took the building back from the Germans and found the charred remains of these heroes, including Zoya Rokovanova, a patriot of the motherland, who remembered the words of Arnold Meri when he said that Komsomol members don't retreat, that they don't get taken prisoner, and that the only way they leave the battlefield is on a stretcher. Zoya Rokovanova fulfilled her duty. She knew that being a captive of the fascists would have been worse than death, and she decided to burn rather than be taken prisoner.

Lieutenant Colonel Afanasy Matveyevich Svirin (Deputy commander for political affairs, 308th Rifle Division): Daily bulletins from the Sovinformburo kept our soldiers informed of the operations of our forces on all fronts. They also knew about the work going on behind the front lines. We didn't get newspapers often, but we had our own radio. We typed out the bulletins and sent out duplicates to the units.

КОМСОМОЛЬСКАЯ ПРАВДА

Орган Центрального и Московского комитетов ВЛКСМ

Воскресенье, 15 ноября 1942 г. ЦЕНА 15 КОП.

«Враг уже испытал однажды силу удар
Красной Армии под Ростовом, под Моск
под Тихвином. Недалек тот день, когда
узнает силу новых ударов Красной Арм
Будет и на нашей улице праздник!»

Герой Сталинграда Борис Шонин

ОТ СОВЕТСКОГО ИНФОРМБЮРО

Headlines in *Komsomolskaya Pravda* read "Hero of Stalingrad Boris Shonin," November 15, 1942.

Each deputy political officer had the plan for the day's political work. If there was going to be a battle the next day for some building or other, the political officer would write a plan that covered three points: (1) preparatory work before the battle, (2) work to be done during the battle, and (3) outcomes of the battle and conclusions drawn from it.

We often made use of press reports from England and America on the resilience of Stalingrad. We did everything we could to get these reports to all the men and officers. Each political worker tried to make the soldiers aware of everything that was being printed by our own press about Stalingrad. The party-political apparatus—comrades Sovchinsky, Belugin, Sidorov, Petrakov—and workers from the political division—comrades Kheruvimov, Polyansky, Maksin, Ingor, and others, could always be found in the trenches with the soldiers. The entire party-political apparatus was decorated for its work.

When I came to the unit the first thing I wanted to know about was the daily life of the soldiers, whether they were being fed. In Stalingrad we had our own bathhouse where we washed. I remember once when the general and I went there to bathe, and a locust[104] came and started dropping bombs. We'd dug our bathhouse where Germans had buried their dead, and there was an awful stench of corpses. But despite that and the bombers we continued bathing.

The political apparatus was not only occupied with propaganda. Many took part in battles and went on the attack. Petrakov, for one, fought and went on the attack, comrade Kheruvimov took part in a bayonet charge, and Major Sidorov, deputy commissar for political affairs, took out two tanks with an antitank rifle and annihilated many fascists. He and Kalinin were wounded in the same battle. I can't think of a single political worker who didn't play an active role in the fighting. [. . .]

The party committee worked right in the trenches, where they accepted new members into the party. We didn't make our comrades on the front lines recite the Party's formal rules and program. Acts of heroism were enough to prove your faith in the party and receive your card.

As part of the twenty-fifth anniversary of the Red Army, we resolved to send a letter to comrade Stalin from the defenders of Stalingrad, which was signed by all the soldiers of the 62nd Army. There was heavy fighting going on when we did this. Our ranks were greatly reduced in number that day. Some three hundred wounded lay on the bank, but there weren't enough boats to get them across, and it was risky on account of the bombing.

Chamov called and said he only had seventeen men left. A sapper battalion was sent over. They pushed the enemy back.

In Stalingrad we lived day by day. The Military Council [of the front] ordered us to hold out for another two days, and we stayed to the end. There wasn't a single man among us who would have tried to cross to the other bank. In that entire period there were only twenty-four cases of desertion. I instructed the divisional prosecutor to keep an eye on certain people.

The first thing I'd do was ask the soldier whether he was getting enough to eat, was he getting his vodka, and then I'd get to talking with him about politics. Usually the soldier would say he was getting enough but didn't have an appetite [. . .]

We put together the letter to comrade Stalin over four nights, moving from trench to trench. Every one of our soldiers signed the letter. I remember it was a cold night in October, raining and windy. You'd get to a trench, cover it with your overcoat to keep out the wind, light a match, and then read out the part with the soldier's oath to comrade Stalin. And the soldier would sign the letter.

Captain Mikhail Lazarevich Ingor (Politruk, 347th Rifle Regiment): These men understood their commanders with barely a word, with a single glance. When they signed that letter, they knew they weren't just writing their names. They were each writing: "Dear comrade

Stalin, my name is Soldier so-and-so, I've killed however many Germans, and I swear—and so on."

Lieutenant Colonel Afanasy Matveyevich Svirin (Deputy commander for political affairs, 308th Rifle Division): We had a copy of the letter from the defenders of Tsaritsyn,[105] and we distributed it as widely as possible. There were a few comrades still alive in Stalingrad who had signed that letter.

The words "stand like stone, for there is nothing for us beyond the Volga" were particularly moving for the soldiers. One soldier repeated those words, "There is nothing for us beyond the Volga," with such intensity and sincerity that when I got home I thought: such patriotism, such love for this place where he is now, where comrade Stalin once was!

Here's how we'd instruct the soldiers: "See that little hill over there? We've got to take it, even if it is little, because there's a big hill on the other side, a great expanse of land, and there are houses and whole families. Every one of these little hills, even if they seem insignificant to us, is important because of what comes after."

It wasn't a coincidence that they fought for every window, every staircase. [. . .]

Our female medics really proved themselves. Back in Kotluban the girls dragged the wounded out under heavy mortar and artillery fire, and fire from the air. They didn't want to dig in. Nothing frightened them, they'd sit cross-legged on the riverbank. You ask them, Why haven't you dug in? They say, Why bother when we're about to move forward?

Female medics are much better than men. They're better at carrying out the wounded, better at dressing wounds, and they even carry the weapons of the wounded. About 40 percent of our girls have been decorated with orders or medals. Some five hundred of them have been decorated in this division.

This one girl, Stoylik, who used to work for the railway, acted so heroically and recklessly, she couldn't have put herself more in harm's way. She's the one who pulled the wounded officers out of the water after their motor launch was destroyed.

All of this resilience and self-sacrificing work was the result of the education and training given to all our fighters. [. . .]

The divisional commander did a lot for the division's combat training, working like a man devoted to his homeland, sparing neither his time nor his health. I ought to mention that during our time in Stalingrad the two of us didn't have a single glass of vodka. Gurtyev is an exceptionally caring and loving person who is dedicated to his work. He denies himself everything, won't allow any kind of luxury. He's always on the same level as everyone else. He was brave in battle. In Stalingrad our command post was buried more than once, and we had to be dug out. [. . .]

In Stalingrad we picked up four spies suspected of passing on the locations of our command posts. One of them was a major whose family was still in Stalingrad. He had decided he must search for his family, but he ran into the Germans. They gave him a choice: either he would give them information or they'd kill his wife. Another was a twelve-year-old boy. I talked with him for four hours before he confessed. He didn't want to give any names. I think that we lost the 339th Rifle Regiment's headquarters because of him. He told me how he worked out the locations of our headquarters and command posts by noticing the wires leading away from them, the number of runners, and the barbers that were nearby. Finally, at dinnertime he would see whether the food was coming in mess kits or on plates.

We interrogated one woman, a spy who had been coming to us for a while. She wouldn't confess for a long time, but then she told us that when the Germans arrived they took [her] two girls as hostages and gave her five hundred Soviet rubles, all so she would extract information from us.

Lieutenant Colonel Alexei Stepanovich Smirnov (Chief of the divisional political section): We admitted people into the party on the march, without slowing down. [. . .] In October and November we admitted about 360 new members in Stalingrad. Usually we took people who had shown real heroism. We held them up as examples for all of the units. We'd print their portraits and send them to the front lines. That's how it was, for example, with Kalinin. Exceptional people were immediately recognized in the army. We'd produce six or seven leaflets. All this work was done by individual party members who had stayed with us. Sometimes you'd have a building being pressed from all sides, but we could still hold them because of the influence of the political workers. For two days comrade Zalipukhin, deputy commander of 1st Battalion, and a group of sixteen men held off an entire subdivision of some three or four hundred Germans. They held their building until the last moment. These men from the 347th Rifle Regiment had only four antitank rifles, a pistol, and a machine gun. In a lot of places our men were forced to retreat, but here they held their ground, even though the Germans were coming closer, and they could hear the roar of their engines. [. . .]

In Stalingrad the party-political work went somewhat differently than at Kotluban. There were fewer political workers. In Kotluban, the communists at the lowest level of organization played a crucial role by quickly bringing people together and setting goals. But the situation in Stalingrad was such that all this work was done differently.

Here the crucial role of the party organizations was to make the dispersed forces as productive as possible, at a time when there might be fifteen to seventeen men left in a battalion. Communication between political workers and individual party members was quite difficult to arrange because there was effectively nothing separating us from the Germans. There were certain characteristic features of our agitation work. The political division tasked instructors with making sure that Party workers were placed at the most vulnerable locations. Our workers were always in these areas during attacks and assaults. [. . .]

We had two-way radio communication with the other side of the Volga. Every day we got reports on the international situation. We printed Informburo bulletins and distributed them to the divisions. To do this we had we had special club workers—including Subochkin, the projectionist—postal workers, and photographers, who would print fifteen to twenty copies of the Informburo materials and distribute them to the regiments. There was no other literature. There was a time when we'd get two-day-old papers from Moscow. But when the air post stopped we'd only get the papers after eight or nine days, so we just used the bulletins from Informburo.

We lost people every day. By the end of the battle our division had only three or four hundred men west of the Volga. Out of 780 party members there were no more than three hundred by the time we got to Stalingrad, and only a handful of them stayed in Stalingrad. [. . .] Despite being wounded, chief of staff Dyatlenko wanted to get his party membership card, and he eventually joined us, still limping, and was able to do excellent work.

Junior officer Fugenfirov was seriously wounded. He'd already been approved by his primary organization, but he hadn't yet been processed at the bureau level. As he was dying he talked about his membership card, wondering whether he'd been admitted into the party.

Senior Sergeant Nina Mikhailovna Kokorina (Nurse, assistant deputy for political affairs, 347th Rifle Regiment): I became a candidate for party membership on October 14. I was admitted during the heavy fighting in the city itself, when we were trying to cross Skulpture Street. They took me, company commander Alexeyev, and

Shuvanov, a medical orderly. The next day we were supposed to go to the divisional party committee. Shuvanov was killed on the evening of the 15th. Alexeyev was seriously wounded and taken to the east bank of the Volga. I was the only one left. But I still decided to go to the ceremony. I went with Pogrebny, the deputy commander for political affairs. The command post was in a tall red building that was more or less intact. On our way there we started getting shot at and bombed by the Germans. But there were people waiting for us. Somehow or other we had to go get our party documents. We walked through ruins, across the railway line. There was rumbling all around, submachine guns were firing. We made it to our headquarters, but no one had come from divisional HQ. We waited a while before heading back. During the return trip I fell behind and got a bit lost. Here's how it was then: this street's ours, that one's theirs; this building's ours, that one's theirs. I went and took the wrong road. I walked up to this one building and could hear someone speaking German. I'll admit I was a bit frightened, though I did have a gun. I took the path to the right. Someone was standing there. I stood up on tiptoe to look around, and I saw someone with a submachine gun. Turns out it's Pogrebny. I went to him, and he yelled at me. When we got to our command post we heard that the battalion's chief of staff had been wounded. He'd been seen to by some of the girls there. It was a head wound. I changed his dressings, bandaged him up. I got my candidate member's card on the east bank at Bruny. In February 1943 I became an official party member and was chosen to be a party organizer.

Alexander Fyodorovich Koshkarev (Party bureau secretary, 339th Rifle Regiment): How did we conduct our party-political work in Stalingrad? [. . .] We introduced a new idea: every soldier had to start a personal account of how many Germans he'd killed. This was essentially a stimulus for socialist competition: to see who could kill the most Germans. We would check these accounts, and if a comrade didn't have any dead Fritzes, we'd have a talk with him, make him feel the shame.

Alexander Dmitriyevich Stepanov (Battalion commissar, 1011th Artillery Regiment): The political and educational element as the regiment was being formed. Well, I can remember it all as if it were today—those ninety convicts who came to us. People in rags, hungry, covered in lice—real cons, as they would say. They frightened me at first, and I wondered how I could educate them, what kind of assignments they could take. I can remember going to inspect the barracks where these men were, and I saw four of them playing cards on top of their bunks, naked. As soon as I entered they got down and put away the cards. I said, "Hand over those cards!" They gave me some old cards, but the ones I'd seen were brand-new. Those weren't the ones they gave me. When I spoke to the duty officer about this, he said: "I don't know why, but it seems that the best men play cards." And these men said: "We're only playing a game of Fool." Shafranov and Gavronsky were among those four. They both had interesting fates.

Shafranov is now a party member in the regiment, a decorated field officer, one of our finest commanders. Gavronsky deserted while the regiment was being formed. He was rounded up near Stalingrad and shot.

Of all the ninety convicts who came to our regiment, only two of them were unable to reform themselves and ended up being shot. All the rest were reeducated and turned into good honest soldiers. [. . .]

At Stalingrad the political staff did a lot of work to clear the criminal records of these men I'm talking about. About 25 percent of the men in our regiment had previous convictions. All of them except for a few got their criminal records expunged because of brave conduct during combat. We regarded this as another way to encourage people to do good work. I should also give credit to the regiment's command and political staff for issuing state decorations properly and in good time. I've got to say that, on the whole, every accomplishment in the regiment was recognized with an award from the regimental commander or, for regular soldiers, from the relevant authority. Fifteen percent of the regiment were issued and presented with decorations. That's a total of 150 men.

I awarded Captain Trifonov, the party bureau secretary, two Orders of the Red Banner, but we still haven't received the actual medals. [. . .]

I'd like to say something about the men's welfare. Even though people were constantly being shot at and bombed by the enemy, there was still good order in the regiment: the men were shaved and getting haircuts, and they wore clean tunics and trousers. We built a bathhouse, a canteen, and even set up places where the soldiers could mend their tunics, underclothes, and so on. Of course there were times when we were eaten by lice, but we got rid of them quickly.

We accepted 120 people into the party at Stalingrad. Captain Trifonov played an especially important role in this. Every one of them was accepted into the party by him, he was the one who made it all official, and he did all of this while in the field.

Lieutenant Colonel Andrei Sergeyevich Chamov (Commander of the 347th Rifle Regiment): The divisional commander, General Gurtyev, is first and foremost an extremely modest man. That's his most prominent trait. At first glance he even seems positively inoffensive. A very simple man, sincere and caring. You might have won ten battles, but if you let a single man go without food, then you're a complete disgrace. I was in the Ravine of Death one day when the general, taking no heed of the danger, walked up to me along with Smirnov, the head of the political department. They spent half a day with me observing the men fight. We were some 150 meters from the front line. They were constantly monitoring the situation, trying to arrive at a meticulously detailed understanding of the enemy, to find out what steps ought to be taken. In these practical matters the divisional commander let his regimental commanders take the initiative, gave them a lot of independence, and always considered their opinions.

There was one occasion I could see there was nothing I could do to assist the divisional commander, nothing I could give him: I had already staked all I had. I wasn't going to say this to him. I said that everything was just as it should be in war: they're shooting—and so are we. But in fact they'd nearly broken through my left flank. I reported this to the division's chief of staff, but I knew they couldn't do anything, so I decided just to do whatever I could. Somehow Gurtyev overhead our telephone conversation and asked what was going on. He wasn't in a position to help. He said: "Think about what you can do, but know that I've got nothing for you. I'm on my own and can't give you a thing."

He was demanding, but to just the right degree. I'd say he had a civilized way of being demanding. He was extremely tactful when he asked you to do something, and this demanding, exacting manner was in some inspiring way linked to far-seeing conviction. People respected and valued him on account of this. He never raised his voice.

His personal staff thought very highly of him. Wherever he went, the first thing he did was visit the canteen and ask how much food they were getting and what they were having for dinner. The soldiers would say: "We'll have a good dinner today—the general's here." But actually the dinner was prepared the same as always. He asked our cook how he dished out the soup. The cook said two fingers from the rim. "Fingers come in different sizes: big and small. See that you make it two small fingers."

It was a good thing that he knew the men, not only the officers but also the regular soldiers. He's got an exceptionally good memory: he knows everyone by name. He likes when everything is in order and by the book. Very particular when it comes to following regulations.

Everyone respects him for his modesty, his sincere way of dealing with people when he's asking them to do something, and for the fact that he really knows his stuff. Nothing bad can be said of him.

Major General Leonty Gurtyev

Genrikh Aronovich Fugenfirov (Commander of the 1011th Artillery Regiment): He's an extraordinary man. The general never yells or swears, but if he simply changes the tone of his voice, that means you've got to do better, do a better job of following his command. The general's commands are always carried out. It's not only the officers who love him, but also the men, who know him well because he's always driving around to see the units. He is thoroughly acquainted with the soldiers' daily lives, never goes past a kitchen without dropping by to sample what they're eating. The men love him. Once I was with him in a car. He spoke about his soldiers with such love. He swears and yells at a soldier, as if he himself were an old sergeant-major, and then he says: "That man will make a fine soldier, a great warrior."

Major General Leonty Nikolayevich Gurtyev (Commander of the 308th Rifle Division): We all kept it together, and during the worst of it, when it seemed there was no way out, we would pick up our weapons and be ready to keep going to the end. No one even thought of leaving. If we looked toward the Volga, it was because we were expecting reinforcements or ammunition. Everyone felt this sense of duty. It meant a lot to us that the army commander was there with us. The soldiers would often walk along the shore in the open, the girls always joking. Mortars were falling all around, but they'd sit and relax—after all, it's hard work carrying out the wounded. They didn't like people who were afraid. [. . .] They didn't like this one doctor because she was nervous, even though she was very skilled and attentive, and she'd always stay in the field to dress the wounded. She wrote me a letter afterward, telling me her impressions of a rally and parade in Stalingrad, where she stayed after we'd left.

Or take the sapper battalion. Apart from doing the primary duties, they also fought alongside us, heroically proving themselves at the crossing. We had these small canoes, and it wasn't easy crossing the Volga at night—even when it was calm—and they ferried over the wounded, ammunition, and reinforcements, all the while under constant bombardment. It's true that we used another crossing, and in the beginning there was a foot bridge over the Volga, but it was destroyed early on, and the boatmen helped us a great deal with their selfless work. They were decorated, their heroic work was noted.

Senior Sergeant Nina Mikhailovna Kokorina (Nurse, assistant deputy for political affairs, 347th Rifle Regiment): After the war I think I'll stay in the army and go to the military academy. I've been here a few days, but I miss them, I wonder how they're doing there without me. Before I joined I wanted to go to university to study history and philology. I really like spending time in the archives, just going there and wandering around.

Lieutenant Colonel Afanasy Matveyevich Svirin (Deputy commander for political affairs, 308th Rifle Division): Our division has its own Siberian traditions. Right now we're preparing a booklet called "Siberians in the Defense of Stalingrad."[106] [. . .] All of our party-political work is built on the foundation of our combat experience and on the traditions of the greatest men.

VASILY GROSSMAN'S "IN THE LINE OF THE MAIN DRIVE"

The Moscow historians were not the first to take an interest in the soldiers of the 308th Rifle Division. In November 1942 Vasily Grossman spoke with Colonel Gurtyev and several of his soldiers. His conversations[107] formed the basis of a November 25 article in *Red Star* titled "In the Line of the Main Drive." The piece describes how the advancing Germans destroyed the 351st Regiment on October 4. The article appears below in its original form.[108] The content is consistent with the testimony given in the Stalingrad transcripts, a sign of the meticulous care Grossman took with the material. At the same time the article showcases Grossman's masterful storytelling.

In his narrative, the impressive will of the soldiers kept the division together. This will welded the troops into a "complete, miraculously constructed, unified body" that performed acts of heroism as a "commonplace and daily habit." The Moscow historians were no doubt familiar with Grossman's piece, and it may be what led them to search for the surviving soldiers of the 308th Rifle Division in April 1943.

Vasily Grossman in Stalingrad, 1942

IN THE LINE OF THE MAIN DRIVE

Vasily Grossman

The regiments that formed Colonel Gurtyev's Siberian division took up their positions at night. The factory had always looked grim and severe. But could there have been any grimmer picture in the world than that seen by the men of this division on that October morning in 1942? Massive dark workshops; the gleaming wet rails, already touched here and there by traces of rust; a pile-up of broken boxcars; mountains of steel pipes strewn about the vast, square-like factory yard; hills of red slag; coal; the mighty smokestacks, which in many places had been struck by German shells. Dark craters covered the paved grounds, the result of aerial bombardments. Steel fragments ripped apart by the force of the blasts were scattered all around like thin strips of calico.

The division was to make its stand at this factory. Behind them was the cold, dark Volga. Two regiments defended the factory, and a third defended the area of a deep hollow that ran through the factory complex toward the river. The Ravine of Death, as it was known to the men and officers of the regiment. Yes—behind them was the ice-covered Volga, behind them lay the fate of Russia. The division was to fight to the death.

That which had been dispersed over two fronts during the 1914–1918 world war, and which in the past year had been brought to bear on Russia alone along a 3,000-km front, had now been brought down like a sledge hammer on one point: Stalingrad and the Caucasus. And as if that weren't enough, here, in Stalingrad, the Germans had again increased the pressure of their offensive. While no longer increasing the intensity of their offensive in the southern and central parts of the city, they were directing the full firepower of countless mortar batteries and thousands of guns and aircraft on the northern part of the city and on the factory still standing at the center of the industrial area. The Germans presumed that men were by nature incapable of withstanding such strain, that no hearts or nerves could survive this wild hell of flame and shrieking metal, of trembling earth and frenzied air. Here, concentrated in one place, was the entire diabolical arsenal of German militarism: superheavy and flame-throwing tanks, six-barreled mortar tubes, fleets of dive bombers with wailing sirens, anti-personnel and high-explosive bombs. Here the sub-machine gunners had explosive rounds, and artillery- and mortar-men had incendiary shells. Here was all of the German artillery, from the small-caliber antitank weapons to the heavy long-range guns. Here both day and night were lit by fires and flares, here both day and night were dark from the smoke of burning buildings and German smoke grenades. Here the roar of battle was as dense as the soil, and the brief moments of silence were still more terrifying and ominous. And while the world bows before the heroism of the Soviet armies, who themselves speak with admiration of the defenders of Stalingrad, here, in Stalingrad itself, the soldiers say with reverence:

"What we do is nothing. But those guys holding the factories—they're something else!"

To the soldier, the phrase "in the line of the main drive" carries dread. No words are more terrifying in war. It was no accident that Colonel Gurtyev's Siberian division was the one defending the factory on this gloomy autumn morning. The Siberians are hardy people, stern, accustomed to cold and hardship, taciturn, ordered and disciplined, and blunt-spoken. The Siberians are a reliable, sturdy lot. In strict silence they hacked into the stony earth, cut embrasures in the workshop walls, and constructed bunkers, trenches, and communication lines.

Colonel Gurtyev, a lean fifty-year-old, had abandoned his second-year studies at the St. Petersburg Polytechnical Institute to volunteer in the Russo-German war in 1914. He served in the artillery and saw action against the Germans at Warsaw, Baranovichi, and Chartorysk. He has devoted twenty-eight years of his life to military matters—both to actual fighting and to the training of officers. His two sons are also taking part in this war; both are lieutenants. His daughter, a university student, and his wife remain in far-off Omsk. On this solemn, terrible day, the colonel thought about his sons and wife and daughter, and about the dozens of young officers he had trained, and about his long, labor-filled, and modest life. Yes, the time had come when the principles of military science, morality, and duty—all that he had steadfastly taught his sons, students and comrades—would be put to the test. The colonel looked with emotion into the faces of his Siberian soldiers—men from Omsk, Novosibirsk, Krasnoyarsk, Barnaul—at those with whom he was destined to repel the enemy's attack.

The Siberians moving into that great line of defense had been well prepared. The division had been well schooled before coming to the front. Colonel Gurtyev had trained his men carefully and cleverly, and was ruthlessly critical. No matter how harsh the training—long marches, simulated night attacks, sitting in trenches while tanks are driven over you, the long marches—he knew that war itself would be a great deal harsher and more difficult. He believed in the perseverance and strength of the Siberian regiments. He had tested these qualities during their long march, which they had completed almost without incident: there had just been one soldier who had accidentally dropped his rifle from a moving troop train. The soldier had then jumped off, snatched up his rifle, and ran the three kilometers to the next station to catch up with his train. Gurtyev had further tested his regiment's staunchness on the steppe near Stalingrad, where these untried men calmly fought off a surprise attack by thirty German tanks. And he had further tested their endurance during the final march to Stalingrad when they covered a distance of two hundred kilometers over two days. Nevertheless, the colonel looked anxiously into the faces of these soldiers who had come to the main line of defense, and who were now in the line of the main drive.

Gurtyev believed in his officers. His chief of staff, the young and indefatigable Colonel Tarasov, could plan complex battles day and night, poring over maps in a bunker as it quaked under the blasts. His directness and merciless judgment, his way of looking facts in the face, of seeking the truth in any military situation, no matter how bitter it might be, were all founded on a faith that was strong as iron. In this lean young man, who had the face, speech, and hands of a peasant, dwelled an indomitable force of thought and spirit. Svirin, Gurtyev's second-in-command and chief political officer, had a strong will, a sharp mind, and an ascetic modesty; he could stay calm, cheerful and smiling at times when smiling was beyond the power of even the calmest and most cheerful of men. Regimental commanders Markelov, Mikhalyov, and Chamov were the colonel's pride: he trusted them as he did himself. Everyone in the division spoke with love and admiration of Chamov's quiet courage, of Markelov's unbending will, and of the remarkable kindness of Mikhalyov, the regiment's favorite, a tender and sympathetic man who cared for his subordinates like a father and simply did not know the meaning of fear. Yet it was still with anxiety that Colonel Gurtyev looked into the faces of his officers, for he knew what it meant to be in the line of the main drive, to hold this great line in defense of the city of Stalingrad.

"Can they take it? Will they hold out?" the colonel was thinking. Barely had the division managed to dig trenches into Stalingrad's rocky soil and establish their headquarters in a deep tunnel bored into a sandy cliff along the Volga, barely had they managed to run communication lines and begin the tap-tap-tapping of radio transmitters linking their command posts to the heavy artillery over on the east bank—barely had the night's darkness yielded to the light of dawn when the Germans opened fire. For eight hours on end the Ju-87s dive-bombed their defenses. For eight hours, without a moment's rest, came wave upon wave of German aircraft. For eight hours their sirens howled, their bombs whistled, the earth shook, and the remains of brick buildings tumbled to the ground. For eight hours the air hung heavy with smoke and dust while lethal shell splinters whistled by. If ever you have heard the shriek of air made incandescent by an exploding bomb, if ever you have experienced a lightning ten-minute German air raid, then you will have some idea of what it must be like to be subjected to eight hours of unrelenting attacks by German dive-bombers.

For eight hours the Siberians threw everything they had at the German aircraft. A feeling akin to despair must have possessed the Germans. The factory was burning. It was shrouded with black dust and smoke—and yet from it still came the crackle of rifle fire, the roar of machine-gun volleys, the quick bursts of antitank rifles, and the measured firing of the antiaircraft guns. The Germans brought in their heavy regimental mortars and artillery. The monotonous sputtering of mortars and the screams of the shells joined the wailing sirens and the rumbling bomb blasts. In grim, austere silence the soldiers of the Red Army buried their fallen comrades. This was their first day, their housewarming. The German artillery and mortar batteries continued through the night.

That night at his command post Colonel Gurtyev met two old friends he hadn't seen in over twenty years. At last parting they were young, unmarried men, but now they were gray and wrinkled. Two commanded divisions, the third a tank brigade. When they embraced one another, everyone nearby—their chiefs and staffs and adjutants, the majors from the operations section—could see tears in the eyes of these gray-haired men. "What are the chances!" they said. And there was in fact something majestic and touching about this meeting of old friends at this dread hour, amid the burning factory buildings and the ruins of Stalingrad. They must have all been on the right path, for it had brought them together once more as they fulfilled this great and difficult duty.

The German artillery rumbled through the night, and the sun had barely risen over the battle-scarred earth when forty dive-bombers appeared, and again the sirens began wailing, and again a black cloud of dust and smoke rose over the factory, covering the earth, the workshops, and the broken boxcars. Even the tall smokestacks sank down into the black fog. That morning Markelov's regiment emerged from its dugouts. In anticipation of a decisive blow from the Germans, he left his cover, his sanctuary, his trenches; he left his concrete and stone bunkers and attacked. His battalions advanced through mountains of slag, through ruined buildings, past the factory's granite administration offices, past the rail line, through the park on the outskirts of the city. From above came the full fury of the Luftwaffe. An iron wind struck them in the face, yet they kept moving forward. The enemy was likely possessed by a superstitious fear: Are these men coming towards us? Are these mortals?

They were mortal indeed. Markelov's regiment advanced one kilometer, took up new positions, and dug in. Only in Stalingrad does one know what a kilometer truly means: one thousand meters, one hundred thousand centimeters. That night the Germans attacked the regiment in overwhelming force. Battalions of German infantry, heavy tanks, and mortars showered the regiment's positions in a hail of lead. Drunken submachine-gunners crept forward like madmen. The story of how Markelov's regiment fought will be told by the corpses of the Red Army men and by their comrades who listened to the clatter of Russian machine guns and the blasts of Russian grenades for two nights and one day. The story of this fight will be told by burned-out German tanks and by the long rows of crosses topped with German helmets, arranged by platoon, company, and battalion. Markelov's men were indeed mortal, and while few of them made it out alive, every one of them had done his duty.

On day three the German aircraft hovered over the division for not eight but twelve hours. They remained there after dark, when the Stukas' sirens howled out from the deep blackness of the night sky, and high-explosive bombs rained down onto the flaming red earth like the heavy and regular blow of a hammer. German artillery and mortars hit the division from dawn until dusk. One hundred German artillery regiments were operating in Stalingrad. Sometimes the Germans fired heavy barrages, and at night they maintained a devastating and methodical rate of fire. The artillery worked together with the trench mortar batteries. Several times a day the German guns and mortars would fall silent, and the crushing force of the dive bombers would disappear. Then came an uncanny silence. The lookouts would shout "Attention!" and the men at the outposts would grab their petrol bombs, anti-tank soldiers would open canvas bags of armor-piercing bullets, machine-gunners would wipe down their weapons, grenadiers would reach for their boxes of grenades. These brief moments of silence did not signify a respite. This merely preceded the attack. Soon the German tanks would come, indicated by hundreds of clanking tracks and the low roar of their engines, and the lieutenant would yell: "This is it, comrades! Sub-machine gunners coming in on our left flank!

Sometimes the Germans would come as close as thirty to forty meters, and the Siberians could see their dirty faces and torn greatcoats, hear them shout threatening words in mangled Russian. After the Germans were pushed back, the bombers returned, and the artillery and mortar batteries would once again send barrage after barrage onto the division.

Much of the credit for repelling the German assaults should go to our artillery. Fugenfirov, commander of the artillery regiment, and the commanders of his battalions and batteries were present on the front line together with the battalions and companies of the division. They were in radio communication with the firing positions, where dozens of powerful long-range guns on the east bank breathed in unison with the infantry, sharing their anxieties, misfortunes, and joys. The artillery worked wonders. It covered the infantry positions in a cloak of steel. It tore apart like cardboard boxes those superheavy German tanks that the anti-tank crews couldn't handle. Like a sword the artillery cut down the German infantry who used their tanks as cover. The artillery blew up their ammo dumps and sent German mortar batteries into the air. Nowhere else in the war has the infantry felt the friendship and power of the artillery or as they have in Stalingrad.

In the space of a month the Germans launched 117 assaults on the regiments of the Siberian division. On one terrible day the German infantry and tanks attacked twenty-three times. All twenty-three attacks were repelled. On all but three days that month German aircraft circled overhead for ten to twelve hours. This took place along a front line about one and a half to two kilometers long. All of mankind could be deafened by this noise; an entire nation could be consumed and annihilated by this fire and metal. The Germans thought that they could break the morale of the Siberian regiments. They thought they had subjected these men to something beyond the limits of what human hearts and nerves can withstand. But surprisingly these men did not waver, nor did they lose their minds or heart or nerves; they instead grew stronger and more at ease. These reserved, sturdy Siberians became even more grim and reserved. The men's cheeks were sunken, and there was a sullen look in their eyes. Here, in the line of the German's main drive, even during those brief moments of rest, you could not hear singing or music, nor any friendly banter. Here the men endured superhuman conditions. There were times when they had not slept for three or four days on end; once, while talking to his men, the gray Colonel Gurtyev was pained to hear one soldier say quietly: "We've got everything we need, comrade colonel—nine hundred grams of bread, and they're bringing us hot meals in thermoses twice a day, even though we don't feel like eating."

Gurtyev loved and respected his men, and he knew that if a soldier "doesn't feel like eating" then he really must be having a hard time of it. But now Gurtyev was content. He knew that there was no force on earth that could move these Siberian regiments from their positions. Both man and officer were enriched by this great and brutal experience of war. Their defenses were strengthened and better than before. In front of the factory workshops rose a vast system of engineering works: bunkers, communication trenches, foxholes. These defenses extended far beyond the workshops. The men learned to maneuver quickly underground, to concentrate or scatter, to use the communication lines to move from warehouse to trench and back again, depending on where the attacking German tanks and infantry appeared.

Along with experience came moral steeling. The division had transformed itself into a wonderfully complete and unified body. The men themselves couldn't sense the psychological changes they had undergone during this month-long residence in hell, on the leading edge of the great defense of Stalingrad. They thought they were just as they'd always been. During the odd spare moment they'd wash themselves in underground bathhouses, and they still received their hot meals in thermoses. Makarevich and Karnaukhov, who, unshaven, looked like simple country postmen, would come to the front line under fire with their leather satchels, bearing newspapers and letters from far-off Omsk, Tyumen, Tobolsk, and Krasnoyask. As before, they thought about their work as carpenters, blacksmiths, and peasants.

They jokingly named the six-barreled German mortar the Fool, and they called the wailing dive-bombers the Screechers or the Musicians. The men believed they were still the same; only the new arrivals from the lower bank looked at them with reverence and awe. It is only from some distance that one could appreciate the iron strength of these Siberians, their indifference to death, their calm determination to endure their difficult lot: to continue to defend Stalingrad to the very end.

Heroism had become the norm. Heroism was the style of this division and its men, a commonplace and daily habit. Heroism was everywhere and in everything. Not only in the feats of the soldiers, but even in the work of the cooks, who peeled potatoes under the burning flames of incendiary shells. Great heroism was seen in the work of the female medics, schoolgirls from Tobolsk—Tonya Yegorova, Zoya Kalganova, Vera Kalyada, Nadya Kasterina, Lyolya Novikova, and many of their friends—who bandaged and carried water to the wounded in the pitch of battle. Yes—from an outsider's perspective, heroism could be seen in each of these men's routine actions, such as when Khamitsky, a communications platoon commander, was sitting calmly, reading a book as a dozen howling dive-bombers pounded the ground; or when Batrakov, a commuications officer, carefully wiped his glasses, filled his field bag with dispatches, and set off for his twelve-kilometer journey along the Ravine of Death with the calm disposition of a man departing for his Sunday constitutional; or when the gunner Kolosov, after being buried up to his neck in dirt and debris in his bunker, turned to deputy commander Svirin and burst out laughing; or when the staff typist Klava Kopylova, a stout ruddy-cheeked girl, started typing a field order in a bunker only to be buried and dug back out, after which she went to do her typing in another bunker, was again buried and dug out, and then finally completed the document in a third bunker before taking it to the divisional commander for his signature. These were the sorts of people who were in the line of the main drive.

After nearly three weeks the Germans launched a decisive assault on the factory. Never had there been such preparations for an attack. For eighty hours their airplanes, heavy mortars, and artillery pounded the area. Three days and three nights were made into a chaos of smoke, fire, and thunder. It went quiet all around, and then the Germans attacked with heavy and medium tanks, regiments of infantry, hordes of drunken submachine gunners. The Germans managed to break through to the factory, their tanks stood beneath the walls of the workshops; they got past our defenses, cut off our divisional and regimental command posts from the forward lines. Without direction, it seemed that the division would lose its ability to resist, and that the command posts, now directly in the path of the enemy, would be destroyed.

But then an extraordinary thing happened: every trench, every bunker, every foxhole and fortified shell of a building transformed itself into a stronghold with its own command and communications. NCOs and regular soldiers took command and repelled the attack with skill and cunning. At that dark and difficult hour, commanders and staff officers fortified their command posts and repelled the enemy's attack like ordinary soldiers. Chamov fended off ten assaults. After defending Chamov's command post, one officer—an enormous, red-haired tank commander—having spent all his shells and cartridges, jumped to the ground and started pelting the approaching submachine gunners with stones. The regimental commander himself manned a mortar-tube. The division's favorite, regimental commander Mikhalyov, died when his command post was hit by a bomb. "They killed our father," said the men. Mikhalyov's replacement, Major Kushnaryov, moved his command post to a concrete pipe that ran beneath the workshops. Kushnaryov, his chief of staff Dyatlenko, and six officers fought at the entrance to this pipe for several hours. They had a few boxes of grenades, and with these they repelled all the attacks of the German submachine gunners.

This unimaginably fierce battle went on for several days without a break. They no longer fought for a particular building or workshop, but for each individual step of a stairway, for a corner in a narrow corridor, for a single workstation, for the space between workstations, for a gas main. Not one man in the division took a single step back during this fight. If the Germans managed to occupy a location, that meant that every Red Army soldier there was dead. Everyone fought like that red giant, the tank commander whose name Chamov didn't know, or like the sapper Kosichenko, who pulled pins from grenades with his teeth because his left hand was broken. When a soldier died it was as if he transferred his strength to the living. There were times when ten bayonets did the work of a battalion in holding the line. Time after time the Germans would take a workshop from the Siberians, and again the Siberians would take it back. It was during this battle that the pressure of the German offensive reached its peak. This was the moment of their greatest potential in the line of the main drive. But it was as if they had tried to lift some unbearable weight; they over-strained the spring that

Mass grave of soldiers at the Red October factory, 1943

powered their battering ram. The pressure of the German attack began to subside. The Siberians had held out against this superhuman pressure.

One cannot help wondering how such great perseverance was forged. It was said to be a combination of their national character and recognition of of their great duty, of a rugged Siberian perseverance, of excellent military and political training, and harsh discipline. But I'd like to mention still another quality that played a significant role in the great and tragic epic: the surprisingly good morale, the intense love that connected all the men of the Siberian division. All of the commanders were imbued with a Spartan spirit of modesty. You could see this in the small things: in the way they refused the hundred-gram vodka ration throughout the battle at Stalingrad, in their reasonable and straightforward leadership. I could see the love that connected these men of the division in the grief they felt when speaking of their fallen comrades. I heard it in the words of a private from Mikhalyov's regiment. Asked how he was doing, he said: "What difference does it make? Our father is gone."

I could see it in the tender meeting of the gray Colonel Gurtyev and the medic Zoya Kalganova, who had just returned after being wounded for the second time. "Hello, my dear girl!" he said softly as he walked toward her with open arms. It was the way a father would greet his own daughter. This love and faith in one another worked wonders.

The Siberian division did not leave the line, nor did they even once look back; for they knew that behind them was the Volga and the fate of their country.

THE LANDING AT LATOSHINKA

On January 1, 1943, Vasily Grossman was recalled to Moscow after reporting for *Red Star* in Stalingrad since September 1942. In his diary he describes the sadness that suddenly befell him on New Year's Eve. While everyone around him was celebrating, Grossman thought of a devastated battalion that he believed had been forgotten: "On this holiday, I recalled the battalion that had crossed over to Gorokhov to divert the blow to itself. It was destroyed to the last man. Who will remember the battalion on this holiday? No one is remembering those who had crossed the river that foul October night."[109] Grossman spoke with sailors from the Volga flotilla during his work as a war correspondent in Stalingrad; from them he is likely to have heard about the battalion's fate. In June and July 1943 the Moscow historians interviewed forty-six members of the flotilla.[110] Many mentioned the doomed battalion, which met its end while attempting to storm a village held by the Germans north of Stalingrad on the western bank of the Volga. Some of the sailors had ferried the soldiers to the other side of the river; others had watched helplessly from the eastern bank as each wave of the assault faltered in a barrage of enemy fire. The sailors seemed deeply stirred by what they witnessed, and most struck a sober tone.

Much of the testimony from soldiers interviewed after February 2, 1943, had passed through the prism of Soviet victory. In the case of the sailors from the Volga flotilla, the focus lay on a failed operation, though quite a few sought to wrest meaning from the event—including Grossman, who attributed to it an objective that had never been intended. The battalion was part of the 300th Rifle Division. Supplied with reinforcements from Bashkiria, Kazakhstan, and Uzbekistan, the division had been awaiting deployment since mid-October.[111] On October 27 General Yeryomenko ordered the division to send a fortified battalion across the Volga to retake the village of Latoshinka from the 16th Panzer Division.[112] From there it was to push south toward Rynok and assist Colonel Sergei Gorokhov's 124th Rifle Brigade.[113] The 1,200-man contingent had been backed against the Volga in hedgehog formation since being cut off from the rest of the 62nd Army when the Germans took the Tractor factory.[114] The second part of the mission was to take advantage of the first lull in the Wehrmacht's drive to eliminate the remaining Soviet positions since October 14. Yeryomenko's daring operation embodied the aggressive spirit that came to dominate Soviet military thinking under Stalin's sway.[115] The November 1 report of the Soviet military staff described the maneuver succinctly: "The reinforced battalion of the 300th Rifle Division entered combat at 4:00 A.M. to occupy the Latoshinka district." On the same day the Wehrmacht reported that "The attempt of several Soviet battalions to cross the Volga to the north of Stalingrad failed completely. A large number of Russian swift boats were drowned, the bulk of the Russian forces was destroyed or taken prisoner."[116] On November 1 the military council of the Stalingrad Front sent a telegraph to Moscow informing the Soviet high command that the enemy had positioned powerful infantry and armored vehicles in Latoshinka, threatening the undermanned and underequipped Soviet battalion. Unable to contact the unit's commander, the military council decided to withdraw the battalion to the eastern bank under the cloak of night. After incurring considerable losses, it had fulfilled its purpose of "drawing enemy forces."[117] On November 4 Latoshinka appeared again in a Soviet military staff report—"The battalion of the 300th Rifle Division, fighting, had fallen back behind the railroad and continued combat in the Niskovodnaya embarkation area"—before being expunged from the annals of the Red Army.[118]

Latoshinka had been in German hands since August 23. A column of the 16th Panzer Division commanded by General Hans Hube crossed the Don on August 23 and by the following afternoon had reached the Volga, forty miles farther east. This enabled the creation of the northern cordon that Gurtyev's 308th Rifle Division tried to breach in September. A history of the German division describes the moment the panzers arrived at the river's "preeminent western bank":

> "Quiet and majestic, the broad, black current carried the barges upriver; beyond it, the Asian steppe stretched infinitely in every direction; the faces of the men showed pride, elation, and astonishment. [. . .] The men entrenched themselves in the outlying villages of Dachi and Latoshinka tucked among the vineyards. After weeks of fighting in the treeless steppe, they hoped for a few days of rest in this luscious magical garden full of walnut trees, oaks, sweet chestnuts, potatoes, tomatoes, and wine."
>
> But this idyll did not last long.
>
> "Within a few days the region north of Stalingrad lay in ruin and the fighting had become relentless."[119]

The chronicle goes on to portray the Soviet landing at the end of October. In contrast to Russian historical sources, it emphasizes the superior numbers of the Soviet force:

> On the night of October 30, the Russians tried again to get a foothold in Latoshinka. Already in the early evening, the men of Stehlke's combat group were roused by a commotion on the other side of the Volga. At midnight the gunboats and tugs began to near the shore. Gerke's armored group opened fire on the Volga train station. Three boats, carrying fifty Russians each, sank; others were damaged and turned around. Three boats managed to land at Latoshinka, on the northeastern edge and in the south. The troops clung to the shore despite machine gun and artillery fire, pushed through to Latoshinka and attacked. Lieutenant Wippermann (16th Antiaircraft Tank Unit) and his troop

> held out despite superior enemy attacks and managed to inflict casualties on the opponent. Sixty Russians shifted their line of attack southward toward Rynok. Under fire from the 2nd Combat Engineers 16, the group was destroyed except for some small pockets, and the command collapsed.
>
> The northern enemy group fought its way to the company command post of the 3rd Combat Engineers 16. But Senior Lieutenant Knoerzer and his company held fast. During a heavy exchange of fire, the division prepared a systematic counterattack to destroy the enemy troops who had landed. When the initiative started, the Russians came out with all guns blazing. But it was no use. At the company command post, fifty-six Russians put up their hands; by 1:00 P.M. thirty-six more prisoners had been captured.
>
> In the meantime, the Russians in the north landed with reinforcements and more powerful ordnance. Crying out "Hurrah!," they attacked to the south, but over the day nine tanks pushed them back to Latoshinka's northern edge.
>
> In the next days, the remaining invaders were killed or captured, the attacks being fended off from Rynok. On the evenings of November 2 and 3, several landing attempts with larger ships were thwarted. A new purge rooted out the last nests of resistance. The brave combat group under the skillful leadership of Major Strehlke, far inferior in number to the enemy, had taken command of the situation: four hundred men of the 1049th Rifle Regiment of the 300th Division from Bashkiria were bagged. Lieutenant Gerke received the Knight's Cross for bravely defending his men.[120]

Looking at the German and Soviet accounts side by side, we can see why the landing failed. Contrary to Yeryomenko's expectations, the Soviet assault did not come as a surprise: several attempts to land in the preceding weeks ensured that the soldiers of the 16th Panzer Division were on guard. Another factor was the lack of coordination among the Soviet troops. In particular, the battalion received no artillery support as it tried to build a bridgehead. Ordered on October 31 by the high command of the Stalingrad Front to help the soldiers of the 300th Rifle Division who had landed on the western bank, the chief of staff of the 66th Army asked why his staff had not heard about the landing. Two days earlier, he explained, the 66th Army and the Volga flotilla had also tried to advance to Colonel Gorokhov from the north.[121] The sailors' stories also detail the disastrous decision by the commander of the 300th Rifle Division, Colonel Ivan Afonin, to send wave after wave of ships loaded with soldiers into German fire; anyone who resisted was threatened with summary execution. Afonin likely feared that he would be reprimanded for cowardice if he acted otherwise. Yet the commanders involved in the operation displayed a tenacity which suggested that they had internalized Stalin's "not one step back" command. Interestingly, the issue of valor in combat had an ethnic component: the mostly Russian sailors of the Volga flotilla criticized the non-Russian soldiers of the 300th Rifle Division for their poor fighting.

On November 9 General Yeryomenko drafted a report for Stalin in which he accounted for the failure of the commanding officers and divisional commander responsible for the operation. (He attributed it to their lack of experience.) In the report Yeryomenko noted that only 169 of the battalion's original 910 soldiers and commanders remained, and he enumerated the loss of equipment in detail. But he also stressed the benefits of the landing operation: "The unit fulfilled the task of drawing away the forces from the Rynok area. The enemy was forced to counteract our landed troops by pulling tanks, artillery, and infantry from the area of Rynok and Spartakovka."[122] In his memoir Yeryomenko devoted just a short paragraph to the events at Latoshinka, repeating the explanation he provided to Stalin.[123] General Chuikov never mentioned the episode; nor did the leading Soviet historian of the battle, Alexander Samsonov.

In his memoir, Isaak Kobylyansky, a former artilleryman in the 300th Rifle Division, described the first attack on Latoshinka. From his position on the east bank, he heard sounds of fighting erupt from the village, and then radio contact was lost. In the evening a soldier who had swum back across the river told of the battalion's sad demise. Kobylyansky was supposed to participate in the second landing attempt, but his boat was incapacitated by German mortar, probably saving his life. "The Latoshinka battalion met a tragic fate," he concludes. "Nearly all of the nine hundred men were taken prisoner, killed, or wounded."[124]

On November 23 the Soviets retook Latoshinka as part of a large offensive. Two days later Captain Pyotr Zayonchkovsky arrived in the destroyed village. His mission was to record the war crimes committed by the Germans. In the enemy positions he found bodies of Red Army soldiers that had been "brutally tortured," presumably under interrogation. (His detailed impressions can be found on page 391.) Several months later representatives of the Extraordinary State Commission for Ascertaining and Investigating Crimes Perpetrated by the German-Fascist Invaders questioned the surviving residents of Latoshinka. They learned that the soldiers of the 16th Panzer Division, after taking the idyllic village, had "set up a love nest in a hole, kidnapped all the pretty girls, and held them there at gunpoint." All the young women in the village were raped.[125]

THE SPEAKERS (in the order they appear)

Yuri Valerievich Lyubimov—Senior lieutenant, navigation officer for a detachment of armored cutters, communications officer for the Northern Group of the Volga Military Flotilla

Yakov Vasilievich Nebolsin—Senior lieutenant, flagship artilleryman, brigade of river ships, Volga Military Flotilla

Sergei Ignatievich Barbotko—Senior lieutenant, commander of armored cutter no. 41

Vasily Mikhailovich Zaginaylo—Deputy commander of the gunboat *Chapayev*

Pyotr Nikolayevich Oleynik—Petty officer 1st class, deputy commander of armored cutter no. 13

Semyon Alexeyevich Solodchenko—Petty officer 1st class, chief helmsman of armored cutter no. 11

Armored boat of the Volga Military Flotilla loaded with troops before a landing, October 1942. *Photographer: A. Sofyin*

Ivan Kuzmich Reshetnyak—Petty officer 1st class, signals officer of armored cutter no. 34

Ivan Alexandrovich Kuznetsov—Lieutenant captain, commander of the gunboat *Usyskin*[126]

Yuri Valerievich Lyubimov (Senior lieutenant, navigation officer for a detachment of armored cutters, communications officer for Northern Group, Volga Military Flotilla): The Latoshinka operation was organized and led by Captain Fyodorov, chief of staff of the Volga Military Flotilla, and Colonel Afonin, commander of the 300th Rifle Division. The landing force was made up of soldiers from the 300th Rifle Division, who were brought in by armored cutter with intensive artillery support from warships of the [flotilla's] Northern Group. The purpose of the operation was to take Latoshinka and link up with Gorokhov's[127] attacking forces, thus improving the situation for soviet forces at this section of the front. The plan was to have two armored cutters go from Akhtuba to the area south of Latoshinka and land a group of men from the 300th Rifle Division. Meanwhile another two cutters were to leave Shadrinsky Bay to land forces on the northern edge of Latoshinka.[128] Both of the first landing groups were meant to have reinforcements brought in on tugboats while the operation was under way. But things went somewhat differently than planned.

One of the armored cutters from the Akhtuba group was having engine trouble, so the other one took two landing parties (about ninety men). The enemy spotted this boat the moment it left Akhtuba. Heavy mortar and machine-gun fire left one man dead and about twenty wounded. They were forced to go back to Akhtuba. But despite that setback, it was important because it drew enemy fire away from the other landing group (from Shadrinsky Bay), which was able to proceed and land unnoticed. They landed without incident and occupied the area from the riverbank to the rail line this side of Latoshinka. Reinforcements were brought in to support the first wave. After the wounded were taken off the boat, the Akhtuba group went back in and made a landing in the area to the north of Latoshinka. In total we landed about a battalion's worth of men from the 300th Rifle Division. The boat from Akhtuba released a barrage of Katyusha (M-13) rockets before landing its troops. But because of poor leadership in the landing party (the battalion lost its commander), the troops broke up into several small groups and lost contact with one another. When the Germans discovered the landing force, they sent tanks in to confront this broken-up, leaderless group and crush it. The landing force didn't offer any kind of organized resistance, to say nothing of offensive operations.

Yakov Vasilievich Nebolsin (Senior lieutenant, flagship artilleryman, brigade of river cutters, Volga Military Flotilla): By the end of October the 300th Rifle Division came to defend the east bank of the Volga from Osadnaya Balka[129] to Srednye-Pogromnoye[130] and started giving artillery support to the 124th Rifle Brigade. On the night of November 1–2, units from the battalion completed a tactical landing at the village of Latoshinka. There were two companies from the 300th Division and one company from the Volga Military Flotilla. By the time they landed, the entire command staff was dead. Their boat went first and was sunk, and all of the battalion commanders died. Leadership on the ground was not established, and the whole landing party was pushed to the northern edge of Latoshinka, where they were rendered ineffective.

Sergei Ignatievich Barbotko (Senior lieutenant, commander of armored cutter no. 41): On October 30 or 31 there was a landing in the area of Latoshinka and Vinovka. The landing operation, in my opinion, was not well planned. There was a gap between the first landing group and the second. The command staff for the landing was on a ferry that sank before reaching the shore. A tugboat carrying artillery and reinforcements arrived very late, which gave the Germans time to regroup. Afonin, the commander of the 300th Rifle Division, boasted that he had 160 field guns to support us with, but none of them fired a single shot during the operation. AC-41 and AC-14 each fired a single volley of rockets. The operation was a failure. The Germans brought in tanks and artillery—they were shooting point-blank at the landing forces and the boats.

Vasily Mikhailovich Zaginaylo (Deputy commander of the gunboat *Chapayev*): The landing party was made up of soldiers from the 300th Rifle Division (Colonel Afonin). The troops landed without any artillery preparation. The landing itself was successful. But instead of having continuous support for the assault, they set a limit on artillery shells. The landing forces had to fight with grenades, without artillery support. The fascists brought in six tanks and artillery, all of which were firing directly at our men. We weren't in communication with the landing party. We didn't know what to shoot at. Captain Lysenko went with AC-23 to better support the operation and establish communication with the landing party. An incendiary shell hit the boat on its way to Latoshinka. Lysenko was seriously wounded and died soon after.

Captain Fyodorov[131] was directing the operation from my observation point. He ordered us to fire on the northern part of Latoshinka with time-fused shells. I let off about forty shells and ceased firing.

Pyotr Nikolayevich Oleynik (Petty officer 1st class, deputy commander of armored cutter no. 13): On October 30 we spent all day at Shadrinsky Bay. Well camouflaged. At night we took on about seventy men with weapons and ammunition (we're rated for nineteen). We got to the opposite shore at half past twelve without drawing much attention. But we ended up two or three hundred meters farther downstream than planned, right under the enemy's nose. Just as the troops were disembarking, we started taking heavy enemy fire. But since the enemy's main firing points were on high ground, and we weren't directly in their line of fire, the shells were all landing astern. But there was a gun firing straight at us from a promontory on our port side. German submachine gunners crept up close and fired at us in the dark.

The landing force, which consisted mostly of Kazakhs,[132] was moving very slowly because they were poorly trained and afraid. We had to force them off the boat. Our sailors unloaded their ammunition. Private Mikhaylov threw nearly all of the boxes onto the bank. It was all unloaded in a few minutes.

When we started heading back we were being shot at by every kind of weapon: mortars, machine guns, cannons, submachine guns. After leaving under enemy fire, we arrived safely at Shadrinsky Bay. We were well camouflaged there during the day. Enemy aircraft were looking but couldn't to find us.

AC-23 (Lieutenant Bytko) was on the south side carrying submachine gunners, but they were unable to land. The cutter took a lot of hits, took losses.

Semyon Alexeyevich Solodchenko (Petty officer 1st class, chief helmsman of armored cutter no. 11): On October 29 AC-11 and AC-13 went to Shadrinsky Bay and were put at the disposal of the 300th Rifle Division. We'd been told we were taking a battalion-strength landing party to Latoshinka. There were two tugboats in addition to the armored cutters. Moroz was in charge of the operation. We went slowly because we had eighty people on board. When they started disembarking, we started taking fire. But the landing went quickly, and we were finished after ten minutes. We got out of there fast, while firing. When we got back we were ordered to make a second run. This time we encountered heavy fire, which we returned. Nine men from the landing party were wounded during our second run. We brought them back. When we got back we learned that the tugboat had unloaded its soldiers but couldn't unload the weaponry. The second tugboat, which was carrying the command staff, was sunk before it could make a landing. The next night only AC-13 was in the operation.

Pyotr Nikolayevich Oleynik (Petty officer 1st class, deputy commander of armored cutter no. 13): The next day we took some submachine gunners that hadn't been taken on AC-23—sixty-eight soldiers and a communications officer from the 300th Rifle Division, who was supposed to gather information and establish communications between the landing party and the division. It was the middle of the night, but the moon made it bright out—we cursed about this and then left for the west bank. The soldiers didn't know where they were going or why. They asked us, but all we knew was the landing site. It was a complete mess. And when we'd finished dropping them off and went back we were instructed to "transfer the landing party," even though we'd completed the operation long ago. The submachine gunners were under enemy fire for about two hours, taking cover behind a wrecked river ferry. The engine wasn't throttled down right away. We were getting shot at, but the shells and mortars were hitting astern. Lieutenant Vashchenko had them muffle the engine. The Germans quit firing soon after. Apparently they'd gone off the scent. The troops landed, the communications officers were waiting for them, and we brought the wounded on board. We took thirty-six men. One of them was a wounded politruk who was part of the first landing. He said that a lot of the landing force got killed, and some had shamefully surrendered.

Our divisional commissar Zhurovko[133] and Seaman Larin walked the riverbank to check on the wounded who wanted to get on the boat. On several occasions they discovered malingers and deserters who had wrapped bandages around their arms or legs to make it look like they were wounded. We brought some of the wounded, and some were brought to us. They came with weapons and were all signed for. They started the engine. Again the enemy started shelling us heavily. We went back to Shadrinsky Bay at full speed.

Yuri Valerievich Lyubimov (Senior lieutenant, navigation officer for a detachment of armored cutters, communications officer for Northern Group, Volga Military Flotilla): I think the main reason for the landing operation's failure was the absence of clear leadership. Captain Fyodorov—who organized the operation—dropped by to give us his "directives" and then left. He didn't show up again, apparently hoping that everything would work out under the leadership of the commander of the 300th Rifle Division. But the rifle divisional commander was not prepared for this kind of operation. During the operation he often gave the most ridiculous orders, and he'd always back them up with the threat of shooting you on the spot. During the day on November 1, for instance, he gave orders for a cutter to take a communications officer to the landing zone, even though it was perfectly obvious that they couldn't go there, that the Germans would shoot them, that they wouldn't make it halfway across the river. And that's exactly what transpired. On his orders, AC-23 was on its way to the landing zone when it was hit in the middle of the river and sunk before reaching the shore.

Semyon Alexeyevich Solodchenko (Petty officer 1st class, chief helmsman of armored cutter no. 11): At 4:00 A.M. we got an order to take two communications officers to the west bank and to clarify the situation around Latoshinka. We were met with heavy fire as we approached. They were shooting at us with machine guns, submachine guns, cannons, mortars. One of the communications officers said this was probably not a good place to land. "Let's back off," he said, "and try upriver." We took direct fire from there too. We moved even closer to shore. But the communications officer wouldn't go. On the third time we came right up to the bank, but the officer refused to get off.

After this refusal we turned around and headed back.

During this operation we got a lot of holes from shells, mortars, and armor-piercing rounds. When we got back to report the situation to the rifle division's HQ, they didn't believe it and blamed everything on the communications officer. At that time AC-23 set down at Shadrinsky Bay. They wanted to send us on the operation, but there wasn't any more fuel. They sent AC-23. Deputy Commander Zhuravkov was on board. As the boat approached the shore, the Germans unleashed a torrent of fire. (We were watching.)

They reversed and turned back, all while returning fire. Soon after that we saw that the boat was listing, but it made it to the east bank and ran aground. A half dozen men were wounded. Seaman Kazakov was killed, the chief helmsman, Vasiliev, died quickly from his wounds, and politruk Zhurakov was wounded and had to be taken to the hospital by force. He ran away from there to get back to his unit. (They wrote about this in the papers.)

Pyotr Nikolayevich Oleynik (Petty officer 1st class, deputy commander of armored cutter no. 13): On the third day AC-11 and AC-13 (Lieutenant Tseytlin was in command of AC-13; now he commands a detachment of two cutters) received the order to pick up the landing force. As we approached the west bank, between thirteen and fifteen tanks appeared. All hell broke loose. It was dark, and we were going in blind. There was such heavy fire when we arrived that there was no way we could get close. The detachment commander ordered us to turn back. We couldn't turn around because our boat, AC-13, had run aground, and AC-11 was right behind. We'd ended up on a sandbar. But we couldn't afford any delays. We took a big hit to the aft machine-gun turret. That was our first breach from a shell. We'd had plenty of bullet holes before that. The shelling damaged our steering. The enemy was thirty meters away. AC-11 was also damaged. But everyone stayed calm. Our commander, Lieutenant Vashchenko, ordered me, as chief helmsman, to move to the secondary helm. But that wasn't working either because the transmission was out. From the outside it appeared that the boat was on fire. The bullets rained down. I told the commander that we'd lost steering. Loza, the chief engineer, overheard me and gave the "full reverse." The boat shook, jerked back, and broke away from the bank. AC-11 had gotten out just a bit earlier.

Semyon Alexeyevich Solodchenko (Petty officer 1st class, chief helmsman of armored cutter no. 11): When we got to the boat and had a look, we found that it had been breached three times by shells and three times by armor-piercing projectiles, and there were a lot of bullet holes from machine-gun fire.

AC-13 also returned and came alongside us. Then this lieutenant colonel from the 300th Rifle Division came over and shouted: "Why aren't you carrying out your orders?" We were running low on fuel. Moroz answered, saying that he "couldn't get out." The lieutenant colonel held a Mauser in his hand as he yelled: "I will shoot you." Then Moroz gave the order to depart. The boats left. The lieutenant colonel walked along the riverbank with his Mauser. Moroz decided to leave AC-11 at Shadrinksy bay and take AC-13 to Akhtuba.

Sergei Ignatievich Barbotko (Senior lieutenant, commander of armored cutter no. 41): We lost AC-34 the next morning. Lysenko, the glorious and courageous Northern Group commander, was on board, and he died a hero's death. The circumstances of his death are as follows: that day Colonel Afonin said that what remained of the landing force should be informed that they were being pulled out. AC-34 and

AC-381 left to pick up the remaining troops. Lysenko tried to explain that the landing party wasn't there and that the boats would be going for no reason. Then Afonin accused Lysenko of cowardice. Not wanting to betray the uniform of a naval officer, Lysenko went out on AC-34 himself. A shell hit and destroyed the steering chain. Without rudder control, the boat ran aground 100–120 meters away from the enemy. The Germans fired incendiary rounds directly at them. AC-41, which was providing cover, fired six volleys, throwing ninety-six shells onto the enemy's firing positions. They took out a six-barreled mortar (a Vanyusha)[134] and a number of emplaced guns.

Nevertheless, the enemy tanks kept firing on the cutter. The troops taken prisoner during the landing operation had given the Germans the positions of our armored cutters. The next day German aircraft launched a raid on those positions, where the cutters, ammunition, fuel, and the gunboat *Usyskin* were all located. One dive-bomber attacked AC-41. Several bombs exploded fifteen to twenty meters away. Three men were killed (a radio operator and two gunners). Such were the losses we sustained during the period of combat operations at Stalingrad. The German artillery fire was very inaccurate, which is why it didn't cause any damage. The mortar fire was more accurate. AC-74, for example, was set on fire by German mortars while it was approaching the bank.

Yuri Valerievich Lyubimov (Senior lieutenant, navigation officer for a detachment of armored cutters, communications officer for Northern Group, Volga Military Flotilla): A small number of soldiers managed to escape and break through to Gorokhov's brigade, which also hadn't started offensive actions in support of the landing. Individual groups from the landing party fought steadfastly against the enemy.

The fight lasted through November 1 and 2. During the landing operation, boats from the Northern Group were at the ready to provide artillery support for the troops. They were waiting for a signal flare. But there wasn't any flare, so they didn't open fire that night. In the morning, when we saw German reinforcements on their way to Latoshinka, we fired at them with Katyushas from the armored cutters and from the guns on the gunboats. The 300th Rifle Division also provided artillery support, not that night, but during the day, when the landing parties were on the defensive.

Those troops weren't really trained (they were made up mostly of national minorities, people who couldn't handle their weapons and lacked discipline).

[. . .] Captain Tsybulsky, chief of staff of the 1st Brigade, came to the Northern Group HQ on November 2. He ordered two armored cutters to go to the landing area at 10:00 P.M. to pick up whatever remained of the landing party, since there was no purpose to their continued presence there. At 12:00 A.M. two armored cutters left Shadrinsky Bay: AC-34 (Lieutenant Glomazdin) and AC-387 (Lieutenant Lukin). The divisional commander, Captain Lysenko, and the detachment commander, Lieutenant Moroz, were both on board AC-34. The boats were caught mid-river by German spotlights, and the enemy immediately opened fire. They concentrated all their firepower on the boats: not only artillery, machine guns, and mortars, but also tanks. They were all firing directly at them. Besides those commanders I already mentioned, and their crews, each boat had five sailors with automatic rifles. There wasn't any way to suppress the enemy fire. Although the cutters did get support from the gunboats of the Northern Group and from the 300th Rifle Division's artillery regiment, none of that had the required effect because they were shooting without making adjustments, based only on the Germans' muzzle flashes.

The cutters couldn't go right up to the shore. They couldn't get closer than fifteen meters, so they were forced to turn back. On the way AC-34 lost control because of a damaged steering chain and ran aground. After seeing this the enemy intensified his fire. The cutter was under direct fire from a close distance. The second cutter (AC-387) tried to pull the first one off the bank, but without success. It was stuck. Because of the heavy enemy fire, nearly everyone on board was either killed or wounded. Captain Lysenko—wounded and bleeding (he'd been hit in both thighs)—told AC-387 to stay put, even while the enemy barrage grew more and more intense. The commander and part of the crew of AC-387 were on board AC-34 trying to rescue those who were hemorrhaging most severely. Detachment commander Moroz was badly wounded by an incendiary round that was burning him alive. The commander of AC-34 was also badly wounded. They were bleeding to death, but there was no one to bandage them and nothing to bandage them with. Lieutenant Moroz dressed his own wounds using a telephone wire. The other end was still connected to the circuit. While their commander and some of the crew were on board AC-34, the rest of AC-387's crew started the motor, backed out, and left, abandoning their commander and comrades to their fate. At around 4:00 A.M. on November 3, Tsybulsky ordered me to take a motorboat to our dying comrades on AC-34, take the wounded and the survivors and get them to shore. I was accompanied by politruk Lemeshko[135] and Lieutenant Peryshkin (commander of the 2nd Detachment of Armored Cutters).[136] The shelling was relentless. When we reached the stricken cutter, we discovered an awful scene of death and destruction. Nearly everyone on board was either dead or wounded, there were pools of blood. Incendiary shells had left some of them covered in blue flames, they were burning alive. Lysenko and Moroz were still alive, but they'd lost a lot of blood. We took them and some of the other wounded onto our boat and gave them first aid. Instead of the recommended six there were fourteen people on our motorboat. We kept getting caught on the riverbed as we moved toward the west bank under constant fire. We promised the ones we left behind that we'd help them soon, that we'd either come back ourselves or send someone else. While we were transferring the wounded from the cutter to our boat, I got hit by three shell fragments in my left arm and leg.

Those comrades who were left behind on AC-34 never got that help. Only the following night did three sailors make it to the cutter in a dinghy. Over the next few nights the dinghy returned several times. They managed to rescue the radio operator Reshetnyak, who was still alive and who had taken sensitive documents and the more valuable instruments and brought them to shore. [. . .]

The heroic Reshetnyak was the only survivor from AC-34. He spent the day of November 3 in the radio room and, despite the devastating enemy fire and repeated aerial bombardments, conducted himself in the most heroic manner. He continued to maintain radio communication with his command post, there among the dead bodies in that scene of total destruction. Reshetnyak was nominated for the title of Hero of the Soviet Union, but was awarded the Order of Lenin. Seamen Belyayev and Zayats, who were the ones who took a dinghy to the wrecked cutter, were also decorated: the first got the Order of the Red Banner, and the second the Medal for Valor. Captain Lysenko was taken to a dugout at Shadrinsky Bay, where he died an hour later, apparently from loss of blood. Moroz died in a hospital two weeks later.

Yakov Vasilievich Nebolsin (Senior lieutenant, flagship artilleryman, brigade of river cutters, Volga Military Flotilla): While approaching the site from Shadrinsky Bay, AC-34 ran aground and was shelled at close range from a battery at Latoshinka. Captain Lysenko, the AC divisional commander, and Lieutenant Moroz, the AC detachment commander, were both on board. The entire crew, including the divisional and detachment commanders, were wounded, and some were killed. All except for the radio operator Reshetnyak. When the motorboat came to remove the crew from the cutter, Captain Lysenko, who had been critically wounded by a thermite shell, told them "not one of us will be taken away, we're going to fight to the death." When he lost consciousness Captain Lysenko was brought to the 300th Division's medical battalion, where he died of his wounds seven hours later.

Ivan Kuzmich Reshetnyak (Petty officer 1st class, signals officer of armored cutter no. 34): During the landing operation at Latoshinka on November 3, 1942, our armored cutter was ordered to scout out the shore and see what the landing parties were doing. AC-34 and AC-379 took part in this operation. On board AC-34 were detachment commander Moroz and Captain Lysenko. Captain Tsybulsky, chief of staff of the 1st Brigade of River Ships, had also arrived at the reconnaissance site. He had his own radio and operator. We were told to maintain contact with this radio, which I did throughout the operation.

At midnight we left Shadrinsky Bay and set a course for the riverbank, which was under enemy control. As we approached the shore, the enemy artillery opened fire. Lieutenant Glomozdin was in command of our cutter. He was demanding and very brave. He never backed down from a mission. No amount of artillery fire was going to make him go back on his decision. Glomozdin decided to land at another location. As we were approaching the bank, an incendiary shell struck the conning tower, which was where the divisional and detachment commanders were located. Volkov, the helmsman, and Tropanov, the signaler, were also there. That shell wounded Captain Lysenko, Lieutenant Moroz, and Lieutenant Glomozdin. It also knocked out our steering. We lost control of the cutter and got stuck in the sand. I was in constant radio contact with Tsybulsky, but when we went aground, the detachment commander ordered me to tell brigade command that we'd gone aground and needed assistance to evacuate the wounded. That message was transmitted to the brigade chief of staff. At the same time I sent a message to AC-379 (formerly AC-44): "Come help pull AC-34 from sandbar and take her to Shadrinsky Bay."

AC-379 received the message and got started on their orders. They tried to tow AC-34, but the boat was so stuck that the steel cable they were using snapped in two. They tried a second cable, but that one also broke. On their third attempt to pull the cutter out of the sand, AC-379 had a mechanical failure. I was instructed by Captain Lysenko to inform the brigade chief of staff about AC-379's mechanical problems. We got a reply saying that a motorboat had been sent for the wounded. Once its engine was back in order, AC-379 came alongside AC-34, inviting their crew to come aboard. But the crew resolved to stay with the ship. Petty Officer Mukhin had taken command [. . .]

The motorboat left after taking some of the wounded. AC-379 also left after they fixed their engine. The crew of AC-34 stayed at their posts. There were also two soldiers and a sergeant from the reconnaissance group. The next shell killed both soldiers and the sergeant.

We kept trying to get ourselves off the sandbank. German spotlights were searching for our boat. Eventually they managed to find out where we were. After that we began taking heavy fire. Soviet U-2s, which were attacking enemy searchlight installations, had reduced the accuracy of the German artillery.

There were ten of us still alive on the cutter (out of thirteen). We got down into the water to try to push off, but it didn't work. Comrade Mukhin—a petty officer 1st class and secretary of the detachment Komsomol organization—took command after Krasavin. He ordered everyone back onto the boat. Then I got in touch with chief of staff Tsybulsky, who had me contact AC-12 and AC-36. They were to come to our assistance. I established communication with them. Those cutters set off, but they were twelve to fifteen kilometers away, but toward daybreak they were subjected to heavy shelling by the enemy. They were ordered to withdraw. Before dawn Mukhin gathered the engineering crew and told them to stay down there until nightfall. Then they would be able get things ready so we could get underway. With help, we could get back to base. The sailors all supported this decision.

I was in the tower, still in contact with Tsybulsky, who sent us a message telling us not to lose heart. There's an exact record of his message in the radio logbook, but I don't know where that is.

We weren't sure why, but from dawn, from about 6:00 A.M. until 1:00 P.M., there was very little enemy fire (there was fog at around ten o'clock). At 12:30 P.M. on November 4 the enemy started to zero in on the cutter. At 1:00 P.M. they began to inflict severe damage. The Germans had four 76mm guns. We were taking direct hits. Two or three shells were landing every minute. At 1:30 P.M. a shell hit the engine room below the waterline. We were badly breached, and the housing of the right engine was damaged.

Petty Officer Mukhin gave orders for the breach to be sealed. When that proved impossible, the crew moved to the aft machine-gun turret. There were about eight men in there. At 2:30 P.M. a shell hit the tower and exploded inside. Seaman Volkov and Petty Officer Svergunov were wounded. Another NCO whose name I can't remember was seriously wounded, and Seaman Vetrov and Petty Officer Shevyrda were both killed. There was a large breach in the tower and water was starting to come in. Petty Officer Mukhin, the helmsman Volkhov, a senior seaman, and a petty officer from engineering decided that, since the situation appeared hopeless, they would try to swim to our side of the river. They got out onto the top deck, grabbed some life preservers, and got ready to jump ship. The radio room hadn't been hit, so I asked if they wanted to come in. None of them accepted my invitation except Volkhov the helmsman, who was still on deck. The others jumped overboard. A German Messerschmitt was flying overhead when he noticed people on deck, went into a dive, and started strafing the ship and the swimmers. Volkov got hit for a second time. Then he jumped overboard. The plane came back around and shot again at the sailors in the water. I never saw my comrades again. They were all killed.

The bridge was destroyed in this attack, and the antenna was damaged. The cutter had no communications. But I was determined to remain until my last breath. The enemy continued this intensive artillery fire until 3.30 P.M. They must have figured that the cutter was completely destroyed, so they stopped firing. But when the smoke cleared they could see it was still there, and they sent four planes to finish us off with bombs. After twelve passes the German planes had dropped a dozen bombs, and we were being shot at from the planes and from the ground. Six or seven bombs hit their target. One exploded above the crew's quarters, another to starboard opposite the fuel tank, a third in the engine room, one on the deck and another in the radio room. But there wasn't any serious damage. The most affected areas were the crew's quarters, the fuel tank, and the galley. At 5:30 P.M. they fired fifty shells but hit nothing because of poor aim.

At 6:00 P.M. the Germans stopped firing. When it got dark I went out on deck. First I went down to the engine room and yelled: "Is anyone alive?" No answer. There were two wounded men in the machine-gun turret. Svergunov and Komarov were badly wounded. I pulled them out of the turret. They were soaked and shivering from the cold. I dragged them to the radio room where I wrapped Komarov in a sheepskin coat. I tore up a sheet to dress their wounds. We started talking about what to do next. After looking at the situation, we decided to wait for help from the other cutters. I was on deck until 9:00 P.M. watching the water, waiting for the Germans to show up. Our cutter was 200–250 meters from the German-occupied riverbank. I had three grenades, a submachine gun, and a revolver. I gave the submachine gun to Seaman Komarov and asked him to open fire if the Germans showed up.

Apart from that, I had to assist my wounded comrades, give them water, dress their wounds. By 9:00 P.M. Komarov was feeling worse. After losing all hope of getting help from the other cutters, and bearing in mind that the wounded were only getting worse, I decided to swim for the east bank, get hold of a dinghy, and return for my comrades. I told Komarov that if the Germans approached he was to shoot at them with his submachine gun. At the same time I put life preservers on them. As I was getting ready to go, I happened to notice this dark spot approaching from a distance. I informed Komarov, saying that he should prepare for a probable encounter with the enemy. I hid in the machine-gun turret. I got my grenades ready and grabbed my submachine gun. That dark spot turned out to be a small boat. We guessed it was German and planned to let it approach to ten meters before shooting. When the dinghy reached that point I yelled: "Who's there?" I heard the familiar voice of my comrades from AC-11 and AC-379. After that we transferred Petty Officer Svergunov and the other wounded to the dinghy. I removed the radio equipment and all sensitive documents and sent the wounded to the hospital at Shadrinsky Bay. At Shadrinsky Bay we met the commander of the other detachment, Lieutenant Peryshkin, who had sent the dinghy out to the cutter. The wounded were taken to the hospital on another dinghy. When Captain Tsybulsky arrived, I gave my report on the cutter's condition and the damage it had sustained. I said there was no point trying to retrieve AC-34, since this could easily lead to the loss of another boat. Tsybulsky gave the order to remove whatever could be taken from the cutter. His men went out to the cutter that night and the following night, and they managed to remove enough parts and equipment to render the boat entirely useless. The bolt assemblies were removed from the guns.

For this operation I was awarded the Order of Lenin by decree of the Presidium of the Supreme Council of the USRR on May 31, 1943. Also by decree of the Presidium of the Supreme Soviet of the USRR, I was awarded the Medal for the Defense of Stalingrad on July 1, 1943.

Ivan Alexandrovich Kuznetsov (Lieutenant captain, commander of the gunboat *Usyskin*): A landing operation was effected at Latoshinka at the end of October. Many of the men in the landing parties were taken prisoner—national minorities, Kazakhs and Uzbeks. It seems that someone had given up our position, because at the end of October the Germans launched an intensive bombardment and mortar attack on our location. I didn't leave my post, but after 2,300 rounds our gun barrels needed replacing, and since there were none available here I was forced to move so that another boat could take my place. The gunboat *Chapayev* took my former position and stayed there for exactly twenty-four hours. It was decided that they would be sent away from there because it was completely impossible to stay—they were being bombed day and night, people were getting wounded and killed.

Vasily Mikhailovich Zaginaylo (Deputy commander of the gunboat *Chapayev*): Some of the landing troops were taken prisoner, and it was because of them that the Germans discovered the positions of our boats.

In the morning the enemy sent nine aircraft to destroy the Northern Group. The bombs came close. But when the planes came on their third approach, the *Chapayev* left its position, and it was this alone that saved her from being sunk. [. . .]

The operation could have been successful if there had been a plan. But not even Gorokhov knew what was going on. So there was no way to assist the operation. The 300th Rifle Division provided no artillery support to the landing forces. Which is why they were almost completely annihilated at Latoshinka.

Yuri Valerievich Lyubimov (Senior lieutenant, navigation officer for a detachment of armored cutters, communications officer for Northern Group, Volga Military Flotilla): They tried to scuttle AC-34, but for some reason it failed to explode, so they left it. There's no need to blow it up—it's nothing more than a mangled, shapeless heap, no good for anything. That winter it was stripped piece by piece, and still now the hull sticks out at the place of her heroic demise, bearing witness to the terrible and bloody things that happened during the great epic of Stalingrad.

THE CAPTURE OF FIELD MARSHAL PAULUS

On January 6 General Konstantin Rokossovsky offered terms of surrender to the surrounded Sixth Army. On January 10, after receiving no response from Field Marshal Paulus, the Soviets began a major offensive. In two weeks they had reduced the size of the *Kessel* considerably, driving enemy troops inside the city limits. On January 26 the Soviets divided the encircled Germans into a southern pocket in the city center and a northern pocket in the industrial district. Soviet leaders suspected that the army high command (AOK 6) was in the southern group but were not sure whether Paulus had fled Stalingrad in the meantime. On January 28, the 38th Motorized Rifle Brigade joined forces with the 29th and the 36th Rifle Divisions and pushed into the city center from the south.[137] In the early morning hours of January 31, German peace envoys approached soldiers from the brigade and led them to a department store basement, where the Soviets were surprised to find Paulus and his staff. The basement had initially been a command post for the 71st Infantry Division under Major General Friedrich Roske.[138] In the final days of January, Paulus and the 250 remaining officers and staff of AOK 6[139] sought refuge there after abandoning their previous quarters—in Gumrak, an airfield west of the city, and in a ravine at the southwest edge of the city.[140] As many of his fellow officers later testified, Paulus had not expressly opposed Hitler's order that the army hold out to the last man, but neither did he enforce it across the board; rather, on January 29 he informed his unit commanders to use their own discretion.[141] Furthermore, Paulus defied Hitler's command to die a "hero's death." As noted in the Introduction, Hitler's promotion of Paulus to field marshal in the early morning hours of January 31 was a roundabout way of telling him to commit suicide or fight to the death, given that no German field marshal had ever been taken alive. Paulus hardly reacted to news of his "promotion." When the Soviets entered the basement, they found him lying in a bed next to Roske's room, where other German officers were negotiating the terms of surrender. Paulus had declared himself a "private" civilian to Roske and his officers, and as such he considered himself not responsible for the German surrender.

On the evening of January 29 Roske reported that the department store could not be held much longer. The army's chief of staff, Arthur Schmidt, urged the officers not to put down their weapons, since the next day marked the tenth anniversary of the Nazi seizure of power. Nevertheless, on January 30 several German officers made contact with the enemy in an attempt to stop the fighting. That evening Colonel Günther Ludwig, the commander of the artillery regiment of the 14th Panzer Division, was received by the battalion command of the 29th Rifle Division. When Ludwig later told Schmidt about his unauthorized actions, Schmidt did not reprimand him; instead, he asked him to arrange for the Soviets to send peace envoys to AOK 6 the following morning.[142]

The Stalingrad transcripts are the first published records to show how the Soviets perceived German efforts to broker a cease-fire and how they responded. They document multiple negotiation attempts between representatives from different units on January 30–31 and explain the confusion that resulted when on the morning of January 31 soldiers from the 38th Rifle Division appeared at the same site to which Colonel Ludwig had asked the command of the 29th Rifle Division to dispatch high-ranking peace envoys. The transcripts also reveal the rivalry between the Soviet units, each wanting to be the first to find Field Marshal Paulus. The interviews contain the reports of proud soldiers of the 38th Rifle Brigade as well as several representatives of the 36th Rifle Division, who came up short in the hunt for Stalingrad's most important trophy.

For most of the Red Army soldiers in the department store basement it was the first time they had seen German officers up close. Informed by Marxist ideas of class, they believed that German generals and officers were all members of the noble elite.[143] Only a few seemed to know that the man they called "General fon Paulyus" grew up the son of a schoolteacher. The supreme high commander of the 64th Army, Mikhail Shumilov, also fell victim to this misconception. The first thing Shumilov did when Paulus arrived at his command post in Beketovka was thoroughly inspect the field marshal's identity card. "The card said," he later explained to the Moscow historians, "that he served in the German army and was von Paulus—the soldier of the German army von Paulus."[144]

The Soviet commanders, most of whom rose from humble origins,[145] were impressed by the German officers' medals and demeanor. Some remarked approvingly on the Wehrmacht's discipline and the respect the officers enjoyed (the implication being that Red Army officers were not held in the same regard). Divisional Commander Roske—one Soviet eyewitness noted his "Aryan blue eyes"—left a lasting impression when he demonstrated his largesse by offering cigars to the "gentlemen" in attendance before the negotiations.[146] But the cultural superiority stereotypically ascribed to the Germans was at odds with the filth and stench Red Army soldiers found in the department store basement. Together with the Nazi racial ideology—Soviet soldiers later recalled that the Germans required their Russian helpers to use separate toilets—this squalor belied the idea of Germany as a great cultural nation.

Postwar German historians have stressed the fatigue and defeatism that prevailed in much of the Wehrmacht during the final days of the battle. The Stalingrad transcripts paint a very different picture, at least in part. Though many captured soldiers called out "Hitler kaput" to avoid being shot, the level of armed resistance the Soviets encountered in "Fortress Stalingrad" was extraordinarily high. Major Anatoly Soldatov explained to historians that at the end of February his soldiers found six Wehrmacht officers in a bombed-out house with a three-week supply of butter and canned food. An NKVD report noted that on March 5, 1943, uniformed German soldiers attacked a senior lieutenant and a sergeant. In a subsequent manhunt Red Army soldiers found and killed eight German officers equipped with pistols and a radio transmitter.[147] The Romanians, Czechoslovakians, and Greeks who fought alongside the Germans expressed relief when captured; for them the war was over.[148] By contrast, many of the Germans, particularly officers, were cavalier, confident that the Germans would eventually prevail.

The interviews below took place on February 28, 1943, and after. Some occurred in Beketovka, where the main headquarters of the 64th Army was located, others at the department store in Stalingrad. The interviews were conducted by Esfir Genkina and transcribed by stenographer Olga Roslyakova.

THE SPEAKERS

38th Motor Rifle Brigade

Major General Ivan Dmitrievich Burmakov[149]—Commander of the 38th Motor Rifle Brigade

Lieutenant Colonel Leonid Abovich Vinokur—Deputy commander for political affairs

Major Alexander Georgievich Yegorov—Chief of the political section

Major Anatoly Gavrilovich Soldatov—Deputy chief of the political section, secretary of the brigade party committee

Captain Ivan Zakharovich Bukharov—Political section instructor

Captain Lukyan Petrovich Morozov—Deputy commander for political affairs, 1st Battalion

Junior Lieutenant Georgy Grigorievich Garin—Reconnaissance platoon commander

Junior Lieutenant Nikolai Petrovich Karpov—Executive secretary for the Komsomol, 3rd Battalion

Junior Lieutenant Nikolai Alexandrovich Timofeyev—Reconnaissance company commander

Senior Sergeant Alexander Ivanovich Parkhomenko—Scout

Junior Sergeant Alexander Semyonovich Duka—Mortar man, 2nd Battalion

Junior Sergeant Mikhail Ivanovich Gurov—Submachine gunner and signaler

36th Guards Rifle Division

Major General Mikhail Ivanovich Denisenko—Commander of the 36th Guards Rifle Division

Guards Colonel Ivan Vasilievich Kudryavtsev—Deputy commander for political affairs

Senior Lieutenant Fyodor Ivanovich Fyodorov—Commander of the 6th Battery, 65th Guards Artillery Regiment

Command Staff of the 64th Army (which includes the 38th Mortar Rifle Brigade and the 36th Guards Rifle Division)

Lieutenant General Mikhail Stepanovich Shumilov—Commander of the 64th Army

Major General Konstantin Kirikovich Abramov—Member of the Military Council

Colonel Matvei Petrovich Smolyanov—Chief of the political section

Captain Yakov Mironovich Golovchiner—Chief of the political section's 7th Section[150]

Major General Ivan Dmitrievich Burmakov (Commander of the 38th Motor Rifle Brigade): We were recently held in reserve for the 64th Army. We were held back for two weeks. Even during this great breakthrough[151] they still held us in reserve. We all resented it. Several times I asked the commander to send us in, but he said: "I know what I'm doing, don't tell me what to do! You get ready to fight!"

Lieutenant General Mikhail Stepanovich Shumilov (Commander of the 64th Army): The front commander ordered us to turn to the northwest again and attack along the Volga together with 62nd Army and clear the city as far as the Long Ravine. [. . .] We cleared the enemy out of all parts of the city south of the Tsaritsa River. But we didn't manage to cross the Tsaritsa. It's such an excellent natural barrier—tall, steep banks. Stone buildings housed the German army's officer and gendarme regiments, who had taken up the defense. Those units offered strong resistance, and we weren't able to get past the Tsaritsa that day.

We had to reorganize the attack some other way, and in any case we'd taken so many losses—riflemen, for the most part—that we needed reinforcements and reserves. They sent in the 38th Motor Rifle Brigade, which was ordered up from the army's left flank. They were to advance along the railroad and force their way into the city center, thereby assisting the attacking forces of the 29th and 36th divisions on the left flank. The 36th Division and the 38th Motor Rifle Brigade managed to cross the Tsaritsa. Nine tanks crossed and started moving toward the center of the city.

[. . .] We didn't have enough manpower, so we brought in the artillery. We'd bring twenty to forty guns—even the 122mm guns—to fire directly at a single building. After one salvo we'd tell the Germans to surrender. If they refused, we'd fire another one or two before telling them to surrender again. Two or three salvoes were usually enough. Their strongholds in the buildings fell one after the other.

Captain Lukyan Petrovich Morozov (Deputy commander for political affairs, 1st Battalion): On January 28, 1943, I got a field order. [. . .] We took it to every soldier, held party and Komsomol meetings, spoke individually with the men. As part of our daily party-political work we studied comrade Stalin's Order no. 345 and his report from November 7. Every soldier knew both of these. This improved their iron military discipline, increased the authority of their commanders, and raised the men's self-awareness.

We held a meeting right before the battle. After the meeting forty-six people applied for party membership. These were the best of our soldiers and officers, everyone who was going into combat. The men and officers had an incredible desire to fight. They all felt responsible for the motherland, knew their duty, and were proving their love and devotion to their country.

Junior Sergeant Alexander Semyonovich Duka (Mortar man, 2nd Battalion): On January 28 we got our orders: engage the enemy in the streets. Before we went I applied for party membership. I'd joined the Komsomol in the 178th Regiment. At nine o'clock we got our battle orders. We set out, taking a break on the way. The one thing I wanted was to know that if I died, I'd die a Bolshevik. So I decided to apply for candidate membership. I handed in my application to the party organization, to Lieutenant—I can't remember his name. During that break there was a party meeting. I wasn't the only one who was applying—eight of us from the battery were nominated. Two of them died in combat. Demchenko and Kovalenko were accepted, as were platoon commander Lieutenant Borisov, Tsukanov, Sergeant Kutyanin, and someone else. All this was around noon. It was freezing cold. They said that we were going into battle that day, that we would prove ourselves in battle and show the Germans they couldn't come any farther into our land. It was our duty to crush them. When I became a party candidate I thought: I must prove myself in this battle. It all happened so fast.

Major Alexander Georgievich Yegorov (Chief of the political section): The enemy was holding the train station. They'd had it for a long time. The walls there were quite thick. It required a lot of painstaking work with the Katyushas and the big guns. They did all right there. And with this we were able to wedge ourselves fairly deep into the enemy formation. The buildings were being defended by very small groups, on the order of seven or eight men. They were using grenades primarily. Our men were given plenty of revolvers. [. . .] Before that they didn't have revolvers—and they were really happy to be given them. Sometimes, especially when you're in a pitch-dark basement, a submachine gun isn't much use. It was so hard to work out who was who that the men had to keep close, elbow to elbow, so they wouldn't shoot each another at night.

The fighting went on day and night.

The darkness helped us because the Germans didn't know how many were in the basements. Brave men like Karpov, Duka—the excellent secretary of 2nd Battalion's Komsomol organization—they'd give the order right away: Company, open fire! Sometimes he'd pretend it was a whole battalion. The German soldier doesn't know Russian very well, but he knows the words for company and battalion. Duka took about five hundred prisoners. Major Soldatov assisted him. Together they took hundreds. They just burst into the basement, and there the Germans all were, stuffed inside like sardines. They could have literally torn Soldatov and Duka to pieces. But what the Germans heard was a strong, determined voice that would allow no challenges or delays. And if they resisted, Duka would toss in a few grenades and create such a panic that they'd all be howling. They would bring whole groups of them out of the cellars at once. Once, though, not far from the candy factory they gave us a bit of a thrashing. Not too bad, but a thrashing all the same. There was a fair number of them, about a thousand men, and we had fifteen. So we decided to attack at night with more noise and more shooting. [. . .]

We had two mortar battalions. Once they got the call saying that some building needed to be shot at, two mortar battalions would start shooting. Can you imagine it? It demoralizes the enemy. And on top of that, they all yell "Hurrah!" Especially at night, and in the basements. When a few of you yell "Hurrah!" at the same time, it makes an impression. The men did it like this: they'd block off a building, take out the firing points. The Germans inside were in a terrible situation. They fought until they were destroyed, until there was no floor, no ceiling. There'd be nothing left but a steel girder. So then the German would get up on that and start shooting. You had to work out which window he was shooting from.

Junior Sergeant Alexander Semyonovich Duka (Mortar man, 2nd Battalion): One night we went to battalion HQ, and the commander gave us a mission. Our 4th Company needed to take this big building and push the Germans out from the basement.

We headed over there. Five men were sent up front with Lieutenant Borisov, our platoon commander. We came up close to the building we were meant to attack. We had to find the 4th Company. The platoon commander sent me to look for them. I found them. I asked for Lieutenant Nechayev, the company commander, and said twenty-five men had come to help him. He showed me that we should take this building from the street, clear it, and then attack the other building from another street.

The Germans were happily throwing grenades from there. Lieutenant Borisov was wounded in the mouth by a shell splinter and had to go to the aid station, so I was the ranking soldier in the mortar battery. There were four of us. We started attacking the building before dawn. We ran across the street to one corner of the building, and from there we went around the other side. We saw someone running away. We kept creeping our way along the wall. We made it. I noticed smoke coming from a chimney and realized they must be in there. Then a second man ran out. Once we were in the courtyard, we [. . .] entered the basement and told the Germans to surrender. I yelled: "Geben Sie Wachen!"[152] and told them to surrender. They said nothing. Not a word. We decided to drop a grenade down the chimney, but then this old Russian man came out from the basement. He said there were civilians down there. There turned out to be eleven Germans, five wounded. We told them to put down their weapons and come out. And they did start coming out one by one. The wounded stayed where they were. Then we searched the basement. They'd brought their wounded to this basement. The woman living there helped them: she cleaned their wounds, bandaged them. While the prisoners were leaving, I was covering my guys in the basement. Then this guy runs out from a corner and shoots.

He killed Sklyarov, our machine gunner, and another soldier who just collapsed there on the basement stairs.

It was just starting to get light outside. We needed to get around to the other side of this submachine gunner. We took turns running—first one, then the second, then the third. Eleven of us got across, one was wounded. It was bright by then. We were spotted by a machine-gunner in another building and he began firing on us. The rest of the men couldn't get across. So there was just eleven of us. We couldn't move forward.

The company commander told us to wait for support. Then our artillery started shooting. The shells were exploding close by, about twenty meters. Then they started hitting another building. We were under such heavy fire that we couldn't move, couldn't do anything. We were in a crater and kept our heads down, while the Germans stayed in the building. A wall came down here, and over there. We had nowhere to go. On one side there was a sniper at a window, and they were shooting from the other side too, and the machine gun was shooting from a third side. We sat like that for twelve hours. Then an infantry company went around and into the rear of the building where the machine gun was firing from. Then a tank rolled up. We started to watch its assault. We waited for the tank to come close enough that we could get behind and move forward. It started to attack another building. We watched as it took one building, moved prisoners, then took another building, until finally they took the building where the machine gun was. We watched the whole thing. Then we started climbing our way out, up one wall and down the next. [. . .] When I ran over there, I saw that the building where the machine gun was had been occupied. [. . .] Then I saw someone run out from another corner of the building with a revolver. I aimed at him. He jumped back so fast I wasn't able to shoot. I went right over, submachine gun at the ready. I went inside. I could see carts and horses. Then these Germans were pushing toward me, shouting. There were also Russian prisoners. I told them to get out of here. These Red Army men got out: "Oh, how we've been waiting for you!" said one. Another said: "There's a hole over there, then some stairs going down to a cellar. That's where their officers are." Then a major came running into the courtyard—I don't know his name—along with Komsomol member Chadov, a senior sergeant. Chadov was busy with something down where the drivers were, and I was here. The major came over to me. I said: "There's Russian prisoners here." He said: "Bring them over." I told them three times to come, but they didn't. God knows what they were doing. I cocked my weapon. I went down the stairs, and one prisoner tells me: "Don't go, don't go, they'll kill you." He grabbed a revolver from someone and came with me. I went down to the basement and opened the door. It's packed full, Germans everywhere, and this was a large basement, two rooms. I could see they've got batteries and headlights from cars, but at the time it was dark. I told them to turn on the lights. At first, when I entered, I shouted: "Bang!" They said: "No bang, no bang!" I stood by the door and told them to turn on the lights. They got them going from the battery. I told them: "Get ready to go." They started tying blankets together. I started sending them out. They started handing over their weapons: they'd bring one from over here, one from over there. I said: "Leave them next to me." They started piling them up. I started searching them, not all of them, but there were sergeant majors there, and I searched them, sent them through quickly. There was more than a thousand of them. The other room was also packed full. I started moving them out of there. We got every one of them out. The major collected them, and I put the weapons together in a pile, and the major sent them out. I went out into the courtyard, where there were cartridges on the ground, drum magazines from submachine guns. I picked them up too and put them in a pile. There was a lot of revolvers, semiautomatics, and other weapons. When I went into the courtyard they could've easily killed me—Bang!—and that would have been that. I went into the courtyard—nobody there. I was all on my own. The major was gone too, and so was the commissar. I went out to the street. I passed the corner where my battalion was attacking, but they'd moved on. While I was trying to work out what was going on, I saw our commissar lying dead in the street. I didn't know where our battalion had gone.

Captain Lukyan Petrovich Morozov (Deputy commander for political affairs, 1st Battalion): At around 5:00 P.M. on the 28th we took possession of two large buildings: the candy factory and a brick building next to the railroad, not far from the crossing. We took those two buildings. The Germans had turned them into a stronghold.

We lost ten men that day to machine guns and antitank rifles.

Seventy Germans were killed, and six hundred taken prisoner. We captured weapons: light machine guns, a lot of grenades and submachine guns. There was a large basement in the candy factory. We took that basement. There was a German hospital there. We took two hundred prisoners. That basically became our command post. When we occupied that basement, up on the right was this big white brick building, just enormous, shaped like the letter L—this was one of the enemy's central strongholds. They'd placed heavy machine guns in the basements, cut embrasures in the walls. You couldn't see any of it from outside. The square was open to fire from multiple directions. To take the building we'd have to launch an assault at night. On the night of the 29th we tried several times to take this L-shaped building. Nothing came of it. By the end of the 30th the building was ours, and we'd taken some eight hundred prisoners. We did lose men there, not just us, but other battalions. We had to surround them on three sides. [. . .] On the night of the 30th our battalion reached the theater. We took a German radio installation and four hundred prisoners. We got vehicles, supplies, and weapons—submachine guns, pistols, rifles. There were a lot of prisoners there. I captured prisoners myself, along with a representative from the special department. In one basement I captured six hundred men, including a Romanian general, a divisional commander. It was just the two of us. We didn't have any men. We had to put them in columns. We got this crowd of soldiers into formation, and then some captain came up and led them away.

Major General Ivan Dmitrievich Burmakov (Commander of the 38th Motor Rifle Brigade): How did we take prisoners? My orders were that they shouldn't wait until all of them started laying down their weapons. If a hundred men put down their weapons, then they're off to the rear. And just one man to go with them. It's a shame to waste manpower. At that time I had around eight hundred prisoners, and by the 30th it was around two thousand. I was already sick of them. I had to use an antiaircraft division, but what you can you do?

Junior Lieutenant Nikolai Petrovich Karpov (Executive secretary for the Komsomol, 3rd Battalion): By then we were attacking during the day. We'd take a building with only ten men, and we'd drag out three or four hundred prisoners. The thing was, all the Germans were in the basements, though they'd keep half a dozen snipers on the roof shooting with submachine guns.

Captain Ivan Zakharovich Bukharov (Political section instructor, 38th Motor Rifle Brigade): Urban combat is very difficult. Every rock is out to get you. The Germans would set up machine guns, camouflage them, and shoot. And to top that off they put snipers on the rooftops. We'd have to run across streets, squares, alleys. We were taking casualties, but not like they were.

Here's what they'd do: They'd settle down in a building, place their machine guns, their sniper-submachine gunners, their mortar men. The rest would stay in the basement to keep down their losses.

And we in turn would place our own submachine gunners and antitank riflemen, who did a good job of destroying those firing points. All of them had grenades. As soon as there was enemy fire, we'd hit that location and take it out. Our men advanced whenever the shooting died down. We were throwing a lot of grenades into basements.

Senior Lieutenant Fyodor Ivanovich Fyodorov (Commander of the 6th Battery, 65th Guards Artillery Regiment, 36th Guards Rifle Division): We started smoking them out of their bunkers. One time we pulled out fifteen Germans and took one aside. We gave him a smoke and sent him back into the bunker to bring out whoever else was there. He went and brought out more people. We didn't do anything to them, but when the others poked their heads out of the bunker, we shot at them.

Lieutenant Colonel Leonid Abovich Vinokur (Deputy commander for political affairs): How were we fighting? We'd shoot five or six times with the big guns and then send an envoy. If they didn't surrender, we'd shoot another five or six times, send the envoy. If that didn't do it, we shot at them again. Then they'd start to line up and beg to be taken prisoner.

Major General Ivan Dmitrievich Burmakov (Commander of the 38th Motor Rifle Brigade): By the evening of the 29th we'd taken around eight hundred prisoners. That evening we captured a German hospital. There were wounded officers, including a regimental commander, a major. This got reported to me. I went right away to ask him where the German group headquarters was located.

There were rumors that Paulus had been flown out.

I asked the major where Paulus was.

He said that Paulus wasn't there.

Somehow that major was dead by morning. Apparently he'd been strangled by our men.

The fighting continued at night. At dawn on the 30th we started to approach and surround the Regional Party Committee building, the building of the Regional Executive Committee, the City Theater, and the buildings to the east. We fought during the day, we fought at night.

Shumilov called me: "Why have you taken so little?" Denisenko has just called to say that he'd taken the theater and the gardens.

"Comrade General, how can Denisenko have just taken the theater? I was in the gardens by the theater and took eight hundred prisoners."

Sure, maybe Denisenko wasn't to blame. It's not easy to know where you are if you don't know the city.

I knew the city, and most of my men knew the city, but these new people didn't.

The fighting continued. We'd take a building and capture 150–200 men. The enemy offered fierce resistance. There were two hundred men defending this building while I was attacking with four hundred. We were all firing away at one another. Their resistance on the 30th was unbelievable. I said: "We're going to need to take every last building."

But we had some tricks up our sleeves. We started sending back prisoners. I telephoned all the battalion commanders, the deputies for political affairs.

I told them if they captured small groups of Germans, twenty or so, then they had to send them back. If the Germans in a building won't surrender, and you've already captured a hundred of them, then take twenty or thirty and send them back. That helped.

Major Alexander Georgievich Yegorov (Chief of the political section): We took 1,500 prisoners, picked out twenty of them, talked with them a bit and then sent them back. Generally, if we captured a single soldier—or two or three—we sent them back, saying that we weren't going to take them one by one. If you want us to take you prisoner, then get your comrades and come on back. I've got to say, this strategy got some fairly good results. [. . .] There was a directive from the army political section that called on us to speed up our shipments of prisoners. It was in connection with this that we launched an assault on the night of January 29–30, at midnight. I left the command post with Colonel Vinokur, the deputy brigade commander, and we arrived just as they had finished occupying the basement of the Univermag department store, which was their hospital. There were about fifty men there: wounded, sick, frostbitten. There were majors, captains. One major asked for my revolver so he could shoot himself—obviously a true believer.

Our men were in high spirits. On January 30 we took the train station. When we were inspecting our units before the attack, we knew for sure that they'd had the right training. These men were ready to fight, they were burning with desire. There was perfect certainty that the task they'd been given the day before would be completed.

But there was still no word on Paulus. We heard he'd flown out. Then, when we started getting large groups of prisoners, the officers told us that Paulus was in some basement with his staff. This of course had its effect on our men and officers. It would be something to capture him. We dragged out a group of two thousand prisoners and brought them to where our command post was. There we carried out a search, sorted them, and pulled out the officers. We got confirmation from this group. Paulus was here in Stalingrad.

Major General Ivan Dmitrievich Burmakov (Commander of the 38th Motor Rifle Brigade): The long and short of it was this: we fought, and we fought, and we fought. In the evening [of January 30] I was told that the building of the Regional Committee, the City Theater, and the adjacent buildings—which we had already surrounded—had agreed to negotiate their surrender, but they asked to wait until 6:00 A.M. Ilchenko reported this to me. I said: "We've got to start immediately!" We sent another messenger. They wouldn't agree. I wondered what the problem was. They asked to hold off until 4:00 A.M.

"Let's give them until 4:00 A.M."

I thought this would be a good chance to lie down, seeing as I didn't get any sleep the night of the 28th–29th. We'd fought all the 29th and all the night of the 29th–30th. We had to get a little rest. After all, there's a limit to a man's strength.

General Shumlilov called: "Sector 101 has been taken."—This was where Paulus was—"Denisenko is there!"

I couldn't take it. I said: "Comrade General, allow me to send my representatives."

I went to check for myself.

Denisenko's men were one and two hundred meters to my left and rear. How could they have taken Sector 101? The unit on my right was occupying Sector 100. I think to myself, it's not possible that they took Sector 101. But if they did, then it's all the more important we attack these buildings.

Major General Mikhail Ivanovich Denisenko (Commander of the 36th Guards Rifle Division): Then the 38th Motor Rifle Brigade was sent to our area. [. . .] It's hard to know who it was exactly that surrounded Paulus's headquarters, but the 38th Brigade got the credit.

Guards Colonel Ivan Vasilievich Kudryavtsev (Deputy commander for political affairs, 36th Guards Rifle Division): Our division captured about six thousand men. Paulus was captured by some new reserve unit that had only just entered combat.

Captain Yakov Mironovich Golovchiner (Chief of the political section's 7th Section, 64th Army): On the night of January 31 the 29th Division entered negotiations with Colonel Ludwig, the commander of the enemy's 14th Panzer Division. At first we spoke via radio, and then he came to our headquarters. We agreed that at 6:00 A.M. on January 31, 1943, the remnants of the 14th Panzer Division would be lined up on the square by the theater, where they would surrender to us. During the negotiations he mentioned that he could mediate negotiations with Field Marshal Paulus, who was in the department store. Now it was clear where Paulus was. Until then this was not confirmed. When this was reported up the chain of command, orders were issued to find Paulus's headquarters right away and to send our people there.

That night the 97th Brigade of the 7th Corps did the following: they got a group of captured German officers and told them to go with our man to Paulus's headquarters and begin negotiations. It was a long time before they agreed. But after the meeting with the officers, two men were chosen: Plate and Lange. They and Lieutenant Vasiliev, chief of intelligence for the 97th Brigade, set off for Paulus's headquarters. They got there, negotiated, and agreed that at 10:00 A.M. they would try to make all the legal arrangements. So he could prove that he'd been there, they gave Vasiliev and pistol and a Nazi banner.

That same night, representatives of the 29th Division (they have a training battalion and a training regiment) were also negotiating with Paulus's staff.[153] At that time I was at the 20th Division's headquarters. When they told me that these negotiations were going on, I went over there. I arrived at the department store building by morning. When I arrived, the building was already surrounded by elements of the 38th Brigade. The sentries outside were from the 38th Brigade, and the ones inside were Germans. As it happened, the 106th Regiment of the 29th Division had gone around the department store and kept going. The 38th Brigade came up and, in orderly fashion, surrounded the building where the headquarters was.

Major General Ivan Dmitrievich Burmakov (Commander of the 38th Motor Rifle Brigade): So, by 4:00 A.M. on January 31, 1943, I'd taken 1,800 prisoners. There were about two hundred officers among them. Then Ilchenko called to say that three of them were battalion commanders. I said: "Question them immediately and find out where their Stalingrad group headquarters is."

Ilchenko called back: "They've confirmed that von Paulus and his headquarters are in the center of the city, in a basement on the other side of Red Square.[154]

I said: "Sector 101."

Right then I called the battalion commanders and deputies and had them get this message to every soldier: locate and encircle this building. I knew that the department store and the hotel were around there somewhere. I told them there was a square. The Square of the Fallen

Warriors. Surround this building immediately. It won't be easy getting in there. Bring in the mortars, open fire, and let's make quick work of it.

Captain Lukyan Petrovich Morozov (Deputy commander for political affairs, 1st Battalion): We destroyed their last stronghold on the approach to the department store and captured forty-eight men, including one translator. I was where the barricade had been built. When our men had occupied the building and started moving the prisoners, I went straight to the battalion and followed the left flank toward the department store. Everything around the gateway was mined. We brought in a heavy machine gun, antitank rifles, submachine gunners. 3rd Battalion and another battalion were advancing on our right. We'd basically surrounded the entire block. Artillery was firing from behind the Volga. When we got to the theater the artillery stopped because we were close enough to the enemy that we might get hit too.

I stayed with the 2nd Platoon. The commander of 1st Company, Captain Savchuk, ran up to me and said an officer was requesting a senior officer for negotiations. "I told them I was an officer, but they said, 'No, we need someone from the high command, go find them, talk to them!'" I went straight to that translator we'd taken with that group of forty-eight and then went to the officer. I said I was the brigade's deputy chief of staff. The translator relayed this to him. He said they needed someone higher up. I told him that I was authorized by our high command. He said there were generals there. Well, all right if that's how things stand! That's when Ilchenko arrived: a senior lieutenant, deputy chief of staff for operations. The brigade commander was having him lead the battle. He was always with us at the battalion, and he gave instructions to our battalion and some others as well. I said: "Well then, comrade Ilchenko, shall we negotiate?" Then Ryabov, an agent from the Special Department, arrived. We set off. We were warned: this area is mined, don't stop. We walked right up to the entrance of the department store basement. There were lieutenants with rifles and submachine guns, and also some machine guns. Someone came out, a duty officer or something. They announced the visitors, saying that we were here for negotiations. We didn't have a white flag, nothing like that. Then Captain Bukharov appeared out of nowhere. He'd already gone in when we were in the courtyard. The Special Department agent left two men in the courtyard. Then Captain Rybak came. Three people went inside: me, Lieutenant Ilchenko, and Captain Rybak, and I suppose Ryabov too.

Captain Ivan Zakharovich Bukharov (Political section instructor, 38th Motor Rifle Brigade): We knew that Paulus was there, we knew that he hadn't been flown out. We'd heard that they had a plane circling all the time, we heard all kinds of things. Paulus's headquarters was in this district. We knew that much, but I wasn't sure which basement he was in. Then this German officer comes out and asks which one of us is the ranking officer. We say we've got captains and a senior lieutenant. We told them they should surrender. We said they were surrounded, and that if they didn't give up we'd throw everything we had at them, that we'd eliminate them down to the last man. He said that he wasn't the one to decide such things, that there were men higher up than him. And then he tells us that Field Marshal Paulus is here. We went up to the main entrance. It was me, Morozov, Ilchenko, and Ryabov, the representative from the Special Department. We went in. The courtyard was packed full of Germans. When we entered the courtyard, we were stopped near the entrance to the basement. The chief of staff came out with a captain who spoke excellent Russian, even knew Russian sayings: "God only knows," "my darling," things like that.[155] He said that Paulus required that we report to higher authorities, officials who could carry out negotiations. We discussed this. We agreed that Ilchenko and I would go and the others would stay. We went to call our battalion command post and the brigade. They told us to leave and report this to the higher authorities. Then I went back to the building. They already knew me there. There were only five of us, not too hard to remember. So I was there, but our men were attacking all around. We were ready for anything. To tell you the truth, it was dangerous being there with them. Any bastard could get you. But at the time it didn't even occur to me to be worried.

Captain Lukyan Petrovich Morozov (Deputy commander for political affairs, 1st Battalion): General Schmidt, the chief of staff, said that they were concerned for the life of the general, that someone might run in and throw a grenade, so he asked if someone would remain at the entrance. Ryabov went. Bukharov was sent to get in touch with brigade headquarters. Now it was just Ilchenko, Captain Rybak—the deputy commander of 3rd Battalion—and me. We started negotiations with Schmidt in a colonel's office that was next to Paulus's room. The general and a translator came in. The translator spoke good Russian. Schmidt asked for Ilchenko's ID. Schmidt said: "May I see your papers?" Ilchenko had said that he was the brigade's chief of staff. But the position listed on his papers didn't correspond with what he'd said. They said they had to have a representative of Rokossovsky, the army commander. Ilchenko said: "I'm the chief of staff now. You're all worried about this small detail, but what matters is the larger picture: what you now have at your disposal, the position you are now in and the position we are now in." But they still demanded a more senior representative. Then Ilchenko said: "I'll go radio for a colonel." He left with Rybak. I stayed in the room with the general and the translator. The general would ask the translator a question, and then the translator would ask me: "Is it true that since they introduced new rank insignia, the Red Army will be known not as the Red Army, but as the Russian Army?" I said: "No, that's not right—the Red Army is not being renamed the Russian Army." I asked him if he knew whether the Red Army was having success on all fronts. "Yes, we've heard that on the radio lately." He asked, among other things, about my rank and position. Then he said: "Do not think that our German army is weak. We are still strong, still very powerful, and we are equipped with first-rate weaponry." I said that, if we were defeating such first-rate weaponry, this was all the more a credit to the Red Army. He said: "You have probably also had the experience of being surrounded." I said that my division had never been encircled. I hadn't personally been in such a situation. He said that they were getting a hundred grams of bread, that they had no other food. Then he asked how long our winter would last. I told him there would be severe frosts until mid-March or so. Then I asked him a question: "You think the German army is so civilized, especially your army staff, but why do you live in such filth?" He replied: "We've been stuck inside lately because of your Katyushas and airplanes. That is the explanation for everything."

They had something like fifty kilos of sausage in there. They pounced on those sausages like jackals: officers pushing soldiers out of the way, soldiers pushing officers.

General Schmidt said through his translator that they were concerned for General Paulus's safety. "We'll give you a captain and ask that you remain by the doors." I said: "Certainly." And I left.

Major General Ivan Dmitrievich Burmakov (Commander of the 38th Motor Rifle Brigade): We opened fire, and then Ilchenko called me out of nowhere to say that Paulus's aide had asked for the most senior officer for negotiations.

"And you're not important enough to negotiate?"

"No," he said, "they only want to talk with someone from army headquarters."

"If they don't want to talk, tell the bastards we're going to throw everything we have at them! Their building will be isolated. Try to get

Colonel Ivan Burmakov and his political deputy, Colonel Leonid Vinokur, in front of the Stalingrad department store, February 1943.

the negotiations started, but if it comes down to it we can talk with grenades, semiautomatics, and mortars."

"Understood!" said Ilchenko.

I called Shumilov right away and told him what was going on. He said: "Stay at your command post for now. Colonel Lukin and chief of staff Laskin[156] are on their way."

That was when Vinokur rushed in. "I'm off!"

"Get going already! Paulus needs to be captured. Do whatever is necessary as the situation unfolds."

I've always been able to rely on Vinokur.

He drove off, and I stayed to wait for Lukin. Just as Lukin arrived I got a call from Ilchenko: "We're already in the department store basement. They're asking for a cease-fire."

I said: "Go ahead and instruct them to cease fire, and I'll call Shumilov."

We stopped firing, and I called Shumilov: "Paulus is asking for a cease-fire. He's also going to order his men to stop."

Shumilov said: "I'll send out the order right away."

But during the negotiations there was still some activity from airplanes and mortars.

Lieutenant Colonel Leonid Abovich Vinokur (Deputy commander for political affairs): When we were surrounding the department store our command post was by the train station. Once we had them surrounded, we decided to ask for the German garrison's immediate surrender. We kept shooting a few shells at a time, and we sent an envoy with a white flag. We knew from prisoner interrogations that the 6th Army's headquarters was there, as was Schmidt, the chief of staff. Ilchenko went as our envoy with a white handkerchief and demanded that they surrender. He went with a translator, one of theirs. They refused. Then the brigade commander ordered three shots from our mortars. The building was already surrounded by all our battalions. Including the 1st Mortar Battalion. They let off three warning shots. We did, of course, do a lot of damage ourselves. The Regional Committee building, for example. We had shelled it very heavily. About fifteen minutes later their representative came and asked for a representative from our high command. Ilchenko told me this on the phone right away. And I headed over there right away. I told Burmakov: "You call Shumilov's staff. I'm going over there now."

Junior Sergeant Mikhail Ivanovich Gurov (Submachine gunner and signaler, 38th Motor Rifle Brigade): They called us from the battalion and said our guys had the building surrounded. Me and the colonel and the political chief got in a car and went over there. We were on our way, and then—Bam!—we're out of gas. It was around nine or ten in the morning, maybe eight. We had a spare can in the trunk. We filled her up and drove over there fast. Then we stopped the car, didn't know where to go. We found some of our men who showed us the way.

Major General Ivan Dmitrievich Burmakov (Commander of the 38th Motor Rifle Brigade): Shumilov gave his order and said that Laskin was coming and that I was to go with him. I waited for Laskin. They called me for the third time. Our men had stopped shooting, but the 57th was still at it. Paulus had asked for a cease-fire. And Vinokur still wasn't there yet. Again I called Shumilov, asked him to make sure the whole front got the message so the 57th would stop shooting. Until that got through to them. [. . .]

The telephone operators were sitting all around us listening, and then they were hearing from everyone: "Paulus! The 38th has got Paulus!" Where? In the basement of the department store. I waited for Laskin.

Lieutenant Colonel Leonid Abovich Vinokur (Deputy commander for political affairs): I got there. Our forces had encircled the entire building. Ilchenko explained the situation. I came because they'd asked for a representative from high command. I brought along Ilchenko, Yegorov, Rybak, Morozov, and a few submachine gunners. We entered the courtyard. We didn't have any white flags. I wasn't about to go there with a flag. We went into the courtyard. As you can see, there's the entrance to the basement. They had submachine gunners posted in the courtyard. They let us past, but kept their weapons at the ready. I've got to admit, I was thinking to myself: Now they've got you, you fool. There were machine guns at the entrance, where some of their officers were standing.[157]

Junior Sergeant Mikhail Ivanovich Gurov (Submachine gunner and signaler, 38th Motor Rifle Brigade): There were German soldiers there, all of them armed. Not many of our guys at all. Ours were down the way a bit. Ilchenko brought us here. We went into the basement. It was almost all officers speaking German. And of course I don't know a word of German. All of them up top were armed, and the ones down in the basement all had guns too.

Major Alexander Georgievich Yegorov (Chief of the political section): At seven or eight in the morning on January 31, Lieutenant

Ilchenko called to say they'd started surrounding the department store building, which, according to our intel, was the location of Paulus's headquarters. There was fierce shooting from their side. The building was nearly encircled. We were going to try to negotiate. The deputy commander [Vinokur] said: "Let's go." We got in the car and headed over there. We couldn't get all the way there in the car, so we got out and walked. When we got to the department store, Lieutenant Ilchenko told us that one of their staff officers had come out and said that Paulus wanted to negotiate, that he wanted someone who could speak on behalf of Rokossovsky. Ilchenko was too junior to negotiate with them. I went with the colonel and posted sentries—both us and them had sentries standing there. We put together a group of officers, eight men. We had grenades in our pockets. We went into the courtyard. It was full of men and officers, lots of them. They stopped us at the entrance to the basement. It was impossible to go any farther. The colonel said: "Negotiations are all very well—but we need to be careful. Make sure that the entire building is surrounded. I'll go."

He walked over and introduced himself as an envoy from Rokossovsky. They asked him for identification. But his papers said that he was Rokossovsky's deputy, a political officer. The Germans questioned this. "These papers," he said, "are out of date. Rokossovsky himself authorized me to conduct negotiations under the terms dictated in the ultimatum. Is that clear?"

What was clear was that this question had already been answered, given the hopeless position they were now in. They gave in. Colonel Vinokur had a report sent back immediately. We had about a battalion's worth of men. The report was sent to the brigade commander and army headquarters.

Lieutenant Colonel Leonid Abovich Vinokur (Deputy commander for political affairs): Through the translator I demanded the immediate presence of a representative from their command. The representative came and asked who we were. "I am the representative of the high command, the political department."

"Are you authorized to negotiate?"

"Yes."

He left and passed this on. After a few minutes they brought me in. It was dark in there. They had a generator from the power station. There was a large radio station in their headquarters. When I went in I said to the adjutant through the translator: "Where are we going? How much farther?"

The adjutant took me by the arm and guided me. I had four submachine gunners with me, plus Ilchenko. The gunners stayed in the corridor.

Junior Sergeant Mikhail Ivanovich Gurov (Submachine gunner and signaler, 38th Motor Rifle Brigade): I went with the commissar to where Paulus was.[158] Then they all got up and said something. The commissar answered them. I don't remember what he said. Then he told me to leave the room. I had an F-1 grenade in my pocket and a German Browning. I thought, "What can I do if they come at us?" The officers couldn't see me. One of them came out of the room, with a medal of some kind, said something. Then he went down to the other end, reported something, and went back to the room. He did this a lot. I figured it wouldn't be a good thing if I tried to stop him. My first thought was that maybe he was running away or something, maybe the commissar would be angry if I let him go. I decided not to do anything. Let him do what he wants, I'm just going to stand here quietly.

But I was still worried about the commissar. I could tell that they were up to something. I wasn't concerned for myself, I don't value my own life very highly.

Lieutenant Colonel Leonid Abovich Vinokur (Deputy commander for political affairs): I went into the room with Ilchenko, we didn't have anyone else. A round table, four chairs, a radio, two telephones. I was greeted by Roske: a short man, very thin, maybe forty-four or forty-five. I could see he was nervous. General Schmidt was sitting on his left. The entire staff was there. When I entered the room, Roske stood up and greeted me. I answered him.[159] He asked if I wanted to take off my coat. I was wearing a sheepskin coat. Even though it was warm in that room, I declined. I said it didn't feel too warm. Then we started talking. Roske let us know right away that he was not negotiating on behalf of the field marshal. Those were literally his first words.

Paulus's room was dark. The filth was unbelievable. Paulus stood up when I went in. He hadn't shaved in a few weeks and he looked defeated.

"How old would you say he is?" Roske asked me. I said:

"Fifty-eight."

"No. He's fifty-three."

I apologized. The room was filthy. He was lying on the bed when I went in. He immediately got up when I got there. He'd been lying there in his coat and cap. He handed over his sidearm to Roske. That was the same weapon I gave to Nikita Sergeyevich [Khrushchev] when he arrived.

Roske did most of the negotiating. Their telephones were working all the time. People had been saying that all their lines had been cut. But none of that was true. We took the telephones ourselves. The station still worked, so we passed it along to the front. The Germans wrote that their garrison was destroyed—none of that was true. [. . .] Roske looked very sharp and clean. He made the best impression of the group.

They didn't say why they were surrendering. On the contrary, he said that they could still resist, that they still had men. But he didn't want any more bloodshed, and in his order he said that he came to this decision because some units had betrayed them.

Chief of staff Schmidt, who looked very neat and tidy, ran back and forth between Roske and Paulus, keeping him informed of the course of the negotiations. I didn't get a good look at him—he was there for three or four minutes at most. All of Roske's other aides looked neat. All of them with dozens of medals. When I asked them to surrender their weapons, Roske gave me his own, Paulus's, and Schmidt's.

Major Alexander Georgievich Yegorov (Chief of the political section): I was in the room with Roske. How did he behave? They knew how to behave. It wouldn't be right to say that his will was broken. He had a great sense of dignity.

Captain Yakov Mironovich Golovchiner (Chief of the political section's 7th Section, 64th Army): Roske was sitting at the table facing us. On his left was General Schmidt, Paulus's chief of staff, sitting on a bed. Facing them was the translator and another one of Paulus's aides and his entire retinue, all in full dress. Vinokur and Lukin were sitting across the table from Roske, and Colonel Lutovin, the deputy political chief, was standing on the left.

What was Roske like? A tall and slender man, with Aryan blue eyes, a rather decisive character, very energetic. He was wearing a general's dress uniform with a Knight's Cross around his neck. He made an impression. Roske was the commander of the 71st Division.

When we all sat down, he took out a pack of cigars and offered them around. The negotiations had begun.

General Schmidt is tall. He doesn't have a very lively face. I'd even say he looked weak-willed. He's maybe fifty-four, dark-haired, unshaven. Paulus could have done with a bit more life in his chief of staff. He kept trying to get one over us during the negotiations, but it didn't work.

Captain Lukyan Petrovich Morozov (Deputy commander for political affairs, 1st Battalion): [. . .] It was the colonel who finally captured General Paulus. Before then they had been asking for a cease-fire. "Who's shooting?" Comrade Bukharov took a car. A German officer was sent with him. They drove around the district trying to get people to stop shooting. Wherever they had a guard posted, we put three or four men with a machine gun. They warned us that they had mines all around: "We'll all get blown sky-high." But that didn't scare us. When the colonel arrived, the whole courtyard was crowded with our men and commanders. General Laskin came later. He arrived when all of this was being wrapped up. Later Paulus and his staff were put in cars and driven away.

Captain Ivan Zakharovich Bukharov (Political section instructor, 38th Motor Rifle Brigade): Then I saw him coming—comrade Vinokur, the political chief. They told him that Paulus had asked for our men to cease fire during the negotiations. Our guns and mortars were still shooting. Paulus asked for our men to stop, and in turn they were telling their own men to stop. Major Yegorov sent me: "Comrade Bukharov, get going." The Germans provided us with an officer, their translator, and a car and driver. We got in the car and drove off. They all had revolvers. We hadn't taken them. I was alone with the three of them. We hadn't thought to take a white flag. We just got in and left. We drove past our troops, and they stayed put. Then this one machine-gunner fired at us. I told the translator to stop the car. I said: "What are you shooting for?"

"Comrade Commander, we thought these Germans had captured you and were taking you away, so I started shooting."

I said: "You've got to stop shooting. We're telling people to cease fire because of the negotiations. We're trying to find a peaceful solution without more bloodshed." We drove over to Major Telegin. We talked, and he came with me. We left the car and went on foot. I said that we'd been instructed by army headquarters to call a halt to our attacks and cease fire because they were in negotiations with Paulus. I drove around to the other units. They had a garrison located in two buildings by the railroad. We drove there. The strip of land between our units and theirs was under fire. But we made it through unharmed. The German major called for an officer and gave him the order. Their sentries were standing behind a wall. I didn't go down to the basement. There were a lot of soldiers. There were machine guns, submachine gunners—and everything was aimed at us. He gave the order to cease fire. Of course, on both sides there were individual snipers and submachine gunners who kept shooting, because they hadn't all gotten the message. After that we drove back.

Major General Ivan Dmitrievich Burmakov (Commander of the 38th Motor Rifle Brigade): Vinokur began the negotiations. Vinokur organized a tour of the units. He sent Bukharov to take care of that. Bukharov said that he'd been put in a terrible position. I told him I understood the dangers. This is war. He went in a German car with two German officers and a driver, and he was sitting in between them. Our guys would see this, think that he was either a prisoner or a traitor, and shoot. [. . .] Laskin arrived. We went over there together. Our men were everywhere. There were loads of soldiers in the courtyard. We got there around 7:00 or 7:30 in the morning—probably more like 7:00. We went into the basement. It was dark.

A crowd of soldiers was in the courtyard. I didn't like this, all of them were armed. I said: "Would you stop here, I have orders for you." I told Laskin to break up the group of German soldiers in the courtyard immediately and to get some of our own submachine gunners in there in case things got out of hand, so we had them covered from all sides.

We went to see Roske. We were introduced, and comrade Vinokur reported the terms of surrender he had given them. Laskin, as the senior officer, gave his consent. They had requested that they retain their sidearms. Vinokur had allowed this. But Laskin did not agree—they needed to hand them over. Then we went to see Paulus. We were told in advance that Paulus was no longer in command. When we arrived we said that the Northern Group should surrender. Vinokur said he'd already brought this up. They said that they had nothing to do with the Northern Group. As of yesterday the field marshal was no longer in command. The group was now operating independently. The field marshal had given up his command, and no one had authority over them.

I went out to the courtyard to check that the submachine gunners were all still at their posts. I could see that my instructions had been carried out. Our men divided them into groups. They divided them into three groups, each of which was surrounded by our men.

Other units had arrived by then. But the very moment the negotiations had been concluded, the 29th Division launched an attack to the right of the hotel building. Our men in the department store yelled out: "What are you doing?"

No one had been shooting, but the Germans had gone onto the attack, opening fire and almost getting some of our men in the department store.

People started gathering on the square.

Even before they had an order I immediately took steps to disarm these groups. But they didn't want to hand over their weapons without an order. I asked Roske to order them to hand over their weapons immediately. He gave the order. They began handing them over. I tried to get rid of these people as soon as possible. I told my men: "If you've got a group together, take them away, push them back to the rear!"

I asked Roske how many men they had. Around seven thousand. I said: "Write out an order to the units and send it out." The translator told him. The order was typed up. The translator came. Roske stood up and asked me through the translator to let his officers to distribute the order. Their officers were afraid of our submachine gunners. I told the translator: "Tell the general that his request will be granted. My officers will be here soon, and they're not afraid of going to the Germans' units."

Before that he'd asked Vinokur to have our representatives drive out to the units. Vinokur said: "Fine, let them go." He gave him Bukharov.

Major Alexander Georgievich Yegorov (Chief of the political section): The deputy commander wrote a message telling me that, according to Roske, there were eight hundred people somewhere around here, including two generals, who wanted to give themselves up. I was to go with this German major and get them.

In came the German major. "I'll be damned," I said to myself. "This area has nothing to do with us, it's the responsibility of the 36th Guards." And in any case, going on your own to take generals is a bit frightening. I thought, this is a German major, and who knows what might enter the head of a German major at the wrong moment? I decided to take all the grenades I could and go with him. I thought: I'll let him go ahead, I'll walk behind. He took me to a bunker. One of our guys was standing there. "What's going on?" "We just came here, we've been under fire. I didn't know what to do. If I move they'll kill me. I don't know where my commander is."

"Why are we waiting for the commander? I'm going in." I let the major go ahead of me. He started yelling something in German at the door, probably so he didn't get shot. We went into the basement, and the smell was terrible. I saw one of our own dead soldiers. I went in.

I asked them who shot this soldier. We kept going. There were three dead German officers. Then, a bit farther on, I could hear some rustling. The major opened the door, and there were four girls, good light, and a wine bottle and orange peels on the table, tinned meat, sausage. Two of the girls were completely drunk. I asked who had shot the soldier. He'd been fully armed. One of them pointed: "That one, the fool!"

"What for?"

"Because he killed those three."

I kept my talk with them brief. I asked the one who still had her wits about her whether anyone else was there. "Nobody, just the three officers."

I looked and saw no generals, just regular officers. Officers were of no use to me when I needed generals.

When we left, the major showed me to another bunker. All right, I thought, let's go. It was about two hundred meters to the second bunker. It was full of soldiers from the 36th Brigade. Nothing for me to do there. So I didn't find the generals. We went back. And that was the end of my mission.

Major General Ivan Dmitrievich Burmakov (Commander of the 38th Motor Rifle Brigade): They distributed the order and reported back. A German officer saluted me and said: "Mission accomplished." He gave his report through the translator. He asked that we wait until eleven o'clock to allow Paulus to gather his things. Paulus's officers and staff would be going with him. I said to Laskin: "I ask that you arrange for the Southern Group staff to stay in place until the handover is complete. I would leave Roske until he gives us the complete surrender, and anyway I need to check out the mine fields."

I asked Roske to call for his mine layers. They had it all on the map, and I asked that their mine layers clear all of it. Vinokur told me later that the building itself was mined. Roske told Vinokur that, whatever happened, he [Roske] was responsible to the Führer for the safety of the field marshal. Anything untoward and we'd all get blown up. I asked that they defuse all of it immediately.

He [Roske] asked that he be given his own submachine gunners and his car. Laskin said that the field marshal would be going in my own car, so there was nothing to be afraid of. I said I'd have a car with submachine gunners going just in front of us. Then we set out. We led all of the soldiers out. They showed us the minefields and cleared the mines. The thing about the building being mined was not true. The corridors were mined, and the entrance was mined, but the building itself wasn't. They entered all the minefields on the map, and at 5:00 P.M. Roske told me that he was ready to go.

Vinokur brought him from his HQ. He'd asked for two cars, and I had two jeeps. I put him in my car and his officers in a truck. We were polite the whole time.

By nine o'clock we'd essentially ended all combat operations. Paulus's capture had completely ended the war in Stalingrad, at least in the southern part of the city. The surrender was immediately followed by a kind of pilgrimage. Representatives of the local authorities were arriving. There were tons of weapons. The men started taking them. By that evening you couldn't find a soldier without two or three revolvers.

Many of the Germans had simply dropped their weapons and gone out onto the square unarmed.

Roske asked for and received permission to say farewell to his officers. I put together a group of officers.

By the way, one of the men there was the city commandant, a Russian. He'd also been in the basement. Roske's translator said that there were a number of officers, including the city commandant, and also eight women, all in the basement. One of the women started crying and asked if she could bid farewell to the commandant. They came to me.

"Comrade Colonel, this bitch would like to know if she can say good-bye to the commandant."

"Is she one of ours?" I asked.

"No, anything but, though she is Russian. The bitch even has the nerve to weep."

That really made me mad. All the other Russian prisoners were packed off either to the special section or to the NKVD.

I'd say Roske is about forty-six, forty-seven. Paulus is older. Roske has five children.

What was Paulus like? He seemed like a cornered animal. He was obviously very unhappy about all that had happened. He was thin, unshaven, sloppily dressed. I didn't like him. His room was filthy. Roske's room was more or less clean. That's where Schmidt was, the chief of staff.

When Paulus was leaving, he asked to be taken out through the back gate. As he was driving away, he looked around with such a stupid, pathetic smile. He was clearly upset.

There was so much filth in the basement, Paulus's room included. The courtyard was a nightmare. We cleared up the mess.

I couldn't believe the filth that Roske had allowed in such a high-level headquarters. I asked him about it. They started talking, and then came the translation: "Your Katyushas and artillery prevented us from going out during the day. We were forced to take care of our bodily functions in the basement. This could only be removed at night, and even then the men were afraid to go out." He blushed slightly. He was clearly a sophisticated man, a seasoned officer.

Major Anatoly Gavrilovich Soldatov (Deputy chief of the political section, secretary of the brigade party committee): [. . .] it was unbelievably filthy, you couldn't get through the front or back doors, the filth came up to your chest, along with human waste and who knows what else. The stench was unbelievable. There were two latrines, and both had written on them: "No Russians allowed." Whether they ever used these latrines is hard to say—the corridors were all one big latrine. There were times when the Germans shot better than us, but we never made latrines out of our living quarters.

Major General Ivan Dmitrievich Burmakov (Commander of the 38th Motor Rifle Brigade): I was surprised when the German radio said that all of them had committed suicide. I ran over there to take a look. Paulus was there in his room, along with my orderlies. There were two submachine gunners, and the four of us. Everything was in order.

When I was getting ready to set Roske's group, I had all of them lay their weapons on the table, Roske included. They all had their weapons until 5:00 P.M. Then they started taking weapons out of their suitcases. They were well able to shoot themselves, and Paulus could even have blown himself up.

On the contrary, Roske was constantly frightened that he was going to be killed, he kept telling me that he was responsible to the Führer for the field marshal's life. He was frightened that there might be some mistake. He asked me to have my own car go ahead of his. Comrade Laskin said: "Don't worry—Paulus will be going in my car." Then Roske stood up and thanked him: "Thank you, thank you."

How could any of them die by their own hand when they're such cowards? They weren't brave enough to die.

I'd just shaved the day before. When I, the commander of the 38th Brigade, was presented as his captor, Roske stood up. He's older than me. He's actually only a little bit older. I may look young, but I'm the same age: forty-four. I've been in the army since 1918. I was among those who fought for Shchors, the Ukrainian. He blushed a little. "Do you recognize me?" I asked him.

"Yes, *gut gut*."

He was a brave one, Roske. He came right out and said that he had some bad commanders. He knew our units well. He was asked a question about one commander. He said he'd acted improperly, poorly. This general knows military matters. Roske was commander of the Southern Group. Schmidt was chief of staff of the 6th Army. Roske led the negotiations. Schmidt acted as intermediary between Roske and Paulus. He kept Paulus informed of the progress of the negotiations and the surrender. He passed on Paulus's personal request that we spare his life, that we not shoot him.

Roske was also taken to Beketovka. He got angry with me. When he was being driven out, I didn't show him the proper respect. I could see he was waiting there for me to come shake hands and so on. He waited awhile in the car, twisting and turning, and I waved at him like it was no big deal.

Lieutenant Colonel Leonid Abovich Vinokur (Deputy commander for political affairs): We sent Paulus away at 11:00 A.M. on January 31, 1943, and at 5:00 P.M. we sent Roske to Shumilov at Beketovka. That's where Paulus had been taken. The Northern Group surrendered the next evening.

Major General Konstantin Kirikovich Abramov (Member of the Military Council, 64th Army): I was still in bed when Shumilov called me at six in the morning saying that Paulus was being taken prisoner, that someone had to be sent. I got dressed and went to see Shumilov at the office. We wondered who to send. We decided on Laskin. When he couldn't be found we sent Colonel Lukin, who was deputy chief of staff and and the chief of the NKVD. He drove off. Then Laskin turned up, and he was sent to Colonel Lukin. By nine o'clock we hadn't heard a thing. We started to worry. Then I went there myself together with Serdyuk.

But we didn't know exactly where the 38th Brigade was, and we didn't know the city, so we missed the 38th Brigade's headquarters and came out onto the square at the department store. We drove around in circles for a while before getting worried that they might already have been sent off to our HQ, so we turned around and went back.

It was about an hour later that Laskin brought Paulus. He delivered him to Shumilov's office. At first Shumilov drafted a list of questions. [. . .] Chief of staff Laskin was walking in front when they brought him in. They drove him over in an Emka.[160] Shumilov was there, and so was I, Serdyuk, Chuyankov, and Trubnikov, the deputy chief of the front political administration. The chief of staff reported: "We've brought von Paulus, field marshal of the German army."

They asked him if he'd like to take off his coat in the hallway. He did. Then Paulus, Shumilov, and Adams came in and shook hands with all of us. Shumilov asked us to sit. We sat. Shumilov asked for Paulus's documents. Paulus produced his service book. Shumilov looked it over,

General Mikhail Shumilov inspects the papers of Field Marshal Paulus. Frames from the Soviet newsreel *Soiuzkinozhurnal* 1943, no. 8.

then asked whether there was a document to show that he was a field marshal. Paulus said he had no such documents, but that his chief of staff would confirm that they had received a radio message saying he was now a field marshal.

Paulus was unshaven, bearded, but he was wearing his iron crosses. Everything was as it should be.

He'd already surrendered his sidearm. He was questioned. They asked whether he had ordered his forces to surrender. He said that he had, that they were surrendering. They asked why he was surrendering. He said they were out of ammunition and food, that there was no point in resisting any longer. When they were being photographed they shook their heads, as if to say no.

The whole thing took four or five minutes. Then we decided to get them some food. Laskin and I took them along. Shumilov stayed where he was. We took them along and said: "Sit down, eat." We talked with them for two hours. Then Shumilov, Serdyuk, and Trubnikov joined us. At first Paulus refused to drink. Then I pushed him to take a glass. He said: "I can't, I haven't eaten." Then he said: "We're not accustomed to drinking vodka." Then he drank a glass, then a second. Shumilov arrived. He drank to our health. We'd been talking for a while already, just sitting there. I asked him why he didn't get out of the encirclement when he was free to leave. He said: "That's for history to decide."

He was asked what his objective had been, how he regarded the destruction of his army. Shumilov told him that we once had the keys to Berlin, but that the Germans had never had the keys to Moscow.[161] And now we were again going to have the keys to Berlin, while they would never have the keys to Moscow. He made a face during this but didn't say a thing. He's fifty-four. He asked me how old I am. I said I was thirty-six. Again he made a face.

Schmidt took part in the conversation. He's an intelligent man, very direct. We didn't really have anything to ask them about. What they could say about their army meant nothing to us because we had them in our grip. And anyway, they knew less about the current situation than we did. Paulus didn't ask any questions. I'm sure he thought we were going to have him shot. We asked him why they destroyed Stalingrad. He said: "You did as much to destroy Stalingrad as we did." We said: "We wouldn't have been doing anything to Stalingrad if it hadn't been for you." He had nothing to say to that.

Shumilov was discreet. Paulus was nervous, his face was twitching, lips pressed tight. He was an old man, nothing more. [. . .] There was something a bit servile and ingratiating about his manner, in the way he praised us, how he smiled and bowed.

When he came to the dining room, he sat down and asked that no one write anything or take photographs. I said that we weren't going to, but that there were people in the other room who were recording everything. But there weren't any photographers.

Lieutenant General Mikhail Stepanovich Shumilov (Commander of the 64th Army): After Field Marshal Paulus was taken to army headquarters, I let him in, and he gave me some information. After that I asked him for something that would prove that he really was Field Marshal von Paulus. He presented me with his service book, where it was written that he was in the German army and that he was von Paulus, a soldier of the German army.

General Shumilov in Stalingrad, January 31 or March 3, 1943. *Photographer: Georgy Lipskerov*

When I'd taken a look at the booklet, I asked my next question, saying that I'd just been told that yesterday or the day before that he'd been given the rank of field marshal, and that I'd like to see documentation to that effect.

He told me that he had no written confirmation but that he had indeed gotten a telegram from Hitler saying that he was now a field marshal. His chief of staff and his adjutant, who had been with him the whole time, would confirm this.

Then I asked him another question: May I report to my government that I've captured not a colonel general, but a field marshal?

He said: "I would ask that you tell your government I am a field marshal."

For the next question, the field marshal was asked to explain why the elite German forces were concentrated in Stalingrad while inferior units, such as Romanians and Hungarians, had been placed on the flanks. I asked whether our high command had gauged the situation correctly when they first defeated these flanks and avoided the elite German forces in Stalingrad. He replied: "That was the mistake of the German army." Incidentally, Paulus never said this himself, but General Roske and the other generals said that after a series of unsuccessful assaults on Stalingrad and Beketovka, Field Marshal von Paulus had asked Hitler for permission to withdraw his forces behind the Don for the winter. Apparently he asked Hitler twice at the request of General Roske and the other generals, but Hitler wouldn't allow his forces to fall back to the Don. That was near the end of October, beginning of November. Before the encirclement.

In answer to the question of whether the surrounded German army could have kept up its resistance, he told me that, after his defenses broke on the Voroponovo—Peschanka—Staraya Dubovka Front, he had thought further conflict was pointless, as their cargo planes had nowhere to land to supply the group with ammunition and food. But, he said, he was a soldier, and he'd been ordered to keep fighting to the last man. Only the complete encirclement of his headquarters had compelled him to surrender.

As for why he hadn't committed suicide—that is something I never asked him.[162]

The German newspapers said that Paulus kept poison and a revolver in every pocket. A search produced only one of these revolvers, and no poison of any kind was found. Paulus was taken unharmed, he wasn't wounded, and he didn't get harassed in any way by our command staff during his capture. He arrived at the 64th Army headquarters with his own car and entourage.

Captain Yakov Mironovich Golovchiner (Chief of the political section's 7th Section, 64th Army): Paulus is tall, slightly bent old man, around sixty, with grayish eyes, very dignified, as you'd expect for a field marshal, unshaved. He was depressed, and he looked unhealthy. According to him, his second adjutant had recently come down with something very bad.

On January 29 Paulus relieved himself of command. On the 31st there was an announcement that the field marshal had turned over command of the Southern Group of forces in Stalingrad to General Roske. Paulus declared himself a private individual via his chief of staff, and he transferred all of his responsibilities to General Roske. [. . .] I spoke with Paulus's staff officers on the road and then here (in Beketovka). They all blamed Paulus for being soft and weak-willed. They said they could have resisted for a substantial amount of time. They still had a lot of men, but he did not show enough resolve. On top of that, they thought, Paulus's staff had made a series of major tactical errors when they were still some distance from Stalingrad. If it weren't for those major errors, then they'd have been able to resist more effectively, they said.

Guards Colonel Ivan Vasilievich Kudryavtsev (Deputy commander for political affairs, 36th Guards Rifle Division): The Germans didn't believe they were surrounded, and their officers weren't telling them about it. They found out it was true when they were left with nothing to eat. They started saying it looked like they were surrounded. Not even the officers knew about the ultimatum, and the soldiers knew absolutely nothing.

Captain Yakov Mironovich Golovchiner (Chief of the political section's 7th Section, 64th Army): Until the very end the German officers were entranced by the confidence they had in their strength, by their confidence in victory. And they maintained control over their men. The soldier obeys his officer without question. [. . .] To the German soldier, anything an officer says or commands is law. They have a very strong sense of discipline.

Senior Lieutenant Fyodor Ivanovich Fyodorov (Commander of the 6th Battery, 65th Guards Artillery Regiment, 36th Guards Rifle Division): Then came the command to stop shooting altogether. All the Fritzes were giving up. The order to cease fire came between nine and eleven o'clock on February 1, 1943. By then they were surrendering by the hundred. They yelled, "Hitler kaput!" Prisoners were being brought out with frostbitten feet, bandaged heads. Most of them were wrapped up in blankets and just went like that. By February 1, I was done using my artillery. But I did use my pistol to finish off their wounded in the basements.

The Square of the Fallen Heroes, with view of department store, March 1943. The sign on the right reads: "Death to the German-fascist invaders and their state, their army, and their new 'order.'"[163]
Photographer: Sergei Strunnikov

Major Anatoly Gavrilovich Soldatov (Deputy chief of the political section, secretary of the brigade party committee): Czechs, Greeks, Czechoslovakians, and of course the Romanians—they all gave up easily, but the Germans were so damned proud. You'd often hear them saying that our success at Stalingrad was all due to chance. Here they've gone and surrendered, and they're still saying these things. Our commandant grabbed one of them by the sleeve, dragged him off, and shot him. He's known for doing that sort of thing.[164]

Lieutenant Colonel Leonid Abovich Vinokur (Deputy commander for political affairs): There was a motorcyclist, someone from army intelligence, and he was there next to a German driver who was wearing a Red Army jacket. I said to the company commander: "Why'd you give him a jacket?"

"He was cold."

"And when exactly did you die so he could pull it off your corpse?"

Major Alexander Georgievich Yegorov (Chief of the political section): We liberated our own POWs here in the Regional Committee building. We decided to get some use out of them right away. We held short interviews, told them that they'd committed a crime for which the legal punishment was a bullet. "The only way you can turn this around is with your own blood." They very joyfully took up their weapons, and we warned them that the least sign of panic or cowardice or attempt to surrender, even if this was only on the part of one or two of them, would result in all of them being shot. Sometimes we got quite a lot out of them.

Colonel Matvei Petrovich Smolyanov (Chief of the political section, 64th Army): The first and most fundamental task was to bring ourselves, our units, and our party organizations back in line. An order came down from Army giving everyone five days' leave. Our task during that leave period was to organize, in addition to the basic activities—getting a shave and a haircut, making repairs—various cultural activities. In line with our party and political work we thoroughly discussed these matters and recommended that we hold a series of meetings with separate worker collectives, at which we would discuss what the experience of the fighting at Stalingrad had taught us. This subject was the central question of all meetings and gatherings.

Major General Ivan Dmitrievich Burmakov (Commander of the 38th Motor Rifle Brigade): N. S. Khrushchev arrived the next day. He knew our brigade well. The first time we met was in Stalingrad. That happened while we were preparing to break out in November. We met on the march and shared our impressions. He kept saying: "Well, boys, don't let us down! You've all done good."

Nikita Khrushchev in front of the Stalingrad department store, February 1943.

Victory rally on the Square of the Fallen Heroes, February 4, 1943.

Shumilov and N. S. Khrushchev arrived the day after Paulus was captured. Khrushchev was hugging and kissing us. "Thank you, thanks to all of you! It's not often you capture a field marshal. Generals you can get, but a field marshal's a rare thing."

It meant a lot to us to have Khrushchev's gratitude. [. . .]

Then he came here, to this basement, and sat down. Chuyanov arrived. Representatives of the local authorities arrived. People began coming in droves. Khrushchev thanked everyone, and Shumilov pointed at me and said: "This is the guy who was angry with me for not ordering him into battle. I know when it's the right time to do that!"

After the rally on February 4 we had a party.

Khrushchev came and praised us again.

I don't mean to brag, but we got them, we did a good job, and I'm pleased that we did this job, I'm pleased that our brigade did so well. To me that's what matters most.

I spoke and welcomed the guests on behalf of our brigade. I think we fought pretty well. Khrushchev stood up and said: "He's just being modest. Thank you for bringing us Paulus!"

They were all there, everyone who had been competing with me for this prize.

Entrance to department store basement, 1944. *Photographer: Samari Gurari*

In February 1943 a cardboard sign was hung at the entrance to the room in the department store basement where the terms of surrender were negotiated. It read: "Here on January 31, 1943, at 7:00 AM the supreme commander of the Sixth German Army, General Field Marshal von Paulus, and his staff, led by Lieutenant General Schmidt, were captured by the 38th Motorized Rifle Brigade." Below were the names of Colonel Ivan Burmakov and his political deputy, Senior Lieutenant Leonid Vinokur. In the same year another sign—identical except for omitting the aristocratic "von" from Paulus's name—was placed at the side entrance of the department store, next to the basement stairwell. As the photograph below shows, it continued to draw visitors in the summer of 1944.

In the basement of the Stalingrad department store.
Photographer: Sergei Strunnikov

In 1951 the sign was replaced by a bronze plaque that painted the events leading up to January 31, 1943 in an epic light. It described the opponent as a "Stalingrad army group [. . .] that was encircled and routed in the great battle of Stalingrad by the glorious Red Army." The plaque honored the 38th Rifle Brigade under the command of Colonel Burmakov, but did not mention Vinokur, whose name had been expunged from Soviet annals in the wake of the anti-Semitic campaigns of the late Stalin era.

The plaque has since been removed, but in the 1990s a local historian dedicated a small museum to the battle in the basement. A few years ago the museum became entangled in a legal dispute with the owners of the department store, who wanted to turn the basement into a restaurant. In May 2012 a judge ruled that the basement was to become part of the state museum complex on the battle of Stalingrad. The new memorial site opened in fall 2012, on the seventieth anniversary of the battle.

3

NINE ACCOUNTS OF THE WAR

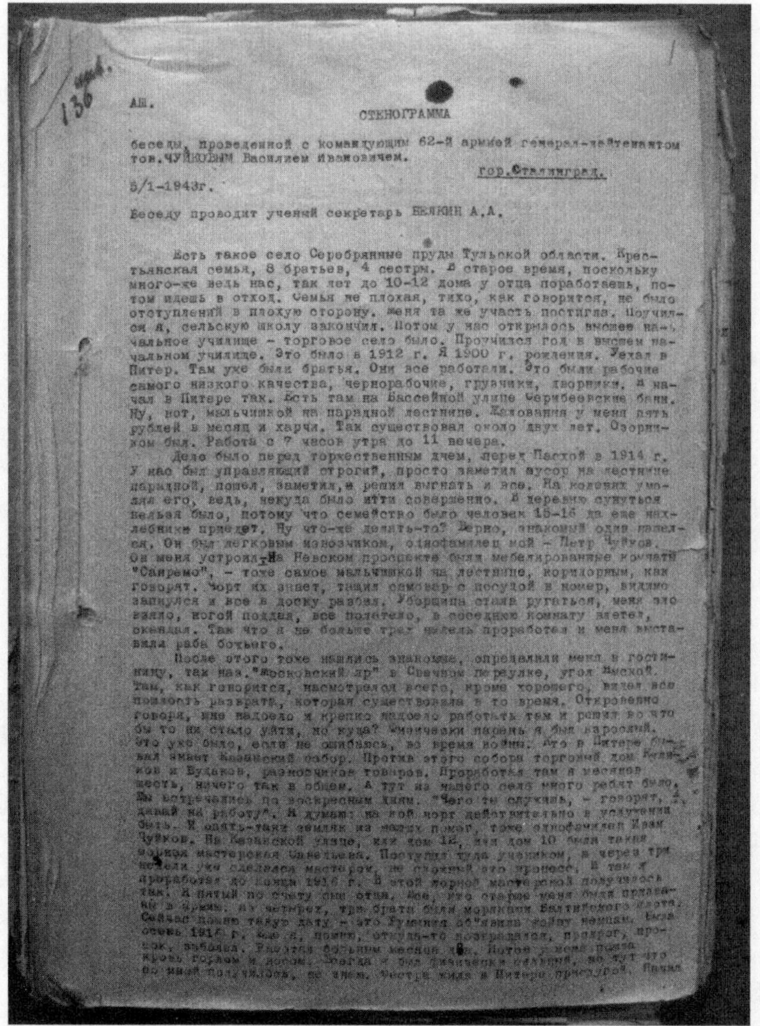

АШ.

СТЕНОГРАММА

беседы, проведенной с командующим 62-й армией генерал-лейтенантом тов. ЧУЙКОВЫМ Василием Ивановичем.

гор. Сталинград.

5/1-1943г.

Беседу проводит учений секретарь БЕЛКИН А.А.

Есть такое село Серебрянные пруды Тульской области. Крестьянская семья, 8 братьев, 4 сестры. В старое время, поскольку много-же ведь нас, так лет до 10-12 дома у отца поработаешь, потом идешь в отход. Семья не плохая, тихо, как говорится, не было отступлений в плохую сторону. Меня та же участь постигла. Поучился я, сельскую школу закончил. Потом у нас открылось высшее начальное училище - торговое село было. Проучился год в высшем начальном училище. Это было в 1912 г. Я 1900 г. рождения. Уехал в Питер. Там уже были братья. Они все работали. Это были рабочие самого низкого качества, чернорабочие, грузчики, дворники. Я начал в Питере так. Есть там на Бассейной улице Черибеевские бани. Ну, вот, мальчишкой на парадной лестнице. Жалованья у меня пять рублей в месяц и харчи. Так существовал около двух лет. Озорником был. Работа с 7 часов утра до 11 вечера.

Дело было перед торжественным днем, перед Пасхой в 1914 г. У нас был управляющий строгий, просто заметил мусор на лестнице парадной, пошел, заметил, и решил выгнать и все. На коленях умолял его, ведь, некуда было итти совершенно. В деревню сунуться нельзя было, потому что семейство было человек 15-16 да еще нахлебники придет. Ну что-же делать-то? Верно, знакомый один нашелся. Он был легковым извозчиком, однофамилец мой - Петр Чуйков. Он меня устроил. На Невском проспекте были меблированные комнаты "Санремо", - тоже самое мальчишкой на лестнице, коридорным, как говорят. Чорт их знает, тащил самовар с посудой в номер, видимо запнулся и все в доску разбил. Уборщица стала ругаться, меня зло взяло, ногой поддал, все полетело, в соседнюю комнату влетел, скандал. Так что я не больше трех недель проработал и меня выставили раба божьего.

Page from the Stalingrad transcripts

GENERAL VASILY CHUIKOV

Lieutenant General Vasily Chuikov (1900–1982) is probably the best-known defender of Stalingrad. He commanded the 62nd Army as it fought from September 1942 to February 1943 against the initially far superior German forces in the city center and the industrial district to the north. At the beginning of October the 62nd held a seven-mile-wide front along the Volga. By the next month the Germans had cut through three of the narrowest sections—just over two hundred yards deep—and advanced to the river. That these dramatic events are widely known owes in good part to Chuikov's own efforts: on the fifteenth anniversary of the battle he published his first account of Stalingrad, which focused on the "legendary 62nd." Despite this memoir and the others he would soon write in rapid succession, Chuikov's interview with the Moscow historians provides a trove of new information and impressions.[1]

The interview took place on January 5, 1943, at the command post of the 62nd Army, near the Red October steelworks. (Chuikov was interviewed again in February or March 1943; parts of that interviews are also shown here.) More so than in later years, Chuikov speaks directly, colorfully, and forcefully. One detects in his mental leaps a nervous tension revealing how close the 62nd Army came to obliteration, and the severe measures Chuikov took to prevent it. He told the historians that on September 14, two days after being put in charge, he shot dead a regimental commander and commissar as their soldiers watched in line formation. The crime? The officers had abandoned their command post without permission. Soon after that, he shot two brigade commanders and their commissars for fleeing to the eastern bank of the Volga. These executions, Chuikov explained, had an immediate effect. In his memoir Chuikov spoke openly about enforcing Stalin's "not one step back" order, but thirty years on he told a different story: the cowardly officers had received nothing more than "a sharp rebuke."[2]

To begin, Chuikov talks about growing up poor in a large family and about his rapid rise in the wake of the 1917 revolution. Following the example of his older brothers, three of whom served in the revolutionary-minded Baltic Fleet, he felt instinctively drawn to the Bolsheviks, whose radicalism and relentlessness impressed him. In Petrograd he joined the armed workers militias of the Red Guards and enlisted in the Red Army immediately after it was formed in January 1918; one year later he became a member of the Bolshevik party. During the Civil War, Chuikov commanded his own regiment (he was only nineteen at the time) and took part in offensives against the White Army in the Urals and in Siberia. His superior and mentor was the divisional commander Vladimir Azin, whom Chuikov likened to the Civil War hero Vasily Chapayev: "A man of military culture, but also like Chapayev [. . .] someone who didn't mind participating in an attack himself, kicking in the face of anyone who wasn't fighting well, who would do what was needed for victory." In Chuikov's telling, the commander had a pronounced physical authority: he pulled rank by punching his inferiors in the face. Like his mentor, Chuikov had a short temper and was inclined to violence, as many of his fellow soldiers testified. But his mouthful of gold-capped teeth—which many western journalists noted on first meeting him—suggests that he had received punches in the face from his own superiors.[3]

After the end of the Civil War, Chuikov visited the Frunze Military Academy in Moscow. (His previous education had been limited to four years of primary school.) Stalin's purges in the Red Army (Chuikov does not mention them in his testimony) did much to promote his ascent. By 1939 he had been named army commander. Chuikov's biography bears the marks of a typical Soviet success story. Like many commanders in the Red Army, he grew up poor in tsarist Russia before acquiring education, respect, and authority in the Soviet system. Not surprisingly, Chuikov passes over the low points of his career, such as the ignominious end the 9th Army met under his command during the Winter War. As punishment he was transferred to China, where he served as a military attaché. In March 1942 he was recalled to serve as deputy commander of the 64th Army, a reserve unit stationed near Tula. In July 1942, the army pushed forward to the Don, where it first did battle against Germany's 6th Army. On September 8 Chuikov was made commander of the 62nd Army.[4]

In providing an account of the battle in Stalingrad, Chuikov describes the emergence of the heroic spirit in the Red Army but also seeks to exemplify it. The general portrays himself as a pivotal hero of the battle and downplays the achievements of his rivals, particularly those of Alexander Rodimtsev, the commander of the 13th Guards Division, who even then was legendary. In *Life and Fate,* Vasily Grossman depicts the infighting among Red Army commanders, each bent on obtaining the greatest accolades. He mentions an incident at the February 4, 1943, victory rally where a "drunken Chuikov leapt on Rodimtsev and tried to strangle him—merely because Nikita Khrushchev had thrown his arms around Rodimtsev and kissed him without so much as a glance at Chuikov."[5] After this incident, the NKVD reprimanded Chuikov for his "unpleasant" behavior.

An internal report from March 1943 recounts a conversation between Chuikov and his deputy for political affairs, Lieutenant General Gurov, in which they dubbed Rodimtsev a "newspaper general" who had good contacts in the press but nothing to show for himself on the battlefield. According to the NKVD informant who wrote the report, these intrigues were the reason why Rodimtsev was the only divisional commander in the 62nd Army who failed to receive a commendation for the defense of Stalingrad.[6]

Chuikov's 64th Army—renamed the 8th Guards Army in April 1943—continued to fight as it moved west, reaching Berlin in 1945. Between 1949 and 1953, Chuikov served as commander in chief of the Group of Soviet Forces in Germany, and in 1955 he was promoted to Marshal of the Soviet Union, the highest rank in the Soviet military. Chuikov later received a special form of immortality in Volgograd. In 1967, a memorial site, crowned with a monumental *Motherland Calls* statue, was erected on top of Mamayev Kurgan and dedicated on the twenty-fifth anniversary of the battle of Stalingrad. On the central axis of the memorial stands a fifty-foot sculpture of a bare-chested soldier. Though the heroic torso is that of a young man, the facial features are those of Vasily Chuikov. As stipulated in his will, Chuikov's body was buried at the feet of *Motherland Calls*.

Vasily Chuikov in Stalingrad

A.S.[7]

TRANSCRIPT
of interview with Comrade Lieutenant General Vasily Ivanovich CHUIKOV
Stalingrad, January 5, 1943
Interview conducted by scientific secretary A. A. Belkin[8]

There's a village called Serebryanye Prudy in the Tula region.[9] A peasant family, eight sons, four daughters. At that time, with these big families, you worked at home for your father until ten or twelve, and then you'd leave to work in the city.

Ours was a good family. We were quiet, as they say. There was never anything bad going on. And I did much the same as everybody else. I graduated from the village school. Then they opened a higher primary school—our village was a trading center. I studied there for a year. That was in 1912. I was born in 1900. Then I went to St. Petersburg. I had brothers there already. They were all working. They all had the lowest kind of jobs: laborers, porters, janitors. That's how I got started in Petersburg. At the Seribeyevskiye baths on Basseynaya Street. I was the errand boy at the front staircase. For wages I got five rubles a month and my meals. I lived like that for about two years. Always getting into mischief. I worked from 7:00 A.M. to 11:00 P.M.

And then, on the eve of a feast day—it was Easter, 1914—I got into trouble. We had a strict boss who happened to notice some trash on the front stairs. He came over, saw it, and fired me right then and there. I was on my knees begging him not to, there was absolutely nowhere else for me to go. I couldn't go back home to the village because there was already fifteen or sixteen people in the family, and I'd just be another mouth to feed. What was I going to do? I got another job through a guy I knew. He was a cab driver with the same last name as me—Pyotr Chuikov. He got me set up at the Sanremo boarding house on Nevsky Prospect doing the same thing as before. I was the boy on front stairs, the hall boy, as they say. God knows what I was doing, but one time I was on my way up to a room with a samovar and some dishes when I tripped and broke everything on the tray. The maid started yelling at me, and I got mad and stomped my feet. Everything went flying, and I ran out of the room. What a scene. So it wasn't more than three weeks before poor little me got sent packing again.

Then I got yet another job through people I knew. They sent me to a hotel, the so-called Moscow Yar on the corner of Svechny Lane and Yamskaya Street. You could find everything there, as they say, except for anything good. I witnessed all the vulgar debauchery that existed at that time. To tell you the truth, I got completely sick of working there, and I decided that I'd leave no matter what. But where could I go? I was still a boy, but physically I was grown up. Unless I'm mistaken, the war had already started by then. [. . .] I'm my father's fifth son. All of my older brothers were drafted into the military. Three of the four were sailors in the Baltic Fleet. That was when Romania declared war on the Germans. The autumn of 1916.[10]

I can also remember that I came back from somewhere soaked through and shivering, and I got sick. I was ill for about two months, but I kept on working. Then blood started coming from my mouth and nose. I'd always been strong and healthy, I don't know what was the matter with me then. My sister was working in Petersburg as a servant. I was just wasting away. I remember waking up at night with my mouth full of blood. I would cough and spit it up for a while, then it would happen again.

Twice I went to the doctor. I couldn't work anymore. Later I found out that my sister had written my father, saying that his boy was dying. After that I got a tearful letter from my father: Come home, there's nobody here now, all your brothers have left, you can help me out at home. As I recall, by early 1917—January—I'd left Petersburg on my last legs. I stayed sick almost all the rest of the winter. The February Revolution found me in Serebryanye Prudy.

By spring I had started to get better and could help with the work. I can't remember exactly when I was completely recovered. I got tired of living in my father's home, so I left to see my brothers in Kronstadt. I made it there. I understood a thing or two about the political situation. The summer of 1917 was a time of political demonstrations. The Left Socialist Revolutionaries[11] held a lot of sway in our village. When my brothers came home, they would tell me everything that was going on. Of course we, the young people, couldn't stand the Socialist Revolutionaries, and people nicknamed us "Bolsheviks." Considering that the Bolsheviks got the blame for anything and everything, that was the role we played. We couldn't be reasoned with. When we were all together, we were a pack of kids you didn't want to mess with. One of my brothers now manages the Sergo Ordzhonikidze machine tool factory in Moscow.

When I got to Kronstadt, I entered a completely new environment. First of all, Kronstadt was a revolutionary city. They were getting ready for October.[12] It wasn't spoken of openly or loudly, but the work was under way. I didn't want to leave, so I signed up in the same training unit as one of my brothers. I learned how to be a sailor—how to swear and eat gruel and wear wide-legged trousers. There were conversations and discussions, and from this I began to form some opinions. My brothers were not party members, but they all had Bolshevik sympathies. Three of them took part in the October Revolution. They wouldn't take me. "Where do you think you're going, kid?" they said. They were part of the group that stormed the Winter Palace, two of them[13] actually fought the cadets who had set up in there. My other brother never left his ship.

We all know how that revolutionary uprising ended. Soon after you got the sense that the old military organization was beginning to come apart. People were leaving the front, leaving the fleet, and we—I think this was in early 1918—all of us ended up in Serebryanye Prudy. We came to the home of our father, whose household now consisted of eighteen people because his older sons had gotten married. The family lived with my father, and then we show up, the scamps, and what's there for us to do? Especially since it's winter.

When I got to my village all the young people came to me. We all did a lot of thinking, but not for long. Around that time they issued the decree on the formation of the Red Army.[14] We all got together. What are we going to do now? Join the army! From our village it was me, Vasily Kuzmich Rykin, Alexei Gubarev, and Yegor Minkin. We went to Moscow. We didn't know where to go. We went up to the first person we saw in an army overcoat and asked him where the nearest military unit was. He turned out to be a good guy.

"What do you want?" he said.

"We want to join the Red Army," we said.

"Do you have documents?"

We went back to our village council[15] to get the right documents showing that we were politically trustworthy. The man recommended that we go to Lefortovo.[16]

He said: "They're putting together some sort of courses there. They might take you."

The commissar in charge of the courses was Segal, if I'm not mistaken. We went there with all our belongings. If we couldn't get work, we might as well study. He talked to us and signed us up right then. They immediately started getting us in line, took us out on walks every Sunday through Moscow to show off the armed forces of the proletariat. We looked pretty good.

Then the Left Social Revolutionaries led an uprising,[17] and we were put in to suppress it. The uprising was crushed. For me it was a baptism of fire. After a while, at the end of July, early August, we graduated. So we had about four months' training. Those were the Red Army's first military instructor courses at the former Alexeyevskaya Academy[18] in Moscow. They sent us to the front. [. . .]

[A long story about Chuikov fighting in the Civil War follows.]

I was admitted to the party in 1919 on the shores of the Vyatka.[19] It was very simple:

"Why should we take you?"

"Why wouldn't you?" And that was that.

Then I was sent on a long trip to China. After that I worked in the Special Far Eastern Army until 1933. Then I worked for a time in Moscow as the head of the Red Army's Officer Training School, until 1935, and after that I studied for another seven months at the Stalin Academy of Motorization and Mechanization. In 1936 I joined the command staff of a mechanized brigade in Bobruysk. In 1938 I was made commander of a rifle corps, then the commander of the Bobruysk Army Group, which then became the 4th Army during the move into Poland. As soon as that campaign was over, they sent me to the Finnish Front. I was leading the 9th Army toward Ukhtinsky. Then that campaign was over. And right when we got back west to the 4th Army, they sent me again to China to be Chiang Kai-shek's chief adviser. I know some English, enough to hold a conversation, and then I started learning a bit of Chinese.

The war found me still in China, and in March 1942 I came home. I was appointed commander of the 1st Reserve Army in Tula. I came here with that army on July 17. [. . .]

My first fight with the 64th Army was not a success. I'm not sure why. We got in on the 17th [of July], and on the 19th we got the order to move in and take up defensive positions, even though 10 percent of our forces hadn't arrived, and by the start of the battle we had 60 percent of our forces at most. The divisions had come two hundred kilometers from the station where they'd disembarked, and then they were going almost straight into combat. The leadership had some strange ideas, and we suffered for it. That's what happened with Gordov.[20] The 64th Army avoided the catastrophe that happened to the 62nd Army on the other shore. I got us out. People called it a chaotic retreat, but I got the army out from under enemy fire. The ones who didn't do this paid dearly, such as the 51st Army and many divisions. But I kept the 64th Army strong. We took casualties, but you can't get anything done without some casualties. I didn't want to leave the front. Whatever happens, happens. Then a group that was made up of the 64th Army and the remnants of the 51st Army was sent to Kotelnikovo.[21] We fought there. They really hit us hard. Front command misjudged the direction of the attack, even though comrade Stalin had told Gordov and everyone else that Tsimlyanskaya[22] was the enemy's main objective.

An enormous German motorized group came out of there and moved from Tsimlyanskaya toward Stalingrad. No one took the appropriate actions. Then they started getting something together to throw at them. They sent me in with my group. At first we were four divisions, then seven. We held the enemy back and made it possible for our troops to move laterally. We foiled the enemy's plan to hit Stalingrad via Kotelnikovo. We slowed them down, took out a large number of tanks and tens of thousands of infantry, especially Romanians, thereby forcing their retreat. We accomplished this primarily with fast troop movements and tough defensive actions. We managed to create a front—otherwise there would have been nothing, just an open gate. [. . .]

On September 11, I was summoned to see Yeryomenko and Khrushchev at front headquarters, where I was told that I was to take command of 62nd Army. My mission: defend Stalingrad. They told me to find out what units were there, since they themselves didn't know exactly.

The Germans were coming in from two directions. The first group was coming at the 62nd Army from the west via Kalach, just north of Spartakovka and Rynok; the second strike force was coming out of the southwest from Tsimlyanskaya and Kotelnikovo. These pincers were coming together on the 62nd Army in Stalingrad, because the 64th Army had withdrawn to Beketovka. The Germans didn't go there. I personally think their strategy was to try and take Stalingrad as quickly as possible, which would demoralize our army so much that we wouldn't know what to do. Stalingrad was important to them as a departure point for the north. Their pincers came together in the area of Karpovka-Nariman, and everything was focused on Stalingrad, where we had only the 62nd Army. The rest of our forces were outside the pincers. [. . .]

After Nikita Sergeyevich[23] told me to go to Stalingrad, he asked me: "What are your thoughts?" Yeryomenko also wanted to know. He's known me a long time. Well, what could I say? I said: "I understand my orders just fine, and I'll carry them out. I'll do what I can. I'll either keep them out of Stalingrad or die trying." There were no more questions after that. They offered me tea, but I declined, got in my car, and drove to Stalingrad.

Our command post was located on Hill 102,[24] and the enemy was three kilometers away. We had communications, telephone and radio. But they were breaking through all over the place, everywhere you looked. The divisions were so tired out and drained from the previous fighting that they couldn't be relied on. I knew I'd be getting reinforcements in three or four days, but I spent those days on pins and needles trying to scrape together enough men to produce something like a regiment to plug the gaps. The front ran from Kuporosnoye and Orlovka to Rynok.[25] The Germans' main thrust was directed at Gumrak[26] and the train station in the center of town, and the second strike was coming on the south side, against Olshanka[27] and the grain elevator.

A division. How many men? Two hundred, from various units. A brigade. How many men? They're saying three hundred. Some divisions were down to only thirty-five men. We had some artillery, not divisional artillery but an antitank regiment.

Those four days were torture, in the fullest sense of the word. The 6th Guards Brigade was completely eliminated on the 13th. Only one tank remained in working order, a T-34. The 113rd Brigade held on to about twenty tanks. They were in the south, and the 6th Guards Brigade had been on the right flank. Colonel Krichman[28] was their commander. They were a fine brigade, but they were on that right flank. There were some other brigades, but they didn't have any tanks, and the Germans were advancing.

General Vasily Chuikov (*second from left*) at his command post. To his left is his chief of staff, Nikolai Krylov; to his right is General Alexander Rodimtsev. Next to him sits divisional commissar Kuzma Gurov. *Photographer: Viktor Temin*
Chuikov's bandaged finger was, according to his son Alexander, not the result of a combat wound but of a nerve-related skin disorder that plagued him chronically in Stalingrad.[29]

When I got to army headquarters I was in a vile mood. I only saw three people: comrade Gurov,[30] chief of staff Krylov,[31] and chief of artillery Pozharsky.[32] Three of my deputies had fled to the east bank. But the main thing was that we had no dependable combat units, and we needed to hold out for three or four days. The divisions had their respective headquarters on the Volga, and we were still forward on this hill. We were in this tunnel alongside the Tsaritsa River, while all the command posts were farther back. This turned out to be the right decision. And then there's one thing that went well, if we can use such a word. We immediately began to take the harshest possible actions against cowardice. On the 14th I shot the commander and commissar of one regiment, and a short while later I shot two brigade commanders and their commissars.[33] This caught everyone off guard. We made sure news of this got to the men, especially the officers. If you go down to the Volga, they said, then you'll find army HQ right ahead of you. And so they went back to their places. If I'd gone across the Volga myself, they'd have shot me when I got ashore, and they'd have been right. The needs of the day determine what needs to be done.

We knew that we could hold out because we knew the enemy had weaknesses of his own. We had detached divisions of thirty-five men, or a group of two hundred, while the Germans rolled right into the city with tanks and other vehicles. On the 14th, when they came into the city, they were getting ready to celebrate. But these detached divisions put them in their place and pushed them back from the riverbank. They'd broken through to the crossing. What could we do? We were completely cut off, there was nowhere to run. We gathered our staff officers, and I got four tanks, and we threw everything we had at them. Rodimtsev's division arrived.[34] We had to at least clear out the landing area. We threw everything at them. The enemy got pushed back to the train station. Everyone stayed in line to the last man. We made it so two of Rodimtsev's regiments could make the crossing safely. They entered the battle from the moment they disembarked at the landing. They didn't know where they were or what was happening; they didn't know whether it was night or day. But we had a sense that the enemy was being reckless, that they were coming at us without taking any precautions whatsoever. Our divisions were small, but we kept at it, we kept cutting them down. We still had plenty of ammunition. All the ammo dumps were here.

During those three days we took out a huge number of enemy tanks. We lost a lot. They got all our guns and crews, but there was nothing we could have done. Everyone knew we had no right to pull back. And the fear of tanks goes away once you've learned how to treat them, and after a while you no longer give a damn about them. Of course there were cowards, men who ran away. But our communications were functioning, we had our liaison officers making sure that every divisional and regimental commander knew that anyone who went back to the riverbank, anyone who came close, was to be shot. The men knew that they had to fight to the last for Stalingrad, and they knew reinforcements were on their way.

The political work was conducted haphazardly, but it was appropriate to the circumstances. During such dangerous times a soldier doesn't need lectures or clever slogans. He needs to know that high command is with him, that his commander is with him. He needs to say that we must kill the Germans and that we will not cross the Volga. Among our commanders and commissars there were both brave men and cowards.

We'd been fighting for three days when Rodimtsev's division arrived, and they'd been fighting for six days in extremely difficult conditions. Sure, they didn't make any gains, but they held that line on the riverbank. The enemy got nowhere in this fighting and started to bypass us, moving toward Mamayev Kurgan. Then we were able to catch our breath. [. . .] At that time the men and officers started realizing that the Germans weren't managing to capture a damn thing, that we could fight and kill them. The men started running with the idea. Soldiers came up with their own slogans. They were starting to feel joy again.

They dropped probably around a million bombs on us, not counting artillery and mortar shells. Our communications were established and worked without interruption. Colonel Yurin was our chief of communications. Even during that brutal bombardment, when everything was exploding, flying, burning, I spoke with every commander on the telephone twice a day, or a dozen times with some of them if they were taking part in an important attack. Our command post had moved to the Barricades factory to the fuel tanks. At that time we were two kilometers from the front lines. We'd sit down to eat, and the enemy would pour down bombs, try to bomb us out. Our soup came to the table with shell fragments in it. Lebedev, a member of the Military Council, told me about a time a shell landed when he was in the latrine. Yes, you'd go into the latrine—and find corpses there.

Supplies reached us only over the Volga and only at night. Our men would go two or three days without eating. There was no way to get anything to them, no time to even think how you might do it. Here's how the wounded got out: if you get wounded, you stay put until night. You're bleeding, but you can't do anything about it because you won't make it if you crawl out of your trench, so you stay there, and tonight someone will find a way to get you out. You couldn't go five minutes without fifteen or twenty airplanes flying overhead. They never stopped bombing, never stopped shelling. Everything kept close to the ground. Their tanks crept forward, with submachine gunners right behind. Their dive-bombers came within forty or fifty meters of the ground. The enemy had a map of Stalingrad and good air-to-ground communication. Their liaisons were excellent. But our soldiers knew that the closer they were to the enemy, the better. They stopped being afraid of tanks. The infantrymen would get in a trench, ravine, or building, and start shooting the enemy infantry who were advancing behind the tanks. The tanks would move through, and we'd leave them to our artillery, which was two to three hundred meters back from the front lines and would fire when they came within twenty to fifty meters. And we didn't let their infantry through. The Germans would think that this area was already cleared, that it was dead ground. But that dead ground came back to life. And we had our Katyushas and our artillery.

The enemy threw one tank division and three rifle divisions against a single two-kilometer section of the front, and there was enough artillery preparation to make your hair stand on end. Their tanks advanced, and more than half stayed with us, disabled. There was no attack like that the next day. They were beaten, and they had some ten to fifteen thousand wounded. We sent back around 3,500 wounded, but who knows how many more stayed behind—not only on the front as a whole but just on that on that two-kilometer meat grinder.

The crossing was under constant fire. The riverbank was ironed flat. It was being shelled the whole time. Comrade Stalin sent Yeryomenko to me to find out how we were holding up. It took him two and a half days to cross over to our bank. His adjutant was wounded in the shoulder, and two cutters were sunk. They crossed at night because of all the planes. Only the cutters were going. The steamers worked at night and hid themselves before dawn, so there wasn't so much as a rowboat on the Volga. They went to Tumak[35] and Verkhnyaya Akhtuba,[36] but they still got hit there. As for our barges—who knows how many of them got sunk?

We didn't have any marine brigades, but we had sailors from the Far East who had come in as reinforcements.[37] They were good men but poorly trained. Their morale was good. You'd give one of them a submachine gun and he'd say: "First time I've seen one of these." After a day he'd know how to use it. There was no shortage of cartridges, they just had to learn what to do with them.

As for the nationalities—there were Russians, many of them from Siberia. Seventy percent were Russian, 10 percent Ukrainian, and the rest were other nationalities. The Russians are the best fighters.

The worst time during the defense of Stalingrad was after Hitler's speech, when Ribbentrop and others announced that Stalingrad was going to be taken on October 14. They took five days to prepare for this. We could feel this. We knew they were bringing in fresh tank divisions, massing new divisions on this two-kilometer section, and in advance of this they were shelling and bombing us more than ever, we could hardly breathe. We stayed in our ravine. They bombed and shelled away, started fires. They knew our army's command post was there. And so were eight fuel tanks. Every one of them was leaking. Fuel flowed down into the dugout of our chief of artillery. Everything caught fire, and it was burning for a whole kilometer along the bank of the Volga. The fire lasted three days on end. We were afraid of being suffocated or being so poisoned by fumes that the enemy would be able to take us alive. We moved to another command post closer to where the enemy would be attacking. And we stayed there. We knew that every extra meter of telephone wires increased the risk of our communications being broken. The most criminal, most dangerous thing for a commander, especially a senior commander, is when you lose control and communications. Most of all, we were afraid of losing control of our troops. I may not be able to send one of my commanders any reinforcements, but it's enough for me to grab the phone and say the right thing, that's all he needs.

I've endured plenty of bombardments and artillery preparations during my life, but I'll always remember the 14th of that month. You couldn't hear individual shells going off. No one was counting the planes. You could leave your bunker and not be able to see five meters ahead of you because of all the smoke and dust everywhere. On the 14th our army headquarters lost sixty-one people, but we still had to stay there. When the enemy launched his attack at eleven o'clock on the 14th, I already knew that we didn't have enough men, and that our only hope was that the men still left would be able to do their job. Just the day before I managed to bring up a single tank brigade, get them well camouflaged and position guards all around them. That night the enemy didn't bomb them. They didn't know we were waiting to ambush them. Our tanks knocked out three columns of enemy tanks. Then our tanks were destroyed, but the fact remains that we put a stop to their attack.

There wasn't anything tougher than that day, though we had something similar on November 11.

The attack was on the 14th, and by the 15th they weren't going to be able to make another one like it. We mobilized our entire army headquarters, our last outpost was on the front lines. We held out for three days until the 138th Division arrived.

People think that urban warfare is a matter of walking down a street and shooting. That's nonsense. The streets are empty, and the fighting is going on in the buildings, in structures and courtyards where you've got to pluck the enemy out with bayonets and grenades. For those fights our men love the Fenya, which is what they call our hand grenade. In urban combat you use hand grenades, submachine guns, bayonets, knifes, entrenching tools. You come face to face with the enemy and slash at them. The Germans couldn't hold out. They'd be on one floor, our men on another. And then there were their tanks. They brought everything they could, but we had the Volga. (Now at last we can walk along the Volga, and it's such a pleasure.)

There were no pauses in combat operations, none at all. On September 13–14 our armies came together and wrestled. We hammered each other. We knew perfectly well that Hitler was not going to stop and that he would keep throwing more and more men at us. But he could sense that this was a fight to the death, and that Stalingrad would keep fighting till the bitter end. Stalingrad was constantly under attack, and this lasted until November 20. When we began to sense they were slacking off, we immediately threw in our forces and launched counterattacks. We didn't leave them alone on Mamayev Kurgan. We attacked them dozens of times. The 37th Division went on the attack around the Tractor factory. There were deadly skirmishes all the time. Up until then we were actively on the defense. Attacking wasn't part of our mission. But our defense was an active defense. We weren't just there to withstand attacks, but to use every minute so we could attack later. Some days the fighting was fiercer, some days it was quieter, but it never stopped. Attacks were always underway. What happened on some days was beyond all imagining.

We were waiting for the enemy's attack before the November holidays. Intel had it that Hitler would be launching a new attack on Stalingrad on November 3. We readied our ammunition and our men. There was no lull in the fighting, but we were still expecting things to heat up. The intel was right. The attack came at the Barricades factory. The enemy was aiming for the north landing, hoping to cut our army in two. But then we were amazed when there wasn't more of an attack on the 3rd, 4th, 7th, and 10th. The fighting continued, but you didn't feel much pressure. Front headquarters was worried. The Germans had a huge concentration of equipment, of weaponry of all kinds. They had two divisions in reserve. We knew all this. Had they discovered we were transferring troops to the right flank? Every day Yeryomenko asked me: "What's going on over there? Have you run away from your sector?" On the 11th the enemy put in the last two divisions that had been in the reserve. We'd basically dragged them in with all our activity. Not to the 64th Army's sector, not against the Don Front, but against us in particular. We had no aerial reconnaissance, but we had some information from agents. [. . .] We got information from prisoners, from the dead, from documents—from things there's no arguing with.

And then after the 20th that enemy air activity came to a sudden halt, like they'd just been cut off, and they also put a stop to every kind of attack. This was not a time to rest. There was fighting going on somewhere, and this bothered us: "What are we going to do, sit here?" We hadn't been given reinforcements, they'd all gone to another section of the front.

This active defense—there were two stages—started on September 12–13 and finished on November 20, 1942. Then we felt that we should attack. We gradually began to capture ground we had lost. They launched massive attacks. They had a hell of a lot of firepower. None of our artillery was in a position to suppress it. With this modern automatic fire, you can crush infantry with only a small amount of manpower. Tanks couldn't move in the city because of all the mines and metal barricades everywhere. After October 14 the enemy tanks hadn't been able to operate because the terrain was too broken up. I wanted to get seven tanks over to the Red October factory. The men struggled and struggled but we couldn't get them through. Craters everywhere. The tanks would fall in and not be able to back out. Everywhere was under fire. Some buildings were burned to the ground, but tanks still couldn't get through.

We had small assault groups that started operations on November 23. Their targets were buildings, basements, factory workshops. These were small but well planned and organized groups with hand grenades. They used all kinds of weapons that I won't go into here. In particular, flamethrowers—as a defensive weapon—and high-explosive shells. We would drag them out onto the streets, set them up and detonate them. There would be a blast radius of a hundred meters, and then our infantry would move in. The Germans couldn't withstand them. Balls of thermite. The long-range artillery mostly shot at enemy firing points, and here we had mortars, antitank guns, and our hand grenades. We used them the most, and they're what worked the best.

The aim of the third stage was to make sure that the enemy forces located here would stay here and not be transferred to other sections of the front. We dragged them into the fight. It was high command's idea that they should be prevented from leaving. We achieved this. Some of their tanks got away, but the divisions we'd been fighting are all still in place, even though they've been shot to pieces. [. . .] We're smashing them. Their morale must be pretty low. We've been up against German divisions for the most part. The commander of these two armies is Paulus, a colonel general.

So: the very first stage of this battle took place beyond the Don. It was two armies fighting there for the most part, the 62nd and the 64th, against the enemy's main attacking forces. We wore them down a lot during that attack. They were already severely weakened by the time they reached Stalingrad. But there they launched aircraft form Crimea and all new forces. The main two strike forces came together near Stalingrad and were directed against the 62nd Army. The 64th Army was resting, doing nothing.

At the second stage, the stakes were total annihilation: either they'd destroy us or we'd destroy them. There was no other way. Every soldier understood that there would be no mercy, that Hitler was not going to stop. I think the enemy's losses were around three to four times higher than ours, for both tanks and infantry, not including airplanes. That was not a pretty sight. Our Stalin's Falcons[38] would only get as far as the Volga before dropping their payload. They'd fly in and drop their bombs. Sometimes they'd hit us and sometimes they'd hit Germans. And then they'd return. But sometimes we'd see several German planes attack one of ours—and that was just awful, we knew that was the end of our boys. Our air forces did good work at night. I don't know who thought up that U-2,[39] but that's one valuable invention. We called that plane the KA: king of the air. It wasn't afraid of anything. And the Germans had such respect for it. They called it death from above. You can take them down with armor-piercing bullets, but it's not so easy to hit them at all.

The third stage, which is where we are now, is to prevent the enemy from leaving, to pin them down with our artillery. On November 22 we knew that the enemy had fallen into the ring. They couldn't get out all the equipment they still had. While they were still wondering what to do, our pincers closed tight. We had sensed that our high command was preparing a major attack, but we didn't know where exactly. We had sensed this from the very beginning of November. We were being given less and less help. We'd been used to talking to people from front HQ every day, but now they'd all vanished. Khrushchev wasn't here, and Yeryomenko came only once. [. . .]

To be honest, most of the divisional commanders didn't really want to die in Stalingrad. The second something went wrong, they'd start saying: "Permit me to cross the Volga." I would yell "I'm still here" and send a telegram: "One step back and I'll shoot you!" The commander of the 112th Division got such a telegram, so did Gorokhov, Andrusenko,[40] Guryev.[41] But Rodimtsev, though he barely made it to my command post, just said: "We'll go down fighting." All the divisional commanders held on to their divisions except for Yermolkin with the 112th,[42] Andrusenko, and Tarasov.[43] Rodimtsev behaved excellently in this regard, as did Gorishny[44] and Guryev. Lyudnikov[45] fought best of all. He got sick before one attack, but at the height of the worst attack on the 11th he went back into battle even though he was sick. He didn't take one step back. Batyuk and Sokolov[46] behaved wonderfully, and Zheludev[47] did well. You pick up the phone, yell at him, and say: "What's going on?" Then he calls for the divisional commissar and gives him an earful. But I very rarely had to talk like that with Rodimtsev, Batyuk, and Guryev.

I couldn't afford not to be harsh with every one of my divisional commanders, I had to be methodical, constantly keeping tabs on them. The absolute worst thing we've had to put up with is when the staffs are lying, and the divisional commander doesn't check up on them, and they give me false reports. There was plenty of stubbornness among the divisional commanders, except for those I mentioned. Sometimes I had to take action to deal with this.

During the most dangerous time, I told Yeryomenko that everything I had was coming apart and that I was losing control. Have the Military Council stay here on the west bank, but let me move my control base across the river. Communication along the shore was breaking up, our radio wasn't working, and it was up to me to reestablish communication between the east bank and west bank, where it would connect with the front lines. I thought it necessary to move our army headquarters there, so I could lead better, and to leave the Military Council here. Then I talked to Krylov and Pozharsky: "You're going over there, and we're staying here." I spoke to them one at a time. They both replied: "I'm not going one step away from you." Rodimtsev might have said the same, Lyudnikov too, and perhaps Guryev or Batyuk. I wouldn't vouch for some of the others. If I'd said, "All right. Go across to the island," then

Divisional commander Nikolai Batyuk (*center*) and General Chuikov (*left*) in Stalingrad, January 1, 1943. *Photographer: Georgy Zelma*

they'd have said: "Thank God, he's letting us go." Some of them are younger than me, some are my age, and some are older. I didn't know them before they were sent to me here. But here you don't need a long history—relationships and bonds are forged in an instant. Every soldier who comes here understands in an instant what his tasks are, he instantly masters the job he is meant to perform. The problem is that many of them don't last long. [. . .]

I don't know the 35th [Guards] Division[48] at all. They weren't defending Stalingrad directly. Guards divisions aren't really all that different. I'm not about to say they fight any better than non-Guards units. They and the others have strengths when it comes to persistence, responsibility, their willingness to die and to defend until the last drop of blood. They also have their faults. Even in the 13th Guards there were deserters, and Rodimtsev had the most people who "voted with their feet." But at the same time, take the 84th, 138th, and 95th Divisions—none of them were Guards. Would the Guards have done any better in their place? It's hard to say. Maybe better, maybe worse.

We have many failings. First of all there's lying, which is the most detrimental thing for us. Lying and the bad leadership that comes from our commanders' not knowing what's what. They don't know something, but they pretend they do. That's good for absolutely nothing. Better to say nothing at all. They're not man enough to say they don't know. This one time I was speaking with Guryev. I respect him as a leader, but sometimes he doesn't think before he opens his mouth. We were about to launch an attack. I'd already checked everything to do with the artillery, who was in charge, how the observation and liaison was organized. I called him: "Comrade Guryev, how are things there?" He said: "Everything's fine, all's well," and so on.[49] I said: "You're lying, that's not right." And I started to lay it out to him.

"That's not possible."

"What do you mean 'not possible'? Get on the phone right now, check it out, and report back to me in half an hour."

Half an hour later he called back: "You were right."

But it's difficult to speak to someone that way if you don't have any hard facts. Usually people just tell you that they've completed this task and that task. Does that mean I should write my report right now? Just wait a minute. I'm sending my own liaisons. They'll go check on things themselves. I'll go to the divisional HQ myself, talk with them, see how the liaison officers are doing, and if they're not up to the task I get rid of them.

My own mistakes? I ought to have pulled back certain units, chosen a more defensible line. But I couldn't do that because I wasn't sure whether they'd stop at that line. That's one. The second relates to how we use our tanks. This wasn't clear then, and it still isn't clear now. There's no point in digging the tanks in and keeping them there simply as guns. You can affect a better ambush with field guns. They're smaller, easy to move, and easier to keep supplied. Tanks ought to be used as mobile groups. Light tanks haven't proven their worth. KVs[50] and T-34s should stay. Their guns and armor make the KV strong, as does their power and off-road capabilities. Aircraft now being what they are, it's impossible to camouflage tanks intended for an important offensive in such a way that the enemy can't find them. But I can't agree with turning tanks into a passive means of defense. A tank will always be a tank, an offensive weapon. Better to replace it in a defensive role with our 45mm cannon. I can drag one of them into a building or an attic, but you can't disassemble a tank, can't drag it out and put it somewhere. We had our tanks set up in the ground, but they ought to have been pulled out and made into some kind of strike force. After we remembered this, we created a few mobile reserves, and they've played their part. [. . .]

We have enough artillery. The guy inside a tank, he's behind armor, but when the bombs are coming he can feel it all that much more, and on top of that he can't see a thing. What's that for a vision slit? We can't even make him a decent vision slit. The German tanks are better in terms of visibility. Our tanks are better that the Germans' when it comes to speed and maneuverability, but they're blind.

Just understand this one thing: all of this has made an impression on our psyches, but you can't go and make generalizations based on our actions. At the same time, we wonder: Could we have done something better? I honestly don't think so. What did we overlook? Here I've got to admit that it was the factories. This is despite the fact that we had an order and the forces—we positioned special sapper units there to fortify them, though this work wasn't coordinated—and we also weren't seeing the same resilience and persistence that the Germans are showing us now. We missed it, even though we could have turned the factories into strong centers of resistance in the city. What kept the units inside the factories from doing this? No doubt it was the enemy aircraft. They were able to build well enough when the factories weren't being bombed. But when they started bombing, the machines and roofs went flying. Reinforced concrete doesn't hold up. They left the factories. Ready-made graves. Bad enough if they'd been dropping small bombs—but, as it was, we had one-ton and five-ton bombs flying around, along with armor plating and steel rails—no one can cope with that. It was mostly Messerschmitt[51] fighters dropping these bombs.

How was this typical of the fighting in Stalingrad? When an officer or soldier comes to Stalingrad and crosses to this side, he's already hardened, he knows his mission, what he's fighting for, why he came here, and what he's got to do. During the entire time we've been fighting for Stalingrad I don't think there's been a case of our units retreating or running away when they ought to have been fighting somewhere. You couldn't find such a company. You stay wherever dawn finds you because you can't move at all during the day. You'd be shot to pieces, so you stay there until dark. We fought to the last. We didn't know retreat. Hitler didn't allow for this, and that was a mistake.

People were different ages, but the bulk of them were thirty to thirty-five. There were young people, especially the sailors who came from the Far East, but there were also a lot of old ones. We screened them, but you can't do anything much on the move. For some reason every soldier understood that he couldn't leave Stalingrad. They knew that the whole country was talking about it, that Stalingrad could not surrender, that Stalingrad was defending the honor of the Soviet Union.

There were a lot of girls: communications workers, paramedics, medical assistants, doctors. They did exceptionally good work, even if you compare a woman with our soldiers. They can't do what a man can do physically, but they outdo men in terms of courage. And in their fortitude, heroism, honesty, and loyalty, not only do they not fall behind, but in many cases they outdo the men. It's true that during heated and difficult combat situations I sent all my female staff workers to the east bank and had them replaced with men, but this was only because of their physical weakness, it had nothing to do with their moral qualities. Whenever you'd go along the riverbank you'd see the work of our medical units. All of our crossings were centralized. The divisions themselves didn't transport anything. There was a mobile unit, a field hospital with surgical facilities. During the fighting we had a working surgical laboratory. One doctor has done two hundred complex operations. And take a look at these so-called nurses. Incredible! They're buried in dust, but they just keep plugging away. I could tell you so many examples of how well these women worked. Looking at percentages, women receive more orders and medals when compared with the men, especially the medical workers. I can't think of a single woman who's been to Stalingrad and hasn't been decorated, and if there is one, she won't stay that way for long.

The peculiarities of the fighting in Stalingrad, in terms of city defense and attacking whole cities, can all be applied to all combat situations. Any populated area can be turned into a fortress and can grind down the enemy ten times better than a garrison.

Ambition is still there, but it's not talked about much.

We don't have heroes who aren't afraid of anything. No one sees or knows what Chuikov does when he's by himself, when there's no witnesses, nobody to see him, to see what's going on in his head. The idea that a commander would go to his subordinates and bare his poor little soul—you could find them, but they're the rejects and failures. We're in a bunker, and shell fragments are flying at us. But what, you just sit there, and that doesn't get to you? I don't believe it. The survival instinct is still there, but a man's pride—an officer's especially—is of vital importance in combat. Lev Tolstoy was right about that.

Here's an example. Shells are flying, whistling, buzzing around—and then there's a hit. Not everyone has the courage not to duck down when a shell's coming. But ducking's not going to protect my head or chest from a shell, so I'm no better off if I duck. Nevertheless, people do it. But my pride doesn't permit this. I never do it. It would be completely different if I were on my own, but I'm never on my own. I don't duck for shells, and I stake my life on that.

Take, for instance, the title of Guards unit, or the honorary titles given to our heroes, the insignia: Don't you think Stalin takes that into account? Grossman puts it this way. You've got some hard-hearted people: a battalion commander who's been fighting all the time. He gets sent on a course, and then someone comes to say good-bye: "Comrade commander, permit me to say farewell. I've given my all." "Oh, so you have. All right then." I told Grossman: That is a valuable commander. In other circumstances they might be all tears and kisses, but here you shouldn't display any weakness. A commander sees thousands of men die, but this can't faze him. He can cry about it when he's alone. Your best friend can get killed here, but you've got to stand there like a rock.[52]

Here's another example. On the 14th [of October] the bunker of the artillery section was destroyed. Nine men were buried, one jumped out, but his legs were stuck. It took two days to dig him out. He was alive. They'd dig, but then the dirt would fall in on him again. It just kills you to see that. But you can't let on that it does.

Or take this. Four men are in a pipe. They're surrounded by eight Fritzes. One of them, wounded, crawls his way through the pipe with a message: open fire on us. We open fire, and the soldiers die along with the Germans. Think that's easy?

If the Germans had taken into account the psychological element, the political factor, the importance that Stalingrad has to every man and officer who comes here, who's gone beyond the point of no return, if they'd taken into account that it wasn't all haphazard and rushed, then they wouldn't have gotten themselves into such a mess.

It was impossible, in Stalingrad, to conduct any strategic or tactical maneuver. All we could do was just sit there. There was no opportunity for any kind of Napoleonic brilliance.

[Second interview]

[. . .] At one point I was livid with our journalists and writers, who seemed to be baiting Hitler on purpose: Stalingrad won't be taken, Stalingrad won't be taken. But the enemy was hitting us harder and harder, and we were sick of it. It's terrible having to take all that. The foreign press, too: Stalingrad won't be taken. A better prize for Hitler! Even without that he was tearing his way in, and now he was being encouraged, he kept hitting us, throwing in fresh troops, and I couldn't get reinforcements. [. . .]

October was the worst time for us in terms of enemy offensive operations. That was when Hitler promised everyone and anyone that Stalingrad would be taken. He really did throw everything at us that they had us on the front. Two, two and a half thousand airplanes were circling not just Stalingrad, but the entire army. They bombed us day in and day out. Mortar and artillery fire never stopped.

What does a thousand airplanes mean? There wasn't a single five-minute stretch when you didn't have twelve, eighteen, thirty airplanes overhead. And they kept dropping more and more bombs. It happened so much that when someone brought you your soup you'd have to scoop the shell fragments out with your spoon. You'd see bits of bombs or stone, they'd landed in the soup on its way to you from the canteen.

In early November the absolute worst thing was the Volga. It was starting to ice up, but the river was still flowing. There was no regular river transport. The armored cutters couldn't get through. In other words, we weren't getting supplies. The planes could only drop supplies at night because they couldn't come out during the day. They were making drops for three days. This was tough for the pilots because our strip of land was so narrow. Sometimes what they dropped would hit the bank, sometimes it would go to the enemy, sometimes to us. They'd fly right up to us and yell: "Hey, where do you want it?" The U-2s were just excellent. We were worn down, nearly out of ammunition. We had limited supplies, limited amounts of food. Got to our last cartridge, despaired, but kept fighting. At that time there we had some stubborn hand-to-hand combat. I think the photographers captured some images. I should say that some of the photographers (this one in particular) didn't hesitate to come with me up to the front lines to take pictures of the fighting twenty-five meters away. We've got an image of our soldiers sticking bayonets into the Germans—that's as real as it gets. No touch-ups there. The battle's raging, and they're capturing it. It's happening right here, and they're getting it on film.

Those were the most difficult days of all. We had a few tons of chocolate in store, and I thought, if we get a bar and some water to every soldier, we'll live through this. We were much more concerned about ammunition. They started bringing things in from Moscow, uniforms and food. To hell with that. I said: "Get me some ammunition, I'm not about to start fighting with socks!" But we eventually got through all that. Not many in the army have gotten frostbitten. We haven't been starving. Not too much in the way of lice. Just now the 64th has had some typhus, but in the 62nd we've only had six suspected cases. Three times a month my men have been going to the baths, the steam baths. They go, hit one another with twigs, feel healthier. All of this is at the riverbank. The bombs are coming, but you're there getting cleaned up, feeling healthy. It's true we went more than a month without the baths, but then we set up several dozen, maybe a hundred. The men are taking baths ten times a month.

We haven't lost control the entire time. We've known pretty well what the enemy is planning to do. Since we know his plans, we can make countermeasures in time. What countermeasures?

We make observations or find out from prisoners that the enemy is going to hit us hard at some location. They're moving in their forces, dragging out their artillery, infantry, tanks, ammunition. We had a group of German forces in an area of about three to four square kilometers. With such a tight concentration of forces, you've just got to attack. You wait until the enemy is nearly ready, and then a few hours before their attack you open fire with your artillery, Katyushas, mortars. For an hour, or two or three, we give them hell. And we watch them, as if it were a movie, we watch their ammunition explode, their vehicles, we see their arms and legs go flying. Nothing remains of that elegant order they wanted to create. We've shattered it. Then they try to put things back in order. We nearly didn't bother counting up their losses. We would just report that the enemy took a loss directly in front of our front line. We really got the better of them with that countermeasure. In some ten to fifteen minutes we shot thousands of shells on that concentrated force. We learned of the results from the prisoners we took. When they start to describe our artillery raid, our operations, you feel a rush of pride. The prisoners say that their hair stood on end, that they sensed they wouldn't be able to take Stalingrad. They were devastated, and taking heavy losses. There was nothing they could do in Stalingrad, because the people defending it weren't people, but some kind of wild animal. "Well," I thought, "good luck to you all!"

Hitler didn't count on the fact that we would resist. When our men entered the city, when scores and hundreds of Germans started to surrender, this boosted our morale. Our men saw that we could hit the Germans and hit them hard. That's the first factor.

The second factor was the orders, and then our propaganda: you can die, but you can't retreat. There's nowhere to fall back to: Stalingrad will decide the fate of the motherland. The men understood this. The men were in such a mood that if they'd been wounded, even with a broken spine, they had tears in their eyes as they were being taken to the east bank. They'd say to their comrades who had brought them out: I don't want to go. Better to be buried here. They considered it shameful to go wounded to the other bank. This echoed comrade Stalin's order.

The third factor was the merciless treatment of cowards and panickers. On September 14 the commissar and commander of the 40th Regiment left their regiment and ran. They were shot right then and there in front of the whole army. Two brigades ran off to the east bank and evaded me for several days. I found them and had their officers and commissars shot. The order was passed through all the units: There will be absolutely no mercy for cowards and traitors.

The fourth factor was that you could look at the Volga and see it was damn difficult to get back across. That's a purely geographical factor.

There were foreign correspondents who were always digging for information: Which units are here? Where are they from? They asked: Are these the Siberian units? I said they were nothing of the sort:

they're Russians, Ukrainians, Uzbeks, Tatars, Kazakhs, and so on. That was the truth. There were people representing all nationalities. There weren't any special or elite units that were created just for Stalingrad. Obviously Russians were in the majority because there's a larger Russian population. The best fighters we have are the Russians, then the Ukrainians, and even the Uzbeks, who'd never fought before.

They did cry a bit on the first and second day, but the situation forced them to follow the example of the Russian and Ukrainians and to fight and die with them. The soldiers had an exceptionally high level of political consciousness.

We'd lie down dead there, but we wouldn't retreat. If it came to it you'd put a bullet in your head. We decided that unless there was an order from above, we wouldn't leave for any reason. In this regard I can attest that the Military Council did not leave, and, if they had, no others would have followed them.

Did we feel we had the assistance and support of Moscow?

What does it mean when N. S. Khrushchev calls on the phone? And he called very often. We know who N. S. Khrushchev is. A member of the Politburo and the Central Committee, someone who can speak directly with comrade Stalin. He didn't pronounce Stalin's name, but the fact that he often called to ask how things are going, how we're feeling—that has meant a lot to us.

"We're fine, not too bad."

"Good, I've got a lot riding on you."

Yeryomenko came here. It took him over two days just to get across the Volga to speak with me. The Volga was boiling and burning, but nevertheless he came over on some sort of cutter. We're old friends.

"Comrade Stalin told me to check in on you, see how you're doing, see what you need." [53]

Things were bad in terms of ammunition and other supplies. There was no supply operation, and we were low on shells. He sent a telegram to Moscow, and the reply came back in a flash, and we could immediately feel the material support. The supply of ammunition and shells meant everything to us. There was aid not only on a material level. If there was something or someone you needed, you always went through Moscow. I only rarely resorted to this, but resort I did.

The wounded were evacuated to the other side. "We're bleeding to death," I wrote to Moscow. "We don't mind dying, and we're fighting bravely. Stalingrad is holding out, so send us more men!"

And they did. They wrote to me directly at my command post.

"Why hasn't Chuikov been given this and that, send him this and that."

We got the papers regularly. A soldier, naturally, is flattered when he reads the pages of central newspapers like *Pravda* and *Izvestiya*, where from the lead article to the very last page they're always writing: "Stalingrad, Stalingrad."

My chief deputy of the medical administration once told me he'd seen a badly wounded soldier. He asked him where he was from and where he was going. The wounded man thumped himself on the chest and said:

"62nd Army. I've been wounded three times, but I'll get better and get back for sure."

We were getting so many parcels from all corners of the Soviet Union. We somehow managed to present these gifts to the men: a few apples, a piece of sausage. But the best soldiers, the ones who really distinguished themselves, they were always getting things. [. . .]

Here's what my wife wrote me: "I know that you're in Stalingrad. It's dangerous there, but I take pride in this struggle for Stalingrad. It looks like it's a duel with the Führer. Hit him hard so his tongue sticks out like it does in the picture (see page 291)." And what do you think people wrote to the soldiers? What did people write to the officers?

With regard to the country as a whole, to Moscow, to the high command, or comrade Stalin himself, I don't have a bad word to say. We felt that we were doomed because we were physically cut off from everything. We felt the full weight of the situation. We felt that we were ready to die if it came to that. But we never felt forgotten or unappreciated. Of course we knew that no one could write openly about the defenders of Stalingrad, that no one could name names. These were military secrets. But when the People's Commissariat of Defense issued a resolution in which the 62nd Army was singled out, every one of our men held his head high and walked with a spring in his step.

In 1943, with comrade Stalin's permission, I took a plane to see my family in Kuybyshev. It coincided exactly with the celebration of the anniversary of the Red Army on February 23. I was invited to the theater. They persuaded me to give a short speech. Marshal of the Soviet Union B. M. Shaposhnikov[54] was there. Many people spoke, and they were greeted cordially, but when the last of them gave me the floor, I stood there like an idiot for five minutes. Every time I opened my mouth, they'd interrupt with applause. I could sense how well they understood our situation and our struggle. . . .

N. A. Dolgorukov, "As it was . . . so it will be!" Soviet propaganda poster from 1941.

GUARDS DIVISION GENERAL ALEXANDER RODIMTSEV

When the battle of Stalingrad began, Vasily Chuikov had yet to make a name for himself. This was in contrast to the lower-ranking and five-year-younger

Alexander Rodimtsev, who was already a highly decorated war hero. Like Chuikov, Rodimtsev stemmed from a peasant family and a childhood shaped by poverty before entering the Red Army at the age of twenty-two and joining the party two years later. Rodimtsev followed an officer's career path and rose quickly through the ranks. In 1936 he was sent to train the International Brigades in Spain. Under his command, the troops scored multiple victories over fascist forces, though he was unable to prevent the collapse of the Spanish Republic and the rise of Franco. On returning from Spain, Rodimtsev received the title Hero of the Soviet Union, the highest distinction in the Soviet Union.

In 1939 Rodimtsev delivered the welcoming address at the Eighteenth National Congress of the Communist party. (That a thirty-four-year-old colonel was selected to give this talk testifies to the large swath that Stalin's purges had cleared among the generals in the previous two years.) In September 1939 Rodimtsev took part in the Soviet invasion of Poland and then in the Winter War in Finland. In the war against Germany he commanded an airborne brigade that broke free from a Wehrmacht encirclement near Kiev. In November 1941 the brigade was expanded into the 87th Rifle Division and received Guards status in January 1942, becoming the 13th Guards Rifle Division.

On September 9, 1942, the division was removed from reserve status and arrived at the Stalingrad Front on September 14. The first battalions of the 10,000-man division crossed the Volga late on the 14th and early on the 15th. They became embroiled in fighting with the Germans as soon as they reached the western banks.[55] By the end of the next week Vasily Grossman had written an article on the 13th Guards Division in Stalingrad. The battle would decide "the fate of the world" and answer the "question of all questions." Grossman portrayed Rodimtsev, since promoted to major general, as the battle's linchpin: "Temperament, strong will, composure, quick reaction, the ability to advance when no one else would even dream of an attack, tactical experience and caution combined with tactical and personal fearlessness—these are the traits of a young general's military character. And the general's character became the character of his division." Grossman asked Rodimtsev whether "he was exhausted by the round-the-clock tension of combat, the round-the-clock thunder of the hundreds of German attacks that had taken place last day, last night, and would continue tomorrow. 'I am calm,' he said, 'this is the way it has to be. I have probably seen it all: how my command post was pounded by a German tank and then a German machine gunner threw in a grenade just to be sure. I threw it out. So here I am, fighting, and will go on fighting till the last hour of the war.' He said it calmly, in a low voice. Then he began asking about Moscow. We actually talked about the current theater season."[56]

Just as Grossman described him, Rodimtsev shows restraint in his interview with the Moscow historians (unlike the hot-tempered Chuikov). He talks cautiously and primarily keeps to the events of the battle, spending most of his time on the September attempt to take Mamayev Kurgan and the storming of the German-fortified "L-shaped house" in early December. Rodimtsev emphasizes the importance of the careful planning and coordination between his regiments for their success and stresses his own military skill. He makes no secret of the heavy losses sustained by his division. By early October, over four thousand men were dead or injured. He mentions that when he ordered the storming of the L-shaped house some of his soldiers—all Uzbeks, he notes—remained on the ground and afterward were shot for their cowardice.

Rodimtsev does not address the defense of the so-called Pavlov House. Only years later did Soviet politicians hype this episode as a grand story of the spirit of Soviet internationalism.[57] Led by Sergeant Yakov Pavlov and Lieutenant Ivan Afanassyev, two dozen Red Army soldiers entrenched themselves in a four-story residential building set off from the street. The soldiers represented up to eleven different Soviet ethnic groups (the accounts vary)—Russians, Belarusians, Ukrainians, Uzbeks, Kalmyks, and others. For almost two months they staved off the German onslaught before troops from the Soviet counteroffensive came to their aid on November 24.[58] In his memoir, published in 1969, Rodimtsev devoted an entire chapter to the Pavlov House; the storming of the L-shaped house received only two pages. The memoir vaunts the soldiers' heroism and the harmonious relations and omits the violence among the ranks and the losses they sustained in combat.[59]

After Stalingrad the 13th Guards Division fought ceaselessly. As before, the division had the task of building bridgeheads, first crossing the Dnieper, then the Vistula, the Oder, and the Neisse. After traversing the Oder in January 1945, Rodimtsev (by then a lieutenant general) was honored as Hero of the Soviet Union for the second time. After the war he worked as a general inspector of Soviet forces and was elected deputy of the Supreme Soviet. Rodimtsev died in Moscow in 1977. Today his daughter Natalya directs a school museum in Moscow devoted to the Great Patriotic War.

TRANSCRIPT
of interview conducted with Major General Alexander Ilyich RODIMTSEV
Commander of the 13th Guards Rifle Division
January 7, 1943
Stalingrad
Interview conducted by scientific secretary A. A. Belkin
Recorded by stenographer A. I. Shamshina[60]

I was born on March 8, 1905, in the village of Sharlyk,[61] in the Chkalov region—formerly the Orenburg region—to a family of poor peasants. Three of my sisters are there now. The youngest of them is forty, the middle one's fifty, and the oldest is sixty. I'm the youngest. Our father died in 1919, our mother in 1929. I was raised mostly by my mother, and then I took care of myself.

I went to the parish school until 1917, then to the upper primary school for two years, until 1919. We had a small patch of land. Then I apprenticed as a shoemaker. One of my sisters went to school, the others got married. Me, my sister, and my mother lived with my sister's husband. I made shoes from 1921 to 1922. 1921 was the year of the famine,[62] and when there was nothing left to eat I started driving a cart.

My mother always said I would come to a bad end. I got into a lot of mischief. She was always crying because I couldn't keep from misbehaving at school. Our teacher kicked me out seven times. I was strong, and I beat up the other kids. We lived right next door to some kulaks,[63] and I was always fighting with the boys. First they'd send out the little ones, then the ones with beards. But these were all clean fights—if they hadn't been, we'd have been up before the community court.

Me and my sister went to school together. She was a serious student. The second she got home she'd be doing her homework. I paid attention in class, but that was it. Never got around to buying slates. The school was around four kilometers away from our street, which was called Otorvanka. It's strange to think, but I didn't have any proper shoes. I never wore boots or anything like that, I just had my bast shoes. Those things wear out quickly. I can remember my teacher always giving me twenty or thirty kopeks so I could buy new ones.

I did all right at school. When I got home, I usually played checkers. We were also very serious about horse riding. I rode horses from a young age, spent fourteen years in the cavalry, then served as a paratrooper, and then I was in the air force.

This one time I was invited to a Komsomol meeting, but when I got there it was just middle peasants and kulaks. This girl ran me out of there and I never went back. I'm extremely sensitive—someone picks on me and I'm not showing up again. It was only after I was in the army that I became a Komsomol member.

In 1921 I started to learn tailoring, shoemaking. In short, I was an apprentice. We had someone from the village, a wealthy man named Lapshin. He had five or six workers, and I also worked for him. I learned the trades, and I got only a scrap of bread, nothing more, no wages of any kind. That went on until 1927. In 1927 I was drafted into the army. Strangely enough, before 1927 I'd never seen a railroad, couldn't even imagine what it was like. I'd heard people talk about it. My brother-in-law, an old soldier, talked about his time in the army, told me how big Moscow was, how there was a Kremlin, and the tsar-bell, the tsar-cannon. It came as quite a shock when I ended up at the Kremlin myself for three years of training.

In 1927 I was drafted into the army and sent to an escort unit in Saratov. I was a regular soldier at first, then a junior officer. This is where I joined the Komsomol. I was chosen by the leader of the company Komsomol organization. Then, as soon as I finished training as a junior officer, I went to the Federal Military Academy at the Kremlin.[64] I was very disappointed at not getting into the cavalry because I loved horses. That was all I cared about. But for some reason the commission didn't take me. Later, after I'd been serving for some time, I wanted to fulfil my dream, to do what I wanted to do.

I was at the academy from early 1929 to late 1931—three years. They took us to Khodynka[65] for the first time, where we were examined. I got an A in math but a D in Russian, because of our unusual dialect. When I went home in 1937 they said something like: "Our Sanka's come home!" Because the dialect was so ingrained I ended up making mistakes when I wrote. I got B's in all my other subjects. I liked gymnastics—the horizontal bar, parallel bars, the pommel horse. I was an amateur athlete, and since I was in good shape I did pretty well. Also did well with military subjects. For three years I stood watch at Lenin's Tomb, the Borovitsky Gates, the Spassky Gates.[66] Then I was admitted to the cavalry school. When we started doing horsemanship drills and jumping, I showed the class what I could do, but the commission decided that my Russian language scores weren't good enough. I said that was nonsense,

I was doing just fine. The squadron commander went to them and said: This guy knows how to ride a horse. I'd started pasturing horses at night by six or seven, and I'd been racing them since I was ten. There was this kulak who had good horses, and they'd put kids in the races, and whoever's horse won would get a sheep.

That was 1927. After that we started training. I finished near the top of my class. I was the deputy cadet commander. Each platoon was led by a cadet commander. I was his assistant for the combat unit, since I'd always been one of the top students. I did well in science: math, physics. History too, and political science. I could quote pages of Lenin word for word, and I still haven't lost all that much. Fiction didn't really interest me. I only developed an interest in that after finishing school. It was only then that I started to read. I was an avid reader of Tolstoy. I've read *War and Peace* three times. I've read *Anna Karenina*, *Resurrection*. In *Anna Karenina*, when Vronsky falls from his horse, I thought: I've raced at the hippodrome. And when there's that obstacle, and his horse falls—I feel for him, and I've come to love the story so much more because I'm a cavalryman too. In *War and Peace* I enjoy reading about the people themselves. But if you look at the way things are now, of course, it's all completely different. Any one of our men is a lot better than heroes from back then. Suvorov was a good man for his time. He had a personal heroism: he picked up his blade and his lance and went forward. Now there's plenty of people like that, and even that's not enough: we've got to organize the battle. Back then there wasn't any kind of coordination. The job of their highest leader was the same as that of a commander of a platoon, a company, a battalion. And now you've even got to be yelling at battalion commanders. [. . .]

[Left out is a longer description of Rodimtsev's experiences in the Spanish Civil War. "That's where I first got a chance to shoot fascists."]

But I was still homesick for Russia when I was in Spain. When I crossed the frontier, I stood on my native soil and said: Yes, now I am in Russia. I never thought I'd be leaving. It was extremely difficult there. We're in a difficult situation now, of course, but the equipment is all the same. There were Messerschmitts. Madrid was destroyed. Not like Stalingrad, of course, but it was still bad. You could see shells landing in the streets. It's true the population didn't get evacuated. In the morning everyone would move out to the field, into dugouts and holes. The people there played a very active role. It was all very democratic. Our people think: Oh, maybe I'll just stay here.

I'm very much against changing into civilian clothing. There was a general who changed out of his uniform and left the encirclement. When he came back, they gave him his army. The instinct for self-preservation is so strong that it supersedes everything. There is nothing else. But there was none of that in my division. One time when I found myself surrounded, the secretary of the party commission changed clothes, and so did the head of operations. I kicked them out of my division right then, brought the brigade together, and announced that these people were no longer with us. There was some criticism over this. They said there might come a time when I would have to do that, but I said that so long as I have any self-respect I would not get down on my knees for anyone, nor would I change out of uniform. It's disgraceful for a military man. I wrote an article about Russian honor—it's going to be in *Red Star*—about the honor of war, about how a warrior should behave, regardless of the situation.[67]

I got back from Spain in 1937 and took some time to relax. I'd been traveling for twenty-five days. I went to the Paris Exposition,[68] saw the delights of Paris, saw how the people lived, what sorts of theaters they had, how the girls behaved. The Moscow Art Theater was there with its actors—the people were interested in this too, to see what it was like. Paris is a nice, very cheerful place. The exposition was there, all lit up. It was extraordinary. Night was like day. I only spent a day in Berlin. Paris is cleaner. Berlin has a sort of dark look to it, all factories and gloom, covered in soot, like Leningrad, especially in the industrial areas. [. . .]

After my time off I was made the commander of the 61st Regiment, where I'd started out as a platoon commander. The previous commander was shot in 1937. Whether he was an enemy or not, I'm not entirely sure. By the time I got to the division nearly everyone had been removed. I started leading the regiment. I was in command for about eight months before leaving for the Frunze Academy.[69] I graduated with perfect scores, a colonel. I'd been a colonel since 1937. I graduated in 1940, after which I was appointed deputy commander of the 36th Division, the same division as my regiment. For about eight months I was a deputy divisional commander on the Finnish Front. The divisional commander often went away—he got sick—so I was often the de facto commander of the division. There I found myself in combat. The cavalry corps had just got there, and on the 12th we were meant to attack Helsinki, cross the Gulf of Finland, and then all of a sudden there was peace.

Before the war they started recruiting for the air forces. Officers and generals were taken from large divisions and sent to the operations faculty. They needed skilled personnel, officers that were not only good pilots but also good tacticians. [. . .] I started flying U-2s. Then we were brought into the airborne forces, and I was made commander of the 5th Airborne Brigade, then the 6th Airborne Brigade. Before the war we were in Pervomaysk,[70] where we were renamed the 3rd Airborne Corps.

In Pervomaysk—when we were still an airborne brigade—we were deployed to Kiev. The enemy had broken through and was threatening Kiev. We got there by train, disembarked, and spent fifteen to twenty days in the area of Darnitsa and Brovary. Then my brigade was moved to Ivankovo. The 5th Army and 26th Corps were there. The enemy broke through. It hadn't yet been decided to use us as infantry. We were all outfitted with automatic weapons—small arms suited to fighting behind enemy lines.

When the enemy got to Stalinka[71] and broke through the front line, Stalin gave us an order: Do not lose Kiev. Our brigades were sent in unit by unit. When I got to Kiev, the 6th and 12th Brigades were already fighting. We joined the battle on August 8, 1941. In fifteen days we pushed them back fifteen kilometers. We fought there for another ten days or so. We were thanked by the government and by the Ukrainian Council of People's Commissars. The Ukrainians had reason to be grateful to me. [. . .]

I was marching on Kharkov. We stopped four kilometers out. The whole division came out, but we took a beating at Peremoga. Then I fought with the 62nd [Army] at the Don. I went in September, on the 14th. I went with this division, though they were already at full strength. All the commanders were still there. That was the 87th Rifle Division. Later they were named the 13th Guards. Their anniversary's on January 19. Things went well for me there too. I had exceptionally good people, all of them from the academies. They all came out as mid-ranking officers. I had ten thousand men under my command. A decent division, with exceptional people, all of them trained. Golikov,[72] the deputy commander of the Western Front, watched as I led my division.

I got my artillery before the 13th [of September]. On September 13 we got our other weapons right on this spot.[73] Front commander Yeryomenko really helped me out there. There were only about two thousand submachine guns. The division was fitted out for the most part. The enemy was already here on the night of the 14th. If I'd been a day later, there wouldn't be a Stalingrad. [. . .]

I've been in worse conditions than in Stalingrad. Here I stayed in a bunker inside a tunnel. There was so little oxygen that matches wouldn't stay lit, but I stayed in that bunker. They threw grenades at our command post, but I figured they wouldn't get to me in my bunker. But back at

Konotop, out in the field, when that tank started coming right for my bunker—that's a whole different thing. After that I was at the command post in a forest. This plane attacked us twenty-seven times, always attacking my command post. All the trees were gone, and there were only two of us left from the bunker. Most of the commanders didn't make it. They were literally jumping out from under tanks, firing as they tried to run away. When I returned to the battalion still alive, I got back to organizing my troops.

It was the same in Kazatskaya, when a secretary of the divisional party committee changed his clothes. I was walking in some bushes, and there was an enemy tank nearby, but it couldn't get me with either its main gun or machine gun. I lay down on the ground when they started throwing grenades. I was with my adjutant and the Special Department representative. They ran off and then came back to me. The men were fighting in an organized manner. The enemy had us surrounded and wanted to take us alive. But an airborne soldier is like this: you give him the order, and he fights. Tanks without people don't do anything, and our infantry was cut off. We were a hair's breadth from being killed. I got myself and my men out of there. That was the one time I was in the encirclement.

And then—Stalingrad.

The enemy was headed straight for the city. Then, when they were taking heavy losses and realized they couldn't get past us, they turned from Orlovka and moved on the factories. It was difficult there as well. My situation improved when we began to bring in fresh divisions.

On September 10 I was already in Kamyshkin when I got an order saying we were going to be trucked over to Srednyaya Akhtuba. Our division still hadn't been equipped, but we were supposed to get weapons soon. I objected, said I wouldn't go without weapons. There were times when my men had been unarmed, and we had had to take weapons off deserters. I was called to the direct line. I had a talk with Vasilievsky. He ordered me go there first and then get my weapons. Stalingrad, he said, was in a difficult situation. We arrived in Srednyaya Akhtuba on the 12th. The weapons still hadn't arrived. We'd been issued some of them, but more than half of my men were still unarmed. On the 12th I reported my situation to front commander Yeryomenko. When I told him all we had was six hundred rifles, he was outraged.

"We need you in Stalingrad right away, right this second. The enemy had broken through and small groups have already entered the city."

I said: "I can't, my men need guns."

"What do you need?"

"Submachine guns."

He gave me 450 (?) submachine guns, twenty heavy machine guns, fifty light machine guns, and about forty antitank rifles. I got all of this on the 12th, got it to the men, and by the night of the 13th the rest of our weapons arrived. On the 13th we were all armed, but we still hadn't been given cartridges or ammunition. We already had our artillery, but that was to stay on the east side of the river. It was impossible to bring it over. There were no tanks.

On the 14th we got the order to cross the Volga and join the 62nd Army, which was under the command of General Chuikov and Military Council member Gurov. We didn't know what the situation was. They gave me a task: I had to send one regiment over at crossing no. 62, and the other two at the central crossing. The first regiment—the 39th—was to take Hill 102, and the other two—the 42nd and 34th—were to cross at the central crossing and clear out the area along the Tsaritsa. One battalion was turned over to the commander of the 62nd Army.

What was the point of giving him that battalion? I think it was to provide security for their headquarters, which was also inside the enemy encirclement.

Yeryomenko had everyone cross to the other side at night, including me and my staff. I had absolutely no idea of the real situation. I had no idea that the enemy had already reached the riverbank. But in the first two waves 1st and 2nd Battalions had to be left to establish a beachhead. We heard that the enemy was on the shore, that the battalion had already engaged them, fighting from the moment they reached dry land. I realized we had to move faster. We were literally giving out ammunition on the barges. The 42nd Regiment embarked right away, around 1,500 men. The engineer started turning some lever back and forth—nothing. The enemy was already shooting at us, with machine guns and artillery. The engineer lost his nerve. We had to shoot him and put someone else in his place. We got back under way. The commander of the 42nd Regiment, Colonel Yelin, made it across. He was the first to lead his regiment in battle.

In the morning I could see that we needed to get the entire division across. I called to get permission from Yeryomenko. That day our headquarters staff made the crossing aboard a cutter. That was about 10:00 A.M. We came under heavy enemy fire, and Colonel Uzky, the chief of our engineering team, was wounded by a mortar. But we got across. The Stalingrad regional NKVD had some men there. They had

A boat full of Red Army soldiers sinks in the Volga, Stalingrad, 1942.

a tunnel. I put my command post there because they had a direct line with Yeryomenko. We had no contact of any kind with Chuikov. That day another barge tried to cross after mine but was hit by enemy fire and sank.

We had aircraft, but they weren't doing very much. Then I crossed, got a sense of the situation, gave the regiments their orders, and went into the attack. Throughout the 14th and most of the 15th I had no contact with Chuikov. Toward the end of the day on the 15th I got to the railroad and took the train station with some losses. Chuikov summoned me. I reached him around 5:00 P.M. On my way there I got a lot of trouble from the planes. I got there, reported that our men had made it, explained our current position. He gave me my objective, and from that moment on we stayed in touch. From then on we remained in contact with high command. [. . .]

The enemy launched a counterattack on the morning of the 17th. After heavy preparation from the air, some forty tanks and about two thousand infantry attacked Hill 102. All those attacks were repelled, and Mamayev Kurgan remained ours through the 17th. The regiment withstood more than eight hundred German air attacks. Dolgov was the regimental commander. I wasn't in contact with that regiment. They were in contact with Chuikov's deputy at the command post at Crossing no. 62 and were getting their orders independently.

The 17th saw still fiercer fighting. There was no question of us organizing any serious attack, of allocating specific forces toward a specific objective. Throughout the 17th we simply swapped the same streets and buildings back and forth. This continued through the 18th, 19th, and 20th.

On the 20th I got a report saying that the enemy had set the train station on fire. The men we had there had given it up and moved to the Communist Grove by Station Square, where they dug in. I can't remember the exact date, but at some point the 92nd Brigade arrived. They were sent to the left flank toward the grain elevator. They were tasked with clearing out the small groups of Germans who had infiltrated the area, and to reinforce their positions there. [. . .]

This building belongs to us, then it's theirs, then it's ours again—it's impossible to say exactly where the front lines are. We lacked any experience with urban warfare. Our weak point, at the very beginning, was our failure to grasp that the enemy had already occupied Stalingrad. We should have prepared ourselves better for urban warfare. We should have assigned specific streets and buildings to specific groups, rather than task them with engaging some division along some line. The Germans were, at this time, in a stronger position. They had been quick to take the House of Specialists and the State bank, and they were still holding on to them. Our men were only thirty meters away, but no matter what I did, I just couldn't retake these buildings. I could have done it at the very beginning, but I didn't want to incur unnecessary losses. I thought I'd get to the railroad and cut them off, then I'd get my reinforcements as scheduled, and then I'd establish a base that would make it impossible for them to hold out. But it all went topsy-turvy. When things got difficult for them, the units to my left retreated to the east bank. That division's commander and commissar were shot.[74] So my left flank, my immediate neighbor, was the enemy.

Up to the 22nd this back-and-forth fighting went on day and night: this building or street is theirs, then it's ours. So assault groups were set up and sent out methodically, so we knew who was supposed to go where. We managed the battle by giving each unit its own street.

[. . .] On the morning of the 20th, at around ten o'clock, the enemy went on the offensive, crushed our forward line, knocked out six guns, and captured the Ninth of January Square. There they took out a few antitank rifles and moved onto Artillery Street. Our soldiers, while losing many men, took out forty-two enemy tanks during this fight and killed around 1,500 Germans, thereby stopping their attack. They were

Soldiers from Rodimtsev's Guards division preparing an attack. Stalingrad, September 1942. *Photographer: S. Loskutov*

unable to advance farther. Panikhin was there, his command post in a sewer pipe. It was a difficult situation. Several enemy tanks had broken through to the Volga, they were moving toward Panikihin, but with heavy artillery fire and antitank weaponry we send them back, disabling some, destroying others. The enemy's attack lost momentum, and they had to fall back.

On the 23rd the Germans tried to improve their position, attacking with a number of small groups. I received modest reinforcements, around five hundred men, and I launched a counterattack, but this achieved no successes in terms of territory because the enemy forces were three to four times the size of our own. I then decided to switch to an active defense while more reserves were brought over. After that, and in coordination with other divisions, I would launch a decisive attack. I was always in contact with Chuikov. He ordered me at that time to move to some sector and defend it. Lieutenant Fedoseyev's 1st Battalion was cut off when our left flank was exposed and an enemy group broke through from the right and surrounded them. By the 2nd that battalion was wiped out. We couldn't reestablish communication with them. Everything we know of their actions comes from reports, from their commander, who was wounded and got out, and a medical orderly. The report said: "Unless the

General Rodimtsev pictured with soldiers from his division. Stalingrad, September 26, 1942.

enemy is walking over my dead body, none of us is going to leave." So this battalion stayed to the last man, dying heroically on that spot.

The fighting was already taking on a different, more local character. There was fighting in every building. The enemy was regrouping his forces. When they saw that they were meeting considerable resistance—and they'd deployed about seventy tanks and a thousand infantry—and that that they weren't going to win here, the enemy moved to the north, to Orlovka, the factory district, by moving around to my right.

Until the 1st things were relatively quiet for us. Then I asked the commander to give me the 39th Regiment, since a new division, Batyuk's 284th, had arrived. On the night of October 1st this regiment was relieved, and I put them on the left flank with the task of protecting the central crossing, Penzenskaya Street, and Smolensk Street, and to prevent the enemy from breaking through to the Volga.

When the regiment was relieved they came here, and the very next day these brave troops withdrew from Mamayev Kurgan, which was then taken by the Germans. From there they could fire on nearly the entire Volga, and they remain in possession of Hill 102 to this day.

I had nothing left. One battalion was wiped out, and the 34th was in a bad way. I lost some four thousand men here. That's not an easy thing to accept. One of our guns took out three tanks. Then the guy manning it was badly wounded, but he didn't take one step back right until a fourth German tank ran over and crushed him. No one retreated or surrendered. Men died, but they did not retreat.

On the 2nd the enemy took the whole of Mamayev Kurgan, putting the entire crossing under enemy fire. [. . .]

Then came our counterattacks to the north. I was ordered to dig in where we were, to hold the line and the streets we'd taken, and switch to a tough, unwavering defense. This was because we were running low on manpower. Any more active operations were out of the question—the units to my left had already retreated to the east bank. I had to make sure the north was secure and prevent the enemy from breaking through our right flank, from reaching the crossing and taking the Volga. There were no more offensive operations. In my sector the enemy was doing the same thing: building a solid defense. Through October, November, and December we improved our positions to keep the enemy from firing on the Volga. We took the L-shaped building and the railway workers building, and there the fighting took on a local character.[75]

While they still held the L-shaped building and the railway workers building the Germans had been able to keep us from crossing the Volga

Soldiers of the 13th Guards Rifle Division storming the L-shaped building. November 1942. *Photographer: Georgy Zelma*

and walking freely there. We were only able to get around in trenches. So the commander set us the task of taking those strongholds: the L-shaped building, the railway workers building, the air force building, and School no. 38. For this task I chose one battalion that was backed up by Panikhin's 34th Regiment. His orders were to take the L-shaped building and School no. 38. The 42nd Regiment, reinforced with two additional battalions, was to take the railway workers building and School no. 38, and then take up position on the Ninth of January Square, where they would dig in. I went to see Yelin at the 42nd Regiment's command post, which was in a mill. You could see a lot from there. The operation was exceptionally well planned. Every soldier knew where he was going and what he had to do. They knew all the angles, which firing points they had to take out, when they had to stop and start firing. I had the artillery put in a heavy ten-minute barrage, during which time our assault was to begin. There was about forty to fifty meters to get to the enemy in the L-shaped building and the railway workers building, and about one hundred meters to School no. 38. We had to run across the Ninth of January Square, which was well covered.[76]

After getting these orders, the men of the 34th and 42nd Regiments started extending their trenches forward, working day and night, until they ended up some twenty to thirty meters away from the enemy. They did most of the digging at night and kept themselves well out of sight during the day. They camouflaged their work by morning, and they got nearly all the way there. They did this over eight days, dug their way some sixty meters. It didn't take that many men; they worked in shifts—two men at a time. They didn't toss the dirt out of the trench but carried it down to the Volga. That was how we prepared for the attack. The attack itself was set for ten o'clock on the morning on December 3. I went to the observation post at 7th Company, 42nd Regiment. The regimental commander was there, while Commissar Vavilov stayed here. He went to the observation post in the pipe. I was able to observe the L-shaped building, the military supply store, and the Ninth of January Square. As for Panikhin, he had been ordered to launch a surprise attack without artillery preparation. He was to get into the L-shaped building at 6:00 A.M., secure it, and start attacking School no. 38 at 10:00 A.M. There was regular shelling that night until 4:00 A.M., when all of our artillery stopped. At 6:00 A.M. the 34th Regiment was to take the L-shaped building by storm. And the 42nd Regiment was to attack at 10:00 A.M. There was meant to be artillery preparation starting at 6:15, with regular shelling until 9:40, to destroy specific enemy firing points. We brought in guns to fire directly at the dispensary. We got a company of flamethrowers, twenty-eight men, and put ten of them with Pankhin at the L-shaped building and eighteen with the 42nd Regiment. Their job was to burn the Germans out of the basements as we were taking these strongholds.

There were many times previously when we'd tried to take these buildings but were unable to hold on to them because we weren't determined enough. The Germans would launch a counterattack, and our men would either retreat to their trenches or die. We had to put together a group that would stay and secure the place after we took it.

The plan itself was well thought out. At 6:00 A.M. a group entered the L-shaped building without firing a single shot. We took control of the top floors at once. There were six of them. Our men went right in and started fighting in the rooms, on all floors. We had control of the top floor and they were down below, and also on the seventh [*sic*] floor. It was hand-to-hand fighting—literally stabbing and smashing. After the fighting was over, we had to take out the bodies, both ours and theirs.

Now, though, it was a matter of getting the rest of the Germans out of the basement. Unless we did this, there'd be trouble later. But there were sixty men down there. In the end we captured seventeen machine guns, eighteen rifles, some submachine guns, flamethrowers, two antitank cannons, some mortars.

At ten o'clock, while I was there, we started the assault on the railroad building. We took it. The men took one prisoner, and the rest of the fascists were corpses. Some of our men were killed, and others went to School no. 38, where the enemy was launching a counterattack on the L-shaped building. I had told Zhukov, the acting commander of the battalion, to put together a proper fire plan. He did a good job organizing things before the attack. He set up the firing points and assault groups, gave the soldiers clear assignments so they knew who was going where and how. But he forgot about a "little detail" of central importance. The assault teams were not going to include heavy machine guns, which were to stay back in a supporting role. He didn't bury them in the ground but hid them on the corners, one on the left and one on the right. When the infantry attacked, these guns were going to suppress the enemy firing points. But Zhukov didn't put them in bunkers, which would have protected them from mortars. When the infantry attacked, the Germans went straight for our machine guns with their mortars. The first was taken out, then the second, but the infantry had already started. They were being cut down by German fire. Then Zhukov went out with his revolver, shouting, "For Stalin, for the motherland—forward!" But we couldn't give him any supporting fire. I was there myself, just sixty meters away, and I immediately had them stop this mess. Eight men were killed there, twenty wounded. We suffered losses because we hadn't weakened the enemy firing points enough, and ours got knocked out.

The second group was led by battalion commander Andrianov. He'd dug in his machine guns. When the Germans began firing back, they could keep on shooting without trouble. The assault group went up, broke through, and began fighting inside the building. And so we managed to take the railroad building. One group went on to School no. 38 but didn't have enough people to finish the job. We thought that they had twenty to thirty men, but it was a whole company there, seventy men.

When I found out that they were fighting at the L-shaped building, I told Panikhin that the building must be cleared out by any means, no matter the cost. Panikhin mobilized his men, organized them. Kutsarenko was his operations deputy. He was told to eliminate the enemy in the basement. There were a lot of them down there. In one basement we broke through the ceiling with crowbars and had at them with three flamethrowers. There were twenty of them there, all of them got burned up. In another cellar they put 250 kilograms of TNT on the floor above and detonated it, and that was the end of them. Then our guys could jump down and take care of the rest. A few of the Germans ran away.

The battle went on for twenty-six hours. By morning we'd completely cleared and secured the building. Now there were only thirty meters between us and the Germans. None of us were able to take School no. 38. This building was very important. You could see all of Stalingrad from there.

We found new ways of doing things. With a bit of thought you can find the right way. The basements were tough to get into, and they were safe from artillery. So we picked our way in with crowbars, broke through, and then had at them—we burned them out of their strongholds and then blew them up.

We dug a fifty-meter tunnel that ran under the railway workers building at a depth of five meters. We placed three tons of TNT in there. Then the assault group was put together. They were to attack just after the TNT was exploded. This didn't go quite as intended. We'd been given reinforcements, but they wouldn't move—they were Uzbeks, extremely bad soldiers. The whole bunch of them were shot. The order was for the assault group to storm the railway workers building immediately after the explosion, with supporting fire. There were Russians too, scouts and old soldiers who knew how to fight. The yell they let out was extraordinarily loud. There were three firing points, and thirty German soldiers and officers This was the end of them. After that it was time to storm the building. Dirt and rock was still in the air a minute and a half after the explosion, and the crater was sixty meters across. The assault groups were there, with twenty meters between them and the building. I'd calculated that they would stay put for ninety seconds after the explosion and then take sixty seconds to cover the ground. If they all rushed in as planned, there would be no problem getting in and taking the building. I gave them two and a half minutes for this. The explosion was on time, and everyone was ready. We even had sappers in place to cut wires and throw chunks of TNT into their embrasures. The sappers and scouts rushed over, cut wires, threw their explosives, but the main storming party didn't move, they all just stayed put. The sappers and scouts were killed, a few were wounded. The platoon commander just lifted them up by their collars and shot them. The Siberians fought best of all.

I got my first decoration in Spain, for Studgorodok, the second was for Guadalajara, the third for Kiev, Kharkov, Tim,[77] and for breaking out from the encirclement, and I got the Hero of the Soviet Union for everything in Spain.

[The Moscow historians interviewed three members of the 13th Guards Division—commander Rodimtsev, nurse Gurova (see the next interview), and a political officer from divisional headquarters, identified only as comrade Koren.[78] The conversation is short and begins with Koren's assessment:]

I was with comrade Rodimtsev for the entire war. He's an open and direct man. That's his most positive characteristic. He says what he thinks, no exceptions. He judges men only by how they fight. If you let him down or get scared, even once, you don't exist anymore. He has a lot of experience. He won't die because of something stupid.

When they were taking the L-shaped building, he was with the 42nd Regiment in the mill, and I was with him there. There was some danger, of course, because the mill was being shelled, but it was a calculated choice on his part: it was the safest place where he could still see everything and manage the battle. The day before, this deputy company commander was killed by a sniper. It was a stupid way to die. But Rodimtsev chose a place where he could see the battle progress and observe what was going on. It was a cold calculation. Though there were times he was beside himself, quite wild. There was this one time when I was working in the regiment. This was when we were headed to the Southwest Front, moving from the Don to the Volga. No one could say we were retreating, we were fighting our way out.

There was another time when we stopped at Olkhovatka[79] and began counting tanks. After we'd got to sixty, we got tired and gave up. They were all German, coming our way. Rodimtsev just didn't believe any of it, got on this horse and rode toward us.

"Where are the tanks, you sons of bitches?"

They were about three hundred meters out.

He said: "Don't worry, they're far away."

There was no command post, just the platoon on the ground, the commander on his horse, just us and him. But we kept fighting inside the encirclement. We were under specific orders to keep fighting. I remember how he changed his uniform and put on medals and orders: "Let's let these bastards see who they're killing." [. . .]

NURSE VERA GUROVA

General Rodimtsev put the number of casualties in his division in the first weeks after arriving at Stalingrad at over four thousand. The account of nurse Vera Gurova gives this number a concrete reality. The twenty-two-year-old Gurova had already been through much—the Winter War against Finland and the heavy fighting as the Soviets retreated before the advancing Germans in the summer and fall of 1941. But nowhere did she see as many wounded as in Stalingrad. (She does not speak of the dead.) Each day, her medic battalion cared for six hundred to seven hundred newly wounded soldiers at the forward aid station. Because of the Volga, the injured could not be transferred rapidly to the field hospital on the other side of the river. They could be moved only at night, and the number who could be transported was limited, given the constant risk of enemy fire. Many of the wounded had to be treated and lodged in the field with whatever was available. General Chuikov writes in his memoir that the surgery unit of the 13th Guards Division worked in a massive drainage pipe on the steep western bank of the Volga. A secret NKVD report confirms the dramatic situation of the injured in September: "Over the course of fighting on September 15 the 13th Guards division suffered four hundred casualties and used up all the ammunition for automatic weapons. The transportation of the wounded to the east bank of the Volga is extremely difficult. The commander of the 13th Guards Division has no means to transport the wounded. The lightly wounded are making rafts, loading the seriously wounded onto them. To cross to the east bank they let themselves be taken by the Volga current. On the other shore they wander around villages, looking for help."[80]

Almost 1 million Soviet women, far more than from any other warring nation, served in the Red Army during World War II, half of them as ordinary soldiers and the other as nurses, phone operators, laundrywomen, or anti-aircraft assistants. Nurses had to assume that they would be sent to the front line and would aid the injured under enemy fire. Like the other medics with whom the Moscow historians spoke, they participated without complaint.

Gurova seemed to welcome the elimination of separate gender roles in war: "I think that a woman in the army is just as useful as a man," she confidently explained. Because of her achievements, Gurova demanded membership in the party although she had not been in the Komsomol.

General Chuikov and other commanders and political officers interviewed in Stalingrad praised the women serving in the army, acknowledging that some showed more stamina than the men. What they did not speak about, and what Gurova only alludes to, was the difficult situation of women in the Red Army. Not only did they have to "man up"; they had to take sexual assaults from superiors in stride. Here again, Gurova internalizes the male perspective and criticizes some of the nurses in her unit for seducing the men. The reality in most cases was the other way around. She speaks proudly of having received the Medal for Battle Merit for the Finnish campaign, though male soldiers had another name for this order when awarded to women: "For Merit in Bed." By the end of the war, the blanket accusations against women in the Red Army became louder. Women who entered into a liaison with officers were known as "campaign women," abbreviated in Russian as "PPSh,"[81] the nickname for the Soviet submachine gun. Doubts about their moral integrity made it difficult for many women to reenter civilian life after the war. In many cases women veterans did not tell their families about their war experiences.[82] Nothing is known about Vera Gurova's later life.

TRANSCRIPTS OF INTERVIEWS CONDUCTED ON THE STALINGRAD FRONT DURING THE DEFENSE OF STALINGRAD

Stalingrad, January 7, 1943
Interview conducted by scientific secretary A. A. Belkin
Stenography by A. I. Shamshina
62nd Army
13th Guards Rifle Division
Nurse Vera Leontyevna GUROVA[83]

I was born in 1920 in Krivoi Rog, in the Dnetropetrovsk region. I'm Ukrainian. I completed my medical training in Krivoi Rog, and then I volunteered on the Finnish Front. I'd specialized as a surgical nurse and I worked there as a senior surgical nurse. For the Finnish campaign I was awarded the Medal for Battle Merit, and for Kiev I received the Order of the Red Star. I got another Order of the Red Star in this division. Colonel Vavilov presented it to me. I was decorated for the fighting at Tim by a decree of the Don Front.

It was bad at Kiev, but not as bad as at Stalingrad. Mortars and shells were exploding all around while we were working, everything was coming down, all while we were trying to do complicated operations. I work in a medical battalion. At Kiev our working conditions weren't as bad. We were in a large hospital, and while the shells could reach us, they didn't bother us as much as they do here. Here we've had six or seven hundred wounded coming in every day. We've had to work day and night. Our building was constantly collapsing. The medical battalion was placed on the other side of the Volga with the second echelon in Burkova,[84] while this place was simply a frontline aid station. I used to be over there, but I've come here as relief because there isn't as much work over there now.

All the complicated operations are done at battalion level under more peaceful conditions. There's no way you could operate on someone here and keep him for four to six days. Right now it's quiet and there aren't many wounded, but we had a lot of them back then.

Most were shrapnel wounds from mortars, shells, bombs. In Stalingrad most of our cases are shrapnel wounds. Before, when we were at Kharkov, our forward aid stations weren't as important because we were able to get the wounded to the battalion station. But in Stalingrad they play a much larger role. We operate on people with abdominal wounds and keep them for a while. They could be dead by the time we got them to battalion. We transfer them on stretchers.

Army command set up this forward aid station during the battle because of the poor transportation. The station had two surgeons and a senior and junior nurse. They gave the men blood transfusions and operated on them, and after a few days' recovery in a dugout the wounded were sent across the river. That's where I was, because the brunt of the workload fell on that section of the medical battalion in the second echelon. We've never experienced anything as bad as we have here. I've never seen so many wounded.

Here I've come to understand that nurses have also got to be affectionate and cheerful. The wounded are watching you. They watch how you behave during bomb raids and react accordingly. I remember one time when we were being bombed just after we'd finished operating, and the men were still on the tables. This was at Kiev. There were a few times when I had to stay with them. At the divisional medical station our operating theater was in a tent. There were a lot of planes in the air. The surgeon finished up and left, but there were still six patients on tables who had to be carried out. That was when the bombing started. We stayed with them, me and another girl, and they looked at us and said: "Go on, save yourselves—we're already wounded."

There wasn't anywhere for us to go. And besides, how could you leave with those men looking at you like that? This happened to me twice. I know the man's wounded and in pain, and he knows that even one piece of shrapnel can do a lot of damage. But the thought of leaving a wounded man doesn't even occur to me. That's what I'm thinking when I go back to the tent to look after him. I came here to save him. I'm not married.[85]

I can say how I felt about my work just the same as any soldier can tell stories about attacking the enemy. There were times when you'd be on your feet two days running without realizing it, doing nothing but seeing to the wounded. As a senior nurse, I understood that I had to be

A nurse in Stalingrad, 1942

both a qualified army nurse and an excellent organizer. So when we move to a new location, the surgeon tasks me, the senior nurse, with making sure our premises are ready. The other senior nurse and I must organize things so everything is ready to go and everyone is in their place. Here I was only assisting during simple operations, so I ended up spending all my time doing organizational work. I had to make sure we had everything we needed to keep the work going. If we ran out of something the surgeons and nurses would have to stop.

There was one patient who made us burst into tears. He was a young lieutenant, born in 1922. This was in Burkovka in October. He was wounded when he came to us, and his legs had to be amputated. He was from Ukraine. His whole family—his mother, his father, his girlfriend—they had stayed there, and he didn't know if they were alive. He was telling us all of this and showing his great hatred for the enemy the whole time before his legs were amputated, while he was being prepped, and afterward he lay on the table for half an hour. The operation was performed under anesthesia. Then we gave him food and water, and he begged us to avenge him for as long as we remained in Stalingrad. Then he was sent to a hospital in the rear.

Very few of the seriously wounded lost their morale or started thinking only of themselves. Most of them stayed in good spirits, perhaps losing it for only a moment during surgery. Afterward a man would start telling us how he got wounded, show his anger and his desire to avenge the motherland. Some of the men with minor wounds show up no longer thinking of themselves as men. Others come with serious wounds without losing faith.

I've been a surgical nurse for five years, and there's no end to the blood. I'd never seen such massive amounts of blood before. I know I should forget about it—this is my job. But of course that doesn't mean I don't sympathize with them, or that I look at them with indifference. I've experienced a lot, but I shouldn't behave in such a way that it affects how I treat the wounded. During a difficult operation, if my mind is elsewhere and I'm not following the operation, I won't get anything right.

I'm not in the Komsomol, but I am applying for membership in the party.

I think that a woman in the army is just as useful as a man, with certain exceptions, of course. But those exceptions exist in peacetime too. Sometimes I'm really offended when people treat a woman with contempt: a woman in the army? I know that I joined the army to do my duty. Let them think what they think.

A LIEUTENANT FROM ODESSA: ALEXANDER AVERBUKH

The following interviews with Senior Lieutenant Alexander Averbukh and Lieutenant Colonel Alexander Gerasimov depict a regiment of the 35th Guards Rifle Division as it defended the city against German panzer troops advancing from the Don in August and September 1942. The division was formed in early August from troops of the 8th Airborne Corps near Moscow and immediately deployed to the Stalingrad Front, where it was to merge with the 62nd Army. The journey to Stalingrad lasted five days and was repeatedly interrupted by enemy air attacks. Almost every station on the route had been destroyed in the bombing. Gerasimov caught sight of the bodies of Soviet soldiers in burned-out railway cars along the embankment. This was the first time many of his soldiers had experienced enemy bombing, requiring that they, as he put it, be "worked over." In the interview excerpts Gerasimov describes the chaos of the following weeks, noting the poor coordination between the army leadership and the commanders in the field and the poor quality of Soviet enemy intelligence.

His regiment was first stationed on the eastern bank of the Don. After a brutal day's march of twenty miles in searing heat—the soldiers had to carry all their equipment and weapons, including a 45mm regiment canon—they reached their destination: Peskovatka. There the regiment was to build a bridgehead on the other side of the river. By that point, the Germans had already massed together multiple divisions on the riverbank, so a new command was issued: stop the German advance near Kotluban, twelve miles farther northeast. Shortly after they were ordered to halt the advancing Germans who had since broken through near the village Bolshaya Rossoshka, eighteen miles west of Stalingrad.[86] In the confusion, they lost contact with the supply train.

Though the regiment was depleted of food rations and ammunition, divisional commander Vasily Glazkov received an order from front command to take a nearby hill. He informed his battalion commanders by telephone that he would personally execute them if they did not succeed. Meanwhile, a telegram from army headquarters arrived praising the soldiers and commanders of the division for their "bravery" and "heroic courage" and urging them to destroy the "fascist pack." Gerasimov had the telegram

A Red Army unit near Stalingrad, August 1942

read to his soldiers immediately before combat began. The regiment took the hill but lost 350 men in the process. A few days later the regiment abandoned the hill when the German 24th Panzer Division pushed past it to the right and left, threatening to surround it. Senior Lieutenant Averbukh's account covers the subsequent withdrawal and continued fight against the 14th and 24th Panzer Divisions in the southwest suburbs of Stalingrad.

The twenty-two-year-old lieutenant was talkative and spoke frankly about his dissolute past as young vagrant and thief. It was not until he entered the institutions of the Soviet state that he became "human." His biography resembles those of the homeless youth in the writings of the Ukrainian reformist educator Andrei Makarenko, men who found their "path in life" through targeted disciplinary and motivational measures.[87] Other Soviet institutions from the prewar era, among them the NKVD, spoke of "reforging": the sometimes violent reeducation of "class enemies" into sensible Soviet citizens. Averbukh's testimony makes clear that Red Army soldiers continued to think in the revolutionary-era categories of transformation and self-realization.

The Averbukh interview is unusual in that it was not conducted by a representative of the Historical Commission, but by a politruk from Averbukh's company, Innokenty Gerasimov.[88] In a letter dated November 1942, Gerasimov came to Isaak Mints with the idea of writing the history of the

Guards regiment. Mints wrote to the reserve administration of the Red Army asking for Gerasimov to be released from service for two months so he could help the commission. The collaboration between Gerasimov and Averbukh recalls the duo of Commissar Furmanov and Commander Chapayev in the Civil War. Just as Furmanov helped the rough-cut Chapayev learn self-control and conscious action, Gerasimov served as a mentor along Averbukh's path to becoming a model fighter. Gerasimov was certainly involved in the decision to induct Averbukh into the party after he was wounded on August 28, an event that at the time marked the climax of Averbukh's personal development.

Dated December 17, 1942, the interviews with Averbukh and regimental commander Alexander Gerasimov (not to be confused with Innokenti Gerasimov) were the first transcripts on the defense of Stalingrad made by Mints's commission. The interviews likely took place in Moscow, where both soldiers had been sent to receive awards: the Hero of the Soviet Union (Gerasimov) and the Order of the Red Banner (Averbukh). The stenographer, Alexandra Shamshina, was part of the delegation that conducted interviews in Stalingrad with many other eyewitnesses of the battle beginning in January.

TRANSCRIPT

of interview conducted with comrade Senior Lieutenant Alexander Shapsovich AVERBUKH

Commander of a company of antitank riflemen, 8th Guards Airborne Regiment

Interview conducted by I. P. GERASIMOV, Hero of the Soviet Union

December 17, 1942

Stenography by Shamshina[89]

(Nominated for Order of the Red Banner)

I was born in Dubossary in the Moldavian SSR, and later I moved to Odessa, where I then lived for many years. When I got to Odessa I was eleven years old. I ran away from home, I was on my own. I met some street children and started being friends with them. The first time I got involved in petty theft I was still going to school. Later I gave up the small stuff and got on to more serious jobs. I became the leader of a gang. I was fourteen or fifteen. I quit doing the stealing myself. They brought all the loot back to me, and I distributed it around, and all the while I was still going to school. I've been everywhere in the Soviet Union. There's not one city in the Soviet Union that I haven't been to.

Then I left secondary school, took some night classes, passed some exams—all while still being a thief. Then it became impossible for me to stay in Odessa any longer. I moved to Tiraspol, where I passed the last of my exams and decided to become a proper human being. I was studying all summer, but I kept up with the drinking, going out, seeing girls. In 1938 I was admitted to an industrial institute. The competition was tough: eight people for every slot. I was one of the top qualifiers. During the second year I decided to quit that life, I wanted to be someone better. I volunteered for the army. All my friends had been locked up. I was the only one left. Then I found new friends and started going out on the town once again.

I loved my mother very much, but I didn't love my father. I loved my little brother. They all had an influence on me. But most of all I loved this girl from the medical institute. She loved me too, but only on the condition that I give up my former life. In Odessa they started calling me Sashka Blot. After that I decided to put aside that former life and started studying. I was doing well at the institute and had stopped stealing; but my old friends were helping me. There were times when I'd be out and I'd see my friends out having a good time—but I couldn't. I loved this girl and decided to give them up.

In 1938 I volunteered for the army. I requested to be in the tank corps, but I didn't get in because of my age. I was enlisted into the local regiment, the 138th Rifles. I spent a year as a private in the personnel office and graduated from the regimental school. Then I was a squad leader. Later, by order of the People's Commissar, those who had completed secondary school and had some third-level education could be sent to a military academy. I thought I might go to the aviation institute. I submitted my application, and it was approved. But just then I was asked to go with a group to the 1st Kiev Artillery School. I liked it there, and I decided to stay. I graduated from that school and stayed on as a platoon leader. I was part of a cadet regiment that left for the front at 9:00 P.M. on June 22 [1941].

We were encamped at Rzhishchev.[90] There was a three-gun salute, and then we set off for the front. (We were all in high spirits before we left for the front.) The first time we were fired on by enemy aircraft was on the 26th. We were in a big forest, so we turned off the road and took cover. We took some casualties—about ten wounded in the regiment.

Nothing serious. But we had more serious casualties in the village of Zhulyany,[91] where the enemy came right up to us. At that time I was the commander of the 1st Cannon Platoon. I've been through a lot, but I've never been a coward. I was worried that I might show my fear in front of my subordinates. This battle ended in success. The enemy was defeated.

The Germans were persistent. My battery fired on them at close range with canister shot. I got wounded. After that battle I was promoted to lieutenant, when we left Kiev for Krasnoyarsk. We were fighting for three months. Our regiment was relieved by other units. [. . .] From August [1942] I was a company commander in an antitank rifle regiment, and I went with them to the front.

I trained my battery when we were still in the rear. I tempered them, had them do night exercises, hundred-kilometer night marches over uneven terrain, through swamps, water, and so on. We had an inspection. During a live-fire exercise my battery got a rating of excellent.

It was a great joy to me when the brigade was named a Guards regiment, first of all because the regiment, not being [. . .] had gotten this Guards title, and second because we were now on our way to Stalingrad, where my mother and sister were living.

On August 5, 1942, we left for the front. My company was made up of three platoons. 1st Platoon was commanded by Junior Lieutenant Kanonetko, 2nd Platoon was commanded by Myasnikov, and 3rd Platoon was commanded by Kopeykin, who had been wounded in one leg. My deputy commander was Junior Lieutenant Novoshitsky, and Gerasimov[92] was the company's politruk. We all left for the front. Classes were organized on the way there. Gerasimov led discussions, and my deputy and I took care of the combat training.

We reached Stalingrad on the 10th. Once we'd gotten off the trains, our company marched to Gavrilovka, where we dug in and took up positions. The first battle started on August 21. I grabbed some newspapers from politruk Gerasimov and drove out to the units to hand them out and talk with the men. But before we'd made it as far as 2nd Battalion, two of our vehicles were disabled by machine-gun fire, and the drivers were wounded. Their hands were all shot up. I dressed their wounds. We decided to run to the battalions, but one of the drivers grabbed hold of me, he wouldn't let me go.

Not too far from our vehicles was an airborne group that had scattered during the bombing. Some of them were wounded. I gathered them all together and put Lieutenant Sosnin in charge. I told him that he was responsible for every one of these men, and that when the bombing stopped he was to report to the regimental command post.

Of course I didn't get a chance to hand out the papers. It was some heavy fighting. I got back to the regimental command post. I was ordered to move forward to find out where the enemy tanks were and destroy them. I went with a detachment belonging to Aratyunyan, a senior lieutenant. At the start of the tank battle it was four of our tanks against eight of theirs. Two of ours were on fire, but the crews couldn't get out. I went with two soldiers, Leonovy and Matyukha, crawled up to the tanks, and pulled out a junior lieutenant and two sergeants. We couldn't get to the second tank because it was too close to the Germans. We also managed to rescue one man who'd been badly burned. Bondar and Karpenko crawled up to the next tank and pulled him out. He was sent to a medical unit in Grechi, and the others went to the 101st Regiment's command post.

Then we shot at the tanks with antitank rifles and they retreated. After that we got the command to fall back, so we did. [. . .]

Then I went to the battalion command post. A very difficult situation had developed there. There weren't any artillery spotters on the front lines. A motorized column was advancing on us, and there were tanks flanking us on our left, where we had antitank crews in place, but we didn't have anyone protecting our right flank. All of this was taking place on Hill 137.2. I took aim, determined the initial deflection and proceeded to destroy the column.

I was calm the whole time because I got so caught up in the work. The column was destroyed. Then I shifted our artillery fire to an infantry column that was coming around our left flank. There were half a dozen tanks and a couple of infantry platoons. We repelled their attacks, we completely eliminated them. Incidentally, it was a warm, sunny day. Two in the afternoon. Clouds of dust and smoke—you couldn't see a thing, the sun could barely get through. The entire column was destroyed. Our men had taken out four tanks and obliterated two infantry platoons.

To mark our success in repelling the German attack, Captain Klashin put together a celebratory dinner on the front line. They brought sour cream and milk, some vodka, and roast mutton. We drank to our having defeated the column. Politruk Klashin even kissed me.

My greatest joy came that same evening after the battle when I was accepted as a party candidate member right there on the front line. That night I went to the command post to see Colonel Gerasimov.[93] He'd been told that I was dead, and everyone was surprised to see me when I showed up safe and sound.

On September 8 I was ordered to defend a particular sector together with Captain Lizunov's battalion. We walked around to have a look at the sector. We really didn't have many people. My company amounted to twenty-two men and six rifles. I took some men from the 20th Tank Destroyer Brigade into my company.

We inspected the firing positions, and everything was just as it should be. Lieutenant Kashtanov and his platoon were assigned to outposts. Lizunov stayed on the left flank, and I went with a platoon to the right. We agreed that in the event of an attack we'd fight to the last, neither of us would make a move without the other. We were going to complete our combat mission or die trying. I briefly explained our task to the men, saying that we had to keep up the defense despite the enemy's superior strength. At night we made sure the soldiers were all fed and then we tried to get some rest.

The first shots came at 4:00 A.M. from a Vanyusha, the six-barreled German mortar system.[94] The enemy launched his attack. There was a continuous wall of tanks with infantry following close behind. We had a platoon of antitank riflemen in trenches, but they weren't in a good position to fire at these tanks because we'd been expecting them to come on the right, while they were actually coming around a hill on the left, so we couldn't get a good line on them. We had to give up on the trenches and shoot at the tanks out in the open. We disabled eight tanks. The Germans towed them back right away. Those tanks were taken out by Privates Nikolayev, Bereznikov, and Nikitin. Even though Nikitin was a quartermaster clerk, he knew how to use a gun.

We fought to the last. When we ran out of ammunition, we used grenades to destroy the tanks. Men were dropping off left and right. We'd lost contact with the battalion. I moved to Lizunov's command post. All I had left was one rifle and eight cartridges. I ordered the men to hold on to them.

I crawled to the command post. On the way the magazine of my Mauser was shattered. I reported the situation to Lizunov. We'd lost all communication with the companies and with regimental HQ. The moment you'd send a runner he'd be dead. But seeing as we swore we'd hold out to the very end, that meant we were going to hold out to the very end. It was just me, Captain Lizunov, and his runner in the bunker. We didn't have anyone else. We weren't in contact with anyone. German infantrymen had passed us by, and we were now in their rear.

They discovered our bunker. I had my Mauser, a pouch of cartridges, and a submachine gun. Lizunov had a submachine gun and three antitank grenades with no fuses. We decided to leave one at a time. I was going to cover him. He'd go two hundred meters, and then I'd go. There were three of us left.

I threw the antitank grenades. They didn't explode. By then Captain Lizunov had run about 150 meters and got hit in the left thigh. He said to me: "Don't come out, they've got it covered. They got me in the leg." I ran over and bandaged him up, but I was tying it so tight that it kept tearing. I was trying to hurry because the Germans were on their way. Eventually we got it tied, but the blood kept coming. I lifted him on my back and crawled about fifty meters. There was an antiaircraft emplacement. I was bracing myself to lift him over the parapet when I took a hit to my right thigh. I'd used the bandages on Captain Lizunov, so I had to go without. Once I'd recovered a bit, we started moving forward, with me helping the captain. We kept moving for two hours. Captain Lizunov was showing little sign of life, but I could hear him whispering, saying that I should leave him and save myself. Obviously I didn't leave him.

We crawled to Verkhnyaya Elshanka,[95] in the area of the radio station. I sat up to get my bearings and got hit again. Submachine-gun fire to the left side of my chest and my left arm. I lost consciousness. I don't know how long I was out. I woke up because it got really cold. It was late, around four in the morning. It was already starting to get light. I could hear people speaking German all around me. I couldn't see Lizunov anywhere. I decided to crawl toward a building. This was on the 9th. I could see there were Germans inside. I decided to shoot myself because I didn't have any strength left, and I didn't want to let them take me alive. I figured there was no way out. I pulled the trigger, but the Mauser was clogged with sand and wouldn't fire. My right arm was still okay. With my right arm I crawled away and by some miracle made it to the divisional command post. It was already midday. There I met Colonel Yudin and the military lawyer Truppe. I didn't manage to find Colonel Gerasimov. I asked for the general. They told me he was dead. I thought they were joking, but it turned out to be true. I gave my report on the situation to the divisional command post.

I wasn't able to get any bandages there. German submachine gunners were already coming right up to the command post. I asked only that the staff give me a weapon or else take me with them. They didn't give me a weapon. The Germans were advancing, and the divisional staff fell back farther. I had to crawl away on my own. On the second day I somehow managed to just about make it to Stalingrad—only three hundred meters left—and then for the first time in my life I cried: Stalingrad was so close, but I couldn't make it. I crawled another 150 meters, and this old man and his daughter picked me up and carried me to their home in Stalingrad. The daughter dressed my wounds and gave me some milk to drink. Her name was Zoya. Later I was sent across the Volga. I kissed both the man and his daughter good-bye. He cried for me like I was his own son. After that I was in the hospital.

REGIMENTAL COMMANDER ALEXANDER GERASIMOV

The following excerpt from the testimony of regimental commander Alexander Gerasimov begins where the interview with his company leader, Averbukh, leaves off. A battle on September 8 all but destroyed two Soviet regiments; Averbukh was seriously injured and Vasily Glazkov, the commander of the 35th Guards Division, was killed.[96] By September 12, according to information provided by General Chuikov, only 250 soldiers in the 35th Guards Divisions were still fit for action.[97] Gerasimov's regiment absorbed the remaining soldiers and began a retreat. On September 20 the grain elevator at the city's southern edge in which they had found temporary refuge was surrounded by German and Romanian troops. The new divisional commander ordered the regiment to push through the German lines to the divisional command post at the mouth of the Tsaritsa. Gerasimov remembers the outbreak very well, the "most remarkable battle" of his Stalingrad experience. The chaos continued to haunt him in his sleep as he lay wounded in a military hospital.

A.S.[98]

TRANSCRIPT
of interview conducted with Lieutenant Colonel Alexander Akimovich GERASIMOV

Commander of the 101st Guards Regiment
December 17, 1942[99]

[. . .] By the evening of the 8th [of September 1942] all of our units had been sent to the outskirts of Stalingrad, where we got the order from the commander of 62nd Army to take up defensive positions inside the city. Then we lost all communication, lost contact with our subunits, lost all liaison with our artillery. It was then that comrade General Glazkov, commander of the 35th Division, was killed. He was first hit in the leg by submachine-gun fire, after which he was put into a car that was then shot from an airplane. That had a strong effect on the battle commanders. But despite the difficult situation, the command staff of the 35th Division managed to bring their units back together and move immediately to defend Stalingrad, specifically its southernmost area, Kuporosnoye. The 35th Division's commander[100] was ordered to defend the area to the south of Kuporosnoye and to cut the Stalingrad-Beketovka rail line. On September 9 what remained of the units was deployed there. The main enemy forces were directed at where the 62nd and 64th Armies met, somewhere between Beketovka and Stalingrad. German tanks and soldiers attacked our units at this junction, pushing eastward from the south.

Our division and those remaining personnel—not much more than a thousand men—kept up the defense of Stalingrad from September 9 to September 21, inside the city itself. There was intense fighting all through this period. My regiment was the only one left in the division. On the 8th, both the 100th and 102nd Regiments were wiped out. Survivors from those regiments were collected and brought into my 101st Guards Regiment. So the division was left with a single combined 101st Guards Regiment, with me in command, and from September 9 to September 21 we conducted defensive operations inside Stalingrad.

I've got to mention that there was about a division's worth of Germans on the front lines in the city, and some Romanians.[101] In Stalingrad Lieutenant Panichkin and his squad took out a platoon of Romanians and captured their commanding officer. He didn't go willingly. I'd ordered Panichkin to take his platoon over to the grain elevator and leave a squad there to cover my flank. He left two of his squads and took another to the area near the elevator. The Romanian platoon was out with their commander on the front line. Panichkin ordered his men to open fire. They started shooting and wounded ten or twelve of them, and the rest ran away. The officer hid behind a building. He didn't get a chance to draw his pistol before Panichkin got to him. Panichkin grabbed him by the arm, started to twist it. The officer screamed. When he turned around, Panichkin hit him in the face. The officer fell. Then Panichkin's men came and held him down. They learned from him that it was Romanians in this area. The Romanians were out front, with rifles, and behind them were the Germans with machine guns. There were times when the Romanians would go on the attack. They'd attack in groups of about fifteen to twenty. They would scream as they ran forward, and the machine guns would provide covering fire. They all had these high-pitched screams, the sound really carried. They'd run up to the forward line. Our guys would rush out, ten or fifteen to their thirty. The Romanians dropped everything they had, including their canteens and ammunition belts, and ran for it. But then the German machine guns started up. They were shooting at the Romanians too. That got them to stop running. They were being shot at from two sides. [. . .]

A small number of us continued defending Stalingrad until the 21st. On the 21st I had just over a hundred men remaining. [. . .]

At around 10:00 P.M. on the 20th I got a written order from the commander of the 35th Division, comrade Colonel Dubyansky, which said: "To the commander of the 101st Guards Rifle Division, Lieutenant Colonel Gerasimov. Two battalions from the 92nd Rifle Brigade are coming to relieve you. Get written confirmation that you've transferred responsibility for the defense area, then continue defending that area together until further notice. [. . .]"

On the night of the 21st I received a second written order. By that time the enemy had already cut me off from my field units on our right flank and had reached the Volga. This meant that I'd been cut off from the divisional command post. The enemy came at us with a mortar battery, with heavy and light machine guns. It was 150–200 people altogether. They had artillery at their disposal from above the Volga and had cut us off from the divisional command post and the field units on the right.

I was handed this order by a messenger who had managed to slip through the German positions and was still in one piece. He was one of the soldiers we'd been given as reinforcements, and I can't even remember his name. The order was from Colonel Dubyansky. Dubyansky also sent me some wine, a little vodka, and two cans of food—to help me keep going, seeing as we weren't getting much in the way of food. Our food was being brought over in small boats.[102] And so Lieutenant Colonel Gerasimov was hereby ordered to gather his remaining men and officers and go to the divisional command post in the area of the Tsaritsa River. At this time the divisional command post was on the Tsaritsa.

It was the most remarkable battle. I couldn't do it again. At my absolute lowest moment I thought: if I don't make it, others will come and tell our story. [. . .]

After getting the instructions from Colonel Dubyansky, the commander of the 35th Guards Division, I sent a runner to go get the commissar. Right then the commissar was with one of the units. He came, and we held a meeting in a dugout. I also had the deputy commander of the 131st Division and the commander of the 20th Rifle Brigade. We ate and drank together, of course. We'd been brought watermelons, sour cream, chickens, eggs, vodka, and fresh apples by boat. We ate well, drank, and started to discuss how we were going to break out. We needed to break through four hundred meters of German combat formations. Since I was the one who had been given the order, I was the one who was to lead the escape of these four staffs. I assumed command of the mission to get the remaining men from these three staffs [*sic*] out of there. The commanders suggested then that we make our way out in small groups of five or ten. We were surrounded and cut off from our units, the enemy had broken through both on our left flank, along the Volga, and on the right, and was also attacking from the main front lines. We had no choice. We had to force our way through their battle formations.

I rejected the idea of having the staffs leave in groups. That would be the end of whatever fighting strength we still had. We decided to fight our way out, using the element of surprise to underpin our plan of action. What were the reasons for this? The enemy was stronger. They had about two hundred men with mortars and machine guns, while I had around seventy, including the commanders. [. . .] We gathered all the remaining men and officers, and I told them our mission. We started crawling our way toward the forward edge of the enemy defenses. I placed a heavy machine gun on my left flank to cover the rail line and prevent the enemy from bringing replacements down to the Volga.

The machine gunner had three belts of ammunition. He was alone. He had no number two. He was in position. I began moving the remaining men and staffs. The Germans spotted us, and we were subjected to heavy machine-gun and rifle fire. Then they sent up flares, and then there was heavy mortar fire. The men were barely visible. I started giving the order to quickly move up to the German combat formations. We made it there. I had to encourage the men to move forward. I ran forward with the commissar and primed two grenades.

What saved us? A railcar was burning on the other side of the German formations, which meant that we could see them while they had a hard time seeing us, because the Germans were looking from the same side as the light. I took advantage of this and immediately pushed everyone into the attack, running out in front with the commissar with pistol drawn, yelling: "Attack! For the motherland! Forward!" and "Comrades, not one step back, only forward!" There were fifteen or so Germans in a large crater. About thirty meters away. I threw a grenade, then a second. You could hear them howling, crying. They yelled: "Rus, Rus!" My men saw me toss the grenade and started running. The flares and mortars had stopped, there was only submachine-gun fire and hand grenades.

When I ran forward, all the soldiers and staff members ran after me. Everyone got tangled up together—us and the Germans—and we were fighting hand to hand. With bayonets. It was dark: you'd run up to someone, see they were one of your own, then move on to the next one. If he was in a short jacket, that meant he was German. Grenades were being used too. They really did throw a lot of hand grenades at us, but we gave as good as we got. We took out more than a hundred of them. Everyone was mixed up, you couldn't make out a thing. Some yelled: "For the motherland!" Others yelled "For Stalin!" Some swore. The whole time I was yelling: "Move forward, stay with me, to the Volga!" You could hear the Germans screaming, their wounded were moaning. Ours would say: "I'm hit, take me with you." Wounded Germans were howling. It was a nightmare.

When I attacked, the Germans stopped firing their rifles and submachine guns, they started fighting only with bayonets and hand grenades. It seems that they'd run out of ammunition, shot all their cartridges, and there wasn't time to reload during the attack. We were also running low. I remember this one lieutenant with a submachine gun whose strap got torn. He grabbed the gun by the barrel and started hitting them in the head with it. The Germans started running. We ran after them. This one German was running behind me. Lieutenant Kulinich says: "Comrade Colonel, a German."

I shot him with my submachine gun, and he dropped. He was running without anything, not even a rifle. This was where Lieutenant Panichkin was killed.

When I threw those two grenades I could see what kind of fight this was going to be. I grabbed a third grenade from my pocket, took my pistol in my left hand, and pulled the pin. There was a group of five to eight Germans. I had just turned around and was about to throw my grenade when a German threw his own grenade, hitting me in the chest. Before it exploded there were sparks: the detonator was burning. It bounced off my chest and ended up about five meters away. I only had time to cover my face with my hands. I should have got down, but I was a bit dazed. Then the grenade went off, and I got hit in my right forearm—two fragments—and above the knee of my left leg.

Then the commissar yelled "Hurrah!" And it was right at that moment that a bullet grazed his tongue, knocked out some teeth, and exited through his chin. A second bullet hit his left cheekbone. He cried out: "Alexander Akimovich, I'm hit."

I said: "Me too. Can you walk?"

"Yes."

"Go on, then. I'll go get some of the others."

Lieutenant Kulinich said he'd also been hit.

I've got to tell you about Private Gulyutkin. When my adjutant Shikhanov went missing on the 8th, I took Gulyutkin, a submachine gunner, as his replacement. He was a small, nondescript, skinny kid, born in 1921 or 1922. Throughout all of the fighting—we went on the attack three times—he was always right behind me, didn't leave my side for a second. He was always concerned for my safety and would warn me: "Comrade Colonel, you're risking your life, you could get yourself killed—we'd be worse off without our commander."

In one of those attacks, in the area of the sawmill, where we were reinforced by comrade Nazarov's sapper company, I gave the order to attack the enemy. The company commander couldn't get his men to move. They were under heavy fire from mortars, machine guns, submachine guns. This was in the evening. The buildings were on fire. My hat blew away in the wind. I was going around without it, and I asked them: "Why aren't you moving forward?" I drew my pistol.

"Move out!" I yelled. "Attack at once!" The enemy had come to 150 meters from our positions.

But they wouldn't go. I ran out in front of the company, stood there with pistol in hand: "Comrades, follow me! Let's go! Attack! Hurrah!"

They looked at me. You could see a kind of smile appearing on their faces. They all got up, and the entire company followed me on the attack. Private Gulyutkin said: "Don't run out in front, there's machine guns."

He always kept himself between me and the enemy, shielding me with his own body. When I yelled "Forward!" he got caught up in the moment, picked up his weapon, and yelled: "Forward!" But then he realized what he was doing and said: "You can't go any farther, it's too dangerous."

There was nothing else I could do, so on I went.

Gulyutkin held on to my left sleeve to make sure he didn't lose me. He held his submachine gun with his other hand as he shielded me with his body. He got wounded in both arms. The same grenade got both of us. When I talk about him, I always think of what a singularly loyal person he was.

When the grenade got us, he didn't say "I'm hit!" but rather: "Are you alive, comrade Colonel?"

"Yes," I said.

I fell over when I got hit. He thought I was dead. I said: "I'm alive. How about you?"

He said: "Hit in the arm, not bad."

He kept at my side with his wounded arm, trying to shield me. I got angry, and said: "Back off, I can't lead with you so close."

And he said: "Yes, you should go first."

Up ahead, everyone was beginning to break through to where our sailors[103] were. I'd been leading the battle for forty minutes without having my wounds seen to. Some of us had got through, and others were still fighting. Finally I reached the sailors, where I was met by the commander of a machine-gun platoon from the 92nd Brigade. He asked me where everyone was. We got a group of eighteen men and sent them back with this platoon commander. They went back to the battle, where they provided covering fire to get the remaining men and the wounded out of there.

I was feeling faint because I'd gone forty minutes without being bandaged. I'd been yelling, my throat was dry after I got hit, I was thirsty. A sailor brought me some water in a helmet. I drank nearly all of it even though it smelled like oil. Then they called a medical assistant to dress my wounds. We were back with our comrades. We started to fall back to the divisional command post. By then I wasn't able to walk. The commissar and I had to be carried. We arrived at the command post and reported to the divisional commander that our staff had gotten out. I gave my report by way of messenger because I still had half a kilometer left to go. I was given permission to move to the other side of the Volga and put my men under the command of Lieutenant Pavlov. The division was withdrawn from the front line on the 25th. I'd already been taken on the 23rd to a hospital in Saratov. All that first night in a proper bed I was still fighting the Germans. [. . .]

Throughout the fighting Panichkin was always at my side. He was a brave commander. If you asked him to take some men and get them into position, he would do it right when you wanted and then report back. Especially brave. He died in that battle and was nominated for a decoration. Gulyutkin was also sent up for a decoration.

During the period of combat operations at Stalingrad the regiment eliminated about three thousand enemy personnel, about sixty tanks, three aircraft, about twenty-eight armored vehicles. We took out about 150 trucks, and also two mortar batteries and a dozen or so field guns.

We didn't take any prisoners because our men and officers are trained paratroopers. When you're behind enemy lines, you can't take prisoners, you can only kill. That's how our men were trained. Which is why our officers and soldiers didn't take any prisoners, why they killed. Once Captain Teltsov said he'd captured eighteen men. I reported this to the divisional commander, who told me to send them along. I asked Teltsov where the prisoners were. He stood there, smiling, and said: "The report was mistaken, they've all been shot."

It turns out that Teltsov had personally ordered them to be shot. In that whole period we had eight prisoners, including two officers: a pilot and a Romanian. The Red Army takes no prisoners. I got an earful from divisional commander Dubyansky: "Why didn't you take any prisoners?"

Everyone had the same excuse: "They tried to escape, so we shot them."

THE HISTORY INSTRUCTOR: CAPTAIN NIKOLAI AKSYONOV

Captain Nikolai Aksyonov and the sniper Vasily Zaytsev, the respondents in the following two interviews, both belonged to the Siberian 284th Rifle Division. (After showing exemplary valor in the battle of Stalingrad, it was renamed the 79th Red Banner Guards Division.) The division was formed in December 1941 from soldiers in the military districts of Tomsk, Novosibirsk, and Kemerovo.[104] Following heavy losses in eastern Ukraine and outside Voronezh, the division was recalled to the Urals in early August 1942, where it replenished its ranks with new local recruits and several thousand sailors from the Pacific Fleet. On September 6, while the division was still conducting training exercises, its commander, Colonel

Divisional commander Nikolai Batyuk

Nikolai Batyuk, received the order to deploy immediately to the Stalingrad Front.[105] The division reached Stalingrad on September 18; the Germans had already taken Mamayev Kurgan.[106] The battle had also spread to the central ferry slip on the west bank of the Volga, forcing the division to cross at a spot to the north, near the Red October factory. On September 20 Batyuk's soldiers were loaded onto barges and conveyed across the river. "Right off the bank" recalled Batyuk in his interview, "we received our combat objective and started fighting, not even knowing our bearings."

Some of Batyuk's men had the mission of retaking Mamayev Kurgan; others were to help the 13th Guards Division, which had been forced to move northward after the Germans captured the central ferry slip on September 22. The Soviets recaptured Mamayev Kurgan, but on September 28 it passed back into German hands. Batyuk's soldiers nevertheless clung to the southern and eastern slopes of the hill, blocking the path to the industrial district and the Volga.[107] The Red Army did not gain complete control of the hill until January 16, 1943.[108]

Captain Aksyonov, a deputy regimental commander in the 284th Rifle Division, led a resupply unit into the burning city on September 30. He portrays the battles his regiment faced in minute detail: the defense of Mamayev Kurgan, the January offensive, and the defeat of the Germans. Before the war Aksyonov taught history at the Tomsk Pedagogical Institute, and he employed his historical knowledge to mobilize his soldiers. In the midst of the battle he recalled his lectures on the Civil War and the battle of Tsaritsyn. He told his troops how Joseph Stalin led the defense of the city from Mamayev Kurgan. Given in the regiment's shelter at the foot of the hill, his talk was so rousing that some soldiers jumped up, eager to examine the trenches from 1918. From that point on the soldiers spoke of Mamayev Kurgan as a "sacred place, the place where Stalin had been."[109]

This story shows how the cult of Stalin had morphed into a cult of military genius by the time the war began. Stalin was no longer just the best and most loyal student of Lenin; he single-handedly led Russia's defense against the foreign invaders.[110] Aksyonov was one of many eyewitnesses to promote Stalin's military legend. In his interview he expresses delight that Stalin was promoted to Marshal of the Soviet Union in March 1943. Among the photographs he submitted to the Historical Commission (some of which he took himself) were several pictures of the building that housed the 10th Soviet Army during the battle of Tsaritsyn. One photo is a close-up of a bullet hole–riddled commemorative plaque informing visitors that comrades Stalin and Voroshilov worked in there in 1918.

Aksyonov's testimony is vivid and detailed, and his account of the storming of Mamayev Kurgan has a cinematic quality. No less dramatic are his memories of September 30, 1942, the day he first entered the burning city, and of February 25, 1943, when after 149 uninterrupted days of fighting he crossed the Volga and was astonished to see an undamaged wooden house.

COMMISSION ON THE HISTORY OF THE GREAT PATRIOTIC WAR

May 5, 1943
Interview conducted by comrade Belkin
Stenography: comrade Laputina
Nikolai Nikitich AKSYONOV
Guards captain, 1047th Regiment, 79th Guards Red Banner Division
Deputy chief of staff for operations[111]

I was born in 1908 in the village of Podoynikova, in the Pankrushikhinsky district of the Altai region. I joined the army on September 8, 1941. I was awarded the Order of the Red Banner for my part in the defense of Stalingrad. Before the war I was a teacher at the Tomsk Pedagogical Institute.

We got to Stalingrad on September 30, 1942. About ten kilometers out I could already see a massive wall of smoke, and the glow from the city was getting brighter as we approached. The entire city seemed to be on fire. The fires looked especially intense at the Red October factory and the oil refinery, which was right where our division was located. I got to the riverbank just as it was getting dark. Stalingrad looked particularly terrifying then. Everything was burning. Oil was flowing out of broken tanks at the refinery and coming down to the banks, and this wall of fire was reflected in the water, making flames appear still taller than they really were. It was a very difficult situation.

We crossed the river at night. The barge we were crossing on got shelled by the Germans. As it happened, the rope connecting us to the tug boat broke, and while the tug went to shore for another rope, we were anchored in the middle of the river with the Germans still shelling us. The whole crossing took us about two hours. We had wounded men on the barge. Mortar shells were exploding close by. The Germans were launching flares that completely lit up the river, but there was nothing we could do—that was particularly unpleasant.

On the night of October 1 we got to our regiment. The next morning I went out to the front line to get to know all the combat units in our sector. I saw all kinds of terrible things there. At the very end of September the Germans bombed our division's positions, especially the refinery, which we were defending. Many of our men were killed: they lay out in the open all over the place, lots of dead bodies in craters, and there were a lot of dead civilians—women and children by the boats, by the buildings, all over the place.

I headed straight for the Metiz factory.[112] It was on fire. There was a smell of burning and of dead bodies; it was hot, dusty, smoky—that's what it was like there. There was fighting going on in 1st Battalion's sector.

I was with Petersky, the chief of staff, and Benesh, the commander of the 1st Battalion, and we surveyed the regiment's entire sector, relocated our machine-gun emplacements in a way that made better sense and returned to our command post by the end of the day. The command post was located on the west bank about three or four hundred meters from the front line.

Starting from September 30, I was in Stalingrad for 152 days on end, never leaving. Very few people went back to the west bank for any reason. You could say that those five months I spent in Stalingrad were the equivalent of five years of normal life.

I learned that we had around five hundred casualties on the first day of fighting, and on October 5 we had 1,300 men. There were companies with only twenty to twenty-five men left.

In early October we were always having to repel counterattacks in two areas of our sector: the Metiz factory and the infamous Mamayev Kurgan, Hill 102.

Our forward line was around fifty to sixty meters away from the Germans, in some places up to one hundred meters. That kind of close distance was rare. It happened most often when we were fighting in the streets, which quickly led to the rise of the hand grenade. Attacks were usually repelled with grenades, along with other kinds of weapons. In our sector the Germans outnumbered us by a factor of five or six. We were basing that on our reconnaissance, observations, and information from other sources, and also the Germans were sending out wave after wave of squads. It wasn't unusual for them to come at us four or five times a day.

[. . .] The toughest fighting in our sector broke out in mid-October. As a historian, I tried to draw comparisons to battles I know from history: Borodino, Verdun during the Imperialist War,[113] but none of that was right because the scale of the conflict in Stalingrad makes it hard to compare it to anything. It seemed as if Stalingrad was breathing fire for days on end. Our Ilyushins[114] did show up, but they took a lot of losses. The Messerschmitts shot them down quickly. The Germans suffered great losses from our U-2s at night, but that wasn't until November. We called them the "gardeners," and they did us a lot of good. They crossed the Volga from east to west, and before they got to enemy lines they cut their engines. Then they dropped their bombs. Once they were back on our side they started their engines again. That's why the U-2 was so hard to catch. But the Germans bombed us at night too.

I remember once having to go to from the meatpacking plant[115] to our command post. We'd just left when the Germans launched flares and started bombing us so much the buildings shook. The night raids really get to you. During the day you can see where they're coming from and work out where the bombs are going, so you don't get too worked up over it. You get used to it eventually.

By the way, it was here that I first saw our bombers attacking with Katyushas, though they didn't come very often at all. On the whole, we had a very slight air presence in Stalingrad, and what we did have was weak. I couldn't say why.

I don't know why, but almost everyone in the division had diarrhea. We were drinking unboiled water, and the Volga was polluted with oil, dead bodies, bits of wood, and so on. The diarrhea was wearing everyone out. I had it myself. General Chuikov, the army commander, had this cook called Boris who joked that he could cure us with his general's dry rusks. General Chuikov had made his command post in the same place as ours, and his kitchen and ours had amalgamated, which is why he was saying that.

In mid-October we reinforced our front line. The Germans weren't pressing us on Mamayev Kurgan. Actually it was us who was pressing them. Mamayev Kurgan was divided into two areas. The eastern [slope] was ours, and they held on to the western slopes, and on top of that the Germans had the water tanks, or the "devil's domes," as they were known. They had their main observation posts in those tanks, and all their artillery observers were safe inside, even though they were right on our front line. So the Germans were in control of the dominant position on the hill. And that's why the subsequent battle for Mamayev Kurgan was really a battle for these tanks. Whoever controlled the water tanks controlled Mamayev Kurgan.

[. . .]

We were never short of ammunition. The ammunition supply weakened only when the Volga started icing over, but until then we always felt that we had enough. Our supply of ammunition was brought across from the east bank on rickety little boats. Our divisional relay point was on the east bank. Each regiment had to transport its own food and supplies across the river. The army had a forward supply unit on the west bank, but it did little to keep us supplied with ammunition.

We had orders from Chuikov and the divisional commander saying that we needed to have our own way of getting across the river. All the barges were broken up, burned, and sunk. There were even large cutters sticking nose-up on the riverbank. The only means of transport we had was these tiny boats. At first our regiment had seven boats, but then this went up to ten, and then we got two pontoons—actually, one part of a pontoon. We jokingly called these boats Korobkov's flotilla. Korobkov was the deputy chief of staff for logistics, the one who created this "flotilla." He's a former teacher and school principal, a great organizer and administrator. He's alive and well, and was given the Medal for Battle Merit. Those rickety boats were the best way we had of crossing the Volga.

I remembered how, back in 1918, comrade Stalin issued an order to remove all the vessels from the river near Stalingrad and send them to the north. That was at the most critical period when the Germans were approaching the city, and we could not fall back.[116] When I was in Stalingrad we didn't have any way of crossing the river, and we never had such an order. Sometimes the cutters would come at night to evacuate the wounded. That was only up until the ice came. After that, all of our clothing, ammunition, equipment, the wounded—everything was taken on those small boats. We couldn't use any other form of transport to supply the regiment because even these rickety boats were getting shot at by mortars and machine guns, and a barge definitely would have been shot up. So the most durable transport turned out to be these tiny boats.

The Volga started icing over on November 9 and was frozen solid by December 17. We were completely fed up with it. This was the hardest time for our army. It was really difficult for the boats to make their way there and back through the ice floes. They'd get stuck, people would be having to move from one little block of ice to the next. There were times when the current took the boats downriver toward the German shore, and then they'd have to either ditch the boat or dump the cargo and try to steer the boat out of danger. One of our boats was taken about three kilometers past Stalingrad, and we were looking for our men for five days. On the whole, the "beautiful Volga" tried our patience and got on our nerves. We did not love the Volga back then. In the morning everyone would ask: Has it frozen over yet? And the Germans, as we learned from prisoners, were also anxiously hoping that the Volga would ice over soon. They knew we were having difficulties, and their plan was to make use of the ice for an offensive.

On November 11 the Germans launched an attack on the sector of the Metiz factory, but nothing came of it.

[. . .] We took a second German prisoner and brought him to regimental HQ. This was the first one we got to talk in Stalingrad. He was a private. He was wounded, and so the men brought him in on a stretcher, but since it was November and the men still hadn't gotten gloves, they kept dropping the stretcher to warm their hands. He had internal injuries, but since this was our first captured German, they started to revive him. The doctor, Krasnov, tried hard to bring him back so he could be questioned. And he did get better, even managed to say that he was a private 1st class in the 216th Regiment, but we didn't get anything else out of him. He died. The second prisoner had more to say. We learned that our division was up against the Germans' 295th Division. That prisoner was very disrespectful and defiant. He came right out and said he was a member of the Nazi party. We sent him to our army HQ, after which he was sent to front HQ. He still considered himself a winner and didn't let on that he was anything other than happy. Though he did tell us how difficult things were for them with clothing at this time. By the end of November we'd already gotten our winter uniforms, but the Germans still hadn't gotten theirs by the end of the battle, though they did keep hoping that they would. [. . .]

The snipers in our regiment played an important role in our active defense of Stalingrad. The snipers appeared in Colonel Metelyov's regiment during the heaviest fighting for Stalingrad, in October. The pioneers of the sniper movement in the regiment were Alexander

Kalentyev—a Siberian from the Urals—and the sailor Vasily Zaytsev, who is now a Hero of Soviet Union. Altogether there were forty-eight snipers in the regiment. During the fighting in Stalingrad, in the streets and on Mamayev Kurgan, they eliminated 1,278 Germans. The role of leader for these forty or so best snipers in the regiment belonged, of course, to Vasily Zaytsev. He was an excellent shot, and he quickly perfected the art of sniping and of being a lone warrior. He actually did the job of a regimental instructor, and he went around to all the units in the regiment. Soon he had a lot of students. The most successful sniper movement was developed in Captain Kotov's 2nd Battalion. That battalion was defending the Metiz factory on the southern slope of Mamayev Kurgan. There was this sense that every soldier and officer in Stalingrad was itching to kill as many Germans as possible. In Stalingrad people felt a particularly intense hatred for the Germans. That was one of the reasons for the sniper movement in our regiment. There were a lot of soldiers who wanted to become snipers, which is why we had snipers using ordinary rifles rather than sniper rifles. Zaytsev would take the best of them, and his main selection criteria were courage, resourcefulness, and composure. Zaytsev went around to the units in the regiment and questioned their commanders, observed the men on the front line, and selected his snipers. Then he trained them. After showing them the scope and doing some target practice, Zaytsev would take his marksmen out to the firing positions. Zaytsev developed the surest and most reliable way to train snipers: he demonstrated what a sniper does right on the front line.

A lot of people went to the front line on their own initiative. Krasnov, the doctor, would sneak out there—he had a count of eight dead Germans.

Izvekov, a medic, would be dressing the wounded in a bunker on the front line, and then he'd run over to the firing positions and shoot at the Germans with his rifle. His count was twenty-one dead Germans.

Zekov, a medic from the 2nd Battalion, became a sniper, so then he had two qualifications: he was a medic and a sniper. His count was forty-five dead Germans. He was given the Order of the Red Star. He had one unfortunate incident—he killed one of our own pilots. One of our fighter planes rammed a German bomber. Two men came down in parachutes. The first one came down on our side. He was on fire, and there was a trail of smoke coming up from his parachute. We didn't know whether he was one of us or one of them, and as he got closer to the ground they could hear him screaming. Zekov had a deadly hatred of the Germans, and he decided that this was the German pilot. He shot at him and killed the man in the parachute, who turned out to be our own pilot, twice decorated. Zekov was absolutely crushed, and it affected the regiment deeply. We buried the dead pilot. Zekov was tried and given a ten-year sentence, which was to be served out on the front line. Zekov was brave and energetic, a real fighter. Being a medic didn't really suit him. While serving out his sentence on the front line, he started eliminating Germans together with Zaytsev, and by the end of the battle he'd killed forty-five Germans. His criminal record was wiped clean, and they gave him the Order of the Red Star.

Even the commander's adjutants would sneak out to try their hand at sniping.

As soon as the chief of staff got to the front line, he would shoot every one of the machine guns. This was also something I did myself. We'd often have to inspect the machine-gun nests. You'd go to the front line for inspections, to check the battalion's combat readiness and, above all, the automatic weapons. I loved shooting the machine guns.

Zaytsev taught his men individually, in groups, and also at meetings of the sniper detachment. The sniper detachment raised the level of our defenses even more, strengthening our resistance. In a very short span of time our snipers brought heavy losses to the enemy, forced them to keep low, and kept them from moving about in the open. Another reason the snipers did so well was that they spent extended periods of time covering literally every approach, every bunker and trench. The second a German tried to take a look around, he'd get a bullet from one of our men. Colonel Metelyov's regiment was famous in Stalingrad and on the entire Stalingrad Front for being a sniper regiment. The exploits of our regiment's snipers were constantly being written about in the papers. That encouraged and inspired the snipers, and also got word of their experiences to soldiers in other units. Zaytsev was a skilled agitator: he was a strong and persuasive speaker. Since he was a member of the Komsomol bureau, he would tour the subunits on Komsomol business, and at the same time he promoted the sniper movement.

The daily reinforcement of our forward defensive line played a major role in the active defense of Stalingrad. I, for example, was moved from regimental headquarters and specially assigned to the 1st Battalion at Mamayev Kurgan. The battalion commander was Lieutenant Georgy Benesh. I was there at Mamayev Kurgan every two or three days, and the two of us were always busy strengthening the front line. [. . .]

Commander Benesh was a truly brave man: a scout, a sniper, and an excellent tactician. He never thought about death, he laughed at death. When he was asked whether he was afraid of dying, he said that he carried death around with him up until the fighting at Kiev, and after Kiev he banished it from his heart. This one time, the two of us were on our way to the front line. We climbed up Mamayev Kurgan and came under German machine-gun fire. We had to lie down. I yelled at him: "Get down!" He was always cracking jokes and he said to me with a laugh: "If Benesh is going to die fighting for Stalingrad, then he's going to die on his feet." He liked messing with people. When we made it to the front line, I couldn't see anyone around, but Benesh was all ready to shoot his sniper rifle. I put up the periscope and started looking. They started shooting my periscope right away, the Germans were following us that closely. I moved to another location. But Benesh popped out and started shooting. I saw that he'd taken off his cap and was looking over the top of the periscope. A German jumped out from behind a tank and started running for the water tank. Benesh got him. He said that made eleven Germans he'd killed.

I was out with him several times, both during the day and at night, and he never had any regard for his safety. You could say it was criminal, how little he took care of himself. And he died for nothing, he died stupidly. He was moving from one building to another, and he was killed by a random mortar shell. He'd been with the medic Rada Zavadskaya. He told her: "You and me, Rada, defending Stalingrad." Benesh was a poet. He was Vasily Grossman's step-nephew. He'd recently asked me to look for Grossman, but I never managed to do it. Benesh was nominated for a medal, and the order for his promotion and decoration came three days after he died. He was decorated for the fighting at Kastornaya.[117] On the subject of Grossman I should say that when he spoke with our regimental commander, he didn't so much as ask about Benesh, and he showed no interest in his diary.[118] His diary was burned. There were a lot of complaints in it about cowardly commanders, and a lot of poetry and outspoken words. Benesh was buried in a cemetery on the riverbank. Since then that cemetery has been known as the burial place for the commanders of the 1047th Regiment.[119]

[Interview continues, May 8, 1943]

No one wanted to take Mamayev Kurgan as much as Benesh, and no one talked about it as often. I remember how you could go up to him at night, "Let's go to the front," and he'd say: "Let's go." He was always going there.

The men in Batyuk's division were the only ones at Mamayev Kurgan from September 21 to January 12. We took heavy losses there. The Germans wanted to push us off the hill completely. We wanted to take those water tanks at any cost because Mamayev Kurgan was the dominant height in the city. On a clear day you could see it about ten kilometers away. It rose about eighty meters above Stalingrad. At the beginning we were having to shoot upward. That's the most hazardous and awkward combat situation: the reverse slope defense. It's impossible to set up a successful fire plan. We were constantly having to try to get up to that ridge, and we considered it a victory if we managed to push the Germans back to gain five to seven meters in a night. [. . .]

An interesting thing happened on October 18. I was in good spirits. As I was looking out over the city I could sense the whole of Stalingrad, and I started thinking about Tsaritsyn, the defense of Tsaritsyn, which I'd only recently given a lecture on at the pedagogical institute. And now here I was defending Stalingrad myself. I told my comrades about these recollections, and I told them how in 1918 Mamayev Kurgan was comrade Stalin's command and observation post. Not many of them knew that. They knew that Stalin had been in Tsaritsyn, that he defended Tsaritsyn, but they didn't know any details. Benesh wanted to know more. He dragged me into the bunker of Lieutenant Litvenenko, where about fifteen people had gathered, and I began telling them about the defense of Tsaritsyn. I delivered an ad hoc lecture for an hour. The story was still fresh in my mind and well suited to the occasion. When they were leaving the bunker, they all wanted to see the trenches from 1918. Benesh used this story, and he asked me to tell other companies about the defense of Tsaritsyn. Afterward the men better understood the symbolic meaning of the defense of Stalingrad. The fact that Stalin had been here went deep into the hearts of these men, and it inspired them. Benesh wanted to take Mamayev Kurgan all the more after hearing that story. We jokingly referred to Mamayev Kurgan as the sacred place, the place where Stalin had been.

On November 20 our division and the entire 62nd Army got the order to attack. The men and officers received that order with great enthusiasm. [. . .] Our regiment was the unit from the division that was slated to attack Mamayev Kurgan and the water tanks. Benesh was gone by then. Zhidkikh was now the commander of 1st Battalion. 2nd Battalion was in the Metiz factory, and 3rd Battalion was advancing with us on the south slope of the hill. But the most important task was to be completed by the 1st Battalion of the 1047th Regiment. By then we'd already developed some new offensive tactics. We understood by then that small assault groups were much more successful. All the battalions and regiments attacked in small assault groups, and that was the only way we could attack, even though Mamayev Kurgan was like being out in the country more than in a city or even a village.

The first attacks were unsuccessful, and we were taking a lot of casualties. The men threw themselves into the assault. Officers broke every rule and ran out in front, but they were still unsuccessful. Out of twenty men in the battalion only four or five would be left. The rest were either killed or wounded. We attacked three or four times that day, at different times of the day: early morning and sunset, during the day and at night. We tried everything and had nothing to show for it. In those early days we attacked with tanks. Two tanks went behind the water tanks—one was destroyed, the other went missing. Our three remaining tanks were immobilized. One broke down, and the other two were on fire.

Incidentally, not much was accomplished during our heaviest stage of artillery preparation. Our artillery support was often inaccurate, and there was some friendly fire. On the 20th, 21st, 22nd, 23rd, 24th, and 25th we were fighting constantly for the water tanks. I spent the first few days at our headquarters. The commander and chief of staff were there the whole time. On the 26, 27th, and 28th, I was on the front line at an observation post with the battalion commander, Lieutenant Ustyuzhanin. Three battalions attacked the water tanks over the course of five or six days. We hit them from the sides. On the sixth day we managed to move about two hundred meters north of the water tanks and pose a real threat. That weakened the Germans' position. Now we could strike them on their flanks. 3rd Battalion moved to the south where they could hit them from the side, and 2nd Battalion was to the west of the water tanks, where they could hit them straight-on. That way we were able to hit them from three sides, but even with that we still weren't able to take the water tanks. Then, on January 10, 1943, we took them, and Mamayev Kurgan was ours. We wanted to know what these things were like in terms of their layout. I also climbed into these tanks. The walls were made of reinforced concrete, about a meter thick, and they were buried in dirt on the outside so that they looked less like tanks than hills. There were two of these, with partitions on the inside, where the water had been. They'd cut a lot of embrasures in the tanks, and these were hard to get at. The whole thing was a pillbox the Germans had set up for artillery. They had at least twenty machine guns there. There were great positions for the German snipers, who killed a lot of our officers. [. . .]

The first snow came to Stalingrad on the 28th. The day before there'd been wind and rain. Our overcoats were frozen solid. Everyone was cold and miserable. Lieutenant Salnikov, 1st Battalion's deputy commander for operations, was sent to the front line to make sure everything was in order. He ended up crawling from one trench to another trying to encourage the men. They got ten men as reinforcements. They brought them breakfast at dawn. Salnikov promised that they'd be getting their winter gear that day, and he ordered company commander Shevelyov to prepare for the attack. We were supposed to attack together with the division's training battalion, which was attached to us, and with the 1st Battalion of the 1043rd Regiment. When everything was nearly ready, Salnikov went out to the front line. He wanted to take another look to see that all the men were where they needed to be. It was already light out. A German sniper took aim and shot Salnikov in the head. And that's how Salnikov, one of our most loyal Old Bolsheviks, was killed.

We attacked again at ten o'clock on the 28th, but we didn't take the tanks that time either. The training battalion was almost completely destroyed—there were only a few men left. You could say that after that attack our division's training battalion ceased to exist. Some of the commanders were sent to our regiment, some to divisional HQ. [. . .]

The offensives in December were also pretty rough. We had very few gains, but our operations in the city did finally contain the enemy, and that was important for the units attacking from the west: to prevent the enemy from maneuvering now that they were encircled.

Our regiment was sent over to the northern slopes of Mamayev Kurgan. We were defending the area between the railway line, which lay on the east side of the hill, and the water tanks. In November our regiment's path to Mamayev Kurgan was obstructed by those water tanks we weren't able to take. Now what was in our way was the Unnamed Height, which was one of the heights on the north side of Mamayev Kurgan. We had to take this height, and anyway it was keeping us from taking the tanks. It was a bit taller than the other heights, and the Germans were very solidly entrenched there, with no fewer than thirty machine guns and a whole system of communication trenches and bunkers. What's more, they had a nice approach to the hill where they had clean lines of sight from their many bunkers. At night they would slip out and improve their defenses, and, when necessary, send in reinforcements.

On January 12–13 the 1043rd and 1045th regiments finally took the water tanks and began moving toward the western slopes of Mamayev Kurgan. The Germans dominated Mamayev Kurgan from that Unnamed Height, so we had to take that height.

1st Battalion's commander at the time was Captain Zhidkikh, and his deputy was Lieutenant Bolvachyov.

For one whole day we got ready to storm the height. Small assault teams were formed. At 1:00 P.M. on January 14, these assault teams attacked the pillboxes and bunkers in waves from the front and a little from the right flank.

I was at 2nd Battalion's command post, about seventy meters from the forward edge, on the railway line. Small groups went into the attack, forty men in total. The Germans obviously outnumbered us, both in men and machine guns. We had more mortars. Until 1:00 P.M. it was just the usual shooting from both sides. It was a cold, frosty day. We didn't have any artillery preparation. It was quiet all around. You could tell that the Germans were holed up in their bunkers, not expecting an attack, since it was an unusual time for an attack. We had five cannons set out in the open. They started shooting at the bunkers where there was smoke. The attack was delayed by half an hour. One group of submachine gunners in white camouflage ran the hundred meters and rushed the German trenches, splitting up and attacking the bunkers from both ends. The Germans jumped out of the bunkers, and our men found themselves right up next to them. One assault group was led by Private Antonov, another group was led by Sergeant Kudryavtsev, the third by Lieutenant Babayev, and the fourth group by Lieutenant Maksimov. All of them distinguished themselves that day and in the coming battles.

I felt like this wasn't real fighting, that this was all just for practice. After four months in Stalingrad we had become so used to danger, so numbed by danger, that it often seemed as if these were just exercises rather than combat. This time was like that: it felt like a training mission. Our men were wearing white camouflage, but the Germans didn't have any, and you could easily pick out their dark figures. You could see people's breaths in the cold air.

Antonov burst into the trench, grabbed a rifle by the barrel, and started hitting Germans in the head left and right. By the way, we didn't use bayonets in Stalingrad, all of them got tossed aside. I ordered our big guns to shoot just above the Germans' heads to cut off any approaching groups. Then men took Antonov's gun-swinging as a sign to cease fire. A sniper yelled at me, telling me to stop shooting.

Through my binoculars I could see Antonov beating the Germans, and Kudryavtsev's group coming from the opposite direction and throwing grenades at the Germans in their trenches. That's when the intense grenade fight began. Then Maksimov's group threw themselves into the fight. The whole thing took about fifteen to twenty minutes. The Germans still hadn't had time to recover and hadn't really started shooting. It seemed strange that there was all this hand-to-hand combat, that the Germans weren't shooting. There wasn't any fire from our side, either, nothing from the machine guns or mortars. But that was because we didn't want hit our own men. All the fighting took place in the German trenches.

When our men went up the hill in their camouflage, the Germans threw reinforcements at them from above. Then our machine guns, mortars, and artillery opened fire, and that kept the Germans from holding them back. That day we took most of the height, but not all of it.

[. . .] We took possession of the entire hill on January 16. We knocked the Germans back down the western slopes. The fighting lasted two days. Afterward we raised a red flag with the words: "For the Motherland, for Stalin!" The slogan was written by the regiment's propagandist, Captain Rakityansky. [. . .]

We said it was a historic day: January 26, the day we met up with the Don Front. An unforgettable day, an unforgettable meeting. I was

"The Red Flag Flies on Mamayev Kurgan," 1943. *Photographer: Georgy Zelma*

at regimental HQ. It wasn't easy staying at headquarters when both the commander and chief of staff had left for the front line. I couldn't leave because I was on the phone with the observation post.

At 10:00 A.M. I heard from 1st Battalion's observation post that Shavrin, a scout, had seen nine tanks approaching Mamayev Kurgan from the northwest. We had the idea that these ought to be ours, but we were worried that maybe the Germans might be trying their luck, disguising themselves in our uniforms. It was impossible to know right away whose tanks they were. After a few minutes the scout said now it was fourteen tanks. Then he saw a red flag on the lead vehicle, and we knew right away that those tanks were Russian, not German.' We'd put up red flags on the Unnamed Height, on the water tanks, and on the boxcars. That way approaching units would be able to identify us. Everyone was on their guard then. We were nearing the historic moment when the two fronts came together.

At 11:00 A.M. Captain Kotov, commander of 2nd Battalion, reported that his men had gone up to the lead vehicle. The men greeted one another and exchanged kisses, and for a moment they forgot about the war. It seemed as if we weren't at war. I asked whose unit it was. Captain Kotov said that it was the lead vehicle of a Colonel Nezhinsky. Then he sent his major to meet our regimental commanders. The meeting took place at the flag pole on the Unnamed Height. There was also a meeting on the western slopes of Mamayev Kurgan. A brief rally was organized, and they were officially received by our division's political chief, Colonel Tkachenko. They wrote about this in *Pravda*.

When this meeting took place between the two fronts—the 62nd Army and the Don Front—the encircled enemy forces were split in half. From then on there were two encircled groups: a southern group in the center of the city and a northern group, centered on the Barricades factory. The commander of the Don Front had apparently decided to destroy these groups in turn. First it was to be the southern group in the center of the city, which was much stronger and was rumored to be where Paulus was, which turned out to be the case. [. . .]

On January 28 we finished the operation, and by order of the divisional commanders our regiment was sent to the northern slopes of the Long Ravine near Ryazhskaya and Artillery streets. Our mission was to break the enemy defenses in the Long Ravine and move toward the center of the city along the railway line.

We fought all day on the 28th and took a lot of casualties, but we didn't take a single meter from the Germans. We'd come up against some of their long-standing defensive positions. The Long Ravine was fortified with many firing points and emplacements, the slopes were mined and covered in barbed wire, and we weren't able to take it. [. . .] The divisional commander ordered us to do anything necessary to complete our mission, but we had only a few men.[120] [. . .] The men were worn out. Some slept while the others manned the machine guns and other weapons. The battalion commanders also slept. [. . .] I looked after the men, made sure they were well fed and were getting enough to drink. We prepared all night. Ustyuzhanin and I had a clear idea how strong the German's defenses were. We couldn't overpower them by brute force, but we were betting that their morale was hanging by a thread. We needed to organize everything and prepare a coordinated attack so we could make a quick strike on the Germans, demoralize them, and take them prisoner. Other regiments were betting on the same thing.

The regimental commander sent me to our command post, where I acted on his behalf and explained our upcoming mission in detail, not as an order but as a decision for each battalion commander to make for himself. [. . .] Some of our scouts managed to get far behind enemy lines and chanced upon the German battalion commander's command post, where he was with his adjutant. The other Germans were in bunkers on the front line. As soon as the adjutant jumped out and started shooting, our men started throwing grenades. Then the battalion commander came out with his hands in the air. He was a neat, robust officer in a greatcoat that didn't fit well. And I've got to say, he was the only German wearing a greatcoat.

That was when the assault groups crossed the defensive lines, flanking the Germans and throwing grenades. That caught them off guard. They started running away one by one. When we found out we had the German commander, we took him to a high place, gave him a sheet, and ordered him to signal his men to surrender. It was getting light out. The German commander waved the sheet, telling his men to surrender. German soldiers started putting up their hands and giving themselves up by the dozen. Scouts and officers disarmed them and stacked their weapons in a pile. At first there were sixty men, and after some time more than a hundred had surrendered.

The 1043rd and 1045th Regiments came just in time to share the prisoners. That morning our regiment took 172 prisoners. At the time that was the most prisoners ever taken by a regiment. Afterward, though, there were still more. I took prisoners, took their weapons. Our guys had a bit of fun with them. The Germans were wrapped up in all kinds of things. One of them had a blanket on each foot. Others wore sheets and looked like scarecrows. We got them in formation and took them to our regimental command post. I gave a report to our divisional commander, and they congratulated us on our successes. I also reported this to army commander Chuikov when I passed by his command post.

Then a cameraman came and told us to climb up the steep bank. He chose the best place for filming, with Stalingrad in the background, and up front there were prisoners on the slope along with the battalion commander in the bad coat. I was walking behind swinging a whip. That was one of the more interesting days in the history of our regiment.

We crossed the Long Ravine, and since there weren't any strong enemy defenses we were able to move into the center of the city.

Our successes continued on January 30 as our division moved to the Ninth of January Square. The Germans were still holding out. There hadn't been any instances of entire German regiments surrendering. They were broken, but still they weren't surrendering entire units. The northern group even pushed back part of our encirclement, and there was a certain amount of danger. [. . .]

The Germans set up a perimeter defense around the Central Hotel. German officers were standing at all the entrances. They were incidents when they'd stick out a flag of surrender from the second floor, and when you went to get your prisoners they'd shoot from the other floors. After that we took a Polish prisoner who we were able to use as a truce envoy. He went about a dozen times and brought out groups of fifteen to twenty Germans. He was a good propagandist, and only too willing to pick out German officers and snipers to be shot.

On the 30th, at the end of the day, the divisional commander asked what should be done with that officers' house: destroy it or leave it. The radio message was something like this: "Ask the commander what is to be done with their garrison at the Central Hotel: leave it or destroy it." The army commander ordered us to destroy the garrison. What ended up happening was that we left some of our men, and the rest of the division moved in to occupy the central areas of the city and the train station. At 2:00 P.M. on the 31st the division reached the Stalingrad train station. We took the station and met the 64th Army, which was coming up to the center from the south. You could say that by 2:00 P.M. on the 31st, the southern group of encircled Germans was done for, but the officers in the Central Hotel were still holding out.

The commander again heard reports about the difficulties of storming the Central Hotel. His orders were to take it immediately, and

Prisoners of war in Stalingrad, 1943. *Photographer: Natalya Bode*

he gave us five tanks for the job. We had four or five assault groups in our regiment. Maksimov, Babayev, and Kudryavtsev proved themselves again, and they were later given awards. When the tanks rolled up and started firing point-blank at the building, our assault groups broke inside, but even there the Germans continued to resist. About one hundred of them were killed, and sixty surrendered. We captured their hospital. I couldn't believe it was a hospital. The orderlies were wearing new overcoats, absolutely spotless. I guessed that they were officers in disguise, though they did everything they could to show they weren't officers and had nothing to do with defending the building.

This last remaining German stronghold in the center of the city fell at 4:00 P.M. on the 31st. Our artist did a sketch of the building.

Our regiment's single greatest loss came on the 31st. A mine killed Captain Vasily Ivanovich Rakityansky,[121] the regiment's propagandist, a fearless soldier who had been wounded twice on the front line. He was a Siberian too. He'd been a second secretary in the Narymsk City Party Committee. He was a writer and a political worker. What he wanted most that day was to go with the men to the front line, and once they had taken the stronghold, he had a red flag ready to go. He'd set things up with the cameraman: Rakityansky was going to take the red flag and place it on the hotel. The cameraman was already getting ready to film when Rakityansky stepped on that mine. A pointless way to die.[122] [. . .]

On February 1 the whole division moved from the center of the city to go fight against the northern group. [. . .] On the night of the 2nd we got orders to advance toward the airport and the parachute tower and then turn right toward the Barricades factory. It's interesting to note that the soldiers started attacking even before they got the order. They could see things were going pretty well, that the Germans weren't shooting much, that they were surrendering, and so they started attacking about half an hour before the order. By the time the regimental commander arrived, the fighting had already begun. The Germans were putting up a good fight, especially at the Barricades factory, but we attacked swiftly and in full strength. That day we took more than eight hundred prisoners. Throughout the fighting in Stalingrad we took 1,554 prisoners. At that point we were trying to take out isolated centers of German resistance. The Barricades factory was well defended. We captured regimental commanders, chiefs of staff. At the end we were interrogating the officers. I remember being in a bunker when they brought me this deputy chief of staff for their 113th Division, a major. We'd captured their deputy chief of staff for logistics and the commandant. These prisoners answered deviously, trying to be loyal. During the interrogations they didn't remember everything right away, they'd get things wrong. But others would jump in to correct them, and they seemed sincere, as if they were trying to demonstrate their sincerity. One major was wearing a Red Army cap with a swastika. One soldier from our headquarters platoon pulled the cap from his head, ripped off the swastika, threw it at him, and tossed the cap to the side.

We also took the Barricades factory. That was the last stronghold of the northern group. The Barricades factory fell at 1:30 P.M. on February 2. Just after 3:00 P.M. all our operations had ended, and our division went to the banks of the Volga.

You can consider 2:30 P.M. a historic moment, the time when the guns stopped firing in the battle of Stalingrad. When I heard that on the telephone, I wrote this in my diary: "Glory to the victors! Today, at 2:30 P.M. on February 2, 1943, the last of the fighting in Stalingrad ended at the Barricades factory. The final shot of this great battle rang out at that historic moment. Today the guns are quiet. Stalingrad has been successfully defended, and thousands of Germans are plodding their way across the Volga. They have witnesses firsthand our ability to fight and win. I know that our descendants will remember this battle far into the future. Only now, as the pressure begins to subside, can I begin think of just how much we've done in Stalingrad."

A few words on the prisoners. They were demoralized. At first we were looking them over one by one, but then we lost all interest. They were already saying "Hitler kaput," to which one of our men remarked: "It's not November [1942] for you anymore, now the whole bunch of you is kaput."

One time we did a search of some prisoners. There were about seventy of them. I started talking to them through an interpreter. The regimental commander came and asked what I was talking to them about. I said I was asking them whether they'd seen the Volga. It turned out that most of them hadn't. Then the regimental commander turned to them and said, via the interpreter, that today they would finally be crossing the river. And within half an hour there was a line of prisoners stretching across the Volga. [. . .]

We were in Stalingrad until March 6. We took a short break after the fighting, and then we started studying. Our task was to examine the German systems of defense. We gathered our intel from the field. The commanders climbed around all the enemy bunkers, trenches, and firing points to identify our own shortcomings and to arrive at some

Red Army soldiers in the ruins of Stalingrad, February 1943.

conclusions based on our combat experiences and to get something we could make use of down the line.

All this intel was collected and summarized by the headquarters staffs. The staffs were working especially hard. I reported my information to the regimental commander, and the regimental commanders gave their reports to the divisional commander, and the divisional commander invited the division's entire command staff—down to the battalion commanders—to come hear his detailed analysis of the information. The walls of the club were covered in maps and the organizational charts of regiments and divisions. The divisional commander himself gave a very interesting report on his own division's combat ability. [. . .]

On February 25 I crossed the Volga for the first time in 156 days. I was up in front with the officers. When we reached the village of Krasnaya Sloboda, the first thing we were struck by was a house that was entirely intact. Smoke was coming from the chimney. We were so used to bombed-out buildings that seeing an entire house was a rare thing, it really stood out. We even stopped to take a look. [. . .]

Many of us received orders and medals for Stalingrad. Some were decorated posthumously. Three battalion commanders in our regiment were the first in the division to receive the Order of Alexander Nevsky for their struggle against superior enemy forces, for their experience and resourcefulness in tactical matters. The Order of Alexander Nevsky was awarded to Captain Kotov, Captain Nikiteyev, and Captain Ponomaryov.

February 10 was a momentous day for the division. That was the day the government issued a decree that awarded the 284th Division the Order of the Red Banner. We celebrated to mark the occasion.

March 2 was also significant. That's when we learned that Colonel Batyuk was being promoted to major general.

But the most important day in the history of our division was March 5, the day we heard on the radio that we were being renamed: from now we were the 79th Guards Division. [. . .]

On February 24, the day I got the Order of the Red Star, I managed to get a car and go take pictures of Stalingrad, anything I thought worth photographing. At that time they were collecting the bodies of dead Germans. In the center of the city I met this civilian and I asked who he was. He said he ran the military department of the Stalingrad City Committee and that he was in charge of collecting the bodies. I asked how many they'd collected. That day they'd collected 8,700 German corpses in the city. I started taking pictures. There were piles of German corpses, two or three hundred, even six hundred piled on top of one another. Nothing in Stalingrad stood out as much as those mountains of bodies, those thousands of truckloads of bodies. I also photographed the bombed-out buildings, the field hospitals where wounded Germans still lay. I went into on German hospital in the City Theater. They were all mixed together: the sick, the wounded, and the dead. There was an awful stench. I found it hard to keep myself from finishing off the wounded.

When we left Stalingrad on March 6, we passed through what used to be the lines of the encirclement. Scattered over dozens of kilometers there were cars, tanks, guns of every caliber, mortars, and lots and lots of bodies. The battlefield was a vast cemetery with no graves. Again we were assured of just how great this battle of Stalingrad was.

Sometimes you'd see a village in an open field, and you'd think maybe you could make a stop. But as you get closer it turns out that it's just a heap of vehicles that looks like a village. So there were cemeteries for equipment too.

We had a rally in the field on March 7, when we found out that comrade Stalin was being given the rank of Marshal of the Soviet Union. That made us all very happy. We'd said it before, that it would be nice to see him in uniform.

All of comrade Stalin's documents and orders made a great impression on us. When things were at their worst, we knew that we weren't alone. I remember in October—our worst month—I was walking at night with my orderly, Korostylyov, and we had to wait in a

After the battle. *Photographer: Sergei Strunnikov*

crater for the shooting to stop. I asked him, jokingly, whether he thought Stalingrad could hold out. He said: "I don't think Stalin's got it wrong." He said this straightforwardly but with a strong belief that Stalin was thinking a lot about those of us who were in Stalingrad.

We felt this especially strongly when we heard they were bringing out the new Medal for the Defense of Stalingrad and giving three cities the honorary title of Hero City.[123]

Our regiment's clerk responded to one of Stalin's decrees (from November, I think) like this: "Nothing brings order to my thoughts like this decree." In that way comrade Stalin's decrees brought order to both the activities and thoughts of our men. We always felt that he cared for us, and we could always sense his wisdom.

In Stalingrad I became a member of the party. In Stalingrad I became a captain and received the Order of the Red Banner.

[Signature:] N. Aksyonov, May 20, 1943

[Handwritten] Transcript read. Major Aksyonov, March 5, 1946

SNIPER VASILY ZAYTSEV

The name Vasily Zaytsev will be familiar to many readers thanks to the 2001 film *Enemy at the Gates*. Yet many parts of the story it portrays are fictitious, aside from the fact that Jude Law, tall and lean, bears no resemblance to man he plays. (The real-life Zaytsev had a stocky build.) According to the film, Zaytsev learned to shoot on wolf hunts with his grandfather. But as he told historians, he acquired his skills while hunting squirrels with his father, mother, brother, and sister. The goal was to shoot as many squirrels as his mother needed to make a fur coat for his sister. In the film, Zaytsev is "discovered" by a commissar, who feeds tales of the sniper's accomplishments to the army newspaper. But the real Zaytsev was not discovered by a commissar; he followed the example of other Stalingrad snipers whose kill totals were widely publicized within the Red Army. Finally the film leads us to believe that the Germans, after repeatedly failing to kill Zaytsev, sent in their most experienced sniper, Major Erwin König, to go head-to-head with the Russian marksman amid the rubble of the Tractor factory. While Zaytsev claimed to wage a three-day duel with a German master sniper he referred to as "Major Koning," there is no evidence that a sharpshooter by this name ever existed.[124]

Consistent with comments by Major Aksyonov mentioned above, the sniper movement in Stalingrad began during the heaviest fighting in October 1942. The use of snipers, like shock troops, was among tactics the 62nd Army command preferred in street fighting. The snipers in the regiment of Guards Lieutenant Colonel Metelyov, of the 284th Rifle Division, caused quite a sensation. According to Aksyonov, forty-eight snipers in the regiment killed 1,278 Germans.

The first sniper to make a name for himself in the regiment was Alexander Kalentyev. He had been trained as a sniper but worked as a liaison officer in the regimental staff. In a conversation with an army newspaper at the beginning of October, he explained that the widely published deeds of other Soviet snipers inspired him to follow suit. He approached the main line of battle and "killed ten Fritzes, my first pack of ten." Kalentyev announced that he would multiply his total by November 7, the twenty-fifth anniversary of the October Revolution.[125] He managed to kill twenty-four enemy soldiers before a German sniper bullet struck and killed him.[126] From the Main Political Administration Kalentyev and other Red Army soldiers on the Stalingrad Front received small journals for recording the number of soldiers they killed and the amount of equipment they destroyed. On the title page of each journal stood the words of Ilya Ehrenburg: "Unless you've killed at least one German in a given day, your day has been wasted."[127]

During October sniper propaganda spread. Notable snipers vowed publicly to up their kills in honor of the anniversary of the revolution. Army leadership encouraged them to train other soldiers and create a sniper movement.[128] Newspapers routinely published the snipers' totals. An article from October 21 had as its headline nothing more than "66" printed in bold; it called for a "socialist competition" on the occasion of the upcoming anniversary. One headline pointedly asked, "Sniper Sytnikov has killed eighty-eight Germans. What about you?" Soldiers who had yet to make a kill were publicly shamed.[129] The campaign proceeded in the style of 1930s shock work. Sytnikov mentioned that before the war he had been active in the Stakhanovite movement as a miner. When he heard about the competition for the anniversary celebration, he thought he could follow the Stakhanovites' example and exceed his previous kill targets.[130] In the 1930s the Stakhanovites were celebrated as "excellent people" (*znatnye lyudi*) of the new socialist era. A variation stuck in Stalingrad: any sniper with more than forty kills was considered an "excellent shooter."[131]

The political apparatus not only prodded soldiers to distinguish themselves in "socialist competitions" but also fanned the flames of hatred toward the Germans. The hate they cultivated bore much fruit. In his interview Aksyonov commented that every soldier and commander in Stalingrad "burned" to kill as many Germans as possible. He believed that this hate was the foundation for the sniper movement in the 284th Rifle Division. Anatoly Chekov, a sniper in the 13th Guards Division, made it clear in his October 1942 interview with Vasily Grossman that hatred was what drove him. Chekov recalled his feelings after he shot his first German: "I felt terrible: I had killed a man! But then I thought back to our own dead and started slaughtering them without mercy. [. . .] I have become a beastly man: I am killing them, hating them as if my entire life is supposed to be like that. I have killed forty people—three in the chest, the rest in the head."[132] Zaytsev too reported that his main driving force was hate.

Zaytsev's name first appeared in the army newspaper on November 2. He was described as a new arrival on the Stalingrad Front who quickly became one of the most accurate marksmen in the army, someone who sets off "each morning at dawn to 'hunt Fritzes.'" It approvingly cited his kill total—116 Germans dead—and the fact that he took other soldiers under his wing.[133] Four days later, with the upcoming anniversary of the revolution in view, the newspaper reported that Zaytsev already had 135 kills. It also recorded the totals of his students who fulfilled "their obligations honorably": one had killed twenty Germans; another, twenty-five; a third, thirty-three.[134] After the anniversary, the newspaper urged the snipers to continue their "fierce competition" with unabated force.[135]

By the time the battle of Stalingrad was over, Zaytsev had killed 242 Germans, more than any other sniper in the 62nd Army.[136] On January 15, 1943, he suffered an eye injury and spent three weeks in a military hospital. On February 22, while visiting an eye specialist in Moscow, Zaytsev learned that he was to be honored as Hero of the Soviet Union. Before the award ceremony—President Mikhail Kalinin would confer the title in the Kremlin on February 26—he received a letter from Professor Mints inviting him to the Institute for the Study of the Great Patriotic War. Zaytsev thought he had to deliver a lecture on the sniper movement in Stalingrad and was nervous when he arrived poorly prepared, especially because the editor in chief of *Pravda,* Pyotr Pospyelov, was present. As he wrote in his memoirs: "I'm answering questions, talking about my comrades, without looking in my notebook where the theses of only the first part of the report are. An hour passes by, then another. I start wondering why no one is asking me to begin my lecture. Finally, they come to the conclusion that my report has scientific value. I am dumbfounded: what value, I haven't read out a single thesis from my notebook!"[137]

Because no stenographer was on hand to record the interview with Mints, Zaytsev was invited to the institute again in April 1943, when the following transcript was produced.[138] In August 1943 a supplementary interview took place. A revised text of the interview was published the same year in brochure form.[139] Zaytsev's testimony is the only eyewitness account of the battle published by the Historical Commission. There are considerable differences between the published and unpublished versions of the interview. The brochure's editors abridged or reworked many passages without indicating the changes. They either embellished or eliminated sections in which Zaytsev came across as less than heroic. For instance, in the original interview Zaytsev claimed to shoot his first German soldier at a distance of 250 feet. In the brochure it became 2,500 feet. Or consider Zaytsev's standoff with the German sniper (the climactic scene in *Enemy at the Gates*). In Zaytsev's telling, he shot his opponent after he had put down his weapon. The brochure portrays the episode differently: the armed German "loses his head" when Zaytsev jumps out of the ditch and fells him with "holy Russian bullets."[140]

Zaytsev continued to fight on the front for the duration of the war. By the time he saw Berlin, he had attained the rank of captain. After the war he headed a sewing machine factory in Kiev. He died there in 1991. In 2006, in accordance with his wishes, his body was moved from Kiev and interred in a grave on Mamayev Kurgan.

The high reverence the Red Army paid to its snipers did not extend to enemy snipers, who were regarded as mass murderers; those captured were separated from the other prisoners and executed.[141] Consider what happened when Colonel Ivan Burmakov, supervising the capture of 71st Infantry Division staff on January 31, 1943, granted Fritz Roske's request to be allowed to say good-bye to his officers:

> His commanders were coming up to him, he was kissing them all and shaking hands. Suddenly an unsightly, sniveling Fritz came up. Here the gesture actually was on Roske's part. Ilchenko was standing next to me. [Lieutenant Fyodor Ilchenko spoke German and acted as a translator.] So that German comes up. Roske is shaking his hand, kissing him. I ask who that is. Roske replies that it is the best machine gunner in his army who has killed 375 Russians. As soon as I heard "375 Russians" I surreptitiously stepped on the foot of Ilchenko, who was standing next to me. So that sniveling Fritz had barely left the basement before he was done in, before he could take aim at number 376.

COMMISSION ON THE HISTORY OF THE GREAT PATRIOTIC WAR

Transcript of interview with comrade V. G. ZAYTSEV
April 12, 1943
Interview conducted by comrade Krol,[142] commission research assistant
Stenography by comrade Roslyakova
Vasily Grigorievich ZAYTSEV: Hero of the Soviet Union, Expert sniper[143]

I was born into a peasant family on April 23, 1915, in the village of Yeleninksky, which is in the Agapov district of the Chelyabinsk region. My father was a forester. Until 1929 I was raised in the forest. I spend my entire childhood in the forest. There I learned how to shoot, and I hunted rabbits, squirrels, foxes, wolves, wild goats. I probably love the forest so much because I spent my entire childhood in the forest. Which means that I've never been lost in a forest, even if it was one I'd never been to. I've never gotten lost. In 1929 my father joined a collective farm. I went there with my parents to our village, Yeleninsky. [. . .] In the summer I tended cattle, I was a herdsman. The Construction Technical School was in Magnitogorsk. I was getting ready to go there at the same time. I still hadn't made up my mind where to study. I'd only decided that I must study something. I wasn't all that interested in construction, but I did want to learn. I was embarrassed to be tending cattle. But I kept doing it and went to school at the same time. I'd let in the cows and tie the horse on a long rope. Then I'd sit under a bush to study. I spent the summer of 1929 tending cattle, and that winter I began my studies at the Construction Technical School. If someone had asked me where I wanted to go, I'd have told them straight out that I wanted to go to the aviation institute. I wanted to be a pilot, but these days both my health and my vision are shot. So in 1930 I entered the Construction Technical School. I was an excellent student. In my second and third years I received prizes. My overall grade when I left was "excellent." I graduated from there in 1932. When I was young I was so small, so skinny and weak. While I was at that school we built the first and second blast furnaces in Magnitogorsk. I built blast and puddling furnaces. And I worked there as a trainee. The workers were old. They had no sense of the theory, but they had a lot of experience. You'd be giving them instructions, and they'd say: "You're just a kid—I've been doing this my entire life, and here you are telling me what to do." I didn't like that. It made me feel bad, so I left. I'd been working there three months. Plus it was dirty work. It was hot, and you had to wear all those hot clothes. I started a bookkeeping course. In Shadrinsk I completed a nine-month course to become a bookkeeper. When I finished, they sent me to the Kizilsky district of the Chelyabinsk region. From 1933 I worked as a bookkeeper for the Kizilsky region Community of Consumer Cooperatives. I liked this careful, exacting work. I was a bookkeeper there until 1936. [. . .] I enlisted in the military through the Komsomol and joined the Pacific Fleet. I'd been a Komsomol member since technical school. In February 1937 I joined the Pacific Fleet. [. . .] Our unit was based in Vladivostok. It's a unique city, in the mountains. When you compare Vladivostok to Chelyabinsk, Sverdlovsk, Shadrinsk, or Tyumen, it seems rather unpleasant. It's not a clean place. There are lots of Chinese, Koreans. I didn't really like them at first, but after I'd spent some time there I got used to the city, got used to the navy, and now I miss the Far East terribly. I'd jump at the chance to serve in any tundra in the Far East. I just love the region. The surroundings are beautiful there, and the city itself is great, I really came to like it. Of course it's a harsh climate, but I loved that city. If I'm still alive after the war I'll definitely go serve in the Far East, although they send you back from there after six years, and I've already lived there seven years.

By order of the Military Council of the Pacific Fleet, those who graduated with top marks from the Military Supply School were given the rank of quartermaster-technician, 2nd class. This order was communicated via telegraph, and the written document was meant to come later. I had the job and standing of a midgrade officer, but I was still a regular seaman. They put me in charge of a department. I was made a bookkeeper in the 4th Submarine Brigade in Vladivostok. From 1939 to March 1941 I served as a bookkeeper with the rank of quartermaster-technician 2nd class. But when they started looking into promotions, it turned out that my rank hadn't actually been properly recorded. It turned out that the order from the People's Commissariat giving me the rank of quartermaster-technician 2nd class was never issued. This upset me, and it was only the beginning of a lot of red tape. I'd been a midgrade officer for six months, and now I was just a regular seaman. Throughout my service I'd never had so much as one disciplinary action, not from the party, the Komsomol, or the service. The Military Council had expressed its gratitude for my work. I'd done nothing wrong the entire time, I had done my job with exceptional discipline. They reached their conclusion: I was to turn in my officer's uniform and go back to wearing that of a simple seaman. Orders are orders. They denied my request, put me back to barracks, and extended my term of service. I wrote a letter to comrade Stalin. Fifteen days later I got a reply. The reply, written on behalf of comrade Stalin, said: investigate this and file a report. Then everything was sorted out quickly and I was given the status of an extended service man. I was taken from an ordinary seaman and given the grade of a reenlistee with ten years' worth of service. [. . .]

When the Germans began their approach to Stalingrad, we petitioned the Military Council to allow Komsomol sailors to go voluntarily to defend Stalingrad. I volunteered for Stalingrad. [. . .] Our unit was formed in Krasnoufimsk that September. On September 6, 1942, we arrived in Krasnoufimsk. On the 7th we were transferred straight from one troop train to the next before leaving for Stalingrad. There were a lot of men on the train, around five thousand of us. In Krasnoufimsk we were assigned to Batyuk's division, back when it was a regular rifle division. We received our training on the way there, in the railcars. Here's how I learned to use a machine gun: I put a machine gun on an upper bunk and had a machine gunner tell me about it, show me how it works. I was a commander and he was a soldier, but he was the one teaching me. There I was made the commander of a supply platoon, but I turned that down to be a regular soldier, a rifleman. I picked up a gun and went as a rifleman. I had been a very good shot even while I was still in the navy.

We arrived in Stalingrad on September 21–22. On September 20–21 we were in Burkovka. At that time all of Stalingrad was burning. From morning until 7:00 P.M. there were air battles between our planes and the enemy's. One after another planes crashed and burned. The whole city was on fire. From the other side of the Volga you could see the flames, the tongues of flame that all merged together to form one enormous ball of fire. The wounded walked and crawled. They were being transported across the Volga. Seeing all this has a profound effect on a new arrival. It filled us with hatred and rage.

We'd already cleaned our weapons and fixed bayonets. We were just waiting, waiting impatiently. We were on full alert. We were carrying our ammunition, mortars, machine guns. We arrived at the Volga in secret and crossed on the night of September 21–22. We were given a representative from a Guards division, but I can't remember which one. After we crossed the Volga, we were standing on the riverbank. The Germans were already in the city by then. They spotted us at 6:00 A.M. and attacked with heavy mortar fire. There were twelve fuel tanks. We occupied the area around them. We took those twelve fuel tanks. Then sixty enemy aircraft flew in and started attacking us. They blew up the tanks, and we got covered in gasoline. We fell back to the Volga, where we dunked ourselves in the water as we ripped off all our burning clothes. We were left only in our undershirts. Some were even naked, and some covered themselves with their tarps. With rifles at the ready, we went on the attack. We forced the Germans out of the factory area, from the Metiz factory and the meatpacking plant. There we dug in. After a while the Germans attacked, but we held back every one of their assaults.

After those early battles the battalion commander took me on as his adjutant. I was the adjutant to the battalion commander, his right-hand man. During the fighting our battalion was scattered, and the Germans managed to disrupt our combat formations. The battalion commander ordered me to gather our men together and contact him. I had my own adjutant, and the two of us began gathering the men and putting the companies back together. We could only account for around seven men in each company. Later, when we were done, there were around sixty or seventy in each of the companies. We organized our battle formations. One of our units was getting held up in the Long Ravine and had begun to retreat. I went over there with my orderly. The battalion commander gave me orders to keep the enemy at bay and hold the line. I followed his orders and held the line. We attacked, repelled the Germans, and straightened out the line. We stalled the German advance. After those battles, when we were on the defensive, command nominated me for the Medal for Valor. On October 23, 1942, I received the Medal for Valor.

The Germans started sending out snipers to pin down our movements. Once I was with the battalion commander, Captain Kotov, and we saw this German jump out. He gives me an order: "There's a German over there: kill him." I bring up my rifle, fire, and the German drops. About eighty meters, and I killed him with an ordinary rifle. People got pretty excited. Everyone knew me there, and I already had a lot of authority over the men. They joked about it, but they were impressed. We could see another one coming out to help the first. The one I'd killed was probably carrying a message. Someone yelled: "Zaytsev, Zaytsev, there's another one coming, get that one too." I brought up my rifle, shot—and he fell. That's two of them in the space of half an hour. I was beginning to like this. I stood at the window and looked. Another German was crawling out to the two dead men. I shot and killed him.

The sniper Vasily Zaytsev (*right*) and his students move into an ambush position in Stalingrad, December 1942

Two days later I got my own sniper rifle with a telescopic sight. Captain Kotov gave it to me on behalf of the regimental commander, Colonel Metelyov. I started learning how to shoot with this rifle. We had one sniper in our regiment, Alexander Kalentyev. He helped me get to know this sniper rifle. I went around with Kalentyev for three days, observing his movements, seeing how he worked with his rifle. Lieutenant Vasily Bolsheshchapov helped me learn the mechanical aspects of the rifle. After that I began staging ambushes and was having a lot of success. Operating on my own would make it easier to keep tabs on the Germans. On top of that, there were a lot of people hunting for me. The Germans already knew who I was.

I decided to recruit more snipers and train them. Since I was killing three or four Germans every day, I started looking for students. I took on five or six students. We had lessons in a forge. They learned the mechanical aspects of the rifle in a ventilation pipe at the Metiz factory. We'd get to the forge, I'd show them how to shoot, and then we'd go out to lie in wait for the enemy. I recruited about thirty students altogether. Once I was convinced they could handle their weapons skillfully, I'd take them with me on an ambush—one, two, three days. These people got used to shooting. They studied the enemy's defensive positions, his activities, and so on. I chose these people myself. They were my friends, and I loved them. We shared everything: sometimes we didn't have much in the way of food, and you'd have to share whatever biscuits or tobacco you had. When people see that you are open and honest with them, they develop affection for you. I hope that if someone comes to love me, they won't ever give up on me, and I won't give up on them. I taught them to remember my every word. This is how I recruited and trained my students.

It's not that difficult to assess someone's fighting qualities at the front. A sniper has got to be daring, cold-blooded, and persistent; he must master his weapon, be a competent tactician, and have good eyesight. These are the qualities that determine whether someone can be a sniper. I taught them and went out with them on ambushes.

In one area, at Mamayev Kurgan, we needed to take this one bunker that was keeping us from moving around—crossing from one district to another, bringing out food and ammunition. Command gave us the task of taking this bunker. Our infantry had tried several times, but their attacks had failed. German snipers were in the area. I sent two snipers from my group, but they missed, got wounded, and were put out of action. The battalion commander ordered me to go there myself and take two other snipers with me. I set off. I encountered a skilled German sniper. I stuck a helmet out from a trench, and he shot it immediately. I had to work out where he was. This was very difficult to do because he'd shoot and kill you the moment you try to take a look. Which means you've got to trick him, outsmart him. That is, you've got to use the right tactics. I put my helmet on a parapet, he shoots, and the helmet goes flying. I hunted him for five hours. I had to resort to the following method. I took off one of my mittens, put it on a board, and stuck it up out of the trench. The German thinks that someone is putting his hands up in surrender, that he doesn't want to fight. The German shoots. I take down the glove and see where it has been shot through. Based on the holes I work out where he's shooting from. If the glove is shot from this side, that means he's over here. If he's somewhere else, then the glove has a hole on the other side. This shot indicated the direction he was shooting from. I grabbed a trench periscope and started looking. I found him. Our infantry was right on the front line. They'd only have to go thirty meters to reach that German bunker. I'd tracked him down. He got up to observe our infantry. To do this, he put down his rifle. Right then I popped out of the trench, shouldered my rifle, and shot. I got him. Then I opened fire on the embrasures in the bunker, where their machine guns were firing from. I started shooting at the embrasures to keep the machine gunners from getting to their guns. Then our infantry rushed the bunker. We took it without any losses.

Here there was only one good tactic: I had to outsmart my opponent. That kept us from losing anyone and let us achieve our objectives.

On one hill there was a company that had been cut off by German snipers and machine guns. It wasn't easy getting there. Command was trying to find out where the enemy was hiding. They went out two or three times but couldn't find them. Colonel Metelyov, our regimental commander, asked me to locate the enemy firing positions, find where the snipers were hiding, and clear the approach. I set off with two of my men, privates Nikolai Kulikov and Dvoyashkin. We left at 5:00 A.M., before dawn. During the day you can't see the flashes, you can't see where they're shooting from, which is why you've got to work at night. We dropped into a trench, rolled a large cigarette, and made a kind of a cross out of sticks. Then we wrapped rags around it to produce something resembling a face. We gave him a helmet, stuck the lit cigarette in his mouth, put coat on, and showed him off. The German sniper sees a man smoking a cigarette. When someone shoots in the dark you can see the flash clearly. That's how I was able to locate the German sniper. When Kulikov held up this stick decoy, the German started shooting at it. He'd shoot, Kulikov would lower it, and then he'd hold it back up again. The German would think he hadn't got him, so he'd start shooting again. By that time I'd managed to pinpoint the locations of the German emplacement and the snipers. I wasn't able to take out the snipers. I could only find out where they were. I got in touch with our antitank artillery. They destroyed the German bunkers and killed the snipers. That was how we got to the company that had been cut off.

You've got to be resourceful. You've got to find the right tactical approach to outwit the enemy. Killing him doesn't take long. But outwitting him, thinking about how to get the better of him—that's not so easy.

Here's another example. We were trying to take this concrete bridge. After several attempts we still hadn't succeeded. Our attacks had all gone wrong. I snuck off with a group of four snipers to the Germans' flank. Actually, we slipped right through to his rear. We climbed up into the bombed-out buildings. When our guys started attacking, the Germans would run out and throw grenades. It was then, when they emerged from their cover, that we began picking them off. They spotted us and brought out one of their guns. We killed the whole crew. In about two hours the four of us killed twenty-eight Germans. That was on December 17, 1942. Our infantry managed to occupy that heavily fortified bridge. The bridge had withstood so many assaults, a lot of direct fire, but it couldn't be destroyed. The concrete was around six meters thick. Hit it with a shell—and all you do is leave a dent in it.

Between October 5, 1942, and January 10, 1943, I had 242 dead Germans on my account. I had trained a total of thirty snipers. I had established a new movement, a sniper school. In the March 15, 1943, issue of *Red Fleet* there was an article by Guards Captain Aksyonov in which he described my work.

I'd gotten a lot of harassment in the navy. The conditions were just unbearable, and even wise people told me: "Zaytsev, if I were you, I'd shoot myself." But I survived and loved the navy despite all the morons—they weren't all that bad, but the quartermaster service really was completely full of morons.

Here's another example. The Germans were bringing in reinforcements. I don't remember the date, but by then I was already in a different regiment. I was there with some students. There were four others working in another district. I was at an observation post with the commander. A messenger shows up looking for me. He says: Comrade Zaytsev, German activity has been reported in such-and-so observation sector. They're sending in reinforcements. I went out with my snipers to take a look at these reinforcements. I called up the other four, so that made six of us, counting me and my student. We ran over there, went into a bombed-out building, and ambushed the Germans as they were moving in formation. We let them come to about three hundred meters before we started shooting. It worked out perfectly. There were about ninety to a hundred of them. They weren't expecting this. They didn't know what was going on, and they stopped: first one drops, then a second, then a third. You need two seconds to shoot. Our SVT rifle holds ten rounds.[144] All you do is squeeze the trigger and it loads the next round. In about half an hour the six of us killed forty-six Germans. That was my most memorable ambush. After we were finished, our artillery and mortars cleaned up the rest.

I remember this one interesting moment. The guys often laugh about this when we meet up. It was the first time I suffered a concussion. I'd climbed into a collapsed furnace. The building had burnt down, all that was left was this one furnace and a chimney. I'd climbed in and was shooting from inside it, but the Germans saw me, and then they hit the chimney with their mortars. I was buried under a pile of bricks, and my rifle was broken. I'd killed a lot of Germans from that furnace. When I got buried I was wearing large boots—size 45—and I couldn't get up. My tarp, which had been torn in half, was wrapped around my feet. I pulled my feet out, but the boots stayed put. By the way, I'd been lying there unconscious for two hours. When I came to, I dug myself out from under the bricks and pulled my legs out, but those boots, like I said, stayed there in the furnace. I threw out all the bricks, thinking: "To hell with them if they kill me." I slung the broken rifle around my neck, wrapped my feet in rags, grabbed the boots with my hands, and ran with no shoes down the alley. The men laugh about this. It would have made a fine photograph. For some reason the Germans didn't shoot me.

Here's another one. It was in the Long Ravine. The Germans had a kitchen there. In a cellar. It was evening, getting late, the sun had set. We were in this building having a smoke. And we see this big German come out from somewhere. They had these enormous insulated pots. The German comes out all in white—a cook, apparently—and he starts washing out the pot. It was a distance of about four hundred meters. He was right out in the open. Someone says: "Zaytsev, shoot him!" I raised my rifle, and just as he grabbed the pot by the rim to look inside I shot him in the head. His head went right into the pot as he dropped. The soldiers said: "The enemy has resorted to the use of tinpot weaponry." We got a kick out of that.

I first started shooting when I was about twelve. I've still got one brother. When we were kids we hunted partridges, grouse. I was a good shot even as a kid. Our father taught us to shoot squirrels. He had us shoot them while they were jumping from one tree to the next. We went hunting a lot: my father, my mother, my sister, and my brother and me. It was fun. If you shoot a squirrel with a shotgun, you tear everything up and ruin the pelt. We had a sister, and me and my brother decided to kill enough squirrels to make her a fur coat.

But we had to shoot them with a single pellet, so we had to practice this art. We made our own pellets. They were similar in size with what you get in a small-caliber TOZ rifle.[145] I was about twelve then. Once I'd gotten good at shooting, my father gave me a hunting rifle. But we still shot squirrels for our sister's coat, about two hundred of them. My sister is older than me. My brother was born in 1918. My mother and sister could shoot too. My mother isn't someone you want to mess with. The forest there was mostly pine with the occasional birch. I can shoot with either eye. The vision in my left eye is still good. My right eye's not that great.

I was seriously wounded once. I've got a piece of shrapnel under my right eye, and another one near the corner of my eye, also on the right. The splinter under my right eye can't be removed because it's under the mucous membrane. It doesn't bother me, but I see red circles when I look down and then back up again. There's another splinter in my left eye. I couldn't see much of anything for five days. My whole face got burned.

I did some hunting in the Far East. I hunted wild boars, bears, bison, lynx, wolves, foxes, pheasants. I was also a good shot in the military. I was a good shot as a kid, and so were my parents. I probably got it from them. My mother's an old woman now, wears glasses, but she'll still go out and shoot. A grouse will perch somewhere in a birch tree, and she comes out, takes a shot, and it's dead. Then she goes home and plucks it.

I found out I was going to be made a Hero of the Soviet Union on February 23, 1943. I'd been called to see comrade Shcherbakov, the head of the Main Political Administration. When I got to his assistant, Captain Vedyukov, I still didn't know about the award. When I got there they congratulated me. The decree granting me the award was made on February 22, 1943. On February 26 I received the Order of Lenin. Mikhail Ivanovich Kalinin handed it to me. Now I'm going to study in Solnechnogorsk.

Snipers usually hide out in buildings. When our forces were outside the city, we had to operate in the field. You've got to study the terrain in advance. You find out where the enemy will be and how he'll get there, you locate the best place for an ambush, study the enemy's defenses.

When you're hunting for enemy officers or soldiers, you disrupt their activities, make it impossible for them to stand up or bring in ammunition, say, or food. You find out when they do these things. You get there and stay put, deciding which weapon would be a better choice: your submachine gun or your rifle. If there's a lot of them, you won't get everyone with the rifle, but with the submachine gun you can mow them all down. Sometimes you shoot from one position and then move to another. They start shooting back at your position, but you're already gone, you're somewhere else. You've always got to prepare several firing positions in advance. And make a lot of decoys to thoroughly confuse the enemy. He shoots but doesn't hit the target. I would shoot, for example, from underneath a dead body. You can also shoot from behind rocks.

How was I wounded? I was lying in wait. The Germans spotted me. None of them could get me. I wasn't letting any of their snipers get up. I was under a railcar. They decided to shoot at the car, hoping I'd be hit by some of the flying bits of metal, splinters, fragments, and so on. So that's

Zaytsev is accepted as a candidate in the Communist party, Stalingrad, October 1942.

what they did. They fired directly at the car. Fragments from the car flew right at me. A shell exploded up above. My face was burned up, I had shrapnel wounds, all my clothing was torn, my knee was dislocated, and my right eardrum was ruptured. Basically, I was very seriously wounded.

I joined the party in October 1942.[146] There was one occasion when me and my men were surrounded. There's the Volga, but you can't get anything across. We were in an encirclement. No hope we'd make it. That's what I was thinking, but I was in command and I couldn't say that to the men. It was an extremely difficult situation. I was a chief petty officer at the time. After that first battle I received a government award, the Medal for Valor.

We were in a terribly difficult situation. We had a representative from the Red Army's Main Political Administration.[147] I told our commanders that there was "no land for the 62th Army on the other side of the Volga. This is our land, and we will defend and hold it."

From six or seven in the morning until seven in the evening the Germans bombed and they bombed. There were [. . .] air raids every day. There was shelling and mortar fire. The six-barreled mortars rumbled all day without a break. Night bombers came after dark to drop more and more bombs. Is there any hope in such a situation? People are getting wounded, killed. But it's a great time for storing up hatred. When you capture a German, you feel there's nothing you couldn't do to him—but he has value as an informant. You grudgingly lead him away.

While we were in the area of the Metiz factory the Germans dragged out this woman (to rape her, no doubt). A boy yelled out: "Mama, where are they taking you?" She shouted—not far from us—"Brothers, save me! Help me!" How does that affect you when there's nothing you can do to save her? You're on the front line. You don't have enough men. If you rush out to help her you'll be slaughtered, it'll be a disaster. Or another time you see young girls, children hanging from trees in the park. Does that get to you? That has a tremendous impact.

We didn't know fatigue. Now I get tired just walking around town, but then we had breakfast around 4:00 to 5:00 A.M. and dinner around 9:00 to 10:00 P.M., going without food all day without getting tired. We'd go three or four days without sleeping, without even feeling sleepy. How can I explain this? You're in a constant state of agitation, the whole situation is having a terrible effect on you. Every soldier, including myself, is thinking only of how he can make them pay more dearly for his life, how he could slaughter even more Germans. You think only of how to harm them even more, to spite them as much as you can. I was wounded three times in Stalingrad. Now I have a nervous system disorder and I'm shaking all the time. I find myself thinking about it a lot, and these memories have a strong effect.

I was a political group leader at the Voroshilov Battery and a bureau member in the Komsomol organization. I got good marks in the history of the party and in the history of the peoples of the USSR. I studied party history in 1939–1940. I enjoyed party history, but most of all I liked the history of the Civil War. I did a lot of reading. I read Furmanov's *Chapayev,*[148] read about Parkhomenko,[149] Kotovsky,[150] Suvorov,[151] Kutuzov, the Brusilov Offensive.[152] That was all while I was in the navy. I read Zazubrin's *Two Worlds,*[153] *Bagration,*[154] *Denis Davydov* (the first partisan),[155] Sergei Lazo—that was a big book.[156] I really liked Stanyukovich's sea stories[157] and Stendal's *The Red and the Black*. I've read Novikov-Priboy,[158] *War and Peace, The Hunchback of Notre-Dame.*[159]

Bookkeeping is good, calm, quiet work. It takes you into the depths of life. You feel like you're in charge, that something depends on you. I like that. It's independent work, and whatever you do, you must apply to your life.

General Chuikov and Commissar Gurov inspect Zaytsev's sniper rifle. *Photographer: Georgy Zelma*

[. . .] Colonel Vedyukov arrived from the Main Political Administration. On the 23rd I was summoned to General [. . .]. There was to be a presentation.[160] I was still in the field, lying in wait. I got word that I was being called in to receive a government award. Snipers and sailors were there with me. Everyone knew me. Word spread: Zaytsev was getting a government award. I asked my sailors: "Well, guys, anything for me to pass along?" We knew that Colonel Vedyukov was with us on the front line. I said: "What should I tell comrade Stalin from us Komsomol sailors? Colonel Vedyukov is here, he'll be going to Moscow and will pass along the message." They told me what to say.

I said: "All right, I'll say—" And I told them.

"That's right, off you go."

Off I went—and soon enough it was all in the papers.

I joined the party during the most difficult period. In October the Germans wouldn't let up. I already had some students then. I was always agitating for the party. I thought it was about time to get ready to join the party. They advised me to. I thought: How can I join the party when I don't know the program? I read the program and wrote my application

Captain Zaytsev is congratulated by fellow soldiers on receiving his epaulets, February 1943.[161]

right there in a trench. Two days later I was summoned to a party commission. By then I'd killed sixty Germans. I'd been decorated. That was after the 23rd [of February].

[. . .] Headquarters work is the worst thing in the army. I just got out of working as a quartermaster, and now I'm having to do the same sort of thing again. I thought: people are fighting. I wanted to do something so history would know that I existed; otherwise you live, trample the earth, and then everything goes dark.

You don't have to use a sniper rifle. A sniper rifle has a telescopic sight with 4x magnification. But with an ordinary rifle, a distance of two hundred meters is still just two hundred meters. Your accuracy isn't as good, but if you know how to shoot that doesn't matter. I had thirty snipers but only eight sniper rifles. The rest used ordinary rifles. Say you're in a city, inside a building, next to a small embrasure. With a scoped rifle you need a larger embrasure, and if the embrasure is large, then the enemy can see you. So there are times when it's better just to use an ordinary rifle.

A SIMPLE SOLDIER: ALEXANDER PARKHOMENKO

On February 28, 1943, Esfir Genkina, assisted by stenographer Olga Roslyakova, interviewed several commanders and soldiers of the 38th Motorized Rifle Brigade who had captured Field Marshal Paulus and his staff on January 31. They brought the interviewees to the Stalingrad department store so that they could relay on site how the capture had taken place (pages 222–261). While in the department store, Genkina encountered Alexander Parkhomenko, a private who had been quartered there together with his company since the beginning of February. Parkhomenko had played no role in the capture of Paulus. The interview with him appears to have been unplanned and differs from many of the others, which involve decorated soldiers and high-ranking officials. As such, it gives a good impression of how a simple soldier in the Red Army talked and thought.

Parkhomenko's remarks are straight to the point. He measures the events of the battle within his own radius, in contrast to the sweeping panoramas provided by the generals and staff officers. And unlike Vasily Zaytsev, Parkhomenko does not tell a hero's story. On the contrary, he confesses that whereas others were brave he was not. His descriptions of the fear he weathered in battle are revealing. He speaks about his weaknesses ("I was a complete coward, but I didn't know it at the time") in the past, signaling that he, as a good Soviet citizen, had learned to conquer his baser instincts. Also noteworthy is his description of the "inexperienced" lieutenant, who, equipped only with petrol bombs, attacked several German panzers and died. Parkhomenko thought little of suicide missions, which he considered a means to display one's readiness to die. (In early 1943 communist agitators did not praise suicidal bravery as much as they had in the first phase of the war, though it continued to be one of several competing models of behavior in battle.) Parkhomenko was in line with army commander Shumilov, who valued military skills and sought to conquer his opponent with cunning instead of confronting him in a head-on manner.[162]

64TH ARMY

(38th Motor Rifle Brigade)
Alexander Ivanovich PARKHOMENKO[163]

I was born in 1921 in the Far East, in the area of the Far Eastern railway. I finished engineering school in Vladivostok. Since 1942 I've been a member of the Komsomol. I joined the navy in September 1939. In 1941 I went back home because I was ill, and I noticed that there wasn't anyone my age there. I started asking relatives and friends: Where is everyone? They said they'd all left for the front. Seeing that all the others had left, I started wishing I could go too. I started writing to my commanders. But they wouldn't let me go: Stay here, we'll do our fighting here.[164] A marine brigade was being formed, and they took me. That was on February 22, 1942. They sent me to the regimental troop school at the Rozengartovka station.[165] I was a student there for about five months. I left with the rank of senior sergeant.

We left for the front on June 12, 1942. We got there, to Stalingrad, on June 28. They filled out our marine brigade with extra personnel from the infantry. From Stalingrad we headed straight toward the Don. We weren't acquainted with the military situation. To us it seemed dreadful. At night when the planes flew in, the flares went up, and the bombing began—I couldn't take it. I'll tell you the truth: other men are brave, but I'm not.

We got to Vertyachy[166] and took up positions. Then we went out with the intelligence officer. Basically, we were on patrol. He ordered me to scout out the enemy forces. We'd been assigned to the third echelon, which was right in Vertyachy. We crossed to the other side of the Don. Now we weren't really familiar with some of the infantry uniforms, and it was night—you couldn't see a thing. There was a patrol walking up ahead, he was not Russian and he was wearing this strange kind of jacket. We shouted at him: "Password!" He didn't know it. Since he didn't know, we started shooting. So did he. The enemy brigade advanced, and we moved to meet them. They opened fire on us. We were under machine-gun fire from two directions, and then it stopped all of a sudden. We radioed our brigade. Everyone in the brigade was ready, they wanted to attack. We'd read in the papers that the enemy launched psychic attacks, marching in columns.[167] When I looked, I could see a column moving either toward or away from the front line. We immediately sent up signal flares and got on the radio. They told us on the radio that these were our own men.

After that we were on the other side of the Don. Our brigade went on the offensive on July 15 and suffered heavy losses. They made me adjutant to the intelligence officer. We attacked the enemy in the area of the villages of Tinguta and Peskovatka.[168] We didn't have any vehicles, so we had to get there on foot. We'd just joined the fight and were taking losses when we were sent back. Orders came from high command, so we went to Tinguta and dug in. The defensive line ran from Tinguta to Peskovatka to Ivanovka. All our battalions were there. We were at the command post with the intelligence officer.

On August 23, 1942, we were hit by a heavy air raid. At first there were four planes: two would bomb while the others reloaded. Then the first pair would fly off while the other two attacked. The dust rose up. The German tanks advanced through this dust. The airplanes were constantly circling overhead. And you know how unbelievable the dust is Stalingrad. It's incredible, and there's no water, no nothing. [. . .] We were attacked by German tanks. On August 24 tanks came from the area of Blinkino and concentrated in the area of Sarepta. The intelligence officer was ordered to ascertain the enemy strength in the area of Sarepta. We went to carry out this order. This was when the intelligence officer got hit. As adjutant, I was ordered to deliver him back to the unit, regardless of whether he'd been hit or torn to pieces, and if that didn't work I was to give my own life trying to save the valuable documents he had with him. I grabbed both him and the documents and took them to brigade headquarters. He was seriously wounded. I was very careful with him. We had just reached the brigade commander when he died. Nothing else to do: I had to go back to the company and continue our work. Lieutenant Khodnev was made the new intelligence officer. We got into a BOB-I armored vehicle and went to scout out the enemy forces in the area of Blinkino station. We found out what they had there and came back. The enemy's strength had been established. They had three armored vehicles. These were scouts in the vehicles, maybe paratroopers. We drove to Blinkino station, parked, and set off on foot to secretly observe the tanks. Their tanks weren't well camouflaged, they were just sitting on top of a hill.

An inexperienced lieutenant from another unit was also trying to find out how many tanks the enemy had. They wanted to torch those tanks. Someone said: "Get down!" Petrol bombs hit the tanks, which turned around and fired at them—and that was it, the whole platoon was neutralized. But the lieutenant, he jumped into a trench when the tanks started coming. A tank drove over there, went back and forth five times to run him over. This was reported to command when the tanks left. The intelligence officer was Lieutenant Kuzin, who also got killed.

In late August we got to Stalingrad and took up defensive positions on the Volga. The brigade was supposed to be in communication with the left flank. We took an armored car out on reconnaissance. This was on August 27. By that time the enemy was already at the Tractor factory, and they were firing on the Volga with machine guns. While were out, I became gripped by fear and lost it. I was a complete coward, but I didn't know it at the time. Fifteen dive-bombers were attacking our vehicle. I figured that if one them dropped a bomb, it would be the end of me. So I ordered them to stop the vehicle so we could escape into a ravine. One of the planes went into a dive, and I got shot in my left hand and both legs. The driver was okay. I climbed into the turret and he drove us back to our unit. We made it, but I couldn't get out. They sent me to Beketovka. There was a field hospital there. I stayed there until evening. Then they moved me to the island, and from there they sent me to Field Hospital no. 2209 in Shchuchy. I stayed there for five days. Then I was sent to Leninsk. From Leninsk I was supposed to be evacuated to the far rear. They started loading me into a railcar. But the moment I was on the train, enemy aircraft came flying in, bombing and burning nearly everything. They sent me to Kapustin Yar. I stayed in the hospital there. I was there from August 27 to October 26. On October 26 I was sent to the 178th Reserve Regiment in Solyanka. On the same day I was assigned to the 38th Brigade. They put me in intelligence again. I was deputy commander of intelligence. On November 3 we went to the front. My legs were weak, so I couldn't keep up. In view of this, Major Belyayev made me chief of the supply depot. I ran the supply depot and ferried ammunition from the east bank to the west bank. We supplied ammunition throughout November. Our ammunition depot also took in captured weaponry. From there we went straight to Beketovka. In Beketovka I was sent beyond our advance units on reconnaissance.

[. . .] We left there on January 28 to go on the offensive near Stalingrad. I went with Sharin, Kiselyov, and Klimov to scout out the entire left flank. The 2nd Battalion of 57th Army was active in this area. We struck the enemy head-on. After that we were on the defensive. What did we do while we were on the defensive? There were German planes in the air, and we started shooting flares at them. They started dropping things on our positions: thermoses with chocolate, bread, ammunition. They dropped all kinds of food to us, they dropped rations on Beketovka many times. We were always getting things from their side.

Soldiers of the 13th Guards Rifle Division after the battle, February 1943.
Photographer: G. B. Kapustyansky

On January 31 I was at the command post. We were at the hospital for water transport workers. By then our forces had General Paulus surrounded. I got up early and went to see. I went with a politruk to find a car. We found one with gas, with everything. Then we went back to the company commander. Then we changed our quarters and began to live in the basement of this department store.

CAPTAIN PYOTR ZAYONCHKOVSKY

One of the top experts on the Wehrmacht at the Stalingrad Front was Captain Pyotr Andreyevich Zayonchkovsky, the head instructor for enemy propaganda in the 7th Section of the political department of the 66th Army.[169] The 66th Army was stationed north of Stalingrad and took part with other Soviet armies in the failed bid to break through the German cordon north of Stalingrad in September 1942. It took the army until January before it was able to advance to Stalingrad. Though their units had been decimated, on February 2 they took the Tractor factory from the Germans. After the north *Kessel* surrendered, Zayonchkovsky led the interrogations of captured German officers and soldiers. The interrogation reports are presented in the next chapter.

The thirty-nine-year-old captain earned his post in the enemy propaganda unit due to his good German language skills, which he acquired at home and in the Cadet Corps prior to the revolution. Enemy propaganda required thorough knowledge of the enemy—the names of the commanders (which Zayonchkovsky shouted through a bullhorn to urge German surrender) but also of the ways the Germans thought and acted. The objective was to "break down" the morale of the enemy soldiers.[170] In his interview Zayonchkovsky analyzed the soldiers of 6th Army, their social background, and their "political and moral state." He describes in detail how the confidence they expressed in letters and diaries in the summer of 1942 gave way increasingly to exhaustion and resignation in the face of heavy Soviet resistance. He believed that the Soviet antiwar propaganda had a great effect, especially after the Germans were encircled. He criticizes the Germans' "robber morality" and lists the baby carriages and infant clothing he found in the abandoned shelters of the Germans. Zayonchkovsky took these thefts as evidence of the enemy's degeneracy: only a morally unhinged soldier could commit such militarily useless crimes against the civilian population.

Zayonchkovsky's comments on Soviet military leadership are similarly astute: the poor coordination between units, the pitiful performance of the air force during the first phase of battle, and the widespread lack of discipline among the troops. At the same time, he notes approvingly the high levels of discipline and order among the Germans.

Before Zayonchkovsky volunteered for the front in 1941, he had studied history at the university and subsequently earned his doctoral degree. His testimony is that of not only an eyewitness but a historian. He consulted letters and diaries of captured or killed German soldiers and checked the sources thoroughly. At one point he remarks that a German letter he cites was not sent by mail but personally handed to the addressee—the implication being that the author could speak openly without fear of military censors. For Zayonchkovsky, the historian, this gave the letter a high value as a historical source.

For historians today, the beginning of Zayonchkovsky's testimony is especially interesting. He proudly announces that he is a descendant of Russian admiral Pavel Nakhimov, who in 1853 destroyed the Osman fleet in the battle of Sinop and later defended the besieged city of Sevastopol in the Crimean War. By World War II the name Nakhimov had come back into favor; in 1944 Stalin created the Nakhimov Medal for members of the Soviet fleet. This was in keeping with the Soviet regime's decision in the late 1930s to cultivate the Russian tradition. (The name "Great Patriotic

War" was chosen as part of this strategy.)[171] Before the late 1930s Zayonchkovsky would not have been able to make these remarks about his family without fearing incarceration or worse. As a descendant of an aristocratic family he had been one of the "former people" in the founding years of the Soviet Union, someone who could neither vote nor study and was suspected of helping the counterrevolution. Concealed behind Zayonchkovsky's brief remark in the interview that he had "worked for seven years as a carpenter in a factory, joined the party in 1931" was a young man's attempt to gain acceptance in the Soviet system. Zayonchkovsky attended the Cadet Corps in Moscow. When it closed in 1918, he transferred to the cadet school in Kiev. In the following years he worked for the fire company and the railroad and at the above-mentioned engineering works.[172] Other young people deemed "class enemies" at this time tried to cleanse their "contaminated" past through "resocialization." It may be the case that Zayonchkovsky worked in a factory in order to develop a proletarian mentality.[173] He likely lied about his family background when joining the party.

While working at the factory, Zayonchkovsky completed a night school course in history at the prestigious Moscow Institute for History, Philosophy, and Literature (IFLI). In 1937 he completed his studies and three years later defended his dissertation (*kandidatskaya*) on the Cyril and Methodius society, a secret association of Slavophiles in the nineteenth century.

After the battle Zayonchkovsky continued to work in the enemy propaganda unit of the 66th Army (renamed the 5th Guards Army on May 5, 1943). After sustaining a head injury in December 1943 he was discharged from the army with the rank of Guards major and returned to his profession as a historian. From 1944 to 1953 he headed the manuscript division of the Lenin State Library in Moscow. From 1948 on, he taught history at Moscow State University. (He was made professor in 1950 after completing his doctoral work.) He wrote eight monographs and edited a multitude of source editions, primarily on political and military aspects of the closing years of the tsarist period. In his field of research there was no one better. The multivolume bibliography of prerevolutionary Russian memoirs and diaries he edited remains an indispensable aid for historians.[174] During his tenure as professor he supervised numerous doctoral candidates from the Soviet Union as well as from American and Japan. In 1968 he received Harvard University's MacVane Prize for European History and in 1973 became an honorary member of the British Academy. However, he was never permitted to travel abroad to accept his awards. During his life Zayonchkovsky's source-based methodology made him ideologically objectionable because it operated outside the prevailing framework. This "positivist" perspective shaped the testimony he provided in Stalingrad.

On September 30, 1983, Zayonchkovsky died of heart failure in the Lenin State Library while working on a history of the Russian officer corps.

TRANSCRIPT
of interview with Major Pyotr Andreyevich ZAYONCHKOVSKY
May 28, 1943
Interview conducted by comrade G. N. Anpilogov[175]
Stenography by A. I. Shamshina[176]

I was born in 1904. My father was an army doctor[177] who came from a noble family.[178] My grandmother was a cousin of Admiral P. S. Nakhimov.[179] I'm from a long line of officers. My great-grandfather received the Cross of St. George[180] for Borodino,[181] and I spent three years in the cadet corps.

From a very young age I was brought up on the heroism of the Patriotic War of 1812. I can remember, for instance, being six or seven and knowing all the heroes of that war. The traditions of the Nakhimov family played an important role, of course. We kept a number of letters. One in particular was from Nakhimov to my grandfather, written after Sinope. I gave it to the Military Historical Archive.[182]

Red Army soldier Pyotr Zayonchkovsky, 1942

I was expected to become a naval officer, of course. In the beginning I went to the 1st Moscow Cadet Corps. The traditions and honor of the Russian army, the honor of the Russian officers—that made a strong impression on me. I remember 1917, the October Revolution. What did my father think of it all? He must have been more or less in line with the Kadets and the Octobrists.[183] I was thirteen years old. I figured I could get along with the Bolsheviks so long as they kept the epaulets. I can remember a time in November [1917] when my father was swearing, saying that they were getting rid of them. He started crying, I was crying, and my younger brother, who was eleven, was also crying. I was glad when they came back again.[184] These traditions played an important role in our family.

My father never was in the army. He was a doctor, and he died in 1926. My mother is a pensioner. Did my father buy in to the Soviet platform? Of course not.

My father was sick for a long time. So the burden of responsibility for the family fell on me. I was still finishing school. My father died after I graduated. I was always doing correspondence courses, and that's how I graduated from the institute and completed my graduate studies. I spent four years working as a plane operator in a factory. I joined the party in 1931. In 1940 I defended my dissertation, and it was 1937 that I graduated from the institute. In December 1941 I volunteered for the army. I joined the home guard on July 3. After a few days our regiment was given leave until further notice. Then I was sent to work for the aerial reconnaissance and warning services. It seemed I wasn't fit for anything better than sitting in a tree looking for airplanes. I was unlucky and ended up in the Political Administration of the Siberian Military District. A doctorate? You can be a lecturer. I spent three months as a lecturer. I asked the head of the political administration to either let me go or send me to the front. I didn't join the army so that I could hang around in Novosibirsk. And because a unit was being formed at that time, I was made an enemy propagandist in the 315th Rifle Division. We left for Kamyshin, a town in the Stalingrad region, as part of the 8th Reserve Army.

The 8th Reserve Army's headquarters was in Saratov. Soon I was transferred to the army political department as an officer in 7th Section, which dealt with work among enemy troops. On August 26—which was after the German's 14th Panzer Corps broke through at Vertyachy, crossed the Don and reached the Volga—the 8th Army was called to the front and renamed the 66th Army. [. . .]

Our army got to the front on September 4, and that night we took up position on a twelve-kilometer line running from the west bank of the Volga to the area of the village of Yerzovka, sixteen kilometers north of the Tractor factory. The army joined the battle on September 5. Our task was to break the German defenses along this twelve-kilometer stretch. The army was made up of six rifle divisions: the 64th, 299th, 231st, 420th, 99th, and 84th. We also had two tank brigades and two rocket regiments. Our assault, which lasted eight days and cost us heavy casualties, did not result in any real successes. We were unable to move forward or break through the German defensive line. Our losses were staggeringly high. We lost nearly all of our tanks and a great number of men. On top of that, looking at it from an army-level perspective, there was a whole series of bad mistakes. For example, we started fighting without any intel on the terrain or the battle. We ought to have taken a day or two to bring our troops in line. After all, they'd just come a long way. Some of them had marched from Saratov. But taking a broader view, it must be said that a one- or two-day delay might have cost us Stalingrad.

The Germans were taking extremely heavy losses. I can quote from a letter we found on a dead soldier. The letter was written on September 23. The letter belonged to Private 1st Class Hubert Hüsken, Field Post 06388. It was addressed to Franz Dahlin, a friend in Germany. He didn't intend to mail it but rather to have someone deliver it in person.

> Dear Franz,
>
> Greetings from your friend Hubert! I'm finally getting around to writing you a few lines. You know how it is with letters, especially here, where there are things we can't write about. Many of the men in our company are gone. Of 180 there are only 60 left. Our first taste of battle was especially brutal. Sprenger will tell you all about it. The war is very different from what I thought it would be. It doesn't seem so important to me anymore. Everyone has to experience it for himself. The fighting on the Don wasn't as bad, but there was often a lot of hand-to-hand combat.
>
> A great battle began on August 22 around Stalingrad, right down to the Volga. We moved from the Don to the Volga in a single day, we were already there by 7:00 P.M. On the first day the Russians completely lost it. Ten of us took 150 of them prisoner, and sixty of them were girls aged eighteen to twenty—there's no way you're going to win a war like that. But by the next day they'd pulled themselves together, and then something started coming at us from all directions, something unimaginable, and it's been like that up to this day.
>
> Second Battalion was supposed to head north to keep the Russians from getting into Stalingrad. It was about ten kilometers from our positions to the outskirts of the city. But I've got to tell you, it wasn't that easy. Their tanks broke into our

> sector every day, and that put all our units in a panic. So you can imagine why we had such losses. In one division's sector the Russians had dug in around a hundred tanks. It gradually got to the point where your nerves couldn't take it. I've never been in a situation like this. We're not getting anything, everything is late, even the food. The Russians captured all of the canteen equipment and other things that were brought in by 5th Company, which was on our left. That company was disbanded yesterday. They only had twenty-seven men left. Twenty-six men from the 7th Company were sentenced to hard labor for cowardice and retreating in a panic. The same thing happened with 1st Battalion, which was left with even fewer men. We have four men left in our unit, and I'm in charge. Now you have an idea of how things are. Every day we wait to be relieved, which we hope will happen soon. We haven't washed in four weeks.

I've got to say that this letter is typical. It describes the mood of the German soldiers. We have a great number of letters and diaries from dead soldiers, and I use this one as an illustration.

A few words on the enemy. The 6th Army's main attack force was the 14th Panzer Corps, which included the 16th Panzer Division and the 3rd and 60th Motorized Infantry Divisions. The 14th Panzer Corps was led by Lieutenant General von Wietersheim.[185] [. . .] I want to emphasize that all these divisions were made up of Germans only. Also, there weren't any Sudeten Germans. The Germans in these divisions were exclusively from northwestern and western Germany, Westphalia, Saxony, Brandenburg, Prussia. The soldiers were between twenty and twenty-five years old and had spent many years in the Hitler Youth school.[186] That was what ensured their morale and political reliability.

One shortcoming of our September operation, for which there is of course no objective excuse, was the severe lack of cooperation between our tanks and infantry. One small example will confirm this. Private 1st Class Johann Weingrann, of the 79th Panzer Grenadier Regiment, 16th Panzer Division, said the following about his capture on September 25: "The Russians broke through our defenses. Their tanks came in the evening. We were in our bunkers. The tanks stopped for a while and then moved back. After some time, before morning, the tanks returned. There wasn't any infantry, and it was something like two hours later that the infantry arrived and took us prisoner."

A second shortcoming was our disposition in depth, which led to massive and unnecessary losses. Finally, there were cases of divisions failing to take up position until it was light. [. . .]

Our air force was weak. Throughout September the Germans ruled the skies unchallenged. Our planes were not up to much; there were few and they accomplished little. They rarely hit their targets. There were times when they bombed not only our own forward positions but also our divisional command posts. On September 7 nine of our planes bombed the command posts of the 64th and 231st Divisions.

On September 13 the army moved into an active defense. But by the end of September our section of the front was extended some twelve kilometers because we were given more divisions, including both the 38th and the 41st Guards Divisions. These Guards divisions were formed somewhere near Moscow out of brigades of paratroopers who had already fought behind enemy lines. They had exceptional personnel. They fought the Germans near Kletskaya,[187] and they literally fought like lions. When they were assigned to our army, they had 5,000–5,500 men each. They got reinforcements sometime in the last week of September. These reinforcements had not been specially chosen, so these Guards units saw a lot of self-inflicted wounds among the reinforcements, and there were some who crossed over to the Germans. I've seen how hard that is on the Guards. It's hard for them to see their Guards banner being soiled by these incidents, which they had absolutely nothing to do with. That shows you how important it is not to put just any reinforcements into a Guards unit. Perhaps they ought to create some sort of Guards reserve regiment.

I've got to say, there still isn't any real system for reinforcements in the Red Army like there is in the German army. In the Russian army, ever since 1812, our regiments have had two active battalions—the first and third—and one—the second—in reserve. The Germans do the same thing, but they also have special reserve battalions that supplement a particular division. That way, a soldier gets to know his division even when he's in the rear. He's trained by officers who are in that division, he learns their traditions, and by the time he gets to his unit, he already knows it, and this has a significant impact on the unit's cohesion. We don't have that.[188] Perhaps it's too much to have divisions keep a reserve regiment in the rear, but in any case it's essential that a soldier knows where he's going. Let's say you have a wounded man, an officer who winds up in an army hospital—it's a big hassle for him to get back to his division. But when a German is wounded, he goes back to his reserve regiment in the rear, and after six months he's back in his own unit, his own company. We ought to give this serious consideration. We do not have a clearly defined system of reinforcement. [. . .]

I'd like to talk about the Germans' morale and political reliability. As I said earlier, this was stable at the beginning, for a number of reasons. But the Germans were taking very heavy casualties in September, and to a certain degree this put them in a state of extreme fatigue. They were constantly hoping that once they took Stalingrad, the 14th Panzer Corps would spend the winter in France. They lived by that hope. It should also be mentioned that the fighting in September and October made them very receptive to our antiwar propaganda. We found our leaflets on the prisoners, on the dead. The German prisoners told us that one of the leaflets—"Daddy Is Dead"—left a particularly strong impression. It has a picture of a four-year-old girl. She's holding a letter, and there's also a dead German soldier. One prisoner told me that one of his comrades sent that leaflet home with someone he knew.

In general, the social propaganda, whose goal was to denounce Hitler's regime, didn't do much good,[190] but our antiwar propaganda was more successful. With the anti-war propaganda they can come to their own conclusions—and you know how dull and narrow-minded the Germans are.

In mid-October I made broadcasts from a field radio near the Volga and the Dry Ravine. We made those broadcasts from a bunker 180 meters from the Germans. As soon as the loudspeaker started up, I would

"Daddy is dead." "Blame Hitler! He did it!" Soviet leaflet disseminated in Stalingrad.[189]

see movement along their communications trenches. The Germans rushed to get closer to the loudspeaker. As a rule, they stopped shooting during the broadcast. They started shooting again afterward.

There was a very interesting case in that same sector in the middle of November, before the encirclement, which I ought to talk about. On the morning of November 19, Lieutenant Duplenko, the commander of the 2nd Battalion, 197th Rifle Regiment, 99th Division, noticed a soldier climb out of the German trenches, curse, and throw his rifle to the ground. A while later two more soldiers climbed out and did the same thing. Then Duplenko went and yelled: "Fritzes! Over here!" The Germans came about forty meters and stopped. Duplenko left with two submachine gunners to meet them. They arrived. The Germans offered him a cigarette. He took one of their cigarettes and then started communicating in gestures. Then he grabbed both of them by the hand and started moving toward our trenches. The Germans went about twenty meters. But this sergeant of some kind came out of the German trenches and started shouting something at them. They started freeing themselves, saying: "Rus, night . . . ," and walked away. Duplenko left. No one shot at anyone else. Preparations were made for that night. That regiment's intelligence chief and Lieutenant Makarov, the instructor who was responsible for working with enemy troops, lay in wait for the Germans. Since this might be a provocation, two dozen scouts and submachine gunners were put in position. What happened that night was most unexpected. The Germans didn't come straight along the front—this was on the bank of the Volga—but rather went down to the Volga and then started to make the climb. They were unarmed. Our sentry held out his hand to the first German—and there he was. And then the reconnaissance company's commissar gave the order to shoot. Apparently they'd been asleep and had had a shock when they woke up and saw Germans. The Germans ran back. The next morning we found eleven duffel bags with blankets and all of their things. [. . .]

During our offensive in October the Germans took especially heavy losses. This was confirmed by prisoner statements and a number of documents we have in our possession. So, for example, the captured rifleman Johann Schmitz—from the 8th Company, 8th Motorized Infantry Regiment, 3rd Motorized Division—said that on the 18th, 19th, and 20th, the 8th Regiment took heavy losses, mostly from artillery. According to Schmitz and other POWs, the companies were left with around twenty-five to thirty men. The Germans were surprised by how determinedly our units fought. An unsent letter was found on the body of a Sergeant Steinberg, who had written: "The Russians who defend this sector are especially fierce and determined. They really understand the importance of this city and what consequences its fall will bring."

Among the sergeants you can find fairly well educated Germans, often with higher education, usually with a secondary school degree.

So that's how things were before the encirclement. In mid-November, when the Germans were hit at the Don and to the south of Stalingrad, the ring started closing in on the 6th Army. From November 19 the Germans were frantically moving units from Stalingrad to the Don. On November 20, 21, and 23, I saw lines of German vehicles with infantry moving west. On November 17 the 16th Panzer Division, except for some small individual units, was pulled out and sent to Kalach to prevent our forces from closing the ring. That evening and night of November 22 I witnessed the constant explosions in the German rear. At the same time the Germans were launching fierce barrages, particularly at our left flank. I wasn't able to get to the front line myself. You had to go four hundred meters across the steppe, which was impossible. It was like that until 5:00 A.M., and then it went quiet. By 8:00 A.M., when our scouts moved up to the German trenches, no one was there. On our army's left flank, along a line some eight to ten kilometers west from the Volga, the Germans had all left. On November 23 the 99th Division just walked into Tomilin, Akatovka, Vinnovka, and Latoshinka, and that day they met up with units of the 62nd Army. It was only after that meeting near Rynok that the 99th Division met stubborn German resistance as they attempted to take a dominant height. Nevertheless, the height was taken. They didn't have a single fatality the entire time.

[. . .] On our right flank the Germans were their usual selves. It was a hasty withdrawal: they blew up stockpiles and vehicles, torched bunkers, buried things in the ground. In the Dry Ravine, for example, we dug up a stockpile of uniforms, boots, and so on. German battalions and rear units had been there. I visited most of their bunkers. That was the first time I'd been in a German bunker. We found shocking things there, things that summed up the nature of German plundering only too well. One example should be enough. I get that the logic of victory and the logic of war might lead someone to take a feather bed or some warm things, maybe a mirror. But why on earth would you bring a child's stroller down there? And to top that off, the nearest village was ten kilometers away. Or baby clothes—I've seen them myself, in a bunker. It's like something out of the Bible. The clothes you can at least send back to Germany, but what are you planning to do with a stroller?

I heard things from civilians. A peasant woman's ragged old shirt is hanging out to dry. A German comes and stuffs it in his pocket. He's got no use for it, but his need to loot and steal is so out of control that he's got to take everything, regardless of whether he needs it or not. [. . .]

As evidence of the Germans' confusion and panicked withdrawal in November, we have both the statements of prisoners and some captured diaries and other documents. Here I quote excerpts from the diary of the soldier Heinz Gossman, Field Post 12387 Z.

> November 21. Yesterday they woke us suddenly at 3:00 A.M., and at 5:00 A.M. we started our withdrawal. The Russians have broken through in the Italian and Romanian sectors. The Italians and Romanians abandoned everything and took off, and now we're the ones who have to take care of their mess. At 5:00 P.M. the Russians cut the road we needed to get out. At 6:00 P.M. we were surrounded. Three guns, our only means of defense, were destroyed.
>
> 8:00 P.M. After a two-hour siege we eventually found a way out. Any vehicles that were out of fuel were destroyed.
>
> November 22. 6:00 A.M. Finally the road is clear again. We can dare to go. The road is covered with the bodies of horses left by the Romanians. Nearly all the animals have frozen to death. Scattered everywhere are guns, ammunition, vehicles, and everything else that the units had. After being shelled three times we made it to the crossing at the Don. At 1:00 P.M. we made it safely to Karpovka, but here the Russians are pushing up from the south.

The diary entries of Corporal Horeski, who was killed at the end of November, were to the point:

> November 23. Running from the Russians from one place to the next.
>
> November 26. The Russians have broken through, we're moving on.
>
> November 27. Stopping at the ravine. Building bunkers again.
>
> November 28. The bunkers were almost finished, but then we left in the morning. Everything's shit.
>
> December 1. Surrounded again. Not much food, the supply routes are cut off.
>
> December 2. We're not getting any mail and we can't send any. Hoping we can get out of this trap.

The Germans, as I mentioned earlier, were destroying their equipment and stockpiles. Sergeant Rudolf Bormann, from the 4th Company, 267th Regiment, 94th Infantry Division, said so in his statement. They burned a depot near Orlovka with an enormous amount of food and clothing. They destroyed food stores that were there for Christmas, including a lot of wine. Whatever wine the officers couldn't drink was destroyed.

The diary of Private 1st Class Heinz Werner from the 24th Panzer Division, who was captured at the time of surrender, contains the following:

> November 22. Because of the lack of fuel, at one airfield we blew up twenty of our own planes.
>
> November 23. Most of our vehicles and tanks were blown up this morning.

In the early days of the encirclement the Germans were literally thrashing about like rats in a sack. They were throwing everyone into the front line: supply personnel, clerks, even sick and lightly wounded soldiers from the hospital in Kalach. Soldiers from the 1st Cavalry in the Romanian division, who had fled after their defeat and wound up in the encirclement, were also seized and sent into the German units, three to five men per company. Among the prisoners were clerks, supply personnel, and other noncombatant staff. Somehow we got hold of the master of ceremonies from the largest variety show in Berlin. He said: "You know, captain, I've never found myself in such a comic situation as I have here with you."

However, the German commanders managed to quell this panic and confusion by early December. General Paulus issued an order saying that the army's task was to hold Stalingrad at all costs—that this city would play a decisive role in the outcome of the war. His order ended with the words: "Hold on. The Führer will get you out!"[191] This order was quoted in an address written by Hitler in a pseudo-Napoleonic style: "Comrades, you are locked in and surrounded. This is not your fault. I will do everything to free you from your situation, because the battle for Stalingrad has reached its apogee. You have hard times behind you, and it will only get harder. You must defend your positions to the last man. Retreat is not an option. Anyone who leaves his post shall bear the full force of the law."[192]

In this way the Germans managed to secure a defensive perimeter and establish some relative order by the beginning of December.

Turning now to the question of atrocities. On November 26 I was told to go to the 99th Division in the area of Akatovka-Vinnovka-Rynok to conduct propaganda work and to document atrocities. I should mention that on November 1–2 elements of the 300th Division conducted a landing operation on the west bank of the Volga.[193] This operation did not end well. Some died on the river but the rest managed to get to shore, where all of them were either slaughtered or taken prisoner. I visited some of the German bunkers in the area. This was not the precise location of the failed landing, and this confirms that the bodies I found there were not of men who had died in battle, but of men who had died as a result of brutal torture. For instance, there was the body of a Red Army soldier whose skin had been pulled off his right hand together with his fingernails. His eyes were burned out, and there was a wound on his right temple from a hot iron. The right side of his face had been covered in some kind of fuel and set on fire. I have the report and a photograph.

If I may digress, I'd like to highlight two things. First of all, when I got to the place where the bodies of these tortured men were, some of them had already been buried, and I had to dig them up. We had buried the bodies of these heroes in a pit, and there were no grave markers. Unfortunately, this was not an isolated case. We don't respect the dead, and despite strict directives from GlavPURKKA and the People's Commissariat of Defense, our treatment of corpses is disgraceful. We haven't been able to develop a proper respect for the dead.

Now I'll move on to the work we did to demoralize the enemy forces during the encirclement. Beginning in December, such work was conducted on a large scale. [. . .] Verbal propaganda took up a particularly large part of it. We spoke to the Germans every day using field radios and megaphones. The main document we used in our propaganda was an appeal to German officers and soldiers that was signed by General Yeryomenko and General Rokossovsky. This was the first appeal to their officers. The document said, for example, that there were many times in military history in which brave men and officers found themselves in a hopeless situation and surrendered. This wasn't an act of cowardice, but of good judgment.

During this period we were giving the Germans daily reports through the megaphone, the latest bulletins from Informburo. Usually they stopped shooting, though they would open fire again at the end of our talk. There was an increase in the number of men who surrendered or came over to our side. Our propaganda was getting better by the day. I

A Soviet soldier megaphones a German translation of the newscast *Final Hour* to the enemy. *Photographer: Leonidov*

can tell you this: On the night of January 10–11, I went to the front line with Quartermaster-Technician Gershman, a translator from the 116th Division, to speak about Paulus's refusal to surrender. It was morning, around 6:00 A.M. We arrived at the front line. Since we were advancing, we were some way away from the Germans, about two hundred meters. You can't talk to the Germans at two hundred meters. The two of us went past our forward line into no-man's land, eighty to one hundred meters from our trenches, and we started talking. The Germans were sending up flares around then, and we could see a group of German soldiers listening to us about fifty to sixty meters away. It was scary, to be honest. Be we said our bit once, then again, and the Germans didn't shoot, even though they could see us. After we'd been through it twice we ran back. They didn't shoot at us then, even though it would have been easy to kill us.

Sending back prisoners was a particularly effective method. This method was in wide use from mid-December. Usually after capturing them we'd take them directly to the battalion or regimental command post, feed them, and then send them back just like that. Just go tell the truth about how you were captured. That had a strong effect, since the German propaganda had them all convinced that the Russians would gouge out their eyes, cut off their ears, and so on.

I remember a Private 1st Class Werner, who was captured at the end of December. He was a musician and composer, and a member of the Nazi party since 1928. I questioned him in a bunker and then brought him to another bunker where the prisoners were. He was limping from a small wound in his leg. It was slippery. We were going uphill. I held him by the arm to help him. I said: "Do you know who I am? I'm a commissar." I'm not sure what was wrong with him, but he immediately backed away from me.

As I was leading him to the bunker with the Germans we were sending back to the front line that night, I told him about life in Russian captivity. I introduced the others to Werner and had them tell him what they'd seen. That evening when I went into the bunker, Werner had a favor to ask: "Captain, would you allow me to tell my comrades what I've seen here today?" And Werner got in front of the microphone that night and spoke to the men two hundred meters away in the same trenches he'd been in the night before.

But our propaganda did, of course, owe most of its success to the fact that our military victories had put the Germans in a very difficult position.

We used two means of communication to talk to the Germans. Once a cat came into one of the bunkers of the 149th Brigade, and he'd come all the way from a German bunker about sixty meters away. The cat came because the Germans had nothing for him to eat. We used this cat in our work to demoralize the enemy troops. First we tied a leaflet to his tail and sent him to the Germans. After a while the cat returned. We did this a few times, and then we made him an apron that could hold about a hundred leaflets. For two weeks he would go over to the Germans and come back empty, until the Germans shot him in the back legs, and he arrived, dying, at our bunker.[194]

The Germans regularly listened to our broadcasts and read our leaflets. There are numerous reports of this from prisoner statements. One day after the surrender I wanted to see how effective our propaganda had been, so I stopped a group of about five hundred prisoners in Dubovka. After telling them about the situation on the front—we had just taken Rostov—I asked how many of them had read our leaflets and listened to our radio shows. All but a few of them raised their hands.

In the final days before the surrender, at the time of the assault on the Tractor factory, we used a radio with a powerful loudspeaker to provide the Germans with more information about the military situation, and to relay the "Final Hour"[195] program. All this could be heard throughout the grounds of the Tractor factory.

A few words on heroism. It's no exaggeration to say that throughout the fighting at Stalingrad, the men and officers—with a few exceptions, of course—showed great heroism. I was often on the front line with them, and the men never stopped asking me questions: How long are we stuck here for? When are we going to attack?

One negative aspect of this heroism—if you can put it that way—is its rash, senseless aspect, and a readiness to take what is at times completely unnecessary risks. Here's the kind of thing that happens during the day on the front line: "Vanya, give me a smoke," and Vanya gets up and runs straight over to his comrade. Or people are walking as if everything is quite normal in places where they really need to crawl, and they die one after the other.

Much has been said and written about the heroes of Stalingrad. I have something to say about one army heroine, Marusya Kukharskaya,[196] who carried out 440 wounded soldiers. I saw her on the battlefield. She is indeed fearless. She was sitting in a bunker and doing some counting: "Well," she said, "another sixty and I'll be a Hero of the Soviet Union." Then there was Captain Abukhov,[197] a battalion commander in the 1153rd Regiment, 343rd Division, whose battalion held off several dozen tank counterattacks, even though he was down to thirty men. In mid-January he was accidentally killed by an exploding mortar shell. And there were the artillerymen of the 803rd Artillery Regiment, 226th Division, who dragged their guns themselves throughout our entire advance from the steppe ravine at Yablonevaya, where they had initially taken up position, to the Stalingrad Tractor factory. Because of the snowdrifts the horses were useless, and the men themselves didn't really grasp what a heroic act they were performing. They didn't see anything special about it, and it became part of their normal life.

I want to talk about the strength of the Germans' mechanical discipline. Despite the recognized success of our propaganda and the demoralization of the encircled units, the fact remains that the general mass of soldiers followed their officers' commands without question. This increased the difficulties we faced while eliminating this group. And it shows us the power of this mechanical discipline. It's clear enough, if you talk to individual German soldiers, that none of them really want to fight. Nevertheless, all it takes is one sergeant yelling "Fall in!" and they form up in ranks and stay there. I've seen this myself. On the night of February 2–3, there were a number of regiments that had surrendered and were being taken prisoner, and they concentrated in the area of the Stalingrad state farm, a few kilometers from the Tractor factory. We took them there, counted them up, gave them 250 grams of bread each, assigned them an escort, and sent them on to Dubovka. That night was extremely cold. I remember going to one of the regiments, about a thousand men. They were standing around, all disorganized. I ordered them to fall in and yelled: "Sergeants, over here!" I said we had to get them in groups of ten, which were to get two loaves of bread each. Then they would wait for their escort. They ended up waiting for several hours. At times you could hear an inhuman wail. That was the ones who were freezing. They fell, and they died, but the men stayed in formation. They'll line up as soon as you get a sergeant in there. The strength of that mechanical discipline was very rightly noted by Ehrenburg.[198]

During the surrender there were a lot of amusing and interesting things. For example, there was General von Lenski's farewell speech to his officers in the 24th Panzer Division. They were already at the 343rd Division's command post, and he asked the divisional commander, General Usenko, for permission to say good-bye to his officers. One of his division's regimental commanders, Colonel von Below, had the officers line up, reported to von Lenski, and then stood on the right side. Von Lenski walked up to his officers and gave the following speech: "Gentlemen, I thank you for always precisely following my orders during our time fighting together. You did your duty to the end. I wish you all a safe journey." This speech, in the spirit of Napoleon's Farewell to the Old Guard, had a strong effect on his officers. Many of them cried.

Then we put the officers in vehicles and sent them off. I approached one of the German staff officers. It was a colonel sitting there. I said: "Colonel, I need to put a few officers in here with you."

He told me in broken Russian that there was a lot of stuff in there, and he doubted there'd be enough room. He smiled. I asked him: "How do you know Russian?"

"Well," he said, "this is the second time I've made this trip. I was captured in 1915 and spent three years in Krasnoyarsk. It seems I'm headed in the same direction."

On January 22, under pressure from our forces, the Germans started falling back to Stalingrad. I was there on the 23rd and 24th, when we saw the endless flow of vehicles moving toward the Stalingrad Tractor factory. A very large number of Germans were concentrating there. We thought that there were three thousand of them, but then, as everyone knows, we took around five thousand prisoners.

On the 23rd, 24th, 25th, and 26th, our units approached the factory from the west. On the north side we took up position right at the edge of the factory grounds. One battalion from the 149th Rifle Brigade was located in the so-called Boots—the factory grounds. There was a brick factory there. We'd taken a pit and a few shacks on the hillside. Everything else belonged to the Germans. From the 25th to the 26th our forces approached the factory from the west. We had nearly surrounded the Tractor factory. Moreover, our units to the south had divided the southern and northern parts of the factory.

The assault on the Tractor factory began on January 27. On the night of the 26th I was told by a member of the Military Council and the head of the political department to go make contact with the Germans and ask for their surrender. The Germans were in possession of the Tractor factory, and there were several small ravines running toward it—the area called New Park. They held those ravines. Our bunkers were on the other side of Mokraya Mechetka,[199] which was where the German bunkers were. I went there knowing the name of the German battalion commander. That was the 274th Regiment, and its commander was Kannengiesser. Under international law I could only speak to someone of equal rank. It was about fifty meters to their bunkers. I started to say that I was Zayonchkovsky, an officer of the Red Army, speaking on behalf of the army commander. I invited Captain Kannengiesser to negotiate. I was in a trench, and I'd emerged just a little so I could speak through the megaphone. Nothing. I tried again. A machine gun started shooting at me. I started to egg him on: "You're a German officer, obviously a brave man, so how is it that you're too afraid to answer?" They shot again. Then I turned to the soldiers. I didn't want to talk to that sonofabitch when he was captured six days later, so I just sent the translator. He claimed that he hadn't heard me, that he was at his command post. He was lying. I had asked the Germans to shoot three times in the air, but they didn't shoot. He said that he couldn't possibly shoot at the Captain! So we got nowhere.

The assault on the Tractor factory was set for January 27. We had very few men. On the night of January 26–27 the Germans left the ravines and fell back all the way to the Tractor factory. Here's how we found out. I was talking to them all night long. At 6:00 A.M. I returned to the command post and lay down in a bunker. An hour later the company commander woke me to say: "Listen, captain, you did well—here are some captured deserters." They happened to be three Romanians. These Romanians said that the Germans were gone. We didn't believe them. But an hour later this German showed up, another deserter—and, he made out, "a former Komsomol member." His name was Otto, and he had a large stash of pornographic cards and various other items necessary for love.[200] He confirmed that they were all gone. I said: "Okay, you go on ahead, and we'll follow. Keep in mind that if you're lying, we going to put a bullet in your head." The place was empty when we arrived. They really had left.

The assault on the Tractor factory began at noon or one o'clock. I was on the northern side. We went down the Mokraya Mechetka ravine and managed to take a number of small buildings that were on the slopes. They put up a strong resistance. We were taking extremely heavy fire from a machine gun and everything else. We had almost no artillery shells, but we had a lot of rifle and machine-gun cartridges.

Something terrible took place there. You couldn't imagine how many of our planes were there, thirty to thirty-five of them coming in wave after wave. I'd never seen so much artillery in my life. They were really piling up the cannons, and all of them were shooting at the Germans. Everything was there, even rockets, absolutely everything. This was not the wisdom of our commanders, but of comrade Stalin himself. It was brutal. We had no men, ten per battalion, couldn't we get some reinforcements? We had no one. But this assault was really an air and artillery assault. If we'd had ten thousand infantrymen we wouldn't have needed them.

You can't really talk about a fight for the Tractor factory itself because there no longer was a Tractor factory, just a few individual buildings. The force of the artillery fire and aerial bombardment left all the basements packed with wounded soldiers. In those final days the Germans had no communication between the regiments. All their communication lines were severed by artillery fire, and this contributed to their surrender. The Germans were astonished, they kept asking where our infantry was. The Germans were in different buildings, shooting. There was no front line as such, but their firepower was still substantial. They kept on firing for all they were worth.

On the morning of February 2, when the surrender was already under way, our tanks moved right up to them, and they started to surrender in an organized manner. Our infantry, between you and me, had all been killed. Did we still have fifteen thousand men left? Yes, if we include those in the rear, we certainly did. Each division still had four thousand, but that's because of the artillery, and they barely had any casualties. There were mortar men, communications companies, and medical battalions—but as for combat soldiers, there were almost none left. Eventually the 149th Brigade held the line at the Boots. The front there was roughly two hundred meters long. There were perhaps thirty men left. The Tractor factory was taken primarily through the actions of our artillery and air force, not by our infantry.

The infantry was unable to advance, but the powerful artillery fire that fell on the Tractor factory made it impossible for the Germans to keep resisting. The Tractor factory was a red-hot cauldron into which so much steel and iron kept flying that it was impossible to withstand. [. . .]

The NKVD chief for the Tractor factory district really is a fearless man. I don't know his name. First of all, he never evacuated but stayed the whole time in Spartakovka and Rynok. When the Germans entered Rynok for half a day, none of the residents knew where he was. Starting in January, or even in December, he lived in Spartakovka, right here, some two hundred meters from the Tractor factory, and he ran an intelligence network of residents from the factory district. Every day we got reports on the number of Germans being sent in. We received an unexpected telegram from the political department of the 49th Division saying that a woman and a lieutenant had been sent in. It turned out that the NKVD chief had been telling us this every day from the Tractor factory. He lived there, he helped get the leaflets and his female agents carried them. This man really was there all the time. Rynok and Spartakovka were part of his district. There may not have been anyone living there, but that was his district. He did his work on the front line as an NKVD man. He kept in touch, made contact with the army, and was always with the brigade's commander and commissar. But he only kept in touch—he never interfered with our assignments. Before the war he received the Order of Lenin.

I saw the director of the Tractor factory at a battalion command post. This was during the assault, before the surrender. He had come back to Spartakovka, and so had a few other men. People were already getting ready to rebuild.

4

THE GERMANS SPEAK

German prisoners of war in Stalingrad, January 1943

GERMAN PRISONERS IN FEBRUARY 1943

General Field Marshal Paulus was taken prisoner by the Soviets on January 31, 1943. The same day German soldiers in the southern pocket laid down their weapons. Two days later the northern pocket, commanded by Karl Strecker,[1] finally surrendered. As tens of thousands of Germans soldiers were marched off to captivity, the Soviet intelligence service got to work. On February 5 Captain Zayonchkovsky and his colleagues, Majors Koltynin and Lerenman, began to interrogate soldiers and officers captured in the northern pocket. After the war, Zayonchkovsky submitted the reports of the interrogations, along with other documents of his activities on the Stalingrad front, to Isaak Mints's Historical Commission. Besides tying in almost seamlessly with events in the department store basement and in the military staff of General Shumilov, the reports are a thrilling read. The statements of named German prisoners immediately after their capture reveal their state of mind and show how the Soviets treated the prisoners and what information they sought from them.

Shortly after the battle of Stalingrad ended, Zayonchkovsky, by then a major, delivered a lecture to military intelligence staff about the purpose of "political interrogation of prisoners of war."[2] As head instructor, Zayonchkovsky was responsible for training the new intelligence staff added in February and March 1943 to cope with the growing tide of prisoners. The primary task of the interrogating officer, he stressed to the audience, consisted in identifying the "political-moral" state of the Wehrmacht soldiers. What did the prisoners think about the war? Did they still believe in German victory? How disciplined were the troops? To what extent was fascist ideology anchored in the Wehrmacht? The political officers of the Red Army believed that the enemy troops, like their own soldiers, were guided by ideological convictions that fostered strong military morale. The aim of political interrogation was to uncover the cracks in the soldiers' loyalty to National Socialism, cracks that the military intelligence then had to exploit on the battlefield to bring down the political and moral scaffolding of the enemy. Because Zayonchkovsky and his staff specialized in enemy propaganda, the interrogations also had to contain detailed questions about the influence of Soviet messages on German soldiers. The Soviets wanted to learn which techniques worked and which needed to be improved. (Several soldiers told them that the initial leaflets dropped by the Red Army came off as primitive and caused much amusement. One soldier said he did not understand why the Soviets called the Germans "fascists.")

In his lecture Zayonchkovsky detailed the different forms of questioning. He argued that individual interrogation—one interrogator and one subject—was best, as prisoners were more likely to talk when alone than in the presence of fellow soldiers or superiors. Interrogators must not fraternize with the prisoners lest it damage the Soviet officers' "honor and dignity." Only in exceptional cases, such as when interrogating high-ranking officers who held vital information, was it advisable to adopt a more relaxed style over a cup of tea. To make a strong impression the interrogating officers had to show the prisoners how much they knew about them, such as by dropping information about the prisoner's unit and the name of his divisional commander. Each question had to be carefully considered. For instance, German soldiers asked whether they belonged to the Nazi party could not be expected to answer truthfully. Instead, the question should be, "When did you join the Nazi party?"

Almost all the following interrogations took place between February 5 and 9 in the staff headquarters of the 66th Army located in Dubovka, thirty miles north of Stalingrad. The prisoners provided information about the final weeks in the Stalingrad pocket and the circumstances that led their units to surrender. They made statements about the Wehrmacht's combat effectiveness and the strength of the Red Army. The reports contain a wealth of previously unknown information on the final days of the battle, such as the different ways Generals Strecker and Arno von Lenski[3] dealt with their units as they showed signs of disintegrating. They reveal the horrendous living conditions of Russian prisoners in German captivity and the terror felt by the penned-in soldiers of the 6th Army as the artillery barrages and air attacks began.

Judging by the reports, the Germans who continued to fight in the face of hunger, exhaustion, and mass death did so out of a mixture of spite, obedience, and ideological conviction. An especially strong motivating factor was fear of capture. In this respect, the Soviet information campaign during the first weeks of the encirclement was ineffective: Wehrmacht soldiers dismissed the images of well-fed and well-clothed German soldiers in Soviet prison camps as empty propaganda. During the final weeks, the Soviets began to give German prisoners tobacco and bread and allow them to return to their units, a tactic that apparently convinced many Wehrmacht soldiers that capture was not tantamount to death.

Despite these interesting details, the interrogators were unable to arrive at a reliable picture of the German mood in the final days of the Stalingrad battle for the simple reason that the general situation and the specific interrogation protocol did not encourage reliable statements. The testimony by the German Senior Lieutenant Otto Conrady shed light on the problem. An intelligence officer in the 389th Infantry Division, Conrady noted that the Soviet prisoners he questioned in the summer and fall of 1942 stated that they fought only under threat of violence and received nothing to eat for days at a time. But his divisional commander rejected the information as nonsense: the strong resistance the 389th Infantry Division encountered in Stalingrad belied the statements of the Red Army prisoners. We can thus assume that all prisoners, Soviet and German, told their interrogating officers, at least to some extent, what they wanted to hear.

All the more disconcerting, then, are the many expressions of pro-Nazi sentiment recorded in the reports. For instance, general staff officer Herrmann Lüben believed that thanks to Nazi conditioning German soldiers would still win the war, but he worried that the "blood purity" of the German *Volk* had been jeopardized, and put the main share of the blame for Germany's military failures in Stalingrad on its—non-Aryan—Italian and Romanian allies. The testimony of platoon leader Ernst Eichhorn (24th Panzer Division) leaves a particularly lasting impression. Perhaps to ingratiate himself with the Russians, Eichhorn expressed his surprise at the good treatment received by German prisoners and recounted how his men wondered why the Germans and Russians were even fighting. In the next sentence—the last of the interrogation report—Eichhorn added that for him and the other German officers it was clear who was really at fault for the war: the Jews, who had taken over everywhere save for Germany. That Lerenman, the interrogating officer, was Jewish appears to have exceeded his powers of imagination.

REPORT

on the political interrogation of POW Senior Lieutenant Max Hütler

Dubovka, February 6, 1943

Interrogated by Major Koltynin, head of 7th Section, Political Department, 66th Army, and

Quartermaster-Technician 2nd Class Gersh, interpreter, 99th Rifle Division[4]

Max Hütler,[5] senior lieutenant, adjutant in the 544th Infantry Regiment, 389th Infantry Division. German. Age: 34. Native of Westphalia. Married. Member of the National Socialist party. Forestry researcher, instructor at the University of Göttingen. Reserve officer. Home address: *Göttingen University*.

The prisoner stated: "From the very beginning of the Stalingrad operation it was clear to me—and not only me but nearly all of the officers—that our high command was taking a big risk by driving in such an enormous wedge. The Russians were obviously going to try to cut through this wedge, surround our forces at its tip, and move in behind us. But we thought our commanders knew what they were doing. We thought they had enough reserves and would be able to hold our flanks. I still can't understand why they didn't bring more men to the flanks. We had reserves, plenty of them. The whole thing confuses me. When your army broke through our defenses at the end of November 1942, people started to panic. But we didn't know who exactly was spreading this panic. Soldiers weren't the only ones losing their heads. A lot of officers were too, especially the commanders of large units.

"By Christmas we understood the utter hopelessness of our situation. There wasn't any help and there wasn't going to be any. Each of us realized this, but we were afraid to admit it. We knew that we were doomed. But despite this most of us didn't even think of surrendering. We'd been tasked with holding back as many Russian troops as possible, troops that would otherwise be sent toward the Caucasus and Rostov. That's what we told the men. They knew what was going to happen to them, and, as you know, it was a small number of worthless men who laid down their arms and surrendered without being ordered to. The main corps of soldiers had been thoroughly instilled with a sense of duty, and they were prepared to give up their lives. Those were the men who held everything together. We weren't bothered by the small groups. They didn't present any danger to us.

"You say that every soldier is still a man, and as such he puts great value on his life and holds on to the idea of returning to his homeland, to his family, his wife, his children. That's true. But still the homeland takes precedence. Each of us is able to sacrifice himself for his homeland. This has been drilled into all of our soldiers. When they were in the encirclement, all of them knew they still had to do their duty, and they did.

"During the two months that we were surrounded there wasn't a single order related to discipline or increasing our monitoring of the regular soldiers. The only thing I know of was on January 27 or 28, 1943—I don't remember the exact date—when General Strecker issued an order stating: (1) Immediately open fire on anyone who moves away from his unit and toward the enemy; (2) anyone who takes supplies for himself from airdrops will be tried by court-martial; (3) anyone who is insubordinate or refuses to follow orders will be tried by court-martial.

"So why did we surrender? First of all, the main force that was with Field Marshal Paulus surrendered on January 30, 1943 [*sic*], so continued resistance was senseless. Our group wasn't able to draw in enough Russian forces to justify the sacrifice. We did our job for as long as we could, and if we could have held your armies back for another two or three weeks, then we wouldn't have put down our weapons, we'd have kept fighting. Second, we had so many wounded that they impaired our ability to fight. They were packed into every other building. All of them would have been killed by artillery fire if we'd resisted any longer.

"How do I judge the current military situation in Germany? Germany is in the middle of a very difficult crisis, but this isn't a defeat. There's still another 2 million or so who can be drafted. But if your offensive continues at the same pace for another two months, then our crisis might turn into defeat."

The prisoner also said that one of the signs by which you could determine who would win was Turkey's entry into the war. Turkey would join the side of the victors, but only when it was absolutely clear who the victors would be.[6]

"I was a National Socialist before the army, and now I'm a soldier. There aren't any National Socialists in the army, just soldiers.

"I was a company commander from April to October 1942. What you've been saying about the brutal treatment of Russian POWs—this is the first I've heard of it.[7] There was nothing like that in either my company or my regiment. There may be exceptional cases, but they'd have been just that: exceptions. It's prohibited. It's the same thing with the local populations. We have orders that make violence against the local population an arrestable offense. We're likewise prohibited from taking valuables from civilians—or any of their things, for that matter. Sometimes we're given permission to take foodstuffs. The packages with boots, dresses, and so on, that some of us sent back to Germany—those were things that had been found in destroyed or burned-out buildings.

"Russian soldiers are pretty good soldiers. They're much better at defending than attacking. And here, where they defend in small groups, they do a lot better than they do as a large mass. You have good snipers."

Major Koltynin, Head of 7th Section, Political Department, 66th Army
Quartermaster-Technician 2nd Class Gersh, Interpreter, 99th Rifle Division

REPORT

on the political interrogation of POW Sergeant Helmut Pist, 21st Panzer

Grenadier Regiment, 24st Panzer Division
Dubovka, February 9, 1943
Interrogated by Captain Zayonchkovsky, senior instructor, 7th Section, Political Department, 66th Army
Pist, Helmut. Born on January 11, 1916, in Schwarzenau (Province of Posen). Graduated from the *gymnasium*. Profession: agronomist. Lutheran. German. Member of the Hitler Youth. Drafted in 1937. Home address: *Krefeld am Rhein, Prinz Fridrich Karl Str., 139.*

When asked about the state of his unit during the final days of the encirclement, Helmut Pist stated the following:

"In early January the regiments in our division no longer existed as such. Individual groups were created that went by the names of the officers in charge. For example, a group was made up out of the 21st and 26th Regiments, and it was commanded by Colonel Brendahl. They also set up these so-called alarm groups. Those groups were different sizes. The one I was in, for example, had fifty men. We were led by Lieutenant Hermanns, and we were located in Orlovka. Morale was low. Many were criticizing the government, blaming it for giving up on us. Our food was getting worse by the day. By around January 20 we were getting fifty grams of bread per day. The air-dropped food supplies were being taken by whoever found them, despite strict orders and the threat of being shot. So there was very uneven food distribution in the units. Discipline was worsening every day, and there was more and more talk of surrender. On around January 25 Lieutenant Koars from divisional HQ told us that General von Lenski, our divisional commander, had issued an order giving freedom of action to the commanders of all units—that is, he was letting them surrender. But that order was canceled a day later.

"Your leaflets didn't have much success among the men before the encirclement, but then the situation changed, especially in January, when the men read them with real eagerness. We were actually looking for the leaflets you were dropping from the air, the ones with maps showing the situation on the front.

"Those last days in Stalingrad were horrible: thousands of dead bodies, and the wounded men dying in the streets because the hospitals were overcrowded, and on top of that we were taking heavy fire from your artillery and aircraft. The surrender wasn't organized. Our bunker was fifty meters from our divisional HQ, but even though we were so close to them, we only learned about the surrender after the Russians had already showed up. We came out of our bunker and put down our weapons. War in Russia is not what it is in the west. During the French campaign in 1940, our squadron was always out in front, and only two of our guys got killed."

Major Koltynin, Head of the 7th Section Political Department, 66th Army
Captain Zayonchkovsky, Senior instructor, 7th Section Political Department, 66th Army

REPORT

on the political interrogation of the POW Ernst Eichhorn, cavalry officer in the 9th Company, 24th Panzer Regiment, 24th Panzer Division

Dubovka, February 5, 1943

Interrogated by Major Lerenman, instructor, 7th Section, Political Department, 66th Army

Ernst Eichhorn. Home address: *Regensburg an der Donau, Luitpoldstrasse 11a.* Field Post no. 11468.

German. In the army since 1935. Not a member of the National Socialist party. On the Russian front since June 1941. Completed cavalry school in Hanover. Born in 1902. Campaigned in Poland, the Netherlands, Belgium, France. Not married.

One reason the surrounded German forces in Stalingrad surrendered was that the front was closing in. Maneuvering was impossible. A massive force was concentrated in this small area with no airfield. That resulted in enormous losses from artillery and airplanes. Another reason was the bad state of the food and fuel supplies. In the final days the men were getting one hundred grams of bread, a bit of horsemeat, forty grams of lard, a daily portion of broth (two liters), and four cigarettes.

They were down to a small number of artillery shells, but there was plenty of ammunition for the infantry. Tanks were turned into pillboxes. Because of that the whole regiment was operating as an infantry unit.

The officers of the 24th Panzer Division understood that the encircled units were in an extremely complicated and difficult situation, but they didn't consider it hopeless.

The order to surrender came through divisional command. It was given verbally, and then envoys were sent out, and units from the 24th Division laid down their arms. But the order to surrender came as a surprise to everyone. Up to the very end, most of the officers were still hoping to get help from the outside. The men never questioned their orders, both during the encirclement and when they were told to surrender. That's how the German soldier is trained: to do something only when he's ordered to. Communication with the outside world was maintained right up until Russian units took the airfield at Pitomnik. There was no postal service after that.

The idea was widespread in the German army—among both men and officers—that being captured by the Russians meant poor treatment, torture, and death. The men and officers had all read the Russian leaflets where it said that prisoners were treated well. There were some with photographs that showed the lives of the prisoners in Russia. But no one believed it, they figured it was just propaganda. During the advance many of them had seen the bodies of men who'd been shot in the head and so on. That convinced us that the Russians were shooting prisoners.

All of the officers in the 24th Panzer Regiment think highly of the Russian artillery. They're accurate and don't scrimp on shells. If there hadn't been any artillery at Stalingrad, and it was just infantry attacking the surrounded forces, then the Germans could have easily fought them off and resisted longer. The Russian infantry doesn't deserve any specific praise. They lack the spirit for an effective offensive. The Russians were a lot better in 1942 than at the beginning of the war. But the German fighter planes are better than the Russian ones. There are a lot of young, inexperienced pilots in the Russian air force. The tanks are very effective. The T-34 is an excellent piece of machinery. Russian tanks are very well armed. And their crews are very highly trained.

The reason for the successful offensive against the surrounded German army was the simultaneity of the attacks from the north and south, and later from the west. On top of that, the Romanian units, which were positioned on the upper Don, ran away. The success of the Russian assault was also facilitated by a certain amount of panicking in the German units. We began destroying stores of food and military equipment in the first days of the encirclement.[8] That complicated the situation for the surrounded forces.

During our advance on Stalingrad there was talk among the officers that the Russians were counting on the winter, that they were going to time their own offensive for the winter. The German commanders thought the Russians were too weak and downplayed the likelihood of a Russian offensive. The German commanders thought they'd have already won by the time winter came. The officers remembered that this wasn't the first time that their general strategic plans had been upended. It wasn't clear then—though it's obvious now—that the plan was unrealistic. You just can't count on simultaneous offensives on Leningrad and Stalingrad while also planning to take the Caucasus. It's too much. The German commanders were planning to take Stalingrad and then move down the Volga to Astrakhan. But they never took Stalingrad. To get to Astrakhan they had to try to cross the Kalmyk Steppe,[9] and that entailed increasing losses for the German army.

If the Red Army continues its offensive as it is doing now, especially if they take Rostov and Kharkov, then that will be of great significance to the outcome of the war.[10] Holding on to Kharkov and Rostov is the most important thing for the German army.

A second front in Europe is inconceivable. German forces are on standby in northern France, and the coast is fortified. An attack from Spain became impossible once the Germans took southern France. Nor could American and English forces land in Italy. The German navy wouldn't allow it. To land in Europe, you'd have to plan extensively, but still it couldn't happen.

"Germany has enough reserve forces and materials," said the prisoner. "We can fight on as much as we like."

The Russian leaflets often made the men and officers laugh. Russian propaganda hasn't really taken into account the particular psychology of the German soldier, his unique sense of discipline. "So, for example, I saw one leaflet that called on soldiers to kill their officers because they were better fed and didn't have to fight," said the prisoner. "Another leaflet told them to kill all the fascists and join the Russians. First of all, officers and soldiers eat the same food. And we don't understand the word 'fascist,' which makes us think of the system of government in Italy."

During the surrender, German officers were worried about their own futures. People said that, if you were going to surrender, give yourself up to the Americans, the British, the French. It's perfectly safe being a prisoner with them.

The prisoner asked: "Why are you going to so much trouble over us? We weren't expecting such good treatment, especially from Russian officers. If your goal is to encourage German officers to surrender, then that's very clever. Being allowed to send letters home was very effective in that regard. Now our soldiers say: 'As prisoners we can see that the Russians aren't bad people. Who knows why this war got started, why there's so much bloodshed.'

"To us officers it's clear that the war came about because of the Jews, who seized leadership roles in the governments of all nations except for Germany."

Major Koltynin, Head of 7th Section, Political Department, 66th Army
Major Lerenman, Instructor, 7th Section, Political Department, 66th Army

REPORT

on the political interrogation of POW Lieutenant Herrmann Strotmann, adjutant, 1st Battalion, 79th Panzer Grenadier Regiment, 16th Panzer Division

February 9, 1943

Interrogated by Captain Zayonchkovsky, senior instructor, 7th Section, Political Department, 66th Army

Strotmann, Herrmann. German. Catholic. Not married. Born May 18, 1918, in Münster. Bank employee. Home address: *Münster, Westfalen, Hermannstrasse 50.*

He was drafted as a regular soldier in 1938. In 1941 he was made an officer. He was a company commander in the 79th Regiment from September 5 and throughout October 1942, and since September he has been an adjutant in the 1st Battalion under Major Wota.

"During the fighting to the north of Stalingrad (south of the village of Yerzovka), from September to November, the 79th Regiment lost between 80 and 90 percent of its men. Reinforcements were constantly being brought from the rear, but that entailed a significant drop in quality. [. . .] Most of our losses were the result of your mortars, which we called the *böse Waffe.*"[11]

When asked about the state of his unit in the encirclement, Strotmann stated the following: "The Stalingrad operation was risky. At first we thought we'd take Stalingrad in five weeks. That didn't work out, and we couldn't fall back because that would have left the Caucasus group wide open. Our commanders' great mistake was attacking in late autumn, which meant we weren't able to dig in and get ready for winter on the front lines. You took advantage of this both last year and this year. If we'd stopped at the Don, then we'd have been able to make the right preparations. Then this catastrophe wouldn't have taken place. The main reason for our surrender: lack of food, men, shells, and also the impossibility of it all—it was physically impossible for us to continue fighting. The quality of our soldiers was very low (most of them had just been brought in in from the rear). We were starving, and most of us were frostbitten. Even the officers were so exhausted and hungry they could barely stand up. There's a limit to what a man can take, and we reached that limit on February 2. We surrendered. The surrender was spontaneous. At 6:00 A.M. I was told that Russian tanks were at our bunker. I cried, got out of the bunker and laid down my weapon."

Moving on to a question about our propaganda, Strotmann said that the quality of our leaflets had significantly improved as of late. "At the very beginning," stated the lieutenant, "they were quite primitive. For example, you reported that we'd lost 4,100 guns at Stalingrad, but there weren't that many guns in the whole army."

Lieutenant Strotmann concluded with the following: "Every soldier believes in victory, but to tell you the truth, if America enters the war, then we'll have a hard time winning."

Major Koltynin, Head of 7th Section, Political Department, 66th Army
Captain Zayonchkovsky, Senior instructor, 7th Section, Political Department, 66th Army
[Zayonchkovsky's signature]

REPORT

on the political interrogation of POW Sergeant Wilhelm Vugeler, 3rd Company, 79th Panzer Grenadier Regiment, 16th Panzer Division

Dubovka, February 9, 1943

Interrogated by Captain Zayonchkovsky, senior instructor, 7th Section, Political Department, 66th Army

Vugeler, Wilhelm. German. Lutheran. Born on March 1, 1916, in Nienburg/Weser. Member of the National Socialist party since 1934. Completed public school. Profession: commerce. Home address: *Nienburg/Weser bei Hannover, Quellhorststrasse 10.*

"There were eighty to a hundred men in our company when we got surrounded, and we were losing fifteen to twenty every day. Reinforcements were constantly coming in from the rear. Our situation improved a bit after December 30 because we built dugouts and were taking fewer casualties. I was transferred to the rear on January 4. In mid-January the remnants of the 16th Panzer Division were assigned to the 24th Panzer Division. All that was left of the 16th Panzer Division was the rear units.

"The men were feeling worse every day. Until January we were hoping to get help, but then in January, when we started retreating, our morale plummeted, and by the time we'd retreated right into the city, most of the soldiers understood the hopelessness of our situation. Still, the men were terrified of being captured by the Russians.

"I've read the Russian leaflets, and even listened to your radio broadcasts during the Christmas holidays. We were at the railroad northwest of Orlovka. All the men listened carefully to your broadcasts. Many of us started doubting that our officers were really telling us the truth. But our counterpropaganda was effective, so we didn't believe you entirely.

"On February 1, I was wounded near the Tractor factory and wound up in a field hospital. On February 3, at 3:30 A.M. (Berlin time), the chief physician announced that the hospital was being handed over to the Russians in two hours. So I was captured."

Major Koltynin, Head of 7th Section, Political Department, 66th Army
Captain Zayonchkovsky, Senior instructor, 7th Section, Political Department, 66th Army

REPORT

on the political interrogation of POW Sergeant Heinz Hühnel, 12th Company, 554th Regiment, 389th Infantry Division

Army Headquarters

Interrogated by Major Lerenman, instructor, 7th Section, Political Department, 66th Army

Heinz Hühnel. Home address: _____. Field Post no. 40886.

Born May 27, 1908. Education: Eight years of public school, Commercial High School. Married. Member of the National Socialist party since 1933.

Throughout the interrogation, Hühnel, a member of the National Socialist party since 1933, tried to convince the interrogator that he had become a new man after being taken prisoner. He claimed to have broken with Hitler's party. He explained that he wanted to study our state and ideological systems, that he wished to return to Germany as this new man or even remain in Russia to advance new ideas, to lead people toward communist ideology. He stated that he used to be far removed from politics. He fell under the influence of the mass psychosis of the National Socialist party, which, in addition to pressure from his wife's family, led him to become a member. Now, after being a party member and seeing the true nature of National Socialism in Germany, he concluded that Hitler's fascism was an ideology of conquest and enslavement.

What the Germans said about communism and Russia turned out to be completely wrong. Seeing what Russia was really like during the war [several words illegible] situation.

When they were first surrounded, the men hoped they would break out quickly. They expected help, but some soldiers understood even then that the situation was serious. They were thinking that they'd have to spend the winter in the encirclement before breaking out in March or April. The men's spirits were falling by the day. They turned in to dull, automatic task-doers, completely stupefied.

Few even considered the possibility of running away because they were certain that being captured meant being shot. The men read the Russian leaflets, but few believed them.

Hühnel talked about a German soldier who returned from Russian captivity. He said that at around 8:00 P.M. on January 8 a certain Holzapfel appeared in the company's bunker. He said he'd been a prisoner of the Russians for twenty-four hours. He'd been fed, given a lot of bread, offered tobacco. Holzapfel said he'd only seen German prisoners being treated well, that he saw how well dressed the Russian soldiers were, how well armed they were. Among those present was the commander, Sergeant Polte. He cut him off, saying that it was all propaganda, that they'd fed him on purpose, that it wasn't really like that for prisoners. Polte brought Holzapfel to the battalion commander, Captain Bitermen. No one saw Holzapfel after that. Who knows where he disappeared to.

Three days before the Holzapfel incident there was talk among the soldiers that someone had come back from Russian captivity saying their prisoners were being treated well.

After Holzapfel's disappearance people were saying that there must be some truth to his story. The prisoner stated: "I told the men to calm down. Let's see what happens. Maybe we'll be surrendering. Don't be afraid, just do what you're told." On January 10, when units of the Red Army were beginning an attack, Hünel apparently ordered everyone to get dressed and head out: "I had seven men and two machine guns at my disposal. We were supposed to defend ourselves—and we could have—but when the Russians came, I ordered my men to put their hands up. Six of the seven did so, and the last one ran to the telephone to tell the company commander what was happening. He was killed by the approaching Russians, and the rest gave themselves up."

All the men are ready to surrender, but they've got to have an order. Very few of them will surrender without an order from their superiors. They've grown so dull and weak that they've lost the ability to think for themselves. Another reason German soldiers don't surrender is because they consider it cowardice and a betrayal of their comrades. But if they're ordered to surrender, then whoever gave the order takes on the responsibility.

Supervision had to be stepped up because of the recent decline in morale. Everything possible was being done to reassure the men. The officers were always saying: Just wait, it's all going to get better soon. At the beginning of January all the German newspapers published Göring's speech where he said that everyone in the encirclement at Stalingrad would be going on leave and getting some sort of package from the Führer. He said that food was coming from the Ukraine and that the soldiers had nothing to worry about.

The men read that speech, and many of them laughed bitterly. All of them had spent the summer fighting in units that had taken heavy losses. Promises of relief came and went without anything happening. The units in the encirclement had been promised help before, but none had come. That made this speech impossible to believe.

The men had recently begun to notice that those who showed dissatisfaction or a "harmful disposition" would be monitored. The Nazis volunteered to keep an eye on other soldiers because they wanted to gain favor through espionage. No one was ordered to spy on other soldiers, but the Nazis considered it their duty.

The soldiers often tell one another that the officers live for themselves, that they're more interested in medals than the affairs of their company or the fate of their men.

Major Koltylin, Head of the 7th Section, Political Department, 66th Army
Major Lerenman, Instructor, 7th Section, Political Department, 66th Army

REPORT

on the political interrogation of POW Sergeant Karl-Heinz Pütz, 64th Regiment, captured on January 10 by units of the 343rd Rifle Division

January 11, 1943

Interviewed by Captain Zayonchkovsky, senior instructor, 7th Section, Political Department, 66th Army

Born on May 15, 1924, in Cologne. Home address: *Cologne, Nippes, Escherstrasse 21.* Father: Electrician. Completed primary and secondary school. German. Catholic.

He joined the army in September 1941 and was placed in a reserve motorcycle battalion stationed in Iserlohn. He worked as the battalion's small-arms armorer. He arrived on the Russian front in September 1942 in the 64th Regiment of the 16th Panzer Division.

When the Russians were surrounded, the prisoner was in an independent detachment that was formed mostly out of units from the 16th Panzer Division. The detachment included two battalions of soldiers from the 64th and 79th Regiments and the 16th Motorcycle Battalion, and also one battalion from the 544th Regiment of the 389th Division.

The first battalion, which is where Pütz was, had forty-five to fifty men. There were about as many men in the second battalion. The infantry battalion was around 150–200 men. Captain Dornemann was in charge of the detachment. The first battalion had only one officer, Lieutenant Schlippa, who'd flown in straight from Germany on January 1. According to the prisoner, cargo planes are still bringing in ammunition, food, fuel, and also replacement officers.

The detachment occupied the area from Hill 137.8 to the southern slopes of Hill 139.7.

Food: The men are currently getting two hundred grams of bread per day—four hundred grams every second day—forty grams of canned meat, and cold soup without the least bit of fat (the horses have all been eaten). Vitamin tablets are also given out daily. During his time in the encirclement the prisoner once received eighty grams of butter. Three hundred grams of chocolate were issued on Christmas, and one hundred grams for New Year's. "The men are starving," said the prisoner. "What they gave us today for seven men is roughly equal to the daily rations of an entire battalion."

The heating situation is also very bad: wood is brought in once a week, but only enough for one day, to heat a stove two or three times.

The men use timber from unoccupied bunkers for heating. But there's not much of that. A lot of people have frostbite. For example, twenty-five to thirty men in the battalion got frostbite on December 25. Now they're all with the baggage train since the hospital is full.

Morale is low. Most of them men think the situation is hopeless, though the officers do try to reassure them, saying that help is on the way, that the main forces of the German army are no more than forty kilometers from the encirclement.

The men are afraid of being captured by the Russians because the officers have convinced them they'll be shot. Pütz learned the truth of the matter from the soldier Holzapfel, who visited him in his bunker on the night of January 9. Pütz was on duty at the time and saw Holzapfel cross over from the Russian side. Holzapfel came into the bunker all excited, and he started telling them right away about the good conditi[...] in Russian captivity, and then he took some bread out from his pocket and shared it around. There were seven men in the bunker, along with a sergeant from the infantry battalion that Holzapfel belonged to.

The sergeant asked Holzapfel to come with him to the baggage train. The next night another soldier told him: "That redhead Holz will be shot for betraying his country." The soldiers sympathized with Holzapfel and blamed him only for not being careful enough.

Regarding the circumstances of his own capture, Pütz said the following: "On January 10, when the attacking Russians were coming right up to our bunker, the sergeant told us that resistance was futile and that we had to surrender. When we put our hands up, we started taking fire from the other bunkers. I got hit, and my comrade Private 1st Class Hilbeck was killed."

Captain Zayonchkovsky
[Signature]

REPORT

on the political interrogation of POW Major Herrmann Lüben, deputy chief of staff and chief of logistics, 389th Panzer Division

Dubovka, February 5, 1943

Interrogated by Major Lerenman, instructor, 7th Section, Political Department, 66th Army

Major Herrmann Lüben. Born in 1908. In the army since 1939. Graduated from the General Staff Academy in 1940. Home address: *Deutsch-Eylau, Hindenburgstrasse 32.*

The prisoner worked for the German Ministry of War, after which, according to him, he took part in the design and construction of military fortifications in the Netherlands (after the German occupation). He was in France. He participated in the campaigns against Poland, Belgium, and the Netherlands, and he was involved in the disbanding of the French army. While working for the general staff, Lüben took part in and even directed the formation of new military units.

As part of his duties, Major Lüben rotated through a diverse range of officer circles in the German army.

During his interrogation the prisoner said that, because of the blows struck by the Red Army against the German war machine, the top brass were trying even harder to align their officer corps with the National

…that in mind, they were propagandizing the theory that …f the National Socialist party which were responsible …he German army. And for the same reason the older … were sympathetic to the political opposition, were …generals who were clear supporters of Hitler.

The prisoner said that recently, in light of the failure of the German army's strategic plans in Russia, there is now a pressing need to merge the officer corps with the leadership of the National Socialist party. [. . .]

From the moment Hitler and his government took power they had the support of the vast majority of the officer corps. For a time the German army's military successes in Europe increased Hitler's authority. But the war with Russia—the collapse of their reckless plans to march on Moscow, to break through to Rostov and Stalingrad—has significantly undermined Hitler's prestige. [. . .]

An idea has been circulating among the officers that there are favorable and unfavorable seasons for Germany; that is, many believe that Germany can and will be victorious in a summer campaign but that winter favors the Red Army.

The prisoner confirmed that the officer corps held such a view of the high command's strategic plans, but that they did not go so far as to express their disagreements openly. Many of the generals, including General Brauchitsch,[12] opposed the plan to advance on Rostov and Stalingrad, but they expressed their disagreement only by suggesting alternative plans. All discussion of the matter stopped when they received their orders. But among the other officers criticism of the risks involved in taking Stalingrad was heard all the more strongly. Describing the situation on the fronts and his own outlook on the war, the prisoner stated: "The defeat at Stalingrad and the Red Army's advances to the west and southwest have come as a heavy blow to the German army, but this isn't enough for us to start talking about a real turning point at the front, or about the beginnings of a German defeat. If the Red Army manages to take back Rostov and Kharkov, then that would be a strong indicator of a turning point. Then you might begin to say that the fortunes of war have turned against the German army." The prisoner concluded: "But it's hard to believe that the Red Army could manage to take those cities."

During his interrogation Major Lüben said that it was wrong to think that Germany has exhausted its manpower or reached its limit. Because of the policy of using foreign workers and POWs in its industries, Germany can call up 10 or perhaps 12 million men, counting both men who of military age and those who have until now been granted exemption. Also, the German army can still bring in large numbers of men from the hospitals.

The prisoner nevertheless stated that productivity is low among foreign workers and POWs who are forced to work. And there is also the problem of blood purity. There are special laws that prohibit these groups from associating with the rest of the population, but the preservation of blood purity is still precarious, and this has become a problem. The next thing that gave the prisoner hope of a favorable outcome to the war was his trust in the unwavering discipline of the German army. Despite obvious tactical and strategic miscalculations, the level of discipline in the Germany army—according to the prisoner—gives them the possibility of later offensive operations when the time is right.

The main reason for all their misfortune, he thinks, is the weakness of their allied armies. The tragedy of the Italian army is that their junior officers have not been properly trained and assigned to the right positions. The educational system in the Italian army does not encourage, but rather discourages the formation of junior officers who will play a decisive role on the battlefield. The Romanians make good soldiers, you can get things done with them. But before the war their officers spent their time in cafés doing business of their own. They weren't training their men, which is why the Romanian army is seriously flawed. "Yes, it's too bad we have to work with such allies," concluded Lüben. He accounted for the increasing numbers of Germans who were surrendering by saying that they have been let down by their allies, and he denied any lack of discipline in the German army. [. . .]

Concerning relations with the populations of countries occupied by Germany, the prisoner said the following: "In France there have been a number of occasions of people shooting at German soldiers in the streets, but we don't expect any uprising in France. The French have always been a frivolous people, and now they've learned nothing from their defeat. They just sing and dance as they did before."

In response to the suggestion that the prisoner might only have seen life in France from the window of a café or German restaurant, he said that he was giving his own impressions and that he didn't know the feelings of the general masses. He also came across displays of ill will toward the Germans in Belgium and the Netherlands. He said that it had to do with people in commerce and industry whose businesses were disrupted when the Belgian and Dutch colonies were seized.

German soldiers and officers thought bad things about Russian captivity not only because surrender is considered cowardice and treason,

but also because very little is known about how prisoners are actually treated in Russia. If POWs were able to write home, then people would think better of them, even in the army. That would dispel all the rumors that are circulating about being taken prisoner in Russia.
Major Koltylin, Head of the 7th Section, Political Department, 66th Army
Major Lerenman, Instructor, 7th Section, Political Department, 66th Army

REPORT
on the political interrogation of Senior Lieutenant Otto Conrady, chief of intelligence, 389th Infantry Division
Dubovka, February 7, 1943
Interrogated by Captain Zayonchkovsky, senior instructor, 7th Section, Political Department, 66th Army
Senior Lieutenant Otto Conrady. Born March 13, 1904, in Berlin. Father: police officer. German. Catholic. Graduated from the law faculty of the University of Berlin in 1926. Married, four children. Has recently worked as a senior prosecutor in Hamm (Westfalen). Home address: *Hamm Westfalen, Ostenallee 93.*

He was drafted into the army on August 26, 1939. He was in the reserves from December 12, 1939, until November 1940, when he was reactivated. Since July 1940 he has been working as the chief of intelligence for the 389th Infantry Division.

The intelligence unit at a divisional headquarters consists of the chief, O-3 (an aide), two translators, one draftsman, and two clerks (the last three are enlisted), as well as one sergeant major.

When asked about his division's situation during the final days of the encirclement, Lieutenant Conrady said the following: "From mid-January we knew our situation was hopeless, but we kept up the defense because our mission was to keep these Russian armies at Stalingrad so they couldn't take part in other offensives. It was a difficult sacrifice, but we had to do this for our country. Lately we were completely out of artillery shells and mortars. We had enough rifle and machine-gun ammunition. The food situation was awful: one hundred grams of bread per day, about one hundred grams of canned meat, some soup.

"After Field Marshal Paulus surrendered on January 31 there was absolutely no point in us continuing to resist. There wasn't any surrender order in our division. Everything happened on its own (to a certain extent). Ten days before the surrender our headquarters was spread out over three locations. The intelligence unit was south of the Tractor factory, near the 305th Infantry Division's main medical station. At around 7:00 A.M. (Berlin time) three Russian tanks approached the building we were in, and we surrendered. I don't know what the situation was in other divisions. After surrendering, we were taken to Orlovka, and on the way we got robbed by Russian soldiers, who took everything we had. To be fair, the Russian officers forbade this, but they couldn't keep track of everyone. What can I say? *A la guèrre comme a la guèrre*. War is war."

Moving on to his evaluation of the Stalingrad operation, Conrady said that, even at the beginning, many officers thought it was rather risky. The flanks of the group moving on Stalingrad were exposed. This was okay at the beginning of the operation because they were expected to take Stalingrad extremely quickly before moving northward on the Ilovlin—[illegible]—Volga line, thereby creating a single front from the Volga to the Don and farther west. The Russians' stubborn defense of Stalingrad created another situation that eventually brought them to ruin. [. . .]

When he was describing the strengths of our Russian army, Lieutenant Conrady praised our generals highly, particularly Marshall of the Soviet Union Zhukov, who led the operations in the south.

"You learned a lot during the war and turned out to be excellent students." Later, when he described the strength of the Red Army's resistance, he said: "Red Army units have put up a stubborn resistance, but the bravest opponent we encountered was in August, when we were fighting on the Don at Dobrinskaya. It was the Krasnodar Officer School (Krasnodar Military Academy—Captain Zayonchkovsky). They fought like lions. When we had captured about a hundred of them, our divisional commander, General Janeke,[13] lined them up and said that he had seldom seen such brave soldiers." In his descriptions of the individual forces, Lieutenant Conrady said that the Russian artillery and mortars were very good, but that our air force was weaker than theirs: "Your air force did us very little harm, even recently it hasn't caused much damage."

When asked about how much the intelligence unit and the divisions knew about the forces they were up against, Conrady stated: "We were always in a rather awkward position: we obtained our basic information from prisoners and defectors. Since June 1942 we've had about thirty thousand of them, 95 percent of whom testified to there being strong anti-Soviet sentiments in the army: the soldiers only fought out of fear, there was a famine, and soldiers in the army would go without food for four or five days. That gave us the impression that your army was on the verge of collapse. On the other hand, we saw the stubborn resistance by Red Army forces. What was this about? I still can't account for it. I often found myself in the awkward situation of presenting transcripts of prisoner interrogations to the general. Several times he said: 'What sort of nonsense are you feeding me? Don't you see these Red Army units are putting up a fierce resistance?'"

Moving on to the question of propaganda among enemy forces, Lieutenant Conrady said that this was undertaken by a special department in the army intelligence unit. This department of propaganda printed and distributed leaflets, and they also used two or three vehicle-mounted mobile radios. This department was staffed by officers, a few translators, and a few sergeants and other NCOs. When asked about the effectiveness of our own propaganda, Lieutenant Conrady said: "Your propaganda is not very effective because it influences only the morally unstable units, and even during the encirclement our men were entirely under the control of their commanders, right up to the last days. We had some who deserted and went to your side, but they were only isolated cases. I think your leaflets had the greatest influence, and as for your radio broadcasts, I'd imagine that they were not very effective. As far as I know, no one listened to them.

"We knew that that you had recently been sending over a lot of prisoners. That of course is the most effective method. After questioning them, we usually moved the prisoners you sent us to other units on other sections of the front."

To conclude, Lieutenant Conrady was asked about the activities of the propaganda companies. The propaganda companies, Conrady said, are attached to each army. They number between 100 and 120 men. They do the following: publish the army newspaper, for which there is a special editorial team and print shop; photograph combat scenes to send to the rear and also shoot film to send to the rear (they would have as many as fifteen photographers). They also make audio recordings of men and officers telling stories of individual episodes, as well as voice recordings of people talking about various events from life at the front (there were up to ten speakers). The propaganda companies almost never work with active units on the front. It's only when a unit is brought back to recuperate that the propaganda companies show films, hold different kinds of lectures, and also organize appearances by cabaret acts brought in from Germany.

Major Koltylin, Head of the 7th Section, Political Department, 66th Army
Captain Zayonchkovsky, Senior instructor, 7th Section, Political Department, 66th Army

REPORT
on the political interrogation of POW Bredahl, Waldemar, interpreter, 389th Infantry Division
Dubovka, February 6, 1943
Interrogated by Captain Zayonchkovsky, senior instructor, 7th Section, Political Department, 66th Army
Bredahl, Waldemar. Born in 1904 in St. Petersburg.

Lutheran. Not married. His father was an engineer who owned a stone-planing factory in St. Petersburg. He studied at the St. Petersburg High School. In 1918 he moved to Estonia with his parents, where he lived until 1940. In 1940 he settled in Germany (Posen). Profession: sales representative, worked for the *Untech* [?] company in Posen. Drafted on October 2, 1942. Arrived at the front on November 4, 1942, as an interpreter for the 389th Infantry Regiment's prisoner collection point.

When asked about their disposition in the last days of the encirclement, Bredahl said: "On January 22 we fell back to Stalingrad, and most of the officers could see that further resistance was useless and would only result in a purposeless loss of life. Among themselves the officers said this openly and were even surprised that their commanders hadn't begun negotiating a surrender. Toward the end that was all they talked about. As for the men, they didn't know the real situation, so they kept hoping we'd get help. The main reason that we surrendered was that we'd exhausted all our resources, and also that our situation was hopeless because we couldn't count on getting help from anywhere. On February 1 the headquarters commandant Captain Stegner called for me and ordered me, the interpreter, to go out with a white flag to announce that this building was a field hospital and would offer no resistance. On February 2 at around 8:00 A.M. there was a cry: 'Translator, come on out, there's three Russian tanks at the door.' The Russian tank crews started taking our weapons and watches right away."

"As for discipline," Bredahl stated, "I don't know of many times when it broke down, though it did decline in the final days before the surrender. For example, I saw some soldiers who'd been sent to the front lines show up just an hour later back at the command post. Nor did they follow subsequent commands to go back to the trenches."

When asked about the Red Army, Bredahl said: "Your artillery is very effective, and your mortars are good too. As for the air force, it's not as strong as ours. First of all, your airplanes are scared of our fighters, which often shoot them down, and, second, they rarely hit their targets, though lately they've been able to feel more at home since our antiaircraft artillery hasn't been operating. Regarding the Red Army's commanders, the opinion circulating among our officers is this: the Russians learned how to fight from us, the Germans, and now they can fight pretty well."

When he spoke about the condition of Russian POWs, Bredahl testified that on January 13 his divisional command issued an order that called for two prisoners to be shot for every one that ran away. That order came in response to a rapid rise in the number of escapees in January. According to Bredahl, the order was not carried out. "Your POWs had tough conditions. They weren't getting any bread at all recently, but before the encirclement they were getting rations of 370 grams of bread and horse soup."

Major Lerenman, instructor, 7th Section, Political Department, 66th Army
Captain Zayonchkovsky, senior instructor, 7th Section, Political Department, 66th Army
[Zayonchkovsky's signature]

A GERMAN DIARY FROM THE *KESSEL*

Among the documents collected by the Historical Commission in Stalingrad were two excerpts from the diary of a German private 1st class. Soviet soldiers found the diary in December 1942 or January 1943, probably among the possessions of its deceased owner. The diary was turned over to the military intelligence unit of the 62nd Army, and several extracts were translated into Russian. The preserved sections of these translations begin on November 22, when the soldier's regiment, stationed in Kalach-on-Don, was attacked by the spearheads of Operation Uranus from the north and southeast. The joining of these spearheads in Kalach completed the Stalingrad *Kessel*. The diary documents the ensuing confusion, the Germans' failed attempts to break out of the pocket, their eastward retreat toward Stalingrad, and how the men fought while subsisting on near-starvation rations. The excerpts end on December 18. By then the diary's author sensed that death was near and wrote nostalgically of home and family. The final entries are a moving testament to the depths of human anguish.

The desperation Wehrmacht soldiers experienced in the *Kessel* has been well known in Germany since the publication of the anthology *Last Letters from Stalingrad* (original: *Letzte Briefe aus Stalingrad*) in 1951.[14] Less well-known is how the Soviets responded to these enemy voices in distress. Following the presentation of the diary excerpts, I discuss how they were read and utilized by Red Army propagandists.

TRANSLATION

From captured documents received by the 7th Section, Political Department, 62nd Army, January 1 1943

Diary of a private 1st class in the 10th Company, 578th Regiment, 305th Infantry Division

November 22—Left Kalach at night.

November 23—Russian planes, constant air raids.

November 24—Got up at 3:45 A.M. and started the difficult march, over sandy ground, to the Don. Constant shooting. On the steep bank of the Don there were Russians. You could see them perfectly. I was always hearing shells exploding. At night we left those positions. Spent the night on frozen ground.

November 25—We lost a unit. Bombs, pilots, artillery.

November 27—A hasty retreat over the sand. We're surrounded, it's so cold. I'm frozen stiff. They're shelling us.

November 28—It's dark, and we're all loaded up, ready to leave. Me and eight of my own. No one knows where we're going.

November 29—We wait for some time on the highway, don't know what to do next. I'm terribly hungry. There have been problems lately with food. What's going to happen? Other neighboring units are cooking, and here I can't even get a spoonful of soup. We kept going. Stopped in a ravine. Started looking for our company. In the next village it was a complete mess: Romanians, Russians, Germans. After a long search we found our company.

November 30—Early in the morning we got to our platoon. We entrenched in the cold ground. Brutal fighting day and night. Russian tanks broke through by evening, and we had to defend against them. Air raid, mortar fire. I haven't eaten in thirty-six hours. Now I've got 1/8 loaf of bread, 1/16 can of tinned meat, a few spoonfuls of pea soup and a sip of coffee.

December 1—Spent the night in a trench: same rations. Mortars exploding constantly. Frightfully cold. We were on the front lines, then we came back. At the nearest village we slept in a barn. Right in the muck and manure. Everything is wet, terribly cold.

December 2—Shelling in the morning. Some killed and wounded. I barely made it. All my stuff got stolen: All I've got left is what I had on me. We marched twelve kilometers, we're dead tired, starving. Another whole day without food. I've lost all my strength.

December 3—Again we march, again no water. Can't get anything to drink. I feel terrible. I've been eating snow. Tonight we didn't find any quarters. It's snowing, I'm completely soaked, water in my boots. We managed to find a dugout. I'm staying there with six other comrades. We cooked up a little horsemeat in snow water. What will the future bring? We're surrounded. 1/12 loaf!

December 4—Heavy march, nineteen kilometers. Everything covered in ice. We got to Gumrak, spend the night in railcars.

December 5—It keeps getting worse. So much snow, my toes are frostbitten. I am so hungry. This evening after a long march we entered Stalingrad. We were welcomed by exploding shells. We ended up in a cellar. Thirty of us. Absolutely filthy, unshaved. We can barely move. There's very little to eat. Three or four cigarettes. A dreadful, savage group of men. I am so unhappy! All is lost. People are fighting constantly, everyone's on their last nerve. The mail's not getting through, it's terrible.

December 6—Same as yesterday. We're lying in this cellar, barely allowed out in case the Russians see. Now at least we're getting 1/4 loaf daily, a can of meat for every eight men, a little butter.

December 7—Everything's as it was. Lord, please help me get home in one piece. My poor wife, my dear parents. How difficult it must be for them! Almighty God, make this come to an end. Let us have peace again. That we may go home soon, go back to a human life.

December 9—Our servings at dinner were a bit bigger, but we got only 1/12 loaf, 1/12 can. Yesterday was my wife's birthday. I'm depressed. Life has lost all meaning. The arguments and fighting never stop. Hunger can have that effect.

December 10—I haven't eaten anything since yesterday. Just some black coffee. I have lost all hope. God, will this go on for long? The wounded are here with us. We can't send them anywhere. We're surrounded. Stalingrad is hell. We boil the flesh of dead horses. No salt. A lot of us have dysentery. Life is so terrible! What have I done to deserve such punishment? Thirty men are packed into this cellar, at two o'clock it starts to get dark. The night is long. Will there be a day?

December 11—Today we got 1/7 loaf, some lard, and we're meant to get some more hot food. But tonight I collapsed from weakness.

December 12—Still in Stalingrad. We've been given a new unit. The food situation is still very bad. Yesterday I brought in some horsemeat. Today, unfortunately, there's nothing. I keep hoping I can keep going. It should get better. There was quite a storm last night: artillery fire, shells. The earth shook. Our NCO went off to fight. We'll be following him soon. We have people here with dysentery. I am so hungry. If only it were a little easier. If we weren't sick or wounded. God help me. The guns are shooting constantly. You can hear the whistle of incoming shells. Today I wrote a letter. I hope that my family gets it soon. Right now I can see my wife so clearly before me.

December 13—This evening we got rice flour and 1/16 can. I was happy to have it. Nothing new apart from that. I'm feeling very weak, very dizzy.

December 14—I'm still feeling faint. No help to be had. There are a lot of wounded here who aren't being looked after. All because of the encirclement.

I smoked my last cigarette. Everything is coming to an end. The things I've gone through this past week—it's too much. I'm always so terribly hungry. This past year in Russia was nothing compared to what's going on right now. This morning I ate 1/7 loaf, a tiny piece of butter. They've been shelling us since last night. What a harsh existence! What a terrible country! I am putting all my hope with God. I have lost my faith in mankind.

December 15—We're needed at the front. We stumbled and crawled our way through the trenches and the ruins of Stalingrad. We crossed paths with a seriously wounded soldier being carried out. We arrived at the command post. Then we went down into a factory basement, and then most of our unit went out to fight. Only thirteen of us remained. I was the highest-ranking one there. There was dirt and debris all around. No way out. Everything shifting and cracking under the Russian artillery fire.

December 16—I'm still here. They bring the wounded down here. In the cellar it's dark both day and night. We built a fire right on the floor. At 4:00 P.M. the food delivery came: soup, 1/8 loaf, a little butter, a bit of canned meat. I ate all of it at once and lay down. Twenty-four hours until the next meal. On December 15 I sent a letter by airmail. I hope it gets there by Christmas. My poor, dear wife and parents.

December 18—The day goes by, just like all the other ones. We eat in the evening. Once every twenty-four hours we get food, then there's nothing. I had to drag in a wounded man. We searched for a long time before finding the doctor, who was also in the basement of a building that had been completely destroyed. I found a dead man when I got back to my trench. It was Rill, I talked with him three days ago. I'm sitting in this trench with another soldier. He's a twenty-year-old from Austria, he has dysentery, the stench is unbearable. Constant shelling. My ears hurt, and I'm really cold. Fifty meters away is the Volga. We're right next to the enemy. I don't care about anything anymore. I can't see a way out of this hell. The wounded aren't taken away, we just leave them in the villages, inside the encirclement. All I can hope for is a miracle. Nothing else can help. Our artillery have gone completely silent, they've probably run out of ammunition. I'm starving, I'm frozen, my feet are like ice. Neither one of us says a thing—what's there to talk about? We're approaching the happy Christmas holidays. What wonderful memories I have of it, childhood. [. . .]

My dear parents, I greet you from far away. Thank you for everything you've done for me. I'm sorry if I've caused you trouble. I never meant to. My poor Mama, what will you do? My sweet sister, it's hard for me to think about the times we played together, from the bottom of my heart I wish you happiness in your future life. There is no one I love as much as you, my sweet wife, my blonde Mitzi. I would give anything to know that we were going to meet again. If that is not to be, let me thank you for all the happy hours you have added to my life.

I don't know whether these lines will ever reach your hands. Writing relieves me of the loneliness and emptiness. May God give you strength and comfort if something happens to me. But I don't want to think about that. Life is so beautiful. Oh, if only we could live in peace! I'm still not able to come to terms with death, but that diabolical music of battle, bringing death, just keeps going and going.

It's day now, the sun is shining, but the shells are constantly exploding all around. I am completely exhausted. Is it possible to survive this? Everything is moving, like in an earthquake.

Graves of German soldiers in Stalingrad, 1943. *Photographer: Natalya Bode*

In Soviet hands the diary acquired a life of its own. The Russian translation was done by Major Alexander Shelyubsky, the director of military intelligence for the 62nd Army. This was similar to Zayonchkovsky's position in the 66th; like his colleague, Shelyubsky was a historian by trade and spoke fluent German.[15] During the battle of Stalingrad he drafted reports at several-week intervals on the "political and moral state" of the German forces that fought against the 62nd Army. The reports addressed specific divisions and commanders and, drawing on captured documents and prisoner statements, presented a detailed picture of the mood in the 6th Army. Shelyubsky appended his January 5, 1943, report to the diary of the German lance corporal.[16]

Shelyubsky also spoke with the Moscow historians and provided his assessment of the enemy.[17] The soldiers fighting against the 62nd Army were almost all from "elite squads" and "cadre divisions" consisting of "pure-blooded Aryans," not from their Romanian or Italian divisions, who in Soviet experience did not fight as well.[18] Until the beginning of October the German soldiers held the hope of "taking Stalingrad by storm." They believed that the large German offensive initiated by the 305th Infantry Division in the industrial district represented a turning point: "let the thunder of victory roar!"[19] "That's how one could describe the mood in the division. It entered combat around October 14. In two or three days its losses were tremendous. That division was thrown against the Barricades works. After such a morale boost along the lines that everything is good here, that Stalingrad is ours, when they started to be worked over by us they simply didn't understand what was going on. We tried to make them understand and dropped various leaflets." This passage shows that Shelyubsky sought to gauge the mood of the enemy strategically and find ways to influence it.

Shelyubsky explained how the pervasive fatalism in many letters in October 1942 gave way to desperation after the 6th Army was surrounded in November. He saw this development as an expression of the Germans' deficient "moral" stability. In particular, he noted that the many thefts and other forms of assault on the civilian population had "become so routine for German soldiers and officers that prisoners of war tell about this without any embarrassment."[20] He was also struck by the Germans' inability to withstand hunger:

> Another aspect that played a great role in the morale of the surrounded enemy has to be noted here: food. Germans don't know how to starve. Our Russian soldier not only during the Patriotic War but also the Civil War and all other wars knew how to starve. Germans cannot do that: when they fight, they are used to stuffing themselves like pigs. That can be proven by their letters. It is almost disturbing: all they talk about is food. I have interrogated dozens of prisoners of war and so did my workers. There wasn't a case where a prisoner did not start with food. Eating is their priority. Their entire brain is filled with chow. Toward the end the situation was very tough for them. The rations would be as low as one hundred grams of bread.

Shelyubsky and other political officers of the Red Army read the German messages through Soviet-tinted glasses, projecting onto the enemy their ideas of what constitutes a soldier. In their view, a soldier's will was firm and "healthy" when it served a higher purpose: the "fight against fascism" and the "liberation of enslaved peoples." An army that did not espouse such aims and merely conquered, pillaged, and destroyed could produce nothing but moral cripples. The inability of Paulus and the other captured German generals to identify the army's higher aims—they claimed that as members of the military they were not in charge of political questions—was interpreted by their Russian interrogators as weakness. The discipline of the Wehrmacht commanded the Soviets' respect, but when it came to political conviction they saw the Red Army as superior.

From Shelyubsky's report the diary of the German lance corporal made its way into the Soviet media. On January 25, 1943, short excerpts were read over Soviet radio and appeared in *Pravda* several days later.[21] The newspaper mostly keeps to Shelyubsky's translation, but presents the diary as a fight to survive within the Wehrmacht, stressing the infighting between the soldiers and their frayed nerves. In place of the drama of the soldier left to his fate is the moral decay of the German army. *Pravda* even goes so far as to falsify a passage. In Shelyubsky's original the lance corporal writes, "I see no way out from this horrible hell [. . .] I can only hope for God's miracle." The newspaper invents another perspective: "I see no way out of this horrible hell but capture."

As the end of the battle of Stalingrad neared, Shelyubsky, Zayonchkovsky, and the other enemy propaganda officers strengthened their efforts to convince German soldiers to surrender. They aimed to dispel the widespread belief among the Germans that Soviet captivity meant torture and death. The dogged resistance of the Germans, fueled mostly by fear of imprisonment, fanned the flames of hatred among the Soviets. As the Stalingrad transcripts document, there were scores of instances in which German soldiers were beaten or shot by Red Army soldiers after they surrendered.

5

WAR AND PEACE

ON FEBRUARY 4, 1943, A THREE-DAY PERIOD OF NATIONAL MOURNING BEGAN in the German *Reich*. All cinemas and theaters were closed, and solemn music was broadcast over the radio. The reports from Stalingrad, Joseph Goebbels recorded in his diary, shocked Germans. "We must do everything to help the *Volk* overcome this dark hour."[1] The same day *Pravda* reported the Soviet victory and the demise of a German army once 330,000-men strong. *Pravda* extoled the "historic fight" for Stalingrad as the one of the greatest battles in human history, in terms of both the size of the armies and the scale of destruction.[2] The army newspaper *Red Star* wrote, "Achieving such victory, especially in the conditions of modern combat, is possible only with highest military skill and with first-class troops. The Red Army has achieved such a victory."[3]

The Red Army's burgeoning self-confidence had already become apparent in early January 1943, when a government decree reintroduced epaulets, which had been reviled since the revolution as symbols of the imperial Russian army. A secret NKVD report from the Don Front noted that some soldiers wondered why the army campaigned against the golden shoulder pieces only to reinstate them with great ceremony; others sensed the pressure of the Soviet Union's Western allies and feared that the Red Army would devolve into a "bourgeois capitalist" military force. But many more soldiers seemed to welcome the decision, finding it only logical that the Red Army adopted some of the customs of their allies, as well as of the Wehrmacht, whose recognition they sought. Commissar Levykin of the 284th Rifle Division explained to the representatives of the Historical Commission the enthusiasm for the reform: "We didn't register a single negative incident of the kind that had taken place in 1918 or 1919.

The attitude has changed completely. Even before the epaulets arrived, troopers were already sewing the loops for them onto their uniforms. Some, jokingly, were saying that without epaulets they felt like plucked chickens."

Thousands of Red Army soldiers were promoted after the battle—including almost every officer interviewed by the historians—and regiments, divisions, and whole armies received Guards status. By June 1943, 9,602 soldiers in the 62nd Army (by then renamed the 8th Guards Army) had received medals for valor in battle. At the decoration ceremonies the political administration gave important speeches and cadre departments kept a record of every soldier who received a medal.[4]

The wave of commendation ignited controversy about who deserved the greatest praise for victory. Vasily Grossman registered the dispute with his customary acumen. In May 1943, several months after being recalled from Stalingrad, Grossman met the commanders of the 62nd Army on the Kursk steppes, where they had been placed on reserve status. Here is his account of the meeting:

> Lunch on the terrace of Chuikov's dacha. An orchard. Chuikov, Krylov, Vasiliev, two colonels—members of the Military Council. The meeting is not warm; they all are seething. Lack of satisfaction, frustrated ambition, insufficient decorations, hatred for anyone distinguished by more generous decorations, hatred toward the press. The film *Stalingrad*[5] is referred to with curses. Not a word about the fallen, about a monument, about memorializing those who did not come back. Each is talking only about himself and his accomplishments.
>
> The next morning at Guryev's. The same picture. No modesty at all: "I did, I overcame, I, I, I." Other commanders are mentioned without respect; some kind of womanish gossip: "I was told that Rodimtsev said something or other" [. . .] The overall idea is this: "Ours are the only accomplishments, the accomplishments of the 62nd, and in the 62nd itself I am the only one, the rest just happened to be there." Vanity of vanities—all is vanity.[6]

Stalin repeatedly tried to defuse the dispute, which continued to smolder long after the war ended. Following the victory parade of June 24, 1945, the Soviet dictator offered a widely noted toast in the ceremonial hall of the Kremlin "to the simple, common people, the 'little bolts' that are keeping active our great state mechanism in every branch of science, economy and military affairs. They are numerous, their name is Legion for there are tens of millions of them. These are modest people. No one writes about them, they have no ranks, no titles, but these are the people that hold us the way the base holds the top. I'm drinking to the health of these people, of our esteemed comrades."[7] Stalin's gesture was a calculated attempt to deflate the egos of the marshals, generals, and officers in attendance. In addition to keeping watch over the conferral of distinctions, Stalin was careful to preserve his own spot at the top of the glory hierarchy. On June 27, 1945, Stalin received the rank of Generalissimus of the Soviet Union, a position created especially for him. During the victory parade mentioned above his deputy Marshal Zhukov rode on a dashing white horse, inspecting the troops. According to some observers, Zhukov's horse was too white and his stance too proud for Stalin's liking. Soon Zhukov was accused of "Bonapartism" and demoted to leader of Odessa's military district.[8]

As a Soviet victory over Germany became increasing certain, the war chroniclers came to the fore. They were already sure of the form history had to take: Tolstoy's *War and Peace*. Just as the Red Army drew on prerevolutionary traditions, Soviet culture by that time found sustenance in a nineteenth-century novel. The iconoclastic spirit of the Soviet avant-garde had become passé. Large runs of Tolstoy's magnum opus were printed from 1941 onward and inspired thousands of readers accustomed to finding answers to life's questions in literature. As literary critic Lidiya Ginzburg observed, Soviets everywhere, even Leningraders left starving in the siege, avidly read *War and Peace*. They read in order to size themselves up vis-a-vis Tolstoy's heroes, Ginzburg commented, "not the other way round—no one doubted the adequacy of Tolstoy's response to life." Tolstoy had said "the last word as regards courage, about people doing their bit in a people's war"; this was the standard by which Soviet readers measured themselves. Whoever had energy enough to read, Ginzburg wrote, "would say to himself: right, I've got the proper feeling about this. So then, this is how it should be."[9] When interviewed by the historians, Chuikov revealed that he gauged his own performance based on Tolstoy's generals; General Rodimtsev reported reading the novel three times.

The People's Commissariat for Education printed brochures with instructions on how to make *War and Peace*—notorious for its length and complicated plot—accessible for soldiers. A 1942 study on the reading habits of Red Army soldiers concluded that Tolstoy's novel was the most discussed in the military.[10] By the close of the war, the parallels between the War of 1812 and the Great Patriotic War had become clear to every Soviet reader: enemy invaders had advanced into the heart of Russia only to be violently crushed by the Russian people. Tolstoy's novel, which ends in 1815, presents Alexander I as "the pacifier of Europe."[11] Soviet military leaders in 1945 believed they had liberated Europe from the scourge of fascism. Now the question was, who would be the Soviet Tolstoy, who would write the *War and Peace* of the twentieth century?[12]

One of the frontrunners for the honor was Vasily Grossman. Since 1943 he had been working on a two-volume war epic.[13] Modeled after *War and Peace*, the novel incorporated his own experiences but also aimed to be a chronicle of the war in its entirety. Like Tolstoy, Grossman tried to distill the spirit of a historical epoch. He borrowed Tolstoy's technique of tying together individual protagonists through family connections. The first volume, completed in 1949, told the history of the war from its outset until September 1942 and concluded with a description of Commissar Krymov's night crossing of the Volga into the burning city of Stalingrad. In August 1948 Grossmann submitted the first installment of the work to the journal *Novy Mir* (New World), where it was to be serialized as *Stalingrad*. For four years the book remained in limbo as Grossman rewrote the text at least three times in an effort to satisfy his critics—editors at *Novy Mir*, directors of the Soviet Union of Writers, members of the Central Committee and the Politburo, and military officers.[14]

Konstantin Simonov, the editor in chief at *Novy Mir* when *Stalingrad* was first submitted, complained about Grossman's strict historical perspective: his portrayal of the war in 1942 makes no reference to its outcome. For Simonov, this was unacceptable. The book ought to propagate optimism among contemporary readers.[15] Other critics objected to the title, which laid claim to a historical objectivity that the narrative's multitude of subjective viewpoints could not fulfill. The figure of the physicist Viktor Strum—clearly identifiable as a Jew—particularly incensed the critics. The writer Mikhail Sholokhov alluded to this subject when he rang up *Novy Mir*'s new editor in chief, Alexander Tvardovsky (he succeeded Simonov in 1950), and barked: "Whom did you entrust writing about Stalingrad? Have you taken leave of your senses?" Sholokhov believed that Grossman, a Jew, should not be writing about a quintessentially Russian topic like Stalingrad. Sholochov's views are just one expression of the anti-Semitic campaigns that had been erupting in the Soviet Union since the late 1940s.

Surprisingly, however, the novel did eventually appear in serial form in the summer and fall of 1952, earning Grossman a nomination for the Stalin Prize. But the January 1953 revelation that Jewish doctors in the Kremlin had been conspiring to kill Stalin triggered a backlash. On February 13, 1953, a scathing criticism of Grossman's novel appeared in *Pravda*, penned by Mikhail Bubyonnov, one of his rivals in the race to become the Soviet Tolstoy. Grossman's earlier supporters publicly turned against him.

But then Stalin died on March 5, 1953, and the tide turned once again. Not only was the doctors' trial halted; the criticism of Grossman subsided and some of his colleagues privately apologized for their remarks. Grossman, for his part, continued work on the second part of his novel—retitled *Life and Fate* in 1949[16]—but now he intended to write it as a literary reckoning with Stalin. Grossman was the first critic to emphasize the resemblances between Stalin's regime and the totalitarian ideology of the Nazis, describing the extent of Soviet anti-Semitism and the similar ways in which both states grind individuals into dust). By the time he finished the work in 1959, it could not be published. The Central Committee secretary in charge of ideological affairs that questioned Grossman compared the novel, were it to be released, to a nuclear bomb. (The secretary claimed he hadn't read the book.) Other political officials who were consulted believed that the book could not be published "for the next 250 years."[17] In 1964 Grossman died bitter and alone following a battle with stomach cancer. After his death, a copy of the manuscript was smuggled abroad and published. It appeared in 1988 in the Soviet Union as part of Mikhail Gorbachev's campaign for transparency known as *glasnost*. Today *Life and Fate* is viewed internationally as a grand literary account of the twentieth century. The preceding volume, which appeared under the title *For a Just Cause,* has remained in the shadows since it appeared.[18] Despite the ruptures that accompanied their publication, the volumes, when read side by side, reveal their underlying Tolstoyan conception. They show how strongly Grossman remained committed to the belief, despite his growing criticism of the Soviet state, that the mass heroism of Red Army soldiers decided not only the battle of Stalingrad but also the war as a whole.[19]

Grossman's conviction is conveyed in the one place no one would suspect—the monumental memorial atop Mamayev Kurgan. Had Grossman lived long enough to see its 250-foot *Motherland Calls* sculpture with extended sword (the memorial was dedicated in 1967), he would likely have seen it as further evidence of an all-powerful state that manipulates people like pawns in a political chess game. Nevertheless, Grossman's words can be found at the memorial. Some are engraved on a wall that visitors must pass on the way to *Motherland Calls*: "An iron wind struck them in the face, yet they kept moving forward. The enemy was likely possessed by a superstitious fear: Are these men coming towards us? Are these mortals?" The words are from Grossman's essay on the regiment that perished while defending the Barricades plant against the Germans (see pages 192–203).

On the other side of the wall is the Hall of Military Glory. From the center of the floor a large white marble hand reaches upward, cupping a torch with an eternal flame. The walls of the circular pantheon are lined with banners bearing the names of 7,200 Red Army fighters—officers and soldiers, men and women—who fell at Stalingrad. (The names were chosen at random from the death roll.)[20] Below the domed ceiling runs an inscription responding to the question posed on the outside wall: "Yes, we were mortal and few of us survived, but we all discharged our patriotic duty to our sacred Motherland." This is also drawn from Grossman's essay, but the words have been modified. The original version was simpler: "They were mortal indeed, . . . and while few of them made it out alive, every one of them had done his duty." Despite the melodramatic backdrop created by the monument's designers, the words convey the idea of a people's war invoked by Grossman during the battle of Stalingrad. Yet nowhere in the museum is Grossman identified as the author of these lines, and no museum guide seems aware of their origin.[21]

Isaak Mints's Historical Commission faced problems similar to the ones Grossman did. Its attempts to publish the chronicle of the Great Patriotic War encountered resistance for years; ultimately, Soviet censorship prevented the history from ever seeing the light of day, ensuring that the authors were mostly forgotten. Until 1945 the commission had worked fervently on collecting documents from the war. Mints wanted to record its entire history, including not only the main combat operations but also the partisan resistance movement, the war economy, Soviet culture, everyday life on the front, and the German occupation. When the Soviet Union declared war on Japan in August 1945, Mints sent several commission staff members to interview Red Army soldiers in the Far East.[22] In December 1945 the executive committee of the Academy of the Sciences dissolved the commission and created in its place the Sector on the History of the Great Patriotic War, an eighteen-person research group led by Mints under the auspices of the society's Institute of History. The following year Mints was inducted into the Academy of Sciences, the crowning achievement of his career.[23]

The documents that have been preserved indicate that the research group's staff worked assiduously through 1947, submitting multiple book projects to the Military Publishing House. At the top of the list was a documentary account of the battle of Stalingrad on the occasion of its fifth anniversary, described as "an instructive history book written by the participants themselves." The other projects included a book on the battle of Moscow, a study of women at the front, and an encyclopedia of three thousand Soviet war heroes. But the publisher was noncommittal and the works never appeared in print.[24] Mints seemed to understand that if he ever wanted to see them published, Stalin would have to be portrayed as a leading figure in every area of the war.[25] This of course went counter to the spirit of the wartime interviews, in which the respondents talked about their own thoughts and deeds and the collective was emphasized. But with the Stalin cult rampant again after 1945, the voices of individual soldiers had become anathema to the regime. An award-winning 1949 film about the battle of Stalingrad adhered perfectly to the prevailing expectations. The film shows the commanders of the 62nd army in dire straits as German fire bears down on them. Their only hope is that Stalin will come to the rescue. The film then cuts to the Kremlin, where Stalin calmly masterminds the defense, ordering up fresh troops and planning the encirclement of the Germans. The other members of the supreme command—generals, officers, soldiers—are all portrayed as cogs in the wheel who follow Stalin's orders as he leads them to victory.[26]

There was another reason why the interview transcripts from the war fell out of favor. Like Grossman, Mints was a Jew and had to contend with growing anti-Semitism in the Soviet Union. But Mints was swept up by the tide of hate earlier than Grossman, and he paid a higher price. Anti-Jewish sentiment began to hold sway in Soviet public life already during the war. A popular expression, "The Jews are fighting the war from Tashkent," implied that Jews used money and connections to flee far from the front, while Russians had to take the fall on the battlefield. In truth, Jewish soldiers in the Red Army fought with extraordinary dedication, as their high casualty rate and many commendations prove. Yet the party leadership suppressed this data,[27] just as it did the enormous suffering Germans inflicted on Soviet Jews. (Postwar newspapers described the Holocaust as a mass murder of "innocent Soviet citizens.") People like Grossman and Ilya Ehrenburg, who as members of the Jewish Anti-Fascist Committee had been documenting German crimes against Jews, were eyed suspiciously. Any special interest in Jewish affairs was contrary to general Soviet objectives, and their proposed "black book" did not receive permission for publication. Meanwhile the party had begun praising ethnic Russians as the best and most devoted soldiers in the Soviet Union. This propaganda spread after the war as the Soviet leadership took a stand against the western allies, condemning foreign influences and stressing Russian values as the measure of all things. In the Russocentric Soviet cosmos of the late Stalin era, Jews were regarded as suspicious nomads, "rootless cosmopolitans" intent on undermining Soviet patriotism.[28]

In 1947 Mints published a seventy-page booklet titled *The Great Patriotic War of the Soviet Union*. It does not mention the work carried out by his Historical Commission during the war. Instead, Mints falls all over himself praising the "great Russian people" who in the course of the war revealed "the concentrated force of its talents." It concludes with an ode to Generalissimus Stalin, the "brilliant, ever-bright star that will always shine in the history of the Soviet country."[29] Mints was obviously trying to present himself as a Russian patriot, yet the book could not offset a wave of public accusations that were being made against the author at the time of its release.

Their instigator was Arkadi Sidorov, one of Mints's closest associates on the Historical Commission. Sidorov was several years younger than Mints. They had met in 1924 while attending an upper-level Communist party school.[30] Like him, Sidorov had joined the Communist party during the Civil War. But whereas Mints rose quickly from one influential position to the next, Sidorov struggled. For a while he worked in the editorial department of Mints's project on the history of the Civil War. In 1936 he was barred from the party but reinstated several months later. During the reinstatement hearing Mints was summoned to provide character testimony but never appeared—something that Sidorov resented.[31] As the war began, Sidorov was finishing his doctoral work at the Institute of History of the Academy of Sciences.[32] When panic broke out in Moscow on October 14, 1941, and the population began to flee the city en masse, he decided to join an armed communist militia. Soon the unit was absorbed into the Red Army. During the battle of Moscow Sidorov was wounded and put on reserve status after a hospital stay. (By then he was a battalion commissar and had attained the rank of major.) In May 1942 Mints recruited him as a permanent staff member on his commission.[33] After the war Sidorov supervised a working group in Mints's sector on the History of the Great Patriotic War.

In November 1947 the journal of the Central Committee's Department of Propaganda and Agitation published a review by Sidorov sharply criticizing a lecture series edited by Mints on early Soviet history.[34] The previous June, Mints had been relieved as director of the Civil War history project; in 1948 he was forced to resign from Moscow State University. In early 1949 the campaign against the "rootless cosmopolitans" reached its zenith. Anti-Semitism raged in many areas of Soviet theater and classical music.[35] It also extended into the academy and affected Mints in particular. His research group at the Institute of History was branded a hostile

Jewish gang. Higher-ranking staff assembled for several days to ascertain the group's members and decide on sanctions. One of the group's main detractors was Sidorov. Mints looked on as events unfolded and was subject to humiliating "self-criticism."[36] He lost his job at the institute and was relegated to a teaching position at the Moscow State Teachers Institute. Sidorov assumed Mints's professorship in Soviet history at Moscow State University, and in 1953 he was named director of the Institute of History.[37]

Sidorov did not rise alone. The decommissioned Red Army major led a phalanx of doctoral candidates, mostly war veterans. All over the Soviet Union, former Red Army soldiers entered universities in droves, and with high expectations. With their experience on the front, self-confidence, and the Communist party books in their pockets, they aggressively claimed for themselves positions in the university administration.[38] Mints's fate is not without irony. During the war he invoked the heroism of simple Red Army soldiers and helped them find a voice and become conscious of their historical role. After the war, the very soldiers whose confidence he helped strengthen were outraged at the "Jewish clique" occupying the positions in the Soviet state that they now wanted for themselves. They had an aversion not only to Mints and his staff but also to the very documents they had collected. They believed these materials were permeated with a bourgeois, empirical spirit that lacked Russian patriotism. No one in those years continued Mints's editorial work, and the commission's documents sank into obscurity.

Siderov took great pride in ousting Mints from the university. And until his death in 1966, he continued to speak pejoratively about Mints, calling him a "parasite," a hypocrite, a shifty person "who everywhere he appeared would always surround himself only by Jews." (He saw Mints's English skills as further evidence of his inadequate "Russianness.")[39] Nevertheless, after Stalin's death Mints experienced a rehabilitation.[40] Unlike Grossman, who worked though his ordeals on the page, Mints remained for the most part silent.[41] Starting in the 1950s, he turned his research to the October Revolution, in line with a Soviet regime intent on passing over the Stalin era and returning to its revolutionary beginnings.[42] In the course of this volte-face Stalin's name was wiped from the textbooks and his body removed from Lenin's Tomb. In 1961 Stalingrad was renamed Volgograd.[43]

In 1984 surviving members of the Historical Commission got together for a night of reminiscing. At eighty-seven, Mints was the oldest one in the group. Mints admitted to his former staff a wish of his that had never been fulfilled: "When I was younger I dreamed that we would publish a gallery of the Heroes of the Soviet Union, but that never got under way." Even more than Grossman, Mints retained a heroic and romanticized view of the war, which he himself helped form during the war years. It had originated in the matrix of his mentor Maxim Gorky and all those ordinary workers who raised themselves to HUMAN BEINGS "in capital letters."

Before his death Grossman made several copies of his censored novel and hid them with friends. Had he not done this, *Life and Fate* would never have seen the light of day. The KGB seized not only the manuscript in Grossman's apartment but also the carbon paper and the ribbon from the typewriter on which the text had been written.[44] Mints used a similar strategy to safeguard his documents for posterity. After Stalin's death Mints learned that the archive of the Soviet Ministry of Defense in Podolsk outside Moscow had requested the interview transcripts from his commission. The request was in keeping with the trend of the time: centralizing all documents pertaining to the war and monopolizing their interpretation. Mints knew that everything the military archive collected would be lost in the long run. (The dissolution of the Soviet Union did little to change things. Russia's Ministry of Defense, the new guardian of the history of the Red Army, has released only a fragment of the estimated 5 million documents from the World War II era.) After Mints received the call from Podolsk, he had the presence of mind to hide the interviews. For several years they were stored in the basement of the Uskoye Sanatorium of the Academy of Sciences. Later they were moved to the basement at the Institute of History. Institute staff, a veteran of the Historical Commission among them, put the archive in order and prepared summaries of its contents.[45] These notes ultimately laid the trail that led to the publication of the Stalingrad interviews.

German prisoners of war in Stalingrad. *Photographer: Georgy Samsonov*

ILLUSTRATION CREDITS

Pages ii–iii, 14, 62, 349, 427—FotoSoyuz Agency, Moscow
Pages 98, 127, 135, 301—Gosudarstvennyi arkhiv Volgogradskoi oblasti, Volgograd
Page 75—Gosudarstvennyi istoricheskii muzei, Mosocwo
Page 110—http://denis-balin.livejournal.com/3324012.html
Page 260 (top)—http://dr-guillotin.livejournal.com/110602.html
Page 386—http://propagandahistory.ru/83Sovetskie-propuska-v-plen-dlya-nemetskikh-soldat/
Page 291—http://soviet-art.livejournal.com/987.html
Page 71—*K istorii russkikh revoliutsii* (Moscow, 2007)
Pages 41, 46, 64, 66, 85, 146, 149, 158, 165, 166, 167, 178, 191, 202, 254, 258, 263, 266, 332, 370—NA IRI RAN, Moscow
Page 381—*P. A. Zayonchkovskii. Sbornik statei i vospominanii k stoletiiu istorika*, ed. L. G. Zakharova (Moscow, 2007)
Page 11—Personal archive Tatyana Yeryomenko, Moscow
Pages 281, 304, 314, 352, 441—RIA Novosti, Moscow
Pages 34, 39, 48, 88, 93, 105, 116, 126, 129, 131, 132, 140, 169, 208, 259, 260 (bottom), 272, 303, 306, 317, 345, 364, 372, 373, 378, 392, 399—Rossiiskii gosudarstvennyi arkhiv kinofotodokumentov, Krasnogorsk
Page 253—*Soiuzkinozhurnal* 1943, No. 8
Page 354, 355—Tsentral'nyi arkhiv goroda Moskvy, Moscow
Page 240—Volgograd State Panoramic Museum "Battle of Stalingrad"
Page 193—http://www.lechaim.ru/ARHIV/104/lazarev.htm
Page 257—www.retro.ru
Page 102—www.stalingrad-battle.ru

MAPS

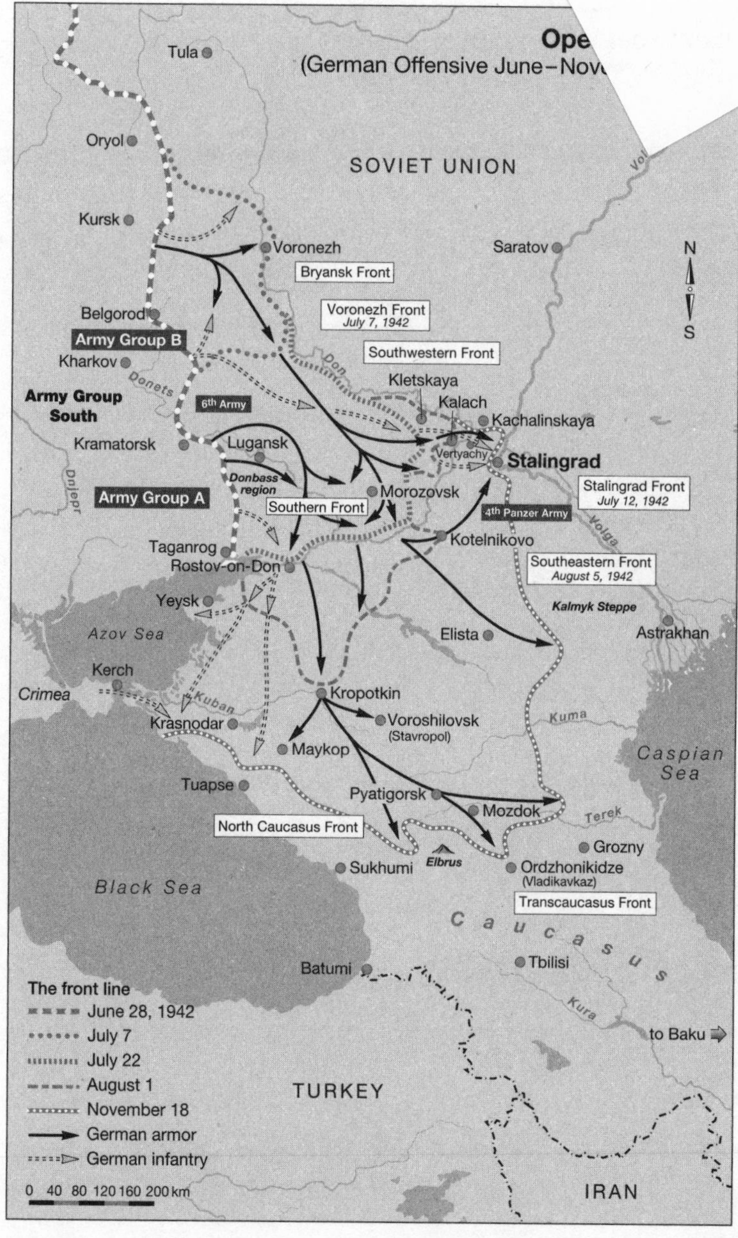

SOVIET UNION
Tula
Oryol
Kursk
Voronezh
Saratov
Bryansk Front
Voronezh Front
July 7, 1942
Belgorod
Army Group B
Kharkov
Southwestern Front
Don
Donets
Kletskaya
Army Group
South
6th Army
Kalach
Kachalinskaya
Kramatorsk
Lugansk
Vertyachy
Stalingrad
Stalingrad Front
July 12, 1942
Dniepr
Army Group A
Donbass
region
Southern Front
Morozovsk
4th Panzer Army
Volga
Taganrog
Rostov-on-Don
Kotelnikovo
Southeastern Front
August 5, 1942
Yeysk
Kalmyk Steppe
Azov Sea
Elista
Astrakhan
Kerch
Crimea
Kuban
Kropotkin
Krasnodar
Voroshilovsk
(Stavropol)
Kuma
Maykop
Caspian
Sea
Tuapse
Pyatigorsk
Mozdok
Terek
North Caucasus Front
Grozny
Sukhumi
Elbrus
Ordzhonikidze
(Vladikavkaz)
Black Sea
Transcaucasus Front
Caucasus
Batumi
Tbilisi
Kura
to Baku
TURKEY
IRAN
The front line
June 28, 1942
July 7
July 22
August 1
November 18
German armor
German infantry
0 40 80 120 160 200 km
N
S

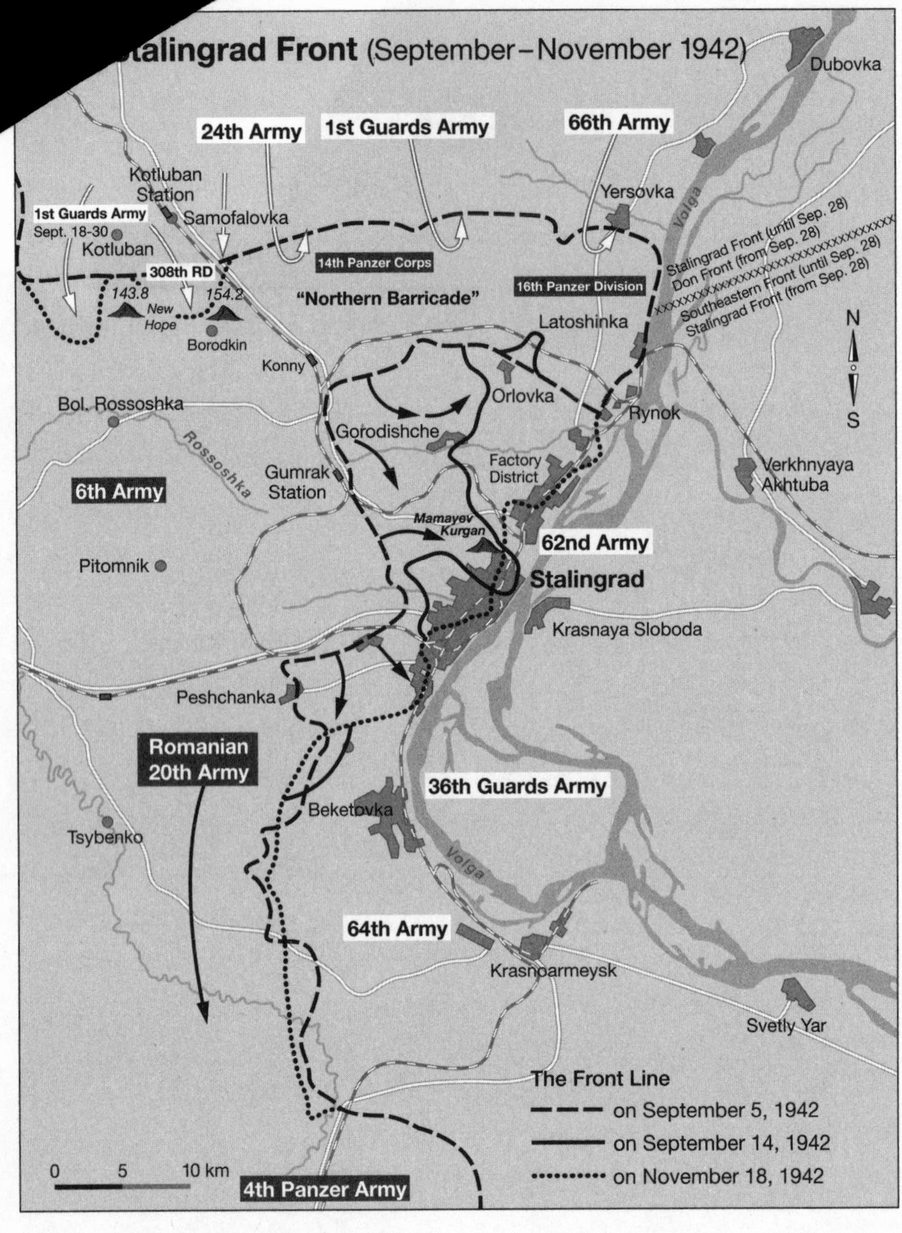

Stalingrad Front (September–November 1942)
Dubovka
24th Army
1st Guards Army
66th Army
Kotluban Station
Samofalovka
Yersovka
1st Guards Army
Sept. 18-30
Kotluban
14th Panzer Corps
308th RD
143.8
154.2
New Hope
Borodkin
"Northern Barricade"
16th Panzer Division
Stalingrad Front (until Sep. 28)
Don Front (from Sep. 28)
Southeastern Front (until Sep. 28)
Stalingrad Front (from Sep. 28)
Latoshinka
Konny
Orlovka
Rynok
N
S
Bol. Rossoshka
Rossoshka
Gorodishche
Gumrak Station
Factory District
Verkhnyaya Akhtuba
6th Army
Mamayev Kurgan
62nd Army
Pitomnik
Stalingrad
Krasnaya Sloboda
Peshchanka
Romanian 20th Army
36th Guards Army
Beketovka
Tsybenko
Volga
64th Army
Krasnoarmeysk
Svetly Yar
The Front Line
on September 5, 1942
on September 14, 1942
on November 18, 1942
0
5
10 km
4th Panzer Army

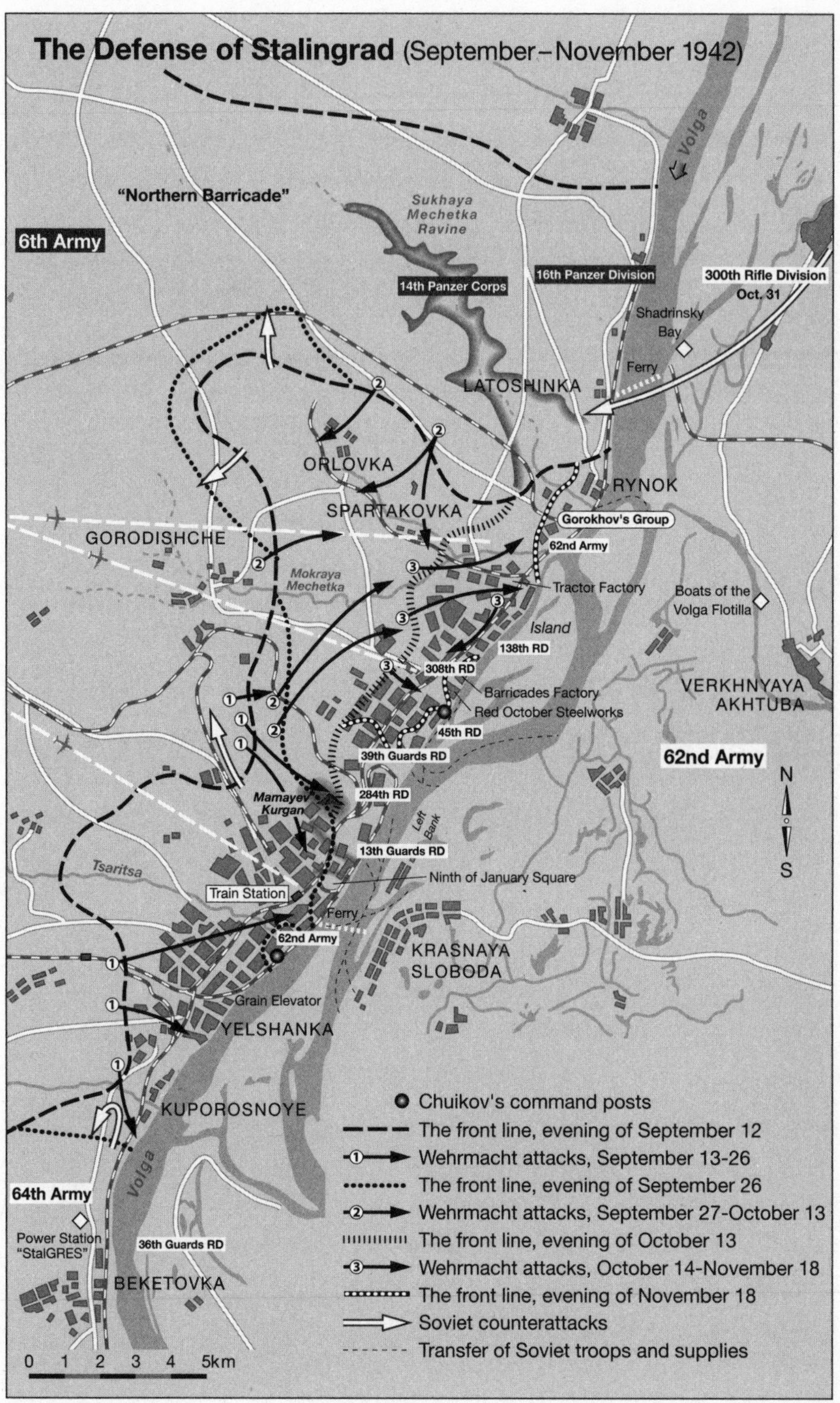
The Defense of Stalingrad (September–November 1942)
"Northern Barricade"
6th Army
Sukhaya Mechetka Ravine
Volga
14th Panzer Corps
16th Panzer Division
300th Rifle Division Oct. 31
Shadrinsky Bay
Ferry
LATOSHINKA
ORLOVKA
RYNOK
SPARTAKOVKA
Gorokhov's Group
GORODISHCHE
62nd Army
Mokraya Mechetka
Tractor Factory
Boats of the Volga Flotilla
Island
138th RD
308th RD
Barricades Factory
Red October Steelworks
VERKHNYAYA AKHTUBA
45th RD
39th Guards RD
62nd Army
Mamayev Kurgan
284th RD
Left Bank
13th Guards RD
Tsaritsa
Ninth of January Square
Train Station
Ferry
62nd Army
KRASNAYA SLOBODA
Grain Elevator
YELSHANKA
KUPOROSNOYE
Volga
64th Army
Power Station "StalGRES"
36th Guards RD
BEKETOVKA
N
S
0 1 2 3 4 5km
Chuikov's command posts
The front line, evening of September 12
Wehrmacht attacks, September 13-26
The front line, evening of September 26
Wehrmacht attacks, September 27-October 13
The front line, evening of October 13
Wehrmacht attacks, October 14-November 18
The front line, evening of November 18
Soviet counterattacks
Transfer of Soviet troops and supplies

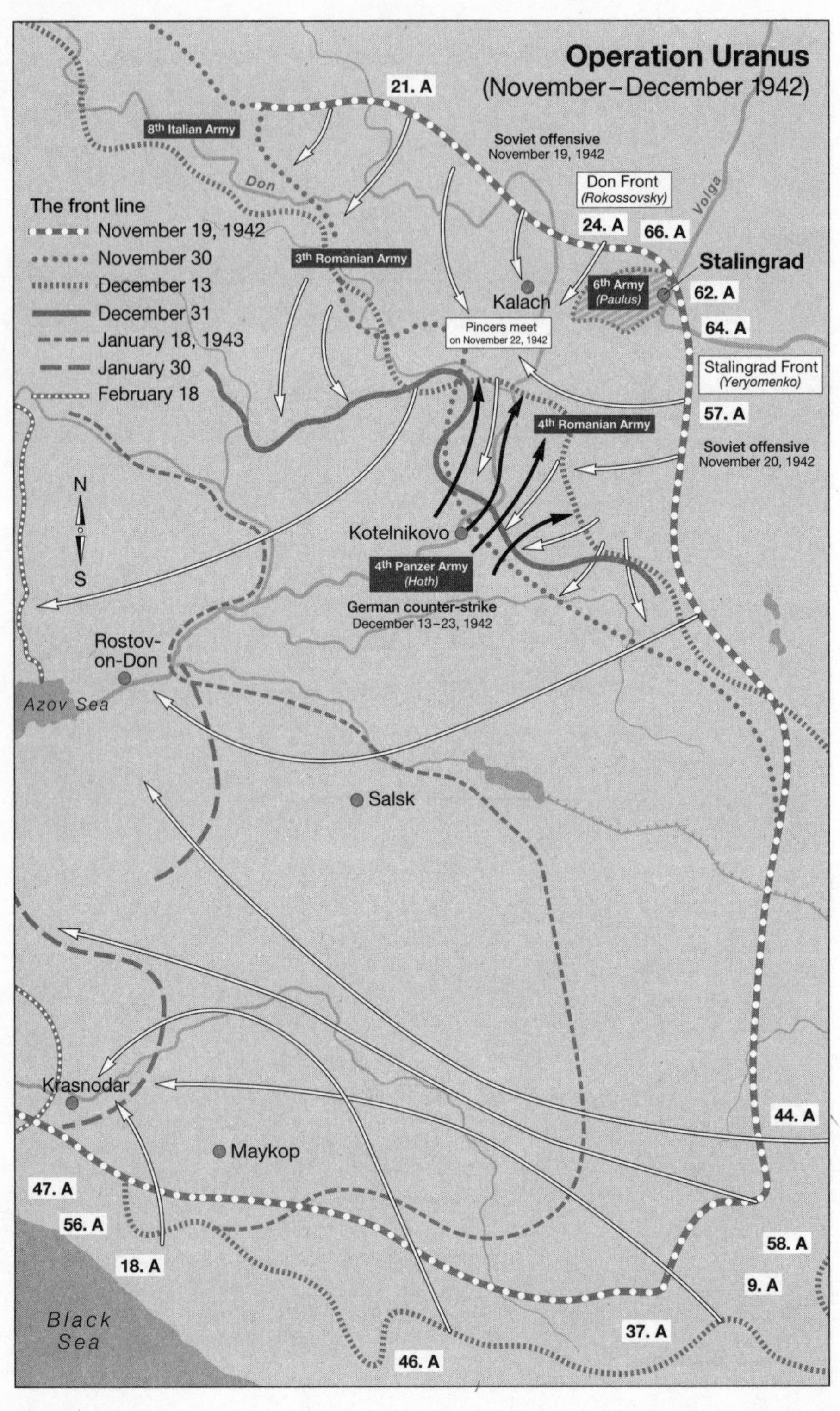
Operation Uranus
(November–December 1942)
21. A
8th Italian Army
Soviet offensive
November 19, 1942
Don
Don Front
(Rokossovsky)
Volga
The front line
November 19, 1942
November 30
December 13
December 31
January 18, 1943
January 30
February 18
24. A
66. A
3th Romanian Army
Stalingrad
6th Army
(Paulus)
62. A
Kalach
64. A
Pincers meet
on November 22, 1942
Stalingrad Front
(Yeryomenko)
57. A
4th Romanian Army
Soviet offensive
November 20, 1942
N
S
Kotelnikovo
4th Panzer Army
(Hoth)
German counter-strike
December 13–23, 1942
Rostov-
on-Don
Azov Sea
Salsk
Krasnodar
44. A
Maykop
47. A
56. A
58. A
18. A
9. A
Black
Sea
37. A
46. A

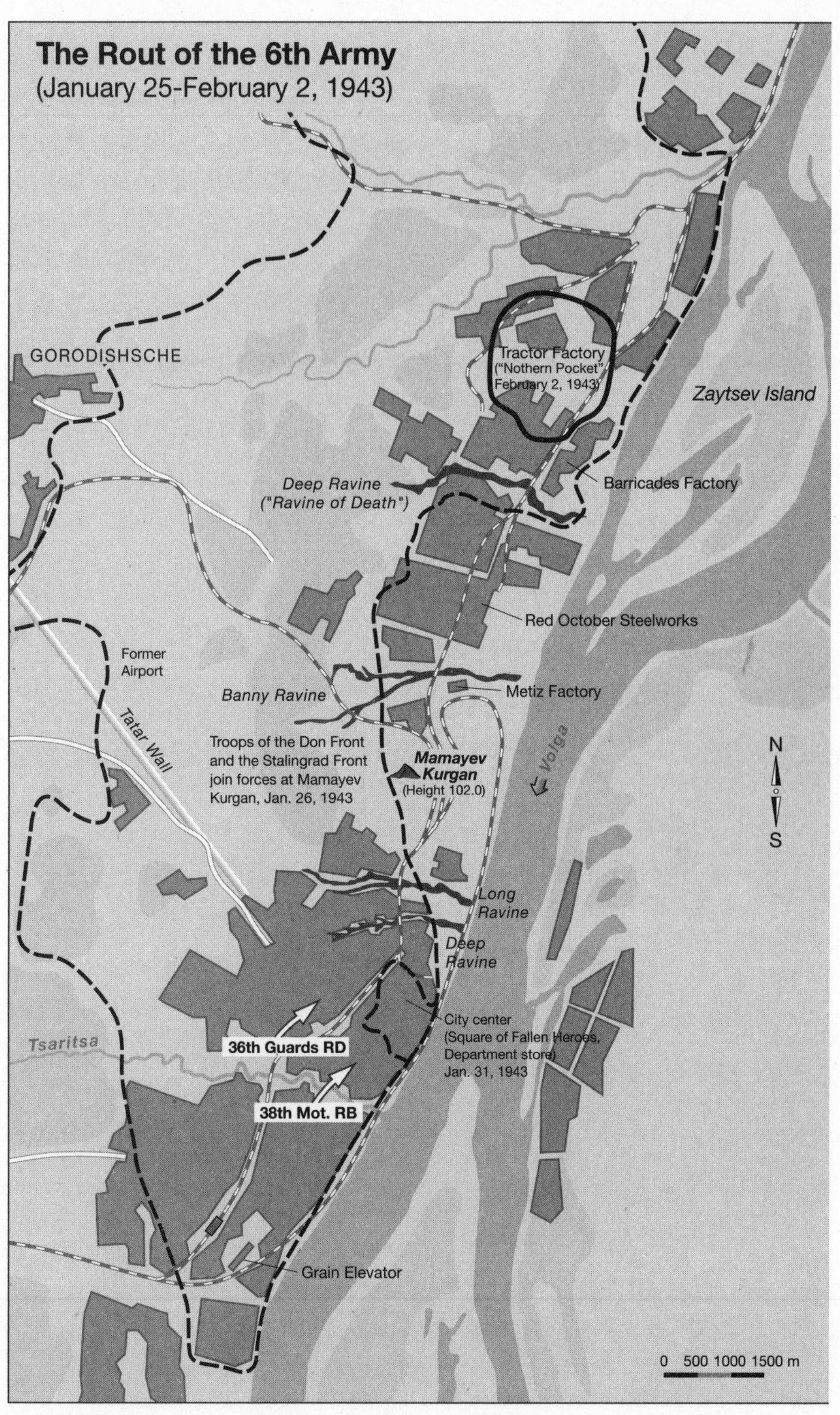
The Rout of the 6th Army
(January 25-February 2, 1943)
GORODISHSCHE
Tractor Factory
("Nothern Pocket"
February 2, 1943)
Zaytsev Island
Deep Ravine
("Ravine of Death")
Barricades Factory
Red October Steelworks
Former
Airport
Tatar Wall
Banny Ravine
Metiz Factory
Troops of the Don Front
and the Stalingrad Front
join forces at Mamayev
Kurgan, Jan. 26, 1943
Mamayev
Kurgan
(Height 102.0)
Volga
N
S
Long
Ravine
Deep
Ravine
City center
(Square of Fallen Heroes,
Department store)
Jan. 31, 1943
Tsaritsa
36th Guards RD
38th Mot. RB
Grain Elevator
0 500 1000 1500 m

ACKNOWLEDGMENTS

This book has been a collaborative endeavor from start to finish, and I want to thank all the institutions and people that have helped produce it. I want to begin by thanking the directors and staff of the Russian and German institutes who jointly supported the work on the transcripts. On the Russian side, these are Andrei Sakharov and Lyudmila Kolodnikova (until December 2010) and Yuri Petrov and Sergei Zhuravlyov (starting in 2011) of the Institute of Russian History of the Russian Academy of Sciences. Sergei Zhuravlyov, in particular, was always on hand with help and advice, as were the institute's archive specialists, Yelena Maleto and Konstantin Drozdov. On the German side, I am particularly grateful to Bernd Bonwetsch, the founding director of the German Historical Institute in Moscow. His engagement and diplomatic talent were indispensable. I also owe much to his successor team—Nikolaus Katzer, Victor Dönninghaus, Sandra Dahlke, and Brigitte Ziehl—for their steady support and energetic efforts. In addition I want to express enormous gratitude to the Fritz Thyssen Foundation and its director, Frank Suder, for their generous and beneficial support of the project. For nearly three years the foundation funded a small group of researchers who sorted and studied the Stalingrad transcripts, along with many other documents from the time of the battle.

My research staff—Darya Lotareva (Moscow), Svetlana Markova (Voronezh), Dina Fainberg (London), and Andrey Shcherbenok (Moscow)—all did outstanding work in assessing and scanning the transcripts and making them available on the group's intranet site. Svetlana Markova typed out many hundred pages and Darya Lotareva performed large parts of the archival work and researched the hitherto virtually unknown story of the Historical Commission's origin. The entire staff discussed which documents should appear in the book and in what form. We met once in Moscow; all other communication took place via intranet and Skype. I owe all of them thanks for a very gratifying collaboration.

Omer Bartov set me on this path many years ago. I told him of my idea to examine Soviet and Nazi German ideologies in dialogue. "Why don't you write on Stalingrad?," he suggested.

During my research I spoke with Tatyana Yeryomenko, Natalya Matyukhina (née Rodimtseva), Bode Roske, and Alexander Chuikov, and I thank them for sharing memories of their fathers and for documents related to the battle of Stalingrad, some of which found their way into this book. In addition, Albert Nenarokov provided revealing details from the life of his mentor Isaak Mints not found in any of his published biographies.

Bernd Bonwetsch, Paul Clemens, David Glantz, Igal Halfin, Peter Holquist, Katinka Patscher, Jan Plamper, Lennart Samuelson, and Gerd R. Ueberschär read sections of the manuscript and supplied helpful input. For their useful comments and suggestions I want to thank Michael Adas, Svetlana Argastseva, Antony Beevor, John Chambers, Andrei Doronin, Mark Edele, Alexander Epifanov, Ziva Galili, Sergei Kudryashov, Jackson Lears, Yan Mann, Zohar Manor-Abel, Annelore Nitschke, Serguei Oushakine, Ingrid Schierle, Wulf Schmiese, Joyce Seltzer, Yelena Senyavskaya, Matthias Uhl, Lyuba Vinogradova, Amir Weiner, and Larisa Zakharova, as well as the participants at conferences in Moscow, Los Angeles, Zurich, Princeton, and Paris, where I presented different pieces of the project.

I want to acknowledge the support of Rutgers University, which granted me leave to complete this book, and Sylvia Nagel, who offered expert assistance on multiple occasions as the manuscript was first prepared for publication.

The book originally appeared in German in the fall of 2012. For the English-language edition I have reworked significant portions, incorporating newly published archival material as well as criticisms and suggestions from other scholars, many of them listed above. For work on the English edition I am heavily indebted to the work of several translators: Christopher Tauchen has done a masterful job, translating all Russian original passages into English. He received advice from Robert Chandler, the translator of Vasily Grossman's *Life and Fate* and an unsurpassed authority on literary Stalingrad. Vitaliy Eyber translated the Russian passages in the first chapter. Dominic Bonfiglio did not merely translate my chapters and sections from German into English; he actively intervened to straighten out my sometimes convoluted thoughts.

I feel lucky to be working with PublicAffairs. Its publisher, Clive Priddle, displayed strokes of genius on repeated occasions, including with the choice of the English title. His team, around Melissa Raymond, Maria Goldverg, and Chris Juby, has been exemplary. I am also grateful to the copyeditor, Chrisona Schmidt, for very effectively dealing with a manuscript that at one point consisted of three different languages.

This book would likely not exist, and certainly not in its present shape, were it not for the continuing presence of three very dear people. In 1984 my father, Hannspeter Hellbeck, encouraged me to learn Russian and study Russian history. He himself had learned the language as a seventeen-year-old soldier in World War II. Later he embarked on a career in West Germany's Foreign Ministry, where he wanted to study Russian but reconsidered when he saw the packed classrooms. He instead became an expert on China. Among the books he gave me was the first German edition of Vasily Grossman's *Life and Fate*.

Katinka's love, humor, and sense of cool, even as a mother, nurture and ground me.

Thinking of our young son in relation to the horrors described in this book, I hope that life, new life, will trump what Grossman saw as our fate.

NOTES

CHAPTER 1: THE FATEFUL BATTLE

1. Evgenii Kriger, "Eto—Stalingrad!" *Izvestiia*, October 25, 1942; see also M. Galaktionov, "Stalingrad i Verden," *Krasnaia Zvezda*, October 3, 1942, p. 4.

2. Jens Wehner, "Stalingrad," in *Stalingrad*, ed. Gorch Pieken et al. (Dresden, 2012), pp. 19–20.

3. Richard Overy, "Stalingrad und seine Wahrnehmung bei den Westalliierten," in *Stalingrad*, ed. Gorch Pieken, pp. 106–117, at p. 113.

4. In fall 1942 British postal censors reported that virtually every letter checked by them lauded the Russians. Philip M. H. Bell, "Großbritannien und die Schlacht von Stalingrad," in *Stalingrad. Ereignis-Wirkung-Symbol*, ed. Jürgen Förster (Munich, 1992), pp. 350–372, at p. 354.

5. *Meldungen aus dem Reich. Die geheimen Lageberichte des Sicherheitsdienstes der SS 1938–1945*, 17 vols., ed. Heinz Boberach, (Herrsching, 1984), 12:4720; January 28, 1943.

6. Yitzhak Arad, *Belzec, Sobibor, Treblinka: The Operation Reinhard Death Camps* (Bloomington, IN, 1999), pp. 173–177.

7. Soviet writer Vasily Grossman was the first to link Himmler's visit to the death camp to the Soviet victory at Stalingrad. Grossman was with the Red Army when it entered Treblinka in August 1944. Based on interviews with eyewitnesses and former camp workers he produced a harrowing account of the Nazi death camp. Vasily Grossman, "The Hell of Treblinka," in *The Road: Stories, Journalism, and Essays* (New York, 2010).

8. Alexander Werth, *The Year of Stalingrad: An Historical Record and a Study of Russian Mentality, Methods, and Policies* (1947; Safety Harbor, FL, 2001), p. 438. A British correspondent reported from Stalingrad for the *Daily Telegraph* as early as January 18, 1943. Bell, "Großbritannien und die Schlacht von Stalingrad," p. 350.

9. See https://archive.org/details/WartimeRadio1943.

10. Alexander Werth, "Won't Survive Two Stalingrads," *Winnipeg Tribune*, February 12, 1943, p. 1; Henry Shapiro, "All of Stalingrad Ruined by Battles," *New York Times*, February 9, 1943, p. 3.

11. Werth, *Year of Stalingrad*, pp. 443–446. In spite of these constraints, Alexander Werth was able to conduct and reproduce verbatim in-depth conversations with Generals Vasily Chuikov and Alexander Rodimtsev, two famous figures at Stalingrad whose much more detailed testimony figures in the present book. Werth, *The Year of Stalingrad*, pp. 456–460, 468–470.

12. Nauchnyi arkhiv Instituta Rossiiskoi istorii Rossiiskoi Akademii nauk (NA IRI RAN).

13. To illustrate the breadth of the interview corpus, Chapter 1 features many excerpts of voices from soldiers whose full transcripts did not enter the volume. A comprehensive online publication of the Stalingrad transcripts is planned.

14. The best military histories of the battle are, from the Axis side, Manfred Kehrig, *Stalingrad: Analyse und Dokumentation einer Schlacht* (Stuttgart, 1979); from the Soviet side, A. M. Samsonov, *Stalingradskaia bitva*, 4th ed. (Moscow, 1989); and from the two sides in interaction, David M. Glantz, *To the Gates of Stalingrad: Soviet-German Combat Operations, April–August 1942* (Lawrence, KS, 2009); Glantz, *Armageddon in Stalingrad: September–November 1942* (Lawrence, KS, 2009); Glantz, *Endgame at Stalingrad: Book Two: December 1942–February 1943* (Lawrence, KS, 2014).

15. See the diary entries and letters of Ursula von Kardoff und Rudolf Tjaden in Walter Kempowski, *Das Echolot: Ein kollektives Tagebuch, Januar und Februar 1943*, 4 vols. (Munich, 1993); Friedrich Kellner, *Vernebelt, verdunkelt sind alle Hirne: Tagebücher 1939–1945*, ed. Sascha Feuchert et al. (Göttingen, 2011).

16. Vasily S. Grossman, *Gody voiny* [The War Years] (Moscow, 1989), p. 5. A Soviet writer and journalist, Grossman (1905–1964) reported to the front voluntarily in summer 1941. As a war correspondent he

reported for the newspaper *Red Star* (*Krasnaya zvezda*), including the battle of Stalingrad and the battle of Berlin.

17. Printed verbatim in *Prikazy narodnogo komissara oborony SSSR. 22 iiuniia 1941 g.–1942 g.* (=*Velikaia Otechestvennaia*, vol. 13) (Moscow, 1997), pp. 276–279.

18. *Die Tagebücher von Joseph Goebbels: Im Auftrag des Instituts für Zeitgeschichte und mit Unterstützung des Staatlichen Archivdienstes Russlands*, ed. Elke Fröhlich, pt. 2: Diktate 1941–1945, vol. 5: Juli–September 1942 (Munich, 1995), p. 353; see also Bernd Wegner, *Der Krieg gegen die Sowjetunion 1942/43*, in *Das Deutsche Reich und der Zweite Weltkrieg,* vol. 6: Horst Boog et al., *Der globale Krieg*, vol. 6; *Die Ausweitung zum Weltkrieg und der Wechsel der Initiative*, ed. Militärgeschichtliches Forschungsamt (Stuttgart, 1990), p. 993.

19. Lazar Brontman, *Voennyi dnevnik korrespondenta "Pravdy": Vstrechi, sobytiia, sud'by, 1942–1945* (Moscow, 2007), p. 57. Diary entry for August 30, 1942. See also Rebecca Manley, *To the Tashkent Station: Evacuation and Survival in the Soviet Union at War* (Ithaca, NY, 2012), pp. 74–75, 132–133.

20. Glantz, *Armageddon in Stalingrad*, p. 119.

21. For the Soviet military, "front" designated what Germans referred to as an army group.

22. Colonel general Andrei Ivanovich Yeryomenko (1892–1970) was appointed commander of the Southeastern Front and the Stalingrad Front on August 12, 1942. On September 28, 1942, the Southeastern Front became part of the Stalingrad Front.

23. Lieutenant General Konstantin Konstantinovich Rokossovsky (1896–1968) commanded the Don Front between September 1942 and January 1943.

24. For more, see Kehrig, *Stalingrad*, pp. 86–119.

25. "Das ist der Unterschied," *Das Schwarze Korps*, October 29, 1942, pp. 1–2.

26. Johannes Hürter, *Hitlers Heerführer: Die deutschen Oberbefehlshaber im Krieg gegen die Sowjetunion 1941/42* (Munich, 2007), pp. 326–340.

27. Facsimile of the order at http://www.historisches-tonarchiv.de/stalingrad/stalingrad-kampf 175a.jpg.

28. General field marshal Erich von Manstein (1887–1973) was commander in chief of the Army Group Don between November 1942 and February 1943. The 6th Army formed part of this army group.

29. The Turkic term "Kurgan" means burial mound. Mamayev Kurgan is named after the Tatar military commander Mamai, who is buried there. On military maps the elevation was labeled "Hill 102.0."

30. Werth, *The Year of Stalingrad*, p. 465.

31. Between August 21 and October 17, 1942, the 6th Army recorded 40,000 deaths, as well as an estimated 100,000 deaths up until November 19. In addition, there were an estimated 30,000 deaths in the 4th Panzer Army. Glantz, *Armaggedon in Stalingrad,* p. 716; Rüdiger Overmans, "Das andere Gesicht des Krieges: Leben und Sterben der 6. Armee," in Förster, ed., *Stalingrad: Ereignis—Wirkung—Symbol*, p. 446. 113,000 survivors: Manfred Kehrig, "Die 6. Armee im Kessel von Stalingrad, in Stalingrad," in Förster, ed., *Stalingrad,* p. 109. Overmans estimated the number of Romanian allies in the *Kessel* as only 5,000 (Overmans, "Das andere Gesicht," pp. 441–442). Soviet loss figures in G. F. Krivosheev, *Soviet Casualties and Combat Losses in the Twentieth Century* (London, 1997), pp. 125, 127; S. N. Michalev, *Liudskie poteri v Velikoi Otechestvennoi voine 1941–1945 gg. Statisticheskoe issledovanie* (Krasnoiarsk, 2000), p. 17–41; for higher estimates, see B. V. Sokolov, "The Cost of War: Human Losses for the USSR and Germany, 1939–1945," *Journal of Slavic Military Studies* 9 (March 1996): 152–193. Sokolov contends that the precise numbers given in divisional and army staff reports, which Krivosheev uses for his analysis, embellish the horrendous actual casualty rates in the Red Army. These, he writes, can be established only indirectly.

32. *Stalingradskaia ėpopeia: Vpervye publikuemye dokumenty, rassekrechennye FSB RF: Vospominaniia fel'dmarshala Pauliusa; Dnevniki i pis'ma soldat RKKA i vermakhta: Agenturnye doneseniia; Protokoly doprosov; Dokladnye zapiski osobykh otdelov frontov i armii* (Moscow, 2000), p. 404.

33. Christian Gerlach, "Militärische 'Versorgungszwänge,' Besatzungspolitik, und Massenverbrechen: Die Rolle des Generalquartiermeisters des Heeres und seiner Dienststellen im Krieg gegen die Sowjetunion," in *Ausbeutung, Vernichtung, Öffentlichkeit: Neue Studien zur nationalsozialistischen Lagerpolitik,* ed. Norbert Frei et al. (Munich, 2000), p. 199; T. Pavlova, *Zasekrechennaia tragediia: Grazhdanskoe naselenie v Stalingradskoi bitve* (Volgograd, 2005), p. 521; S. Sidorov, "Voennoplennye v Stalingrade. 1943–1954 gg.," in *Rossiiane i nemtsy v epokhu katastrof. Pamiat' o voine i preodolenie proshlogo,* ed. Jochen Hellbeck, Lars-Peter Schmidt, Alexander Vatlin (Moscow, 2012), pp. 75–87.

34. For critical reflections on this, see Michael Kumpfmüller, *Die Schlacht von Stalingrad: Metamorphosen eines deutschen Mythos* (Munich, 1995); Wolfram Wette and Gerd R. Ueberschär, eds., *Stalingrad: Mythos und*

Wirklichkeit einer Schlacht (Frankfurt, 2012); Wegner, *Der Krieg gegen die Sowjetunion 1942/43*, pp. 962–1063.

35. See *Letzte Briefe aus Stalingrad* (Gütersloh, 1954); Kempowski, *Das Echolot*; *Feldpostbriefe aus Stalingrad: November 1942 bis Februar 1943*, ed. Jens Ebert (Göttingen, 2006).

36. Enlightening in this regard is Bernd Boll and Hans Safrian, "On the Way to Stalingrad: The 6th Army in 1941–1942," in *War of Extermination: The German Military in World War II, 1941–1944*, Hannes Heer and Klaus Naumann, eds., (New York, 2000), pp. 237–271.

37. *Stalingrad: Eine Trilogie*, directed by Sebastian Dehnhardt and Manfred Oldenburg.

38. Erich von Manstein, *Lost Victories*, trans. Anthony G. Powell (Chicago, 1958), p. 289.

39. *Feldpostbriefe aus Stalingrad*; *Es grüsst Euch alle; Bertold. Von Koblenz nach Stalingrad: Die Feldpostbriefe des Pioniers Bertold Paulus aus Kastel* (Nonnweiler-Otzenhausen, 1993); *Stalingrad* (1993), directed by Joseph Vilsmaier. Recent publications accentuate the ideological conditioning of everyday life at the front: Mark Edele and Michael Geyer, "States of Exception: The Nazi-Soviet War as a System of Violence, 1939–1945," in *Beyond Totalitarianism: Stalinism and Nazism Compared*, ed. Sheila Fitzpatrick and Michael Geyer (Cambridge, MA, 2008), pp. 345–395; Peter Fritzsche, *Life and Death in the Third Reich* (Cambridge, MA, 2008), pp. 143–154.

40. Inge Scholl, *The White Rose: Munich 1942–1943*, trans. Arthur R. Schultz (Middletown, CT, 1983), p. 93.

41. Manstein, *Verlorene Siege*, pp. 303–318; Heinrich Gerlach, *Die verratene Armee* (Munich, 1957).

42. Jochen Hellbeck, "Breakthrough at Stalingrad: The Repressed Soviet Origins of a Bestselling West German War Tale," *Contemporary European History* 1 (2013): 1–31.

43. Susanne zur Nieden, "Umsonst geopfert? Zur Verarbeitung der Ereignisse in Stalingrad in biographischen Zeugnissen," *Krieg und Literatur/War and Literature* 5, no. 10 (1993): 33–46; Diaries and letters by Martin Fiebig, Paulheinz Quack, Martin Rahlenbeck, Wilhelm Saak, Hildegard Wagener and others in Kempowski, *Das Echolot*. Ian Kershaw asserts that the Führer cult in the German population had faded before Stalingrad, and for this reason he believes that the defeat in Stalingrad accelerated the loss of popular support for the regime. Ian Kershaw, *The "Hitler Myth": Image and Reality in the Third Reich* (New York, 1987), pp. 188–190. Michael Geyer und Peter Fritzsche, however, reference other connections between the Nazi regime and the population, which were created during Stalingrad and intensified in the further course of the war: Germans increasingly began to see themselves as victims of a massive disaster. This national and European victim perspective was orchestrated by the Nazi leadership. See Michael Geyer, "Endkampf 1918 and 1945: German Nationalism, Annihilation, and Self-Destruction," in *No Man's Land of Violence: Extreme Wars in the 20th Century*, Alf Lüdtke and Bernd Weisbrod, eds. (Göttingen, 2006), pp. 52–53; Peter Fritzsche, *Life and Death in the Third Reich* (Cambridge, MA, 2008), pp. 279–280.

44. Ronald Smelser and Edward J. Davies III, *The Myth of the Eastern Front: The Nazi-Soviet War in American Popular Culture* (New York, 2008), p. 69; David M. Glantz, "The Red Army at War, 1941–1945: Sources and Interpretations," *Journal of Military History*, July 1998, pp. 595–617.

45. Horst Giertz, "Die Schlacht von Stalingrad in der sowjetischen Historiographie," in *Stalingrad: Mythos und Wirklichkeit*, p. 214; Samsonov, *Stalingradskaia bitva*.

46. See especially the multivolume series *Russkii arkhiv: Velikaia Otechestvennaia*, ed. V. A. Zolotarev (Moscow, 1993–2002), with numerous documents from the Central Archives of the Russian Ministry of Defense. A planned volume on the battle of Stalingrad (vol. 4, pt. 2) has not appeared in the series. *Organy gosudarstvennoi bezopasnosti SSSR v Velikoi Otechestvennoi voine. Sbornik dokumentov*, 5 vols. (Moscow, 1995–2007), draws on documents from the FSB archives. *Stalingradskaia ėpopeia*, also prepared by archivists in the FSB, features abundant new material and is indispensable reading for any student of the battle. The same applies to the documents presented in *Velikaia Otechestvennaia voina. 1942 god*, ed. T. V. Volokitina and V. S. Khristoforov (Moscow, 2012). See in addition numerous documents published in the periodicals *Rodina* (since 1988) and *Istochnik* (1993–2003).

47. Konstantin M. Simonov, *Raznye dni voiny: Dnevnik pisatelia*, 2 vols. (Moscow, 2005); Grossman, *Gody voiny*. See also Vasily Chkalov, *Voennii dnevnik: 1941. 1942. 1943* (Moscow, 2004); Nikolai N. Inozemtsev, *Frontovoi dnevnik* (Moscow, 2005); Boris Suris, *Frontovoi dnevnik: Dnevnik, rasskazy* (Moscow, 2010); *Poslednie pis'ma s fronta*, 5 vols. (Moscow, 1990–1995); Alexsandr D. Shindel', ed., *Po obe storony fronta: Pis'ma sovetskikh i nemetskikh soldat 1941–1945 gg.* (Moscow, 1995). See the rather mundane letters from General Rokossovsky to his family: "'Posylaiu miaso, muku, kartofel', maslo, sakhar i t. p.' O chëm pisal s fronta Konstantin Rokossovskii" ["'I am sending you meat, flour, potatoes, butter, sugar, etc.' Konstantin Rokossovsky reporting from the front"], *Diletant* 2012, no. 2: 58–62. With a few exceptions, chains of letters written by a

single author, a crucial source for the study of individual experience, have not been published. Exceptions include: *Iz istorii zemli Tomskoi 1941–1945: Ia pishu tebe s voiny . . . Sbornik dokumentov i materialov* (Tomsk, 2001); *Pis'ma s fronta riazantsev-uchastnikov Velikoi Otechestvennoi voiny, 1941–1945 gg.* (Riazan', 1998).

48. In 2007 the Defense Ministry launched a website devoted to all Soviet personnel who were killed or went missing in action during the Great Patriotic War and its aftermath. The searchable site includes scans of documents from various archives that shed light on the fate and place of burial of a given soldier. To date, more than 16 million scans of documents have been made available, though the site does not state how many service men and women have been registered. It continues to be expanded. www.obd-memorial.ru.

49. Antony Beevor, *Stalingrad* (London, 1999), p. xiv.

50. Ibid., p. 431.

51. John Erickson, "Red Army Battlefield Performance, 1941–1945: The System and the Soldier," in *Time to Kill: The Soldier's Experience of War in the West, 1939–1945*, ed. Paul Addison and Angus Calder (Pimlico, 1997), p. 244; Frank Ellis, "A Review of Antony Beevor and Luba Vinogradova (ed. and trans.), "'A Writer at War': Vasily Grossman with the Red Army 1941–1945," *Journal of Slavic Military Studies* 20, no. 1 (2007): 137–146.

52. *Stalingradskaia ėpopeia*, p. 222.

53. Beevor, *Stalingrad*, p. 200.

54. Ibid., pp. 87–88.

55. Speaking in October 1942, in the immediate wake of being liberated by Soviet troops, a Russian woman from a village near Rzhevsk had this to say about the Germans (she was talking to other villagers and was not aware that a Soviet newspaper correspondent was listening): "Well, we once thought that these Germans were cultured people. [. . .] But how shamelessly they undress in front of women, how they splash about in the trough, how they pollute the air when they are seated at the table, and how they urinate inside the hut! Is this what they call culture? Then they chase after girls and young women like wild stallions. Fall over them. [. . .] This is the culture of convicts. Shameless. [. . .] Are they like this in their own country as well?" Aleksei Surkov, "Zemlia pod peplem," *in Publitsistika perioda Velikoi Otechestvennoi voiny i pervykh poslevoennykh let* (Moscow, 1985), pp. 135–141. Interviewed by the historians in Stalingrad, Lt. Col. Pyotr Molchanov of the 36th Rifle Division said: "The Germans prepared, obviously, to attack us. They pulled together their soldiers and attacked. To attack they did the following: they laid aside their uniforms, rolled up their shirt sleeves, many in their underwear, like bandits. So they attacked us."

56. Catherine Merridale, *Ivan's War: The Red Army 1939–45* (London, 2005), p. 320.

57. Merridale, *Ivan's War*, p. 94.

58. Even Merridale concedes that "most [Soviet soldiers] were more deeply saturated in their regime's ideology than soldiers in the Wehrmacht, for Soviet propaganda had been working on its nation's consciousness for fifteen years by the time that Hitler came to power in Berlin" (*Ivan's War*, p. 12).

59. Catherine Merridale, lecture to the Harriman Institute, Columbia University, http://www.c-spanvideo.org / program/191531-1.

60. *The People's War: Responses to World War II in the Soviet Union,* ed. Bernd Bonwetsch and Robert W. Thurston (Urbana, IL, 2000); Elena S. Seniavskaia, *Frontovoe pokolenie: Istoriko-psikhologicheskoe issledovanie, 1941–1945* (Moscow, 1995); Amir Weiner, *Making Sense of War: The Second World War and the Fate of the Bolshevik Revolution* (Princeton, 2001); Lisa A. Kirschenbaum, *The Legacy of the Siege of Leningrad, 1941–1995: Myth, Memories, and Monuments* (New York, 2006).

61. Roger Reese's recent study, for instance, lists a range of individual motivations to fight while deemphasizing the mobilizing reach of the Soviet regime. Roger R. Reese, *Why Stalin's Soldiers Fought: The Red Army's Military Effectiveness in World War II* (Lawrence, KS, 2011).

62. Overy, *Russia's War,* pp. 187–189; Merridale, *Ivan's War,* p. 160; Timothy Colton, *Commissars, Commanders, and Civilian Authority: The Structure of Soviet Military Politics* (Cambridge, MA, 1979), pp. 4–5, 60, 68; Mawdsley, *Thunder in the East: The Nazi-Soviet War, 1941–1945* (London, 2005), p. 213. Colton and Mawdsley emphasize the pervasive presence of the party in the army. Roger Reese is ambivalent: Roger R. Reese, *The Soviet Military Experience: A History of the Soviet Army, 1917–1991* (New York, 2000), pp. 78, 126.

63. Stephen Kotkin, *Magnetic Mountain: Stalinism as a Civilization* (Berkeley, CA, 1995), pp. 198–225.

64. Jochen Hellbeck, *Revolution on My Mind: Writing a Diary Under Stalin* (Cambridge, MA, 2006); Hellbeck, "Everyday Ideology" *Eurozine*, February 22, 2010; Hellbeck, ed., *Tagebuch aus Moskau, 1931–1939* (Munich, 1996); Karl Schlögel, *Moscow, 1937* (Cambridge, MA, 2012).

65. Anna Krylova, *Soviet Women in Combat: A History of Violence on the Eastern Front* (New York, 2010).

66. Regarding these character ideals, see Katerina Clark, *The Soviet Novel: History as Ritual* (Chicago, 1981).

67. Lazar Lazarev, "Russian Literature on the War and Historical Truth," in *World War 2 and the Soviet People,* ed. John Garrard and Carol Garrard (New York, 1993), p. 29; Bernd Bonwetsch, "War as a Breathing Space," in *The People's War,* pp. 137–153. Elena Iu. Zubkova, *Obshchestvo i reformy, 1945–1964* (Moscow, 1993), p. 19; Merridale, *Ivan's War,* pp. 338–340. Most of these studies cite post–Stalin era memoirs as evidence for Soviet society's emancipation from the party during the years of the war.

68. Vasily Grossman, *Life and Fate,* Robert Chandler, trans., (New York, 2006).

69. *A Writer at War: Vasily Grossmann with the Red Army, 1941–1945,* Antony Beevor and Luba Vinogradova, ed. and trans. (London, 2006), p. 34.

70. Vasily S. Grossman, *Gody voiny* (Moscow, 1989), p. 263.

71. Grossman again used Commissar Shlyapin as a template for *Life and Fate.* Captain Grekov, the defender of House 6/1 and a commander who preaches "democracy and toughness," bears recognizable traits of the commissar.

72. On Grossman's horizons during the war and their development in the postwar period, see Jochen Hellbeck, "The Maximalist: On Vasily Grossman," *The Nation,* December 20, 2010.

73. The proportion of military in the Communist party had grown to 55 percent in January 1944. Colton, *Commissars, Commanders, and Civilian Authority,* p. 16.

74. *Ideologicheskaia rabota KPSS na fronte, 1941–1945 gg.* (1960), pp. 253–254. On October 14, 1944, the Central Committee criticized the lack of "political resilience" among many Red Army soldiers who were new to the party, and it ordered the Main Political Administration to intensify its "ideological and political education." The decree was issued on the eve of the Red Army's offensive into East Prussia; Soviet leaders must have been concerned over the political reliability of their own soldiers after entering enemy lands. A prominent victim of the new hard line was the later dissident Lev Kopelev, who served as a specialist for enemy propaganda in the Red Army. In April 1945 in Germany he was accused of "bourgeois humanism" and served almost ten years.

75. Robert MacCoun et al., "Does Social Cohesion Determine Motivation in Combat? An Old Question with an Old Answer," *Armed Forces and Society* 32 (2006); Thomas Kühne, *Kameradschaft: Die Soldaten des nationalsozialistischen Krieges und das 20. Jahrhundert* (Göttingen, 2011). The thesis was first advanced by Edmund Shils and Morris Janowitz, "Cohesion and Disintegration in the Wehrmacht in World War II," *Public Opinion Quarterly,* Summer 1948, pp. 280–315, based on their interviews with German POWs. Samuel Stouffer et al., *The American Soldier* (Princeton, NJ, 1949) seemed to support this with American GIs. For a skeptical perspective, see Omer Bartov, *Hitler's Army: Soldiers, Nazis, and War in the Third Reich* (New York, 1991), especially pp. 29–33.

76. Morris Janowitz and Stephen D. Westbrook, *The Political Education of Soldiers* (Beverly Hills, CA, 1983), pp. 196–198. For the same reason, the Red Army did not follow the German model of a reserve army (*Ersatzheer*), which ensured that recovering soldiers would rotate back into their regionally identified units (see p. 385 for a Soviet officer suggesting that the Red Army adopt the German model). At a meeting with western correspondents in early 1943, Alexander Shcherbakov, the head of the Red Army's Main Political Administration, became irritated when one of the journalists talked about a Russian tradition of military bravery: "Don't talk to me about the Russian soul," Shcherbakov retorted, "Let me recommend you to study the Soviet man." Karel Berkhoff, *Motherland in Danger: Soviet Propaganda during World War II* (Cambridge, MA, 2012), p. 206. Nazi leaders upheld the notion of *Landsmannschaft* in part because of its racial essence: their common soil would help forge the German recruits into Aryan fighters.

77. Jürgen Förster, "Geistige Kriegführung in Deutschland 1919–1945," in *Die deutsche Kriegsgesellschaft 1939–1945,* vol. 1, *Politisierung, Vernichtung, Überleben* (*Das Deutsche Reich und der Zweite Weltkrieg,*vol. 9/1), ed. Jörg Echternkamp (Munich, 2004), p. 567.

78. Toward the end of the war Wehrmacht units fighting in the east had casualty rates approximating those the Red Army had suffered all along. According to Omer Bartov, the decimation of the primary groups prompted military commanders to increasingly rely on ideological indoctrination to mold troupe cohesion, which in turn explained the "barbarization" of German warfare in the east. Omer Bartov, *The Eastern Front, 1941–45: German Troops and the Barbarization of Warfare,* 2nd ed. (New York, 2001). Critics contend that Bartov's thesis explains little, as fighting on the Eastern Front had been exceptionally violent from the start. Mark Edele and Michael Geyer, "States of Exception: The Nazi-Soviet War as a System of Violence, 1939–1945," in *Beyond Totalitarianism,* pp. 345–395, at p. 357. The ideological work conducted in

the Wehrmacht paled against the comprehensive political conditioning that prevailed in the Red Army and other communist armies. For the latter, see Alexander L. George, *The Chinese Communist Army in Action: The Korean War and Its Aftermath* (New York, 1967); Shu Guang Zhang, *Mao's Military Romanticism: China and the Korean War, 1950–1953* (Lawrence, KS, 1995), pp. 14–18; William Darryl Henderson, *Why the Vietcong Fought: A Study of Motivation and Control in a Modern Army in Combat* (Westport, CT, 1979).

79. Reese, *The Soviet Military Experience*, p. 4.

80. Orlando Figes, *A People's Tragedy: The Russian Revolution, 1891–1924* (New York, 1998), p. 601.

81. Figes, *People's Tragedy,* p. 597.

82. Reese, *The Soviet Military Experience*, p. 4; Mark von Hagen, *Soldiers in the Proletarian Dictatorship: The Red Army and the Soviet Socialist State, 1917–1930* (Ithaca, NY, 1993).

83. Peter Holquist, "What's So Revolutionary About the Russian Revolution?" in *Russian Modernity: Politics, Knowledge, Practices,* ed. David L. Hoffmann and Yanni Kotsonis (New York, 2000), pp. 87–111; Von Hagen, *Soldiers in the Proletarian Dictatorship*; Reese, *The Soviet Military Experience.*

84. Peter Holquist, *Making War, Forging Revolution: Russia's Continuum of Crisis, 1914–1921* (Cambridge, MA, 2002), pp. 232–240; Holquist, "Information is the Alpha and Omega of Our Work: Bolshevik Surveillance in Its Pan-European Context," *Journal of Modern History,* September 1997, pp. 415–460. Military censors read only a portion of the letters sent to Red Army soldiers from the "rear."

85. Ortwin Buchbender und Reinhold Sterz, eds., *Das andere Gesicht des Krieges: Deutsche Feldpostbriefe, 1939–1945* (Munich, 1983).

86. Dietrich Beyrau, "Avant-garde in Uniform," manuscript (Tübingen, 2011); Colton, *Commissars, Commanders, and Civilian Authority,* p. 42.

87. A. G. Kavtaradze, *Voennye spetsialisty na sluzhbe Respubliki Sovetov, 1917–1920 gg.* (Moscow, 1988), pp. 170, 177.

88. *Kremlevskii kinoteatr 1928–1953. Dokumenty* (Moscow, 2005), pp. 951–981.

89. Krylova, *Soviet Women in Combat,* pp. 67–68.

90. Compare the interview with Captain Mikhail Ingor of the 308th Rifle Division: "It was October 4. The situation was scary. The Hitlerites used their tanks to mount a 'psychic attack' against the command post of the 339th Rifle Regiment" (NA IRI RAN, f. 2, razd. I, op. 71, d. 3). See also interview with Alexander Parkhomenko, pp. 374–375. An interview with a given soldier is archivally referenced only after its first mention.

91. Isaak Babel, *1920 Diary*, ed. Carol J. Avins (New Haven, 1995), entries for July 14 and August 28, 1920. In *Red Cavalry,* Babel's collection of short stories from the Civil War, Timoshenko is immortalized as divisional commander Savitsky.

92. Evan Mawdsley, *The Russian Civil War* (London, 1987), pp. 88–92.

93. Iu. F. Boldyrev u. V. P. Vyrelkin, "V ogne grazhdanskoi voiny. Tsaritsyn i bor'ba na iugo-vostoke Rossii. 1918 g.," in *Aktual'nye problemy istorii Tsaritsyna nachala XX veka i perioda grazhdanskoi voiny* (Volgograd, 2001), p. 42.

94. A. L. Nosovich (A. Chernomorchev), *Krasnyi Tsaritsyn. Vzgliad iznutri. Zapiski belogo razvedchika* (Moscow, 2010), pp. 28–29. The author was introduced to the Red movement already in the spring of 1918 and served as chief of staff in the Northern Military District. In October 1918 he fled, to forestall detection. He published his notes in the journal *Rostov on Don.*

95. See the announcement in *Pravda,* March 28, 1942.

96. Quoted in Samsonov, *Stalingradskaia bitva*, p. 153.

97. *Pravda*, November 11, 1942, p. 1. *Krasnaia Zvezda,* November 11, 1942, p. 1.

98. *Dokumenty o geroicheskoi oborone Tsaritsyna v 1918 godu* (Moscow, 1942).

99. *Pravda,* May 2, 1931, p. 1.

100. Cited in Richard Overy, *The Dictators: Hitler's Germany and Stalin's Russia* (New York, 2004), p. 465.

101. Overy, *Dictators,* p. 464.

102. V. A. Somov, "Dukhovnyi oblik trudiashchikhsia perioda Velikoi Otechestvennoi voiny," in *Narod i voina* (Moscow, 2010), pp. 333–335; David L. Hoffmann, "Mothers in the Motherland: Stalinist Pronatalism in Its Pan-European Context," *Journal of Social History* 34, no. 1 (2000): 35–54; Hoffman, *Cultivating the Masses: Modern State Practices and Soviet Socialism, 1914–1939* (Ithaca, NY, 2011).

103. Hellbeck, *Revolution on My Mind,* pp. 92–93; Schlögel, *Moscow, 1937* pp. 136–152. Oleg Khlevnyuk sees fear of war as the main trigger of the great terror in the 1930s: Oleg Khlevnyuk, "The Objectives of the Great Terror, 1937–1938," in *Stalinism: The Essential Readings*, ed. David Hoffmann (Oxford, 2003), pp. 81–104.

104. Vsevolod Vishnevskii, *Poslednii reshitel'nyi* (Moscow, 1931), cited in Overy, *The Dictators,* p. 462.

105. Overy, *Dictators,* pp. 469f., 474–476; Reese, *Soviet Military Experience,* pp. 85–92.

106. Reese, *Soviet Military Experience,* pp. 86–88; Mawdsley, *Thunder in the East,* p. 20f.

107. NA IRI RAN, f. 2, razd. III, op. 5, d. 37a, 37b.

108. Mawdsley, *Thunder in the East,* p. 43.

109. Ibid., p. 29.

110. Ibid., pp. 58–59.

111. The T-34 is a medium Soviet tank that was built from 1940. Steve Zaloga/Leland S. Ness, *Red Army Handbook: 1939–1945* (Stroud, 1998), pp. 162–169. The Pe-2 is a Soviet bomber developed by Vladimir Petliakov that went into production in 1941. Soldiers gave it the nickname "Peschka." Valerii Bargatinov, *Kryl'ia Rossii: polnaia illiustrirovannaia ėntsiklopediia* (Moscow, 2005), pp. 493–494.

112. Mawdsley, *Thunder in the East,* p. 85.

113. Mark Harrison, *The Soviet Home Front, 1941–1945: A Social and Economic History of the USSR in World War II* (London, 1991), pp. 127–132.

114. Figures from Mawdsley, who doubts the German information about 3.35 million prisoners of war (Mawdsley, *Thunder in the East,* p. 86).

115. Glantz, *Colossus Reborn,* p. 549f.

116. On November 30, 1939, the Red Army attacked Finland after it rejected Soviet territorial claims. The war ended on March 13, 1940, with Finland ceding 11 percent of its land area. During the Winter War the Red Army showed great strategic and tactical weakness. It purchased a victory, however, with enormous loss of life.

117. Compare A. A. Cherkasov, "O formirovanii i primenenii v Krasnoi armii zagradotriadov," *Voprosy istorii* 2 (2003): 174–175.

118. *Sovetskaia propaganda v godу Velikoi Otechestvennoi voiny,* ed. A. Ia. Livshin and I. B. Orlov (Moscow, 2007), p. 306.

119. Colton, *Commissars, Commanders, and Civilian Authority,* pp. 16–17, 21.

120. *Istoriia kommunisticheskoi partii Sovetskogo Soiuza,* vol. 5, bk. 1, 1938–1945 (Moscow, 1970), p. 284.

121. NA IRI RAN, f. 2, razd. III, op. 5, d. 8, l. 50–58.

122. Nikolai Glamazda, interview (NA IRI RAN, f. 2, razd. III, op. 5, d. 9, ll. 24–34); see also Lieutenant Colonel Afanasy Svirin, interview, pp. 148–192.

123. Vasily Zaytsev, interview, pp. 360–373.

124. NA IRI RAN, f. 2, razd. III, op. 5, d. 9, ll. 24–34.

125. NA IRI RAN, f. 2, razd. III, op. 5, d. 11.

126. NA IRI RAN, f. 2, razd. III, op. 5, d. 2a, l. 42–70. On hate as a motivation in the Red Army and its effects, see Amir Weiner, "Something to Die For, a Lot to Kill For: The Soviet System and the Brutalization of Warfare," in *The Barbarisation of Warfare,* ed. George Kassimeris (London, 2006).

127. See Grossman, *Gody voiny,* p. 355; Chuikov, interview, pp. 266–290.

128. *Partiino-politicheskaia rabota v Sovetskikh Vooruzhennykh silakh v gody Velikoi Otechestvennoi voiny 1941–1945 gg. Kratkii istoricheskii obzor,* ed. K.V. Krainiukova, S. E. Zakharova, and G. E. Shabaeva (Moscow, 1968), p. 215.

129. A. M. Vasil'evskii, *Delo vsei zhizni* (Moscow, 1973), p. 233.

130. Fritz, Fritzes: slang for German soldier.

131. NA IRI RAN, f. 2, razd. III, op. 5, d. 9, l. 35–55.

132. NA IRI RAN, f. 2, razd. III, op. 5, d. 14, l. 117–126.

133. On Duka, see p. 227–231.

134. Glantz, *Colossus Reborn,* p. 380; *Istoriia kommunisticheskoi partii Sovetskogo Soiuza,* vol. 5, bk. 1, 1938–1945 (Moscow, 1970), p. 318.

135. Reese, *Soviet Military Experience,* p. 70; *Stalingradskaia ėpopeia*; V. Khristoforov, *Stalingrad: Organy NKVD nakanune i v dni srazheniia* (Moscow, 2008).

136. Overy, *Dictators,* p. 473; Glantz, *Colossus Reborn,* pp. 383–385.

137. The anonymous letter writer built on Stalin's support, because he portrayed the behavior of the NKVD men as undermining the spirit of Stalin's single command in October 1942. Of his fate nothing more is known. *Sovetskaia povsednevnost' i massovoe soznanie, 1939–1945,* A. Ia. Livzhin and I. B. Orlov, eds. (Moscow, 2003), pp. 109–110. By the time of this letter, the NKVD Special Departments had become incorporated into a new counterintelligence organization called SMERSH (Russian acronym for "Death to Spies"), founded in April 1943. Vadim J. Birstein, *Smersh: Stalin's Secret Weapon. Soviet Military*

Counterintelligence in WW II (London 2011),

138. See pp. 233–238.

139. See note 62.

140. *Sbornik zakonov SSSR i ukazov Prezidiuma Verkhovnogo Soveta SSSR. 1938 g.–iiun' 1956 g.* (Moscow, 1956), pp. 200–201.

141. The order is printed in *Stalingradskaia ėpopeia,* p. 423. See also Colton, *Commissars, Commanders, and Civilian Authority,* pp. 14, 60; Glantz, *Colossus Reborn,* pp. 381–382.

142. Lieutenant Colonel Dubrovsky and battalion commissar Stepanov, interviews.

143. See the interview with Major General Burmakov, commander of the 38th Rifle Brigade, regarding the collaboration with his political deputy Leonid Vinokur. See also the photo that shows Burmakov und Vinokur side by side (p. 240).

144. Divisional commander Levykin und brigade commissar Ivan Vasiliev, interviews.

145. Colton, *Commissars, Commanders and Civilian Authority,* p. 59.

146. NA IRI RAN, f. 2, razd. III, op. 5, d. 16, l. 14–52.

147. Amnon Sella explains the price of such operations. Among the fallen Soviet soldiers in the first six months of the war were 500,000 members and candidates of the Communist party. In total, 3 million Soviet communists perished in the Great Patriotic War. Amnon Sella, *The Value of Human Life in Soviet Warfare* (London, 1992), pp. 157–158.

148. NA IRI RAN, f. 2, razd. III, op. 5, d. 8, l. 29–49. In his discussion of the Soviet assault troops in Stalingrad, Beevor overlooks this political aspect (*A Writer at War,* pp. 154–169). During the Civil War units of the Red Army considered unreliable were filled with communists to strengthen the combat force. Reese, *The Soviet Military Experience,* p. 72.

149. During the Civil War, party comrades were celebrated as the "ferment" of the Red Army. Beyrau, "Avantgarde in Uniform."

150. NA IRI RAN, f. 2, razd. III, op. 5, d. 4, l. 29–31.

151. "Geroicheskii Stalingrad," *Pravda,* Oktober 5, 1942, p. 1.

152. Agitators were party activists who specifically trained poorly educated soldiers, using simple and graphic means. Berkhoff, *Motherland in Danger,* p. 3.

153. The battle for Tunisia, which began in November 1942, was part of the North African Campaign waged by British, American, and French troops. It would end in May 1943 with the rout of the Axis forces. More than 230,000 German and Italian soldiers were taken as prisoners of war. The Western Allies referred to their victory as "Tunisgrad."

154. NA IRI RAN, f. 2, razd. III, op. 5, d. 16, l. 62–74.

155. NA IRI RAN, f. 2, razd. III, op. 5, d. 8, l. 85–93.

156. Captain Ivan Maksin, 308th Rifle Division, interview, pp. 145–182.

157. "Comrade Koren," interview, p. 310.

158. Petrakov, interview, pp. 145–162.

159. Zayonchkovsky, interview, pp. 381–398.

160. NA IRI RAN, f. 2, razd. III, op. 5, d. 3a, l. 1–3.

161. Afanassyev described the first combat action of his artillery battery at defensive battles in the Crimea in September 1941. NA IRI RAN, f. 2, razd. III, op. 5, d. 15, l. 37–46.

162. See p. 149.

163. NA IRI RAN, f. 2, razd. I, op. 80, d. 14. In 1941 Soviet psychologist M. P. Feofanov wrote: "In a person without self-control fear escapes the control of his will. It takes the place of reason [. . .] lowers the will to the lowest level, the level of impulsive will." M. P. Feofanov, "Vospitanie smelosti i muzhestva," *Sovetskaia pedagogika* 1941, no. 10: 62. See also V. A. Kol'tsova, Iu. N. Oleinik, *Sovetskaia psikhologicheskaia nauka v gody Velikoi Otechestvennoi voiny (1941–1945)* (Moscow, 2006), p. 108.

164. This emphasis, and along with it the education of fearlessness, had a prerevolutionary pedigree. General Mikhail Dragomirov (1830–1905) sought to inculcate a theory of morale among Tsarist troops that was built on similar principles. Dragomirov believed that the essence of victory was to impose one's own will on the enemy. He also regarded the bayonet attack as the decisive action in battle. The parallels with Bolshevik ideas of a "psychic attack" and the Soviet preference for the Hoorah battle call in infantry attacks are obvious. Bruce Manning, *Bayonets Before Bullets: The Imperial Russian Army, 1861–1914* (Bloomington, IN, 1992), p. 41; Jan Plamper, "Fear: Soldiers and Emotion in Early Twentieth-Century Russian Military Psychology," *Slavic Review* 68, no. 2 (2009): 259–283. For fear conditioning among American and British soldiers in the two world wars, see Joanna Bourke, *Fear: A Cultural History* (Emeryville, CA, 2006), pp. 197–221.

165. NA IRI RAN, f. 2, razd. I, op. 71, d. 15. See also Lt. Col. Alexei Kolesnik (204th Rifle Division), interview: NA IRI RAN, f. 2, razd. III, op. 5, d.12, l. 22–25.

166. The penalties threatened in Order no. 227 were nothing new. Blocking units and penal companies had been with the Red Army since its creation in 1918. Abolished after the Civil War, they were revived in military campaigns in the Far East in 1938 and 1939, and then in the Winter War with Finland. They appeared again in various sectors of the German-Soviet front starting in late June 1941. V. O. Daines, *Shtrafbaty i zagradotriady Krasnoi Armii* (Moscow, 2008); Cherkasov, "O formirovanii i primenenii v Krasnoi armii zagradotriadov." What was new about Order no. 227 was its reach: it was to be read to all soldiers of the Red Army. Stalin referred to Order no. 227 as a copy of disciplinary measures that the German army applied to its own soldiers in the fighting around Moscow. For this reason historian Mikhail Miagkov claims that in December 1941 the German side formed blocking detachments. M. Iu. Miagkov, *Vermakht u vorot Moskvy 1941–1942* (Moscow, 1999), pp. 218–219. The relevant literature contains no mention of such measures: Christian Hartmann, *Wehrmacht im Ostkrieg: Front und militärisches Hinterland, 1941/42* (Munich, 2009); Hürter, *Hitlers Heerführer.* The blocking units in the Red Army were abolished in October 1944.

167. Ordinary soldier offenders were dispatched to penal companies; officers charged with cowardice or desertion were sent to separate penal battalions.

168. NA IRI RAN, f. 2, razd. III, op. 5, d. 14, l. 112–116; see also below, pp. 57–59.

169. NA IRI RAN, f. 2, razd. I, op. 57, d. 1, l. 1–11.

170. NA IRI RAN, f. 2, razd. I, op. 80, d. 3.

171. NA IRI RAN, f. 2, razd. III, op. 5, d. 2a, l. 29–41.

172. NA IRI RAN, f. 2, razd. I, op. 80, d. 32.

173. Alexander Shelyubsky, interview, NA IRI RAN, f. 2, razd. III, op. 5, d. 2a, l. 101–133.

174. Order no. 227 addressed this problem squarely: "There is a lack of order and discipline in the companies, regiments, and divisions, with the armored force, the flying squadrons. This is currently our biggest deficiency. We need to introduce in our army the strictest order and an iron discipline, if we want to save the situation and defend our homeland successfully." *Prikazy narodnogo komissara oborony SSSR*, p. 277.

175. See interviews with Pyotr Zayonchkovsky und Alexander Shelyubsky.

176. Acting in this manner, Kurvantyev meticulously implemented Stalin's Order no. 270 of August 1941, which called on Red Army soldiers, regardless of their rank, to shoot their commanders if they abandoned their positions.

177. Ayzenberg, interview.

178. NA IRI RAN, f. 2, razd. III, op. 5, d. 12, l. 22–25.

179. Alexander Stepanov, interview, pp. 146–188.

180. Soldiers and officers from the criminal units who "atoned for their guilt in the struggle against the German aggressors" received a certificate of rehabilitation: http://rkka.ru/idocs.htm, see under: dokumenty/lichnye/Spravka ob iskuplenii viny. Beevor claims that the promise of forgiveness extended to punished soldiers was a fiction because those in the criminal units were allowed to bleed to death. The case he cites, of officers of the 51th Army who were accidentally sent to a penal battalion, makes clear, however, that the Main Political Administration monitored the situation. Beevor, *Stalingrad,* p. 85.

181. On loss estimates, see John Erickson, "Soviet War Losses," in *Barbarossa: The Axis and the Allies,* ed. J. Erickson and D. Dilks (Edinburgh, 1994), p. 262; see also Alex Statiev, "Penal Units in the Red Army," *Europe-Asia Studies*, vol. 62, no. 5 (July 2010): 721–747, at p. 740.

182. NA IRI RAN, f. 2, razd. III, op. 5, d. 14, l. 160–170.

183. More than one million criminals were conscripted into the Red Army over the course of the war. Most of them were drafted before Order no. 227 was issued and sent to regular units. Beginning in October 1942, most gulag prisoners were sent to penal companies. Statiev, "Penal Units in the Red Army," p. 731; see also Steven A. Barnes, "All for the Front, All for Victory! The Mobilization of Forced Labor in the Soviet Union During World War II," *International Labor and Working-Class History*, Fall 2000, pp. 239–260.

184. NA IRI RAN, f. 2, razd. III, op. 5, d. 9, l. 56–61.

185. Glantz, *Colossus Reborn,* pp. 547–551.

186. The author wrote "Cossacks" but almost certainly meant Kazakhs. First, this addresses the confusion of this nationality with other Central Asian ethnic groups (Uzbeks and Turkmen) and, second, the questionable loyalty of Cossacks, especially the Don Cossacks, who supported the White Army in the Civil War. In World War II Cossacks fought in the Red Army as well as on the side of the Wehrmacht. For this reason, they were grouped into separate statistics by the NKVD. RGAMO, f. 220, op. 445, d.

30a, l. 483. R. Krikunov, *Kazaki: Mezhdu Gitlerom i Stalinym. Krestovyi pokhod protiv bol'shevizma* (Moscow, 2005); Rolf-Dieter Müller, *An der Seite der Wehrmacht: Hitlers ausländische Helfer beim "Kreuzzug gegen den Bolschewismus" 1941–1945* (Berlin, 2007), pp. 207–212.

187. The 45th Division, a unit comprising 10,000 soldiers in spring 1942, consisted of 6,000 Russians, 850 Ukrainians, 650 Uzbeks, 258 Kazakhs, and smaller numbers of Belarussians, Chuvash, and Tatars. Overall, it was made up of twenty-eight nationalities. Serov, interview.

188. Karpov, interview, pp. 225, 232; see also Captain Lukyan Morozov, interview, pp. 225–246.

189. NA IRI RAN, f. 2, razd. III, op. 5, d. 11.

190. Bukharov, interview, pp. 225–246.

191. Rodimtsev, interview, pp. 294–310.

192. NA IRI RAN, f. 2, razd. I, op. 53, d. 1b. German divisional staff officers at Stalingrad kept track of the numbers of Soviet deserters crossing the lines. Their records showed a disproportionate number of non-Slavic deserters, Central Asian and Caucasian soldiers in particular. Ellis, *Stalingrad Cauldron*, pp. 315–319.

193. On Russian nationalism in war and its relationship to Soviet patriotism, see Weiner, *Making Sense of War*; David Brandenberger, *National Bolshevism: Stalinist Mass Culture and the Formation of Modern Russian National Identity, 1931–1956* (Cambridge, MA, 2002).

194. NA IRI RAN, f. 2, razd. III, op. 5, d. 29, l. 29–35.

195. NA IRI RAN, f. 2, raz. I, op. 80, d. 29.

196. V. S. Khristoforov, "Voina trebuet vse novykh zhertv: Chrezvychainye mery 1942 g.," in *Velikaia Otechestvennaia voina. 1942 god* (Moscow, 2012), pp. 173–222, at p. 192; *Stalingradskaia ėpopeia*, pp. 222–224. The latter source has figures that extend to mid-October 1942.

197. "Dokumenty organov NKVD SSSR perioda oborony Stalingrada," *Velikaia Otechestvennaia voina. 1942 god*, p. 456; V. S. Khristoforov, "Zagraditel'nye otriady," in *Velikaia Otechestvennaia voina. 1942 god*, pp. 473–494, at p. 486; *Stalingradskaia ėpopeia*, p. 223.

198. These words are from an appeal in the Red Army newspaper that detailed how Order no. 227 was to be implemented without mentioning the secret order by name. "Za nepreryvnuiu boevuiu politicheskuiu rabotu!" *Krasnaia zvezda*, August 9, 1942, p. 1; see also Khristoforov, "Zagraditel'nye otriady," p. 477.

199. Igal Halfin, *Terror in My Soul: Communist Autobiographies on Trial* (Cambridge, MA, 2003); Halfin, *Stalinist Confessions: Messianism and Terror at the Leningrad Communist University* (Pittsburgh, PA, 2009).

200. Already in November 1941 General Zhukov ordered the commander and the commissar of a division that had shrunk from the Germans to be shot in front of their unit. Zhukov also ordered that all commanders and political officers of the Red Army be informed of his action. Mawdsley, *Thunder in the East*, pp. 114–115.

201. See, for example, Daines, *Shtrafbaty*, pp. 131–135.

202. Mark Edele, *Soviet Veterans of the Second World War: A Popular Movement in an Authoritarian Society, 1941–1991* (Oxford, 2008), pp. 115–117.

203. Khristoforov, "Voina trebuet vse novykh zhertv," p. 183.

204. Statiev, "Penal Units in the Red Army," p. 744. This approach, Statiev writes, once more referenced the revolutionary political culture inside the Red Army. Most other modern armies sentenced penal soldiers to long prison terms.

205. The latest publications by General Valentin Khristoforov, head of the Archives of the FSB, document many abusive practices within the wartime Red Army. The author comments on them with outrage. This is a notable departure from his earlier works, which celebrate the "Chekists" for their "patriotic" work. Khristoforov, "Voina trebuet vse novykh zhertv," pp. 204–210; Khristoforov, *Stalingrad. Organy NKVD nakanune i v dni srazheniia* (Moscow, 2008).

206. Krivosheev gives a precise number: 157,593 people; a similar number ("more than 157,000 death sentences") is cited by Vladimir Naumov and Leonid Reshin and has been widely accepted by scholars as the number of executions actually carried out inside the Red Army. Vladimir Naumow and Leonid Reschin, "Repressionen gegen sowjetische Kriegsgefangene und zivile Repatrianten in der USSR 1941 bis 1956," in *Die Tragödie der Gefangenschaft in Deutschland und der Sowjetunion, 1941–1956*, ed. Klaus-Dieter Müller et al. (Cologne, 1998), pp. 335–364, at p. 339; Merridale, *Ivan's War*, p. 136. But Krivosheev adds that a special court order suspended more than 40 percent of all death sentences and had the convicts join penal units instead (Krivosheev, *Rossiia i SSSR v voinakh XX veka*, p. 302). Elsewhere in the same publication, Krivosheev writes of "135,000 executed soldiers" (ibid., p. 43). Of the death sentences, Naumov and Reschin believe that most were given in the early phase of the war and affected soldiers who had been temporarily

encircled by the Germans or taken captive.

It remains unclear whether executions on the spot performed by commanders on the battlefield in response to soldierly infractions entered the statistics of the NKVD or not. Various authorities—military courts, SMERSH, and "Special commissions" (*Osobye soveshchaniia*)—were authorized to order executions, and the grand total may not be known to the present day. Military procuracy records and other hitherto classified documents will certainly shed more light on the matter.

207. *Stalingradskaia ėpopeia,* p. 380.

208. Stimulants such as alcohol and psychotropic drugs were used in many armies in World War II, but only the Red Army administered them by decree. A. S. Seniavskii and E. S. Seniavskaia, "Ideologiia voiny i psikhologiia naroda," in *Narod i voina: 1941–1945 gg. Izdanie podgotovleno k 65-letiiu Pobedy v Velikoi Otechestvennoi voine* (Moscow, 2010), p. 160; Sonja Margolina, *Wodka: Trinken und Macht in Russland* (Berlin, 2004), pp. 68–70.

209. NA IRI RAN, f. 2, razd. III, op. 5, d. 8, l. 15–28.

210. NA IRI RAN, f. 2, razd. III, op. 5, d. 5, l. 18.

211. NA IRI RAN, f. 2, razd. III, op. 5, d. 14, l. 43–63.

212. These sentences are carved into the walls of the Stalingrad battle memorial at Mamayev Kurgan. Compare Jochen Hellbeck, "War and Peace for the Twentieth Century," *Raritan,* Spring 2007, pp. 24–48.

213. Grossman, *Gody voiny,* p. 321.

214. On Shumilov, see pp. 226–254. The fifty-five minutes mentioned by Shumilov cover the entire operation that he describes, with the mock attack in the middle.

215. NA IRI RAN, f. 2, razd. III, op. 111, d. 1.

216. Svirin, interview, p. 149. The Panfilov men inspired one of the earliest myths of the Great Patriotic War. Twenty-eight soldiers were alleged to have destroyed eighteen enemy tanks in the defense of Moscow; all of the men were killed. Later investigations revealed that at least six of the Panfilov men had survived and one of them worked as an auxiliary police officer for the German occupiers as the war progressed. It was also found that a war correspondent for *Red Star* invented the number twenty-eight as well as some of the last words of these Soviet "heroes." N. Petrov and O. Edel'man, "Novoe o sovetskikh geroiakh," *Novyi Mir* 6 (1997): 140–151.

217. See pp. 316–317.

218. See pp. 209–213, 222.

219. Gordov was arrested in 1947. The Soviet secret service had bugged his apartment and recorded a conversation between Gordov, his wife, and his deputy, Major General Filipp Rybalchenko, in which Gordov held Stalin responsible for postwar economic and social problems in the Soviet Union. He also talked about a need for more democracy. Gordov and Rybalchenko were charged with treason and the "restoration of capitalism" and executed in 1950. They were rehabilitated in 1954, one year after Stalin's death. R. G. Pikhoia, *Sovetskii Soiuz: Istoriia vlasti. 1945–1991,* 2nd rev. ed. (Novosibirsk, 2000), pp. 39–41.

220. In the language of German military psychologists in World War II, Zaytsev would have been considered a "war trembler"; the western Allies spoke of shell shock. Paul Lerner, *Hysterical Men: War, Psychiatry, and the Politics of Trauma in Germany, 1890–1930* (Ithaca, NY, 2003). The Soviet psychological discourse in World War II interpreted war injuries in a physiological manner. The treatment aimed to develop psychological resources such as the will and the moral consciousness. S. Rubenstein, "Soviet Psychology in Wartime," *Philosophy and Phenomenological Research,* December 1944:181–198. See the already noted case of the Komsomol Ilya Voronov.

221. Merridale, *Ivan's War,* pp. 56–58, 199, 262; Oleg Budnitskii, "Evrei na voine: Soldatskie dnevniki," *Lekhaim,* May 2010, http://www.lechaim.ru/ARHIV/217/budnitskiy.htm; Mark Edele, "Toward a Sociocultural History of the Second World War," *Kritika* 15 (2014), no. 4: 829–835.

222. Ever since the signing of the Anglo-Soviet alliance on May 22, 1942, Soviet officials vocally pushed Great Britain and the United States to open a "second front" in western Europe before year's end, to ease the burden on the Red Army, which was practically fighting the Axis forces alone. This second front would not materialize until June 1944. See *Allies at War: The Soviet, American, and British Experience, 1939–1945,* ed. David Reynolds, Warren F. Kimball, A. O. Chubarian (New York, 1994).

223. *Stalingradskaia ėpopeia,* pp. 233–234, report of October 21, 1942. Soviet wartime diaries are a rare but interesting source because they show individual thoughts in evolution. Stepan Kalinin, commander of the Volga military district, kept a diary in which he harshly criticized leadership deficiencies and supply problems in the Red Army in 1941 and early 1942. When he heard of Order no. 227, he read it as a long overdue moral call to order and was relieved. (Kalinin was accused of conducting "anti-Soviet propaganda"

and arrested in 1944.) Khristoforov, "Voina trebuet vse novykh zhertv," pp. 178–190. In similar ways, Vasily Grossman used his diary to expose party and military officials who drank and partied instead of leading. He also criticized ordinary civilians who put their personal needs over those of society. All along he retained a moral, Soviet perspective on the war. See also the diaries mentioned in note 47, and the confiscated diary discussed in *Stalingradskaia ėpopeia*, p. 207.

224. Khristoforov, "Voina trebuet vse novykh zhertv," p. 197. The report was dated September 30, 1942.

225. Ibid.

226. Elizabeth Astrid Papazian, *Manufacturing Truth: The Documentary Moment in Early Soviet Culture* (De-Kalb, IL, 2009).

227. The words of Sergey Tretyakov are cited in Maria Gough, "Paris: Capital of the Soviet Avant-Garde," *October,* Summer 2002: 73; see also *Literatura Fakta,* ed. N. F. Chuzhak (1929; Munich, 1972), pp. 31–33; Tretyakov's notion of the "operative" strongly influenced Walter Benjamin; see especially his essay, "The Author as Producer" (1934), in Walter Benjamin, *Reflections: Essays, Aphorisms, Autobiographical Writings,* Peter Demetz, ed. (New York, 1986), pp. 220–238

228. Frederick C. Corney, *Telling October: Memory and the Making of the Bolshevik Revolution* (Ithaca, NY, 2004), pp. 112–113, 126.

229. Katerina Clark, "The History of the Factories as a Factory of History," in *Autobiographical Practices in Russia,* ed. Jochen Hellbeck and Klaus Heller (Göttingen, 2004), pp. 251–254; Hans Günther, *Der sozialistische Übermensch: Maksim Gor'kij und der sowjetische Heldenmythos* (Stuttgart, 1983), p. 92; Papazian, *Manufacturing Truth,* p. 137.

230. On the political background of the editorial work in the Gorky Project, see Sergei Zhuravlev, *Fenomen "Istorii fabrik i zavodov": Gor'kovskoe nachinanie v kontekste epokhi 1930-kh godov* (Moscow, 1997); Josette Bouvard, *Le métro de Moscou: La construction d'un mythe soviétique* (Paris, 2005).

231. Zhuravlev, *Fenomen,* p. 176. Gorky floated other documentary projects: the history of Soviet cities, the history of the village, the history of culture and everyday life, and other subjects. Zhuravlev, *Fenomen,* p. 175.

232. Elaine MacKinnon, "Writing History for Stalin: Isaak Izrailevich Mints and the *Istoriia grazhdanskoi voiny,*" *Kritika: Explorations in Russian and Eurasian History* 6 (2005), no. 1: 20–21.

233. MacKinnon, "Writing History for Stalin."

234. Papazian locates the end of the documentary movement in the early Stalin period with the promulgation of socialist realism as a compulsory aesthetic. The spirit was continued, however; it showed itself not only in the work of the Mints commission during the war, but also in the documentary project *A Day in the World,* which was first launched in 1935 and revisited twenty-five years later. M. Gor'kii and M. Kol'tsov, eds., *Den' mira* (Moscow, 1937); *Den' mira: 27 sentiabria 1960 goda* (Moscow, 1960). The 1960 project in turn inspired the East German writer Christa Wolf to start a similarly conceived documentary diary. Christa Wolf, *Ein Tag im Jahr: 1960–2000* (Munich, 2003).

235. In 1930, the commander of the Cossack Corps, Vitaly Primakov, married Liliya Brik, formerly the lover of the poet Vladimir Maiakovsky and a well-known muse of the artistic avant-garde. A few years later, Primakov was hit by the purges in the Red Army and confessed under torture to participating in an anti-Soviet fascist conspiracy. He was executed in June 1937. We learn nothing about these circumstances in the recently published diary of Isaak Mints, which excludes the years of Stalin's terror and is generally patchy. I. I. Mints, *"Iz pamiati vyplyli vospominaniia": Dnevnikovye zapisi, putevye zametki, memuary akademika AN SSSR I. I. Mintsa* (Moscow, 2007); see also *K istorii russkikh revoliutsii: Sobytiia, mneniia, otsenki. Pamiati Isaaka Izrailevicha Mintsa* (Moscow, 2007).

236. Vividly portrayed in the diary and in the short stories of Isaak Babel, another Jew who fought in the Red Cossacks. Babel, *Konarmeiskii dnevnik 1920 g.*; Isaak Babel, *Red Cavalry* (New York, 2003); MacKinnon, "Writing History for Stalin," pp. 11–13.

237. A. P. Shelyubsky, "Bol'shevik, voin, uchënyi. (K 70-letiiu so dnia rozhdeniia akademika I. I. Mintsa)," *Voprosy istorii* 1966, no. 3: 167–170; see also Mints's autobiography in *K istorii russkikh revoliutsii,* pp. 221–222.

238. A laudatory review of the second volume appeared in *Pravda,* January 13, 1943, p. 4.

239. MacKinnon, "Writing History for Stalin," p. 29.

240. Ibid., p. 6, n. 2.

241. In the style of Istpart, the surviving members of the commission came together in 1984 for an evening of remembering the Great Patriotic War and reminisced about the founding and work of the now virtually forgotten commission. Naturally, a stenographer was present to transcribe the oral memories.

"Vstrecha sotrudnikov Komissii po istorii Velikoi Otechestvennoi voiny AN SSSR," *Arkheograficheskii Ezhegodnik za 1984 g.* (Moscow, 1986): 316–319. A tape recording of the meeting is preserved in the Russian State Archive of sound recordings. RGAFD, f. 439, op. 4m, no. 1–2. All citations refer to this recording.

242. Jochen Hellbeck, "Krieg und Frieden im 20. Jahrhundert," afterword in Wassili Grossman, *Leben und Schicksal* (Berlin, 2007), pp. 1069–1085.

243. The letter to the Central Committee that Mints remembered writing in July 1941 could not be found in the archives. But there is evidence of other documentary projects pursued by other institutions at the same time. On July 15, 1941, the Soviet People's Commissariat of Education called on all museum staff to collect materials on the Great Patriotic War. The call was followed by Order 170 of November 15, 1941, "On the Collection of Documents and Objects of the Great Patriotic War." T. Timofeeva, "Istoricheskaia pamiat' i ee pamiatniki," in *Rossiiane i nemtsy v epokhu katastrof*, pp. 122–134, at pp. 127–128. Regardless of the Red Army's disastrous losses over the first months of the war, Soviet scholars appeared to believe that historical certainty was on their side and that the war would end victoriously for them.

244. Rodric Braithwaite, *Moscow 1941: A City and Its People at War* (New York, 2006); *Moskovskaia bitva v khronike faktov i sobytii* (Moscow, 2004).

245. E. N. Gorodetskii and L. M. Zak, "Akademik I. I. Mints kak arkheograf (K 90–letiiu so dnia rozhdeniia)," *Arkheograficheskii ezhegodnik za 1986 god* (Moscow, 1987): 136.

246. Mints, *Iz pamiati,* pp. 41–42.

247. *Moskovskaia bitva v khronike faktov i sobytii,* p. 246. Mints, *Iz pamiati,* p. 42 (diary entry for December 11, 1941). On the history and activities of the commision: D. D. Lotareva, "Komissiia po istorii Velikoi Otechestvennoi voiny i ee arkhiv: rekonstruktsiia deiatel'nosti i metodov raboty," *Arkheograficheskii ezhegodnik za 2011 g.* (Moscow, 2014): 123–166; A. A. Kurnosov, "Vospominaniia-interv'iu v fonde Komissii po istorii Velikoi Otechestvennoi voiny AN SSSR (Organizatsiia i metodika sobiraniia)," in *Arkheograficheskii ezhegodnik za 1973 g.* (Moscow, 1974): 118–132; B. V. Levshin, "Deiatel'nost' Komissii po istorii Velikoi Otechestvennoi voiny, 1941–1945 gg.," in *Istoriia i istoriki: Istoriograficheskii ezhegodnik za 1974 g.* (Moscow, 1976); E. P. Michailova, "O deiatel'nosti Komissii po istorii Velikoi Otechestvennoi voiny sovetskogo naroda protiv fashistskikh zakhvatchikov v period 1941–1945 gg.," in *Voprosy istoriografii v Vysshei shkole* (Smolensk, 1975), pp. 352–359; I. S. Archangorodskaia and A. A. Kurnosov, "O sozdanii Komissii po istorii Velikoi Otechestvennoi voiny AN SSSR i eë arkhiva. (K 40-letiiu so dnia obrazovaniia)," in *Arkheograficheskii ezhegodnik za 1981 g.* (Moscow, 1982): 219–229; A. M. Samsonov, "Vklad istorikov AN SSSR v izuchenie problemy Velikoi Otechestvennoi voiny," *Vestnik AN SSSR* 9 (1981): 84–93; E. V. Vasnevskaia, "Vospominaniia-interv'iu o bitve pod Moskvoi," in *Arkheograficheskii ezhegodnik za 1983 g.* (Moscow, 1985): 272–277; I. S. Arkhangorodskaia and A. A. Kurnosov, "Istorii voinskikh chastei v fonde Komissii po istorii Otechestvennoi voiny AN SSSR," in *Arkheograficheskii ezhegodnik za 1985 g.* (Moscow, 1986): 174–181; A. A. Kurnosov, "Memuary uchastnikov partizanskogo dvizheniia v period Velikoi Otechesvennoi voiny kak istoricheskii istochnik. (Opyt analiza memuarov po istorii Pervoi Bobruiskoi partizanskoi brigady)," in *Trudy MGIAI, t. 16* (Moscow, 1961): 29–55; A. A. Kurnosov, "Priemy vnutrennei kritiki memuarov. (Vospominaniia uchastnikov partizanskogo dvizheniia v period Velikoi Otechestvennoi voiny kak istoricheskii istochnik)," in *Istochnikovedenie. Teoreticheskie i metodicheskie problemy* (Moscow, 1969), pp. 478–505.

248. Mints, *Iz pamiati,* p. 42.

249. Arkady Lavrovich Sidorov (1900–1966). Historian at the Institute of Red Professorship (1928). On Sidorov's later life, see Chapter 5.

250. Mints, *Iz pamiati,* p. 46f.

251. NA IRI RAN, f. 2, r. 14, d. 23, l. 16, 213

252. NA IRI RAN, f. 2, r. 14, d. 7, l. 23–24; see also A. A. Kurnosov, *Vospominaniia-interv'iu,* p. 122.

253. Mints, *Iz pamiati,* p. 49.

254. In February 1943 the Academy of Sciences registered the commission's new status, but the Communist party withheld approval in spite of Alexandrov's petitioning to Shcherbakov for support. RGASPI f. 17, op. 125, ed. chr. 204, l. 2.

255. Clark, "History of the Factories," p. 251, n. 1.

256. Mints, *Iz pamiati,* pp. 52–53.

257. Shelyubsky, "Bol'shevik, voin, uchënyj."

258. I. I. Mints, "Dokumenty Velikoi Otechestvennoi voiny, ikh sobiranie i khranenie," in *80 let na sluzhbe nauki i kul'tury nashei Rodiny* (Moscow, 1943), pp. 134–150. Many of these sources cited by Mints are kept in the archives of the Institute of Russian History of the Academy of Sciences (NA IRI RAN, f. 2).

259. NA IRI RAN, f. 2, r. 14, d. 22, l. 45.

260. A. A. Kurnosov, "Vospominaniia-Interv'iu," p. 121.

261. NA IRI RAN, f. 2, razd. XIV, d. 7, l. 34–41 (no date given).

262. Kurnosov, "Vospominaniia-Interv'iu," p. 125, 132.

263. NA IRI RAN, f. 2, razd. XIV, d. 7, l. 34–41.

264. Ibid.

265. The figures refer only to the interviews done in Stalingrad in January-March 1943. Numerous other Stalingrad witnesses were interviewed in later months and at other venues.

266. Kurnosov, "Vospominaniia-Interv'iu," p. 126.

267. E. V. Vasnevskaia, "Vospominaniia-interv'iu o bitve pod Moskvoi," in *Arkheograficheskii ezhegodnik za 1983 g.* (Moscow, 1985): 272.

268. NA IRI RAN, f 2, razd. III, op. 5, d. 4, l. 1–2 (Batyuk); razd. I, op. 71, d. 11 (Pavlov); on Fugenfirov, Koshkaryov, Rivkin, Smirnov, Stepanov, and Svirin, see pp. 145–146.

269. Ensign Arnold Krastynsh, interview. NA IRI RAN, f. 2, razd. I, op. 80, d. 3.

270. The 4,930 transcribed interviews counted by Kurnosov were conducted from 1942 to 1944 and do not include the transcripts produced by the commission in 1945. Kurnosov, "Vospominaniia-Interv'iu," p. 131; also see *200 let AN SSSR: Spravochnaia kniga* (Moscow, 1945), p. 252.

271. Two large-scale interview projects launched in the United States and Great Britain during the 1930s suggest that the documentary impulse of the Mints commission may have been part of a larger cultural phenomenon: The Federal Writers Project in the United States, enacted by the Works Progress Administration in 1935, employed several thousand writers who collected information—much of it by way of oral histories—about American history, folklore, and everyday life. David A. Taylor, *Soul of a People: The WPA Writers' Project Uncovers Depression America* (Hoboken, NJ, 2009). Britain saw the founding of Mass-Observation in 1937, a nongovernmental project that sought to gauge and activate the political pulse of ordinary Britons in response to the rise of fascism. See James Hinton, *The Mass Observers: A History, 1937–1949* (Oxford, 2013).

272. S. L. A. Marshall, *Island Victory* (New York, 1944).

273. S. L. A. Marshall, *Men Against Fire: The Problem of Battle Command in Future War* (Washington, 1947).

274. Roger J. Spiller, "S. L. A. Marshall and the Ratio of Fire," *RUSI Journal: Royal United Services Institute for Defence Studies,* August 1988: 63–71; Richard Halloran, "Historian's Pivotal Assertion on Warfare Assailed as False," *New York Times,* February 19, 1989. An official commissioned by the US Army Center of Military History describes Marshall's interview technique as groundbreaking. Stephen E. Everett, *Oral History Techniques and Procedures* (Washington, DC, 1992).

275. *Notes and Statement by the Soviet Government on the German Atrocities* (Moscow, 1943), p. 19.

276. Molotov's "outrageous note" was a "typical Jewish" attempt to blame Bolshevik atrocities against their own people on the Germans, Goebbels recorded on January 8, 1942. A day later, he noted that "when it comes to atrocities, the Bolsheviks have so much to answer for that their own atrocity reports can't elicit a dog from behind the stove." *Die Tagebücher von Joseph Goebbels.* Part 2: *Diktate 1941–1945*, vol. 3: *Januar-März 1942,* ed. Elke Fröhlich (Munich, 1995), pp. 70–71, 79.

277. Mints, *Iz pamiati,* pp. 52, 54.

278. Shchegoleva was an astute observer. Her diary commented on the corrosive anti-Semitism and the bigotry of the occupiers who made disparaging comments about all things Russian and Soviet. When the Germans left Yasnaya Polyana after six weeks, they had turned the holy place for Shchegoleva into a stable, and human excrement covered the balconies of Tolstoy's apartment building. Only by a hair did the museum workers succeed in extinguishing the fire started by the Germans during their retreat. The diary was serialized in *Komsomol'skaia Pravda*: December 18–24, 1941. A copy is in NA IRI RAN, f. 2, r. VI, op. 4, d. 2.

279. *Sovetskaia propaganda v gody Velikoi Otechestvennoi voiny,* pp. 204–205.

280. E. Genkina, *Geroicheskii Stalingrad* (Moscow, 1943); V. G. Zaitsev, *Rasskaz snaipera* (Moscow, 1943).

281. Genkina, *Geroicheskii Stalingrad,* p. 76.

282. Cultural anthropologists and philosophers refer to this incompatibility as the Rashomon effect. Karl G. Heider, "The Rashomon Effect: When Ethnographers Disagree," *American Anthropologist,* n.s., March 1988: 73–81; Marvin Harris, *Cultural Materialism: The Struggle for a Science of Culture* (New York, 1979), pp. 315–324.

283. The interviews with Chuikov, Rodimtsev, and Aksyonov each run up to 10,000 words; they are presented with cuts.

CHAPTER 2: A CHORUS OF SOLDIERS

1. Leningrad was to be strangled and starved.

2. Figures from the files of the archive of the Russian Defense Ministry (Pavlova, *Zasekrechennaia tragediia,* p. 166). Based on German sources, Beevor counts 1,200 and 1,600 aircraft sorties on August 23. Beevor, *Stalingrad,* p. 103.

3. Hubert Brieden, Heidi Dettinger, and Marion Hirschfeld, *Ein voller Erfolg der Luftwaffe: Die Vernichtung Guernicas und deutsche Traditionspflege* (Nördlingen, 1997), p. 72.

4. Beevor, *Stalingrad,* p. 69; Janusz Piekalkiewicz, *Luftkrieg 1939–1945* (Munich, 1978), p. 138. A smaller number (1,500 dead) is cited in Rolf-Dieter Müller and Florian Huber, *Der Bombenkrieg 1939–1945* (Berlin, 2004), p. 248.

5. Pavlova, *Zasekrechennaia tragediia,* p. 167; Beevor, *Stalingrad,* p. 106.

6. Pavlova, *Zasekrechennaia tragediia,* pp. 154–160; interview with D. Pigalyov.

7. Pavlova, *Zasekrechennaia tragediia,* p. 137f.

8. Ibid., p. 139.

9. Ibid., pp. 143–148.

10. Ibid., pp. 140–141, 159f., 166.

11. Beevor, *Stalingrad,* p. 106; Overy, *Russia's War,* pp. 166, 351 (n. 22) with further references. Volgograd historian Tatiana Pavlova considers these figures understated (Pavlova, *Zasekrechennaia tragediia,* p. 186).

12. See p. 108.

13. Pavlova, *Zasekrechennaia tragediia,* p. 202.

14. Ibid., p. 211. None of those assembled on the evening of August 23 admits to being the "defeatist" who proposed mining the plants. Yeryomenko in his memoirs makes Chuyanov responsible for it; he in turn writes that the representatives of the ministries had made the proposal, and that he had spoken out against it. See A. I. Erëmenko, *Stalingrad: Zapiski komanduiushchego frontom* (Moscow, 1961), p. 139; A. S. Chuianov, *Stalingradskii dnevnik (1941–1943),* 2nd rev. ed. (Volgograd, 1979), p. 157.

15. Pavlova, *Zasekrechennaia tragediia,* pp. 221–222.

16. Ibid., pp. 226–229.

17. Ibid, p. 225.

18. *Stalingradskaia bitva. Ėntsiklopediia,* p. 214.

19. *Stalingradskaia bitva. Ėntsiklopediia,* p. 148. The Red October factory produced steel again starting in July 1943; the Barricades munitions plant took up production again in the autumn of 1944.

20. For an account of the fighting, see Grossman's story "In the Line of the Main Drive," pp. 192–203.

21. *Stalingradskaia bitva.* Ėntsiklopediia, pp. 374–376; Hans Wijers, *Der Kampf um Stalingrad. Die Kämpfe im Industriegelände, 14. Oktober bis 19. November 1942* (Brummen, 2001), p. 26.

22. Chuianov, *Stalingradskii dnevnik,* p. 254.

23. René Fülöp-Miller, *The Mind and Face of Bolshevism: An Examination of Cultural Life in Soviet Russia* (New York, 1965); Mark Steinberg, *Proletarian Imagination: Self, Modernity, and the Sacred in Russia, 1910–1925* (Ithaca, NY, 2002).

24. Kirschenbaum, *Legacy of the Siege of Leningrad,* pp. 64–65.

25. Source: NA IRI RAN, f. 2, razd. III, op. 5, d. 14, 21, 22; Chuianov, *Stalingradskii dnevnik,* S. 90, 100f., 150, 212f., 380f. For Chuikov, see p. 266. Mikhail Vodolagin was interviewed in Stalingrad in June 1943.

26. Since 1936 Stalingrad had consisted of seven districts. The Yermansky district was located in the city center.

27. A kymograph is a device that produces graphical representations of physical processes (e.g., heartbeat, breathing, muscle contractions, etc.).

28. This is a reference to the M-13, or BM-13, multiple rocket launcher built by the Soviet Union during World War II. Soviet soldiers affectionately called the rockets "Katyusha"; German troops referred to them as "Stalin's organ" or "Joseph's organ," prompted by the resemblance of the launch array to a church organ and the sound of the rocket motors. Zaloga and Ness, *Red Army Handbook,* pp. 211–215; "Katiusha," *Voennyi ėntsiklopedicheskii slovar',* S. F. Akhromeev and S. G. Shapkin, eds. (Moscow, 1986), p. 323.

29. The Soviet government decreed the creation of destruction battalions on June 24, 1941. Formed on a volunteer basis and staffed by trusted Soviet activists, their task was to guard lines of communication and industrial objects against saboteurs and enemy agents. The battalions received military training and worked under the oversight of the NKVD or local party officials. Many units formally joined the Red Army over

the course of the war. S.V. Bilenko, *Na okhrane tyla strany. Istrebitel'nye batal'ony i polki v Velikoi Otechestvennoi voine 1941–45 gg.* (Moscow, 1988).

30. A machine and tractor station (MTS) was a state enterprise for ownership and maintenance of agricultural machinery for use on collective farms. Agricultural equipment and technical personnel were scarce and thus shared by collective farms in a given region.

31. Demchenko is alluding to the disintegration within the Red Army.

32. Alexei Adamovich Goreglyad (1905–1985) served as representative of the People's Commissar of the Tank Industry at the Stalingrad Tractor factory (July-September 1941) and was later promoted to people's commissar. K. A. Zalessky, *Stalin's Empire. A Biographical Encyclopedic Dictionary* (Moscow, 2000).

33. Olga Kuzminichna Kovalyova (1900–1942) began working at the Red October factory in 1927. *Stalingradskaia bitva. Ėntsiklopediia,* p. 193.

34. In 1940 Pravda reported on four women who toiled in one of the blast furnaces of the Magnitogorsk Metal Works: Tatiana Mikhailovna Ippolitova, and her subordinates S. S. Vasilieva, L. Spartakova, and P. Tkachenko, *Pravda,* January 7, 1940.

35. German military sources mention nothing about this.

36. Pigalyov in his interview mentions 57 aircraft.

37. Viktor Stepanovich Kholsunov (1905–1939), a native of Tsaritsyn, commanded a squadron of the International Brigades in the Spanish Civil War and was awarded the Hero of the Soviet Union in 1937. He was killed in a flying accident. The monument in his honor was built in 1940. Restored after the war, it still stands at its original location in the city center. *Stalingradskaia bitva. Ėntsiklopediia,* p. 432.

38. Settlements south of Stalingrad. On September 13, the German attack through Yelshanka to the Volga River split the 62nd Army from the 64th Army, which was stationed farther south. Samsonov, *Stalingradskaia bitva,* pp. 175–183.

39. Pavlova writes that Chuyanov and his staff had left the city on the evening of September 13. Pavlova, *Zasekrechennaia tragediia,* p. 230.

40. Probably an error. Major General Stepan Guryev commanded the 39th Motor Rifle Division. Major General Vasily Sokolov commanded the 45th (74th Guards) Rifle Division in the 62nd Army.

41. Lavrentiy Beria (1899–1953) headed the Soviet security and secret police apparatus (NKVD) during World War II.

42. On their retreat from Napoleon, Russian military commanders gathered in the village of Fili near Moscow in September 1812 and debated whether they should confront the invader or cede Moscow to him. Leo Tolstoy describes the gathering in *War and Peace.* Asserting that losing Moscow did not mean losing Russia, commander Mikhail Kutuzov decided to leave the capital to Napoleon. In regard to Stalingrad the Soviet regime argued conversely.

43. Society for the Assistance to Defense, Aviation, and Chemical Construction: a popular volunteer organization in the Soviet Union that existed from 1927 to 1948. See also p. 30.

44. The "Rally of the Victors" took place on February 4, 1943, on the Square of Fallen Heroes. In attendance were thousands of Red Army soldiers as well as party and city officials.

45. Kotelnikovo: a village 190 kilometers southwest of Volgograd. Kotelnikovo was captured by the Wehrmacht on August 2, 1942. It was from here that General Hoth's panzer group sought to break through to the encircled German troops at Stalingrad in December 1942. Hoth's attempt failed, and Soviet forces took Kotelnikovo on December 29, 1942.

46. In the first weeks after the liberation of the city, the NKVD arrested 502 "traitors, agents, and accomplices" of the Germans, including 46 agents, 45 espionage suspects, 68 police employees, and 172 individuals who had voluntarily assisted the German armed forces (*Stalingradskaia ėpopeia,* pp. 406–407). In the surrounding villages, 732 arrests had been made by July 1, 1943. Pavlova believes that many more collaborators were not punished by the Soviet authorities. Pavlova, *Zasekrechennaia tragediia,* pp. 412, 547.

47. These numbers are given, respectively, by Gerlach, *Militärische "Versorgungszwänge," Besatzungspolitik und Massenverbrechen,* p. 199; and Pavlova, *Zasekrechennaia tragediia,* p. 460.

48. Pavlova, *Zasekrechennaia tragediia,* p. 291.

49. Ibid., p. 460.

50. Ibid., p. 461; *Pravda* and *Izvestiia* from October 17, 1942, citing German attacks in the area of the Barricades munitions plant on October 4, 1942.

51. The Germans, Speidel claimed under further interrogation, also tried "at all costs to get the Cossacks on their side" (Pavlova, *Zasekrechennaia tragediia,* pp. 307, 468). While Stalingrad itself was largely populated

by Russians, many Cossacks lived in the villages and on the farms in the area. German occupation officials emphasized the "consanguinity" of the Cossacks to the Aryan peoples and styled Pyotr Krasnov—the commander who had directed the attack against Red Tsaritsyn in 1918 and who was living in German exile—as a liberator of the Cossacks from the Bolshevik yoke. In the summer of 1942 this propaganda fell on open ears. Later, the picture changed when the Germans failed to abolish the collective farms, as they had promised they would, and when the villagers witnessed the mistreatment of Soviet prisoners of war. The Soviet leadership had evacuated able-bodied men from the Cossack settlements in the Volga-Don region to prevent a possible collaboration between Cossacks and Germans. That was one of the few instances of the timely evacuation of the civilian population. Pavlova, *Zasekrechennaia tragediia,* pp. 321–331, 359; R. Krikunov, *Kazaki.*

52. *Stalingradskaia ėpopeia,* p. 396.

53. Pavlova, *Zasekrechennaia tragediia,* pp. 316–319, 363–364.

54. Communists could survive if they were willing to denounce fellow party members. Speidel probably died in late 1943 in the Beketovka prison. Pavlova, *Zasekrechennaia tragediia,* pp. 314, 467, 469, 478–479.

55. Pavlova, *Zasekrechennaia tragediia,* pp. 304–305; Gert C. Lübbers, "Die 6. Armee und die Zivilbevölkerung von Stalingrad," *Vierteljahrshefte für Zeitgeschichte* 54 (2006), no. 1: 115.

56. Gert Lübbers refutes Christian Gerlach's claim that the evacuation ordered by the quartermaster general of the army was aimed to extinguish Stalingrad's civilian population. But his attempt to humanize the policies of the military government seems anachronistic: the sources Lübbers cites speak in a language of bureaucratic calculus. Relying on Russian archival sources, Tatiana Pavlova describes in detail the inhumane conditions of the evacuation. Gerlach, "Militärische 'Versorgungszwänge,' Besatzungspolitik, und Massenverbrechen," pp. 200–202; Lübbers, "Die 6. Armee und die Zivilbevölkerung von Stalingrad," pp. 110–119; Pavlova, *Zasekrechennaia tragediia,* pp. 485–508.

57. Pavlova, *Zasekrechennaia tragediia,* p. 496 (G. Scheffer, Feldpost 45955).

58. *Stalingradskaia ėpopeia,* p. 394. Pavlova estimates the remaining population in the city as 30,000. Pavlova, *Zasekrechennaia tragediia,* p. 527.

59. Pavlova, *Zasekrechennaia tragediia,* pp. 347, 527, 530–531.

60. Ibid., p. 533; *Stalingradskaia ėpopeia,* p. 394.

61. Pavlova, *Zasekrechennaia tragediia,* p. 539.

62. NA IRI RAN, f. 2, razd. III, op. 5, d. 22, l. 66–71.

63. The grain elevator on the southern outskirts of Stalingrad was built in 1940. It was at the time the tallest building in the city. It fell to the Germans after heavy fighting on September 22, 1942, and was recaptured on January 25, 1943. Made from concrete, the elevator is one of few surviving prewar buildings in Volgograd today. *Stalingradskaia bitva. Ėntsiklopediia,* p. 456.

64. The Ninth of January Square, today's Lenin Square, was located in the northern center of Stalingrad near the Volga River and was fiercely fought over during the battle. Both the L-shaped house and Pavlov's House bordered on the square. See Rodimtsev, interview, pp. 305–309; *Stalingradskaia bitva. Ėntsiklopediia,* p. 305.

65. On Kotluban: Glantz, *Armageddon in Stalingrad,* pp. 37–58, 168–183.

66. Glantz, *Armageddon in Stalingrad,* p. 701; Chuikov, *Srazhenie veka,* p. 247.

67. Glantz, *Armageddon in Stalingrad,* p. 980.

68. Glantz, *Armageddon in Stalingrad,* p. 174. On September 30, 1942, General Rokossovsky became commander of the army group fighting in the north, which was now called the Don Front. In his memoirs, he comments on the uninspired operations of his predecessor, Yeryomenko, who kept throwing rifle divisions into frontal attacks for twelve consecutive days. Konstantin K. Rokossovsky, *Velikaia pobeda na Volge* (Moscow, 1965), p. 157.

69. Georgy K. Zhukov, *Vospominaniia i razmyshleniia* (Moscow, 2002), 2:78.

70. Wegner, *Der Krieg gegen die Sowjetunion,* p. 981.

71. Glantz, *Armageddon in Stalingrad,* pp. 44, 50–51., 55, 177.

72. Ibid., pp. 322, 327–329.

73. Ibid., p. 359.

74. Fighter pilot Herbert Pabst, cited in Wegner, *Der Krieg gegen die Sowjetunion,* p. 995.

75. Glantz, *Armageddon in Stalingrad,* p. 542.

76. Ibid., pp. 542, 670.

77. Ibid., p. 636; see also the interview with divisional commander Ivan Lyudnikov.

78. Führer command of November 17, 1942, concerning continuation of the conquest of Stalingrad by the 6th Army; cited in Wegner, *Der Krieg gegen die Sowjetunion,* p. 997.

79. NA IRI RAN, f. 2, razd. I, d. 1–3, 5–8, 11, 14. The Moscow interviews were conducted by E. B. Genkina and transcribed by O. A. Roslyakova; the interviewer in Laptyevo was P. M. Fedosov and the stenographer M. P. Laputina. Major Pyotr Mikhailovich Fedosov (1897–1974) was a battalion commissar during the Great Patriotic War. He served on the Historical Commission since its creation in December 1941. Fedosov's daughter, herself a former staff member of the Institute of History of the Russian Academy of Sciences, has researched his wartime work for the commission: E. P. Fedosova, "'Privezennyi material mozhet sluzhit' dlia napisaniia istorii . . . '," *Arkheograficheskii ezhegodnik za 2011 g.* (Moscow, 2014): 167–176.

80. Leonty Nikolayevich Gurtyev (1891–1943) was appointed major general on December 7, 1942. He died on August 3, 1943, during the fighting for Oryol and was posthumously awarded a Hero of the Soviet Union.

81. The State Fishing Trust.

82. The Russian Red Cross Society was established in 1854. In 1923 it was renamed the Union of Red Cross and Red Crescent Societies of the USSR (the Soviet Red Cross). Its activities included teaching first aid skills to the general population and providing medical training to nurses.

83. Nina Kokorina ended the war in Berlin. After the war she lived in Sverdlovsk, where she led the female veterans association. She died in January 2010. N. Kriukova, "Chizhik: Medsestra iz soldatskoi pesni," *Tiumenskie izvestiia,* January 27, 2010.

84. Cheka (1917–1922) and GPU (1922–1934): predecessor organizations of the NKVD (and later, KGB), the Soviet state security police.

85. From 1917 to 1932, the Supreme Soviet of the National Economy was the central authority for managing industry. It was dissolved in 1932, and its functions were transferred to branches of the People's Commissariat.

86. Kumylga—a railway station on the Uryupinsk–Volgograd line.

87. Samofalovka—a village near Kotluban.

88. From these heights Tsaritsyn was defended in the summer and autumn of 1918.

89. Arnold Meri (1919–2009) was an Estonian soldier who volunteered to serve in the Red Army after the Soviet invasion of Estonia. In July 1941 he was wounded in the defense of Pskov and awarded the Hero of the Soviet Union. From 1945 to 1949 he chaired the Estonian Komsomol organization. In 2003 the Estonian prosecutor indicted Meri for genocide. He was accused of deporting 251 Estonian civilians to Siberia after the war. Meri denied the allegations. Russian president Medvedev awarded him the Medal of Honor posthumously in 2009.

90. In all likelihood, Ilya Nikolayevich Kuzin (1919–1960) was the leader of a group of demolitionists in a Volokolamsk partisan detachment that spent six months behind enemy lines near Moscow. Kuzin personally conducted about 150 acts of sabotage. He was declared a Hero of the Soviet Union on February 16, 1942.

91. Zoya Anatolyevna Kosmodemyanskaya (1923–1941) was a Komsomol from Moscow who voluntarily joined the guerrilla movement after the outbreak of war. Their task was to burn down German accommodations behind the front lines. Kosmodemyanskaya was discovered by a Russian guard and handed over to the Germans. She was tortured and then hanged publicly. Petrischchevo, the village where she died, was liberated on January 22, 1942. The journalist Pyotr Lidov reported the partisan's story a few days later in *Pravda,* and the article became famous. Kosmodemyanskaya was awarded the Hero of the Soviet Union on February 16, 1942.

92. Weapons are camouflaged behind the defense line. Two to three guns with armor-piercing munitions wait until the enemy completes his assault only to experience massive fire from two sides. The fire starts a counterattack by troops emerging from the trenches. See "Kinzhal'nyi ogon'," *Bol'shaia sovetskaia ėntsiklopediiantsiklopediia,* 2nd ed. (Moscow, 1953), 21:11.

93. Spartak was a popular Soviet sports society of industrial cooperatives (established in 1935).

94. For more on Nikolai Kosykh, see *Sibiriaki na zashchite Stalingrada* (Novosibirsk, 1943).

95. On September 18, 1942, Commissar Petrakov wrote his daughter a letter: "My black-eyed Mila! With this letter I am sending you a cornflower [. . .] Imagine: here the battle rages, enemy projectiles explode, everything is destroyed and yet here grows a flower [. . .] And then the next explosion, and it has torn the cornflower. I have removed the flower and put it in my shirt pocket. The flower grew and wanted the sun, but the force of the explosion has destroyed the flowers, and if I had not picked them up, they would have been trampled. Just what the fascists do with the children in the occupied villages around;

they kill and crush the children [. . .] Mila! Your Papa Dima will fight to the last drop of blood against the fascists, to the last breath, so the fascists will not treat you like this flower. What you do not understand, your mom will explain." The letter was first published in 1957 in *Rabotnitsa*. That same year saw the inauguration of the Soldiers Field memorial west of Volgograd. Among the mass graves stands a bronze statue of a girl holding a cornflower in her hands. At her feet is a triangular stone in the shape of a Red Army letter. On it are carved Commissar Petrakov's words to his daughter. *Stalingradskaia bitva. Ėntsiklopediia*, p. 355.

96. Georgy Maximilianovich Malenkov (1901–1988), one of Stalin's closest aides, was a member of the State Defense Committee during the war. In this capacity Malenkov traveled to Stalingrad in August 1942 to inspect the city's defenses.

97. Kirill Semenovich Moskalenko (1902–1985). Commander of the 1st Guards Army.

98. Boris Petrovich Shonin (1918–1942), assistant chief of staff of the 339th Rifle Regiment of the 308th Rifle Division, recipient of the Red Star and the Lenin orders. Shonin's deeds were documented by Captain Ingor, the interviewee: M. Ingor, *Sibiriaki: Stalingradtsy* (Moscow, 1950), pp. 22–26.

99. Vasily Anufriyevich Zhigalin (1910–1942). Senior lieutenant, assistant to the regimental chief of staff. Fell on October 27, 1942, in Stalingrad (details at www.obd-memorial.ru).

100. Semyon Grigoryevich Fugenfirov (1917–1942). Assistant to the regimental chief of staff. Died of his wounds on October 29, 1942, in Stalingrad (details at www.obd-memorial.ru).

101. A reference to an open letter to Stalin sent by hundreds of Red Army soldiers fighting at Stalingrad on the eve of the revolutionary holiday in November 1942. The soldiers swore to defend Stalingrad to the last drop of their blood. The letter was published in *Pravda,* November 6, 1942, p. 1.

102. Probably Prokhor Vasilievich Kayukov (1914–1942), who died in Stalingrad in October 1942, according to www.obd-memorial.ru.

103. Captain Ingor writes that before the war Zoya Rokovanova taught Russian literature at a school. At the front she hosted readings under the motto "Life Is Magnificent!" The readings featured the life of revolutionary writer Nikolai Chernyshevsky (1828–1889), whose writings supplied the motto. Rokovanova had books shipped from Omsk to prepare for the readings. After the readings, she distributed written summaries among the soldiers. M. Ingor, *Sibiriaki—gurt'evtsy—gvardeitsy* (Omsk, 194?), pp. 44–46. The publication date on the volume, 1941, is a misprint.

104. That is, German aircraft, probably a Focke-Wulf fighter bomber.

105. The "Call by the participants in the defense of Tsaritsyn to the defenders of Stalingrad" was published in the army newspaper *For Our Victory. Za nashu pobedu*, October 2, 1942.

106. The book was published in 1943 under the title *Sibiriaki na zashchite Stalingrada* (OGIZ, 1943). It included the stories: A. Svirin, "Sibiriaki v boiakh za Stalingrad"; V. Grossman, "Napravlenie glavnogo udara"; V. Belov, "Bogatyri Sibiri"; M. Ingor, "Leitenant Boris Shonin"; M. Ingor, "Artillerist Vasily Boltenko"; V. Belov, "Vasily Kalinin," and others.

107. Grossman, *Gody voiny*, pp. 388–399.

108. *Krasnaia zvezda,* November 25, 1942, p. 3. Grossman talked with the soldiers of the 308th Rifle Division before the beginning of the November 19, 1942, counteroffensive. In later editions the essay was slightly altered to foreshadow the Soviet victory. Grossman, *Gody voiny,* pp. 49–61.

109. Grossman, *Gody voiny,* p. 365.

110. Most of the interviews were conducted on the ships of the Volga flotilla, which were scattered after the battle of Stalingrad: to conduct the interviews, the historians had to travel to Kuibyshev (now Samara), Saratov, Sarepta (near Stalingrad), and Chorny Yar (near Astrakhan).

111. The division was refurbished after it lost 80 percent of its personnel fighting in eastern Ukraine in summer 1942. Isaac Kobylyansky, "Memories of War, Part 2," *Journal of Slavic Military Studies,* December 2003,:147. In April 1943, the division was renamed 87th Guards Rifle Division.

112. *Stalingrad 1942–1943. Stalingradskaia bitva v dokumentakh* (Moscow, 1995), p. 192. Latoshinka today borders on the northern outskirts of Volgograd. During the war, the village was often called Latashanka. The spelling has been standardized here.

113. Tsentral'ny arkhiv Ministerstva oborony Rossiiskoi Federatsii, f. 1247. op.1. d.10. l. 105.

114. Samsonov, *Stalingradskaia bitva,* p. 240.

115. Glantz, *Armageddon in Stalingrad,* p. 522.

116. Apparently the maneuver was postponed for twenty-four hours. See also Oleynik, interview.

117. The Soviet general staff and German Wehrmacht reports are cited from *Stalingradskaia bitva. Khronika, fakty, liudi* (Moscow, 2002), 1:827–842.

118. *Stalingrad 1942–1943,* pp. 187–188. The document bears the signatures of Yeryomenko, Khrushchev,

and Varennikov.

119. *Stalingradskaia bitva. Khronika, fakty, liudi*, 1:842.

120. Wolfgang Werthen, *Geschichte der 16. Panzer-Division, 1939–1945* (Bad Nauheim, 1958), pp. 106–108, 110.

121. Werthen, *Geschichte der 16. Panzer-Division,* p. 116; Glantz, *Armageddon in Stalingrad,* pp. 521–524.

122. *Stalingrad 1942–1943,* pp. 183–184, 187; see also Zaginaylo, interview.

123. *Stalingrad 1942–1943,* p. 192.

124. Erëmenko, *Stalingrad*, p. 248. A recent Russian publication identifies the losses of the landing operation but also points out that the Soviet battalion "had destroyed 10 to 15 enemy tanks and up to an infantry battalion of the enemy." In addition, it notes that the action successfully concealed Soviet preparations for Operation Uranus. (*Stalingradskaia bitva,* pp. 224–225). That, however, had not been the stated goal of the landing maneuver.

125. Isaak Kobylianskii, *Priamoi navodkoi po vragu* (Moscow, 2005), chap. 5.

126. NA IRI RAN, f. 2, razd. I, op. 80, d. 3, 7–8, 12, 16, 28, 32, 80. Those interviews that bear dates were recorded between July 18 and 28, 1943. The Interviewers were Vasily A. Divin, Filipp St. Krinitsyn, and Nikolai P. Mazunin, and the stenographers Ye. S. Dassayeva and V. Shinder. The latter, the record notes, was a sailor of the Red Fleet.

127. Colonel (and as of December 1942, Major General) Sergey Fyodorovich Gorokhov (1901–1974) commanded the 124th Independent Rifle Brigade and the Northern group of the 62nd Army.

128. Shadrinsky Bay is on the eastern bank of the Volga, opposite the settlement, located on the river's western bank.

129. Today the village is located near the Volga cargo port.

130. Sredne-Pogromnoye is a village on the left bank of the Akhtuba.

131. At another point in the interview, Zaginaylo said about him, "Fyodorov is an amazingly quiet commander; he does not shout, is not nervous, but explains the order clearly."

132. Oleynik possibly confused Kazakhs and Bashkirs. Before the landing maneuver the division was resupplied in Bashkiria, probably with local recruits.

133. Nikolai Nikitich Zhuravkov (1916–1998).

134. This refers to the six-tube 15cm Nebelwerfer 41, which Soviet soldiers called Vanyusha, in contrast to their Katyusha.

135. Anton Grigoryevich Lemeshko. Lieutenant of the Guards, Commissar of the Northern Group of the Volga Flotilla.

136. Probably Ivan Mikhailovich Pyoryshkin.

137. The brigade fought since September 1942 at Stalingrad, first as part of the 64th Army, later in the 62nd, 57th, and 51st Armies before being restored to the 64th Army in January 1943. See Burmakov, interview; *Stalingradskaia bitva. Ėntsiklopediia*, p. 401.

138. Friedrich Roske (1897–1956). Previously regimental commander in the 71st Infantry Division. Succeeded General Alexander von Hartmann as divisional commander on January 26, 1943, after his death. According to several witnesses, Hartmann had sought a "hero's death": he walked up to the battle line, standing tall, and was shot in the head. Kehrig, *Stalingrad,* p. 533; Torsten Diedrich, *Paulus: Das Trauma von Stalingrad* (Paderborn, 2008), p. 289.

139. Akte Dobberkau (p. 2), in RMA Hirst Collection, Hoover Institution Archives (Stanford University), Box 10.

140. Diedrich, *Paulus,* p. 285.

141. Ibid., pp. 289–291.

142. Kehrig, *Stalingrad,* p. 542f.

143. In 1860, 65 percent of the officers of the Prussian army came from the nobility. Until 1913, the share of aristocratic officers in the Imperial Army stood at 30 percent. In 1918, 21.7 percent of generals were aristocrats. After the Nazis took power, the percentage declined again. In 1944, 19 percent of all generals were of noble origin. Bartov, *Hitler's Army,* p. 43.

144. The scene in Beketovka was captured in the documentary film *Stalingrad* (dir. Leonid Varlamov, 1943). The speaker dubbed the German commander correctly as "Friedrich Paulus." Yet in his 1972 memoir Leonid Vinokur repeated the title "Von Paulus." L. Vinokur, "Plenenie fel'dmarshala Paulyusa," *Raduga: Organ Pravleniia Soiuza pisatelei Ukrainy* 1972, no. 2: 145–148.

145. Army General Shumilov came from a poor peasant family, as did Captains Ivan Morozov and Lukyan Bukharov. Both negotiated with Generals Schmidt and Roske in the department store basement. See

interviews with Shumilov, Morozov, and Bukharov.

146. Fritz Roske, "Stalingrad," manuscript, 1956. From the private archive of Bodo Roske, Krefeld. Presented in abbreviated form in *Die 71. Infanterie-Division im Zweiten Weltkrieg 1939–1945,* ed. Arbeitsgemeinschaft "Das Kleeblatt" (Hildesheim, 1973), pp. 299–300.

147. Cited from the television documentary *Stalingrad: Eine Trilogie* (2003). The commandant of Stalingrad reported that a group of Germans was seized in a shelter on March 11, 1943 (Demchenko, interview).

148. On the role of European volunteers who joined the Wehrmacht, see Hans Werner Neulen, *An deutscher Seite: Internationale Freiwillige von Wehrmacht und Waffen-SS* (Munich, 1985); Müller, *An der Seite der Wehrmacht.*

149. Burmakov was a colonel during the battle and was only promoted to major general on March 1, 1943.

150. NA IRI RAN, f. 2, razd. III, op. 5, d. 11, 14–15.

151. A reference to Operation Ring, which was initiated on January 10, 1943. See pp. 11–12.

152. Duka wanted to say, "Hand over your weapons!" ("*Geben Sie Ihre Waffen!*"), but he mistakenly said: "Hand the guards!"

153. This is confirmed by Kehrig in *Stalingrad,* pp. 542–543.

154. Red Square was adjacent to the Square of Fallen Heroes. Several German wartime maps show only Red Square in the city center, omitting the larger Square of Fallen Heroes. Red Square was abolished in the course of the postwar reconstruction of Stalingrad.

155. This could have been Boris V. Neihardt, translator with the 51st Army Corps. In view of a possible surrender to the Soviets, Neihardt was ordered to serve Paulus and the Army Command on January 22, 1943. Kehrig, *Stalingrad,* p. 539.

156. Ivan Andreyevich Laskin (1901–1988) was the 64th Army's chief of staff between September 1942 and March 1943. In 1941, Laskin had commanded a rifle division at the Southwestern front and successfully broken through a German encirclement. In December 1943, the NKVD learned that the Germans had in fact captured and interrogated Laskin, before he managed to escape again. (After his escape he had remained silent about this fact.) The major general, who had received Soviet and American decorations for his role in the capture of Field Marshal Paulus, was arrested, accused of treason and espionage, and—after prolonged interrogations that stretched over years—sentenced to a fifteen-year prison term. The basis for this harsh treatment was Stalin's Order no. 270 of August 1941. Laskin was freed as part of an amnesty in 1952 and rehabilitated in 1953. Naumow and Reschin, "Repressionen gegen sowjetische Kriegsgefangene und zivile Repatrianten in der USSR 1941 bis 1956," p. 339.

157. In his 1972 memoir Vinokur describes his arrival at the department store consistent with the facts described here, but he gives a different slant to the encounter with the hundreds of armed German soldiers in the courtyard of the store: "The Germans huddled in a corner together talking to each other. You could only understand single word fragments: "Kamrad, Kamrad, Hitler kaput! Paulus kaput, kaput." Our officers and soldiers were talking boldly, courageously, with dignity. It seemed as if the capture of fascist generals was an everyday thing" (L. Vinokur, "Plenenie fel'dmarshala Pauliusa," p. 146). Vinokur's 1943 interview conveys how threatened he felt surrounded by armed Germans. The memoir hides this feeling and gives an anachronistic image of the defeated Germans trying to ingratiate their superior Soviet opponents.

158. Paulus was in a different room. Gurov confuses the exceedingly tall field marshal with Roske, who was shorter: "Roske was tall and thin. Paulus was shorter, but had a fuller build."

159. In the final part of the interview Vinokur again refers to the scene: "I was speaking through the interpreter. I went into Roske's room. I said: [*sic*]. He said the same thing. He liked that. He asked if I would sit down." It would be nice to know what word or words Vinokur used when he greeted the German officer. The stenographer did not say, perhaps wisely?

160. Emka: Soviet M-1 limousine, colloquially referred to as "M-type."

161. During the Seven Years War, Russian and Austrian troops occupied Berlin for a few days in October 1760.

162. Probably Shumilov was asked if he had asked Paulus why he had not committed suicide.

163. To establish a spatial and moral "new order" in Europe and the world was the explicit goal of the Axis powers: Germany, Italy, and Japan. Mark Mazower, *Dark Continent: Europe's Twentieth Century* (London, 1998), pp. 143–146.

164. The reference is probably to Major Demchenko, the city commandant of Stalingrad. See p. 92.

CHAPTER 3: NINE ACCOUNTS OF THE WAR

1. W. I. Chuikov, *Legendarnaia shestdesiat vtoraia* (Moscow, 1958); Chuikov, *Nachalo puti*, ed. I. G. Paderina (Moscow, 1959); Chuikov, *Vystoiav, my pobedili. Zapiski komandarma 62-i* (Moscow, 1960); Chuikov, *180 dnei v ogne srazhenii. Iz zapisok komandarma 62-i* (Moscow, 1962); Chuikov, *Besprimernyi podvig. O geroizme sovetskikh voinov v bitve na Volge* (Moscow, 1965); Chuikov, *Srazhenie veka* (Moscow, 1975); *Stalingrad. Uroki istorii. Vospominaniia uchastnikov bitvy*, ed. W. I. Chuikov (Moscow, 1976).

2. Chuikov, *Srazhenie veka*, pp. 108–109.

3. Walter Kerr, *The Russian Army: Its Men, Its Leaders, and Its Battles* (New York, 1944), p. 144; Werth, *The Year of Stalingrad*, p. 456.

4. Richard Woff, "Vasily Ivanovich Chuikov," in *Stalin's Generals*, ed. Harold Shukman (London, 1993), pp. 67–74.

5. Grossman, *Life and Fate*, p. 660.

6. *Stalingradskaia ėpopeia*, p. 390; see also Chuikov, *Srazhenie veka*, pp. 257–258.

7. Initials of the stenographer, Alexandra Shamshina.

8. NA IRI RAN, f. 2, razd. III, op. 5, d. 2a, l. 1–28.

9. Serebryanye Prudy, in Moscow province, is Chuikov's birthplace. Today it features a Chuikov Museum as well as a memorial bust (by artist Yevgeny Vuchetich) and another monument (by artist Alexander Chuikov, Vasily Chuikov's son).

10. Romania and Germany declared war on August 15, 1916.

11. The party of the Left Social Revolutionaries existed from 1917 to 1923 and had formed an oppositional circle in the Socialist-Revolutionary party. Its members wanted to withdraw from World War I, transfer land to the peasants, and terminate cooperation with the Provisional Government.

12. The October Revolution, 1917.

13. The names Ilya and Ivan are written in the margin in pencil.

14. The decree, signed by Lenin, was published on January 15, 1918.

15. The village soviet occupies the lowest rung of the soviet system; at its upper end is the Council of People's Deputies.

16. Lefortovo: a district in Moscow's east, home to barracks and military academies.

17. The insurrection of the Left Socialist Revolutionaries began on July 6, 1918, with the assassination of the German ambassador in Moscow, Count Wilhelm von Mirbach-Harff.

18. The Alexeyevskaya Military Academy was founded in 1864 and located in Lefortovo.

19. A river that rises in the western foothills of the Urals and flows into the Kama, the largest tributary of the Volga.

20. For Gordov, see pp. 63–64.

21. Kotelnikovo: a settlement located 190 kilometers southwest of Volgograd.

22. Tsimlyanskaya: a village in the Volgograd region.

23. Nikita Sergeyevich Khrushchev.

24. That is, Hill 102.0, or Mamayev Kurgan.

25. Orlovka and Rynok were villages north of Stalingrad and formed part of the city's outer defense perimeter.

26. Gumrak: village northwest of Stalingrad.

27. Correct: Yelshanka.

28. Mikhail Naumovich Krichman (1908–1969). From June 1942 to April 1943 he commanded the 6th Guards Tank Brigade.

29. Interview with Alexander V. Chuikov, Moscow, November 11, 2009.

30. Kuzma Akimovich Gurov (1901–1943). Lieutenant general. Member of the Military Council of the Stalingrad Front.

31. Nikolai Ivanovich Krylov (1903–1972) was appointed chief of staff of the 62nd Army in August 1942. Until the arrival of the new army commander, Chuikov, he commanded the army for more than a month. He received the Hero of the Soviet Union award twice in 1945. See N. I. Krylov, *Stalingradskii rubezh* (Moscow, 1969).

32. Nikolai Mitrofanovich Pozharsky (Pozharnov) (1899–1945). From September 1942 artillery commander of the 62nd Army.

33. See p. 280, note 43.

34. See pp. 292–293, and Rodimtsev, interview, pp. 298–301.

35. Tumak: bend of the Volga below the settlement of Krasnaya Sloboda, which served as an important crossing point for the 62nd Army.

36. Verkhnyaya Akhtuba: a village east of Stalingrad.

37. Among them was sniper Vasily Zaytsev. See Zaytsev, interview.

38. Stalin's Falcons: slang for Soviet fighter pilots.

39. Polikarpov U-2 biplane. Built in 1927, it was used as a trainer aircraft and crop duster and in war as a reconnaissance aircraft. The aircraft flew slowly, had no technical equipment, and offered its two-man crew, who flew in an open cockpit without helmets, weapons, or parachutes, no protection. Losses were consequently high. Among Germans the nightly raids were feared. They referred to the bombers as "nuisances" or "sewing machines." Kempowski, *Das Echolot,* p. 556.

40. Korney Mikhailovich Andrusenko (1899–1976), who fought in the Red Army since 1918, commanded the 115th Independent Rifle Brigade during the battle of Stalingrad. Chuikov reprimanded Andrusenko for retreating without authorization on November 3, 1942, following a devastating German attack. Andrusenko was demoted in rank and made regimental commander. For more details on Andrusenko's complex war biography, see: *http://www.warheroes.ru/hero/hero.asp?Hero_id=4530.*

41. Stepan Savelyevich Guryev (1902–1945). Commander of the 39th Guards Rifle Division.

42. Ivan Efimovich Yermolkin (1907–1943). Commander of the 112th Rifle Division.

43. Lieutenant Colonel P. I. Tarasov, commander of the Independent 92nd Rifle Brigade, had moved his command post without authorization from the center of Stalingrad to an island in the Volga on September 26 in the course of a German attack. A military tribunal accused him of cowardice, pointing out that his irresponsible behavior (as well as that of the brigade commissar, G. I. Andreyev) had prompted the troops to leave their defense positions. Both the commander and the commissar were executed on October 9, 1942 (Daines, *Shtrafbaty*, p. 133). Tarasov and Andreyev must have been one of the two brigade command teams that Chuikov personally executed in front of the brigade's assembled soldiers (see pp. 273, 288). Chuikov's memoirs make no mention of their names.

44. Guards Lieutenant General Vasily Akimovich Gorishny (1903–1962). Commander of the NKVD's 13th Motor Rifle Division. Hero of the Soviet Union (1943).

45. Colonel General Ivan Ilyich Lyudnikov (1902–1976). Commander of the 138th Rifle Division, which led the fight for the Barricades munitions plant. Hero of the Soviet Union (1943).

46. Possibly Afrikan Fyodorovich Sokolov (1917–1977). Captain chief of staff of the 397th Antitank Regiment of the 62nd Army. Hero of the Soviet Union (1945).

47. Major General Viktor Grigoryevich Zholudyev (1905–1944). Commander of the 37th Guards Division, which fought for the Stalingrad Tractor factory. Hero of the Soviet Union (posthumously, 1944).

48. The division was formed in August 1942 near Moscow on the basis of the 8th Airborne Corps. See the interviews with A. P. Averbukh und A. A. Gerasimov.

49. The text comes from the French song "Everything Good, Beautiful Marquise," which Russian entertainer Leonid Utyosov used in his repertoire. In the song the Marquise asks what happened to her estate after her absence. Everything is good, they say, and so on, to the small matter of the death of her gray mare.

50. The KV is a heavy Soviet tank named after Marshal Kliment Voroshilov. German soldiers called the tank "Dicker Bello" due to its strong armor.

51. The German fighter Messerschmitt Bf 109 (Me-109).

52. Vasily Grossman interviewed Chuikov in December 1942. His brief notes are concordant with Chuikov's present statements; for example, "Final conversation [with Chuikov] about cruelty and callousness as principles. A dispute. His last, surprising sentence: 'Well, what the heck, I cried, but alone. What do you say when four Red Army soldiers directs fire onto themselves! You cry, but alone, alone. Nobody. Has. Ever. Seen me cry.'" Grossman, *Gody voiny,* p. 357.

53. While in Stalingrad, Grossman also spoke with front commander Yeryomenko and asked him about his opinion of Chuikov: "Chuikov I suggested. I knew him; he cannot be swayed by panic. 'I know your bravery, but it comes from drinking, this bravery I do not need. Don't make any rash decisions, you like to make them.' I helped him when he panicked." The writer's notebook portrays the front commander in unflattering ways: Yeryomenko claims that he had been the first to come up with the idea of encircling the Germans in a pincer operation, and he repeatedly underlines his closeness to Stalin (Grossman, *Gody voiny,* pp. 350–353). A chapter in Grossman's Stalingrad novel describes the front commander's visit with Chuikov: Yeryomenko felt like a "guest" who had come to see the "master of Stalingrad." Grossman, *Life and Fate,* p. 56.

54. Boris Mikhailovich Shaposhnikov (1882–1945). Deputy people's commissar of defense of the USSR (1942–1943).

55. Alexander I. Rodimtsev, *Gvardeitsy stoiali nasmert'* (Moscow, 1969), pp. 7–10.

56. Vasily Grossman, "Stalingradskaia bitva," September 20, 1942, in Grossman, *Gody voiny*, p. 29.

57. On October 18, 1942, *Izvestiya* reported on the house but did not mention Pavlov. Speaking to historians, Rodimtsev described the hostilities he conducted as a commander. The defense of the Pavlov house may have been controlled below his command level.

58. The destroyed Pavlov house was rebuilt in July 1943, to great propaganda fanfare. Located on 61 Penzenskaya Street, the building appears as "House 6/1" in Vasily Grossman's novel *Life and Fate*. See *Stalingradskaia bitva. Ėntsiklopediia*, pp. 136–137, as well as the television documentary *Iskateli: Legendarnyi redut* (dir. Lev Nikolaev, 2007).

59. The "house of the soldiers' sacrifice," in A. I. Rodimtsev, *Gvardeitsy stoiali nasmert'*, pp. 85–105, 133–134, 138.

60. NA IRI RAN, f. 2, razd. III, op. 5, d. 6, l. 1–7.

61. Sharlyk is a village in the Orenburg region and birthplace of Alexander Rodimtsev. A street and a school are named after him and a bust of him exists there. In 1967, a school museum of military glory was opened, and Rodimtsev loaned it his uniform jacket, cap, and binoculars.

62. The great famine in Russia (1921–1922), brought about by the Civil War and a drought, cost about 10 million lives. It particularly affected the agricultural region between the Volga and the Urals, including Orenburg.

63. Kulaks: pejorative Soviet-era reference to wealthier peasants who were considered "class enemies" of poorer peasants.

64. Today, the Moscow Military Academy.

65. The Khodynka field, located northwest of Moscow, was used for military instruction and target practice.

66. Students of the Federal Military Academy had the exclusive right to stand guard at the Lenin mausoleum.

67. The article could not be found in *Red Star*.

68. The International Exposition dedicated to Art and Technology in Modern Life, held from May through November 1937. Set up at the foot of the Eiffel Tower, the exposition was noted for the visual confrontation between the German and Soviet pavilions, which faced each other.

69. The M.V. Frunze Academy of the Staff of the Red Army. Since 1998 known as the General Military Academy of the Russian Armed Forces.

70. A city in southern Ukraine.

71. Stalinka (today Chernozavodskoye): town in the Poltava region, Ukraine.

72. Filipp Ivanovich Golikov (1900–1980). Commander of the 1st Guards Army on the Southeast and Stalingrad Fronts. From September 1942 deputy supreme commander of the Stalingrad Front; from October 1942 commander of the front.

73. The division was reinforced and newly equipped after suffering heavy losses in the battle of Kharkov. Many of the reinforcements were officer trainees without combat experience. During the reorganization, the division was ordered to Stalingrad. Krylov, *Stalingradskii rubezh*, pp. 128–129.

74. Rodimtsev's memoir contains nothing about the shooting.

75. According to Samsonov, the L-shaped house (in Russian: "*G-obrazny dom*") and the Railway Workers house, which stood seventy meters from each other on Penzenskaya Street, were multistory buildings with massive cellars. After taking the two houses, the Germans converted them into veritable fortresses. The buildings had great tactical value because they controlled the area. Samsonov, *Stalingradskaia bitva*, pp. 265–266.

76. For a detailed description of the storming of the L-shaped house and the Railway Workers house, see W. I. Chuikov, "Taktika shturmovykh grupp v gorodskom boiu" (Assault group tactics in city fighting), *Voennyi vestnik* 1943, no. 7: 10–15. The storming of the L-shaped house was filmed by Valentin Orlyankin and is shown in the documentary *Stalingrad* (dir. Leonid Varlamov, 1943).

77. Tim is a town in the Kursk region.

78. The conversation, like the one with Rodimtsev, took place on January 7, 1943, in Stalingrad. The interviewer was A. A. Belkin, and the stenographer was A. I. Shamshina. NA IRI RAN, f. 2, razd. III, op. 5, d. 6, l. 8–8 ob.

79. Olkhovatka: probably a village in the Voronezh region.

80. Chuikov, *Srazhenie veka,* p. 350; *Stalingradskaia ėpopeia,* p. 196.

81. PPSh stands for Pistolet Pulemyot Shpagina and is a Soviet submachine gun. It was developed by Georgy S. Shpagin.

82. This renders all the more valuable the interviews that Svetlana Aleksievich conducted with female veterans of the Great Patriotic War during the 1980s: Svetlana Aleksievich, *War's Unwomanly Face* (Moscow, 1988).

83. NA IRI RAN, f. 2, razd. III, op. 5, d. 6, l. 9–10.

84. Burkovka: a settlement on the eastern side of the Volga and location of a 62nd Army field hospital.

85. Maybe Gurova answered the question of her marital status. Since the interviewers' questions are not included in the transcript, the degree of their intervention in the conversation is difficult to gauge.

86. *Stalingradskaia bitva. Khronika, fakty, liudi,* 1:417, 427; *Stalingradskaia bitva. Ėntsiklopediia,* p. 402. Today Rossoshka is home to a German war cemetery which was set up by the German War Graves Commission in 1999. An estimated 50,000 German soldiers are buried there. A Russian war cemetery is located on the other side of the street.

87. On Makarenko, see James Bowen, *Soviet Education: Anton Makarenko and the Years of Experiment* (Madison, 1965).

88. Innokenti Petrovich Gerasimov (1918–). Details at *Geroi Sovetskogo Soiuza: Kratkii biograficheskii slovar'* (Moscow, 1987), 1:319; *Stalingradskaia bitva. Khronika, fakty, liudi* 1:74–75.

89. NA IRI RAN, f. 2, razd. III, op. 5, d. 38, l. 36–37.

90. Rzhishchev: a town southeast of Kiev.

91. A settlement on the southwestern edge of Kiev.

92. Political officer Innokenti Gerasimov, who conducted the interview with Averbukh.

93. Regimental commander Alexander Akimovich Gerasimov, not to be confused with the eponymous political officer (see note 88).

94. This refers to the six-tube 15cm multiple rocket launcher Nebelwerfer 41, which Red Army Soviet soldiers called the "Vanyusha" (little Vanya), in contrast to their own "Katyusha" (little Katya) rocket launcher.

95. Verkhnyaya Yelshanka: a settlement south of Stalingrad.

96. The blood-stained uniform of Major General Vasily Glazkov (1901–1942), shot through in 168 places, is now displayed in the Volgograd Panoramic Museum.

97. Chuikov, *Srazhenie veka.* Glantz writes that on September 11 the division still counted 454 soldiers. Glantz, *Armageddon in Stalingrad,* p. 85.

98. Initials of Alexandra Shamshina, the stenographer.

99. NA IRI RAN, f. 2, razd. III, op. 5, d. 38, l. 25–32. The transcript does not indicate who conducted the interview.

100. After Glazkov's death, Colonel Vasily Pavlovich Dubyansky (1891–?) assumed command of the 35th Guards Rifle Division.

101. The 35th Guards Division fought against the German 14th and 24th Panzer Divisions, as well as the Romanian 20th Infantry Division. Glantz, *Armageddon in Stalingrad,* pp. 64, 93.

102. Gerasimov's regiment was located south of the German forces that had reached the Volga on the southern edge of Stalingrad. The only open way to reach the division command was by boat.

103. The sailors of the Volga Military Flotilla who controlled the river crossing.

104. *Stalingradskaia bitva. Ėntsiklopediia,* p. 127; see also the interview with divisional commander Batyuk.

105. Interview with Alexander Levykin, commissar of the 284th Rifle Division.

106. "Donesenie OO NKVD Stalingradskogo fronta v NKVD SSSR o khode boev v Stalingrade, 16. 9. 1942," in *Stalingradskaia ėpopeia,* p. 196.

107. William Craig, *Enemy at the Gates* (New York, 1973), p. 120.

108. This date is given by Aksyonov in his interview. According to another source, the hill was not fully under Soviet control until January 26: Kratkie svedeniia ob osnovnykh ėtapakh boev 62. Armii po oborone gor. Stalingrada, NA IRI RAN, f. 2, razd. III, op. 5, d. 3, l. 5.

109. As a history teacher, Aksyonov felt an affinity to Isaak Mints's historical commission. The State Historical Museum in Moscow has an oil lamp made from a grenade shell with the inscription: "To the history professor Dr. Mints in memory of the defense of Stalingrad from Captain N. N. Aksyonov." *1943 god. Voina glazami ochevidtsev. Vystavka iz sobraniia Gosudarstvennogo Istoricheskogo muzeia pri uchastii Tsentral'nogo muzeia Vooruzhennykh Sil* (Moscow, 2003), p. 8.

110. On the Stalin cult in the Soviet Union, see Jan Plamper, *The Stalin Cult: A Study in the Alchemy of Power* (New Haven, CT, 2012).

111. NA IRI RAN, f. 2, razd. III, op. 5, d. 4, l. 3–16 ob. The long interview began on May 5 and was continued on May 8.

112. Metiz: acronym for "Metal Products." Established in 1932 as the Stalingrad steel mill, the factory was located at the foot of Mamayev Kurgan.

113. Imperialist War: this is how Lenin and other Soviet Marxists referred to World War I.

114. This refers to the Il-2, a Soviet fighter plane, which was built under the direction of Sergey Ilyushin and came into use during the war.

115. The plant was situated on the slope of Mamayev Kurgan.

116. In accordance with Soviet wartime propaganda Aksyonov represents the defense of Tsaritsyn as a struggle against the Germans. Yet German occupation troops in the Ukraine did not participate in the attack on the city in 1918.

117. Kastornaya: railway junction on the Kursk-Voronezh route. In July 1942, heavy fighting took place there.

118. Letters written at the time by Grossman indicate that he was, in fact, very concerned about Benesh. See *A Writer at War*, pp. 203–204.

119. Signed: "Viewed on May 12, 1943, N. Aksyonov."

120. Corrected by hand to "none."

121. Rakityansky was born in 1913. This is confirmed at: http://www.obd-memorial.ru/html/info.htm?id=9413438.

122. The following was deleted: "and we felt very sorry about him."

123. A Stalin order of May 1, 1945 formally declared four Soviet cities "Hero Cities": Leningrad, Stalingrad, Sevastopol, and Odessa. The number later rose to twelve.

124. See also Frank Ellis, *The Stalingrad Cauldron: Inside the Encirclement and Destruction of 6th Army* (Lawrence, KS, 2013), pp. 270–284.

125. *Na zashchitu rodiny,* October 5, 1942, p. 2.

126. Kapitan N. N. Aksënov, "Rol' snaiperov v oborone Stalingrada" (manuscript), NA IRI RAN, f. 2, razd. III, op. 5, d. 26, l. 2.

127. Words from an article by writer and journalist Ilya Ehrenburg (1891–1967). Il'ia Erenburg, "Ubei!" ["Kill!"] *Krasnaia zvezda,* July 24, 1942.

128. Chuikov, *Srazhenie veka,* pp. 174–175.

129. *Na zashchitu rodiny,* October 21, 1942, p. 1; October 26, 1942, p. 1; October 30, 1942, p. 1.

130. Ibid., October 26, 1942, p. 1.

131. "*Znatnyi snaiper,*" Beevor, *Stalingrad,* p. 203, with a reference to the archive of the Russian Defense Ministry.

132. Grossman, *Gody voiny,* p. 387.

133. "Snaiper Vasilii Zaitsev," *Na zashchitu rodiny,* November 2, 1942, p. 1.

134. *Na zashchitu rodiny*, November 6, 1942, p. 1.

135. Ibid., November 14, 1942, p. 1.

136. Zaytsev, interview, p. 367; NA IRI RAN, f. 2, razd. III, op. 5, d. 27, l. 44; *Stalingradskaia bitva. Ėntsiklopediia*, p. 151. A Moscow archive has Zaytsev's Stalingrad "combat account" for the period from October 5 to December 5, 1942. The booklet countersigned by Captain Kotov lists 184 killed "Hitler soldiers" (RGASPI-M, f. 7, op. 2, ed. 468).

137. Zaitsev, *Za Volgoi zemli dlia nas ne bylo,* pp. 105–106.

138. Captain Aksyonov may have played a role in facilitating the interview with Zaytsev. On March 9, 1943, he wrote an essay on the role of snipers in the defense of Stalingrad (NA IRI RAN, f. 2, razd. III, op. 5, d. 26, l. 1–20). Presumably this text was in front of the historians who talked with Zaytsev in April; that would explain the concordance of the narrated episodes. Aksyonov's essay, or parts of it, appeared in the newspaper *Red Fleet* on March 15, 1943 (see p. 367).

139. Vasilii G. Zaitsev, *Geroi Sovetskogo Soiuza. Rasskaz snaipera* (Moscow, 1943).

140. Zaytsev's 1981 memoir also departs from the 1943 interview on multiple counts. Zaitsev, *Za Volgoi zemli dlia nas ne bylo.*

141. *Stalingradskaia bitva. Ėntsiklopediia*, p. 151; *Geroi Sovetskogo Soiuza: Kratkii biograficheskii slovar'*, 1:524.

142. Raisa Ivanovna Krol' worked for the commission beginning in 1942.

143. NA IRI RAN, f. 2, razd. III, op. 5, d. 4, l. 17–26.

144. Zaytsev describes the sniper modification of his automatic rifle, the Tokarev SVT-40.

145. Probably the TOZ 8 sports and hunting rifle that was produced by the Tula Weapons Factory.

146. In the published interview: "In October, something very important happened in my life. The Komsomol handed me over to the ranks of the Communist Party." Zaitsev, *Rasskaz snaipera,* p. 8.

147. The political officer in question must be Colonel Vedyukov.

148. On Furmanov and Chapayev, see pp. 25–28.

149. Alexander Yakovlevich Parkhomenko (1886–1921) was a Civil War hero. Vsevolod Ivanov published his biography in 1939.

150. Grigori Ivanovich Kotovsky (1881–1925) was a Soviet commander during the Civil War. Zaytsev probably read V. Shmerling's book *Kotovsky* (Moscow, 1937).

151. Alexander Vasilievich Suvorov (1730–1800), the last Generalissimo of the Russian army and one of the most distinguished commanders in Russian military history.

152. Brusilov offensive: a vast and successful Russian offensive against Austria and Germany during World War I, under the command of General Alexei Brusilov. Zaytsev probably read the book by L. V. Vetoshnikov, *Brusilovskii proryv: Operativno-strategicheskii ocherk* (Moscow, 1940).

153. Vladimir Yakovlevich Zazubrin (1895–1937) was a Soviet writer whose novel about the destruction of Admiral Kolchak, *Two Worlds,* was published in 1921.

154. Pyotr Ivanovich Bagration (1765–1812) was a general in the Patriotic War of 1812. Zaytsev probably refers to S. B. Borisov, *Bagration. Zhizn' i deiatel'nost' russkogo polkovodtsa* (Moscow, 1938).

155. Denis Vasilievich Davydov (1784–1839) was a Russian poet and military commander who led a guerrilla movement during the Patriotic War of 1812.

156. Sergey Georgyevich Lazo (1894–1920) was a Soviet commander in the Civil War. See *Sergei Lazo. Vospominaniia i dokumenty* (Moscow, 1938).

157. K. M. Staniukovich (1843–1903), *Morskie rasskazy* (1934).

158. Alexei Novikov-Priboi Sikych (1877–1944) was a Russian-Soviet writer and student of Maxim Gorky. In 1932 he published his most famous novel, *Tsusima,* followed by part 2 in 1941.

159. The supplementary interview with Zaytsev begins after this passage. It was recorded on August 23, 1943. The interviewer was Raisa Krol'; Alexandra Shamshina transcribed.

160. On that day Chuikov presented Zaytsev with the Medal for Valor.

161. Epaulets were denounced as a sign of counterrevolution and abolished in the Russian army in December 1917. In January 1943 they were reintroduced by the Red Army.

162. See pp. 62–64.

163. NA IRI RAN, f. 2, razd. III, op. 5, d. 14, l. 154–159. The interviewing historian and the stenographer are not identified.

164. Until December 1941 the Soviet government readied itself for a Japanese attack in the Far East. After the attack on Pearl Harbor and the US declaration of war against Japan, the specter of a two-front war became less likely, and by early 1942, twenty-three divisions and nineteen brigades of the Red Army were deployed from the Soviet Far East to the European theater. Glantz, *Colossus Reborn*, p. 154.

165. Rozengartovka: train station in the Khabarovsk region.

166. Vertyachy: a hamlet in the Don bend, west of Stalingrad.

167. Regarding the concept of the psychic attack, see pp. 25–26.

168. Tinguta and Peskovatka: settlements in the Stalingrad region. The distance between them is more than one hundred kilometers.

169. For the activities of the 7th Section, see Norman Naimark, *The Russians in Germany: A History of the Soviet Zone of Occupation, 1945–1949* (Cambridge, MA, 1995), pp. 17–20.

170. See A. Epifanov, "Sovetskaia propaganda i obrashchenie s voennoplennymi vermakhta v khode Stalingradskoi bitvy (1942–1943 gg.)," *in Rossiiane i nemtsy v epokhu katastrof,* pp. 67–74

171. For the appropriation of imperial Russian traditions in Soviet prewar and wartime culture, see Kevin M. F. Platt and David Brandenberger, eds., *Epic Revisionism: Russian History and Literature as Stalinist Propaganda* (Madison, WI, 2006).

172. This and the following biographical details are taken from L. G. Zakharova, "Pëtr Andreevich Zaionchkovskii: Uchënyi i uchitel'," *Voprosy istorii* 1994, no. 5: 171–179; Terence Emmons, "Zaionchkovsky, Petr Andreevich," in *The Modern Encyclopedia of Russian and Soviet History,* ed. George N. Rhyne, vol. 55 (Gulf Breeze, FL, 1993), pp. 185–186.

173. Hellbeck, *Revolution on My Mind*; Orlando Figes, *The Whisperers: Private Life in Stalin's Russia* (London, 2008), pp. 64, 196–199.

174. *Istoriia dorevoliutsionnoi istorii Rossii v dnevnikakh i vospominaniiakh. Annotirovannyi ukazatel' knig i*

publikatsii v zhurnalakh. Nauchnoe rukovodstvo, redaktsiia i vvedenie professora P. A. Zaionchkovskogo, 5 vols. in 13 pts. (Moscow, 1976–1989). Several of Zayonchkovsky's monographs have appeared in American translation, including *The Abolition of Serfdom in Russia* (Gulf Breeze, FL, 1978).

175. Grigori Nikolayevich Anpilogov (1902–1987) was a Soviet historian. He served on the Historical Commission from 1942 to 1945.

176. NA IRI RAN, f. 2, razd. III, op. 5, d. 54, l. 1–7.

177. This refers to Andrei Cheslavovich Zayonchkovsky (1862–1926). His brother was Nikolai Cheslavovich Zayonchkovsky (1859–1918), a senator, and later deputy Procurator of the Holy Synod.

178. The Zayonchkovskys, a noble family of Polish origin, owned the estate Mikhailovsky in the government of Smolensk. The farm was located near the village Volochek, today Nakhimovsky.

179. Pavel Stepanovich Nakhimov (1802–1855). Admiral. Commander of the Black Sea Fleet squadron during the Crimean War, 1853–1856.

180. The George Cross is a Russian order of merit, which was founded in 1769 by Catherine II.

181. The battle of Borodino (August 29, 1812) took place near Moscow and was one of the key moments in the Patriotic War of 1812.

182. Today it is the Russian State Military Historical Archive, or RGVIA.

183. The Kadets (Constitutional Democrats) were a bourgeois-liberal party in prerevolutionary Russia. The Octobrists formed a party farther to the right that supported the reformed Tsarist state after the Revolution of 1905.

184. See p. 363, note 161, and pp. 431–432.

185. Gustav Wietersheim (1884–1974). Lieutenant general of the infantry and commander of the 14th Panzer corps at Stalingrad. After the corps incurred heavy casualties in September 1942, Wietersheim suggested a partial withdrawal to the Don. Army commander Paulus accused him of defeatism and Wietersheim was demoted.

186. Hitler Youth: the youth organization of the Nazi party in Germany.

187. Kletskaya: a train station located 230 kilometers northwest of Stalingrad on the banks of the Don.

188. See p. 22, note 76.

189. Soviet enemy propagandists produced the "Daddy Is Dead" leaflet in a variety of forms because it proved extremely effective. In a June 1942 meeting with Red Army propaganda specialists, GlavPURKKA head Alexander Shcherbakov discussed the leaflet at length. He had been told, Shcherbakov said, that there was not a single German POW who did not know about the leaflet, and that many enemy soldiers were clutching it in their hands as they surrendered to the Red Army. Shcherbakov's reasoning was interesting: German soldiers were brutal, fully conforming to Hitler's ambition to produce a beastly and cruel new generation, but they were also sentimental. Shcherbakov urged the assembled specialists to work on the enemy's soft spot and produce more "sentimental" propaganda. M. I. Burtsev, *Prozrenie* (Moscow, 1981), pp. 100–102. An exact image of the leaflet as described by Zayonchkovsky could not be found.

190. Zayonchkovsky is referring to propaganda that appealed to German soldiers, as sons of workers and peasants, to turn against a Nazi regime controlled by capitalists.

191. For the full wording of the order, see p. 10, note 27.

192. Hitler's address to the soldiers of the 6th Army was dated November 26, 1942, and is referenced in Kehrig, *Stalingrad*, pp. 264–265.

193. See "The Landing at Latoshinka," pp. 203–222.

194. Elsewhere in Stalingrad, too, cats were used to deliver Soviet propaganda. The intelligence department of the 62nd Army reported on two soldiers of the 149th Independent Rifle Battalion who noticed "that a cat living in their shelter from time to time visited the shelters of the Germans. They decided to use the cat to transport fliers to the adversary. They wrapped the cat with leaflets and shooed it forcibly to the Germans. In this way the cat took about one hundred leaflets to the Germans. The fact that it returned without leaflets suggests that the German soldiers read our leaflets and care about them." Unlike Zayonchkovsky's story, this report ends without the heroic death of the cat. It is interesting to note that the animal had to be shooed to the Germans; by itself it would not go there. NA IRI RAN, f. 2, razd. III, op. 5, d. 3a, l. 27 ob. Report of January 5, 1943.

195. A Sovinformburo broadcast.

196. Maria Petrovna Kukharskaya (Smirnova) (1921–2010) was a medical educator who joined the front as a volunteer in 1941. She held the rank of lieutenant at the end of the war. See Iu. A. Naumenko, *Shagai, pekhota!* (Moscow, 1989); *Akmolinskaia Pravda,* September 28, 2010.

197. Captain Nikolai Dmitriyevich Abukhov (1922–1943) commanded the 1st Rifle Battalion, 1151st Rifle Regiment, 343rd Rifle Division. See Iu. A. Naumenko, *Shagai, pekhota!*

198. Ehrenburg produced hundreds of columns during the war, filled with scathing observations on Nazi German "culture." To make his point, Ehrenburg often quoted from captured German letters and diaries. See Jochen Hellbeck, "'The Diaries of Fritzes and the Letters of Gretchens': Personal Writings from the German–Soviet War and Their Readers," *Kritika: Explorations in Russian and Eurasian History* 10 (2009), no. 3: 571–606; Peter Jahn, ed., *Ilya Ehrenburg und die Deutschen* (Berlin, 1997).

199. Mokraya Mechetka is a river that flows through the area of the Tractor factory. The riverbed is transformed seasonally into a ravine.

200. Soviet observers frequently commented on the pornographic images that they found in the pockets of German POWs or in abandoned trenches. "You want to wash your hands after touching any of these Germans' things," Vassily Grossman subtly remarked in his war diary. Grossman, *Gody voiny*, pp. 261–262. Talking with the Moscow historians, Major Anatoly Soldatov was more explicit: "There were a lot of obscene magazines that they left behind—such obscenities that you rarely see on photographs. An official edition, mind you." Soldatov might have had in mind *Ostfront-Illustrierte*, a magazine that was produced for soldiers of the 6th Army. Its issues were replete with erotic pictures of young German women, in tune with the Nazis' aggressive reproductive aims. A partial run is at Bundesarchiv-Militärarchiv (Freiburg), RWD 9/32. Compare also Dagmar Herzog, *Sexuality in Europe: A Twentieth-Century History* (Cambridge, 2011), pp. 67–94.

CHAPTER 4: THE GERMANS SPEAK

1. General Karl Strecker (1884–1973) commanded the German 11th Corps at Stalingrad. He surrendered on February 2, 1943, as commander of the Stalingrad north *Kessel.*

2. 2 NA IRI RAN, f. 2, razd. I, op. 258, d. 2, l. 8–11.

3. Colonel Arno Ernst Max von Lenski (1893–1986) commanded the 24th Panzer Division at Stalingrad. In January 1943 he was promoted to lieutenant general.

4. Presented here is only a selection of the interrogation transcripts preserved in the archive of the Historical Commission: NA IRI RAN, f. 2, razd. I, op. 258, d. 5.

5. Handwritten insertions in the typewritten transcripts are italicized.

6. Turkey, which had maintained its neutrality, declared war on Germany and Japan on February 23, 1945.

7. See Zayonchkovsky's information about the desecrated corpses of Soviet soldiers, which he found in November 1942 near Latoshinka (pp. 207, 391).

8. During the first days of the encirclement German commanders in the *Kessel* readied themselves for a breakthrough to the west, and they ordered food and military supplies to be destroyed.

9. Kalmyk steppe: desert-like area southeast of Stalingrad.

10. The Red Army liberated Rostov on February 14 and Kharkov on February 16, 1943. On March 15 Kharkov again fell into German hands and was finally liberated on August 23.

11. *Böse Waffe* (German): evil weapon.

12. General Walther von Brauchitsch (1881–1948, promoted to general field marshal in 1940) was the commander-in-chief of the German Army from 1938–1941. He was sacked by Hitler after the failed Moscow offensive and spent the remainder of the war in enforced retirement.

13. Erwin Jaenecke (1890–1960), Lieutenant general and commander of the 389th Infantry Division. He was flown out of Stalingrad as one of the last higher officers.

14. See Jens Ebert, "Organisation eines Mythos," in *Feldpostbriefe aus Stalingrad,* pp. 333–402.

15. Shelyubsky crossed paths with Isaak Mints during the war and appears to have joined the Historical Commission shortly after the war ended. See Sheliubskii, "Bol'shevik, voin, uchënyi"; A. P. Sheliubskii, "Bol'shevistskaia propaganda i revoliutsionnoe dvizhenie na severnom fronte nakanune 1917 goda," *Voprosy istorii* 1947, no. 2: 67–80.

16. NA IRI RAN, f. 2, razd. III, op. 5, d. 3a, l. 1–48.

17. NA IRI RAN, f. 2, razd. III, op. 5, d. 2a, l. 101–133.

18. Schelyubsky: "Among our [sic] German divisions, who fought against us, there were also several small Austrian units. The Austrians came in first after the Germans."

19. These are words from a poem by Gavriil Derzhavin (1743–1816), which became the unofficial

Russian national anthem of the late eighteenth and early nineteenth centuries.

20. NA IRI RAN, f. 2, razd. III, op. 5, d. 3a, l. 14–15.

21. "Vechernee soobshchenie 25 ianvaria," *Pravda,* January 26, 1943, p. 3; see also "Pis'ma okruzhennykh nemtsev," *Pravda,* January 10, 1943, p. 4.

CHAPTER 5: WAR AND PEACE

1. Quoted from Kempowski, *Das Echolot,* 3:173.

2. *Pravda,* February 4, 1943, p. 1.

3. *Krasnaia Zvezda,* February 4, 1943, p. 1.

4. The list with the 9,602 decorated soldiers is signed by the head of the cadre department in the political administration of the 62nd Army. NA IRI RAN, f. 2, razd. III, op. 5, d. 3, l. 1.

5. The documentary *Stalingrad* (dir. Varlamov). Grossman collaborated on the screenplay. See also p. 224, n. 144.

6. Grossman, *Gody voiny*, p. 369 (entry for May 1, 1943).

7. *Pravda,* June 27, 1945, p. 2. Stalin's use of the screw metaphor is often viewed as an expression of his cynical views toward the Soviet people. That may be, but there is evidence that Soviet citizens readily described themselves in the very same terms. In September 1943 an engineer at Moscow's ZIL factory noted in his diary: "The news gets better every day. There is growing confidence that we will end the war this year. What magnificent events we are witnessing! And what a joy to think that you are a tiny little screw in these events." V. A. Lapshin, entry for September 7, 1943, in Somov, "Dukhovnii oblik trudiashchikhsia perioda Velikoi Otechestvennoi voiny," p. 342. For the cynical interpretation see, among others, Seniavskaia, *Frontovoe pokolenie*, p. 4.

8. I. S. Konev, *Zapiski komanduiushchego frontom* (Moscow, 1991), pp. 594–599; Laurence Rees, *World War II Behind Closed Doors: Stalin, the Nazis, and the West* (New York, 2010), pp. 395–398.

9. Lidiya Ginzburg, *Blockade Diary,* trans. Alan Myers (London, 1995), p. 3.

10. N. N. Gusev, *"Voina i mir" L. N. Tolstogo: Geroicheskaia ėpopeia Otechestvennoi voiny 1812 goda, Bloknot lektora* (Moscow, 1943); A. Rashkovskaia, "'Voina i mir', prochtennaia zanovo," *Smena* (Leningrad), February 3, 1943; James von Geldern, "Radio Moscow: The Voice from the Center," in *Culture and Entertainment in Wartime Russia,* ed. Richard Stites (Bloomington, 1995), p. 53.

11. Leo Tolstoy, *War and Peace*, trans. Richard Pevear and Larissa Volokhonsky (New York, 2007), p. 1137.

12. Ilya Ehrenburg, *Letopis' muzhestva: Publitsisticheskie stat'i voennykh let* (Moscow, 1974), p. 355; L. Lazarev, "Dukh svobody," *Znamia* 9 (1988): 128.

13. Benedikt Sarnov, "'Voina i mir dvadtsatogo veka," *Lechaim,* January 2007, http://www.lechaim.ru / ARHIV/177/sarnov.htm. *War and Peace* was, as Grossman acknowledged, the only book that he read during the war years. *A Writer at War,* pp. 54–55; see also Grossman, *Gody voiny,* p. 287.

14. Grossman was fortunate that the Central Committee of the party called on General Rodimtsev as a military expert. He remembered Grossman's war reports from Stalingrad and had a favorable view of the writer (RGALI, f. 1710, op. 2, ed. chr. 1, entry from May 31, 1950). Twelve versions of the novel are preserved in Grossman's estate. Grossman compiled a diary to document the twisted road that his manuscript traveled.

15. RGALI, f. 1710, op. 1, ed. khr. 106, l. 26; see also f. 1710, op. 1, ed. khr. 152.

16. RGALI, f. 1710, op. 1, ed. khr. 37, title page.

17. John Garrard and Carol Garrard, *The Bones of Berdichev: The Life and Fate of Vasily Grossman* (New York, 1996), pp. 355, 358.

18. The book is forthcoming under its original title, *Stalingrad,* in the New York Review of Books Classics series (trans. Robert Chandler).

19. Grossman's daughter remembers how committed her father was to the mythology of the Soviet people's war. The family often sang war songs at evening gatherings. Inevitably the evening reached its high point: with his unmusical voice, her father intoned the famous song of the "holy war" (1941). The song moved him so powerfully that he had to stand up. "Father stands hunched over, his hands on his hips, as if he were in a parade. His face is solemn and serious. 'Rise up, rise up great country / to the last battle [. . .] This is a war of the people / a holy war.'" *A Writer at War,* p. 348.

20. Sabine R. Arnold, *Stalingrad im sowjetischen Gedächtnis: Kriegserinnerung und Geschichtsbild im totalitären Staat* (Bochum, 1998), p. 293.

21. How Grossman's words came to be included in the war memorial is unclear. Surviving witnesses

supply conflicting information. Compare Arnold, *Stalingrad im sowjetischen Gedächtnis,* p. 294.

22. NA IRI RAN, f. 2, razd. XIV, d. 22, l. 210.

23. *K istorii russkikh revoliutsii,* p. 224. According to a different source, the decision to dissolve the commission and its transformation in the sector was made on September 15 or November 15, 1945. NA IRI RAN, f. 2, "Prikazy po Institutu istorii za 1945 g.," no call number, l. 119; Levshin, "Deiatel'nost' Komissii po istorii Velikoi Otechestvennoi voiny," p. 317. The sector worked in the same place as the commission before it, in the house on Comintern Street.

24. Many documents were kept secret even after the war due to their detailed descriptions of military operations and fighting. Gorodetskii and Zak, "Akademik I. I. Minc kak arkheograf," p. 142.

25. NA IRI RAN, f. 2, unsigned folder on the activity of the sector in the year 1946, l. 71–72 (July 25, 1946).

26. *Stalingradskaia bitva* (dir. N. Petrov, 1949).

27. *Kratkaia evreiskaia Ėntsiklopediia,* vol. 1 (Jerusalem, 1976), pp. 682–691; *Dopolnenie 2* (Jerusalem, 1995), pp. 286–291.

28. Yuri Slezkine, *The Jewish Century* (Princeton, NJ, 2004), pp. 297–313; Gennadi Kostyrchenko, *Out of the Red Shadows: Anti-Semitism in Stalin's Russia* (Amherst, MA, 1995).

29. I. Mints, *Velikaia Otechestvennaia voina Sovetskogo Soiuza* (Moscow, 1947).

30. It was the Institute of Red Professors in Moscow, led by historian Mikhail Pokrovsky (1868–1932).

31. A. L. Sidorov, "Institut krasnoi professury," in *Mir istorika: Istoriograficheskii sbornik,* vol. 1 (2005), p. 399; see also K. N. Tarnovskii, "Put' uchënogo," *Istoricheskie zapiski* 80 (1967): 207–251, at p. 223.

32. His doctoral thesis examined the war economy of the Russian empire during the First World War. Sidorov submitted the work in December 1942; it appeared in full only after his death. A. L. Sidorov, *Ekonomicheskoe polozhenie Rossii v gody Pervoi Mirovoi voiny* (Moscow, 1973). Compare Tarnovskii, "Put' uchënogo," pp. 226–228, at p. 244.

33. Tarnovskii, "Put' uchënogo," p. 225; NA IRI RAN, f. 2, razd. XIV, d. 22, l. 18–19; d. 23, l. 14, 23, 56; Mints, *Iz pamiati vyplyli vospominaniia,* p. 50. Sidorov conducted many interviews for the commission. In fall 1943 he talked with dozens of residents of Kharkov shortly after the liberation of the city; in 1945 he interviewed Red Army soldiers who had taken part in the assault on Königsberg and the liberation of Czechoslovakia. For his service in the Red Army, Sidorov was awarded the Order of the Red Star. Tarnovskii, "Put' uchënogo," pp. 225–227.

34. Prof. A. Sidorov, "O knige akademika I. Mintsa 'Istoriia SSSR'," *Kul'tura i zhizn'* 33 (1947): 4; compare V. V. Tikhonov, "Bor'ba za vlast' v sovetskoi istoricheskoi nauke: A. L. Sidorov i I. I. Mints (1949 g.)," *Vestnik Lipetskogo gosudarstvennogo pedagogicheskogo universiteta. Nauchnyi zhurnal. Seriia Gumanitarnye nauki* 2011, no. 2: 76–80. That Sidorov's review appeared in *Kul'tura i zhizn'*, a highly political magazine, suggests that the campaign against Mints was supported or controlled from above. Mints seems to have fallen out of favor because, among other reasons, in the book discussed by Sidorov he had claimed that some of his editorial staff on the history of the Civil War had laid the "foundations" of the history of Soviet society. Yet only one publication could claim such a role: the 1938 *The Short Course of the History of the Communist Party* that was ascribed to Stalin. Mints was also accused of neglecting the work on the history of the Civil War. Indeed, only two volumes had been published so far. Since 1942 Mints had incorporated the entire staff into the Commission on the History of the Great Patriotic War. *K istorii russkikh revoliutsii,* pp. 224, 251.

35. Detailed in Kostyrchenko, *Out of the Red Shadows,* pp. 179–221.

36. In this connection Mints also wrote to Stalin and Malenkov, confessing various errors and offenses in his scientific work. *K istorii russkikh revoliutsii,* p. 251.

37. Kostyrchenko, *Out of the Red Shadows,* pp. 198–199. Sidorov's obituaries are silent about the campaign against "cosmopolitanism," and Sidorov's participation in it. Tarnovskii, "Put' uchënogo"; P. V. Volobuev, "Arkadii Lavrovich Sidorov," *Istoriya SSSR* 3 (1966): 234–238. In 1959 Sidorov relinquished his position as director for health reasons. His works are listed in Tarnovskii, "Put' uchënogo," pp. 245–251.

38. Edele, *Soviet Veterans of World War II,* pp. 61, 129–136; A. M. Nekrich, "Pokhod protiv 'kosmopolitov' v MGU," *Kontinent* 28 (1981): 304–305; Tarnovskii, "Put' uchënogo," p. 229.

39. Sidorov, "Institut krasnoj professury," pp. 397, 399–400.

40. On his seventieth birthday Mints was awarded the Order of Lenin, the highest award of the Soviet Union. The leading Soviet historical journal published a tribute to his life's work. It was written by the Stalingrad veteran Alexander Sheliubskii, the former head of the intelligence department of the 62nd Army. Sheliubskii mentioned the Historical Commission, founded by Mints during the war, and expressed his regret that its documentary record remained virtually unexplored. Sheliubskii, "Bol'shevik, voin, uchënyi,"

p. 168; see also *K istorii russkikh revoliutsii,* p. 277. For his work on the history of the battle of Stalingrad, Samsonov (himself a veteran of the battle) had access to the documents from the Mints commission, but he made virtually no use of them.

41. His posthumously published diaries are anything but instructive. Mints, *Iz pamiati vyplyli vospominaniia.* Mints's estate in the archives of the Academy of Sciences is currently not available.

42. The main outcome of this work was the *History of Great October,* volume 1 of which appeared on the fiftieth anniversary of the October Revolution (I. I. Mints, *Istoriia Velikogo Oktiabria,* 3 vols., Moscow, 1967–1973). In 1968 Mints drew a straight line from his work in the 1930s as a responsible editor of the history of the Civil War to his research on the history of the Revolution after the war. He passed over his activity during the war. "Nashi interv'iu: Akademik I. I. Mints otvechaet na voprosy zhurnala 'Voprosy istorii,'" *Voprosy istorii* 1968, no. 8: 182–189, at p. 187. Mints's collected writings are listed in *K istorii russkikh revoliutsii,* pp. 280–330.

43. In 1957 the third volume of the *History of the Civil War in the Soviet Union* appeared, but without Mints's involvement. The volume devotes eight pages to a description of the battle of Tsaritsyn in the summer and fall of 1918. Stalin is mentioned just three times. The main actors in this account are the workers of Tsaritsyn, the "Tsaritsyn Central Committee" (to which Stalin belonged), and Stalin's colleague Voroshilov. *Istoriia grazhdanskoi voiny v SSSR,* vol. 3 (Moscow, 1957), pp. 250–257.

44. Robert Chandler, "Introduction," in Grossman, *Life and Fate,* pp. xv–xvi.

45. RGAFD, f. 439, op. 4m, N. 1–2 (Memories of Nadezhda Trusova); see also p. 73, n. 247.

INDEX

Matthias Stausberg

JOCHEN HELLBECK, professor of history at Rutgers University, is preparing a book on the German occupation of the Soviet Union during World War II. He directs a team of Russian, Ukrainian, and Belorussian scholars that uncover and examine wartime records on the Soviet experience of Nazi occupation. Hellbeck regularly travels to Russia and Ukraine to document popular memories of the Second World War. His website, facingstalingrad.com, features portraits and interviews taken with German and Russian veterans who fought at Stalingrad. Hellbeck's previous book, *Revolution on My Mind*, explored personal diaries written in the Soviet Union under Stalin. He lives in Brooklyn, NY.

CHRISTOPHER TAUCHEN is a freelance translator and editor. He lives in State College, PA.

DOMINIC BONFIGLIO lives in Berlin and works as a freelance translator of German prose.

PublicAffairs is a publishing house founded in 1997. It is a tribute to the standards, values, and flair of three persons who have served as mentors to countless reporters, writers, editors, and book people of all kinds, including me.

I. F. Stone, proprietor of *I. F. Stone's Weekly*, combined a commitment to the First Amendment with entrepreneurial zeal and reporting skill and became one of the great independent journalists in American history. At the age of eighty, Izzy published *The Trial of Socrates*, which was a national bestseller. He wrote the book after he taught himself ancient Greek.

Benjamin C. Bradlee was for nearly thirty years the charismatic editorial leader of *The Washington Post*. It was Ben who gave the *Post* the range and courage to pursue such historic issues as Watergate. He supported his reporters with a tenacity that made them fearless and it is no accident that so many became authors of influential, best-selling books.

Robert L. Bernstein, the chief executive of Random House for more than a quarter century, guided one of the nation's premier publishing houses. Bob was personally responsible for many books of political dissent and argument that challenged tyranny around the globe. He is also the founder and longtime chair of Human Rights Watch, one of the most respected human rights organizations in the world.

• • •

For fifty years, the banner of Public Affairs Press was carried by its owner Morris B. Schnapper, who published Gandhi, Nasser, Toynbee, Truman, and about 1,500 other authors. In 1983, Schnapper was described by *The Washington Post* as "a redoubtable gadfly." His legacy will endure in the books to come.

Peter Osnos, *Founder and Editor-at-Large*

31192020775332